A Publication Sponsored by
the Society for Industrial and Organizational Psychology, Inc.,
A Division of the American Psychological Association

Other books in the Professional Practice Series sponsored
by the Society and published by Jossey-Bass include:

Employees, Careers, and Job Creation
Manuel London, Editor

Organizational Surveys
Allen I. Kraut, Editor

Performance Appraisal
James W. Smither, Editor

Individual Psychological Assessment
Richard P. Jeanneret and Robert F. Silzer, Editors

Evolving Practices in Human Resource Management

Responses to a Changing World of Work

Allen I. Kraut

Abraham K. Korman

Editors

Foreword by Manuel London

Jossey-Bass Publishers • San Francisco

Chapter 11: material from Thomas and Ely (1996) is reprinted by permission of *Harvard Business Review.* From "Making Differences Matter: A New Paradigm for Managing Diversity" by David A. Thomas and Robin J. Ely, Sept/Oct 1996. Copyright © 1996 by the President and Fellows of Harvard College; all rights reserved.

Chapter 11: material from Schuler, R. S., Fulkerson, J. R., & Dowling, P. J. (1992), Strategic performance measurement and management in multinational corporations, *Human Resource Management, 30* (3), is reprinted by permission of John Wiley & Sons, Inc.

Chapter 11: material from Trompenaars, F., *Riding the Waves of Culture,* 1993, McGraw-Hill, is reprinted by permission of The McGraw-Hill Companies.

Chapter 11: material from Fulkerson, J. R., & Schuler, R. S. (1992), Managing worldwide diversity at Pepsi-Cola International, from S. S. Jackson (editor), *Diversity in the workplace: Human resource initiatives* (pp. 248–276), is reprinted by permission of The Guilford Press.

Chapter 12: material from *Best Practices in Leading Downsized Organizations: Proceedings of a Conference, April 5–7, 1995* is reproduced by permission of the Center for Creative Leadership, Greensboro, NC, copyright 1996. All rights reserved.

Library of Congress Cataloging-in-Publication Data

Evolving practices in human resource management : responses to a changing world of
   work / Allen I. Kraut, Abraham K. Korman, editors : foreword by Manuel London.
      p.   cm. — (Professional practice series)
   "A joint publication in the Jossey-Bass business & management series and the
Jossey-Bass social and behavioral science series."
   Includes bibliographical references and index.
   ISBN 0-7879-4012-7
   1. Personnel management.   I. Kraut, Allen I.   II. Korman, Abraham K.
III. Series.   IV. Series: Jossey-Bass business & management series.   V. Series:
Jossey-Bass social and behavioral science series.
HF5549.E89   1999
658.3—dc21   98-32342

FIRST EDITION
HB Printing

A joint publication in
The Jossey-Bass
Business & Management Series
and
The Jossey-Bass
Social & Behavioral Science Series

Society for Industrial and Organizational Psychology
Professional Practice Series

We dedicate this book to the memory of our esteemed friend and colleague Richard J. Campbell, a past president of the Society for Industrial and Organizational Psychology, who was a wonderful example of an effective scientist-practitioner anticipating as well as responding to the changing world of work.

Contents

Part Three: Perspectives on the Future and How to Get There

Foreword

This volume is part of the Professional Practice Series, which is sponsored by the Society for Industrial and Organizational Psychology. The books in the series address contemporary ideas and problems, focus on how to get things done, and provide state-of-the-art technology based on theory and research from industrial-organizational (I/O) psychology. They try to cover the needs of practitioners and those being trained for practice.

Four earlier volumes in this series, developed under the senior editorship of Douglas W. Bray, were published by Guilford Press and are now distributed by Jossey-Bass. The first book, *Working with Organizations and Their People* (1991), which was also edited by Douglas W. Bray, examines the role of I/O psychologists as practitioners involved in evaluation, training, and organization development. The second book, *Diversity in the Workplace* (1992), edited by Susan E. Jackson, offers cases and methods for creating and assessing a diverse workplace, managing workplace diversity through personal growth and team development, and developing strategic initiatives to manage workplace diversity. Abraham K. Korman's *Human Dilemmas in Work Organizations: Strategies for Resolution* (1994) considers the expanding world of the human resource (HR) practitioner. Readings describe programs for employee assistance, stress management, marginal performers, reorganization, employee ethics, and elder care. Ann Howard's *Diagnosis for Organizational Change* (1994) focuses on organizational diagnosis for design and development. Chapters in the volume examine the assessment of human talent for staffing and training and also provide an overview of the high-involvement workplace with a consideration of organizational cultures, reward systems, and work teams.

As the new senior editor of the Professional Practice Series under our new publisher, Jossey-Bass, I edited *Employees, Careers, and Job Creation* (1995), which examines ways in which HR development programs contribute to an organization's viability and growth in tough economic times. It describes programs that help employees maintain their value to their firm or find new employment after organizational downsizing. It shows how organizations, government, and universities can work together to help employees create new ventures and career opportunities.

Allen I. Kraut, an editor of the current volume, also edited *Organizational Surveys: Tools for Assessment and Change,* which appeared in the series in 1996. It demonstrates the value of surveys in diagnosing individual and organizational strengths and weaknesses, communicating organizational culture and expectations, and evaluating HR policies and programs. Cases describe best practices and methods by which organizations share items and compare results. The book shows how to link survey results to measures of organizational effectiveness such as customer satisfaction, financial performance, and employee turnover. It also addresses such tough issues as holding managers accountable for survey results and judging the validity of the survey results.

James W. Smither's book *Performance Appraisal* (1998) provides state-of-the-art methods for performance management. It recognizes the strategic, systemic role of a performance appraisal process that evaluates employees on behaviors that are important to organizational success and ties the appraisal results to rewards and development. It addresses current legal and societal issues in appraisal, including equal employment opportunity and disability legislation and judicial rulings. The goal is to design a performance appraisal process that is fair and applies in different organizational situations (such as teams) and contexts (multinational corporations). New forms of appraisal are described, such as 360-degree (multisource) survey feedback and self-assessment. The book shows how to increase rater accuracy and use appraisals for employee development. Overall, the book is a valuable resource for practitioners who want to evaluate and revamp their appraisal systems to meet the changing needs of their organizations.

The next volume, *Individual Psychological Assessment* (1998), edited by Richard P. Jeanneret and Robert F. Silzer, focuses on the evaluation of a few highly qualified candidates for executive positions. Organizations are learning, sometimes the hard way, that seat-of-the-pants selection methods such as search committees and do-it-yourself interviews are insufficient for executive selection. Individual assessment is especially difficult these days because of the increasingly complex nature of organizational leadership. Leaders are coaches, developers, negotiators, change agents, communicators, educators, and visionaries as well as strategic planners and organizers. Chapters in the book offer a theoretical framework for assessment, describe methods, and give examples of ways that assessment has been used. Other chapters debate whether assessment should focus on behavioral dimensions or the "whole person" and show how feedback on assessment results affects both the individuals assessed and the organization.

The current volume, edited by Allen I. Kraut and Abraham K. Korman, explores how changes in the work world during the last two decades have altered the nature of human resource management (HRM). Economic, global, and marketplace changes have led to flatter organizational structures, reengineered jobs, team processes, and methods for continuous, customer-driven quality improvement. The chapters in this volume show how the practice of HRM and I/O psychology has adapted to these challenges and contributed to organization development. Readers will learn how work is changing and about the new implicit contract between employers and employees. The chapters—all written by expert practitioners who value research—describe success stories and emerging strategies in key areas of HRM such as career development, recruitment and selection, performance appraisal, teamwork, leadership development, and organizational surveys. Chapters examine how HRM will continue to enhance employees' work involvement and take advantage of diversity in the multinational, fast-paced organizational environment. The book is invaluable for understanding how strategic HRM helps organizations change and meet future challenges.

My editorial board contributed to this effort by setting the direction for the series and ensuring the high-quality results represented here. I would like to thank board members Lawrence Fogli, Nita French, Catherine Higgs, Allen Kraut, Edward Levine, Kenneth Pearlman, and Walter Tornow. I am also grateful to the Society for Industrial and Organizational Psychology for sponsoring the series and supporting this volume.

December 1998   MANUEL LONDON
State University of New York   *Series Editor*

Preface

This book originated with several conversations not long ago about how the world of work has changed since we entered it a few decades ago. Some of these talks took place with colleagues in school hallways, others at professional meetings or in clients' offices. Much of what we spoke of was obvious in the daily headlines; topics varied from layoffs where there had never been any before to the creation of and recruitment for exotic new occupational specialties. Far more interesting but far less obvious was the enormous change going on in the practice of human resource management (HRM) and the areas of industrial-organizational (I/O) psychology that support or influence HRM.

A few publications pointed in a deeper and more meticulous way to some of these changes. Examples include Howard's edited volume on *The Changing Nature of Work* (1995), Bridges's intriguingly titled book *JobShift: How to Prosper in a Workplace Without Jobs* (1994), and professional symposiums like Pearlman's *Is "Job" Dead? Implications of Changing Concepts of Work for Industrial-Organizational Psychology Science and Practice* (1995). Clearly, something was in the wind.

There is little argument that fundamental changes have taken place in the world of work, especially during the last two decades. These changes are transforming HRM. Downsizing, growth of part-time and contract jobs, telecommuting, and the renewed emphasis on "employment at will" agreements have all generated a new work environment. These changes are fueled by increased competition, globalization, and high rates of technological innovation.

These factors are having dramatic impacts and will continue to do so, pushed by the realities of a more diverse workforce and the growth of two-paycheck families and single-parent responsibilities. All of this has created a world of work characterized by high levels of anxiety and uncertainty, temporary relationships, decreased mutual commitment between employers and employees, and less emphasis on long-term career growth sponsored by employers.

However, although many of the bedrock assumptions about jobs, careers, and work in America have been transformed—probably forever—what is not clear at this time are all the implications of these changes for the most basic assumptions and practices of human resource (HR) managers. These assumptions and practices often mirror the views and activities of the I/O psychologists who lead and support HR managers.

In this book we explore the changes that have been taking place and the impact they have had (and will have in the future) on HRM concepts and practices. In particular we share the views of working I/O psychologists who so often play a key role in thinking about and shaping these practices. Our goal is to examine the impact of these environmental and technological changes on the concepts and practices used by HR practitioners and I/O psychologists as both groups try to enhance organizational effectiveness and employees' sense of personal and social fulfillment through work.

Audience

We think the audience for this book falls into three groups:

- *HR executives, generalists, and specialists* who want to gain a more sophisticated perspective on these issues and be in a position to enhance their future activities.
- *I/O psychologists,* both researchers and practitioners, who are facing the new challenges. Among these may be consultants, internal staff members, and faculty members conducting research projects.
- *Faculty and students* in fields where these issues are likely to be addressed, including those in graduate and advanced undergraduate courses in organizational behavior, I/O psychology, and industrial and labor relations.

Overview of Contents

A few of the chapters in this volume are conceptual in orientation, exploring the fundamental changes taking place but with an eye to the affected HRM practices. Most are written by practitioners to illustrate ongoing or completed actual projects that reflect emerging practices and responses to continuing forces for change. The authors try to specify the fundamental concepts and assumptions that guide practice in the areas they discuss, from the past, the present, and the future. They also share "success stories" about new practices that meet the needs of the changed circumstances. Although many of the changes have been dramatic, a number of organizations have responded in clever and effective ways, which are described here.

The first part of the book explores the major forces for change, namely, the shifts in demographics, economics, laws and government regulations, and technology, as well as in attitudes and values, that have had an impact on the world of work. It also looks at some of the overall effects of these changes. In prior years assumptions of long-term employment were sometimes so encompassing that they were described as "womb to tomb." But changes in the world of work have had a significant effect on work-related motivation and employer-employee expectations. New and profoundly different types of psychological contracts are being developed and implemented.

The second part of the book looks at specific practice areas, ranging from the nature of jobs themselves to recruitment and selection. It also examines new ways of working together: in teams, with more worker involvement, with greater diversity in the United States and abroad. Some chapters focus on how performance is managed and how leaders and managers are groomed, developed, and selected to fulfill their evolving roles. All the chapters consider past assumptions underlying HRM practice and what has changed to make new practices desirable.

The last section looks to the future, including a chapter on how to help organizations cope with the extraordinary impact of downsizing, mergers, and reorganizations. The unique role of organizational surveys in measuring and guiding change is also reviewed. The shifts in the use of surveys is a metaphor for much that has happened: a shift from merely assessing employee satisfaction to being a lever for organizational transformation. In the last chapter, Benjamin Schneider looks to the future with the provocative question, "Is the sky really falling?"

Acknowledgments

Many people have helped us bring this volume together. We are thankful for the guidance provided by members of the series editorial board: Lawrence Fogli, Nita French, Catherine Higgs, Edward Levine, Kenneth Pearlman, and Walter Tornow. The series editor, Manuel London, has been especially helpful. In addition, we have been aided in one or more chapters by helpful input from William Byham, Michael Hoppe, Laura Iemma, Angela Lynch, Maria Park, Melvin Sorcher, Anna Marie Valerio, Richard Wellins, and Paul Yost.

We are most grateful for the contributions of the chapter authors themselves. By sharing their knowledge and views with us, these very busy and successful practitioners and scholars will vastly enrich all the readers of this volume.

December 1998   ALLEN I. KRAUT
Rye, New York

ABRAHAM K. KORMAN
New York, New York

References
Bridges, W. (1994). *JobShift: How to prosper in a workplace without jobs.* Reading, MA: Addison-Wesley.
Howard, A. (Ed.). (1995). *The changing nature of work.* San Francisco: Jossey-Bass.
Pearlman, K. (Symposium chair). (1995, Apr.). *Is "job" dead? Implications of changing concepts of work for industrial-organizational psychology science and practice.* Paper presented at the Tenth Annual Conference of the Society for Industrial and Organizational Psychology, Orlando, FL.

The Authors

ALLEN I. KRAUT is professor of management at the Zicklin School of Business, Baruch College, City University of New York, and president of Kraut Associates, a human resource consulting firm specializing in opinion surveys. During his twenty-five years at IBM, Kraut held senior posts in personnel research and management development and was responsible for employee opinion survey research in the United States and overseas. Kraut earned his Ph.D. in social psychology at the University of Michigan. He is a fellow of the American Psychological Society and a diplomate of the American Board of Professional Psychology. In 1995, he received the Society for Industrial and Organizational Psychology's Distinguished Professional Contributions Award for his work in advancing the usefulness of organizational surveys.

ABRAHAM K. KORMAN is the Wollman Distinguished Professor of Management at Baruch College, City University of New York. Earlier, he was on the faculty of the University of Oregon and New York University. He is the author of seven books and over fifty articles in the areas of work motivation, leadership, executive stress, and intergroup relations in work settings. He has served as a visiting faculty member at universities in Great Britain, China, Israel, Egypt, Canada, the Netherlands, South Africa, and France, and has made many presentations to professional and managerial groups worldwide. He has over thirty years experience as consultant to such companies as Amstar, Beatrice Foods, Fairchild Industries, RCA, IBM, American Airlines, Unilever, and the *New York Daily News*. He holds a Ph.D. in industrial psychology from the University of Minnesota.

Cristina G. Banks is a principal and co-owner of Terranova Consulting Group (formerly Human Resource Solutions), a full-service management consulting firm. She holds a doctorate in industrial-organizational psychology from the University of Minnesota (1979) and has twenty years' experience in management consulting. The former director of undergraduate programs, she is currently a senior lecturer for the Haas School of Business at the University of California, Berkeley, and is also director of corporate communications and programs for the Center for Organization and Human Resource Effectiveness (COHRE) there. A past president and founder of Leadership California, a nonprofit organization designed to develop and promote women leaders in California, she now serves as a director on the board of Whole Foods Market. Banks also teaches in international executive education programs human resources and is an active member of several professional organizations, including the America Psychological Association, the Academy of Management, the Society of Industrial-Organizational Psychology, and the Northern California Human Resources Council. Her research interests include strategic planning, performance management, organizational change and restructuring, executive development, and leadership.

Gerard A. Callanan is a vice president with the Federal Reserve Bank of Philadelphia. He also serves as an adjunct assistant professor of management at Rider University. He received his Ph.D. in organizational psychology from Drexel University (1989). A member of the Academy of Management, his research has appeared in the *Journal of Vocational Behavior* and *International Journal of Career Management*. He is the coauthor (with Jeffrey H. Greenhaus) of the second edition of *Career Management* (Dryden Press, 1994).

Scott L. Eggebeen is director, People Processes & Systems, Booz Allen & Hamilton, and is active worldwide in state-of-the-art human resource management, organizational development, and change. Eggebeen is also an adjunct professor at New York University. He was formerly vice president, Executive Resources, at Merrill Lynch and staff director, Research and Mechanization, at NYNEX. He has extensive experience in succession planning, executive assessment and development, testing, employee opinion surveys, appraisal, compensation, and employee relations, and is an active member of the American Psychological Association and the Metropolitan

New York Association for Applied Psychology. His Ph.D. in psychology is from Columbia University.

John R. Fulkerson is currently vice president of organization capability and training at Kmart Corporation. From 1983 to 1997, he held various positions as a vice president with PepsiCo. He is professionally focused on issues related to leadership and organization capability and change. He received his Ph.D. from Baylor University.

Cristina B. Gibson is research assistant professor of management at the Center for Effective Organizations at the University of Southern California. Gibson's research interests include communication, interaction, and effectiveness in teams; the impact of culture and gender on work behavior; social cognition; and international management. She has contributed to numerous books on human resource theory and practice and her research has appeared in the *Journal of Management, Journal of International Business Studies, Journal of Cross-Cultural Psychology, International Executive, Advances in International Comparative Management,* and *Journal of Managerial Issues.* She is the recipient of numerous awards recognizing her research, including grants from the Thomas J. Watson Foundation for International Research and the Carnegie Bosch Institute for Applied International Management. In 1996, she received a four-year research grant from the National Science Foundation to investigate the implementation of teams in multinational corporations.

Jeffrey H. Greenhaus holds the William A. Mackie Professorship in the Department of Management at Drexel University. He received his Ph.D. in industrial-organizational psychology from New York University (1970). A member of the Academy of Management and the American Psychological Society, his current research focuses on career dynamics, work-family linkages, and the management of diversity. His research has appeared in the *Academy of Management Journal, Academy of Management Review, Human Resource Planning, Journal of Applied Psychology, Journal of Organizational Behavior, Journal of Vocational Behavior,* and *Organizational Behavior and Human Decision Processes.* Former associate editor of the *Journal of Vocational Behavior,* he is coauthor (with Gerard A. Callanan) of the second edition of *Career Management* (Dryden Press, 1994) and coeditor (with Saroj Parasuraman) of *Integrating Work and Family: Challenges and Choices for a Changing World* (Quorum Books, 1997).

George P. Hollenbeck is a Houston-based consultant in leadership development who has held positions in human resources (Merrill Lynch, New York), executive development (Fidelity Investments, Boston), and executive education (Harvard Business School). He teaches leadership at Texas A&M and Boston University. After receiving his Ph.D. from the University of Wisconsin, he joined IBM. He was a Cattell Fund Fellow at the University of California, Berkeley, and attended Harvard Business School's Advanced Management Program. His writings include *How to Design an Effective System for Developing Managers and Executives* (with Maxine Dalton) and *CEO Selection: A Street-Smart Review,* both published by the Center for Creative Leadership. With coauthor Morgan McCall, Hollenbeck is engaged in studying leadership in international executives.

Bradley L. Kirkman is an assistant professor of business administration in the Joseph M. Bryan School of Business, University of North Carolina, Greensboro. He received his Ph.D. in organizational behavior from the University of North Carolina, Chapel Hill. His current research interests include work team effectiveness, international management, organizational change and development, and organizational justice. His articles have appeared in journals such as the *Academy of Management Journal, Academy of Management Review,* and *Journal of Organizational Change Management,* and he has contributed chapters to *Research in Organizational Change and Development* and *Trends in Organizational Behavior.*

Katherine J. Klein is an associate professor of industrial and organizational psychology at the University of Maryland. She received her Ph.D. from the University of Texas. She serves on the editorial boards of the *Academy of Management Review* and the *Journal of Applied Psychology.* Her research focuses on innovation implementation in organizations and on levels of analysis issues. She has published several articles and chapters on these topics and is currently editing a book, with Steve Kozlowski, on multilevel theory and research in organizations.

Edward L. Levine is professor and chairperson, Department of Psychology, University of South Florida, Tampa, Florida, where he administers one of the largest departments on campus. Over his career at USF he has served also as director of the Ph.D. program in industrial and organizational psychology and as associate chair. He received his Ph.D. in psychology from New York University and is certified as a diplomate in his field by the American Board of Professional Psychology. Levine has conducted research and published widely in such areas as job analysis, communication, and staffing. In addition, he has worked extensively as a consultant and trainer.

Karen E. May is a principal at Terranova Consulting Group and has over ten years of experience as an educator and consultant in the fields of industrial psychology and human resource management. She received her Ph.D. in industrial-organizational psychology from the University of California, Berkeley. She has worked extensively in the areas of employee selection and training, job design, performance appraisal, leadership, work process redesign, self-directed teams, and small business issues. As a consultant to businesses in multiple industries, she has gained extensive experience with human resource problems and works with client organizations to link their human resource decisions and systems to their business strategies. May lectures nationally and internationally in human resource management and executive leadership development for the University of California, Berkeley, Extension Programs, and for California State University, Hayward.

Morgan W. McCall Jr. is professor of management and organization at the Marshall School of Business, University of Southern California. Earlier, he was director of research and a senior behavioral scientist at the Center for Creative Leadership. He authored *High Flyers: Developing the Next Generation of Leaders,* coauthored *The Lessons of Experience* and *Whatever It Takes,* and was a developer of the management simulation "Looking Glass." He received the 1997 Marion Gislason Award for Leadership in Executive Development given by the Executive Development Roundtable at Boston University. He is a Cornell Ph.D. and a fellow of the Society for Industrial and Organizational Psychology.

Joseph (Joel) L. Moses is managing director of the Applied Research Corporation, a leadership selection and development consulting firm he cofounded in 1989. Known for his work on senior level assessment centers while at AT&T, Moses's recent work has focused on identifying leaders for evolving organizations resulting from mergers, acquisitions, and joint ventures. He was president of the Metropolitan Association of Applied Psychology and served on the executive board of the Society of Industrial and Organizational Psychology. A Baylor University Ph.D., he is a fellow of the American Psychological Association and the American Psychological Society and holds a diplomate from the American Board of Professional Psychology.

David M. Noer heads his own consulting and training firm in Greensboro, North Carolina. A leading thinker, speaker, and researcher on leadership and organizational competencies in the new millennium, Noer is the author of a wide range of academic and popular articles, book chapters, and research. Among his five books, the most recent are *Breaking Free: A prescription for Personal and Organizational Change* (Jossey-Bass, 1996) and *Healing the Wounds: Overcoming the Trauma of Layoffs and Revitalizing Downsized Organizations* (Jossey-Bass, 1993).

R. Scott Ralls is the director of economic development for the North Carolina Community College System. In this role he is responsible for coordinating North Carolina's customized job training programs, Small Business Assistance Network, and Worker Training Tax Credit. He received his Ph.D. from the University of Maryland. His previous research has focused on computer training and aging issues, and he is the author of the 1994 Department of Labor report, *Integrating Technology with Workers in the New American Workplace.*

Hannah R. Rothstein is associate professor of management at Baruch College, City University of New York. She received her Ph.D. in industrial-organizational psychology from the University of Maryland in 1980. Before coming to Baruch, Rothstein worked as a personnel research psychologist at the United States Office of Personnel Management, where she conducted research on personnel selection and participated in the development of meta-analytic methods. Her current interests include recruitment, selection, job redesign, and dispute resolution in changing organizational environments.

Lise M. Saari is program director, Global Employee Research, at IBM Corporation. She has strategic responsibilities for employee research and surveys and leads the global team of research and survey experts. Saari earned her Ph.D. in organizational psychology from the University of Washington in 1982. Before joining IBM, she was senior manager, People Research, for the Boeing Company; before that she was research scientist at Battelle Research Institute, where her experiences included research projects in Europe through Battelle's London and Geneva offices and in Asia. She has made a variety of conference presentations, including a Society for Industrial and Organizational Psychology professional workshop on using employee opinion surveys to make breakthrough organizational change. She is on the editorial review board of *Personnel Psychology, Innovations in Research-Based Practice,* and is a former member of the Mayflower Group's board of governors.

Juan I. Sanchez earned his Ph.D. from the University of South Florida, Tampa. He is director of graduate studies and associate professor of psychology at Florida International University, Miami. His job analysis research has been awarded by the International Personnel Management Association and the National Society for Performance and Instruction. He has consulted with private organizations and government agencies in the United States, Europe, and Latin America. Currently a member of the editorial board of the *Journal of Applied Psychology,* he has published in refereed journals such as the *Academy of Management Journal, Journal of Applied Psychology, Journal of Vocational Behavior, Group and Organization Management, Journal of Occupational and Organizational Psychology,* and *Journal of Applied Social Psychology,* among others.

Benjamin Schneider is professor of psychology at the University of Maryland and chair of the Industrial and Organizational Psychology Program. He has taught at Michigan State University and Yale University and, for shorter periods of time, at Bar-Ilan University

(Israel, on a Fulbright), University of Aix, Marseilles (France), and Peking University (People's Republic of China). He holds a Ph.D. in psychology and his academic accomplishments include more than eighty journal articles and book chapters, six books, and appointment to the editorial review board of the *Journal of Applied Psychology* and other journals. His most recent book (with David E. Bowen) is *Winning the Service Game* (Harvard Business School Press, 1995). Professional recognition for his accomplishments include election to president of the organizational behavior division of the Academy of Management, and president of the Society for Industrial and Organizational Psychology. In addition to his academic work, he is vice president of Organizational and Personnel Research, a consulting firm.

Virginia L. Smith-Major is a doctoral student in industrial and organizational psychology at the University of Maryland. She received her B.A. in sociology from Indiana University, Bloomington. Her research interests include work-family conflict, culture and leadership, and organizational diversity.

Michael F. Tucker is president of Tucker International, an international human resource development company headquartered in Boulder, Colorado. Tucker International works with a select group of multinational organizations on issues of expatriate assessment, intercultural training, and multicultural team-building. He is the author of the *Overseas Assignment Inventory*. He received his Ph.D. in industrial-organizational psychology from the University of Utah in 1969.

Changes in the World of Work
Signs and Root Causes

CHAPTER 1

The "DELTA Forces" Causing Change in Human Resource Management

Allen I. Kraut
Abraham K. Korman

The world of work in which human resource management (HRM) operates has changed dramatically in the last half century. Not surprisingly, therefore, the HRM concepts and practices being created and carried out today are also increasingly different from those of the past. Planners and practitioners who understand this and who also have a way to anticipate the coming changes and needed HRM practices of the future will provide their organizations with a strategic competitive advantage.

It is our view that virtually all the changes we see in HRM concepts and practices are in response to changing social, economic, and business environments. We therefore need to understand these influences on our work setting because many of those factors that have affected us in the recent past will continue to do so in the future, though perhaps in different ways. By examining these forces, we will be better able to understand what challenges we need to cope with today and those that are likely tomorrow.

In this chapter, we look at the major forces affecting the world of work. We will also lay out a framework to help examine them. Although much of what we present can be seen as a description of past events, the framework will also be useful as a blueprint for periodically doing an environmental "scan" of the forces that are likely to have an impact in the future.

The Five DELTA Forces

We believe that the significant environmental forces influencing HRM policy and practice fall into five sets:

- *Demographics* refers to those aspects of the quantity and quality of the workforce itself that are determined by birth rates, participation by women and minorities, immigration, migration, and education.
- *Economics* covers issues like the basis of the national economy, productivity and labor rates, inflation, and the increasing importance of competition and participation in a global economy.
- *Legal and regulatory issues* include civil rights legislation and laws covering safety and health, plant closings, and so on, as well as government deregulation in some industries.
- *Technology* involves the obvious and the subtle shifts caused by new products such as computers, fax machines, cellular phones, fiber optics, robots, space satellites, and various drugs and medicines.
- *Attitudes and values* refer to subjects as varied as the psychological contracts formed with employers, notions about careers and commitment, feelings about extending employer benefits to cover unmarried partners, and so on.

These five forces can easily be remembered by the acronym DELTA. This seems appropriate because the symbol for the Greek letter *delta* is used in mathematics to represent change. This five-part framework, as shown in Exhibit 1.1, will help us to grasp the relevant issues. But at the same time, we must recognize that many of these forces are complex and often all are operating at the same time. It may be useful to examine each of them now.

Demographics

The flow of people, recorded in a society's vital social statistics, are major if sometimes invisible forces in our work lives. Trends in the

Exhibit 1.1. The DELTA Forces of Change
on the Human Resource Environment.

Demographics
- Workforce makeup, age, education, gender
- Migration, immigration, birthrates

Economics
- Wage rates, inflation, competition
- Growth, level of development

Legal and Regulatory Issues
- Equal opportunity, safety, benefits
- Labor relations, plant closings, dismissals

Technology
- Communications and transportation
- Computers, lasers, fiber optics, and breakthroughs

Attitudes and Values
- Work ethic, business conduct guidelines
- Loyalty to company, career views

birthrate make interesting social history, but they are also important to human resource planners because nearly all the workers who will enter the workforce during the next two decades have already been born. Birth statistics tell us how many people there will be to employ. For example, Americans born during the low birthrate years of the 1930s formed a relatively small cohort. Yet they entered the workforce during the 1950s and 1960s, a long period of unparalleled growth and expansion in the post–World War II economy. Being much in demand, these workers stepped onto an escalator to career growth and prosperity that often seemed to exceed their individual work achievements. Similarly, we can see important if not always recognized demographic influences on the career patterns of other well-known age cohort groups.

The Baby Boom

Beginning in 1946, returning veterans of World War II started their families in earnest. The extraordinary surge in the population, called *the baby boom,* saw the number of newborns jump from 2.9 million in 1945 to 3.8 million a year later. This high birthrate continued until about 1964. The baby boomers started joining the workforce in the mid-1960s, providing an ample supply and in fact creating much competition for the available openings. Selection of the best available candidates from the many applicants became an important issue. As the baby boomers have aged, their interests and needs have naturally changed. In the year 2000, they will range in age from about thirty-six to fifty-four, with cares and thoughts now on midcareer issues, medical benefits, retirement planning, and fears about Social Security.

The Baby Bust and Increased Participation of Diverse Workers

The shortage of entry-level workers during the early 1990s was foretold by the low birthrate of the 1970s. Starting in 1964, when oral contraceptives became widely available, the birthrate declined significantly and it dropped still more sharply in 1970, when abortion became legal. Thus, the effects of a new technology—contraceptive drugs—and the Supreme Court's legal decision on abortion combined to reduce the birthrate during that decade to an even lower one than in the era of the Great Depression.

The result, called the *baby bust,* means that the children born during the 1970s form another relatively small cohort, again much in demand, as they enter the workforce some two decades later. Combined with a healthy economy in the late 1990s, this situation puts a premium on effective recruitment. In addition, this relative shortage of workers has coincided with and fostered the increased participation in the workforce of certain segments of the population: women, minorities, and immigrants. As a result, the diversity of the American workforce has reached a level unparalleled in our history.

Women

One of the most fundamental shifts in work patterns over the last few decades has been the increased participation of women, a trend documented by rather startling statistics. The number of women in America who are in paid employment surged from eighteen million in 1950 to sixty-five million in 1998, based on data from the U.S. Department of Labor and the Census Bureau. Similarly, the proportion of all women who work has increased over that time from 34 percent to 60 percent, so that women as a percentage of the total workforce have gone from 30 percent to 47 percent of all workers.

Equally remarkable is the range of occupations that women now work in. No longer restricted to traditionally female jobs such as secretary, nurse, and teacher, they have entered all fields in great numbers. Women are found among the professional ranks of accountants, programmers, engineers, lawyers, physicians, managers, and executives and are visible in some traditionally blue-collar jobs, such as police officer and mail carrier. This pattern is also seen in the educational achievements of women who moved from a small portion of academic degrees earned to now make up about half of all college and professional school graduates. The long and short of it is that women are distributed widely throughout the workforce and are there to stay. Rather than taking low-involvement jobs until they marry and then becoming full-time homemakers in an Ozzie-and-Harriet scenario, women have become permanent members of the workforce at all levels.

As a result, there are many more two-paycheck or dual-career families. This in turn has created enormous pressures for flexibility in work arrangements to cope with family needs. It has also led to more employee reluctance to relocate for job advancement and to the need for better child-care arrangements. As a result, even before the states and the federal government created the Family and Medical Leave Act (FMLA), many firms had introduced various child-care support programs, made geographic relocation less of a requirement for career mobility, provided spousal relocation aid, eased rules barring nepotism, and introduced more flexible work schedule arrangements.

Minorities

Ethnic and racial minorities of all backgrounds have also increasingly joined the workforce during the last few decades. In large part, this has come about as traditional discrimination barriers were lowered in response to legislation such as Title VII of the Civil Rights Act of 1964, which forbids discrimination in employment on the basis of sex, race, religion, color, or national origin. HRM has been required to respond proactively to avoid breaking the law in all conditions of employment. This includes recruitment and selection, work assignments, training, appraisal, pay, and promotion. Social enlightenment—that is, a greater acceptance of nonwhites as employees—may have also played a role. And, of course, employers' needs for more people to do the available work has lowered barriers.

Immigrants

Historically, America has been a land of immigrants. This is still so. But it is a surprise to many citizens to learn that during the 1980s more immigrants entered the United States than in any other decade since 1900. In the past, most immigrants to the United States came from Europe. In the last two decades a much higher proportion than previously have come from Asia and Latin America. At the end of the 1990s, this trend is continuing.

The enormously increased diversity of the workforce first made headlines with the publication of Johnston and Packer's *Workforce 2000* (1987). Their report made it abundantly clear that the native-born white men who largely made up the workforce would be increasingly replaced by women, minorities, and immigrants. Although the study was often exaggerated or misquoted, the general thrust of its predictions is proving true. Employers are faced with a diversity in their workforce that is obvious in the workers' appearance but also shows up in their varying work experiences and assumptions. HRM needs to take and has taken the leadership role in many firms in order to promote effective communications and work relationships that may be challenged by this worker diversity.

Economics

Companies today operate in an intensely competitive global economy. For most firms, it has been a huge transition to realize this and operate accordingly. In the years right after World War II, the U.S. economy produced about three-fourths of all the world's goods and services; today it produces less than one-quarter of them. America's economic dominance then, set against the war-weary manufacturing base in Europe and Asia, gave American companies a great advantage in satisfying the enormous consumer demands put on hold during the hostilities. Automobiles, houses, refrigerators, and other such goods could be easily sold, despite qualms about their cost or quality.

For most American companies, this was a highly stable period with relatively little competition. Combined with the command-and-control organizational style that had proven so successful during the war, it led to large bureaucratic organizations mining economies of scale and able to engage in long-range planning. Judith Bardwick (1991) sees this affluence, along with the limited supply of workers born in the 1930s, as leading to a mindset of *entitlement* among management and employees rather than to a more competitive notion of *earning* one's success. This, she notes, is an inappropriate mindset for today's changed circumstances.

Global Forces

By the 1970s European and Japanese plants had been rebuilt, and many new and highly competitive products came in from overseas. Automobiles and television sets were among the most obvious new entrants, and they were soon joined by other well-made and innovative products. The globalization of commerce had begun in earnest. For many American firms that had grown "fat, dumb, and happy," the good times would no longer keep on rolling. Serious competition set in, with market shares being threatened and eroding, and for the first time massive layoffs and cutbacks were seen in industries that had rarely been touched before.

These tradition-breaking layoffs altered the "psychological contract" for many workers (De Meuse & Tornow, 1990). Thousands and thousands of workers were affected, mostly in large companies, during the late 1980s and throughout the 1990s. These shocking downsizings were sometimes euphemistically called "rightsizing," although the effect on the traditional perception of job security was still disastrous. However, not always visible behind the glare of bad-news headlines, an equal number of jobs (if not more) were being created in small and medium-sized companies. All this came about as a result of the increased efforts of companies to respond quickly to competitive pressures. At the same time, the desire to upgrade product and service quality led to HRM being among the leading proponents of Total Quality Management and related initiatives.

Among the effects of this general shift in employment patterns was a much greater willingness to hire people who were already experienced and had the critical and often different skills needed rather than to hire staff right out of college and train them over a longer period of time. Naturally, assumptions about career growth and development were also changing.

Also a result of globalization—at least in part—has been the truly extraordinary pace of mergers and acquisitions over the last two decades. There has been a much greater willingness than in the past to merge related firms and gain market advantages quickly or to acquire desirable organizations and their skills, markets, and products. The need to undertake organizational culture audits and understand how to bring new organizations together rapidly and effectively as result of these trends created important new demands on HRM.

Cost of Labor

The increased global competitiveness is partly responsible for American labor becoming more competitively priced over the last quarter of a century, mainly through stagnation of their wages. In fact, the average American worker earns less today, when adjusted for inflation, than in 1973. The average weekly earnings of non-supervisory workers went down 19 percent by 1995, or almost 1 percent per year. Buying power has actually decreased. Curiously, the average earnings of the typical American family have gone up slightly over that time, about 1 percent in total adjusted for inflation, a trend that is really a reflection of having more two-earner families nowadays than in the past.

One result of these wage trends has been truly extraordinary. Because labor costs are lower here than in their own countries, both Japanese and German auto companies have moved major plants to the United States, giving them a competitive edge in the American market.

But the globalization of commerce has been working in two directions. Just as foreign competitors came to the United States, American firms were expanding overseas. Today, many companies have changed from colonialist *international* firms expanding overseas from a domestic base, to *multinational* firms cloning new versions of themselves in other countries or truly *global* firms where products are made by global teams for global customers. For example, through the use of computer and telecommunications technology, design teams in Ford Motor's European, American, and Asian locations can work around-the-clock on the same project, electronically handing off an ongoing project to colleagues in another continent as the earth rotates.

With increased interaction between staff from different countries, cultural differences have come into play more than ever. The diversity of assumptions and values in different nations has required more training of people on international assignment. It has also raised questions about the applicability of American-based management philosophies in other countries (Hofstede, 1980).

Service Economy

In the meantime, the base of the American economy has shifted from manufacturing to service. From 1950 to 1995, the goods-producing sector shrank from 41 percent to 21 percent of the total, while the service-producing sector of the economy grew to 79 percent of all jobs. This shift has greatly reduced the proportion of jobs that require low-skill workers and increased the need and opportunities for highly literate and well-trained, technologically sophisticated people. One further effect of the drop in the share of workers employed in manufacturing industries like autos and steel has been the reduction in the proportion and power of unionized workers.

Geographic Influences

A movement related to the long-term drop-off in manufacturing in the United States was the relocation of industry and workers from the "rust belts" of the Northeast and Midwest to the "sun belts" in the West and South. These patterns changed the availability of various skills and the employment rates in different areas. For example, California's Silicon Valley has become a mecca for people in the computer industry.

As a result, companies trying to grow or establish new locations have had to be aware of these shifts in worker accessibility. In fact, companies have had to pay attention in recent years as various states in the Midwest and Northeast changed their taxation and education policies in order to retain and attract workers who might be at risk of loss to the sun belt states.

Legal and Regulatory Issues

Both the daily practice of HRM and its strategic importance are influenced strongly by the nation's laws. Nowhere is this clearer than with the Civil Rights Act of 1964. Over time this law, like many others, has been amended by Congress, extended by the case law arising from court rulings, and expanded by the president's executive orders and the Equal Employment Opportunity Commission's guidelines.

Legislation

Antidiscrimination laws were once said to apply to groups traditionally considered as minorities, but with the extension of related laws to protect women, workers over age forty, Vietnam-era veterans, and the disabled, now a majority of workers are protected. Thus, in practice, attention to fairness and nondiscrimination in all aspects of employment is required as "a way of life" for *all* employees in an organization. As these laws open up violators to large financial penalties, the stakes are quite high, and in most firms it is HRM that has taken on the responsibility to ensure compliance. As a sign of HRM's success, many of the actions taken to avoid discrimination, once seen as novel, have become a way of life. This has also been true in the past for other laws. HRM practices regarding child labor, minimum wages, and payment for overtime, considered revolutionary when the Fair Labor Standards Act was first passed in 1938, are standard today.

Many other laws approved in recent decades have profoundly affected the role and function of HRM. These include safety and health practices, funding for retirement and related medical plans, and extension of medical benefits to employees and families of those who leave employment. As a result, HRM has acquired new responsibilities for formulating new practices, educating employees, and keeping extensive records. For example, the increased availability of tax-deferred savings plans (such as 401k's) has given HRM the opportunity to create plans that complement or replace older pension schemes. The government mandate for firms to provide access to health maintenance organizations (HMOs) has been another new responsibility.

Other legislation, such as that requiring early warning of major plant closings, has forced HRM into greater involvement with business planning that may affect employees. Laws and court cases concerning a variety of other issues, such as employee privacy, genetic screening, and illnesses such as AIDS, have had similar effects.

Deregulation

The deregulation of the 1970s in such industries as the airlines and trucking gave rise to many new, low-cost entrants to these businesses. Because many of the new firms were nonunionized and offered lower wages, competition increased greatly while at the same time high wage rates could no longer be as easily passed on to consumers. Two-tier wage systems therefore arose, with new hires being paid a lot less than their predecessors.

Even in unionized companies new work patterns had to be devised to enhance competitiveness. The successful example of Southwest Airlines is generally well known. That company's changed work practices encouraged workers to pitch in wherever needed, so that gate agents and even pilots might move baggage if that were desirable. The breakup of AT&T into multiple companies gave rise to many new firms in the telecommunications industry, and vastly expanded competition. In the near future we will see similarly deregulated competition breaking out among the electric utilities. Here, too, we can expect that HRM will play a key part in trying to gain competitiveness as legal and regulatory requirements change.

In recent years, some deregulation has changed entire industries. For example, the financial services area has been drastically altered, with a blurring of traditional lines between banking, stock brokerage, and insurance activities. This has caused some firms to expand into new product lines and also allowed many mergers of previously unrelated companies. HRM has become heavily involved in combining work activities into new jobs and work groups, with all the related issues such as selection, training, and performance management. In addition, the integration of differing HRM systems among the combined organizations has become a challenge for the affected firms.

Technology

Advances in electronic technology have changed how we work in ways that were scarcely imaginable just twenty years ago. The increased power and lowered cost of computing have made computer chips ubiquitous, increasing our capability for moving masses of information more swiftly, accurately, and cheaply than ever before.

For example, to maximize profit airlines can practice "yield management," based on models of likely sales on a particular flight in different price categories. Combining historical and projected data, they can monitor real-time inputs to price the remaining seats in a way to attract more travelers at the highest prices and fill their seats. Also in an attempt to enhance efficiency, airlines can combine data about the number of passengers and the weight of their luggage on a specific flight as the passengers are boarding, match this information with the temperature and wind conditions applying to that flight, and determine how much fuel is required and even whether any passengers need to be shifted to other seats to balance the plane better. All this is done before the plane's doors are closed for takeoff. It has important implications for staffing, job demands, and training requirements.

Creation of New Jobs

The PC industry itself has become a huge new part of our economy. It is an industry where the type of selling has changed from one of a relatively low volume of high-priced computers to a high volume of low-priced PCs that are sometimes similar enough to other companies' products as to be interchangeable commodities. The industry now often uses entirely new distribution channels, such as retail stores and telephone sales, rather than employing dark-suited sales representatives to call on major companies. To help in these efforts, HRM has had to look at very different types of employees working in different ways. Among them may be articulate but invisible teleworkers who take orders in remote telephone call centers and have working hours that are adjusted to peaks and valleys in call volume from across the nation.

The use of computers has had an impact on every element of how we work, from data preparation, analysis, and presentation to the determination of who sees what data and when. The effect has been to make many things easier and quicker to do, and to provide people with much more (and more useful) data than ever before. This has expanded the need for people in some jobs, such as programmers and systems managers, at the same time it has minimized the jobs of others. For instance, with so much correspondence now being done through e-mail, where addressees respond through their own keyboards, the number of secretaries has been declining.

Organizational Architecture

Some pundits note that computers have changed the structure of organizations themselves. Nadler and his associates (Nadler, Gerstein, Shaw, & Associates, 1992) have observed that information gathering and disseminating used to be among the critical tasks of middle managers in most organizations. With computer-based networks doing much of this work, the need for middle managers has declined. Moreover, computers allow organizations to be designed with entirely different structures. Just as the emergence of structural steel, elevators, and better plumbing permitted twentieth-century buildings to be redesigned in totally new ways, computers and other devices for communicating more widely and quickly permit new and rapidly changing forms of organizational structure to be considered. Flatter, more complex, and even short-term or ad hoc virtual organizations are real and frequent occurrences.

The availability of vastly improved technology has also changed powerful imperatives guiding business. In prior years, *cost* and *quality* were the common mantras. With the pressure of competition and the availability of novel technology, an important new consideration is *cycle time*—the amount of time it takes to create and produce a product or service. In order to meet or exceed your competitors' offerings, you must create new ones in less time than ever. If the cycle time to make a Japanese car is thirty-six months, an American manufacturer's forty-eight-month cycle time means it can never catch up with its competitor.

This has led to entirely new ways of looking at how business operations are conducted. Often called *reengineering*, this is a way of looking at the process by which work gets done and not just accepting the traditional collection of jobs assembled to do the work (Hammer & Champy, 1993). HRM has become one of the key players in reexamining and revising how work gets done. Jobs formerly done by various people have been combined and recombined. Departments as well as jobs have undergone dramatic transformations. The result has been radical change in the makeup of many jobs. Instead of job analyses defining what a worker does, work process analyses are the tools that define work activities. It has also led to many more cross-functional teams, cutting across narrow specialties, to focus on optimum ways to create the total product or service.

Flexibility

The availability of faxes, e-mail, laptop computers, cellular telephones, voice mail, and overnight delivery services has enabled people to work easily from remote locations. The traditional "road warrior" now has more weapons to be effective, to stay in touch with colleagues and vital databases. With this equipment, people can also enter into new work relationships, such as telecommuting from home or satellite locations, and gain more flexibility in work schedules. Under pressure from employees for more flexibility to help them balance work and family obligations, innovative HRM staff in many companies have worked out and continue to explore new ways for people to work.

Attitudes and Values

One subtly occurring change in values has been the gradual recognition that competition has given customers a real choice of what products and services they can buy. The recognition of this new consumerism, with its higher expectations and ability to make better informed choices, has often been translated into a concern for and emphasis on customer satisfaction. Again, HRM has taken a lead role in many firms in educating workers about the importance of customer satisfaction.

Attitudes Toward Work

Attitudes have also changed remarkably about the nature and length of the relationship between companies and their employees. Long-term employment security is no longer promised or implied, and this has changed the degree of mutual commitment that employees and organizations feel toward one another. The consequences are paradoxical for many companies. On the one hand, they want to be freer to shed employees who are not needed; on the other hand, they want to encourage needed employees to stay as long as possible. But employees who know they have no long-term security are often busy looking for better opportunities. Instead of a long-term relationship or even a "marriage," both employees and companies can wind up in a "dating game" as they look for short-term selfish advantage. As an HRM strategy in tight labor markets or when employees with rare skills are involved, some firms have committed themselves for specific contracted periods or offered stock options and incentive-based schemes to hang on to desired individuals.

Nevertheless, at least one organizational survey consortium reports that employee attitudes on job security have become much less favorable in all companies over the last decade, even as other attitudes have remained relatively constant (L. Saari, IBM

Corporation, private communication with the authors, January 1998). As several commentators have noted and as the chapters by Noer and others in this volume note, the *psychological contract* has changed (De Meuse & Tornow, 1990; Rousseau & Wade-Benzoni, 1995). One noticeable effect of this change is in college recruiting, where companies no longer promise long-term careers and actually use "signing bonuses" to get the most talented graduates to join them. In other words, short-term payoffs are being used to make up for long-term inducements.

Nonwork Obligations

Most companies now see family responsibilities as a more acceptable counterpoint to work obligations. Many employees desire flexible work schedules and supervisor support for emergencies and use these criteria to select employers when there is a choice. Some books have become best-sellers because they rate and describe "the best places to work" (Levering & Moskowitz, 1994).

Underlying realities that have helped give voice to such concerns include changes in marriage patterns. Divorce rates have gone up substantially during recent decades, leaving many women dependent on their own efforts for economic well-being and creating many more single parents than in the past. (In addition, unmarried women are more likely to keep their children, eschewing abortion or adoption.) For single parents, work is an economic necessity but it also competes with family for time and energy.

In a related phenomenon, age at first marriage has increased by almost a year per decade for the last half century, so that it is now about twenty-four for women and twenty-six for men. With this shift, many couples now live together without benefit of the clergy's blessing. Their concerns include many mutual career decisions, which may affect accepting a job or relocating. In recent years, this concern has sometimes emerged as a desire for company benefits to be extended to domestic partners. This has been especially noted when homosexual partners, who do not have the option of legal marriage, want such coverage. The open expression of such living arrangements and sexual orientations by workers represents another major shift in attitudes and values.

Outdated Assumptions

This review of the environmental forces affecting industry and HRM indicates that many of the assumptions made in the past about people in the work setting are no longer valid. If the assumptions are no longer valid, then the concepts and practices based on them may also be invalid.

As we indicated in our opening discussion, many of these assumptions arose in the 1950s, and it is these beliefs that need to be reexamined and reevaluated. The following are *outdated assumptions* about the operating environment in most organizations today:

- The competitive environment is stable, with control over new product introduction and no undue pressure for innovation or short development and manufacturing cycle times.
- Jobs are well defined and slow to change, with clear relationships to other such jobs on the career ladder.
- Employment relationships are long-term ("womb to tomb").
- The psychological contract exchanges long-term security and gradual advancement for employee loyalty and sacrifice.
- Workforces are relatively homogeneous, largely white and male.
- Most families are one-paycheck, leading to a "family" orientation, so workers have total dedication to company for overtime, relocation, and so on.
- Organizations are made up of functional "silos" with long time horizons for employee development and there is relatively little need for intergroup cooperation across different functional specialties.

Today's Assumptions

The changes in the environment we have noted, which most companies operate in today, have required a new set of assumptions that are more appropriate for the times and that generate new HRM concepts and practices. These new assumptions may be subdivided according to their application to organizations and to individuals.

Organizations today contrast in several respects with those of the past. The shifts are evident in corporate forms and dynamics:

- More than ever, organizations are likely to be fluid, continually changing, and have many new relationships, from joint ventures, alliances, and partnerships to use of vendors and subcontractors (Greller & Nee, 1989).
- Embattled organizations are continually under pressure to increase outputs, improve cycle time, enhance competitiveness.
- A focus on short-term achievements is an imperative. Corporate acquisitions may often be seen as a better bet than undertaking long-term product development.
- Important skills and talent are to be hired as needed rather than developed internally over a long period. Conversely, unneeded employees should be quickly converted or disposed of.

Individuals have been greatly affected by the signals employers send them. Many of these new attitudes are brutally and acerbically depicted in Scott Adams's comic strip series *Dilbert*. The popularity of the syndicated comic strip and several books about Dilbert (Adams, 1996, for example) testify to the fact that many employees have a less than benign view of their employers. It seems fair to say that many workers now operate (or should operate) with the following assumptions:

- Expect few long-term commitments from employers.
- Accept that career development is mostly your own responsibility.
- It is a good idea to keep a "parachute" handy (through an up-to-date resume and a network of contacts).
- When it comes to job skills and experiences, there is a need for continuous development.
- In general, a certain amount of distrust and suspicion about employers is probably wise.
- Expect and seek quicker advancement when you merit it and don't depend on mere length of service or employer beneficence.

Conclusion

HRM concepts and practices arise from a complex set of forces that form the operating environment for the organizations HRM serves. When the environment is stable, many of the changes are determined by the organization itself, often in a desire to give itself a competitive advantage in attracting, retaining, and motivating employees. Sometimes the concepts and practices arise out of the company founder's personal philosophy and preferences. But the environment has not been very stable during the last two decades.

Many of the operating assumptions on which HRM operates have been severely but gradually challenged in the last two decades in a series of inexorable changes. As a story popular in some management circles puts it, a frog dropped into a pot of boiling water will instantly jump out. But if the frog is placed in a pot of cool water that is gradually brought to a boil, the frog will simply grow warmer and doze off until it is too late. It is the suddenness of change that makes it vivid for people as well.

Many of the shifts noted in this chapter have taken place gradually and in different spheres, and they may not have been given sufficient notice at the time of their occurrence. But when we look back over the last twenty-five years, it is obvious that many principles that were simply taken for granted are no longer true. This is as dangerous for us as the slowly warming pot is for the frog. To be effective, it is necessary for HRM concepts and practices to be lined up with assumptions that are based on the reality of our environments.

For organizations to assess their environments accurately it is useful periodically to go through a disciplined scan of their current and expected environments. In fact, many large firms and some consortia conduct environmental scans on a regular basis. This certainly seems like a healthy practice. We believe that a useful framework for doing environmental scans is one that looks at the DELTA forces around us, that is, the demographics, economics, legal and regulatory issues, technology, and attitudes and values. These are the forces that have greatly affected us in the past and seem the right places to look to for future change.

References

Adams, S. (1996). *The Dilbert principle: A cubicle's-eye view of bosses, meetings, management fads, and other workplace afflictions.* New York: Harper-Collins.

Bardwick, J. M. (1991). *Danger in the comfort zone: From boardroom to mailroom—How to break the entitlement habit that's killing American business.* New York: AMACOM.

De Meuse, K. P., & Tornow, W. W. (1990). The tie that binds has become very, very frayed! *Human Resource Planning, 13,* 203–213.

Greller, M. M., & Nee, D. M. (1989). *From baby boom to baby bust: How business can meet the demographic challenge.* Reading, MA: Addison-Wesley.

Hammer, M., & Champy, J. (1993). *Reengineering the corporation: A manifesto for business revolution.* New York: HarperCollins.

Hofstede, G. (1980). Motivation, leadership, and organization: Do American theories apply abroad? *Organizational Dynamics, 9,* 42–63.

Johnston, W. B., & Packer, A. (1987). *Workforce 2000: Work and workers for the twenty-first century.* Indianapolis, IN: Hudson Institute.

Levering, R., & Moskowitz, M. (1994). *The one hundred best companies to work for in America.* New York: NAL/Dutton.

Nadler, D. A., Gerstein, M. S., Shaw, R. B., & Associates. (1992). *Organizational architecture: Designs for changing organizations.* San Francisco: Jossey-Bass.

Rousseau, D. M., & Wade-Benzoni, K. A. (1995). Changing individual-organization attachments: A two-way street. In A. Howard (Ed.), *The changing nature of work* (pp. 290–322). San Francisco: Jossey-Bass.

CHAPTER 2

Motivation, Commitment, and the "New Contracts" Between Employers and Employees

Abraham K. Korman

Most knowledgeable observers in the field of human resource management (HRM) would agree that its major development as a profession came during the half century or so between the end of World War II and the early 1990s. As organizations employing as many as hundreds of thousands became dominant influences in the world of work and as questions about selection, training, work motivation, and compensation practices became more challenging in a growing, dynamic society, the need for professionally trained, skilled personnel became great. Also, despite occasional downturns in the economy, the professional growth of HRM took place against a general culture of prosperity, a belief that such good patterns would continue and even improve, and an assumption that work organizations should and would share in such growth.

Important too as HRM developed during this era was that the policies and practices developed and implemented were based in large part on the assumption that a desire for personal growth was the most important motivational characteristic of the workforce, along with the belief that more of everything (particularly economic outcomes) is better. Korman (forthcoming) has referred to this pattern as *self-enhancing* motivation and has cited as illustrative of this type of motivation such actions as making choices that match and fulfill one's personal needs, engaging in activities that foster self-growth, attempting to attain high levels of work performance, and working for goals that legitimately enhance oneself in one's own eyes and those of others. Given the cultural context and the assumption of the dominance of this type of motivational pattern, it was a relatively short step for HRM professionals during this era to develop a perspective that reflected them. Characteristic programs of this type included job enrichment, career management and career development, self-appraisals and peer performance appraisals, and income incentives of various kinds.

Less significant as an influence on HRM during this era but still of some importance were programs based on what Korman (forthcoming) has called *self-protective motivation*, defined as the desire to defend oneself from perceived threatening environmental and personal forces that might affect one's sense of identity. Korman suggests that it is this motivational force that underlies the need for personal and job security. Despite its importance, however, this need was generally viewed as less important than employee needs for growth, development, and achievement during the years of prosperity.

There were several reasons for this difference in emphasis. One factor, certainly, was the prosperity and the continued expectations of same. It was not a climate that generated a sense of anxiety, whether warranted or not. Second, the strength and membership of labor unions—organizations that have traditionally made job security a keystone of their efforts—were declining. With the assumption of continued prosperity and the weakness of labor unions, human resource (HR) managers and their allied professionals, such as industrial-organizational psychologists, worried less about providing job security than about providing the opportunity for growth, development, and achievement. Third, theorists on motivation in work organizations generally had a low level of interest in such concepts as anxiety, even though important research findings were beginning to be reported on the significance of such related variables as fear of failure in performance settings (Atkinson, 1964). Instead, theories were popular if they saw people as growth-oriented (for example, Argyris, 1957), desiring meaningful work achievement (McGregor, 1960), and interested in attaining both intrinsic and extrinsic goals (Vroom, 1964; Hackman & Oldham, 1976).

Nevertheless, despite these influences, there was some concern even during these years about providing a greater sense of security for employees. Prominent among those expressing such interest was Frederick Herzberg, an important management writer (Herzberg, Mausner, Peterson, & Capwell, 1957; Herzberg, Mausner, & Snyderman, 1959) who saw in the reduction of anxiety that came with job security a significant approach to reducing job dissatisfaction. In addition, although their membership continued to decrease, labor unions and their emphasis on job security did not totally disappear from the work scene. Far from it. Unions remained strong in some areas, particularly the federal, state, and local civil services, and their presence did much to ensure that job security remained on the table as an employee concern, at least in some instances.

There were, then, these two patterns of HR practice. One, the more influential, assumed that the more important motivational patterns were desires for growth, development, achievement, and self-enhancement. The second, less significant as an influence, assumed desires for job security and self-protection. Both were recognized, and both influenced HRM practices. Less recognized was that the disparity in influence of these patterns of practice encouraged another important underlying assumption. This assumption was that HRM policies and practices could be developed in a manner that would enable the attainment of two goals. The first of these goals was to help organizations obtain their objectives. The second was that HRM could help employees meet their most important needs because the employees' desire to attain positive outcomes (both intrinsic and extrinsic), that is, self-enhancement, and their willingness to work for them were congruent with organizational needs for effective performance. Furthermore, this congruence could be maintained and encouraged because of the continuing expected affluence. In contrast, rarely if ever discussed was that these practices and policies and the assumed congruence between employer and employee depended on these assumptions of continued prosperity and that other approaches would become necessary if the situation changed.

The New World of Work

Now that time has come. A new and different world of work has begun to emerge, one that exists alongside the traditional work setting and that may eventually come to supplant it. It is a world characterized by at least three major trends that have implications for HRM.

- First, *downsizing* is now a frequent key component of managerial decision making, with all the potential short- and long-term anxiety-inducing effects on employee motivation that we would expect.
- Second, the *work-family conflict* is an endemic part of the lives of both employers and employees.
- Third, we live in a world marked by the *extensive use of temporary workers,* part-time employees, and outsourcing.

My goal in this chapter is to examine the effects of these newer trends on work motivation and to propose some of their implications for HRM practice.

Workforce Reduction

Downsizing has become so much a part of the world of work during the past decade that it is a term familiar to almost all who work or who wish to. Table 2.1 lists some of the more dramatic illustrations of downsizing that have occurred in American corporations during the past five years.

Downsizing is a phenomenon that continues to this day. Some of the more recent downsizings announced in 1997 are Eastman Kodak (10,000), Fruit of the Loom (7,700), and Levi Strauss (6,400). Perhaps even more dramatic are the declines in some of the biggest companies. AT&T has shrunk in part as a function of court-ordered divesting but also through downsizing, from 313,000 employees in 1993 to 128,000 in 1998 (Scheisel, 1998). IBM has gone from about 410,000 employees in recent years to approximately 225,000. Downsizing is a fact of the world of work that influences the lives, attitudes, and emotions of millions. That other jobs are

**Table 2.1. Examples of Downsizing Among
Major American Corporations in the 1990s.**

Company	Number of People Let Go
Bell South	11,300
Boeing	12,000
Chemical/Chase	12,000
Citicorp	9,000
CNA Financial	6,000
International Paper	9,000
Kimberly-Clark	6,000
Kmart	6,449
Lockheed-Martin	15,000
Woolworth	9,200

Sources: New York Times, Mar. 22, 1994, p. 19; *New York Post,* Dec. 14, 1995, p. 44;
New York Post, Nov. 18, 1997.

continually being created—and they are—may not significantly affect those concerned about their long- and short-term job prospects.

Work-Family Conflict

Also part of this new world of work is conflict with the family, an inevitable fact of life as our society is increasingly characterized by women in the workforce, dual-career couples, and single-parent families. The increasing presence of women in the workforce contributes to this conflict, a conflict that is among the most serious facing American families and work organizations as we approach the new millennium. It is a problem, both actual and potential, that is becoming increasingly widespread. It is also one of the characteristics of the new world of work that has had and continues to have a major impact on the motivational and attitudinal characteristics of people in the workforce, both men and women.

Noncore Workers

We now also have a work setting marked increasingly by outsourcing agreements between companies, relocation of companies from high- to low-wage areas, globalization, a desire for individuals to develop multiskill capability rather than job specialization, and explosive growth in the use of temporary and contingent employees.

Feelings of ambiguity and conflict have resulted from these changes. On the one hand, there are now new ways for individuals to seek self-enhancement in the world of work, paths that have important implications for the practices and policies HRM may adopt. But on the other hand, the resulting anxiety from these changes has led to a high level of self-protective motivation. The outcome has been a world of work where the two different motivations are assuming equal significance. In other words, it is a world in which the desire and need for security has become as relevant as the need for achievement, growth, and development. It is therefore a world in which both motivational patterns will need to be addressed by HRM, but in different ways than they have been previously.

The remainder of this chapter focuses on meeting these challenges through a two-phase process. Phase 1 proposes new conceptual and attitudinal assumptions for HRM as a field. Phase 2 outlines the types of specific programs that follow from Phase 1 and reflect the changes in the world of work already discussed.

Phase 1: The New Assumptions

HRM needs new and different assumptions on which to base policy and practice. One necessary change, I believe, is to assume no longer that there is a congruence of interests between employees and employers. Sometimes there may be, but sometimes there may not be. Second, we need to assume that the key interpersonal and intergroup relationships in a particular work setting are as likely to be among individuals from different organizations with different investments as they are to be among individuals within the same organization. The following paragraphs elaborate on these recommendations in greater detail.

Because self-enhancement was assumed to be the dominant work motivation during the years of the growth of the field, it is not surprising that HR professionals operated on the belief that it was both possible and desirable to design and implement policies and practices that could and would integrate the goals of both employees and organizations. In fact, one of the major books of this era, and one which served as a sort of conceptual guideline for many, was titled *Integrating the Individual with the Organization* (Argyris, 1964). In a similar vein and serving as further illustration of this assumption of congruence between employer and employee was the growth of job enrichment as a management tool, fueled by the belief that individuals would respond to the challenge of enriched jobs. According to this perspective, the enriched job provided a mechanism for self-enhancement and, in satisfying such desires, the individual would be more highly performance-motivated and contribute more to the attainment of organizational goals.

Now, however, we need to change this assumption. More specifically, we need to view the individual and the organization as separate entities who will be able to integrate their efforts and cooperate with one another under certain conditions but not under others. Furthermore, determining what those conditions might be will be an important objective for HRM professionals in the coming years.

A second assumption about people and organizations during the years of growth and prosperity was that the interpersonal and intergroup relationships HRM needed most to be concerned with were those that took place within the organization, that is, intraorganizational relationships. In other words, the focus was on the relationships between people in different jobs, in different functions, and at different hierarchical levels, but all within the same organization. Although it was recognized that individuals often met with salespeople, suppliers, and others, such meetings with "outsiders" were generally limited to specifically designated occupational groups. Now, however, more attention will have to be paid to relationships between those with primary allegiance to a particular organization and those who may work in that organization but not have primary allegiance to it.

Today, individuals work full-time in an organization to which they have primary loyalty while next to them or with them are individuals on temporary assignments, part-time workers, and people working in joint venture settings and in outsourcing situations. The result may therefore be individuals working together whose allegiances and concerns may involve differences that are highly important to us. Relationships, views, and expectations among those who are all part of one group—or who view themselves as part of the same company or as "insiders"—are different from the types of relationships and communication patterns that develop among those who view themselves as belonging to different groups. For example, Korman (1988) has proposed that in situations in which we find insiders and outsiders, the former are more likely to discriminate and act in a prejudicial manner toward the latter. The result may be unnecessary conflict and sometimes even "tribalistic" patterns, where each group cares only about itself and not about the other or joint goals. Although cases of severe conflict may be extreme—because there are usually some reasons for these different groups and individuals to at least try to work together—the potential for conflict between groups and individuals exists in this new work setting and there will be a need to take account of such possibilities in developing future HRM programs.

These new assumptions, which I believe to be more appropriate for the emerging work setting, suggest the need for new HRM approaches, techniques, policies, and practices that will allow satisfaction of both the self-enhancing and the self-protective motivational processes.

Phase 2: Some Program Suggestions

Programs consistent with the new assumptions need to be developed for HRM as it confronts this new world of work. The remainder of the chapter outlines four such programs, with each discussed in greater detail in the following sections.

- Effective self-career management programs based on the desire for self-enhancement
- Labor pool associations designed to meet needs for both self-enhancement and self-protection

- Performance incentive programs that are not based on organizational commitment, including financial rewards providing direct income as well as health, welfare, and pension benefits
- Insider-outsider training programs

Programs for Self-Career Management

Self-career management programs are designed primarily for those individuals who view themselves as relatively independent professionals or "businesses," rather than as organizationally dependent job holders. These are individuals who can and do make their own decisions about their careers, know their capabilities, and understand where they can find the types of work opportunities where they can "sell" themselves as a business or service. Self-career management is a different way of looking at oneself and one's work capabilities. It is a mechanism for declaring oneself independent of an organizational control system but at the same time being willing to negotiate mutual terms of acceptability concerning work contributions to that system. Self-career management—thus defined as the giving up of relatively permanent organizational relationships in favor of more self-controlled career decision making—has become increasingly recommended to and by HRM professionals as a possible approach to dealing with challenges presented by the emerging world of work, a world still dominated in great degree by the use of downsizing as a management strategy despite continuing questions about its outcomes (for example, Covin, 1993; Kets de Vries & Balazs, 1997).

Clearly, there are reasons for such positive evaluation. Self-career management recognizes the tentative nature of a specific employment relationship while also emphasizing the need for employee skills and meaningful contributions and the opportunity to fulfill the desire for self-enhancement that is so important in the work setting. In addition, for the appropriate individual and the appropriate situation, self-career management also provides an approach to meeting the need for self-protection, because this can be negotiated by the individual involved. The key, however, is in the word *appropriate*. Self-career management is appropriate when the individual has or can develop both meaningful self-knowledge and the types of skills and abilities that are in demand. In addition, self-career management is appropriate when the individual has knowledge of the job market and the freedom to respond to the opportunities available.

A variety of techniques reflect self-career management when it is defined in this manner. Because a number of these are discussed by Callanan and Greenhaus in Chapter Seven of this volume, a review of these approaches will not be repeated here. Rather, my focus will be on the overall role of self-career management as a potential component of HR programs in this new world of work and how its value might be maximized.

Perhaps the most important and first question that needs an answer (for which the HRM professional must provide input) is whether a specific organization should provide financial and other resources for developing and implementing self-career programs for its employees, particularly programs emphasizing personal growth. This is not an easy question to answer. At first glance, there are clearly reasons for companies to undertake such programs. They provide recognition of the frequently temporary nature of contemporary work settings while at the same time encouraging positive relationships between individuals and organizations over the long run. Both of these outcomes may serve the individual and the organization in good stead at once or at some time in the future. In addition, these programs may serve to illuminate and develop skills in the participants not previously realized and thus eventually prove beneficial to the individual and the organization. Finally, such programs help the organization in situations where downsizing may become inevitable. Clearly, preparing individuals to deal with the loss of employment before it happens is to be preferred over sudden notices of termination.

Still, some negative aspects also need to be recognized before a corporate decision is made to undertake a personal growth program encouraging self-career management. One obvious problem is the cost involved. The cost may be considerable, depending on the number of individuals involved and the type of programs chosen. Second, there is the continuing reality that all the benefits the programs may provide to employees may never be of value to the organization that pays for them (and, indeed, may turn out to be of value to competitors). Third, it needs to be realized right from the beginning that such programs are *not* for everyone. They should not be oversold as "the answer" to the problems of the new world of work. Rather, companies need to keep in mind that other programs will be necessary regardless of what they decide about self-career management programs (for more on this, see the following section). To be blunt, self-career management is not and cannot be appropriate for those who have neither the personality nor the technical skills, educational levels, or likelihood of developing the skills to the degree needed to make the approach fruitful. For these individuals, other alternatives will be necessary.

Assuming these pros and cons have been considered and the company decides to proceed with such programs, how might they do so? One possible procedure is to make self-career management programs a voluntary aspect of the HRM process. Such an approach would increase the probability of successful outcomes by making it likely that the individuals participating in the programs possess the skills, abilities, interests, or personality that would enable them to benefit from the programs.

In addition, once the decision to proceed is made, HRM can increase the effectiveness of self-career management programs by generating and making available as much information as possible about the nature of potential and actual career possibilities in a particular job market for those participating in the programs. Self-career management programs are much concerned with personal growth but are not aimed at personal growth alone. They also have career and work-oriented goals. The more work opportunities available that the participant knows about and the more the participant has the time, knowledge, and personal characteristics to carry out a job or career search, the more self-management career programs will be useful. A further advantage of providing job knowledge to those undergoing self-career management is that doing so will help identify those for whom such programs might not be useful, that is, those who will not have job opportunities for the skills they have or are likely to develop. For this latter group, other types of programs will be necessary, perhaps programs of the type we now turn to.

Labor Pool Associations

HRM also needs to begin to develop mechanisms that are appropriate in assisting the adaptation of current and potential employees for whom the concept of self-career management is inapplicable. Among these are the unskilled and semiskilled, immigrant workers, single parents whose job freedom is limited, and people with little growth potential. Two factors concerning these individuals are crucial. First, there are great numbers of such employees and they may, in fact, be increasing relative to the population at large. Second, despite their numbers, economically they are falling farther and farther behind people with higher skill levels, as evidenced by the findings of an increasing disparity in income between those at the higher and lower levels of our population (Uchitelle, 1997; Johnston, 1997).

Yet despite their numbers and this disparity, it is fair to say that little attention has been paid to how the new world of work can meet the needs of these people. For these individuals, basic educational training may have been insufficient, job training opportunities may not be available, and financial resources to keep up skill development may not be there. Also, the habit and encouragement of self-reliance in the occupational sphere may be more foreign to these individuals than those who are higher on the occupational hierarchy. Rather, these individuals may have, perhaps, more of a tendency to rely on traditional employment relationships and organizational reward systems as sources of meeting self-enhancement and self-protection needs. Because the characteristics of the emerging world of work makes this pattern increasingly unlikely, it is even more important to pay attention to helping these groups adapt to the new and different setting.

I suggest a new type of organization be developed with the aid of HR professionals in response to these considerations. Let's call them *labor pool associations*. Such associations can be conceived of as organizations based on cooperative relations among different companies (and perhaps government agencies) that focus on maximizing the human resources available to all of them. As cooperatively managed HR personnel from different organizations, labor pool associations would have several objectives. First, they would keep a continuing registry of individuals and their skills, thus ensuring a labor supply as needed by member organizations, large or small. Second, they would serve as training-retraining-counseling centers for occupational entry and upgrading as desired and available. Third, and perhaps most uniquely, they would serve as "permanent employers" who, besides supplying and making available job and training opportunities, would also provide such "security-type" benefits as health insurance and pension plans. These benefits would be paid into accounts maintained for each individual by the organizations. They would thus replace the security systems traditionally used by organizations, which are increasingly difficult to maintain in this era of downsizing and rapid corporate change.

One step toward this type of organization is the Talent Alliance (TA), an association of companies that has been operating since spring 1997 and includes such members as AT&T, Du Pont, GTE, Johnson & Johnson, Lucent Technologies, NCR, TRW, Unisys, and UPS (Lancaster, 1997). The TA, as Rothstein discusses in this volume in Chapter Four, has several goals. One is to keep individuals employed in companies and settings where they are most needed when they are needed. It is therefore an employee allocation system (or labor pool association) of the type we envision here. A second objective is to increase employee marketability; this is done in a number of ways, including through career growth counselors, training and retraining programs for employees, and strategic planning seminars for corporate management aimed at adapting HR practices to the new world of work.

The TA is, therefore, a step toward the type of organization I suggest here because it has some of the aspects I recommend. However, it lacks at this time a focus on the necessity of meeting the needs underlying self-protective motivation, that is, the desire for the security of health and welfare benefits and pensions. A second possible limitation is that it is designed for the occupational spectrum of relatively big organizations employing large numbers of individuals, a considerable percentage of whom may be at a high technical level. Such organizations are, of course, crucial as major employers and these occupational groups are of legitimate concern. However, I believe that labor pool associations need also be concerned with those individuals who, though working for small, sometimes marginal organizations, nevertheless have traditionally looked to organizations as the mechanisms through which they will meet their needs for both enhancement and protection.

One further note. Labor pool associations may be of value to those for whom self-career management programs are appropriate as well as for those for whom it is not. This is because systems need to be developed to bring individuals and organizations at all levels together for their mutual benefit in this emerging world of short-range assignments as well as long-range jobs and rapidly changing skill and competency demands. Labor pool associations, as we have envisioned them, would satisfy this need.

In sum, we need organizations like the TA and others like it, such as Job Link in Louisville, Kentucky, to meet self-enhancement needs but also to meet the need for self-protection (Richman, 1994). (Job Link is a one-step career center established by the non-profit Louisville Private Industry Council in 1989. It is basically a referral and counseling center that makes training available as a final resort.) We need organizations such as the TA and Job Link because the two major motivations in work settings—self-enhancement and self-protection—increasingly may not be met by individual companies. For some organizations, self-career management will be an appropriate alternative mechanism. However, for others, co-operative efforts like labor pool associations will be needed to help them find qualified workers and to help workers find jobs that meet both self-enhancing and self-protective needs. Key here is the need for cooperative activity among different organizations, including accepting the principle of having these associations serving as an "employer" designed to meet self-protective concerns. This is perhaps a somewhat different perspective from that we are used to, but it is an idea that reflects the new world of work and the needs it has generated.

Nonorganizationally Linked Incentive Systems

Financial incentive systems for performance have long been one of the staples of HRM and there is little reason to think they would or should lose their relevance in the new world of work. On the contrary, they may become even more relevant as other types of in-centives—those that assume organizational links and commitment, such as promotion and transfer opportunities—will become less relevant to those who see their future as falling into the self-career management pattern or who are attaining employment through "labor pool associations."

Purely financial incentives, on the other hand, are not limited to any specific type of setting. Bonuses tied to individual or unit performance are innately transferable (or fungible) and do not have to be linked to any particular organization. That is, the value of financial incentives as mechanisms to self-enhancement are not limited to any particular context and will usually hold their meaning regardless of where they are offered. Financial incentives will, then, retain significance in the new world of work and may become even more significant as the ties of organizational loyalty become less common and less relevant. First, direct monetary income in this changing world of fewer commitments will gain increased significance. Second, incentive programs that enable individuals to meet their needs for self-protection will have increased value. Such needs might be met by developing and applying incentive payments directly into health, welfare, and pension programs even though the employees involved may be temporary workers who frequently change employers. Consistent with the logic underlying the labor pool associations described earlier, HR professionals might well consider developing financial incentive programs using individual "benefit" accounts into which employers (and employees) would contribute based on employment, no matter how temporary or varying that employment might be. These would be financial incentives for performance designed to satisfy self-protection needs by paying into health, welfare, and pension accounts maintained by the labor pool association. In addition to being of value to the individuals involved, such contributions are likely to increase commitment and loyalty to an organization's needs. (One might note that the type of account we are referring to here is somewhat analogous to Social Security accounts. However, there are two major differences. First, these accounts are linked to individual work patterns and individual work behavior in a more immediate manner. Second, these plans focus on health and welfare benefits as much as if not more than pay and pension concerns.)

Insider-Outsider Training Programs

Training programs designed to integrate individuals of diverse backgrounds and views into cohesive work teams are not new. They have been a standard part of HRM programs in recent years as cultural and ethnic diversity has become a major challenge for organizations. Some of these training programs have proved fruitful and some have not.

However, the challenge to HRM here is somewhat different in that the programs we refer to have generally made one major assumption that we cannot make in the new context: that the individuals and groups in these programs, diverse though they may be, all wish to maximize the effectiveness of the same organization, that is, the organization to which they are all committed by reason of employment. In the new world of work, group members may include permanent employees committed to the same organization and work unit as well as temporarily assigned employees who rotate from assignment to assignment within the same organization and are sent to different units with not always consistent goals.

Even more difficult, however, will be dealing with people who are individual contractors or temporary workers who go to different organizations once a specific job is finished. It is not just that there will be changing memberships and changing interaction patterns in these organizational settings. Rather, there are and will also be individuals working together who have different, perhaps even conflicting loyalties. How does one get these groups to work together for some superordinate goal when some are truly insiders and some outsiders?

It is not clear how one proceeds here. Appeals to superordinate goals may not be appropriate over the long run (although they may be for the short run). In addition, the need for emotional cohesion may not be great because the groups may not be conceived of as even quasi-permanent. It is also uncertain which type of development program might be most appropriate and which type of incentive program might be best. One possibility may be the extensive use of financial incentives to integrate such groups into a common effort because financial benefits are not tied to any particular organization or setting. These incentives may be performance-based, perhaps even providing stock options keyed to the length, level, and quality of performance in a particular setting.

We really do not have any answers to these questions at this time, but the potential for conflict between insider-outsider groups within organizations is great, as is the potential for conflict among those with different perspectives who also need to work together, such as suppliers and vendors. Hence, it is in the development of appropriate training and performance incentive programs to meet this need that HRM may make another significant contribution in the new world of work.

Summary and Conclusion

A work setting is beginning to emerge that is radically different from the one that has traditionally provided the context for HRM policies and practices. In this world downsizing is a tool of managerial decision making, work-family conflict is a fact of life for millions and, increasingly, contingent workers, part-time workers, and outsourcing are used. It is a work setting where opportunities to meet self-enhancement and growth needs exist for some individuals but not for all, and where opportunities for self-protection such as job and benefit security are increasingly difficult to come by.

These changes have made it necessary for HRM as a profession to reevaluate its traditional practices and begin to develop and implement programs that meet these needs for self-enhancement and self-protection in the new work setting. This chapter offered illustrations of such programs, including effective self-career management programs based on personal growth principles; labor pool associations for those for whom self-career management is inappropriate; performance incentive programs not based on organizational commitment, including financial rewards of both direct income and health, welfare, and pension benefits; and insider-outsider training programs.

Underlying these recommendations is my view that HRM professionals, regardless of specific training, need to take an active role in meeting the demands of the new world of work. Key to this process is recognizing that the opportunities for meeting and satisfying the primary motivational patterns of self-enhancement and self-protection are no longer what they used to be, whatever level of the occupational spectrum we are focusing on. For the benefit of both organizations and individuals, developing new mechanisms for responding to these changes is a major challenge facing HRM today.

References

Argyris, C. (1957). *Personality and organization*. New York: Wiley.

Argyris, C. (1964). *Integrating the individual with the organization*. New York: Wiley.

Atkinson, J. (1964). *An introduction to motivation*. New York: Van Nostrand Reinhold.

Covin, T. J. (1993, Spring). Managing workforce reduction: A survey of employee reactions and implications for management consultants. *Organization Development Journal, 11*(4), 67–76.

Hackman, J. R., & Oldham, G. (1976). Motivation through the design of work: Test of a theory. *Organizational Behavior and Human Performance, 16,* 250–279.

Herzberg, F., Mausner, B., Peterson R. O., & Capwell, D. F. (1957). *Job attitudes: Reviews of research and opinion.* Pittsburgh: Psychological Service of Pittsburgh.

Herzberg, F., Mausner, B., & Snyderman, B. (1959). *The motivation to work* (2nd ed.). New York: Wiley.

Johnston, D. C. (1997, Sept. 2). Executive pay increases at a much faster rate than corporate revenues and profits. *New York Times,* p. D4.

Kets de Vries, M.F.R., & Balazs, K. (1997). The downside of downsizing. *Human Relations, 50*(1), 11–50.

Korman, A. (1988). *The outsider: Jews and corporate America.* San Francisco: New Lexington Books.

Korman, A. (forthcoming). Self-enhancement and self-protection: Toward a theory of motivation. In H. Thierry, M. Erez, & U. Kleinbec (Eds.), *Individual, group, and cultural perspectives on work motivation.* Hillsdale, NJ: Erlbaum.

Lancaster, H. (1997, Mar. 11). Managing your career: Companies promise to help employees plot their careers. *Wall Street Journal,* p. B1.

McGregor, D. (1960). *The human side of enterprise.* New York: McGraw-Hill.

Richman, L. (1994, June 27). The new force builds itself. *Fortune,* 68–One.

Scheisel, S. (1998, Feb. 8). A leaner company without a crash diet. *New York Times,* p. B11.

Uchitelle, L. (1997, Aug.). Strike points to inequality in two-tier job market. *New York Times,* p. A22.

Vroom, V. (1964). *Work and motivation.* New York: Wiley.

PART 2

Specific Practice Areas
Past, Present, and Future

CHAPTER 3

Is Job Analysis Dead, Misunderstood, or Both?

New Forms of Work Analysis and Design

Juan I. Sanchez
Edward L. Levine

Predictions of a "dejobbed" society—in which the notion of a static job with fixed responsibilities will no longer exist—have received a great deal of attention in the popular press (Bergquist, 1993; Bridges, 1994a, 1994b; Davidow & Malone, 1992). These predictions have also triggered questions about the usefulness of traditional human resource (HR) tools. As one of the very few HR tools that bears the word *job* in its label, conventional job analysis has recently been the object of numerous criticisms. Indeed, it has been accused of being legalistic and establishing rigid boundaries that preclude the type of flexible management that today's dynamic business environment demands (Drucker, 1987; Olian & Rynes, 1991; Young, 1992).

A Future Without Jobs?

Job analysis has certainly had bad press from those calling for innovation in HR management. Should HR practitioners respond to these criticisms by ceasing all forms of job analysis? In this chapter, we argue that the proclaimed obsolescence of job analysis is really the obsolescence of some of the uses that job analysis has served in the past. Without a doubt, the analysis of work—whether packaged into traditional jobs or not—still is and will be a fundamental management tool in a fast-evolving environment. Empirical evidence supports this assertion, suggesting that HR processes informed by work analysis, whether traditional or otherwise, provide value-added for companies that employ innovative management practices (for example, Huselid, 1995). Despite the relevance of work analysis—including numerous features of traditional job analysis—to the transforming conditions experienced by today's organizations, it should be acknowledged that radical changes in the manner in which traditional job analysis is conducted are in order. The term *work analysis* is consistently used in this chapter to emphasize that rather than defining, documenting, and rigidifying job boundaries, the analysis of work should serve to propel the change process. In fact, we advocate using the term work analysis from now on to signify this new focus.

Let us provide a brief road map for the readers of this chapter, which will (1) discuss the basis of traditional job analysis, (2) outline the business trends that have called that basis into question, and (3) propose revisions in traditional job analysis practices in line with these emerging trends. Given the practice orientation of this volume, how-to information will be the primary focus. The chapter will outline how a new approach to the analysis of work may best support HR systems such as selection, training, job design, performance evaluation, compensation, and cost containment.

Before proceeding with a discussion of how this new approach to the analysis of work can facilitate effective management in a dynamic environment, we must critically consider possibly exaggerated predictions of a world without jobs. The renewed emphasis on the "futurology" of a new workplace is not surprising; the Judeo-Christian tradition has always prophesied that the arrival of the new millennium would bring not simply a change of the old order but a complete transformation of social structures (Cohn, 1970). As we approach the year 2000, projections of a new organization of work probably help clarify the new rules of the market and so offer a means to reduce the uncertainty of what some perceive as a new world order.

This chapter too intends to reduce uncertainty about the future. However, because we are not in the prophecy-making business the ideas we report represent our view of the way traditional job analysis must change to serve newly emerging purposes. It is not mere speculation about what the future may bring. The changes of tomorrow's workplace started years ago with the advent of the electronic revolution and the global economy. So instead of attempting to visualize a future landscape that may never materialize, we take the more conservative tack of projecting from changes already well under way. We begin by comparing and contrasting the factors that shaped the job analysis methodology that has been used successfully in the past with their emerging counterparts, which make some traditional forms of job analysis obsolete (see Table 3.1).

The Bases of Traditional Job Analysis Versus Work Analysis

Sanchez (1994) noted how the socioeconomic factors that influenced traditional job analysis are being replaced by new, emerging factors.

Division of Labor Versus Cross-Functional Responsibilities

In the past, the organization of work was dominated by simplified and predetermined job responsibilities that described the "best way" to perform the job. Any deviations from such standard operating procedures were not only unrewarded but at times punished by management and even by labor (Drucker, 1987). In contrast, today's economies of speed demand ever-changing assignments and employee flexibility. In addition, line employees are nowadays called on to perform tasks like quality control that were conventionally reserved for staff employees. The proliferation of downsizing programs, which require survivors to broaden their responsibilities, and of lean, small-sized enterprises, are also forces making boundaries between jobs quite fuzzy.

Table 3.1. Contrasting Factors in Job Analysis.

Traditional Factor	Consequence	Emerging Factor	Consequence
Division of labor and clear-cut labor-management distinction	Preoccupation with job boundary definition and job worth	Cross-functional responsibilities and blurring of labor-management distinction	Diffuse job boundaries and responsibilities
Static jobs	Fixed and long-lasting job requirements	Dynamic work assignments	Work requirements in continuous flux
Minimal interaction with coworkers	Analysis of within-job activities	Maximal interaction with coworkers	Analysis of interactive activities
Accountability to superiors	Importance of incumbent-supervisor interaction	Accountability to internal and external customers	Importance of incumbent-customer interaction
One-way relation to technology	Prescribed job responsibilities	Two-way relation to technology	Self-determined responsibilities
Long-term employment	Static work activities and conditions of employment	Short-term employment	Continuously evolving sets of work activities and conditions of employment
Cultural homogeneity	Emphasis on technical tasks	Cultural diversity	Emphasis on emotional and interpersonal tasks
Tolerance for budgetary slack	Time-consuming analytical procedures	Cost containment	Streamlined analytical procedures

Clear-Cut Labor-Management Distinction Versus Blurred Distinction

Line employees used to be excluded from planning and controlling their own work. The sometimes obsessive preoccupation with detailed job descriptions in the past reflected this adversarial approach to labor-management relations. That is, unions often demanded clearly defined job boundaries to prevent management abuses. The flattening trend observed in today's organizations (fewer management layers, more salaried personnel) fits with the notion of employees assuming responsibilities that were formerly reserved for managers. Because traditional compensation systems offer few incentives for workers to assume enlarged responsibilities within a job, the rise of all-salaried and skill-based pay systems is not surprising. In traditional compensation systems, job analysis provided information about the job that was later used to support job evaluation decisions. It appears that this focus of job analysis needs to shift toward identification of the general sets of knowledge, skills, abilities, and other personal attributes that may be compensable within a framework of enlarged assignments.

Static Versus Dynamic Responsibilities

The economies of scale of the past were based in some settings on stable markets dominated by just a few firms. Job descriptions were long-lasting and the mastery of the specified job responsibilities ensured all the talent needed to perform the job for a long time. In contrast, today's dynamic workplace demands constant changes in responsibilities. In addition, the rapid pace of technological change forces evolving modes of interaction between people and technology, which radically and continuously changes the content of work. For learning organizations adapting to change, job descriptions are likely to be short-lived. Thus, rather than being a once-every-few-years event, a system of continuous work analysis is needed.

Minimal Versus Maximal Interaction with Coworkers

In the past, division and simplification of labor led to isolated workstations, minimal feedback, and little work-related interaction. As a result, job analysis targeted within-job activities rather than inter-actions among staff. The emerging popularity of high-involvement management has resulted in an emphasis on teamwork and self-managed groups. This management philosophy calls for max-imal employee interaction and a cooperative attitude. In contrast to the focus on within-job activities characteristic of traditional job analysis, an emphasis on interactive activities seems necessary under a team-oriented philosophy.

Accountability to Superiors
Versus Accountability to Customers

A hierarchical command-and-control system made the immediate supervisor the party to whom employees were accountable. Su-pervisors were often seen as the only legitimate source of employee appraisals; the thought of having subordinates appraise their su-pervisors often raised eyebrows. Thus, the job tasks that formed the core of employee-supervisor interactions became the primary determinants of employees' performance appraisals and a focus of job analysis. Interactions with other parties, such as coworkers and even customers, took second place in both performance evalua-tions and job analysis. But the ongoing reduction of management layers, together with the management and social trends favoring employee empowerment and a customer focus, have brought re-newed attention to employees' interactions with parties other than their immediate superiors; these interactions have been included in the definitions of *contextual performance* (Borman & Motowidlo, 1993) and *organizational citizenship behavior* (Organ, 1988). These interactions require interpersonal and emotional attributes that have usually been overlooked by traditional job analysis.

In addition to the factors described by Sanchez (1994), the fol-lowing are other contrasting factors calling for new forms of work analysis.

One-Way Versus Two-Way Relationship
with Technology

In the past, technology was imposed on employees who did not have control of the process (for example, in assembly lines). Pre-scribed job responsibilities and little discretion accompanied these jobs, whose description was equally imposed on employees. By contrast, in today's high-tech environment employees often retain control of the process and are allowed to modify it to answer temporary contingencies (such as in just-in-time manufacturing). Flexible technology permits on-line modification of procedures by employees (as in computer-aided manufacturing) who are not the recipients of technology but rather the agents in charge of it. Thus, job responsibilities are often determined by employees on a contingency basis, rather than being externally imposed on them.

Long-Term Versus Short-Term Employment

In the stable economy of the past, organizations often provided assurances, albeit often in an implied manner, of employment for life. Employment stability led to a quid pro quo mentality among employees. Routine jobs seemed more bearable in the face of job security. Changes in job content were rare and, therefore, job descriptions were expected to be long-lasting. In contrast to these long-term employment relationships, today's short product cycles and continuous technological updates demand an ongoing revision of work assignments and consequently of employment conditions (Hall, 1996). Frequent rotation and even geographical relocation are no longer the exception but the rule. As a result, idle job responsibilities portrayed in static job descriptions do not take long to become obsolete. An iterative process of work analysis is needed to keep up with today's fast-evolving work assignments.

Cultural Homogeneity Versus Diversity

A "melting pot" mentality assumed a homogeneous culture and a clearly defined set of social norms. Thus, culturally sensitive interactions and other attempts to manage the emotional aspects of work were ignored or considered superfluous. As a result, job analysis focused on tangible and technical tasks, whereas "softer tasks" involving organizational citizenship behavior such as helping other parties (coworkers and customers, for example) were virtually ignored in job descriptions. Managing the emotional aspects of work (displaying sensitivity to culturally different individuals, for example) is one of today's business necessities, especially in a global market (Rafaeli & Sutton, 1987). Service-oriented work activities centering on managing diversity are considered critical to successful performance and, therefore, should no longer be ignored in work analyses.

Budgetary Slack Versus Cost Containment

The predictability of past business environments contrasts with today's sense of urgency. Budgetary slack or a plenitude of resources permitted detailed job analyses involving multiple meetings and relatively large samples of respondents. But today's fierce global competition has led organizations to streamline their procedures and cost structures. Organizations are reluctant to undertake any activities not viewed as core elements of their competitive advantage. Peripheral activities are often outsourced to subcontractors who can perform them at a lower cost. Along the same lines, professional staff have been reduced significantly and "fat" internal service departments have become rare as professional activities are outsourced to consultants hired on a project basis. As a result, organizations are reluctant to engage in detail-oriented job analyses that need multiple informants and meetings. Such efforts are sometimes seen as superfluous overhead that does not belong in today's lean-and-mean organizations.

In the face of all these changing factors, we maintain that emerging business trends do not proscribe the analysis of work activities. Rather, these trends heighten its usefulness as a tool to reshape organizations striving to meet the new competitive challenges. However, what does seem obsolete are many of the purposes that shaped traditional job analysis, like the detailed documentation of work activities to establish clear boundaries between jobs. Unfortunately, this obsolescence is often interpreted as the obsolescence of the analysis of work per se, whether that be traditional job analysis or the newer forms of work analysis that will be introduced in the next section. This erroneous conclusion should be lamented, because it prevents many organizations from fully utilizing a most powerful tool for change management.

Forms of Job Analysis Versus Work Analysis

To organize this section on the necessary changes in work analysis and design, we use what may be seen as the building blocks of work analysis (Levine, 1983; McCormick, 1976): sources of data; methods of data collection; types of data; and level of analysis. The traditional forms within each category will be compared with the new ways dictated by a changing workplace. In addition, practical examples and applications of the alternatives proposed will be described.

Sources of Work-Analytic Data

Traditionally, job holders have been the preferred subject matter experts (SMEs) in job analysis. But the maximal interaction demanded by new assignments, enlarged and cross-functional responsibilities, and accountability to individuals other than to immediate superiors call for the inclusion of alternate parties, such as internal and external customers, as legitimate sources of work information (Bernardin, 1992). For instance, even though many organizations advocate a customer focus, customers are seldom heard in the process of work design.

The analysis of work activities should serve to pinpoint the primary clients or beneficiaries of each work function; the input of these clients should in turn be solicited in work analysis intended to design the functions. In the retail industry, for instance, it is becoming commonplace to employ focus groups of customers who are consulted on store practices and customer service. However, focus group opinions do not always conform to customer wishes because group dynamics may lead the panel of customers to enunciate imaginary needs. As an alternative to focus groups, corporations like Domino's Pizza, Great Western Bank, and Saks Fifth Avenue rely on professional "mystery shoppers," who regularly visit branches armed with checklists of critical behaviors that employees should display in customer-contact interactions. These mystery shoppers represent an invaluable source of information on the frequency and performance quality of these behaviors, which are thought to have a major impact on customers.

Although alternative sources of work information are no doubt helpful, employees on the front line continue to be the primary source of work data. They possess the most and perhaps the best information about the strengths and weaknesses of current work processes and are therefore best suited to inform others about them. As the following quote illustrates, imposed job descriptions have long neglected this rich source of work information: "My job is to weld the cowl to the metal underbody. . . . My job is all engineered out. The jigs and fixtures are all designed and set out according to specifications. There are lots of little things you could tell them, but they never ask you" (Ginzberg & Berman, 1963, pp. 283–284).

Future assignments that must change in response to uncertain conditions call for the use of panels and other group formats of data collection. Diverse groups representing multiple facets of expertise may outperform individuals in forecasting future-oriented work requirements. The cross-functional nature of many of today's work assignments also demands the representation of various areas of expertise. A project in which one of the authors recently participated involved a high-tech electronics company that assembled panels of individuals from multiple functional areas and remote locations. Working together, these panels were able to identify flaws in current work processes and suggest potential corrections.

Traditional job analysis has assumed that incumbency is a sufficient criterion for the selection of SMEs. However, the nature of work information sought is often overlooked when selecting SMEs. For instance, Jones and others (1997) reported how HR specialists provided more accurate ratings of task trainability than incumbents who, unlike the specialists, were not experienced on training matters. Similarly, judgments of psychological dimensions such as tolerance for stress are often solicited from incumbents. But affective biases are likely to influence ratings of such factors, which should probably be formulated by individuals formally trained in such matters. Because of their sometimes limited exposure to a variety of work environments, job incumbents are not always able to judge the severity of their working conditions. For example, in a recent experience of one of our doctoral students, engine operators working for a cruise line reported that they were not exposed to loud noises at work; a job analyst's visit to the ship's engine room suggested quite the opposite.

The ever-changing nature of work activities reinforces the importance of continuous training and the establishment of a learning organization. Thus, determinations of the trainability of knowledge, skills, abilities, and other personal attributes will be essential. Such judgments may be used to decide between either a selection or a training strategy to ensure the necessary job skills. The incumbents' ratings of difficulty of learning tasks characteristic of conventional job analysis seem unable to meet this challenge because incumbents probably lack experience and expertise on the new systems. The use of external criteria of skill trainability derived in controlled learning situations may be a suitable alternative.

For example, in a project in which one of the authors is involved, a methodology is being developed to facilitate the determination of those components of the job of air traffic controller that should be targeted in selection as opposed to training. The problem is that the job in question does not yet exist because the new traffic control technology is still in the research and development phase. Under such futuristic circumstances, determinations of difficulty of learning need to be based on controlled simulations rather than on conjectures loosely based on an individual's prior job experience. With the constant incorporation of new technology in the workplace, a priori determinations of difficulty of training components will be critical in preventing person-job mismatches. In sum, simple incumbency seems no longer to be a necessary or sufficient selection criterion for SMEs.

Methods of Data Collection

Electronic performance monitoring may provide a rich set of data that is otherwise unavailable. For instance, cable companies are electronically monitoring their mobile maintenance units so that stops and time spent on each service call can be strictly monitored. Truck-leasing companies are installing onboard computers that are synchronized to the truck's engine and therefore able to track speed, idle time, and other important parameters of the driver's performance. In another example, virtually any large or even medium-sized customer service department monitors the calls answered by its telephone representatives using electronic switchboards connected to its phone systems. These data may be electronically stored and analyzed in order to obtain accurate information about parameters that in the past had to be indirectly judged by incumbents (for example, frequency of tasks, number of critical errors per task). However, from a business ethics point of view, electronic performance monitoring is a delicate issue. Indeed, implementation of such systems should attend to employee privacy rights and fair treatment.

Of course, interviews and surveys may be an essential part of work analysis, but the medium through which these are administered is radically changing; note, for example, the increasing use of teleconferencing. On-line surveys are becoming widespread in work analysis, at least among software companies like Microsoft.

We have observed that today's cost-conscious organizations object to the standard job-analytic practice of convening large panels of SMEs. It is not only the large number of incumbents that have to be excused from work that bothers organizations but also the transportation and travel expenses associated with such meetings. Because of global markets, managing remotely is becoming a necessity. For example, in a recent effort to model the knowledge, skills, abilities, and other personal attributes that the managers of its Latin American branches needed, a high-tech company realized that many critical tasks involved managing distant workers. Assembling panels of such remote SMEs is extremely costly.

Although its interactive capacities are still limited, electronic media provide a suitable replacement for face-to-face SME panels. In a recent experience of one of the authors, commercial groupware was used to assemble lists of core skills and associated critical behaviors. Multiple panels of SMEs working independently produced these lists. Panels used groupware to access one another's lists, which were edited until consensus was reached. The time-consuming multiple iterations advocated by group-oriented approaches like the Delphi technique are considerably shortened by the communications capability of electronic media. These and other new technologies can definitely streamline the sometimes tedious process of collecting and refining work analysis data.

Access to electronically stored work analysis data will soon be available not only at the occupational level (for example, the O*NET project being developed by the Department of Labor; Peterson, Sager, & Anderson, 1996) but also at the individual level as more organizations share their results by placing them on their Web pages or by answering ad hoc requests for this type of data posted on the Internet. This virtual database offers a tremendous inventory of just-in-time work analyses and may become an extremely useful departure point for those embarking on similar projects and wishing to benchmark their work analysis practices against industry standards.

Conventional methods of data collection assume that SMEs have prior experience and knowledge of the job. Unfortunately, this assumption does not hold when jobs are new or are being substantially altered. In such cases, no incumbents are available. Several approaches have been suggested to guide the process of future-oriented job analysis. Schneider and Konz (1989) argued that a comparison of present versus future-oriented job-analytic ratings may lend some objectivity to this process. Alternatively, Arvey, Salas, and Gialluca (1992) and Sanchez and Fraser (1994) suggested procedures that rely on empirical linkages between currently performed tasks and worker attributes, like ability to project the new sets of tasks. Assuming that these empirical linkages derived from existing work will hold in the future, information about the tasks involved in the new assignments can be used to estimate the level of attributes demanded by such combinations of tasks. In our opinion, however, unless SMEs have had some prior experience with at least some of the components of the new work assignments, future-oriented ratings may not be useful.

To facilitate realistic projections of future-oriented work requirements, hypothetical scenarios may be put together. Such scenarios should include demographic, social, economic, political, and technological trends (London, 1988, p. 203). Aids such as mental imagery have been proposed to visualize better how future work responsibilities may be constructed. For instance, the job of air traffic controller is changing rapidly with the number of computerized functions. That is, tasks that used to be accomplished from the control tower are being shifted to computer screens operated in a darkroom environment. Although most airports do still heavily rely on the control tower, the pace of technological change is such that by the year 2010 virtually all of these tasks will be performed in a darkroom environment.

To forecast the requirements of tomorrow's air traffic controller, SMEs may be asked to concentrate on the computerized tasks that they currently perform and visualize themselves performing all tasks in a similar manner. Then they should answer questions like, "What will be different?" and "How would this change communications in the control room?" In the near future, expert systems that capitalize on rapid developments in the field of artificial intelligence (Coovert, Craiger, & Cannon-Bowers, 1996) may be able to model SMEs' inferences about future-oriented work requirements.

Types of Data

Tasks and human attributes have been the primary objects of traditional job analysis. To prevent the rapidly obsolete job descriptions that result from excessively detailed, molecular job analyses, some have argued for the use of broader descriptors of both work behaviors and human attributes. In line with this argument, the O*NET project seems to have decided in favor of general worker activities that best resemble the broadly defined sets of tasks or business processes characteristic of today's work assignments (Cascio, 1995). Broader sets of worker attributes (Klimoski & Jones, 1995) that incorporate strategic and team-oriented aspects of work are also needed.

The surge of competency analysis (often referred to as competency modeling) might be explained by this interest in broader descriptors of work requirements. Unfortunately, there is much confusion about what competency modeling actually entails. The term *competency* was made popular by Prahalad and Hamel's influential work (1990) on core competencies, even though these authors referred to organizational rather than individual attributes. Despite their distinct meanings, the terms *competency* and *competence* are sometimes used interchangeably. In fact, whereas competence means demonstrated mastery of or proficiency in a determined function, competency refers to a personal attribute or human capability. Thus, competence assessment involves the observation of worker performance on key work behaviors. Controlled competence assessment in vocational training and employee certification has been refined quite a bit in the United Kingdom (Wolf, 1995). In contrast, because the term competency is closer to a human attribute than to a work behavior, the process of competency modeling appears to signify identifying competencies or broad human attributes needed for performance.

There has been quite a debate about whether competency modeling is superior to or indeed different from traditional job analysis (Barrett & Callahan, 1997; Pearlman, 1997). Perhaps the primary difference between traditional job analysis and competency modeling lies in the level of analysis. That is, competencies are broader sets of human attributes than the narrowly defined knowledge, skills, and abilities (KSAs) of the past.

Unlike traditional worker attributes, competencies do not always have straightforward links to formal tasks (Jackson & Schuler, 1990; Kerr, 1982; Snow & Snell, 1992). Thus, the derivation of competencies should not proceed solely from the analysis of prescribed job responsibilities. In addition, when tasks are in continuous flux and when group-related tasks are more critical than individual tasks, a different manner of deriving human attributes is needed (Cannon-Bowers, Tannenbaum, Salas, & Volpe, 1995; Stevens & Campion, 1994). Indeed, competencies should also be informed by organizational variables (for example, mission, core business values), environmental factors (temperature, location), technology, and types of employee outputs (Levine & Baker, 1991).

To illustrate the need for broader descriptors of human attributes, let us examine customer service work, an area of ever-increasing importance. Although job descriptions usually emphasize task performance or the technical aspects of customer service (Motowidlo & Van Scotter, 1994), contextual aspects such as organizational citizenship (Organ, 1988) and service-oriented behavior are often ignored in traditional job analysis. For instance, traditional descriptions of patient-contact jobs in health care focus on activities like documenting a patient's vital signs and administering prescribed medication. By contrast, what Gronroos (1982) refers to as the *functional quality of services* (that is, the manner in which services are transferred to the customer) is virtually ignored. Descriptors of these interpersonal behaviors and attributes that appear to be critical for team and customer-oriented organizations are sorely needed in work analysis.

To cite another example of insufficient attention to interpersonal behaviors, task analysis has traditionally produced task inventories that resemble "laundry lists" of within-job activities. Interactive activities, which seem most critical in today's cross-functional and interdependent work assignments, have often been neglected. In a recent experience of one of the authors, the quality and openness of the relationship between operators and quality auditors in a pharmaceutical plant, which was found to be a critical determinant of performance, was not reflected in the operators' job description. Today's work analysis should emphasize the description of between-worker interfaces through the incorporation of tools like workflow analysis, which describes dynamic processes involving multiple parties rather than static activities involving a single job title (Levine & Baker, 1991).

Let us illustrate the results of the approach that we are advocating here by first considering a traditional job analysis of the job titled *quality auditor*. This analysis will lead to KSAs such as "numerical ability to perform accurate computations involving unit transformations" and "knowledge of relevant standard operating procedures." By contrast, work analysis that is not constrained by job boundaries and detailed accounts of prescribed tasks may reveal the need for broader competencies such as "constructive communication," which involves nontechnical aspects of the job like the management of trust and the effective delivery of potentially threatening information.

Emotional stability and other personality attributes have received little attention in conventional job analysis, at least when compared with cognitive and technical job specifications. However, interpersonal, team, and customer-oriented attributes seem essential in today's work assignments and therefore should be stressed in work analysis. Organizations are attempting to manage interpersonal and even emotional aspects of work that in the past were left to the employee's discretion (Rafaeli & Sutton, 1987). For example, the manner in which customer service reps handle customer reactions is often "scripted"; employees are given specific responses to use when facing customer reactions. However, not being able to express one's true feelings may result in emotional dissonance and eventually job burnout (Morris & Feldman, 1996). In fact, Hogan, Hogan, and Busch (1984) found that emotional stability was a significant contributor to effective customer service among health care employees.

Still another example of the need to stress personality in work analysis involves work activities requiring adaptation to diverse sets of values and beliefs, which are of ever-increasing relevance given the cultural differences among not only employees but also customers. For example, expatriate managers need to be sensitive to cultural differences in *power distance*—defined as the extent to which individuals in a culture accept and expect an uneven distribution of power (Hofstede, 1980)—so that they keep the appropriate social distance in their interactions. Mistakes in this area can offend local parties and result in important revenue loss. In a similar vein, expatriates need to cultivate personal relationships and friendships with key local parties because in collectivistic cultures emphasizing personal and family ties, business is done only when parties fully know and respect each other (see Hofstede, 1980, for a classification of collectivistic versus individualistic cultures). Employee attributes like self-awareness and tolerance for ambiguity seem essential for competent performance in global markets. Other attributes, like time urgency, may actually be harmful in such circumstances because attempts to move right into business matters may be met with suspicion. Thus, work analysis should describe not only technical and administrative activities but also the manner in which such activities should be carried out.

The descriptors needed to capture the attributes associated with the interpersonal aspects of work remain underdeveloped. Nevertheless, some practices already in effect suggest potentially relevant descriptors. For instance, Jackson and Schuler (1990) suggested describing roles rather than simply jobs. The Disney Corporation uses behavior modeling with its theme park employees to describe their role as actors capable of conveying positive and esteem-enhancing messages to "guests" (Morris & Feldman, 1996). Similarly, a fast-food chain famous for its ethnic food provides restaurant servers with a list of remarks about the manner in which they fixed the items ordered (for example, "This is the fastest [blank] I have ever prepared"), so that customers feel they have received unique, personalized service. The description of these job aids and their purpose should help define the roles that employees are expected to carry out.

Turning now to work redesign, understanding the relationships among employees via work flow analysis should help in reengineering efforts (Hammer & Champy, 1993). Hupp, Polak, and Westgaard (1995) recommend that the assumptions underlying current work processes be challenged and that alternative work flows be mapped. They believe that alternative maps should conform to reengineering principles like organizing systems around an entire product or service. These maps should consist of as few

steps as possible (especially if steps do not add value) and mini-
mize reconciliation and second-party checking (unless there is a
sufficient cost-benefit justification). These ideas about process
reengineering are consistent with work redesign principles that
have been around for decades, such as the need for whole rather
than fractionated tasks and the need to increase employee autonomy (Hackman & Oldham, 1975).

Contrary to stereotypical thinking arguing that increasing technology leads to worker alienation and devaluation, a comparison
of the impact of computerized technology on bank tellers in European countries revealed significant differences in the number of
tasks performed after its implementation (Child & Loveridge,
1990), so that the same technology led to an increase in the number of tasks in some locales and a decrease in others. This finding
suggests that factors such as employee autonomy and skill variety
are not necessarily lost when tasks that were performed manually
are automated and that work analysis can help such redesign
processes.

Because work assignments are becoming knowledge-intensive,
methods of cognitive task analysis have been proposed to map the
mental models used to support performance. Cognitive task analysis is concerned with the description of the cognitive processes and
knowledge structures (sometimes called *schemas*) involved in performing the observable tasks that are the target of traditional task
analysis. As noted by Gordon (1994, p. 68), cognitive task analysis
covers not only entire sets of tasks but also their interrelationships.
Perhaps the most innovative of the descriptors employed in cognitive task analysis is the representation of knowledge and procedures in a graphical format or *structural network,* which describes
factual knowledge in terms of concepts and their interrelationships. Although structural networks can be developed using any
syntax the analyst wishes, the method of concept mapping—where
one uses whatever concepts and labels are relevant to the domain
under study—seems to be the preferred approach (see Klinger &
Gomes, 1993, for a detailed description of this methodology).

In sum, when work assignments are predominantly team-
oriented and cross-functional, understanding whole processes and
their critical between-worker interrelationships is pivotal. Tradi-

tional task inventories are deficient in this respect because they are usually limited to within-job activities. Cognitive task analysis and work flow mapping may provide the information on interrelationships that is missing from traditional task analysis; thus, the latter should be supplemented by these alternative approaches. For instance, Levine and Baker (1991) showed how task and work flow analysis can be fruitfully combined using flow and time charts. They pointed out that because team functions are dynamic, not clearly sequenced, and dependent on environmental or other process factors, the operations and decisions involved in such processes are particularly suitable to combinations of descriptors like task definitions, work flows, and time charts. In a similar application, Wellins, Byham, and Dixon (1994) described how Cape Coral Hospital examined current work processes concerning patient care, unbundled these tasks, and then rebundled them to create multiskilled caregiver teams.

Work redesign practitioners may need to create new rating scales. For instance, task analysis has usually employed scales like time spent, difficulty of learning, and criticality (Sanchez & Fraser, 1992; Sanchez & Levine, 1989). When cost-containment strategies like value analysis are used to identify nonessential work activities that may be outsourced or even eliminated (Townsend & Gebhardt, 1990), new scales may be employed, such as the extent to which tasks or even entire work processes affect the core functions of the job and the extent to which they can be outsourced without a significant impact on the core processes. Other dimensions, like impact of employee error on customer satisfaction, may be used to help the organization improve its customer service (Sanchez & Fraser, 1993).

Work-analytic ratings may also be used to shed light on effective versus ineffective models of job performance. Sanchez, Prager, Wilson, and Viswesvaran (1998) illustrated how SMEs (here, sales employees) may be grouped into clusters according to similarities in their job-analytic ratings. Such clusters were in turn used to identify significant differences in sales performance. An average difference of more than $50,000 in sales was found between sales representatives of two different clusters, each defined by differences in the SME's emphasis on a distinct set of tasks.

Level of Analysis

As mentioned, general worker activities and competencies may replace tasks and KSAs as the units of work analysis. Because molecular tasks are likely to be in continuous flux in today's work assignments, it would be virtually impossible to keep up with every minor change. Competencies, defined as the human attributes underlying the broadly defined sets of worker activities characteristic of today's work assignments, may become the core element of employee selection and training, and through employee certification or skill-based pay, compensation.

It should be noted that in suggesting the use of general worker activities and competencies we do not intend to argue that broader is better, at least in this context. In fact, we concur with Harvey (1991) that the behavioral focus is crucial in work analysis because it provides information about what is done, how it is done, and when it is done. These basics facilitate inferences about the human attributes demanded by one's responsibilities at work. Facing insufficient or even misleading information, SME panels may produce competencies that are influenced by stereotypes and preconceived notions about the job that are unresponsive to organizational realities. One of us has already observed an instance in which the absence of behavioral information led an SME panel to import a list of competencies defined by an industry rival. Such off-the-shelf, armchair work analysis is unfortunate and should be prevented by not skipping the often painstaking but necessary analysis of work behaviors. Otherwise, a costly and time-consuming SME meeting may produce the same output that a single researcher could accomplish in a few hours in the business section of a library.

Although team, organizational, and strategic analyses should provide valuable information on the contextual and organizational aspects of the necessary competencies, behaviorally empty competencies are difficult to measure. Indeed, accurate prediction needed for successful staffing requires that behavioral specificity be built into competencies and performance criteria (Campbell, McCloy, Oppler, & Sager, 1993). In addition, the absence of information on critical and important work behaviors may call into question the job-relatedness of competency-based HR systems. And if their job-relatedness is questionable, it may make such competency-based systems especially vulnerable to legal challenges (Uniform Guidelines on Employee Selection Procedures, 1978; Varca & Pattison, 1993).

Instead of being obsessed with documenting molecular work behaviors to the last detail, work analysis should examine the bulk of the activities performed by employees and then formulate hypotheses that link these broad activity clusters with similarly broad competencies. As noted by Landy, Shankster-Cawley, and Kohler Moran (1995), in many organizational applications of work analysis behavioral information is only the vehicle that takes us toward the ultimate goal of work analysis, which is to understand the human attributes or competencies needed for successful performance.

Summary and Conclusion

We have argued that the so-called obsolescence of job analysis is really the obsolescence of some of the traditional forms and applications of job analysis. Indeed, despite the prominent role that job analysis has acquired in employment litigation, its primary purpose was to be neither a litigation tool nor a mediator between labor and management in disputes concerning job boundaries. The analysis of work was conceived primarily to inform management decisions. We do not call for an across-the-board preservation of conventional job analysis; substantial transformations in the building blocks of traditional job analysis are needed so that work analysis can significantly reduce the uncertainty of an accelerated business environment.

As for the sources of work data, incumbents need to be seen as consultants to the work analysis process rather than as passive informants. That is, incumbents constitute a rich source of data concerning flaws and potential reengineering of current work processes. However, simply engaging in work activities does not qualify one to be a judge of, for instance, psychological attributes. In addition, today's emphasis on teamwork and customer satisfaction dictate that sources such as coworkers and customers be consulted as well.

As for the methods of data collection, electronic performance monitoring offers invaluable data concerning important parameters of work (such as time spent) that used to be estimated in traditional job analysis. Because of qualitative limitations on data gathered through electronic performance monitoring and potential invasion of employee privacy issues, conventional methods like interviews and surveys will still be valid, even though electronic media may speed up data collection and processing. Although the detailed documentation of molecular tasks and job boundaries seems useless when work assignments are in flux, we believe that careful analysis of work behaviors is still necessary to prevent behaviorally empty, unmeasurable competencies. However, broadly defined human attributes or competencies should be informed not only by work behaviors but also by macrolevel descriptors (for example, corporate strategy, context, and roles).

Continuous change demands a system of warnings and databases that can identify and facilitate significant work changes. Electronic performance monitoring provides the opportunity to capture significant work changes on the spot. On-line services like O*NET and expert systems may help in cutting the costs associated with updating work-analytic information.

Finally, let us suggest that a common principle underlies these recommendations: unlike traditional job analysis, instead of being overconcerned with documenting molecular tasks and job boundaries new forms of work analysis should focus on contributing useful inputs to the process of continuous organizational innovation. Knowing what is done and how it is done are necessary steps in determining what should be done and how we should do it. Work analysis is a vehicle that will help us bridge this gap.

References

Arvey, R. D., Salas, E., & Gialluca, K. A. (1992). Using task inventories to forecast skills and abilities. *Human Performance, 5*(3), 171–190.

Barrett, G. V., & Callahan, C. M. (1997, Apr.). Competencies: The Madison Avenue approach to professional practice. In R. C. Page (Chair), *Competency models: What are they and do they work?* Practitioner forum presented at the Twelfth Annual Conference of the Society for Industrial and Organizational Psychology, St. Louis, MO.

Bergquist, W. (1993). *The postmodern organization.* San Francisco: Jossey-Bass.

Bernardin, H. J. (1992). An analytic framework for customer-based performance content development and appraisal. *Human Resources Management Review, 2*, 81–102.

Borman, W. C., & Motowidlo, S. J. (1993). Expanding the criterion domain to include elements of contextual performance. In N. Schmitt & W. C. Borman (Eds.), *Personnel selection in organizations* (pp. 71–98). San Francisco: Jossey-Bass.

Bridges, W. (1994a, Sept. 19). The end of the job. *Fortune,* pp. 62–74.

Bridges, W. (1994b). *JobShift.* Reading, MA: Addison-Wesley.

Campbell, J. P., McCloy, R. A., Oppler, S. H., & Sager, C. E. (1993). A theory of performance. In N. Schmitt, W. C. Borman, & Associates (Eds.), *Personnel selection in organizations* (pp. 35–70). San Francisco: Jossey-Bass.

Cannon-Bowers, J. A., Tannenbaum, S. I., Salas, E., & Volpe, C. E. (1995). Defining competencies and establishing team training requirements. In R. A. Guzzo, E. Salas, & Associates (Eds.), *Team effectiveness and decision making in organizations* (pp. 333–380). San Francisco: Jossey-Bass.

Cascio, W. F. (1995). Whither industrial and organizational psychology in a changing world of work? *American Psychologist, 50,* 928–939.

Child, J., & Loveridge, R. (1990). *Information technology in European services: Toward a microelectronic future.* Cambridge, MA: Basil Blackwell.

Cohn, N. (1970). *The pursuit of the millennium: Revolutionary millennarians and mystical anarchists of the Middle Ages.* Cambridge, England: Cambridge University Press.

Coovert, M. D., Craiger, J. P., & Cannon-Bowers, J. A. (1996). Innovations in modeling and simulating team performance: Implications for decision making. In R. A. Guzzo, E. Salas, & Associates (Eds.), *Team effectiveness and decision making in organizations* (pp. 291–332). San Francisco: Jossey-Bass.

Davidow, W. H., & Malone, M. S. (1992). *The virtual corporation.* New York: HarperCollins.

Drucker, P. F. (1987, Aug. 2). Workers' hands bound by tradition. *Wall Street Journal,* p. 18.

Ginzberg, E., & Berman, H. (1963). *The American worker in the twentieth century: A history through autobiographies.* New York: Free Press.

Gordon, S. E. (1994). *Systematic training program design.* Upper Saddle River, NJ: Prentice Hall.

Gronroos, C. (1982). An applied service marketing strategy. *European Journal of Marketing, 16,* 30–41.

Hackman, J. R., & Oldham, G. R. (1975). Development of the Job Diagnostic Survey. *Journal of Applied Psychology, 60,* 159–170.

Hall, D. T. (1996). Protean careers of the twenty-first century. *Academy of Management Executive, 10,* 8–16.

Hammer, M., & Champy, J. (1993). *Reengineering the corporation: A manifesto for business revolution.* New York: HarperCollins.

Harvey, R. J. (1991). Job analysis. In M. D. Dunnette and L. M. Hough (Eds.), *Handbook of industrial and organizational psychology* (2nd ed., pp. 71–163). Palo Alto, CA: Consulting Psychologists Press.

Hofstede, G. (1980). *Culture's consequences: International differences in work-related values.* Thousand Oaks, CA: Sage.

Hogan, J., Hogan, R. T., & Busch, C. (1984). How to measure a service orientation. *Journal of Applied Psychology, 69,* 167–173.

Hupp, T., Polak, C., & Westgaard, O. (1995). *Designing work groups, jobs, and work flow.* San Francisco: Jossey-Bass.

Huselid, M. A. (1995). The impact of human resource management practices on turnover, productivity, and corporate financial performance. *Academy of Management Journal, 38,* 635–672.

Jackson, S. E., & Schuler, R. S. (1990). Human resource planning: Challenges for I/O psychologists. *American Psychologist, 45,* 223–239.

Jones, R. G., and others. (1997). *Selection or training? A two-fold test of the validity of job-analytic ratings of trainability.* Manuscript submitted for publication.

Kerr, J. L. (1982). Assigning managers on the basis of the life-cycle. *Journal of Business Strategy, 2,* 56–65.

Klimoski, R., & Jones, R. G. (1995). Staffing for effective group decision making: Key issues in matching people and teams. In R. A. Guzzo, E. Salas, & Associates (Eds.), *Team effectiveness and decision making in organizations* (pp. 333–380). San Francisco: Jossey-Bass.

Klinger, D. W., & Gomes, M. E. (1993). A cognitive systems engineering application for interface design. *Proceedings of the Human Factors Society Thirty-Seventh Annual Meeting* (pp. 16–20). Santa Monica, CA: Human Factors Society.

Landy, F. J., Shankster-Cawley, L., & Kohler Moran, S. (1995). Advancing personnel selection and placement methods. In A. Howard (Ed.), *The changing nature of work* (pp. 252–289). San Francisco: Jossey-Bass.

Levine, E. L. (1983). *Everything you always wanted to know about job analysis.* Tampa, FL: Mariner.

Levine, E. L., & Baker, C. V. (1991, Apr.). *Team task analysis: A procedural guide and test of the methodology.* Paper presented at the Sixth Annual Conference of the Society for Industrial and Organizational Psychology, St. Louis, MO.

London, M. (1988). *Change agents: New roles and innovation strategies for human resource professionals.* San Francisco: Jossey-Bass.

McCormick, E. J. (1976). Job and task analysis. In M. D. Dunnette (Ed.),

Handbook of industrial and organizational psychology (pp. 651–696). Skokie, IL: Rand McNally.

Morris, J. A., & Feldman, D. C. (1996). The dimensions, antecedents, and consequences of emotional labor. *Academy of Management Review, 21,* 986–1010.

Motowidlo, S. J., & Van Scotter, J. R. (1994). Evidence that task performance should be distinguished from contextual performance. *Journal of Applied Psychology, 79,* 475–480.

Olian, J. D., & Rynes, S. L. (1991). Making total quality work: Aligning organizational processes, performance measures, and stakeholders. *Human Resource Management, 30,* 303–333.

Organ, D. (1988). *Organizational citizenship behavior: The good soldier syndrome.* San Francisco: New Lexington Press.

Pearlman, K. (1997, Apr.). Competencies: Issues in their application In R. C. Page (Chair), *Competency models: What are they and do they work?* Practitioner forum presented at the Twelfth Annual Conference of the Society for Industrial and Organizational Psychology, St. Louis, MO.

Peterson, N. G., Sager, C. E., & Anderson, L. E. (1996, Apr.). The occupational information network content model: Windows for describing the world of work. In M. A. Campion (Chair), *The occupational information network: Reinventing the dictionary of occupational titles.* Symposium presented at the Eleventh Annual Conference of the Society for Industrial and Organizational Psychology, San Diego, CA.

Prahalad, C. K., & Hamel, G. (1990, May–June). The core competence of the corporation. *Harvard Business Review,* pp. 79–91.

Rafaeli, A., & Sutton, R. I. (1987). Expression of emotion as part of the work role. *Academy of Management Review, 12,* 23–37.

Sanchez, J. I. (1994). From documentation to innovation: Reshaping job analysis to meet emerging business needs. *Human Resource Management Review, 4,* 51–74.

Sanchez, J. I., & Fraser, S. L. (1992). On the choice of scales for task analysis. *Journal of Applied Psychology, 77,* 545–553.

Sanchez, J. I., & Fraser, S. L. (1993, May). *Development and validation of the Corporate Social Style Inventory: A measure of customer service skills.* Report No. 93–108. Cambridge, MA: Marketing Science Institute.

Sanchez, J. I., & Fraser, S. L. (1994). An empirical procedure to identify job duty-skill linkages in managerial jobs: A case example. *Journal of Business and Psychology, 8,* 309–326.

Sanchez, J. I., & Levine, E. L. (1989). Determining important tasks within jobs: A policy-capturing approach. *Journal of Applied Psychology, 74,* 336–342.

Sanchez, J. I., Prager, I., Wilson, A., & Viswesvaran, C. (1998). Understanding within-job title variance in job-analytic ratings. *Journal of Business and Psychology, 12,* 407–419.

Schneider, B., & Konz, A. M. (1989). Strategic job analysis. *Human Resources Management, 28,* 51–63.

Snow, C. C., & Snell, A. A. (1992). Staffing as strategy. In N. Schmitt, W. C. Borman, & Associates (Eds.), *Personnel selection in organizations* (pp. 448–480). San Francisco: Jossey-Bass.

Stevens, M. J., & Campion, M. A. (1994). The knowledge, skill, and ability requirements for teamwork: Implications for human resource management. *Journal of Management, 20,* 503–530.

Townsend, P. L., & Gebhardt, J. E. (1990). *Commit to quality.* New York: Wiley.

Uniform guidelines on employee selection procedures. (1978). *Federal Register, 43*(166), 38290–39309.

Varca, P. E., & Pattison, P. (1993). Evidentiary standard in employment discrimination: A view toward the future. *Personnel Psychology, 46,* 239–258.

Wellins, R. S., Byham, W. C., & Dixon, G. R. (1994). *Inside teams.* San Francisco: Jossey-Bass.

Wolf, A. (1995). *Competence-based assessment.* Buckingham, England: Open University Press.

Young, S. M. (1992). A framework for successful adoption and performance of Japanese manufacturing practices in the U.S. *Academy of Management Review, 17,* 677–700.

CHAPTER 4

Recruitment and Selection
Benchmarking at the Millennium
Hannah R. Rothstein

Key changes in the nature of organizational life challenge many of the bedrock assumptions of traditional recruitment and selection practices, thus threatening the viability of the practices themselves. In the traditional model, the supply of job seekers is plentiful, applicants are hired to perform specific jobs, and employees are expected (and expect) to move up in the organization in a predictable fashion and to remain with the organization for much of their careers (as long as they perform acceptably). Also, the functions of recruitment and selection are handled internally by the organization's human resource (HR) staff. In today's workplace, these conditions are far from universally true.

Current labor market conditions are varied and volatile. In some industries and occupations, the available workforce far exceeds the number of available positions, overwhelming the hiring organization with resumes to sort through and applications to evaluate. In other markets, qualified candidates are increasingly scarce and the primary difficulty for the organization lies in identifying, attracting, and retaining such individuals.

The terms and conditions of employment have also become variable and uncertain. Fewer employees are hired to perform specific tasks, with many selected on the basis of the range of things they can do or learn to do for the organization and some technical experts hired on the basis of a narrow set of skills. Similarly, at the same time that many organizations no longer expect or offer long-term employment relationships with most employees, they have grown dependent on the continuity provided by a critical core group.

Finally, trends in organizational restructuring have deeply affected the operation of HR departments. A new focus on maintaining core businesses and outsourcing other activities has led to the downsizing of many HR departments, with various recruitment and selection functions contracted out to external vendors. The trend toward integration across business functions presses for a synthesis of recruitment and selection activities. Formerly competing organizations have developed strategic alliances for recruitment and selection in order to increase flexibility and adaptability in hiring and employment. As a result of such changes, the role of the HR professional in recruitment and selection has itself changed dramatically.

The objective of this chapter is to examine the implications of changes in the organizational reality for recruitment and selection. First we will survey some of the challenges that the new workplace poses for recruitment and selection; then we will examine the efforts made by industrial-organizational psychologists and other HR professionals to respond to the new conditions. Finally, problems raised by the new state of affairs will be discussed and some concluding remarks about where events seem to be taking the field will be offered.

Challenges Posed by the New Workplace

The challenges posed by the new workplace may be grouped into three sets.

A Two-Tier Workforce

The traditional organizational structure was built on a base of largely permanent, full-time, in-house employees. In today's organization, a relatively small core of employees who perform critical functions retain this status. According to *HR Magazine* (Greble, 1997), only 60 percent of a typical corporation's employees are in the traditional arrangement; the other 40 percent are there through a variety of alternative arrangements, such as temporary employment, independent consulting or contracting, and employee leasing. These "contingent" workers are not a permanent part of the organization but rather come and go as needed for specific assignments. Yet the organization still depends on their performance to achieve its objectives.

Because organizations do not have a long-term claim on these workers, the need for effective methods to recruit contingent personnel quickly is increasing. Furthermore, the importance of accurately assessing potential employees before hire is escalating dramatically. People with whom the organization has little history are brought in to play important and responsible roles; they are expected to be fully functional immediately, with no probationary period, training, or mentoring. In addition, many of these workers do not have the traditional employee's accountability, nor is the organization always able to monitor or supervise them closely. Under these conditions, the cost of hiring the wrong person is very high.

Effective recruitment and selection of employees for the core workforce that provides the organization with stability and continuity has become essential for organizational survival and presents another set of challenges. There is already intense competition for workers who are talented enough to be a part of the core, and this is predicted to become even fiercer. Each member of the core is expected to perform multiple "jobs" and handle multiple responsibilities, as well as to maintain long-term loyalty to the organization. Thus, organizations need to attract and select workers who won't jump ship but who can swim from ship to shore (or ship to ship) as needed, and who can keep their bearings when pushed.

A Shift in Organizational Focus

Successful campaigning by HR professionals and a new focus on economic justification of business activities have led to the awareness that the recruitment and selection of effective performers should be seen as a strategy for achieving organizational growth and success rather than as a fixed cost of doing business. However, along with the improved status of HR activities comes the demand that HR demonstrate the value-added nature of its role. HR departments are feeling pressured to provide cost estimates of recruitment and selection activities and justify those costs in terms of contributions to organizational productivity and profitability. The demand is for cost-effective, value-added recruitment and selection. This shift in perspective has led to greater awareness of the costs of inefficiencies and mistakes, including wasted recruitment dollars, productivity losses, high turnover, worker errors and accidents, damaged relationships with clients or customers, and lost business.

Increased Number and Types of Abilities Needed for Effectiveness

Although the specific knowledge, skill, and ability (KSA) requirements for worker success vary from industry to industry and occupation to occupation, there is a growing consensus about a common core of abilities needed by most individuals to succeed in the changing workplace. They will have to be able to acquire new knowledge and skills continually; adapt successfully to a series of temporary assignments with varying demands; commit to high performance on each job; function effectively as team members; and work well with a variety of other people, including customers.

One result of the expanded requirements for success at work is that HR personnel are being asked to assess and evaluate a broader range of competencies than before. This is certainly good for the selection business, but it also raises a problem. Although valid, cost-effective methods of assessing some of these competencies are widely available, we do not have good measures for many others. This situation provides a golden opportunity for developing new selection tools, but the pressure to produce assessments whether or not valid instruments are available also provides fertile ground for charlatans peddling magic cures to all selection ills. Even well-trained and ethical HR professionals are caught between the need to be responsive to management and the limitations imposed by the current state of knowledge.

A second result of the new requirements for effectiveness is an increasing misalignment between the qualifications of the relevant applicant pools and the demands posed by the jobs they are seeking. According to the *1997 Survey of Human Resource Trends* (Society for Human Resource Management, 1997), 60 percent of employers responding to the survey reported significant skill deficiencies among job applicants. Most common was an undersupply of workers with the intrapersonal, interpersonal, and technical skills required by, for example, team-based structures in high-tech fields. What is often not realized is the degree to which this problem exists at lower levels of the workforce. Information provided by the National School-to-Work Learning and Information Center (1997) indicates that in 1997 over 50 percent of U.S. employers reported problems finding qualified workers for entry-level positions. The primary cause of this situation was said to be the lack of fit between the educational system and the changing nature of work. The center has further commented that "until we as a society fully address the mismatch between what and how students are learning in high school and what they will be required to know and do to ensure successful careers, this figure is likely to continue to rise." Although the mismatch is greatest for students who seek jobs right after high school, employers are increasingly expressing dissatisfaction with college graduates as well.

Responses to the Challenges: Methods, Measures, and Structures

There have been a variety of responses to the three sets of challenges just outlined. Three of the most important are the incorporation of advanced technology throughout the *recruitment process*, from advertising position openings to testing applicants; the search for valid *measurement tools* of applicant competencies in areas such as ability to learn and adapt, self-management, communication skills, emotional resilience, and ability to work in a team; and the development of *new organizational structures* to procure workers, such as cooperative cross-industry staffing alliances and organizations specializing in outsourced staffing functions.

Recruitment Process

An overview and illustrations of key developments in each of these areas will now be presented, beginning with a review of technologically advanced recruitment processes.

On-Line Recruiting

Among the biggest changes in the area of staffing is the growth of
on-line recruiting. According to the Internet Business Network
(1997), a consulting firm specializing in the on-line employment
industry available at *http://www.interbiznet.com/eri,* in December 1996
1.0 million resumes were on-line and 1.2 million job vacancies were
advertised over the Internet. Electronic recruiting takes several
forms. Organizations both large and small post job vacancies on
their own Web sites. (Last year fifty-eight hundred firms listed job
openings on-line. The International Personnel Management Association Assessment Council's own Web site *(www.ipmaac.org)* lists
and provides links to private and public organizations with a strong
recruitment presence on the Internet.) There are currently hundreds of career services Web sites including those of traditional employment agencies who advertise over the Internet as well as others
belonging to exclusively on-line search firms. The U.S. Department
of Labor has an on-line job bank *(www.ajb.dni.us)* that posts jobs
from semiskilled to professional. In addition, third-party firms specialize in helping employers post jobs on controlled organizational
Web sites to which access is limited by the recruiting firm.

One of the critical differences among Internet recruiters is the
method by which their service matches candidates with jobs. So-
called bulletin boards, such as Monster Board *(www.monster.com)*
and Career Mosaic *(www.careermosaic.com),* have served primarily as
on-line job posting and resume listing services whose main objective is to speed the dissemination and exchange of information between job seekers and organizations with jobs to fill, and to provide
an efficient and cost-effective means of reaching a wide audience.
Bulletin boards allow employers to search using key words they
choose but do not participate actively in making matches. Other
types of services take advantage of computer technology to varying
degrees in the method they use to match candidate characteristics
with the requirements of open jobs. The sophistication and validity of different systems and services vary greatly.

The simplest approaches involve the use of key words like *benefits specialist* and *New York metropolitan area* to generate a list of appropriate open positions or suitable job seekers. Variations on this
theme are word matching strategies that attempt to match appli-

cant characteristics to a list of criteria specified by the prospective employer. Unfortunately, the most commonly used criteria—education or years of experience, for example—are the least valid. Electronically capturing items of low predictive validity does little to improve hiring and could lead to the relegation of on-line recruiting to the bin of discarded HR fads.

A relatively sophisticated approach is illustrated by Intellimatch *(www.intellimatch.com),* a service that is available free to job hunters in the general public and to organizations by subscription. Intellimatch uses a structured, skill-inventory approach to both resume construction and position descriptions. Each potential applicant is asked to provide a relatively specific list of skills (for example, test validation, pension fund administration) and for each skill is asked to list the number of years of use, most recent use, and level of proficiency. Employers are asked to describe available jobs using the same list of skills given to applicants. Another approach to matching job candidates with openings is illustrated by Resumix, which uses expert-system technology (information available at *www.resumix.com).* The basic Resumix system is a resume-tracking computer application that organizational clients purchase, not an Internet site (end users are the HR staff of these client organizations rather than job seekers and potential employers). It does, however, contain a feature that allows its clients to post jobs to public recruiting Web sites as well as to view resumes posted to these sites. Resumix uses scanning and imaging technologies to enter resumes into its system. It then uses artificial intelligence to extract key information, which is put into a standardized candidate summary. The extraction technology allows it to categorize candidate information on the basis of broad job categories (for example, software engineering, finance) and somewhat more specific skill areas (dental assistance, staffing), as well as to store summarized personal information and educational and work histories. For internal candidates, proficiency ratings can be attached to the stored resume. Individual clients using Resumix can have the system customized to describe open jobs and collect resume information using any job descriptors or vocabulary they specify. These descriptors can refer to education, training, and experience, or to KSA, depending on the individual employer's wishes. Thus, the potential validity of this system varies with the accuracy and specificity of position descriptions.

This type of approach could be made more effective if a standardized, cross-job, cross-organizational vocabulary of individual characteristics, job specifications, and assessment tools were developed and used to create both applicant descriptions and job listings. Individuals who reported meeting particular job specifications could be given on-line valid tests or assessments of each major characteristic. The tests could be scored immediately, with applicants whose scores exceed the cutoff moving to the next step of the selection process. This would eliminate the needs for each organization to do its own testing and for applicants to be repeatedly tested. A computer-driven strategy that simultaneously capitalized on the technology's capacity to match applicants and jobs, the expanded knowledge base in the area of preemployment assessment, and cooperative assessment arrangements could reengineer the staffing process by integrating recruitment and selection functions.

Despite the advantages it offers, on-line recruiting has disadvantages that must also be noted. One is that direct contact between the applicant and prospective employer usually takes place later than in the traditional process (but visit Texas Instruments's recruiting Web site at *www.ti.com/recruit/docs* to see how this problem can be addressed on-line). To the degree that the employer is interested in a general match between person and organization rather than a fit to a particular job, early exposure of the applicant to the organization's values and culture and of the organization to the applicant's values and goals is an important part of selection, for both parties.

A second disadvantage of on-line recruiting is that it may reduce the access of disadvantaged job seekers to job vacancy information because minority and older applicants are less likely to own, use, or feel comfortable with computers. According to O'Reilly & Associates (1996), of Internet users 67 percent are male, 80 percent are under the age of forty-five, and 74 percent have household incomes above $35,000. *Time* magazine ("World White Web," 1998) has reported that although nearly two-thirds of all white students have visited the World Wide Web, fewer than half of all African American students have done so. In addition, there have been allegations that the key words used in searches are prone to cultural bias. Any employer using Internet or Intranet recruiting must be careful not to produce an adverse impact on minorities or people over age forty.

In addition, the massive proliferation of recruiting sites of varying quality and the volume of electronic resumes that HR departments sometimes receive in response to a posting have the potential to make the system ineffective because of sheer information overload. HR personnel must be able to avoid becoming overloaded with low-payoff activities if they are to maintain the cost-effectiveness of Internet recruiting.

Automating Assessment Activities

A current trend in applicant screening is the paperless application. The paperless application process usually involves a combination of Touch-Tone and interactive voice technology with artificial intelligence software. An example of this is provided by the Automated Prescreening Process (APP) that HReasy, an HR consulting firm, furnishes to its clients (information available on-line at *www.HReasy.com*). However, many organizations operate similar systems internally. Under the APP system, individuals who respond to ads or walk in to apply for a job are directed to call a special toll-free telephone number, which is available twenty-four hours a day, seven days a week. Once they have placed the call, applicants are prompted to enter their social security numbers and telephone numbers to initiate an automated screening interview. Applicants press one key to answer Yes and another to answer No to a set of questions about education, experience, skills, and availability. Those who meet the initial requirement are advanced to a second-level interview. Within minutes of the completion of the interview, managers at the client organization can receive by fax, e-mail, or phone a report on the applicant's qualifications. This report is usually used by the client organization to determine which applicants should be invited to continue with the rest of the selection process. Automation of initial applicant screening has several advantages: it is ready whenever an applicant is, it proceeds more quickly and more objectively than traditional screening, and it reduces demands on both the HR staff and the hiring managers.

There has been a similar movement to automate other parts of the testing process. Coopers and Lybrand has implemented Strategic

Selection Advantage (SSA), an extensive automated, on-line selection battery for initial matching of college students and other entry-level professionals in fields such as auditing, computing, human resources, and actuarial consulting. Anyone with access to the Internet can submit an electronic application by accessing the Coopers and Lybrand recruiting Web site *(www.clspringboard.com)*. The on-line battery includes a basic application form, a biodata inventory, some psychological tests, and a writing sample, which can be completed at one time or in multiple sessions. Applicants are told they will receive a response to their application via e-mail within forty-eight hours. Those who match organizational needs are invited to in-person interviews.

Saville and Holdsworth, Ltd. (information available at *www.Shlusa.com*) has developed a Microsoft Windows–based assessment and reporting system that provides on-screen administration and automated scoring of application forms, aptitude and ability tests, personality questionnaires, interest inventories, and structured interviews on a customized basis. The system can generate narrative reports summarizing the qualifications of each candidate as well as store candidate profiles in a database that can be sorted on a variety of dimensions. In addition to providing the opportunity to conduct remote (off-site) testing, this system supports the integration of graphics, animation, sound, and video into the testing process. The use of multiple media enhances face validity and offers the potential to expand the domain of KSAs that can be tested.

Interactive Simulating

One of the most innovative applications of selection technology is in the use of live telephone call–centered role-play exercises to assess candidates for customer contact positions (for example, customer service representative, account executive, telemarketer, technical assistance provider). The Telephone Assessment Program (TAP) of Assessment Solutions, Inc. (ASI) is a state-of-the-art example of this type of system. In consultation with subject matter experts from the client organization, ASI designs job- and organization-specific simulations to assess candidates' abilities to perform key aspects of the target job. Each exercise is modeled directly on the job and simulates common types of calls the customer representative would receive. In a typical assessment, candidates (at testing centers sponsored by the client) are provided with written background materials, including a simplified set of procedures and guidelines on how to deal with customer queries, and are given time to review these materials. They then receive a series of eight or nine telephone calls from "customers" who are actually trained assessors at ASI headquarters working from a structured script. Each call, which lasts several minutes, is conducted by a different assessor and is designed to evaluate a different but overlapping set of skills. Every assessor uses a structured multidimensional on-line rating form to document and evaluate the candidate's performance. Performance on each dimension, in each call, is compared with the ability level needed to succeed on the job, as predetermined by a job analysis at the client organization. Scores are then mechanically combined, and a dimensional and overall performance report is generated for each candidate.

Advantages of this approach are that it can be conducted remotely with candidates virtually anywhere in the world, it provides a realistic preview of the target job, and it reliably yet relatively inexpensively captures actual samples of behavior using specially trained assessors. Strategically, it focuses on the customer's perspective, which is in line with the new organizational emphasis on customer and client satisfaction. The technique has high face validity and predictive validities (using supervisory rating forms developed for research purposes) ranging from .20s to .40s before correction for criterion unreliability (Seymour Adler, personal communication, January 12, 1998).

Measurement Tools

As mentioned earlier in the chapter, there seems to be a common core of skills and abilities that will define the successful worker of the near future. To function effectively in the new workforce, most individuals will have to be able to continually acquire new knowledge and skills; adjust successfully to a series of temporary assignments with varying demands; commit themselves to and achieve high performance on each job; and work well with a variety of other people, including customers, perhaps as part of a team. In this section, we will examine the approaches that are being taken to the prehire assessment of these characteristics and how well they are succeeding.

Measuring General Characteristics Versus Specific Competencies

Two distinct strategies for selection have emerged. One strategy suggests that in an environment of rapidly changing job demands, selection based on general abilities such as intelligence, conscientiousness, or adaptability will contribute most to the overall effectiveness of the organization. The second strategy suggests that effectiveness is enhanced when selection is based on evaluation of the applicant's ability to perform the behaviors needed to do the job for which he or she is being hired. I suggest that, ideally, the first strategy should be applied to individuals being hired for the core workforce, whereas the second could be used to hire peripheral or contingent workers. At this point in time, however, when we do not have a complete arsenal of selection tools to implement either strategy, we have to use parts of each for both types of workers.

Assessing the Ability to Acquire New Knowledge and Skills

Eighty-five years of research on personnel selection supports the claim that industrial psychologists are very good at measuring the ability to acquire job knowledge. A review of thousands of validity studies (Schmidt & Hunter, 1997) concluded that the best single predictor of job performance, performance in training programs, and the acquisition of job-related knowledge for virtually every job in the U.S. economy, is general cognitive ability. According to the study's authors (p. 8): "When an employer uses general mental ability to select employees who will have a high level of performance on the job, the employer is also selecting those who will learn most from job training programs and will acquire job knowledge faster from experience on the job."

In the changing world of work, employees at all levels will need to go back for formal training many times during their careers in addition to engaging in less formal learning in order to keep pace with workplace changes. Furthermore, many newly emerging jobs demand rapid acquisition of cognitively complex skills. Thus, there is a strong argument to be made that a test of mental or cognitive ability should be part of the selection battery for every job.

Assessing Commitment to High Performance

Staffing experts would like to have job performance–related measures of a variety of personality characteristics that are hypothesized to contribute to success in the new workplace, particularly those associated with responsibility, self-management, adaptability to change, and ability to get along with others. However, despite psychologists' ability to obtain reliable, construct-valid measures of five major personality factors—extroversion, openness to experience, emotional stability, agreeableness, and conscientiousness—only conscientiousness has been consistently linked to job performance. An extensive review recently conducted by Mount and Barrick of the University of Iowa (1995) showed that measures of conscientiousness were consistently valid predictors of performance across a wide spectrum of occupations (professional, police, managerial, sales, and skilled and semiskilled). Employees who are conscientious, that is, characterologically responsible, dependable, organized, and persistent are more successful than those who are not. Conscientiousness is clearly related to one of the primary demands placed on employees in the new workforce: commitment to high performance and the responsibility and self-management to achieve it. It is important to note that conscientiousness was a stronger predictor of performance in high-autonomy than in low-autonomy jobs because many alternative work arrangements (for example, telecommuting, contracting, self-managed work teams) emphasize autonomy. The assessment of conscientiousness, or the related construct of integrity, is becoming part of the selection process in an increasing number and variety of organizations.

Assessing Adaptability

To my knowledge, there are no general measures of emotional resilience or adaptability to change that have been validated for work settings. Martin Seligman (1992) developed a measure of "learned optimism" that captured some aspects of resilience, which showed some early success predicting performance in insurance sales jobs; however, the original validity data are a decade old and no newer evidence has emerged. Measures of the Big Five personality characteristics of emotional stability and openness to experience have been disappointing in this regard, with virtually no cross-occupational validity and limited validity within specific occupations. Joyce Hogan's research on Big Five–based and interpersonal predictors of success in creative, artistic, and socially oriented jobs is promising but still preliminary (Joyce Hogan, personal communication, December 1997).

Nonetheless, stimulated in part by obvious changes in workplace stressors and in part by the publication of Daniel Goleman's book *Emotional Intelligence* (1995), employers are keen to assess the resilience and adaptability of job candidates. Because measures validated for the workplace don't exist, there has been a surge in pseudopsychological assessment by unqualified individuals and firms using untested methods. Many hiring managers (and some HR professionals who should know better) are relying on unsubstantiated measurements of these characteristics to make important staffing decisions. These include clinical assessments of personality by unqualified interviewers or assessors, projective tests with questionable psychometric properties, and even adaptations of a questionnaire originally published in *USA Today* (Peterson, 1997) to illustrate the construct of emotional intelligence for newspaper readers. The professional interests of industrial psychologists and HR professionals are not well served when popularity is substituted for validity in determining an instrument's use.

Assessing the Ability to Work with Others and Function in a Team
The best available measures of interpersonal skills assess focused and job-specific competencies rather than general personal attributes. Measures of the Big Five personality characteristic of extroversion have been used successfully to predict job performance for managerial and sales occupations but not for others in which the interpersonal component is less dominant. As more types of jobs require significant interaction with others, the validity of extroversion for predicting job success may become higher, and more generalizable, but its use as an across-the-board assessment of interpersonal skills cannot be recommended on the basis of the current evidence.

Because the popularity of team-based work structures has grown so rapidly, industrial psychologists are still sorting out the issues involved in selecting for effective team membership, and measures of the ability to work in teams are still in the process of development. A promising approach is being pursued by Stevens and Campion (1994) at Purdue University, who are validating a test that measures KSA requirements for being a team member by having respondents assess and react to hypothetical teamwork situations. Stevens and Campion are concerned with measuring aspects of effective team membership that can be learned or developed rather than with enduring personality characteristics. However, their focus is on the distinctive requirements of working in a team setting and not on the technical, task-related skills required by specific jobs incorporated into the work team. Thus, their instrument is intended for multioccupational, multiorganizational use. Interestingly, their results so far show that individual functioning as part of a work team is related not only to the domains of interpersonal abilities but also to self-management. In the two validity studies conducted to date, scores on the test were significantly related to supervisory ratings of teamwork and of overall performance.

New Organizational Structures

Although organizations have historically relied on employment agencies and search firms to help them recruit prospective workers and on consultants to help choose selection instruments, today there is a move toward placing considerably more of the hiring process on outside experts.

Outsourced Functions

According to *The 1997 Survey of Human Resource Trends* (Society for Human Resource Management, 1997), which surveyed seventeen hundred organizations, 50 percent of respondents outsourced more HR functions than they did three years ago. Recruitment was currently outsourced by 12 percent of all firms surveyed, whereas preemployment testing was outsourced by 15 percent. Among larger organizations and those whose staffing needs fluctuate significantly, these percentages are higher.

The past several years have seen tremendous growth in firms that specialize in full-service "employment processing." Two trends have contributed to the growth in the use of such firms. First is the emergence of a new philosophy of organization that holds that, in order to succeed in the current environment, organizations must focus on their core businesses and distinctive competencies and outsource support functions such as human resources. Second is the pressure to reengineer and demonstrate the cost (and cost-effectiveness) of every activity. Specialized companies whose organizational mission is to provide HR services are in a better position to "price out" each step of the hiring process, and because of experience and economies of scale, provide services at a cheaper price than can the prospective employer.

Several traditional HR consulting firms such as ASI and AON Consulting have now added "employment processing" services for clients who wish to outsource recruitment and selection. An example is provided by the services that ASI performs for one of its major clients, a communications company with over a hundred thousand employees. The client creates and places the initial recruitment advertisements, but everything from this point on to the delivery of qualified candidates is handled by ASI. ASI has thus contracted to implement the client's preexisting selection process. ASI begins by reviewing responses to the ads, which are mailed in, phoned in, faxed in, and in some cases even submitted on-line. They then schedule and conduct initial screening interviews with candidates who meet the client's basic requirements. At the client's option, scheduling and screening are conducted using an interactive voice response system. Based on the results of that interview, ASI selects and schedules candidates for further testing and interviewing, which are conducted by telephone and computer from a remote location. Background investigations, including medical and drug testing when needed, are coordinated by ASI as well. Finally, ASI sends a report to the client in which candidates are listed in order of qualification scores based on mechanically weighted composite criteria developed by the client. ASI handles all paperwork to document applicant flow throughout the hiring process. Finally, because the client organization is usually charged on a per-hire basis, it can reduce fixed costs.

When employment-processing activities are outsourced to industrial-organizational (I/O) psychologists who are trained in selection and assessment, these psychologists may end up facing an unanticipated dilemma. On the one hand, the I/O psychologists are asked to implement a recruitment and selection process designed by the client and are evaluated on the basis of how rigorously they followed the client's specifications. On the other hand, the I/O psychologists have received extensive professional training as independent professionals and may decide that in their professional judgment the client's procedures could be improved. Should a psychologist scrupulously follow the client's procedures if she believes there are more valid, more efficient methods available? Does the psychologist have an obligation to raise the issue and suggest the other methods? What if the client objects? As psychologists depart from traditional consulting roles, these questions will need to be confronted.

Cooperative Alliances

One of the most dramatic responses to the rise in environmental uncertainty has been in the way in which organizations view each other. Traditionally they viewed each other as competitors for the best available workers. HR departments played a zero-sum game, with one organization's staffing gain (a well-qualified new hire) becoming another's loss (a replacement for a qualified worker or the placement elsewhere of the most qualified applicant). Cooperation among organizations in the HR area was rare, generally limited to organizations helping to find jobs for each other's "trailing spouses" in dual-worker families. But with today's need for flexibility and adaptability, many organizations have been increasingly willing to enter into cooperative arrangements with others for various purposes, including broadening their recruiting and hiring reach (getting more value for the money) and securing the services and commitment of contingent workers. Several trends indicate that further cooperation among former competitors for human resources is likely. One reason for the formation of cooperative recruitment alliances has been the increase in the number of small and start-up organizations, which often do not possess sufficient resources to recruit and hire efficiently. By working together, they can purchase more expertise, participate in more activities, and reach a broader applicant market than they can on their own. Of equal benefit, they can maintain more control over the recruiting process than if they rely on an external agency. Because the number of new start-ups is expected to increase, so should cooperative recruiting arrangements.

A second reason for establishing cooperative alliances is to ensure the continuous availability of well-qualified individuals without having to make them permanent employees. This is the case not only for new, small companies but also for the largest and most established. Frequently changing tasks or goals and project-based organizational structures require a fluid workforce. Sharing workers across organizations increases the work-ready labor pool on which an organization can draw. It also provides an advantage in quality control, because the worker does not totally "disappear" after a project is over but instead moves to another organization within the alliance.

The benchmark for innovation in the area of cross-organization cooperation is the Talent Alliance (TA), a nonprofit network of large and small businesses, industry and trade associations, and government groups and educational and academic institutions that began operating in April 1997. Founding members of the TA include AT&T, Du Pont, GTE, Johnson & Johnson, Lucent Technologies, NCR, TRW, Unisys, and UPS. The TA is an HR consortium that attempts to provide cooperative solutions to the many staffing problems emerging from the changing nature of work, including how to manage the consequences of just-in-time hiring effectively, how to meet the increasingly divergent needs and goals of individuals and organizations, and how to reverse the declining proportion of matches between the characteristics of the available workforce and the requirements of the jobs that must be filled.

Underlying this organization's mission is its basic belief that: "Winning globally demands that we as employers ensure that our [U.S.] workforce is creative, competitive, flexible, and innovative. We can accomplish that much more aggressively and economically if we combine forces, drawing on the best of each and every one of our members" (Talent Alliance, 1997).

The primary goals of the TA are to ensure that individuals are employable throughout their working years by developing and maintaining marketable skills, and to make certain skilled workers are available to companies at the time and in the numbers they are needed, for as long as needed. In the short term, the TA is concerned with the redeployment of displaced workers to settings where they are needed. Longer term, it is committed to developing strategies for bridging the gap between employee skills and workplace needs and providing policy-oriented research on workplace trends.

TA programs are divided among several areas, including these:

- A Career Growth Center provides employees of member organizations with access to career planning tools and counselors, as well as to on- and off-line education and training programs for both short- and long-term skill development.
- A Business Growth Center offers member companies diagnostic assessments, seminars, and other materials on strategic employment planning and on improving employment practices, as well as survey feedback on the success of these practices.
- Also featured is an on-line Job/Applicant Matching System, which is available to both individual employees of member companies and hiring managers. This system advises individuals of job openings at all companies in the alliance and provides feedback on how well their skills match jobs in demand. It helps employers manage applicant flow by providing pre-screening assessments and by alerting them automatically when qualified people become available.

The TA maintains an extensive Web site at *www.talentalliance.com*. Although parts of the site are accessible only to member companies and their employees, other parts are open to the public and are worth visiting by readers of this chapter.

Some Concluding Thoughts

The challenges that the changing workplace poses for professionals in recruitment and selection are serious. If they can be met successfully, I/O psychologists and HR managers can become important players in the strategic management process. After years of being viewed as a minor part of the organizational support system, we have reached a point in history when our ability to procure the right personnel and deploy them to the right jobs at the right time is considered critical to organizational success. To profit from this situation, we must show that our participation in these activities adds unique value. In other words, we must show that recruitment and selection jointly conducted by I/O psychologists and HR professionals results in better performing workers and increased organizational effectiveness than recruitment and selection otherwise conducted. But can we show this? I think so, but only if we remember what differentiates us from other management consultants. Specifically, our recommendations and tools should be scientifically justifiable (read *valid*) and our goal should be to promote human welfare at work.

In terms of new structures, the new environment is likely to encourage the continued development of cooperative alliances and consortia. I am hopeful that one result of this will be the development and use of standard-language job specifications and standardized resumes or applications, much like the uniform college application many universities and colleges now share. Another outcome I would welcome is the evolution of a national talent databank or registry. Currently, the TA and the U.S. Department of Labor are each attempting to develop voluntary skill certification systems. Developments such as these could make it easier for workers to endure the frequent job changes we expect for so many of them. Furthermore, a talent registry might overcome some of the problems associated with self-reports, such as intentional or unintentional exaggeration of skills and abilities. Alliances and consortia can also provide the basis for validation studies that extend beyond the tenure of a single job and permit us to look at the predictors of performance across the career span. These might not be identical with predictors of performance on a single job.

In terms of new methods, the new environment means we should be selective in introducing computer-driven recruitment and selection. Although HR can benefit greatly from emerging technology, it must avoid being seduced into ignoring evidence of validity—or its absence. Delivery systems should not be confused with the substance of what is being delivered. We must be vigilant that our ultimate deliverable is valid assessment, not attractively packaged entertainment.

Computer technology could be of immense value if it substitutes multimedia or interactive realistic job previews for early organizational contact for applicants from remote sites.

In terms of new measures, we must make sure not to oversell the implications of what we know and not to claim that we know what we don't. We need to increase what we know about emotional intelligence, resilience, and working in teams before we can offer workplace applications of this knowledge. We need to know more about the overall incidences of different competencies and characteristics in the population and assess the likelihood that organizations will be able to find individuals with the attributes required for success. It is hard to keep pace scientifically in a time of rapid change because of the length of time research can take, but we must do the research nevertheless. To do otherwise would be to abandon our own competitive advantage and risk becoming one of the casualties of the new organizational reality rather than one of its architects.

References

Goleman, D. (1995). *Emotional intelligence: Why it can matter more than IQ.* New York: Bantam Books,

Grehle, T. C. (1997, Feb.). A leading role for HR in alternative staffing. *HR Magazine,* pp. 99–104.

Internet Business Network. (1997). Electronic recruiting news. [http://www.interbiznet.com/eri]

Mount, M. K., & Barrick, M. R. (1995). The Big Five personality dimensions: Implications for research and practice in human resource management. In G. R. Ferris (Ed.), *Research in personnel and human resource management* (Vol. 13, pp. 153–200). Greenwich, CT: JAI Press.

National School-to-Work Learning and Information Center. (1997). Fact sheet. [http://www.stw.ed.gov/FACTSHT/stwlc.htm]

O'Reilly & Associates. (1996). Defining the Internet opportunity. [http://www.ora.com/research/users/index.html]

Peterson, K. (1997, Feb. 18). Signs of intelligence. *USA Today,* p. 1D.

Schmidt, F. L., & Hunter, J. E. (1997). *The validity and utility of selection methods in personnel psychology: Implications of eighty-five years of research findings.* Unpublished paper, University of Iowa, Iowa City.

Seligman, M. (1992). *Learned optimism.* New York: Pocket Books.

Society for Human Resource Management. (1997). *The 1997 survey of human resource trends.* Alexandria, VA: Society for Human Resource Management.

Stevens, M. J., & Campion, M. A. (1994). *Staffing teams: Development and validation of the Teamwork-KSA test.* Paper presented at the annual meeting of the Society of Industrial and Organizational Psychology, Nashville, TN.

Talent Alliance. (1997). About the Talent Alliance. [http://www.talent-alliance.com/about/tfaq.htm]

World white Web? (1998, Apr. 28). *Time,* p. 24.

CHAPTER 5

Our Past, Present, and Future in Teams

The Role of Human Resource Professionals in Managing Team Performance

Cristina B. Gibson
Bradley L. Kirkman

Most Fortune 1000 employees have been affected by the widespread proliferation of work teams. This holds true also for the millions of employees and managers who work outside the Fortune 1000. Recent evidence about the growth in work teams reinforces the notion that they have become a way of life in many organizations (Osterman, 1994; Lawler, Mohrman, & Ledford, 1995). For example, Osterman (1994) found that over 50 percent of the seven hundred firms he studied were using teams and that over 40 percent had more than half of their employees working in teams. As the use of teams continues to grow, human resource (HR) professionals need more knowledge about teams in general and, more specifically, information about the HR practices that enhance team performance. Human resources play a critical role in developing and implementing organizational strategies and structures. Successful HR professionals will be those who can align their organizational HR practices with the unique demands of team-based organizational structures.

In this chapter, we have four objectives. First, we provide HR professionals with a brief history of the use of teams in the United States, reviewing definitions and types of teams, evidence regarding the impact of teams, and the factors that led to their proliferation. Second, we aim to provide the HR professional with tools to increase the effectiveness of teams, discussing the key assumptions underlying supportive conditions for teams. Third, we review modifications in HR practices that are necessary to implement teams effectively. Finally, we discuss potential challenges that HR practitioners may face in implementing teams in multinational organizations; looking to the future, we present guidelines for meeting these challenges. We conclude with some predictions about the use of teams that will likely develop as our team-based organizations continue to evolve.

What Teams Are, How Teams Contribute, and When to Use Them

In general, a work team can be defined as a group of individuals working interdependently to solve problems or accomplish tasks (Manz & Sims, 1993; Sundstrom, De Meuse, & Futrell, 1990). However, a single definition is not sufficient to capture the key differences that exist between the various types of teams being used in organizations. Table 5.1 shows the most common types of work teams and their key characteristics and differences.

A number of key differences between these types of teams will determine the efficacy of HR practices designed to enhance their effectiveness. For example, compensation structures are normally altered for self-managing work teams to include team-based rewards to encourage cooperation between members and motivate them to reach team goals (Gerhart & Milkovich, 1992; Kanin-Lovers & Cameron, 1993). Because self-managing members are working on permanent teams, the effort and expense involved in changing compensation structures is often justified. However, in more temporary teams, such as cross-functional or problem solving teams, other types of HR policy changes (for example, altering an evaluation system to include team behaviors) may be more appropriate to encourage positive behaviors.

Table 5.1. Types of Teams.

Rating	Team Type	Typical Work Performed/ Typical Members	Task Design	Duration
(1)	Self-managing work teams	Day-to-day work activities, including some managerial duties	High autonomy, high task interdependence, teamwork is the job	Permanent
(2)	Work team	Day-to-day work activities	Varies	Permanent
(3)	Management teams	Strategic decision making carried out by top managers	High autonomy, high task interdependence, teamwork is the job	Permanent
(4)	Cross-functional teams	Members of different functional areas assigned to carry out work	Some autonomy, moderate task interdependence, functional responsibility is retained	Until project or assignment is complete
(5)	Problem-solving project teams	Specific tasks designed to improve work processes or meet specific customer needs	Some autonomy, moderate task interdependence, functional responsibility is retained	Until project is complete or problem is solved
(6)	Virtual teams	Members geographically dispersed who seldom meet face-to-face	Extreme autonomy, low to moderate interdependence, functional responsibility is retained	Until project is complete

Note: The team rating (from 1 to 6) indicates the degree to which a team member's time is spent in the team and the life span of the team (for example, 1 = all of the member's time is spent in the team and the team is permanent; 6 = only some of the member's time is spent in the team and the team is temporary).

Our point here is not to review all of the appropriate HR policies for each type of team (see Cohen & Bailey, 1997, for a good review) but rather to acknowledge that our use of the term *work team* includes several different types of teams.

Contrary to popular belief, teams are not a new phenomenon. The origins of teams can be traced to the Tavistock studies of post–World War II (Trist & Bamforth, 1951) and the Swedish sociotechnical movement generally associated with the Volvo Corporation (Pasmore, 1995). The first work teams in the United States were found in the Procter & Gamble Company in the early 1960s, the Topeka work system at a General Foods pet food plant in the late 1960s, and the Rushton Quality of Work Project in Pennsylvania in the mid-1970s. Given that teams were identified as a mechanism for improving employee performance as early as the 1960s, why has it taken over thirty years to implement work teams on a large scale in the United States?

We attribute the recent rise in the interest in and use of teams over the last ten years to three factors: a higher concern for the social component of work; the globalization of the U.S. economy and resulting downsizing; and the early adoption of work teams by highly visible companies such as General Motors, AT&T, General Electric, Xerox, and Motorola. Although many believe that organizations have adopted work teams to improve employee morale or productivity, the forces behind their adoption have been much larger in scale and much more connected to global patterns of international business. Organizations have adopted work teams because many had no choice. Dramatically reduced numbers of managers could not keep up with employee activities on a day-to-day basis.

Furthermore, the increased use of teams can be attributed, in part, to evidence of their success. Work teams have been associated with higher levels of *productivity* (Banker, Field, Schroeder, & Sinha, 1996; Cohen & Ledford, 1994); *quality* (Banker, Field, Schroeder, & Sinha, 1996; Cohen & Ledford, 1994; Wellins and others, 1990); *customer satisfaction* (Wellins and others, 1990); *safety* (Cohen & Ledford, 1994); *job satisfaction* (Cordery, Mueller, & Smith, 1991; Wall, Kemp, Jackson, & Clegg, 1986); and *organizational commitment* (Cordery, Mueller, & Smith, 1991). It should be noted, however, that most of these studies have been conducted with self-managing work teams that have considerable control over their own structure and process. For traditional work teams, much of the evidence of impact has been collected on a case-by-case basis. Wellins, Byham, and Dixon (1994), for example, chronicle the pervasive positive impact teams have had in twenty companies. These companies claim that implementing teams resulted in improvements in bottom-line indicators such as cost savings, quality and service improvement, speed, absenteeism, and turnover.

This is not to say that teams are a panacea. Several studies on the impact of teams have failed to find effects for performance on more quantitative measures, such as productivity (for example, see Wall, Kemp, Jackson, & Clegg, 1986); others report only modest findings for productivity (see Goodman, Devadas, & Griffith-Hughson, 1988). Smaller effect sizes for productivity may be the result of using work teams in contexts where they are not appropriate. Clearly, work teams are not ideal for every task (even if you have a hammer, not every problem is a nail). Work teams are more effective under the right circumstances and situations.

For example, work teams are most effective when there is high task interdependence or a high degree of coordination and collaboration required between team members to accomplish tasks (Shea & Guzzo, 1987). Thus, a group of insurance sales agents who are geographically dispersed and have little interaction with one another to carry out their tasks would most likely be an inappropriate context in which to implement teams. The agents would probably see such an effort as an empty, poorly developed strategy designed to capitalize on a management fad.

Work teams are also more appropriate when the tasks that their members carry out are complex and well designed (Cordery, Wall, and Wright, 1997). If a group's work is routine and unchallenging, of dubious importance, and wholly preprogrammed with no opportunity for feedback, teams will probably not make much difference in productivity (Hackman, 1987). As Johns (1996) has stated, "Taking a bunch of olive stuffers on a food processing assembly line, putting them in distinctive jumpsuits, calling them the Olive Squad, and telling them to self-manage will be unlikely to yield dividends in terms of effort expended or brainpower employed" (p. 257). Work teams, especially those that increase autonomy and responsibility, are most effective when members are given complex tasks that capitalize on their diverse knowledge and skills. Thus, teams should view their tasks as significant, the tasks should require the use of a variety of skills, and members should, where possible, assemble an entire product or deliver a complete service.

The effectiveness of work teams also depends on whether an organization has high integration needs as a result of operating in a complex environment (Mohrman, Cohen, & Mohrman, 1995). Complex environments usually force organizations to serve a wide variety of customers, deal with rapidly changing technology, and satisfy large numbers of different stakeholders. IBM, for example, faces a much more complex environment than McDonald's (compare the rate of change in PCs with that of Big Macs over the last fifteen years). Organizations must simultaneously deal with all of these issues—in other words, differentiate into smaller, more responsive units—and then integrate these widely dispersed efforts and units back into one cohesive organization. Teams will be most effective when a team structure is the best solution to obtaining *the integration* required to accomplish goals in a complex organizational environment (Mohrman, Cohen, & Mohrman, 1995). Without effective integration, the benefits attributed to work teams (increased productivity, higher quality, better job satisfaction) will not be realized.

Thus, companies implementing teams from a "bandwagon" perspective will not realize the benefits to be had from an appropriate fit between teams and context. In fact, many organizations are currently struggling with team effectiveness. We argue that this is the result, in part, of traditional assumptions about work that still prevail. In order to implement teams effectively, assumptions must change. We next discuss these adaptations.

The Need to Adapt Our Assumptions

We discuss the assumptions that shaped the decisions made by HR professionals in traditional hierarchical organizations in three areas: motivation; structure of work; and accountability. Traditional assumptions must be adapted in order to support effective implementation of teams. The old and new assumptions are summarized in Table 5.2. As we discuss each type of assumption, we elaborate on how it must be adapted.

Motivation

The first set of assumptions that must be examined pertain to motivation. National culture helps determine what motivates people. For example, some cultures can be classified as *individualistic,* where people tend to value their own self-interest and welfare over the interests of groups or societies; other cultures are known as *collectivistic,* where people tend to value the welfare of groups more than their own (Hofstede, 1980). Individualists are motivated by the opportunity to gain personal recognition. They resist working in teams more than people from collectivistic cultures (Kirkman, 1996; Kirkman & Shapiro, 1997). Such resistance lowers team effectiveness on outcomes such as productivity, job satisfaction, cooperativeness, and organizational commitment (Kirkman, 1996). It takes time and experience for people to adjust their notions of fairness and equity to include collective accountability. Taking a longer-term focus and understanding the eventual payoffs for early investments in team-based systems is essential for harnessing the motivational power of teams.

Table 5.2. Adapting Our Assumptions.

Domain	Previous Assumptions	New Assumptions
Motivation	• Individual motivation • Individualistic values • Competition • Short-term focus	• Group motivation • Collectivistic values • Collaboration • Longer-term focus
Structure	• Independent work • Quantity is important • Narrow job definitions • Strong organizational boundaries	• Interdependent work • Processes are important • Multiskilling • Permeable boundaries
Accountability	• Individual responsibility • Functional specialization • Vertical reporting structures • Command and control	• Mutual responsibility • Lateral thinking • Horizontal reporting • Self-management

In understanding motivational assumptions, it is also important to consider expectations. Research attests to the importance of collective expectations in determining our level of motivation and subsequently our performance (Bandura, 1997; Gibson, 1995). When we believe we can accomplish objectives as a team, we are motivated to stick with our work tasks and prevail. But sometimes these high expectations get out of hand, to the point that teams hold unrealistic expectations. Cohesive teams often fall prey to this phenomenon, which is referred to as *groupthink* (Janis, 1982). Coinciding with extremely high expectations, teams suffering from groupthink also hold illusions of invulnerability. They ignore important external information sources that might help them adjust their performance to fit the needs of customers better. Teams in individualistic cultures appear to be particularly susceptible to overconfidence (Gibson, 1996). This may be because individualists view their team as an entity in and of itself rather than one that is connected to the external context and are therefore even less apt to use external sources of information to make corrections in their behavior and improve their performance. Particularly in individualistic cultures, team-based organizations need to have systems that help teams set realistic expectations. This allows them to stay motivated while at the same time remaining open to learning from feedback and mistakes.

Work Structure

A second domain of assumptions concerns the structure of work. Traditional work groups were generally formed around common technical or functional skills and areas of expertise (for example, accounting, finance, or production). In recent years, it has become apparent that organizing work around a process (for example, new product development) rather than around a specific task or function is more effective (Dunphy & Bryant, 1996). Doing so often requires extending team members' task skills. Multiskilled teamwork involves teams made up of individuals with multiple and overlapping skills that are deployed around the performance of a whole task, which represents a significant part of a larger work flow. Members are multiskilled so that work can be flexibly allocated among them.

In organizing work around processes, organizational boundaries must often be renegotiated. Increasingly, work teams include external customers and suppliers. For example, General Electric Medical Systems invites representatives from leading health maintenance organizations (HMOs) to serve on its sales and service teams. The American Red Cross has members of communities serving on key committees that set organizational objectives. Eastman Kodak allies itself with key competitors to form market segment task forces. These types of work structures require a whole new notion of collaboration—collaboration with external constituencies. Those who were previously viewed as "them" are now viewed as "us."

The reorganization of work around processes and across boundaries has numerous benefits. For example, multiskilling (the learning of new skills in addition to functional expertise) can result in reduced staffing as fewer workers can perform the same range of tasks. It can create efficiencies through more flexible task assignment. Multiskilling also often leads to lower inventories because there is more effective work flow coordination. It also makes the team more flexible in meeting fluctuating market demand through operational flexibility. Finally, it can lead to a more differentiated response to the needs of particular customer segments and so contribute to strategic flexibility. Multiskilling leads to greater awareness of the whole task and enables the team member to take part in problem solving, innovation, and strategic thinking (Dunphy & Bryant, 1996). These same benefits do not accrue when tasks and organizations are structured under traditional assumptions of static, independent jobs.

Accountability

A third domain of assumptions that shape team effectiveness pertain to accountability. The focus of most HR departments has been on the individual. Individual accountability and responsibility have been the foundation on which all of the business practices in the United States have been built. Furthermore, accountability in traditional work organizations was vested in those with formal positions—the managers and supervisors. Individual employees showed deference to people in these positions. Reporting structures were vertical and a command-and-control philosophy reigned. Skills such as planning, coordination, personnel functions, quality management, health and safety, and boundary management were the domain of managers. But increasingly, these duties are becoming the domain of teams. Managerial responsibility is shifting from individual accountability to collective, mutual accountability. As this has occurred, the notion of self-management has gained acceptance. Self-management grows as the team's operational tasks are delegated to the team itself. Many different terms have evolved to describe and distinguish varying degrees of autonomy, including *self-directed work teams* (Osburn, Moram, Musselwhite, & Zenger, 1990), *empowered teams* (Lawler, 1986; Wellins, Byham, & Wilson, 1991), *self-leading teams* (Manz & Sims, 1987), and *superior work teams* (Kinlaw, 1991). The common distinguishing characteristic of such teams is that they operate with some degree of autonomy.

As nonmanagers become collectively responsible for managerial duties, basic assumptions about the legitimacy of authority are challenged. Team members may begin to question what gives peers the right to set rules for others. They may have difficulty dealing with authority that does not stem from position. Rather than depending on a job description and direction from the manager, people work jointly with coworkers to determine what they do. Because personal success depends on collective success, an individual's fate is tied to coworkers. Feelings of mutual trust and partnership must develop. The organization must help people learn to deal with greater ambiguity, uncertainty, continual change, and collaborative relationships. Both managers and employees in the team-based organization need to adjust to this shift in accountability and responsibility. We discuss the HR systems that increase team effectiveness in the next section.

The Need to Modify HR Practices to Support Teams

In addition to recognizing and adapting the assumptions on which they base their practices, HR professionals must also modify those practices to support teams. The practices to be modified cluster in five areas: recruitment and selection; task design; training; evaluation; and compensation. In the following sections, we summarize the modifications and provide references for practitioners interested in exploring them in greater depth. Table 5.3 presents an overview of the practice modifications.

Table 5.3. Modifying HR Practices.

HR Component	Practice Modification
Recruitment and selection	• Identifying teamwork knowledge, skills, and abilities • Matching people with tasks • Utilizing written, interview, and activity-based techniques
Task design	• Building opportunities for collaboration • Structuring tasks with collaboration in mind • Matching structure with task processes • Building integrating mechanisms
Training	• Developing interpersonal skills • Nurturing collaboration • Obtaining managerial skills • Learning how to share practices
Evaluation	• Evaluating teamwork knowledge, skills, and abilities • Assessing team performance • Using peer and customer evaluation techniques • Involving team members in evaluation
Compensation	• Compensating individual contributions to teams • Rewarding teams • Integrating teams through rewards • Assessing culture congruence

Recruitment and Selection

Working effectively in a team requires a particular set of knowledge, skills, and abilities (KSAs) that were not as critical in traditional organizations. Proficiency is needed in at least five areas: conflict resolution, collaborative problem solving, communication, goal setting and performance management, and planning and task coordination (Stevens & Campion, 1994; Klimoski & Jones, 1995). During recruitment, organizations aspiring to create a workforce of effective team members should clearly communicate the importance of these proficiencies. Doing so provides a realistic job preview and can therefore help to reduce turnover (Wanous, 1989). Recruiting individuals who prefer these activities also makes sense because team members' preferences for teamwork are related to team effectiveness (Kirkman & Shapiro, 1997).

It is also important to consider teamwork KSAs in the selection process. It might seem easy to include measures of KSAs in most selection systems, but most selection instruments focus on basic learning abilities (for example, math, language, perceptual skills) or specific technical abilities (for example, mechanical, electrical, and so on). In the last few years, employment tests designed to measure teamwork KSAs have been under development. Early results suggest that the tests can predict subsequent performance beyond the level of prediction from a large battery of traditional employment aptitude tests (Stevens & Campion, 1994). These initial findings offer encouraging support for such instruments. Interviews might also be a viable method of assessing social and interpersonal attributes that contribute to teamwork. There is evidence that a structured interview designed to measure social KSAs can predict future team effectiveness (Campion, Campion, & Hudson, 1993). Finally, selection techniques that involve collecting biographical information may be another way to assess teamwork KSAs.

Task Design

The second set of practices that must be modified relate to task design. Effective teams are designed around the tasks they perform. Two key considerations are that teams should be relatively self-contained and handle many aspects of their own functioning. First, teams should be collectively responsible for an identifiable and substantial part of the work of the organization. To the extent possible, support services should be included in the team so that it has the resources necessary to accomplish its goals. Members should be multiskilled and dedicated to the team so that they do not have to split priorities. Finally, the team should report as a unit so that members do not have conflicting directions from different managers (Mohrman, Cohen, & Mohrman, 1995).

Second, the team should be responsible for many aspects of its own functioning. For example, it should be able to determine how to apply the team's resources, strategies for completion of work, and quality monitoring. It should also be responsible for working with internal and external customers. Finally, part of the team's task should be performance evaluation. Whenever appropriate skill levels and task conditions exist, team members should be involved in reviewing their own performance and determining their own rewards (Wellins and others, 1991; Zingheim & Schuster, 1997).

Beyond these two fundamental design principles, a third issue is whether teams should be functional or cross-functional. Functional organizations group people by common specialties and break work down into functional packets that translate into individual assignment. Project organizations combine different specialties required to perform the entire project but then break the work down for members of functional groups within the project. Team-based organizations require a shift away from a hierarchical breakdown to focus instead on the lateral distribution and integration of work (Mohrman, Cohen, & Mohrman, 1995).

Whether teams should be functional or cross-functional is a choice to be based on an analysis of the work to be accomplished. Process analysis can be used to determine the sets of activities that have to be carried out and integrated to deliver value to customers (Davenport, 1993). If within an identifiable set of activities coordination must occur across different functional areas, then teams should be cross-functional. In the cross-functional teams members can integrate work across disciplines and make trade-offs that require a multidisciplinary perspective. But if the process analysis indicates that an identifiable set of activities occurs within a functional area, then teams should be functional.

Training

Training constitutes a third set of practice modifications for effective team implementation. There is often a mistaken belief that people who are highly educated have the basic skills to work effectively in team settings. In fact, highly specialized individuals are often used to working alone and may lack some of the basic interpersonal skills necessary for collaboration. Training programs designed for interpersonal skills in teams take one of two approaches: traditional classroom instruction in which a lecturer delivers material about techniques or strategies for working in teams and creative off-site team-building sessions in which teams participate in athletic, artistic, or competitive activities unrelated to their actual day-to-day responsibilities. What is generally missing is the development of hands-on team capabilities, which is best accomplished by treating the team as a whole and applying the training as the team performs its actual tasks (Mohrman, Cohen, & Mohrman, 1995). In this way, the value of the training is established in the context of the work that the team does.

In addition to teaching interpersonal skills, training must focus on establishing the skills necessary for self-management. First, considerable attention must be given to determining an optimal degree of autonomy. Self-managing teams are an appropriate response to situations where performance can be enhanced by taking decisions closer to the organization's environment (Mohrman, Cohen, & Mohrman, 1995). In contrast, self-management is not appropriate when the team is particularly large, when there is a high degree of functional diversity, or when the team is newly formed (Mohrman, Cohen, & Mohrman, 1995). In these situations, the team is faced with a high level of complexity, information-processing requirements are extensive, and managerial tasks are particularly challenging. Having an external leader provide direction in these instances can improve team effectiveness. Perhaps the most substantial costs associated with increasing self-direction in teams are associated with the level of training and development needed to ensure that all or most of the members have the KSAs required to perform what were previously managerial responsibilities. In addition, on some teams employees are asked actually to carry out the training and development of their fellow members (Manz & Sims, 1993).

Another training focus pertains to learning. In a team-based system, multidirectional learning is required across functions, levels, and organizations. This requires norms that are far different from those that prevailed in the traditional organization. For example, learning requires the willingness to surface bad news and act on it. But that will not happen unless the traditional reaction— negatively evaluating the messengers of bad news—changes. Organizations that encourage experimentation and innovation and set up mechanisms for shared reflection can capitalize on this learning potential (Mohrman, Cohen, & Mohrman, 1995). Lateral learning must occur through dialogue and collaboration, and vertical learning must occur between teams at different levels in the organization. Local learning and innovation occurs through trial and error, but broader learning depends on whether organizations establish mechanisms for reflecting on and capturing learning from a variety of experiences.

Evaluation

A fourth set of practices that must be modified involves evaluation. If organizations wish to motivate teamwork, they must incorporate teamwork KSAs into their appraisal systems. It is important that the appraisal system not only reward good team players but also discourage behaviors that are not conducive to team effectiveness. An organization-specific job analysis should be conducted to determine the precise nature of the behavioral and performance measures to be included in the appraisal form for each individual team member. Categories of teamwork KSAs such as conflict resolution, collaborative problem solving, communication, goal setting, performance management, planning, and task coordination could be translated into critical work behaviors or performance dimensions and incorporated into such an appraisal form (Stevens & Campion, 1994).

Equally important, however, is that team behaviors then be assessed. Imagine four teams, each performing the same task. In the first team, each team member is given an individual goal. In the second, a goal is set for the team as a whole only. The third team is given both individual and team goals. The fourth is given no specific goal at all. Which team will do the poorest work? In an experiment that replicated this situation, the team with *individual goals only* was the poorest performer among all four teams. The team with both individual and team goals performed the best (Mitchell & Silver, 1990). Most organizations might claim they have both individual and team goals if they have profit sharing or gain sharing. However, psychologically, these types of "team goals" are often overshadowed by individual goals, because the personal sense of control over performance lessens as one focuses on larger and larger groups, such as the entire organization.

Each team should identify a set of critical measures representing a combination of results and process-oriented outcomes. Focusing only on results (for example, return on sales, revenue growth, and so on) does not help inform the team about which behaviors should be adjusted. Process measures (time spent per call, days before call returned, and so on) identify key behaviors that the team can change in order to improve results. Teams should avoid developing too many measures. If a measure is not critical in guiding the team's behavior, then discard it. Most experts recommend that teams track six to ten performance areas (Meyer, 1994). Finally, in team-based organizations, people are responsible for collective performance at multiple levels. Individual, team, and business unit performance must be evaluated. Optimizing performance at any one level may hurt performance at other levels. The link between behavior at one level and performance at another may be uncertain. People are often concerned that they will not get adequate feedback on how they are performing when the focus is on collective performance. Therefore, appraisal systems should assess behaviors that contribute to performance of other units or other levels within the organization.

Team members should receive feedback from multiple sources, not just a manager. In small teams, each person can receive peer feedback, that is, feedback from all other team members (Saavedra & Kwun, 1993) and, where appropriate, feedback from customers. Customers may be external to the organization (for example, a person who purchases a product or service) or internal (a person downstream in the process who receives the work of the team). It is also critical that feedback be given on multiple levels. It should be provided on individual performance, individual contributions to the team, team performance, and the team's contribution to the organization as a whole. Especially for the latter, feedback from customers and about competitors is critical. Whenever possible, it is best for teams themselves to document their own performance. This documentation should be developed and then discussed regularly at team meetings.

Compensation

A final set of HR practices that should be examined when implementing teams pertains to compensation. Good practices for rewarding team performance require good processes for defining what the performance should be and for measuring and evaluating the performance (Kanin-Lovers & Cameron, 1993). Some researchers have advocated that rewards should be the last component put in place in the transition to teams (for example, see Mohrman, Cohen, & Mohrman, 1995). This argument is made because team rewards are difficult to develop and have to be tailored to the organization.

We recommend that organizations begin by introducing teamwork as a central objective in each individual's performance evaluation. Individual compensation should then be based on the accomplishment of these objectives. This is an intermediary step on the path toward team-based rewards; it allows recognition for teamwork and allows time for the organization to adjust other systems (Harrington-Mackin, 1994). Next, HR professionals can work to change the organizational compensation and reward practices. For example, team awards and team bonuses help team members focus on the performance of their own team. Profit sharing and gain sharing help team members focus on unitwide performance and orient employees to the larger performing unit by making it in everyone's interest to improve the performance of the enterprise as a whole.

We argue that the most effective compensation systems incorporate an element of all three of these approaches (individual rewards, team rewards, and unit rewards). This combination ensures that performance at each level is recognized and encouraged, in turn ensuring that individual behavior is in the best interest of the team and that team behavior is in the best interest of the organization.

Impediments, Facilitators, and Challenges for the Future of Work Teams

HR professionals may face several additional impediments. We see four challenges in particular: the inability of work teams to make a dramatic improvement in organizational performance quickly; the inevitable interteam conflict inherent in team-based organizations; resistance to work teams in foreign affiliates; and North American cultural barriers to working in teams.

Time Lag

The first stumbling block to the further proliferation of work teams in organizations is the time lag between their implementation and positive results on productivity and employee morale. As with most large-scale organizational changes, team implementation may make things worse initially. Employee productivity and morale may drop and absenteeism and turnover may increase (Cordery, Mueller, & Smith, 1991; Manz & Sims, 1993; Wall, Kemp, Jackson, & Clegg, 1986). This time lag is problematic for two reasons. First, many managers focus heavily on quarterly results. Such a focus may cause extreme disappointment in top managers looking to maximize short-term profitability. Second, because the popular press contains so many positive stories about teams, many top managers are likely to be shocked by the initial drop in organizational performance. After reading *The Greatest Team Success Stories* (a fictional title but probably not far off from the real thing!), patience is likely to wear thin by the time improvements in productivity or morale are actually realized. HR professionals need to arm themselves with concrete evidence about what *really* happens when work teams get implemented. They must inform top managers that work teams will not be an overnight success. In fact, many leading researchers have suggested that three to five years is not an unreasonable time frame for work teams to be fully and successfully implemented (Manz & Sims, 1993; Mohrman, Cohen, & Mohrman, 1995).

Inward Focus

The second likely impediment to successful work teams is a common phenomenon in sports. When individuals are divided up, given team names, granted a set of distinct responsibilities, and told to perform well as a team, they naturally tend to become more inwardly focused and concerned about their own team than about others. Football players shout insults, hockey players brawl, and work teams occasionally place their own interests above that of other teams and the organization as a whole. Such interteam conflict can result in lack of cooperation, refusal to assist other teams in need, or worse, outright sabotage of other teams' efforts. In other words, too much team commitment can be detrimental. An unwillingness to communicate between teams destroys one of the reasons that organizations implement teams in the first place: to create a higher level of integration in a complex organizational environment. Inwardly focused teams that fail to collaborate with others or communicate with external customers perform more poorly than externally focused teams (Ancona, 1990).

Several strategies are available to the HR professional for overcoming problematic inwardly focused teams. First, managers should keep teams focused on a higher level, or superordinate, goal. Such a goal can be organization-, plant-, or unitwide. A superordinate goal keeps teams focused on the big picture, lowers competition between teams, and ties everything that all do more closely to overall organizational success. A second strategy is to implement rewards (possibly based on goals) that are tied to the success of a set of teams as whole (a work unit, for example). Unit-level rewards are tricky in that all team members have to know how their contribution affects their rewards (also known as line of sight). A final strategy is to create linking or integrating teams composed of members from each of the competitive teams. Integrating teams tend to dilute original team member loyalties and ensure that each team's concerns are heard (Mohrman, Cohen, & Mohrman, 1995). Regardless of the strategy chosen, ignoring the problem of combative teams will inevitably erode any potential gains to be realized from the implementation of work teams. HR professionals should take a proactive stand by designing strategies to reduce competition *before* the teams are allowed to become inwardly focused.

Resistance

A third impediment may arise when multinational organizations use work teams in their foreign affiliates. Organizations often wish to "export" their management practices because having similar HR practices in each country streamlines operations and reduces costs (Earley & Erez, 1997). For example, the Goodyear Tire and Rubber Company has begun using work teams in Europe, Latin America, and Asia; Sara Lee Corporation currently uses teams in Puerto Rico and Mexico; and Texas Instruments Malaysia has organized its entire workforce into teams (Manz & Sims, 1993; Kirkman & Shapiro, 1997).

Organizational scholars have pointed to national culture as a determinant of the success or failure of management initiatives that are developed in one culture and implemented in another (Adler, 1997; Hofstede, 1980; Erez & Earley, 1993). Some employees may resist management initiatives or react angrily when those initiatives clash with their deeply held cultural values (Adler, 1997).

HR professionals should learn about the cultures in which the company's work teams will operate. Through better understanding of cultural differences comes the knowledge of potential stumbling blocks to successful implementation *before* attempts are made to export work teams. Success stories about work teams in foreign affiliates exist (Manz & Sims, 1993), but that success depends on an understanding of the cultural forces that shape employee reaction to teams.

Values

A final potential impediment to the success of work teams comes from differences in employee preferences and values within the United States. Just as some cultures are more individualistic or more collectivistic than others, individuals *within* cultures also vary on this dimension—even though there is, on average, more variation across cultures than within cultures (Hofstede, 1980). For example, when faced with the prospect of moving to a team-based work environment, some employees in a study conducted in the United States expressed concerns that reflected their individualistic values (Kirkman, Shapiro, Novelli, & Brett, 1996). Their comments included these (p. 56): "Why should someone else's performance affect my pay?" "Will the team get credit for what I do?" "Individual achievement won't count anymore." "My achievement will be diluted by overall team success."

These comments suggest that some employees may resist work teams because they are not compatible with their own work-related values. Tests exist for measuring individualistic and collectivistic values at the individual level (Maznevski & DiStefano, 1995). Other measures such as preference for teams (Campion, Medsker, & Higgs, 1993) could be used as selection tools to evaluate prospective team members *before* they are placed on a team. If the teams are self-managing or autonomous, measures such as need for growth (Hackman & Oldham, 1980) or need for achievement (McClelland, 1985) could be used to assess prospective member preferences for increased autonomy and responsibility. Whatever the measures used, HR professionals need to be aware of the role of individual differences in a team's success or failure in order to select more carefully individuals who are suited to working in a team.

Barring the availability of such individuals, training must attempt to enhance employee receptivity to work teams.

Facilitators

We see three forces that will continue to enhance the use of teams: the sharing of business practices across organizational units and across different organizations, organizational environment trends, and cultural change.

First, in the years during which Total Quality Management enjoyed its heyday (the 1980s), many companies began a practice that had previously seemed contradictory to maintaining competitive advantage: benchmarking HR practices in other organizations. In years past companies viewed their internal operations as sources of extreme value. But with the growth in international competition—especially in automobiles, electronics, and textiles—some businesses in the United States have realized the benefits of sharing information more openly to increase the global competitiveness of entire industries. This realization coupled with the work team success stories in the popular press have fueled an unprecedented exchange of both ideas and visits between companies and even competitors interested in adopting or improving work teams. For example, companies such as General Electric have looked to other seemingly unrelated businesses, such as Southwest Airlines, in order to adapt team-based practices. The benchmarking of HR practices also occurs within industries. Several major semiconductor manufacturers (for example, Intel, DEC, Texas Instruments) have benchmarking agreements that allow for information exchange around HR best practices (Johns, 1996).

Second, in many industries, organizational environments are becoming exceedingly dynamic and complex. Scholars and practitioners alike have long realized the importance of aligning organizational structures with environmental characteristics (Cummings, 1978; 1982). For example, the rapid changes witnessed in the computer industry forced companies such as IBM to restructure to achieve a better organizational structure-environment fit. There is general consensus that increasing environmental complexity will continue for the foreseeable future for organizations in many industries (Jones, 1995). As these changes continue, the use of work teams will continue to serve as an integrated and flexible means of responding to organizational environments.

Finally, regarding cultural change, researchers have suggested that there may be a substantial amount of cross-national convergence of management practices, values, and beliefs as a result of the interactions between organizations across cultures (Ralston and others, 1992). As cultural convergence continues, a common set of values and assumptions may develop across national boundaries. This implies that eventually it may be possible to develop a universal set of best practices that will be appropriate no matter the cultural setting (Teagarden and others, 1995). In other words, less cultural adaptation may be necessary. Thus, HR practitioners in multinational corporations may gradually have an easier time dealing with cultural impediments. We caution, however, that although some convergence is likely to take place, there are fundamental cultural values within nations that will remain stable. Researchers have referred to this phenomenon as the distinction between peripheral and core values (House, Wright, & Aditya, 1997; Trompenaars, 1994). Therefore, it will always be necessary to adapt HR practices to some degree to fit the cultural context if the effectiveness of those practices across national boundaries is to be enhanced.

The Future of Work Teams

We expect the work teams of the twenty-first century to take on new characteristics that are not currently in common practice but exist in the early adoption phase in the Fortune 1000. First, as the environment grows increasingly complex, temporary team structures will supplant more permanent work teams. As the forces outside organizations continue to change, the structures inside organizations will become more fluid. Rather than permanently assigning people to work teams, team composition will shift as projects, problems, or customers demand. Ad hoc teams or project teams will be more prevalent, placing extraordinary demands on employees to be flexible and demonstrate their value to organizations consistently through their team efforts. The challenge for HR managers will certainly involve compensation and evaluation for employees who may be constantly moving from one project team to another without a regular supervisor or team members with whom they have any long-term contact.

Second, the use of multicultural teams (composed of members from different cultures) and globalized teams (composed of same-culture members in a variety of countries) is likely to rise as trade barriers continue to fall (as, for example, with NAFTA and the European Union). National culture plays a strong role in determining employee attitudes and behavior (Adler, 1997). If a significant rise in these more culturally diverse teams occurs—and we feel strongly that it will—then HR managers must familiarize themselves with the cultures in which their organization operates. For example, if peer evaluations are part of the performance appraisal process on a multicultural team, HR managers must identify the key cultural characteristics that may serve as stumbling blocks to these evaluations. If globalized teams are used, it is likely that entirely different compensation systems will be needed depending on the dominant cultural values of the areas in which an organization has business.

Finally, with more telecommuting and flextime there will be less face-to-face time in work teams. We predict that traditional work teams will be replaced by virtual teams, whose members may seldom or never meet in person. Also referred to as "mobile," these teams have no geographic center. The members work out of their homes, automobiles, and clients' facilities and communicate via e-mail, fax, telephone, and videoconference. Team meetings may take place only once each quarter. The challenge for HR professionals is to assist managers in integrating team members, building cohesive teams, and facilitating communication and information exchange without having team members together in one place.

Conclusion

Teams are a powerful design option for organizations that hope to meet the challenges of increased global competition, improve output quality, and address the social needs of the ever-changing global workforce. However, the success or failure of work teams in multinational organizations will depend largely on the HR professional. Effective implementation of teams requires that HR practitioners adapt key assumptions about motivation, structure, and accountability. Adapted assumptions must support lateral thinking, collaboration, interdependence, a focus on process, permeable boundaries, and mutual responsibility.

At the same time, HR practices must evolve to support team-based systems. Modifications in recruitment and selection, task design, training, evaluation, and compensation are all key to the effective use of teams in multinational organizations. Key to effective selection and recruitment for teams is the identification of teamwork KSAs. Critical for task design is the development of teams around task processes and the integration of functional areas. Developing interpersonal, managerial, and learning skills are important training needs in team-based organizations. Finally, effective evaluation and compensation for teams requires a multi-level perspective and a balance between individual and team-based systems.

Numerous impediments will challenge the effective implementation of teams across national contexts, including the inherent time lag between implementation and results, the often tenuous relationships between teams, cultural differences that require adaptations in practices to fit the context, and increasing domestic demographic diversity within nations. To address these potential impediments, HR practitioners can encourage sharing practices within and between organizations, observe and adapt to organizational environmental trends, and maintain awareness of cultural convergence.

HR professionals who can change their assumptions and are adept at modifying basic HR practices will be better poised to face future trends in the use of teams that are just on the horizon. As temporary team structures, multicultural teams, and virtual teams proliferate, these team-savvy practitioners will be able to lead their organizations through successful implementation and use of teams in multinational contexts.

References

Adler, N. J. (1997). *International dimensions of organizational behavior* (3rd ed.). Cincinnati, OH: South-Western College Publishing.

Ancona, D. G. (1990). Outward bound: Strategies for team survival in an organization. *Academy of Management Journal, 33,* 334–365.

Bandura, A. (1997). *Self-efficacy: The exercise of control.* Upper Saddle River, NJ: Prentice Hall.

Banker, R. D., Field, J. M., Schroeder, R. G., & Sinha, K. K. (1996). Impact of work teams on manufacturing performance: A longitudinal field study. *Academy of Management Journal, 39,* 867–890.

Campion, M. A., Campion, J. E., & Hudson, J. P. (1993). *Structured interviewing: A note on incremental validity and alternative question types.* Working paper, Purdue University, Lafayette, IN.

Campion, M. A., Medsker, G. J., & Higgs, C. A. (1993). Relations between work group characteristics and effectiveness: Implications for designing effective work groups. *Personnel Psychology, 43,* 823–850.

Cohen, S. G., & Bailey, D. E. (1997). What makes teams work: Group effectiveness research from the shop to the executive suite. *Journal of Management, 23,* 239–290.

Cohen, S. G., & Ledford, G. E., Jr. (1994). The effectiveness of self-managing work teams: A quasi-experiment. *Human Relations, 47,* 643–676.

Cordery, J. L., Mueller, W. S., & Smith, L. M. (1991). Attitudinal and behavioral effects of autonomous group working: A longitudinal field study. *Academy of Management Journal, 34,* 464–476.

Cordery, J. L., Wall, T. D., & Wright, B. M. (1997, Apr.). *Toward a more comprehensive and integrated approach to work design: Production uncertainty and self-managing work team performance.* Paper presented at the Twelfth Annual Conference of the Society for Industrial and Organizational Psychology, St. Louis, MO.

Cummings, T. (1978). Self-regulating work group: A sociotechnical synthesis. *Academy of Management Review, 21*(3), 625–634.

Cummings, T. (1982). Designing work for productivity of work life. *Outlook, 6,* 39.

Davenport, T. H. (1993). *Process innovation: Reengineering work through information technology.* Cambridge, MA: Harvard Business School Press.

Dunphy, D., & Bryant, B. (1996). Teams: Panaceas or prescriptions for improved performance? *Human Relations, 49*(5), 677–699.

Earley, P. C., & Erez, M. (1997). *The transplanted executive.* London: Oxford University Press.

Erez, M., & Earley, P. C. (1993). *Culture, self-identity, and work.* London: Oxford University Press.

Gerhart, B., & Milkovich, G. T. (1992). Employee compensation: Research and practice. In M. D. Dunnette & L. M. Hough (Eds.), *Handbook of Industrial and Organizational Psychology* (Vol. 3, pp. 481–569). Palo Alto, CA: Consulting Psychologists Press.

Gibson, C. B. (1995). *Determinants and consequences of efficacy: Beliefs in work organizations in the U.S., Hong Kong, and Indonesia.* Unpublished doctoral dissertation, University of California, Irvine.

Gibson, C. B. (1996, Aug.). *They do what they believe they can: Group-efficacy beliefs and group performance across tasks and cultures.* Paper presented at the annual Academy of Management meeting, Cincinnati, OH.

Goodman, P. S., Devadas, R., & Griffith-Hughson, T. L. (1988). Groups and productivity: Analyzing the effectiveness of self-managing teams. In J. P. Campbell & R. J. Campbell (Eds.), *Productivity in organizations: New perspectives from industrial and organizational psychology* (pp. 295–327). San Francisco: Jossey-Bass.

Hackman, J. R. (1987). The design of work teams. In J. Lorsch (Ed.), *Handbook of organizational behavior* (pp. 315–342). Upper Saddle River, NJ: Prentice Hall.

Hackman, J. R., & Oldham, G. R. (1980). *Work redesign.* Reading, MA: Addison-Wesley.

Harrington-Mackin, D. (1994, Mar.–Apr.). The team building tool kit: Evaluating and rewarding team performance. *Compensation and Benefits Review,* pp. 67–76.

Hofstede, G. (1980). *Culture's consequences: International differences in work values.* Thousand Oaks, CA: Sage.

House, R. J., Wright, N. S., & Aditya, R. N. (1997). Cross-cultural research on organizational leadership. In P. C. Earley and M. Erez (Eds.), *New perspectives on international industrial/organizational psychology* (pp. 535–625). San Francisco: New Lexington Press.

Janis, I. (1982). *Groupthink* (2nd ed.). Boston: Houghton Mifflin.

Johns, G. (1996). *Organizational behavior: Understanding and managing life at work.* New York: HarperCollins.

Jones, G. R. (1995). *Organizational theory: Text and cases.* Reading, MA: Addison-Wesley.

Kanin-Lovers, J., & Cameron, M. (1993). Team-based reward systems. *Journal of Compensation & Benefits, 8,* 56–60.

Kinlaw, D. (1991). *Developing superior work teams: Building quality and the competitive edge.* San Francisco: New Lexington Press.

Kirkman, B. L. (1996). *The impact of national culture on employee resistance to teams: A comparative analysis of globalized self-managing work team effectiveness between the United States, Finland, and the Philippines.* Unpublished doctoral dissertation, Department of Management, University of North Carolina, Chapel Hill.

Kirkman, B. L., & Shapiro, D. L. (1997). The impact of cultural values on employee resistance to teams: Toward a model of globalized self-managing work team effectiveness. *Academy of Management Review, 22,* 730–757.

Kirkman, B. L., Shapiro, D. L., Novelli, L., Jr., & Brett, J. M. (1996). Employee concerns regarding self-managing work teams: A multidimensional justice perspective. *Social Justice Research, 9,* 27–47.

Klimoski, R., & Jones, R. G. (1995). Staffing for effective group decision making: Key issues in matching people and teams. In R. A. Guzzo & Associates (Eds.), *Team effectiveness and decision making in organizations* (pp. 291–332). San Francisco: Jossey-Bass.

Lawler, E. E., III. (1986). *High-involvement management: Participative strategies for improving organizational performance.* San Francisco: Jossey-Bass.

Lawler, E. E., III, Mohrman, S. A., & Ledford, G. E., Jr. (1995). *Creating high performance organizations: Practices and results of employee involvement and total quality management in Fortune 1000 companies.* San Francisco: Jossey-Bass.

Manz, C. C., & Sims, H. P. (1987). Leading workers to lead themselves: The external leadership of self-managing work teams. *Administrative Science Quarterly, 32,* 106–128.

Manz, C. C., & Sims, H. P. (1993). *Business without bosses: How self-managing teams are building high-performance companies.* New York: Wiley.

Maznevski, M. L., & DiStefano, J. J. (1995). *Measure culture in international management: The cultural perspectives questionnaire.* Unpublished working paper, University of Virginia, Charlottesville.

McClelland, D. C. (1985). *Human motivation.* Glenview, IL: Scott, Foresman.

Meyer, C. (1994, May–June). How the right measures help teams excel. *Harvard Business Review,* pp. 15–23.

Mitchell, T., & Silver, W. (1990). Individual and group goals when workers are interdependent: Effects on task, strategies, and performance. *Journal of Applied Psychology, 75,* 185–193.

Mohrman, S. A., Cohen, S. G., & Mohrman, A. M., Jr. (1995). *Designing team-based organizations: New forms for knowledge work.* San Francisco: Jossey-Bass.

Osburn, J., Moram, L., Musselwhite, E., & Zenger, J. H. (1990). *Self-directed work teams: The new American challenge.* Burr Ridge, IL: Irwin.

Osterman, P. (1994). How common is workplace transformation and who adopts it? *Industrial and Labor Relations Review, 47,* 173–188.

Pasmore, W. A. (1995). Social science transformed: The social-technical perspective. *Human Relations, 48,* 1–21.

Ralston, D. A., and others. (1992). Eastern values: A comparison of managers in the United States, Hong Kong, and the People's Republic of China. *Journal of Applied Psychology, 77,* 664–761.

Saavedra, R., & Kwun, S. K. (1993). Peer evaluation in self-managing work groups. *Journal of Applied Psychology, 78,* 450–462.

Shea, G. P., & Guzzo, R. A. (1987). Group effectiveness: What really matters? *Sloan Management Review, 3,* 25–31.

Stevens, M. J., & Campion, M. A. (1994). The knowledge, skill, and ability requirements for teamwork: Implications for human resource management. *Journal of Management, 20,* 503–530.

Sundstrom, E., De Meuse, K. P., & Futrell, D. (1990). Work teams: Applications and effectiveness. *American Psychologist, 45,* 120–133.

Teagarden, M. B., and others. (1995). Toward a theory of comparative management research: An idiographic case study of the best international human resource management project. *Academy of Management Journal, 38,* 1261–1287.

Trist, E. L., & Bamforth, K. W. (1951). Some social and psychological consequences of the Longwall method of coal getting. *Human Relations, 30,* 201–236.

Trompenaars, F. (1994). *Riding the waves of culture: Understanding diversity in global business.* Burr Ridge, IL: Irwin.

Wall, T. D., Kemp, N. J., Jackson, P. R., & Clegg, C. W. (1986). Outcomes of autonomous work groups: A longitudinal field experiment. *Academy of Management Journal, 29,* 280–304.

Wanous, J. P. (1989) Installing a realistic job preview: Ten tough choices. *Personnel Psychology, 42,* 117–133.

Wellins, R. S., Byham, W. C., & Dixon, G. R. (1994). *Inside teams: How twenty world-class organizations are winning through teamwork.* San Francisco: Jossey-Bass.

Wellins, R. S., Byham, W. C., & Wilson, J. (1991). *Empowered teams.* San Francisco: Jossey-Bass.

Wellins, R. S., and others. (1990). *Self-directed teams: A study of current practice.* Pittsburgh: DDI.

Zingheim, P. K., & Schuster, J. R. (1997, Spring). Best practices for small-team pay. *ACA Journal,* pp. 40–49.

CHAPTER 6

Performance Management
The Real Glue in Organizations

Cristina G. Banks
Karen E. May

For several decades, industrial-organizational (I/O) psychologists and human resource (HR) practitioners have wrestled with the problems of accurately assessing performance and designing effective performance development tools. We have focused on a number of variables that held promise for increasing measurement effectiveness: designing the "right" format—one that captured appropriate job content, minimized judgmental and perceptual errors, and was user-friendly; framing performance assessment in the context of goal setting—that is, allowing performance assessment to be a matter of setting an employee's annual goals and then measuring the degree of attainment (for example, management by objectives, or MBO); and obtaining assessments from all levels of the organization (superiors, subordinates, and peers) as well as customers (360-degree feedback).

Different performance measurement systems emerged over the years, some more successful than others. But despite these efforts, effective and well-accepted performance measurement systems still elude many organizations. Why?

Measurement of performance effectiveness is a cornerstone for organizations. Upon it rests an organization's ability to select, train, reward, and motivate the right people in the right ways. Performance measurement is often the only source that employees have to learn about the value of their contributions and the areas in which they need to focus more of their efforts. Performance measurement also provides managers the opportunity to shape employee work behavior through training and coaching to build greater capabilities and encourage even higher performance. With such importance placed on performance measurement, I/O psychologists and HR practitioners need to continue efforts to determine how to design better systems. In this chapter, we explore reasons why performance measurement systems have fallen short of expectations and suggest how we might design better ones.

Many of us who have evaluated and designed performance measurement systems have encountered situations like the following, which illustrates the kinds of problems organizations have with typical performance evaluation systems. A senior-level manager in a large public utility—let's call her Theresa—complained, "I just received my annual review from the general manager, and I'm furious! I made all my performance goals, and even exceeded some. I went well beyond the call of duty several times, but all I received was a 'meets expectations!' When I questioned the general manager about his rating of my performance, he remarked, 'You met my expectations, and that's good—my expectations are so high, I don't expect anyone to really exceed them.'"

Theresa felt unfairly rated; the general manager gave her what he thought she had earned. Where was the problem? A reasonable performance assessment process with specific, objective performance goals set mutually a year earlier and multiple assessments of progress toward goals had missed badly. This was surely not the result the general manager intended. How can a well-intentioned and seemingly well-constructed system go so wrong? To begin to answer this question, let's examine what Theresa understood about the evaluation process.

Although Theresa understood the performance dimensions, she was uninformed about the *continuum of effectiveness* underlying these dimensions. Her boss never told her that goal attainment meant "meets expectations" or explained what kinds of work behaviors exemplified "exceeds expectations"—the continuum of effectiveness was in his head. In the absence of this information, Theresa assumed that meeting her goals and then some would merit a rating of "exceeds expectations." When she learned otherwise, she felt betrayed. Her frustration turned into anger and later into disruptive behavior on the job. The general manager learned that it was difficult to deal with Theresa because she was a complainer. Thus, performance measurement failed to communicate to Theresa how well she was performing, and this experience became an impediment to later communications about expectations and performance improvement.

The case of Theresa shows how organizations need to deal with the real underlying issue, turning performance assessment into a management and communication tool, which in turn becomes a *performance management* system. We believe that such a system must have at least three elements to be effective: a well-articulated set of performance dimensions that capture an employee's value to the organization; a behaviorally anchored continuum of effectiveness for each dimension to communicate degrees of contribution; and a structured process for communicating performance feedback. In addition, managers and supervisors must believe that the performance measurement system is necessary for them to do their *own* jobs more effectively. By knowing exactly what kinds of work behaviors are needed from their employees and then managing employees to greater effectiveness through meaningful communication, managers and supervisors will achieve their own productivity and effectiveness targets and enjoy greater opportunity to work strategically on long-term goals and issues. The lack of connection between performance measurement and management's self-interest is at the heart of traditional performance measurement failures.

Critical Importance of Developing Performance Management Systems

Organizations often undergo rapid change to maintain competitiveness. Organizational structures must change, job boundaries must change, the nature of the employment contract must change, work processes must change, and relationships between employees and their supervisors must change (Miles & Snow, 1994). What we once considered as certainties are now uncertainties, including job security, advancement, pay increases, career development, retirement, and benefits. These changes are influencing organizational culture by creating work environments that employees have not experienced before. Paternalistic, family-oriented company giants (for example, State Farm Insurance Companies and IBM) have undergone dramatic cultural change, evolving into innovative, customer-driven, and hard-driving entities. Although changes in culture can be communicated through the CEO and repeated by senior management, real behavior change (which is required for cultural change) does not occur unless it is embedded in performance expectations as expressed through the performance management system. Thus, the performance management system is the glue that ensures that new cultural behaviors "stick" and it binds employee efforts together to create competitive advantage.

We need effective performance measurement now more than ever. Employees still want to know how well they are doing their job (Murphy & Cleveland, 1991). When rewards are attached to performance, many want to know how they can enhance the opportunity for pay increases. Whether employees want feedback, recognition, or pay increases, the integrity and quality of the measurement process become very important and may determine how satisfied they are with their jobs and the organization in general (Murphy & Cleveland, 1995). The integrity and quality of employee recognition programs based on performance measurement may also influence employee behavior and decisions to stay or leave. Even an employee's feelings of self-worth may be wrapped up in others' acknowledgment of his or her efforts, and this in turn may influence work-related behavior. In these times of skill shortages and retention problems, organizations must look at the performance management system as a key lever in developing an effective and stable workforce (Arthur & Rousseau, 1996).

More important, performance measurement that is embedded within a performance management system presents the best opportunity for focusing employee efforts on precisely those priorities and business strategies that underlie competitive advantage (Schneier, Shaw, & Beatty, 1991). Top management can articulate clearly through the performance management system the kinds of behaviors and outcomes desired to drive critical business strategies, and management can shift emphasis in behaviors and outcomes year to year through revisions in the performance management content. Thus, organizational capabilities—those capabilities that underlie an organization's ability to execute business strategies (Ulrich, 1997)—can be created and enhanced by carefully constructing performance dimensions and effectiveness criteria and refocusing them as business strategies change over time. Organizational capabilities will ultimately determine whether organizations grow and compete; without the capacity to engage employees in working smarter, faster, and with fewer resources, organizations will lose their competitive advantage. Thus, performance management is an essential key to ensuring that organizations keep that edge by focusing employee efforts on high-value behaviors and outcomes that execute strategy (Simons & Davila, 1998) and rewarding such performance to ensure its continuance.

Few tools other than performance management are available for engaging employees in critical business issues and directing their efforts in specific ways. However, performance management must be constructed and implemented so that the organization values it and people use it in the manner intended. We will outline the critical elements of an effective performance management system and detail the steps involved in its development. Examples of actual performance management systems in use will be offered for illustration. First, however, we will review traditional performance assessment methods and clearly specify the ways in which performance management is fundamentally different and explain how performance management can yield the kind of results that managers and business owners desire.

Traditional Performance Assessment and Development

For decades, most organizations have used nearly the same approach to performance assessment and development (Murphy & Cleveland, 1995). Particular systems vary across organizations, but most follow a similar process. Elements of a typical process are presented in Exhibit 6.1 (see Latham, Sharlich, Irvine, & Siegel, 1993; Meyer, 1991; and Wexley, 1986, for more detail on typical performance appraisal).

As the exhibit shows, performance measurement is based on a job analysis and rarely includes broader organizational criteria.

Exhibit 6.1. The Typical Approach to Assessment.

Element	Description
Structure	A set of performance dimensions derives from a job analysis
Unit of analysis	Tasks and activities defined in behavioral terms
Content	Important and critical aspects of the job as identified through the job analysis
Measurement method	A rating scale calibrated from "low" to "high" effectiveness
Evaluation criteria	Descriptors that anchor different points along the rating continuum
Specificity of criteria	Ranges from general (for example, "excellent") to specific (for example, "constructs an expert presentation with all relevant facts in appropriate order")
Evaluation frequency	Formal evaluation conducted once per year
Who evaluates	One appraiser, usually a direct supervisor
Focus of evaluation	Comparison between performance expectations (for example, personal goals, performance standards) and actual job performance (for example, typical job behaviors, performance outcomes)
Feedback process	Feedback interview between appraiser and appraisee in which evaluator shares his or her evaluation of the appraisee
Appraiser's role	To reach a mutual understanding of the appraisee's performance effectiveness and areas for further improvement
Appraisee's role	To accept or rebut the appraiser's assessment and to learn in what areas he or she needs to improve
Follow up	Development of a performance improvement plan that includes recommended training and motivational intervention (for example, financial incentives)

Also, performance measurement is usually static; in other words, it captures at one point in time a summary of an entire year of work behavior and performance outcomes. In addition, the focus of the feedback interview is on reaching agreement on the results of the evaluation and determining actions that need to be taken to improve performance.

Underlying Assumptions

The traditional approach to performance assessment fit the needs of organizations when jobs were relatively independent and stable in nature, work processes were primarily procedural and observable, and managers had a relatively small number of direct reports whose job performance could be observed frequently through interaction. Managers controlled the work of subordinates by defining jobs, delegating work, supervising work production, and overseeing work results. Employees were generally considered effective performers when they met the manager's performance expectations (Bernardin & Beatty, 1984).

Variations on the Basic Process

Over the years, practitioners have introduced a number of variations on the basic appraisal process, such as increasing the number of raters beyond the manager (for example, 360-degree feedback), implementing a variety of appraisal formats (mixed standard scales, BARS, BOS), and including a variety of performance criteria (contextual as well as technical performance). But the process has remained generally the same because it served the needs of the organization.

Unfortunately, employees reviewed through this process were often not happy with the results, and managers implementing it often found the task tedious, time consuming, irrelevant to their own jobs, and ripe with potential for conflict. The gap between the intent of performance measurement and the managerial and employee response to the measurement process has been at times so great that some organizations have chosen to drop "performance appraisal" entirely (Meyer, 1991).

Changes in the Work World

To close this gap and to make performance measurement a more meaningful part of a manager's job, we need to examine the ways in which the traditional approach to performance measurement needs to change. How does traditional performance measurement fit within the context of current organizational needs? How can the performance measurement process be modified to complement employee and manager priorities? First, let's consider how changes in the world of work may influence the way we manage and evaluate performance.

Changes in the nature of organizations, the structure of jobs, and the assumptions built into employment contracts affect how individual job performance is defined and managed. These changes challenge many of the assumptions underlying traditional performance measurement, creating an opportunity to redesign the measurement process so that both managers and employees embrace the process and incorporate performance measurement *and management* into their daily work lives.

Changes in Organizational Structure

Changes in organizational structure that are reshaping our approach to performance management include the growing number of flatter organizations along with increasing decentralization and globalization, need for individuals to be flexible and agile, and number of company-to-company partnerships and alliances.

Although flatter organizations are thought to be more versatile and efficient, the people working in them often find themselves with an expanded scope of responsibilities and fewer resources available. In addition, managers may have fewer opportunities to observe performance, whereas employees have increased discretion over their work and how they do it.

Increased decentralization of organizations, like increased globalization, creates a tension between local needs and practice on the one hand and the need for consistency within companies on the other. When decision-making authority is distributed, whether functionally or by geographic region, performance management can be used as a local management tool or as a tool to reinforce overall company principles and objectives as employees are evaluated along dimensions that support the company's business strategies. The challenge is to develop a system that can do both.

An increasing number of company-to-company partnerships and alliances have created new types of work situations in which employees from different companies work side-by-side on the same projects, often in the same location, sharing responsibility for outcomes. These types of working relationships present a challenge for performance management systems when they create incentives for different work behaviors and reward performance based on different criteria.

In sum, flexible performance management systems that vary in content, criteria, frequency, and evaluators are likely to be more effective than traditional performance measurement systems because they can respond to changing organizational forms.

Changes in the Nature of Jobs

Changes in job structure that affect performance measurement include an increase in the use of teams, an increase in the number of people working from home or on the road, rapidly advancing technological knowledge, and fluidity of assigned tasks and jobs (that is, they change as a function of work process improvement).

A great deal of work has been done on evaluating team performance (for example, see Mohrman, Mohrman, & Lawler, 1992), and many organizations are developing systems that measure and reward individuals and teams. Companies face a clear challenge in both the measurement of team-based results and the willingness of employees to accept feedback that focuses on the team and not on themselves individuals.

As more people work from home or on the road, there are a series of challenges to the observation of performance and the delivery of timely and specific feedback. Contact between employees and managers is limited when employees are located in different geographic regions. As Murphy and Cleveland (1995) note, limited opportunity for observation and interaction may lead to an overemphasis on outcomes and results. When interacting on the job with coworkers, customers, and vendors is as important or more important than performance outcomes, observation of work behavior will be essential for evaluating employees' contribution to organizational success. Therefore, inclusion of different observers in the measurement process may address this issue.

Rapidly advancing technological knowledge also tends to limit observation of behavior (Hedge & Borman, 1995). Technology affects where (for example, at home) and how (for example, in semiautonomous work groups) work is performed. In addition, technological advances are occurring so quickly that it may be difficult for managers to stay abreast of those changes and incorporate them into performance criteria and expectations. Although electronic monitoring (for example, electronic time stamps) may allow task accomplishment to be measured, it is likely to provide measurements that are perceived as trivial.

Fluidity of assigned tasks and jobs requires flexibility in a performance management system. Flexibility can be achieved if managers and employees periodically review the performance criteria included in the system; as work assignments or priorities change, they can revise the system to reflect these changes.

Changes in the Nature of Employment Relationships

The nature of employment contracts is changing as well (Arthur & Rousseau, 1996; Osterman, 1996; Cappelli and others, 1997). Employment is no longer assumed to be permanent, stable, or predictable. Including contingent workers, independent contractors, and employees on temporary assignments under managerial direction makes performance measurement and management more complex. These workers are less likely to be well known to the managers and thus more difficult to appraise and manage. As the nature of employment shifts from secure and paternalistic to insecure and independent, employees are less likely to be committed to the organization or to care about performance improvement.

Changes in the Aspects of Performance We Measure

Traditionally, I/O psychologists have advocated that performance measurement should be based on a systematic job analysis from which important and critical dimensions of job performance can be derived (Murphy & Cleveland, 1995; Murphy, 1989). In fact, job analysis constitutes crucial evidence for the defense of performance measurement systems and outcomes in discrimination cases (Bernardin & Beatty, 1984). However, by focusing the measurement content exclusively on the *job* and the *job context,* organizations miss an opportunity to include organizationwide performance criteria. For example, performance criteria have broadened in recent years by including contextual performance factors that support the organizational, social, and psychological environment in which job-specific activities must be performed (Borman & Motowidlo, 1993).

A relatively new set of criteria includes conformance to company values and critical success factors (Bullen & Rockart, 1981). These are organizationwide variables through which employees can also influence business success. As organizations define individual performance more broadly to include such variables, more of these variables will be included within the performance measurement domain.

One of our clients incorporated company values into the performance measurement system for the entire organization. Top management had previously identified the company values as the "eleven attributes of a championship team." Exhibit 6.2 shows three selected values, their definitions, and examples of work behaviors that exemplify each one.

These attributes were incorporated into individual performance assessments by generating behavioral examples of job performance that reflected the quality-of-work behavior the company valued. Managers then evaluated employees on the degree to which they performed their jobs in the manner described by the examples. This added an important missing component to this company's previous performance measurement system. Top management realized they needed to change how people worked in order to achieve better outcomes, so they introduced new performance expectations and criteria to motivate this behavioral change.

Other examples of how new factors have been incorporated into performance measurement systems may be found among companies that have introduced measurements of critical success factors (CSF), factors in a company's business strategy that give it a unique competitive edge and thus separate it from the competition (Bullen & Rockart, 1981). Each company needs to execute these CSFs exceptionally well in order to reap competitive gains, and employees are responsible for their successful execution. By measuring employee behavior that supports their successful execution, a company can increase awareness of the importance of these factors and reward those employees who perform in ways that support successful execution (see Schneier, Shaw, & Beatty,

Exhibit 6.2. Incorporating Company Values in the Performance Measurement System.

Company Value	Definition	Behavioral Example
"Best results come from the best process"	"I must use the best process to achieve best results."	• Plans carefully before initiating action • Effectively executes plans once they have been established and agreed upon • Sets clear deadlines for completion of process
"Will to win"	"A passionate will to win must be present in everything I do."	• Shows real persistence regarding important issues—does not give up • Is effective in motivating others to overcome challenges • Demonstrates strong support for others' projects—not just his or her own
"Commitment to teamwork"	"We must work as cross-functional teams to maximize results."	• Clearly defines the roles and responsibilities of members of the teams he or she establishes or sponsors • Requires timely communication from teams on progress and needed assistance • Seeks to develop all employees as team players—not just a favored few

1991, for a more extensive discussion of CSFs in performance assessment). Examples of two companies' CSFs are Wal-Mart's superior capability in purchasing and logistics, which enables it to compete on an "everyday low price" basis, and McDonald's superior site selection, high-quality service, product innovation, and communications.

CSFs can be translated into job-specific performance measures. Exhibit 6.3 lists several companies that have included CSFs in their performance measurement process.

Any company can capture CSFs and then operationalize them as individual performance criteria where relevant. In this way, individuals can be held accountable for company-level initiatives by including job-specific behaviors that enhance the company's CSF capabilities into performance measurement.

Still another set of new measures include general skills and abilities, or *competencies,* that underlie an organization's ability to innovate, change rapidly, and form key strategic relationships and partnerships with various entities. Perhaps because these factors lack relatedness to specific jobs they are included only infrequently

Exhibit 6.3. Companies That Have CSFs in Their Performance Measurement Systems.

Company	Critical Success Factor	Measure
Federal Express	Customer service	12-Factor Service Quality Index tracks late deliveries, lost and damaged packages, missed pick-ups.
Xerox	Customer service	Service call measures: frequency, responsiveness, length of call, copy quality.
Coca-Cola	Penetrating and operating in foreign markets	Number of days to set up operations in a country.
General Motors	Operating efficiency	Number of direct labor hours to produce a car.
Hewlett Packard	Innovation	Percentage of revenues from products that are two years old or newer.

in traditional performance measurement systems. However, they have increased in importance recently as the perception of their relationship to competitiveness has grown. Some examples of definitions of such competencies follow.

- *Flexibility* is the ability to adapt to different people's needs and styles of communication, to recognize each person as an individual, or to adapt to procedural and organizational changes.
- *Ability to learn* refers to the ability to assimilate and incorporate new information into a knowledge set that increases a skill or knowledge, the ability to gain knowledge and expertise from experience, or the ability to generate new knowledge through study, experience, or data collection.
- *Technological savvy* refers to the ability to use technology to maximize benefit, the ability to innovate using technological solutions in order to improve work outcomes, or the ability to use a variety of technology tools for multiple purposes.
- *Teamwork skills* include the ability to cooperate and collaborate with other members of the team to achieve team outcomes, the ability to gain other team members' support and commitment to the team's work, and the ability to work as a member of a team, including collaborating on work activities, communicating with other team members, resolving conflicts with other team members, delegating tasks, and solving problems.
- More recently, *personality factors* that influence work behavior and performance outcomes also have been added to the performance domain (for example, Barrick & Mount, 1991).

These factors as well as other relevant performance dimensions could be mapped on the "Big Five Personality Factors" to identify relevant aspects of personality in performance effectiveness and to derive behavioral examples to be included within the performance measurement process. (Acknowledgment made to Allen Kraut for his contribution to this point.)

Each of these new performance dimensions adds to the total performance picture in a specific job. In this way, employee effort can be tied directly to a company's competitiveness through business strategy execution and core competency development (Prahalad & Hamel, 1990). The more closely individual effort is tied to organizational success in a performance management system, the more likely managers and supervisors will perceive performance measurement as useful and helpful to their own success. By managing their employees toward higher individual performance, managers and supervisors will be more likely to achieve their own performance goals because these goals are also tied to organizational success. As long as performance measurement at all levels is tied to critical aspects of organizational success, managers and supervisors will be more likely to see the connection between their own success and employee success. Thus, performance measurement will become a personally meaningful process and performance management will become a meaningful tool for obtaining critical organizational outcomes.

Why is it important to make performance measurement and management a personally meaningful process? We believe that one of the factors behind resistance to traditional performance measurement is its lack of personal meaningfulness. It has been well demonstrated over the years that one of the major stumbling blocks to effective performance measurement is the appraiser's unwillingness to provide accurate appraisals (Banks & Murphy, 1985; Murphy & Cleveland, 1995). Unwillingness may be a function of a number of factors, such as desire to avoid unpleasant conversations and confrontation, lack of organizational norms for honesty, and amount of time spent outside of the manager's job to complete an employee appraisal. But when content is meaningful in the eyes of the appraiser, it is in the appraiser's best interest to evaluate employee performance accurately and conscientiously and overcome these barriers. Thus, we can increase not only managers' motivation to appraise accurately but also their motivation to work with subordinates to address performance issues.

The motivation of those being appraised to participate in the process and work with their managers or supervisors on performance issues may also be affected by changes in performance measurement. Today, employees share a sense of job insecurity and often feel the need to take responsibility for their own career management (Arthur & Rousseau, 1996). In the eyes of the individual being appraised, the performance measurement and management system may offer a critical avenue for controlling the future. By engaging frequently in honest discussions of performance effectiveness with their managers, those on the receiving end of an appraisal can learn how to modify their behavior to create the greatest value to the organization. Appraisers may view this opportunity as a hedge against downsizing or becoming obsolete.

We believe that the changes in the world of work have contributed to a fundamental shift in the way organizations perceive and use performance measurement. Changes in measurement content and in employee and managerial interest in performance management have converged to create new forms of performance measurement and management systems.

We now turn to a description of this new form of performance measurement—reconceptualized as performance management—to signify its importance as a management and communication tool.

The Emergence of Performance Management

New forms of performance management began to emerge when business needs changed as competition from abroad increased (Schuler & Huber, 1993). Human resource management in general had to become strategic in order to help organizations operationalize their business strategies and achieve critical outcomes. When this step was taken, there was a greater emphasis on engaging every individual in the success of the organization. Employees were key to improved business outcomes by producing more at higher levels of quality with fewer resources and by continuously innovating in the workplace in an effort to reduce costs and improve product and service quality. More emphasis on employee contributions to overall business success led to a number of changes in the workplace and in particular to changes in the relationship between employees and their managers.

When organizations placed greater emphasis on managing people, they realized that performance measurement had to evolve to meet changing organizational needs (Banks, 1997). Employees need to be engaged fully in their work, but traditional ways of rewarding and motivating performance, such as promotion and advancement, are less available than before. Other trends, such as fading employee loyalty, fewer resources for the development of expensive incentive compensation systems, and instability in the employment contract between employers and employees, contribute to the need for organizations to find a new tool that can continuously sharpen employees' focus on precisely those things that lead to business success.

Organizations have also been in the midst of great organizational change in an effort to meet competitive challenges, and shifts in organizational culture have served as important catalysts for change. As greater shifts in culture were required (for example, shifting from a "knowing" to a "learning" organization; Senge, 1990), there was a need to redefine appropriate job behavior and interactions with people both within (functional peers) and outside (customers) the organization. Thus, companies began introducing cultural change through performance management.

Organizations began to create tools that engaged employees in the enterprise by emphasizing the importance of managers managing people (as opposed to managing tasks) on a continuous basis. Managers and employees began to communicate frequently and in very specific ways, focusing on aspects of performance that contributed significantly to business success. They communicated until they achieved a shared understanding of what it takes to be most effective in the organization.

In sum, organizations moved from performance measurement to performance management to meet competitive challenges. New performance management systems are nimble, can be changed according to business needs, and include organizationwide concerns. They focus on a shared understanding of effective performance through continuous communication and feedback between managers and their subordinates, and then motivate behavioral change by capitalizing on the self-interests of both appraisers and appraisees.

Differences Between Performance Management and Performance Measurement

How does performance management differ specifically from performance measurement and development? Exhibit 6.4 summarizes the major elements of performance management.

Management Versus Measurement

The most obvious difference is the emphasis on management rather than measurement. Instead of viewing the process as an opportunity to measure the effectiveness of an employee's performance over

Exhibit 6.4. Major Elements of Performance Management.

Element	Description
Structure	A set of performance dimensions derived from an *organizational* analysis as well as a *job* analysis
Unit of analysis	Tasks and activities defined in behavioral terms
Content	Important and critical aspects of the job as identified through the organizational and job analyses
Measurement method	A rating scale calibrated from "low" to "high" effectiveness
Evaluation criteria	Descriptors that anchor different points along the rating continuum
Specificity of criteria	Specific (for example, "constructs an expert presentation with all relevant facts in their appropriate order")
Evaluation frequency	A formal evaluation conducted several times a year (e.g., monthly, quarterly, or at the conclusion of assignments or projects); informal evaluation perhaps almost daily
Who evaluates	Everyone who had an opportunity to observe and evaluate performance; can incorporate multiple sources of feedback
Focus of evaluation	Comparison between performance expectations (e.g., personal goals, performance standards) and actual job performance (e.g., typical job behaviors, performance outcomes)
Feedback process	Feedback meeting between appraiser and appraisee whenever either party desires; appraiser shares observations and relates them to performance criteria, appraisee seeks clarification on the observations or on the criteria
Appraiser's role	To understand the performance criteria and to help the appraisee understand how his or her performance fits within the criteria; also to look for ways appraisee can improve performance
Appraisee's role	To understand the performance criteria and to help the appraiser understand how his or her performance fits within the criteria; also to look for ways he or she can improve performance
Follow up	Further observation and feedback on performance; development of plans for further improvement, including training and motivational intervention

the last year, it is seen as an opportunity to collect performance data to help shape the employee's understanding of performance objectives and various avenues for achieving important work outcomes. Performance measurement has been transformed from just a report card to an opportunity for a discussion between manager and subordinate. This discussion is critical for managing the employee's performance—staying informed of his or her progress toward goals and objectives, noting efficiencies and innovations, reinforcing valuable work efforts, and guiding behavior toward higher achievement.

The difference in performance management is that *measurement is continuous,* and it is seen as a means to an end rather than an end in itself. Thus, performance assessment is transformed from a tool for evaluation and review to one that molds performance through continuous feedback. Coupled with effective reward and recognition programs, performance management can shape work behavior to reap the gains desired in the competitive marketplace.

Strategy-Based Versus Job-Based Dimensions

As mentioned earlier, traditional systems derive from a job analysis that focuses on technical as well as contextual factors that underlie performance (Murphy & Cleveland, 1995). Performance management dimensions are broader in scope and explicitly tie business strategy to individual performance. By broadening the scope of evaluation beyond an employee's job duties and responsibilities, important business initiatives (strategies, organizational change) can be operationalized down to the individual level, making the connection between what an employee does and organizational success much more apparent. Managers seeing the connection may be more likely to coach and develop employees to achieve important organizational outcomes. The performance management system provides the avenue through which coaching and development can take place.

Evolving Versus Static Definitions of Performance

Traditional systems are designed to capture job tasks that remain relatively stable over time. In addition, traditional systems emphasize standardization of performance dimensions and criteria, enabling comparisons across incumbents within the same job. In contrast, performance management systems are designed to fit business needs, which are likely to change periodically with the competitive landscape. The definition of the term *performance* needs to evolve as the components of competitiveness evolve. Performance management dimensions are relatively easy to change because of the interactive nature of the system between appraisers and appraisees. Because both parties communicate frequently about performance, modifications in performance dimensions and criteria can be incorporated into the existing system as the need presents itself. An underlying foundation of communication between the two parties provides a natural bridge for evolving definitions of performance.

Shared Versus Single Responsibility for System Development

Traditional systems are usually created by management and presented to employees to inform them of the basis of their evaluations. Even though organizations using traditional systems emphasize the importance of appropriate appraisal content and performance criteria, employees may still perceive the system as unfair and subjective because they did not participate in its development (Giles & Mossholder, 1990). In contrast, organizations using performance management systems often engage both parties to discuss standards and criteria in order to design a system that everyone understands and agrees to. Agreement up front increases the likelihood that the performance management process will be perceived as meaningful and useful to all parties. Conflicts arising from different perspectives on standards and criteria are best resolved early in system development rather than after the first results of the process are communicated. Early resolution of these conflicts will increase acceptance of results later.

Rewards

Traditional systems often pair appraisal results with financial rewards. Performance assessments are needed so that rewards can be distributed to employees in line with performance achievements.

It has been noted that performance appraisals are distorted whenever appraisal results are viewed as a means to deliver certain financial outcomes (Banks & Murphy, 1985; Murphy & Cleveland, 1991). In contrast, performance management systems emphasizing performance improvement through continuous feedback may limit the temptation to distort feedback for greater financial gain. When accurate performance assessment is viewed as critical for achieving important organizational goals and objectives, appraisers may be less motivated to distort feedback. With frequent feedback, there is less opportunity for appraisers to "hide" performance problems from others and thus appraisers are less likely to reward employees inappropriately. More important, if performance management is used as a management tool, rewards may be less of an inducement to distort assessments. Rewards, then, may function as complements to the performance management system rather than drivers of appraisal outcomes.

Management Process Versus Administrative Hurdle

Traditional systems consist of once- or twice-a-year assessments that play a somewhat ancillary role in a manager's job (Cascio, 1993). Whenever performance assessment is perceived as separate from a manager's everyday job, it is likely to be perceived as a lower priority and thus become an administrative hassle. Performance appraisal is often described as an activity best accomplished on airplanes or at home on weekends when there is no other work that can be done, and several appraisals are usually written in one sitting (Murphy, 1993). Performance management cannot be accomplished in this manner. Because it is an ongoing process, performance management is incorporated into the manager's tool kit for getting results from units or departments. Managing the performance of subordinates becomes the job; frequent performance assessments give managers the data they need to make appropriate adjustments.

Case Study

In this section we briefly present an example of how a company developed and implemented a new performance management system based on the concepts presented in this chapter.

A business information services (BIS) department within a Fortune 500 company that consists of 120 employees divided into five functional areas had a performance appraisal system that was unsatisfactory. It required significant manager involvement, including observing and reviewing employees' work, writing narratives, rating three skill areas (technical, social, and business), and meeting with each employee to discuss evaluations and future career development. A few years ago, a company reorganization greatly reduced the number of managers in BIS, resulting in an employee-to-manager ratio as great as sixty to one and averaging over thirty to one. Frustration reached a critical stage when employees experienced greatly reduced time with their managers. In fact, a few hadn't even received an appraisal in over two years.

We developed a new performance appraisal system that achieved the company's original objectives of evaluating performance and developing skills on a periodic basis. The new system would also need to work within the current employee-to-manager ratio constraints. To address this issue, the company created a new position: a feedback specialist, who was responsible for collecting performance data and holding feedback meetings with employees following assessments. This position was filled when the new system was installed. (It should be noted that a feedback specialist may be anyone who has communications and counseling training.) By repositioning the system as a management and communication tool, refocusing assessment content, and facilitating communications, we were able to create a performance management system that met the organization's needs and gained wide acceptance.

The BIS system employs a set of performance dimensions anchored by behavioral examples across positions exemplifying high, average, and low levels of effectiveness. Each employee and manager selects a subset of dimensions most relevant for the evaluation of that employee's work. The feedback specialist e-mails evaluation forms to evaluators nominated by the employee and his or her manager, and evaluators subsequently complete the forms and e-mail them back to the feedback specialist. Evaluators are asked to provide examples of employee performance that match the dimensions and rate the employee using the anchored scales. The feedback specialist then collects the data from the various forms and integrates them into an Excel spreadsheet including both ratings and comments. The feedback specialist consolidates comments, forwards information to his or her manager, and communicates the feedback in person to the employee and makes suggestions for further improvement.

On a yearly basis, the feedback specialist works with the manager to prepare a formal review and then serves as a facilitator when the manager and employee meet for the review. The manager discusses the employee's performance over the year and together the two set goals for the following year. They leave the meeting sharing the same understanding of the level of the employee's performance and direction for next year.

We followed several steps in developing the new system.

1. *Assessing the organization's readiness to build a new type of performance management system.* Readiness means that an organization has identified its goals, objectives, and values and is committed to developing a system that will help direct employee performance toward those outcomes.

2. *Involving top management in the development of the new system.* When organizational leaders are involved in system development, it ensures that meaningful performance dimensions are identified and that acceptance by the rank and file is more likely.

3. *Using company and department values, goals, and objectives to identify critical and meaningful performance dimensions.* Values, goals, and objectives form the foundation of the system. In this case, we identified them by working with senior management and internal experts to determine the areas of performance that, taken together, would lead to organizational success.

4. *Developing behavioral anchors to exemplify the performance dimensions.* Experts from each department unit worked together to develop anchors that exemplified high, average, and low levels of performance for each dimension. Both job incumbents and their managers served as experts.

5. *Determining feedback sources.* Many potential sources of feedback were available, including contractors who work closely with the employee, internal and external customers, team members from inside and outside the department, and project managers from inside and outside the company. Employees, with input from their managers, could identify several qualified sources of feedback for evaluating their performance.

6. *Establishing ownership of the performance management system.* Ownership means taking responsibility for the administration, maintenance, and modification of the system over time. BIS leadership delegated responsibility for the system administration to the feedback specialist, an outside contractor. By locating this responsibility outside the permanent workforce, BIS employees could avoid getting sidetracked with the administrative tasks associated with the system.

7. *Developing a process for collecting performance data frequently.* A method was needed for collecting, combining, and distributing feedback, enabling managers to collect data for coaching and decision making. BIS distributed forms and collected feedback via Lotus Notes. Performance data were compiled and combined using Microsoft Excel.

8. *Training users.* Users participated in training, which included an explanation of the electronic system as well as the dimensions and anchors that were to be used in the feedback process.

9. *Introducing the new performance management system to all employees.* Although some employees were involved in developing the new system, a formal introduction to the system was needed in which each aspect of the system was explained and issues resolved.

At this writing, the system has been working well for over a year. BIS employees were so satisfied with the results that when corporate HR attempted to replace the system with a traditional one, BIS flatly refused. After a series of heated meetings, BIS and corporate reached a compromise: corporate's performance criteria were incorporated into the BIS performance management system.

We believe BIS's adopting the performance management system is representative of a new wave of organizations desiring to turn performance measurement into a management tool. This approach may be particularly attractive to consulting and accounting firms that are interested in evaluating performance when projects and assignments come to an end and in managing their employees toward greater customer service.

Conclusion

In this chapter we have argued that it is important to change the view of performance appraisal from one emphasizing measurement to one emphasizing content and communication. The needs of organizations have changed, putting greater focus on engaging employees in the success of the enterprise. Traditional performance measurement didn't do it; employees and their managers often viewed appraisal as a scorecard, one that was compiled too infrequently and often used as a means to distribute raises. So how can employees be engaged other than through incentive compensation? We believe that the performance management system is a critical tool for increasing employees' awareness of the value of their contribution to the organization's success and for creating a dialogue with their managers that can enhance the contributions that employees can make.

This new approach incorporates different content than traditional approaches. It is more focused on organizationwide initiatives, less on the specific job. The content explicitly ties employee behavior to the strategic objectives of the organization as they are operationalized at that particular level or unit. As also noted, this approach goes beyond mere goal setting. In addition to specifying the goals desired in behavioral terms, the approach details the entire continuum of effectiveness and clearly identifies where "meets goals" falls on the continuum. Furthermore, by operationalizing strategy this approach reinforces behavioral changes on the part of employees. Our experience tells us that by changing the content of the appraisal to critical issues that the organization faces, the perceived importance of the performance review dramatically increases for both employees and their managers.

When the importance of the performance management process increases, there is a greater need for skill in conducting the process properly. In order to serve as a management tool, managers must be trained in its proper use. This means that managers must understand how this system helps them achieve better results through their people, and they must acquire the communication and performance management skills (for example, articulating expectations, observing performance or work products, evaluating the effectiveness of work behavior) to do so. Because the importance of performance management is greater, the need for higher-level performance management skills through effective training increases.

As the importance of performance management increases, the need for employee acceptance of performance appraisal results also increases. The goal of performance management is improved employee performance. This implies that employees must see value in the results of the review and accept the feedback to direct them toward changing in order to be more effective. Thus, as the need for acceptance of appraisal results increases, it is more important to create a system that is perceived as fair and useful.

When the outcomes of the performance management process become more valuable to the organization, there is a greater need for the organization to use the process on an ongoing basis. Rather than conducting appraisals once or twice a year, organizations can benefit from conducting them as often as practical or whenever significant assignments are completed. If performance management including appraisal is woven into the fabric of managers' everyday duties and responsibilities, it is more likely that managers will engage in it on a continuous basis and thereby provide feedback and coaching to employees as needed (for example, monthly or quarterly). In the fast-paced competitive world in which most global businesses run today, ongoing performance management is a valuable tool for staying on course or changing direction, as the marketplace demands. As the value of this process increases, the use of this system is likely to increase as well.

Indeed, cultural change and organizational transformation are unlikely to occur without new values being introduced into the performance management system. Declarations by senior management are insufficient to drive the new behaviors needed for cultural change; rather, these behaviors must be embedded in the performance fabric and woven into daily efforts and priorities. We believe that performance management can be the real glue in organizations by bonding together all the elements of organizational success into a single, aligned process that channels employee performance toward the same organizational goals and reinforces and maintains that alignment through reward and recognition programs. If the power of this tool can be harnessed and used to the fullest, then organizations can better their chances of success in a highly competitive business world.

References

Arthur, M. B., & Rousseau, D. M. (Eds.). (1996). *The boundaryless career.* New York: Oxford University Press.

Banks, C. G. (1997). *Performance management in the twenty-first century.* Paper presented at the Industrial and Organizational Psychology Conference, Auckland, New Zealand.

Banks, C. G., & Murphy, K. R. (1985). Toward narrowing the research-practice gap in performance appraisal. *Personnel Psychology, 38,* 335–345.

Barrick, M. R., & Mount, M. K. (1991). The big five personality dimensions and job performance: A meta-analysis. *Personnel Psychology, 44,* 1–26.

Bernardin, H. J., & Beatty, R. W. (1984). *Performance appraisal: Assessing human behavior at work.* Boston: Kent.

Borman, W. C., & Motowidlo, S. J. (1993). Expanding the criterion domain to include elements of contextual performance. In N. Schmitt & W. Borman (Eds.), *Personnel selection in organizations* (pp. 71–98). San Francisco: Jossey-Bass.

Bullen, C. V., & Rockart, J. F. (1981). *A primer on critical success factors.* Boston: Center for Information System Research, Massachusetts Institute of Technology.

Cappelli, P., and others. (1997). *Change at work.* New York: Oxford University Press.

Cascio, W. F. (1993). *Managing human resources* (4th ed.). New York: McGraw-Hill.

Giles, W. F., & Mossholder, K. W. (1990). Employee reactions to contextual and session components of performance appraisal. *Journal of Applied Psychology, 75,* 371–377.

Hedge, J. W., & Borman, W. C. (1995). Changing conceptions and practices in performance appraisal. In A. Howard (Ed.), *The changing nature of work* (pp. 451–481). San Francisco: Jossey-Bass.

Latham, G. P., Sharlich, D., Irvine, D., & Siegel, J. P. (1993). The increasing importance of performance appraisals to employee effectiveness in organizational settings in North America. *International Review of Industrial and Organizational Psychology, 8,* 87–132.

Meyer, H. H. (1991). A solution to the performance appraisal feedback enigma. *Academy of Management Executive, 5*(1), 68–76.

Miles, R. E., & Snow, C. C. (1994). *Fit, failure, and the Hall of Fame: How companies succeed or fail.* New York: Free Press.

Mohrman, A. M., Mohrman, S. A., & Lawler, E. E., III. (1992). The performance management of teams. In W. Bruns (Ed.), *Performance measurement, evaluation, and incentives* (pp. 217–241). Boston: Harvard Business School Press.

Murphy, K. J. (1993, Spring). Performance measurement and appraisal: Merck tries to motivate managers to do it right. *Employment Relations Today,* pp. 47–62.

Murphy, K. R. (1989). Dimensions of performance. In R. Dillon & J. Pelligrino (Eds.), *Testing: Applied and theoretical perspectives* (pp. 218–247). New York: Praeger.

Murphy, K. R., & Cleveland, J. N. (1991). *Performance appraisal: An organizational perspective.* Needham Heights, MA: Allyn & Bacon.

Murphy, K. R., & Cleveland, J. N. (1995). *Understanding performance appraisal: Social, organizational, and goal-based perspectives.* Thousand Oaks, CA: Sage.

Osterman, P. (Ed.). (1996). *Broken ladders: Manager careers in the new economy.* New York: Oxford University Press.

Prahalad, C. K., & Hamel, G. (1990). The core competence of the corporation. *Harvard Business Review, 68,* 79–91.

Schneier, C. E., Shaw, D. G., & Beatty, R. W. (1991). Performance measurement and management: A tool for strategy execution. *Human Resource Management, 30*(3), 279–301.

Schuler, R. S., & Huber, V. L. (1993). *Personnel and human resource management.* St. Paul, MN: West.

Senge, P. M. (1990). *The fifth discipline.* New York: Doubleday.

Simons, R., & Davila, A. (1998). How high is your return on management? *Harvard Business Review, 76,* 70–80.

Ulrich, D. (1997). *Human resource champions.* Boston: Harvard Business School Press.

Wexley, K. N. (1996). Appraisal interview. In R. A. Berk (Ed.), *Performance assessment* (pp. 167–185). Baltimore: John Hopkins University Press.

CHAPTER 7

Personal and Career Development
The Best and Worst of Times
Gerard A. Callanan
Jeffrey H. Greenhaus

"It was the best of times, it was the worst of times."

When Charles Dickens began *A Tale of Two Cities* with this now-famous phrase, he was concisely describing the human condition in Europe near the close of the eighteenth century. Since the book's publication 140 years ago, Dickens's line has been used countless times to characterize the state of affairs confronted by society. Indeed, this phrase is probably applicable at any given moment in history.

As we near the end of the twentieth century, this memorable dichotomy paints an apt picture of the present-day job market and career prospects for millions of workers. Over the past decade, the landscape of work and careers has seen dramatic alterations that, depending on one's perspective, can be viewed in either a positive or a negative light. For example, all forms of the media have cited the unfavorable consequences of the downsizing trend and the related loss of loyalty, dissolution of the implicit psychological contract between employer and employee, and debilitating effects of

Note: We thank Fran Engoron of Price Waterhouse and John Epperheimer of the Career Action Center for the useful and timely descriptions of their organizations' programs.

job loss. Yet at the same time, the changing landscape of work has produced new opportunities as never before. Increased pursuit of entrepreneurial careers, an accelerating job market with smaller, start-up companies, and new, more flexible work patterns all represent positive changes in the work environment.

The confusion over how we should view the current state of affairs with respect to work and careers is reflected in the inconsistent and contradictory messages given by the popular press and other news media. For instance, in March 1996 the *New York Times* ran a weeklong series on the downsizing of America with front-page articles that discussed, often in gut-wrenching terms, the effects of mass job loss on individuals, families, communities, and companies throughout the United States (Kleinfield, 1996; Rimer, 1996; Uchitelle & Kleinfield, 1996). Yet just three months later the same newspaper heralded the end of the period of what was referred to as "corporate anorexia" with this headline, *Layoffs Are Out; Hiring Is Back* (Uchitelle, 1996). Indeed, by mid-1998 hiring was so strong that the unemployment rate in the United States was the lowest it had been in a quarter of a century. It seems that for every tragic and traumatic story of job loss, there is equally positive news of some pathbreaking entrepreneur striking gold with a new product or an unemployed individual finding a more suitable position in a different work environment.

What is one to make of these conflicting themes? Are we really witnessing a historic shift in the attitudes toward work and its organization? Is the traditional organizational career dead, as some researchers have declared? Are companies so focused on short-term results that they are willing to ignore the personal and career development of their employees?

In this chapter we attempt to make some sense out of the turbulence surrounding the nature of work and its influence on personal and career development programs or approaches. The chapter will provide a brief overview of the historical trends in the meaning of careers and career management; discuss the influences in today's work environment on individual development; review the new conceptualizations of career competencies; offer our recommendations for effective individual career management in light of the new conceptualizations; and review current and emerging career management practices (including examples from contemporary organizations and consulting firms) and their implications for practitioners of industrial-organizational (I/O) psychology and human resource (HR) management.

Overview of Historical Trends in the Treatment of Careers

A recent *Fortune* magazine article (Bridges, 1994) made a bold proclamation that the "job," at least as defined in modern terms, is over, a "social artifact" (p. 62). Other researchers have declared that the traditional form of a career is dead (Hall, 1996). If these views on the demise of the conventional approaches to jobs and careers are true, then the question is, what are the new conceptualizations? And perhaps more important, what does the future hold in terms of the evolution of work and career development?

Before we address these questions, we need to use a historical perspective to understand careers since the development of modern industrial organizations. During the past one hundred years, the concept of career has evolved substantially. Etymologically, the word *career* derives from French and Latin words meaning road or passage. In today's lexicon, the theme of a road or passage is still apparent. A career is normally defined as a pattern of work experiences that span the course of a person's life (Bird, 1994; Greenhaus & Callanan, 1994) and is usually seen in terms of a series of stages that reflect the "passage" from one life phase to another.

Our modern view of careers crystallized during the era of prosperity following World War II. After the war, the United States and the rest of the industrialized world saw unprecedented economic growth. This growth allowed existing organizations to flourish and also permitted the establishment of new firms in record numbers. In this environment, the demand for human capital soared. Workers had job opportunities as never before. Individuals saw their careers in terms of a particular organization, and the concept of an organizational career was born. In this sense, an organizational career entailed a pattern of work experiences spanning a person's life *within a particular organization*.

In order to provide security to the organization and to the individual workers, an unwritten psychological contract developed between the two parties. Psychological contracts serve to specify the contributions an employee believes are owed to the organization, as well as the inducements the employee believes are owed in return from the organization (Robinson, Kraatz, & Rousseau, 1994). Earlier researchers distinguished two forms of psychological contracts: *relational* and *transactional* (MacNeill, 1985).

The traditional view of careers assumes a relational contract between employer and employee. Relational contracts are normally longer-term and usually involve a high degree of commitment. They are based on a promise of job security by the employer in exchange for loyalty on the part of the employee (Robinson, Kraatz, & Rousseau, 1994; Rousseau & Wade-Benzoni, 1995). A transactional contract, in contrast, is shorter-term, predicated on performance-based pay, involves lower levels of commitment by both parties, and allows for easy exit from the agreement.

From a historical perspective, adherence to the relational psychological contract made life simple and predictable for both the employing organization and the individual. As Nicholson (1996, p. 41) states, the relational "psychological contract is one that promises security and the possibility of advancement in exchange for the employee's singular commitment to the organization."

Several themes are apparent when considering the traditional view of work and career. The first is stability. Most existing career theories assume stability in the individual's work environment (Arthur, 1994). Stability takes many forms, including work organizations whose existence is certain, the absence of factors that may make jobs obsolete, and constant opportunity for individual growth and development.

A second theme is that of movement, either through hierarchical advancement or intraorganizational mobility. The standard conceptualization of careers is that the individual employee will have consistent and fair opportunity either to move higher in the organizational hierarchy or to move to other functional areas within the firm to gain broad-based experience for developmental purposes. In addition, many models of career development assume that available jobs will be consistent with the individual's interests, talents, and lifestyle preferences.

In total, the psychological contract based on mutual attraction, presumption of a stable work situation, and expectations for advancement opportunities created an environment that seemed ideal for the organization and the individual. For the individual, it meant having a job that was personally meaningful and in which it was possible to move up the corporate hierarchy in a planned and orderly series of steps, receive attendant rewards, and be loyal to an organization that truly cared about personal development and well-being. For the organization, the standard model meant a steady supply of dedicated workers who would sacrifice at any cost for the good of the organization. This structure gave the organization workers whose behaviors were predictable and also supplied a steady stream of talent eventually to take over new or expanding managerial roles (Rousseau & Wade-Benzoni, 1995). This idealized compact between employer and employee was well depicted in Whyte's *Organization Man* (1956) and in Kanter's *Men and Women of the Corporation* (1977).

Of course, overwhelming evidence accumulated over the past fifteen years shows that the Camelot era of the organizational career—the 1950s, 1960s, and 1970s—has ended. The convergence of a variety of environmental forces has rendered it counterproductive and unsustainable. We will discuss these environmental factors in the next section. For now, suffice it to say that both parties to the presumed relational psychological contract—employees and employers alike—acknowledge its demise. Large-scale, high-profile organizations now demand workers with relevant skills at specific points in time, sort of a just-in-time application of human capital. At the same time, employees have come to understand, albeit slowly, what Arthur (1994) refers to as "the dangers in presumed organizational benevolence" (p. 301). The new reality is that employees no longer see loyalty to a specific company as meaningful or beneficial. Instead, the attitude is that one must at all times look out for one's best career interests, regardless of the consequences for a particular firm.

From all this turbulence over the past two decades a key question from a career development perspective emerges: What portion if any of the prior research on careers remains relevant? To put it differently, can previous theories of career management, which saw career development tasks as narrow, sequential, and methodical activities, be applied in a work world that is uncertain, unbounded, and ever-changing? We would argue, as Arthur (1994) has, that the existing foundation of research and accepted models concerning organizational careers are still relevant in the changed environment of so-called individual or self-centered careers. (We recognize that the term *self-centered* usually has a negative connotation, but we believe it accurately conveys the idea that individuals must be somewhat selfish in managing their careers to maximize their own well-being and worth. This view contrasts with the concept of the traditional organizational career, where individuals were expected to subjugate their own best interests to those of the company.)

Specifically, many existing models maintain that career management is an inherently individual process. In this sense, the individual is ultimately responsible for such career management tasks as pursuing career exploration, setting career goals, devising career strategies, and seeking out related feedback. These standard tasks require the individual to be proactive to complete them, regardless of the level of support received from other parties.

It remains our belief that theories and models of career management that are based on individual actions are still relevant in this era of self-centered careers. In the following section, we present a more thorough discussion of the environmental and individual factors that presently affect personal and career development.

Current Factors Influencing Personal and Career Development

We have stated that the traditional organizational career—which was manifest in an implicit relational psychological contract between employer and employee—has ended. In its place, we find workers who must be more self-reliant in managing their careers, and organizations that must employ, use, and develop employees for short-term performance goals. This shift from organizational to self-centered careers did not occur overnight but rather evolved over the past fifteen years. And the situation is still evolving as both individuals and organizations try to sort out their reactions to the new realities of work.

What factors have given rise to this new world of work and careers? As with any large-scale societal change, researchers can point to the confluence of a number of environmental and individual causes. Several of these factors are discussed in the following section.

Shifts in Employment

Over the past fifteen years significant changes have occurred both in the way people are employed and in the types of jobs they hold. In a recent article (Uchitelle & Kleinfield, 1996), the *New York Times* estimated that 43 million jobs had been lost in the United States during the period from 1979 to 1995. Yet during the same period the *net* number of jobs added by the U.S. economy totaled 27 million, with the number of jobs in the nonfarm sectors rising from 90 million in 1979 to 117 million in 1995. Thus, there has been a significant amount of job turnover and reemergence over this sixteen-year period, even with the economy and the number of jobs growing.

In addition, the pace of job loss accelerated in the 1990s. According to the *New York Times* (Uchitelle & Kleinfield, 1996), during the 1980s average annual job loss was 2.3 million. In the 1990s the number jumped substantially, rising to 3.2 million jobs lost per year on average, or an increase of nearly 40 percent over the 1980s. Finally, the percentage of jobs lost has climbed sharply in the 1990s. For example, in 1979 the percentage of jobs lost during the year was about 1.4 percent of total employment. In contrast, the percentage of jobs lost in 1995 was nearly 2.9 percent, or more than double the 1979 figure.

Changes in Organizations

A number of different arguments have been made as to why so many jobs have been lost in the 1990s. One view is that mass job loss is an economic inevitability reflecting the natural consequence of the substantial investments in information and other processing technology made during the last two decades. New technology has rendered many jobs obsolete.

Another argument for job loss is that corporations had become bloated with excess staff during the halcyon economic days of the 1960s and 1970s. Cutting these slack resources in order to increase efficiency, competitiveness, and the company's stock price became widespread in the 1980s and accelerated in the 1990s. More intense global competition also forced many American organizations to cut their staffing levels and seek out mergers and acquisitions to become stronger economically.

Disagreeing with the economic inevitability argument presented earlier, other commentators have argued that mass layoffs and restructuring are the product of corporate greed. In this view, organizations have callously engaged in mass layoffs and thereby eliminated any sense of mutual loyalty simply for bottom-line, short-term results.

Regardless of the reasons for mass job restructuring, the reality is that a new era is emerging where job security for the individual, at one time taken for granted, is now virtually nonexistent.

Changes in Organizational Structure

In addition to cutting staff, organizations have also changed the way they employ and use their employees. Specifically, the use of contract staff and temporary workers has jumped markedly in the 1990s, as organizations have sought to become more efficient by using their human capital in a just-in-time fashion (Fierman, 1994). For many individuals, working on a contingent basis has become a permanent way of life.

These recent alterations in work organizations and their approaches to staffing "directly challenge the career competencies of affected workers" (DeFillippi & Arthur, 1994, p. 311). The result has been that the playing field for the individual management of careers has changed, with a new set of individual behaviors and actions required. As DeFillippi and Arthur (1994, p. 311) state, "Multiple changes in organizational career contexts reflect a new era of interfirm competition in both national and global markets. The changes reflect not only corporate restructuring and downsizing but also a range of new organizing principles developed in response to the new era. These principles imply distinct changes in the kinds of career competencies to be encouraged." We will discuss these new career competencies in the next section.

Changes in Workforce Characteristics

While organizations have been shifting their levels of and approaches to staffing, the workforce itself has seen dramatic changes over the past two decades. First, the workforce is becoming more culturally diverse. The increasing proportion of women, racial minorities, and immigrants has put pressure on organizations to manage this diversity effectively. Workforce diversity also challenges employees to understand cultural similarities and differences and to work cooperatively with others who may have different values and perspectives. Career advancement could well depend on an employee's ability to thrive in a multicultural environment.

Technological advances and fundamental changes in work have led businesses to require workers who are more literate and who possess requisite technical skills. Unfortunately, the skills of individuals entering the workforce or those available through displacement often fail to meet the requirements of organizations. Thus, businesses and individuals can face a mismatch between the skills demanded and the skills available.

Changes in Individuals

Behavioral scientists point to a number of changes in individual attitudes and behaviors over the past two decades. Some of these changes reflect cultural shifts in beliefs, whereas others are reactions to social forces such as the changes in work and careers. Perhaps the most significant cultural change affecting individuals is the heightened challenge of managing commitments to both work and family. Many two-career couples face new dilemmas in juggling work and family obligations. By necessity, members of such relationships must learn to balance two careers as well as extensive family responsibilities. Individual workers have also adapted to the new work environment by showing a willingness to try new work arrangements. The increasing number of people choosing to undertake entrepreneurial careers is at least partially attributable to the new reality of work and the related alterations in the psychological contract.

In summary, a number of environmental and individual factors are changing the basic foundation of personal and career development and in turn have consequences for organizations and individuals as they attempt to optimize performance and satisfaction. In the next section, we discuss these consequences in more detail, paying particular attention to their influence on the new conceptualizations of career competencies.

New Conceptualizations of Career Competencies

Over the past several years, researchers and the popular press have created a number of different terms to describe the evolving career management focus, all reflecting the view that the once-standard relational psychological contract has ended. These new terms include the *protean* career (Hall & Mirvis, 1996), the *boundaryless* career (Arthur, 1994), career *pluralism* (Brousseau, Driver, Eneroth, & Larsson, 1996), and the *career-resilient workforce* (Waterman, Waterman, & Collard, 1994). In this chapter we have added to this list the term *self-centered* career management. Although there are subtle differences in their meanings, all of these terms are consistent in their implication that individuals must be more adaptable in managing their careers. The new terminology is based on the assumption that the single organizational career, with job security taken for granted, is no longer viable.

In this new environment, standard jobs have been replaced by evolving *work situations* (Bridges, 1994), which require flexibility and adaptability on the part of the worker. Under the old environment, jobs were tailored or structured to reflect the abilities of the workers. In the new work landscape, the individual, as evidenced by the use of the contingent workforce, must be adaptable to the work situation. Companies now have a Darwinian view, ensuring that the fittest or most adaptable are the ones who survive in the organization.

Being adaptable to varying work situations, with multiple employers, requires a new set of career competencies and strategies as outlined in the following paragraphs.

Establish a Clear Identity

A variety of researchers have concluded that the primary building block for career success and fulfillment is the need for one's work to be consistent with one's self-identity. This maxim is even more relevant in the current environment of job instability, where one's personal needs can easily get overlooked. Establishment of a clear self-identity normally involves a process of self-exploration where individuals use standard assessment tools in conjunction with introspection and feedback from trusted others in the social network to understand better their interests, talents, and lifestyle preferences.

Focus on Employability, Not Employment

Employees are responsible for ensuring that their portfolio of skills is transferrable to other work situations and other employers (Arthur, 1994). Individuals should ensure that they have the competitive skills to improve their chances of finding a new position when it is needed (Waterman, Waterman, & Collard, 1994). In this sense, the individual would possess a set of what might be called *portable competencies* that could be applied in any number of organizations or work settings.

Commit to Lifelong Learning

Related to the idea of a portable set of skills is the recommendation that individuals invest in lifelong learning to keep their skills relevant (and thereby transferable). Continuous learning can take many forms. One category would involve pursuing additional schooling; another category could include seeking out assignments that allow new competencies to be learned. A commitment to learning might also involve staying abreast of developments within one's current organization as well as other firms in the industry.

Invest in Reputation Building

It is naturally assumed that people's past experiences and accomplishments bode well for future performance. Therefore, a "focus on building reputation over one's career can provide employability regardless of the changing fortunes of a single employer" (Arthur, 1994, p. 301). Individuals can build a positive reputation by accomplishing such tasks as engineering a turnaround of an unfavorable work situation or showing leadership on a particular assignment. Reputation building is also closely related to image enhancement. Image enhancement is a strategy designed to convey an appearance of success and suitability (Greenhaus & Callanan, 1994).

Maintain a Technical Specialty

The new career conceptualizations are based on the premise that individuals must adapt to a wide variety of jobs and other work experiences as they move through their careers. Nonetheless, there remains a basic understanding that many individuals will also have a technical competency as the basis for their career, especially in the early years (Allred, Snow, & Miles, 1996). Yet, as Schein (1996) cautions, overreliance on technical or functional competence as a career anchor is unwise because it can inhibit flexibility or could make a person's career obsolete as technology changes more rapidly.

Gain Experience in Team and Project Collaboration

A number of researchers have concluded that the use of project teams as a means of organizing and accomplishing work will become more prevalent in the future (Allred, Snow, & Miles, 1996; Bridges, 1994). Therefore, organizations will come to rely more heavily on individuals who have collaborative abilities derived from being members and leaders of teams. Individuals can thus enhance their portfolio of skills and increase their interorganizational employability when they show experience and accomplishments through team and project collaboration.

As this discussion suggests, the new conceptualizations of career competencies have widespread implications for individuals as they go through the sequence of steps in the management of their careers. Although a bit more subtle, there is also a message that organizations must change their HR programs and developmental approaches to ensure a consistent stream of talented employees and improve the prospects for retaining those individuals most critical to current and future performance. Later in the chapter we discuss a number of approaches organizations can use in attempting to maximize individual and firm performance in the evolving work environment.

New Career Realities: Implications for Individual Development

As we have seen, the changing landscape of work has led to new conceptualizations of individual career management. The central theme of these new conceptualizations is that individuals must be more proactive as they attempt to control the direction of their careers. We believe that career management models that are based on the completion of individual tasks (such as the model presented by Greenhaus & Callanan, 1994, p. 18) are quite useful and appropriate in advising individuals. These key tasks include self-exploration and work exploration, goal setting, strategy development, and reappraisal.

Explore Self and Work

We stated earlier that having a clear self-identity is a critical requirement for effective career management. This means that individuals must remain conscientiously attuned to their interests, talents, and lifestyle preferences. In its most simple form, the task involves occasionally taking time to assess what is meaningful in one's life. People change and develop over the course of their lives, not only through such dramatic events as family or work crises but also in more subtle and evolutionary ways. People who manage their careers effectively are sensitive to changes in themselves and sufficiently flexible to make career decisions that are more compatible with their emerging selves (Greenhaus, Callanan, & Kaplan, 1995).

A number of forms of assistance are available to help individuals explore their lives. For example, there are several well-known self-help books on the market, such as Bolles's *What Color Is Your Parachute?* (1996), which can assist individuals in better understanding themselves. Other means of self-exploration include programs at public libraries, licensed career counselors, and insight from family and friends. Also, a number of career consulting and outplacement organizations offer programs in self-assessment for individuals.

The other half of the career exploration process involves maintaining an awareness of internal and external work environments. In a world marked by comparatively higher levels of job insecurity, it becomes increasingly important for individuals to keep up with these changes. This awareness is multifaceted. On the one hand, it means being knowledgeable about factors within one's current employing organization. When people have this knowledge, it can help prevent them from being blindsided by a layoff or help them identify the most favorable career paths within the company. On the other hand, being knowledgeable about the external work environment can assist individuals as they attempt to map out shifts in career direction. For example, standard advice is "to network," or stay in contact with friends, relatives, neighbors, former coworkers, and others in the social network in order to stay current with employment requirements of other employers. Arthur (1994) states that networks are among the primary techniques individuals have to avoid reliance on a single organization and that they also serve as a media through which to accumulate knowledge.

Another mechanism for maintaining awareness of the external environment is job search clubs. Members of job search clubs share tips and advice on looking for a new position, hear experts discuss related job-hunting topics, and provide one another with camaraderie and support (Capell, 1997).

Set Career Goals

Setting career goals is normally a function of the results of the exploration process. Career goals are a general guide for the future, summarizing nothing more than the broad-based work experiences an employee wishes to attain. The career goal is a map of the future that takes into account the tasks that one finds enjoyable and satisfying, provide appropriate rewards, and permit one to achieve a desired lifestyle.

Some question whether the setting of career goals is useful or relevant in today's uncertain work world. This view is based on the premise that the environment is moving so rapidly that it is impossible to set meaningful goals and that the pursuit of a career goal makes one rigid and inflexible, unable to adjust to an altered set of requirements. We believe this view reflects common misconceptions about career goals, specifically that a career goal is defined in terms of a particular job with a specific company and that a career goal is overly instrumental in its use.

In reality, career goals remain an integral part of the career management process. They are useful precisely because they can be stated in less specific terms. They allow an individual to establish an overall road map of the future. Career goals can act as a rudder during times of work turbulence because they take into account the results of the exploration process. Thus, career goals can help steer individuals into jobs and work organizations that are compatible with their personal values, interests, talents, and lifestyle preferences. In addition, career goals can be usefully applied in a current job as a means to improve performance, develop new skills, and enhance one's reputation.

Of course, we recognize that work is an economic necessity, and people sometimes take jobs regardless of compatibility (or incompatibility) with personal factors. Nonetheless, career goals remain a meaningful guide for the future, even if one must temporarily be in a job that doesn't satisfy the goals in the short run.

Devise Career Strategies

Closely linked with setting career goals, career strategies represent the actions an individual takes to improve the chances of achieving career goals. They are the conscious individual choices about which human capital investments to make and which to avoid (Barney & Lawrence, 1989). Career strategies can involve seeking greater competence in one's present job, more extensive work involvement, skill development, opportunity development, mentors and other supportive alliances; they may also involve image building and playing organizational politics (Greenhaus & Callanan, 1994).

We indicated earlier how the new career conceptualizations dictate more active career management by the individual. Developing and implementing appropriate career strategies are integral tasks in the protean, boundaryless, and self-centered career. As Mirvis and Hall (1994, p. 375) state, "Under the transactional contract, the locus of responsibility is squarely on the individual: he or she is employed based on current value" and "This puts added responsibility on [them] to learn new skills, take on developmental projects, and develop further their core identities." In other words, in the new work world of transactional employment contracts, it is essential that individuals pursue learning and developmental strategies that enhance their value to employing organizations. Further, individuals should evaluate potential employers at least in part based on the kinds and amounts of training and development they offer.

Perform Career Appraisal

Career appraisal serves as a catalyst for continuous career management. It involves assessing whether one's career goals are still meaningful and whether established strategies are appropriate to achieve career goals. Further, career appraisal either will confirm that an individual's goals and strategies are consistent with his or her interests and preferences or indicate that changes in goals or strategies are warranted. Accordingly, the feedback from career appraisal can serve as input as one restarts the process of career exploration. For example, many individuals realize after reflection that a corporate career is inappropriate and that an entrepreneurial career is more suitable. This realization can then lead to a new set of career goals and related strategies.

In summary, we believe that the new work and career realities outlined so far make it more important than ever for individuals to be conscientious in completing the career management tasks described.

Current and Emerging Career Management Approaches: Implications for Organizational Practice

Traditional models of career development programs saw organizations as benevolent entities that played an active role in mapping the careers of individual workers (Arthur, 1994). But the new work environment has led many companies to abandon this activist philosophy. A number of researchers have noted how the pendulum of responsibility for career management has moved heavily in the direction of the individual and away from employers (Altman & Post, 1996; Mirvis & Hall, 1994). As Mirvis and Hall (1994, p. 369) state, "It seems likely that the locus of career development responsibility will shift even more so to the individual in part because boundaryless organizations will not be able to meaningfully plan an employee's career. There will be simply too much uncertainty about future organizational needs to chart out prospective career paths and steer people through prescribed developmental sequences."

If organizations are no longer willing or able to play an active, guiding role in charting individual careers, then what should their new responsibilities be? Moreover, what new roles should practitioners—including I/O psychologists and HR professionals—play in helping individuals and organizations respond to the changed landscape of work and careers? Ideally, new corporate developmental programs, as well as the actions of practitioners, would simultaneously work to improve the competencies and performance of organizations while also helping individuals develop relevant skills and competencies.

Based on a review of the literature, the developmental prescriptions (and the related influence of practitioners) can be grouped into several categories as follows.

Create an Environment for Continuous Learning

It has been argued that organizations must be adaptable to quickly changing environments in order to be successful (DeFillippi & Arthur, 1994). This argument implies that organizations will have to make a commitment to learning in order to respond quickly to market conditions. "Learned" organizations will possess knowledge and information that gives them a unique competitive advantage over other firms (Quinn, Anderson, & Finkelstein, 1996). Thus, as Bird (1994) argues, organizations must now become *knowledge creators* in order to improve their competitiveness. This means that "firms must develop their human resources in ways that enhance the supply of information and knowledge available to the firm. In other words, employees add value to the organization by creating information through their work experiences" (p. 328).

As DeFillippi and Arthur (1994) point out, organizations can support employee learning through three approaches. First, they can encourage them to join occupational associations that provide continuing education for their members. Second, they can make a direct investment in their employees through training and development programs within or outside of the firm. Several high-profile organizations have made extensive investments in employee learning. For example, Intel and Motorola each estimates that it spends approximately $120 million per year on employee training (Sanger & Lohr, 1996; Wiggenhorn, 1990). Further, Motorola believes "that at least five percent of each employee's time should be spent on training or education" (Waterman, Waterman, & Collard, 1994, p. 89).

A good example of organizational support for continuous learning through training is provided by Gutteridge, Leibowitz, and Shore (1993) in their description of Ford Motor's Leadership Education and Development (LEAD) program. Ford designed LEAD in conjunction with the University of Michigan. It focuses on the training needs of Ford's three thousand middle managers as they respond to a changed competitive environment. The program emphasizes adult learning principles and concentrates on on-the-job applications.

A third approach to continuous learning is direct support for individual motivation, where the "individual is driven by a desire for greater learning or achievement" (DeFillippi & Arthur, 1994, p. 313) and the company encourages this initiative. An example of organizational support for individual learning is Wiggenhorn's description (1990) of Motorola's in-house school that provides training in functional areas such as engineering and marketing as well as remedial courses in reading and math. The Motorola program is an extensive, ambitious effort to raise the skill levels and the value of its employees.

Provide Opportunities for Self-Assessment and Introspection

We stated earlier that having a clear understanding of one's self-identity, including interests, talents, and lifestyle preferences, allows an individual to seek out jobs and organizations that represent a proper match or fit. Providing people with various self-exploration tools such as the Myers-Briggs Type Indicator was standard in traditional career development programs. Yet in today's environment, organizations must go beyond simple paper-and-pencil exercises and provide employees with tools and information to perform the self-assessment process.

More precisely, in addition to self-exploration exercises, companies should provide information that allows individuals to benchmark their skills and abilities against what the company and the job market in general are demanding (Waterman, Waterman, & Collard, 1994). There are various mechanisms for disseminating this information to employees, including the performance appraisal process, corporate publications and pronouncements, and announced changes in internal requirements. Beyond these standard, formal approaches, however, organizations must be willing to part with sensitive data on strategic decisions that could have a significant influence on individual employee plans.

The move toward greater openness with employees represents a major cultural change for most companies. Organizations traditionally have not been willing to share data on business direction or changes in corporate structure with their employees. As Waterman, Waterman, and Collard (1994, p. 92) state, "Conventional wisdom holds that a company has little to gain by telling employees as soon as it has decided to exit a business or shut down an operation. The assumption is that morale and productivity will suffer, people will abandon ship, and the performance of the operation will deteriorate." But organizations must realize that openness with employees is beneficial because it allows them to seek out developmental opportunities and ensure a fit with the company's direction. It also allows employees whose career interests are at odds with those of the company the opportunity to exit at an earlier time.

How do organizations assist their employees in the self-assessment process? Evidence suggests that most large organizations still rely on in-house career management centers for this purpose. But many organizations now contract out the management of such centers. One of the leading providers of career management services for organizations is the Career Action Center, headquartered in Cupertino, California. The center helps design and staff career centers for such major corporations as Sun Microsystems, Hewlett Packard, IBM, AT&T, and Raychem. A core feature of the Career Action Center program is the promotion of career resilience through lifelong learning. Specifically, the center's approach emphasizes continual learning and adjustment on the part of the employee to ensure that skill levels are consistent with organizational requirements. As opposed to traditional approaches, the program places less emphasis on vertical or hierarchical movement within the sponsoring organization but greater emphasis on individual employability and value through lifelong learning. The Career Action Center maintains strict confidentiality in working with individual employees as a way to gain their trust and confidence.

Respond to Work-Life Issues

The increased participation of dual-earner couples and single parents in the workforce has pressured organizations to help employees balance their work and family commitments. Extensive work-family conflicts have negative consequences for the well-being of employees (Higgins, Duxbury & Irving, 1992). In addition, job candidates are increasingly scrutinizing companies' commitment to work-life balance as a precondition for employment (Shellenbarger, 1997).

Organizations can be responsive to work-life issues in three ways (Greenhaus & Callanan, 1994). First, they can provide dependent care support through such initiatives as on-site or near-site child-care centers, discounts and vouchers, resource and referral systems, and sick leave and elder care programs. Although these programs can be quite helpful, they do not in and of themselves change the way the employer organizes work activities to help employees achieve work-life balance.

Second, organizations can provide progressive work arrangements, such as flexible work schedules, part-time employment, job sharing, and telecommuting. These arrangements give employees more control over the location and timing of their contributions. However, many employees are fearful of participating in such programs because they believe that the stigma attached to such participation can jeopardize their careers (Connor, Hooks, & McGuire, 1997).

Third, organizations can change their cultures to legitimize achievement of work-life balance. This approach is the most difficult to accomplish yet potentially the most powerful in its effects. Bailyn's insightful analysis (1997) identifies three cultural barriers to work-family integration: the beliefs that "putting in time" is a sign of an employee's loyalty, commitment, and productivity; that external control is essential to ensure that employees comply with their job requirements; and that the work-family "problem" is essentially a personal issue (primarily for women with young children) that requires substantial accommodation on the part of the employee.

Dependent care and flexible work arrangements are important ingredients in a comprehensive work-life program. However, to be productive and competitive in today's marketplace, many organizations will require a culture that makes work-family issues central to their strategic planning (Friedman & Johnson, 1997).

Ensure Consistency Between Career Progression and Organizational Expectations

A classic article in the management field is Kerr's "On the Folly of Rewarding A, While Hoping for B" (1975). As the title implies, Kerr makes the point that many institutions have stated goals and expectations that are not supported by the reward system and also notes that the reward system can actually run counter to the stated expectations. This dissonance runs deep in many organizations where the stated expectations for workers (being adaptable, willing to pursue learning opportunities, focusing on customer-relevant competencies) are inconsistent with established career progression and reward systems. More precisely, many companies still use traditional promotional and reward systems that are based more on tenure, political skills, or potential for future promotions than on absolute value to the firm. Correcting this imbalance often requires a formal change process where intrafirm mobility is tied to one's organizational value and commitment to upgrading skills and competencies.

An example of this type of change process is a program implemented by Price Waterhouse, a worldwide professional services firm of over fifty thousand partners and staff members that practices in 118 countries, including ninety offices in the United States. Price Waterhouse is a leading global consultant to top-tier companies offering such services as change integration, information technology consulting, tax consulting and compliance, auditing and accounting, corporate finance and recovery, dispute analysis, and business advisory services.

During the early 1990s the management of Price Waterhouse recognized the need for greater flexibility in its career progression system. The old system in existence up to that point was somewhat rigid and "tenure-based." Further, employee career goals were based on attaining the designation of partner within a set number of years. Those not making partner in that time frame were expected to leave. Based on client demands and other factors, it became obvious that Price Waterhouse needed to change its approach. The company embarked on a multiyear change process that focused on better retention of professionals with specialized expertise, better service to clients, and more varied ways for employees to succeed. In essence, the new program emphasizes a competency-based approach to career progression where employees are expected to develop the abilities needed to perform in more demanding roles. Under the new system, employees can develop expertise in multiple areas or choose to build in-depth capabilities in a single function, with variations based on accumulated experience, demonstrated capabilities, and individual career goals.

Price Waterhouse's revised career progression system was instituted on a national basis beginning in 1995. Because the system represents a major cultural shift, it has taken time to develop management and employee acceptance. Nonetheless, career progression programs of this type, which take into account individual competency and value to the firm, are consistent with the new realities of individual career management. Accordingly, they represent a win-win scenario for the employee and the employer.

Ensure That Career Development Is Consistent with Other HR Processes and Programs

Just as it is critical for job expectations to be consistent with career progression, it is also important for organizations to integrate career development with other HR systems. Gutteridge, Leibowitz, and Shore (1993) note how such HR functions as job posting, performance appraisal, compensation, and succession planning all influence and are influenced by career development. To cite an obvious example, performance appraisal systems should explicitly benchmark the employee's skills against evolving expectations. The performance appraisal should also state what developmental opportunities are available to upgrade the employee's competencies. Waterman, Waterman, and Collard (1994) note that under the new work realities pay systems must support flexibility and adaptability.

Look to Redeployment Before Outplacement

Although many companies see outplacement as an expedient way to reduce staffing levels, other organizations look first to redeployment of workers whose present skills are inconsistent with business demands. Obviously, redeployment requires some further investment in the employee to make skill levels consistent with current and future requirements. Sanger and Lohr (1996) describe a program instituted by Intel to retrain employees so that they can be redeployed in open jobs. Although Intel offers the training, it provides no guaranteed jobs. "Workers are given four months to shop for new jobs within the company. If a worker can't find a new job, he or she has to leave the company" (Sanger & Lohr, 1996, p. 12). In this example, Intel fulfills its responsibility to help employees upgrade their competency level. But in line with the new career conceptualizations, the onus is on the employee to find work, whether within Intel or with some other firm.

Concluding Thoughts

From a practitioner's standpoint, a key task of the HR function is to help foster, implement, and monitor the career management practices as described in this chapter. More precisely, I/O psychologists and HR professionals play a critical role helping individuals bridge the ever-widening divide between traditional organizational careers and the new career conceptualizations. Practitioners can work to ensure that the programs described here are available to help individuals cope with the emerging needs for lifelong learning, adaptability, employability, and development of a clear self-identity. If individual workers, organizations, and practitioners each have a clear understanding of the changed nature of work and careers, and if they collectively make attendant adjustments in their attitudes and behaviors, then we may have to contradict Dickens and merely say that it is "the best of times."

References

Allred, B. B., Snow, C. C., & Miles, R. E. (1996). Characteristics of managerial careers in the twenty-first century. *Academy of Management Executive, 10*(4), 17–27.

Altman, B. W., & Post, J. E. (1996). Beyond the social contract: An analysis of the executive view at twenty-five large companies. In D. T. Hall (Ed.), *The career is dead: Long live the career* (pp. 46–71). San Francisco: Jossey-Bass.

Arthur, M. B. (1994). The boundaryless career: A new perspective for organizational inquiry. *Journal of Organizational Behavior, 15,* 295–306.

Bailyn, L. (1997). The impact of corporate culture on work-family integration. In S. Parasuraman & J. H. Greenhaus (Eds.), *Integrating work and family: Challenges and choices for a changing world* (pp. 209–219). Westport, CT: Quorum/Greenwood.

Barney, J. B., & Lawrence, B. S. (1989). Pin stripes, power ties, and personal relationships: The economics of career strategy. In M. B. Arthur, D. T. Hall, & B. S. Lawrence (Eds.), *Handbook of career theory* (pp. 417–436). Cambridge, England: Cambridge University Press.

Bird, A. (1994). Careers as repositories of knowledge: A new perspective on boundaryless careers. *Journal of Organizational Behavior, 15,* 325–344.

Bolles, R. N. (1996). *What color is your parachute?* Berkeley, CA: Ten Speed Press.

Bridges, W. (1994, Sept. 19). The end of the job. *Fortune,* pp. 62–74.

Brousseau, K. R., Driver, M. J., Eneroth, K., & Larsson, R. (1995). Career pandemonium: Realigning organizations and individuals. *Academy of Management Executive, 10*(4), 52–66.

Capell, P. (1997, Jan. 7). Executives find advice and support in job-search clubs. *Wall Street Journal,* p. B1.

Connor, M., Hooks, K., & McGuire, T. (1997). Gaining legitimacy for flexible work arrangements and career paths: The business case for public accounting and professional service firms. In S. Parasuraman & J. H. Greenhaus (Eds.), *Integrating work and family: Challenges and choices for a changing world* (pp. 154–166). Westport, CT: Quorum/Greenwood.

DeFillippi, R. J., & Arthur, M. B. (1994). The boundaryless career: A competency-based perspective. *Journal of Organizational Behavior, 15,* 307–324.

Dickens, C. (1981). *A tale of two cities.* New York: Bantam Books. (Originally published 1859)

Fierman, J. (1994, Jan. 24). The contingency workforce. *Fortune,* pp. 30–36.

Friedman, D. E., & Johnson, A. A. (1997). Moving from programs to culture change: The next stage for corporate work-family agenda. In S. Parasuraman and J. H. Greenhaus (Eds.), *Integrating work and family: Challenges and choices for a changing world* (pp. 192–208). Westport, CT: Quorum/Greenwood.

Greenhaus, J. H., & Callanan, G. A. (1994). *Career management* (2nd ed.). Orlando: Dryden Press.

Greenhaus, J. H., Callanan, G. A., & Kaplan, E. (1995). The role of goal setting in career management. *The International Journal of Career Management, 7*(5), 3–12.

Gutteridge, T. G., Leibowitz, Z. B., & Shore, J. E. (1993). *Organizational career development.* San Francisco: Jossey-Bass.

Hall, D. T. (1996). *The career is dead—Long live the career.* San Francisco: Jossey-Bass.

Hall, D. T., & Mirvis, P. H. (1996). The new protean career: Psychological success and the path with a heart. In D. T. Hall (Ed.), *The career is dead: Long live the career* (pp. 15–45). San Francisco: Jossey-Bass.

Higgins, C. A., Duxbury, L. E., & Irving, R. H. (1992). Work-family conflict in the dual-career family. *Organizational Behavior and Human Decision Processes, 51,* 51–75.

Kanter, R. M. (1977). *Men and women of the corporation.* New York: Basic Books.

Kerr, S. J. (1975). On the folly of rewarding A, while hoping for B. *Academy of Management Journal, 18,* 769–783.

Kleinfield, N. R. (1996, Mar. 4). The company as family, no more. *New York Times,* p. 1.

MacNeill, I. R. (1985). Relational contracts: What we do and do not know. *Wisconsin Law Review, 3,* 483–525.

Mirvis, P. H., & Hall, D. T. (1994). Psychological success and the boundaryless career. *Journal of Organizational Behavior, 15,* 365–380.

Nicholson, N. (1996). Career systems in crisis: Change and opportunity in the information age. *Academy of Management Executive, 10*(4), 40–51.

Quinn, J. B., Andersen, P., & Finkelstein, S. (1996). Leveraging intellect. *Academy of Management Executive, 10*(3), 7–27.

Rimer, S. (1996, Mar. 6). A hometown feels less like home. *New York Times,* p. 1.

Robinson, S. L., Kraatz, M. S., & Rousseau, D. M. (1994). Changing obligations and the psychological contract: A longitudinal study. *Academy of Management Journal, 37*(1), 137–152.

Rousseau, D. M., & Wade-Benzoni, K. A. (1995). Changing individual-organization attachments: A two-way street. In A. Howard (Ed.), *The changing nature of work.* San Francisco: Jossey-Bass.

Sanger, D. E., & Lohr, S. (1996, Mar. 9). A search for answers to avoid the layoffs. *New York Times,* p. 1.

Schein, E. H. (1996). Career anchors revisited: Implications for career development in the twenty-first century. *Academy of Management Executive, 10*(4), 80–88.

Shellenbarger, S. (1997, Jan. 29). New job hunters ask recruiters: Is there a life after work? *Wall Street Journal,* p. B1.

Uchitelle, L. (1996, June 18). Layoffs are out; hiring is back. *New York Times,* p. D1.

Uchitelle, L., & Kleinfield, N. R. (1996, Mar. 3). On the battlefields of business, millions of casualties. *New York Times,* p. 1.

Waterman, R. H., Waterman, J. A., & Collard, B. A. (1994, July-Aug.). Toward a career-resilient workforce. *Harvard Business Review,* pp. 87–95.

Whyte, W. F. (1956). *Organization man.* New York: Simon & Schuster.

Wiggenhorn, W. (1990, July–Aug.). Motorola U: When training becomes an education. *Harvard Business Review,* pp. 71–83.

CHAPTER 8

Leadership Development
Contemporary Practices

George P. Hollenbeck
Morgan W. McCall Jr.

"There are almost as many definitions of leadership as there are persons who have attempted to define the concept." So wrote Ralph Stogdill only a little more than twenty years ago in his classic review of the leadership literature (1974, p. 259). In 1998 we might be tempted to nod in agreement—certainly the many authors on leadership in these last two decades seemed compelled to provide their own definitions—but agreement would indicate ignorance of the dramatic changes in our views of leadership in organizations and how leadership development takes place.

In this chapter, we take a brief look at twenty years ago and then examine leadership development today, focusing on content, methods, learner, and context, with some conclusions and predictions.

Memories of the Past

Just how long ago 1977 was can be seen if we remember some of the events of that year:

- Jimmy Carter was inaugurated as president of the United States.
- Elvis died, as did Charlie Chaplin and Bing Crosby.
- The Apple II computer (Steve Jobs's "bicycle of the mind") was introduced.

- At year-end, the Dow Jones Industrial Average stood at 871.
- Seattle Slew won horse racing's Triple Crown.

In the world of leadership there were also some notable events:

- Zaleznik's classic *Managers and Leaders: Are They Different?* was published, distinguishing leadership from management. Important books on "transformational" and "transactional" leadership were still a year away (Burns, 1978) or more (Bass, 1985).
- Kotter's *The Leadership Factor* (1988) was eleven years away. Bennis's popular *Leaders: The Strategies for Taking Charge* (Bennis & Nanus, 1985) would not be published for another eight years.
- The Center for Creative Leadership—an organization that in 1996 had a staff of 459 and offered 275 public programs worldwide—had a staff of 39 and offered 4 public programs for 1976–1977, including one session of the Leadership Development Program (LDP). Research for *The Lessons of Experience* (McCall, Lombardo, & Morrison, 1988) had not even begun.
- International communication in 1977 was a chore, at best. There were few if any nonstop flights from New York to Tokyo or Beijing (then Peking) and, hard to imagine today, it was a world with no e-mail, fax machines, or Internet!

Our assumptions of the day included these:

- Organizations needed management more than leadership (McGregor's 1967 classic was entitled *The Professional Manager*). Management was learned in school and in a lifetime career with one company. Succession planning with long time horizons would produce all the senior managers we would need.
- Strategic planning worked because the future would be a linear extension of the past. Large planning staffs confidently reported on directions for the future.
- Decisions should be pushed up to the highest level in multilevel bureaucratic organizations.

- American management and know-how would enable us to control the future in a stable, regulated environment without much competition.
- The study of leadership—theoretical and academic—didn't have much to offer the practitioner.

Today's assumptions show how much things have changed over the last two decades:

- The only certainty is change—linear projections of the future don't help much.
- Leadership, not management, is crucial to effective change.
- Leadership is learned from experience, when it is learned at all.
- Leadership for large-scale change is in short supply.

As for leadership development, today's world includes much of the old—some "old wine" bottled as new—and some that is new and truly exciting. Classrooms, business schools, and traveling gurus are still much in evidence. *Competencies,* now de rigueur, are rebottled versions of dimensions and knowledge, skills, and abilities (KSAs). In contrast, *action learning* combines the old and new by using a training setting to solve business problems, in essence moving on-the-job experience into a systematic learning environment. Finally, some current practice is altogether new—for example, using executive coaches, delivering training through interactive media, and including "world tours" (trips for participants to different countries) in development programs.

Leadership development today is expected to produce specific business results, an expectation that has both good and bad attributes. On the one hand, investments in and visibility of leadership development activities have dramatically increased; on the other, expectations may be too high—development alone cannot hope to solve the competitive challenges of the global marketplace.

Each of the four elements discussed in this chapter—content, method, learner, and context—reflects a shift in perspective from the past.

- The *content* of development has shifted from the theoretical models of the past to here-and-now problems and issues.

- *Methods* used to develop leaders have tilted away from universities and the classroom toward in-house learning, action learning, and real experience.
- The *learner* has moved from background to foreground. No longer assuming that "one size fits all," development is more closely geared to individual needs.
- Finally, the changing *context*—organizational structure, culture, policy, and practices—that surround development demand more and different kinds of leadership and, in turn, development.

Content of Leadership Development

The content of current leadership development can be broken down into three broad areas: developing desired attributes in the leaders themselves, frequently called *competencies;* developing the individual's capacity to solve business problems; and transmitting the organization's strategy or values.

Competencies

The content of leadership development is most often shaped by a list of desired competencies. However defined (see Spencer, McClelland, & Spencer, 1990, for one attempt to define the term and a methodology), competencies have replaced dimensions and KSAs as the building blocks of models for selection, development, and performance management. Competencies or a competency model are also the targets of the leadership development efforts in many organizations. In the next chapter Moses and Eggebeen describe the evolution of the term, and Briscoe (1996) and Wofford (1993) present a number of competency approaches.

These targets of development have changed enormously over twenty years. What was seen as a single dimension of management (only sometimes called leadership and sometimes not present at all) has evolved into multiple competencies. For example, in *Formative Years in Business* (1974), Bray, Campbell, and Grant's assessment dimensions included only one leadership competency, defined as "how effectively can ... this man lead a group to accomplish a task without arousing hostility" (p. 19). By 1982, the AT&T assessment definition of *leadership* had changed to "To what extent can this individual get people to perform a task effectively" *(Advanced Management)*. Note two changes: "man" becomes "individual," and getting results becomes more important than "not arousing hostility."

In the 1990s, AT&T, a much different company with new leadership requirements, defined a "transformational leadership framework" with eight dimensions (Schaffer, 1994) to be applied to high-potential development, as well as to selection, performance management, and career development: learns continuously; thinks strategically; inspires a shared purpose; creates a climate for success; seizes opportunities; transforms strategy into results; builds partnerships; and leverages disagreements.

Another company, Chase Manhattan Bank, developed over three years a set of leadership competencies that specifically relate "to business challenges" for executive leaders (Sontag, 1996): sets strategic vision and direction; manages complexity; drives for results; champions change; leads with confidence; builds high-performance organizations; builds partnerships with customers and colleagues; and promotes shared values.

The similarities in these two sets of competencies may be applauded or criticized, depending on one's view of competency models, leadership, and large organizations. The point is that these reflect the state of the art in developing targets for leadership development and illustrate how much Zaleznik's distinction (1977) between leadership and management has become accepted practice. Both Chase and AT&T no doubt still have *management* training development, targeted against *management* competencies, quite distinct from leadership.

Advocates of competency models welcome the widespread use of explicit behavioral definitions of organizational leadership. The models have not, however, escaped criticisms such as these, which the authors have heard on several occasions: "Executive performance cannot be broken down into a small number of discrete pieces." "So much energy is invested in building the competency model that little energy or money is left for leadership development." "Much of the competency model building is a waste of time and money because similar competencies are 'discovered' across organizations." "Competencies are based on the past rather than the future." "Competencies are static and cannot adapt to changes as quickly as leadership requirements do." "There is more than one kind of effective leader, therefore a model based on one set of competencies is deceptive." "The model inevitably becomes the brainchild of the human resources function, not the line organization where real development takes place."

Despite the criticisms, competencies have become firmly entrenched as a primary source of content for leadership development.

Business Problems

A more direct approach to relating development to business results is to base the content of development directly on a corporation's strategic directions or its pressing problems. For example, if a company's strategic thrust requires partnerships and joint ventures, the content of leadership development becomes performing effectively in creating and leading such organizational arrangements. Similarly, development content might be determined by identifying problems or opportunities, such as anticipating the needs of future customers in as-yet undeveloped international markets, and assigning them to trainees. Note that development has two goals: developing leadership capability *and* moving the business forward. Key issues are how the business problems are identified, how the problem solving process is structured, and what authority is given to the "trainees." (The section on action learning later in this chapter offers a fuller discussion of these issues.)

In practice, the content of a business-focused approach to development varies widely, depending on the business needs of the organization. For example, one company's strategy called for restructuring to give more autonomy to its business units. Consequently it created a leadership development program that began with a presentation on how a strategic business plan should look, followed by coaching business unit leadership teams in developing their own business plans. Presumably the participants both learned a new discipline for crafting strategic plans and created viable plans.

Another organization needed its technical professionals to assume responsibility for leading a significant organizational transformation, including relationships with unions, customers, and nonprofessional employees. They created a development program to expose these new leaders, who until then had operated in narrow silos, to these critical constituencies, including presentations by satisfied and dissatisfied customers and by union presidents whose members were threatening to strike.

General Electric's Workout, a widely publicized program primarily designed with a business purpose—removing unnecessary bureaucracy—had a direct leadership development impact on both managers and their subordinates (Tichy & Sherman, 1993).

Development content may be determined by individual needs rather than by organizational issues: a manager who has difficulty giving candid feedback may be assigned a project to develop and give detailed behavioral feedback to a problem subordinate; a manager having trouble managing upward might be assigned to develop a presentation for a senior executive. Such programs are usually conducted on-line, over time, and under the guidance of a coach, perhaps with a group of peers.

Business-centered thinking about the content of development opens up almost limitless possibilities. It has the advantage of creating both individual learning and immediate business payoff. Still, it is not without limitations. In our experience, the projects chosen for development over time may become less significant; assigning important problems for development purposes may take responsibility away from the decision makers who should be solving them; putting business issues into the development setting may diminish their apparent importance; potential outcomes of the programs can be oversold; some business issues are not amenable to resolution in a program setting; and the approach can be atheoretical to a fault, with little logic to guide an individual's cumulative development.

Shared Strategy, Mission, and Values

The leader's role in defining strategy, mission, and values has become explicit—shared purposes or values appear in both of our example lists of leadership competencies. And so has the recognition that corporate culture is a key element in organizational performance (see Deal & Kennedy, 1982; Peters & Waterman, 1982; Schein, 1985; and more recently, Kotter & Heskett, 1992).

As a result, strategy and mission have become key topics in some leadership development programs (Bolt, 1989). As organizations have pushed decision making down and out, leaders at all levels are expected to identify strategies and missions for their units that support the broader organization.

The emphasis on leadership in contrast to management also brought into focus the personal side of leadership. The leadership challenge (Kouzes & Posner, 1995) to get "ordinary people to do extraordinary things" requires that effective leaders know who they are and what they are about. The continued best-selling popularity of Covey's *Seven Habits of Highly Effective People* (1989) and related personal leadership programs reflect the growth of personal leadership as an important part of a leadership curriculum. With the recognition of the motivational value of a clear personal mission, both for leaders and followers, exercises in defining oneself have become an accepted part of the leadership development process.

Methods of Leadership Development

In this section we will review six contemporary methods for developing leadership: formal educational programs, 360-degree feedback, use of executive coaching, use of action learning, on-the-job learning, and use of technology.

Formal Programs

By the 1970s, formal programs, usually in business schools, were thought of as the primary means to develop leadership. Such programs still flourish and the major universities offer and fill top-of-the-line executive education courses, but universities no longer have the monopoly. This is largely the result of five trends that have shifted both the focus and the options available to corporations that choose to use formal programs.

First, twenty years ago outstanding faculty were concentrated in a few business schools; now they are spread widely across campuses and consulting firms around the world. Whereas the top ten management school professors used for in-house corporate education programs include six from the expected bastions—Columbia, Darden, Tuck, and Wharton—the remainder come from nontraditional sources: two are from USC, one is freelance, and one is from

Hototsubashi (Bongiorno, 1993). The top-rated business schools offering an executive MBA now include places like Emory, Purdue, NYU, Western Ontario, Michigan State, SMU, Texas, USC, Boston University, Illinois, Washington, and Texas (Bongiorno, 1993).

Second, competition for the executive development dollar has led universities to develop programs that are more "relevant" to business problems—most business schools now offer company-tailored contract programs (de Lisser, 1993). Many schools even design internal (to the company) MBA programs for corporate clients—Boston University provides an executive MBA program for forty executives of Daewoo.

Third, MBA programs have incorporated leadership into the curriculum in response, at least partially, to business complaints of "overly analytical" MBAs. As a result, many so-called high-potentials join companies with a leadership development experience under their belts, perhaps taught by the same professors once accessible only through executive education. This trend has even begun to reach undergraduate programs—both USC and Boston University offer undergraduate leadership courses, and the University of Richmond even offers an undergraduate degree in leadership.

Fourth, organizations have created internally run "leadership academies" geared to their specific needs. The major change at General Electric's Crotonville Education Facility over the last twenty years has been a shift from a management and technical training center to a leadership development center. McDonnell Douglas (along with merger partner Boeing), PepsiCo, Sun Microsystems, Ford, and LG Group in Korea are just a few of the companies worldwide with internal leadership programs and even institutions. They can buy the university faculty they want and create their own programs tailored to their own situations. Several consulting firms have sprung up that design tailored programs for corporations and then provide the faculty, drawing on universities, consultants, or other executives.

Finally, public programs, once almost the exclusive domain of universities, are now offered widely by nonuniversity vendors. The Center for Creative Leadership is a recognized leader in this explosion ("Keeping Track," 1993), as are such popular figures as Stephen Covey (Covey Leadership Center), Tom Peters and Jim Kouzes (TPG/Learning Systems of the Tom Peters Group), and new faces like poet David Whyte (*The Heart Aroused*, 1994). Conger (1992) provides an in-depth look at some of these programs.

Wherever delivered, the lecture course has been eclipsed by other pedagogical approaches. Leadership programs usually combine all or most of the methods described in this chapter, including 360-degree feedback, action learning, case studies, and internal and external faculty, all organized around a set of strategic issues. Some programs are timed to coincide with critical transitions in managerial careers (for example, becoming a director), organizational transitions (going global), or leadership changes (when a new CEO takes charge).

One very unusual program has received a lot of publicity in the business press and may serve as a model for future leadership development. An intensive leadership development program for the highest-potential PepsiCo managers that was tailored to Pepsi's strategy was created by Roger Enrico, now CEO of PepsiCo but at the time vice chairman. Conducted in various of his private residences, it began with a five-day seminar led by Enrico followed by a ninety-day action-learning application, and concluding with a three-day workshop to share insights gained. The program was molded specifically to Enrico's view of the leadership qualities required by PepsiCo. One of the greatest benefits for the participants was the opportunity to interact so closely with Enrico (Tichy & DeRose, 1995).

University-run programs have also responded to the new emphasis on global competitiveness, business relevance, and efficiency by shortening the length of attendance, significantly bolstering their international emphasis, and in some cases seeking specialty niches, either in subject matter (for example, total quality) or in geographic region covered (the Pacific Rim).

360-Degree Feedback

The concept of 360-degree feedback has come of age. We no longer need to define it in conversations with executives; most have themselves participated one or more times in a 360-degree process, either as feedback giver, receiver, or probably both. Books have been written about it (Lepsinger & Lucia, 1997; Tornow & London, 1998), special issues of journals have been devoted to it (Tornow,

1993), conferences argue its pluses and minuses, consulting firms offer 360 degrees as one of their products or services, and most of the popular business press has carried articles describing it. Few HR tools have become so popular so fast. At a recent conference of industrial-organizational psychologists, a participant was heard to say, "360-degree feedback is the most important innovation in the field in twenty years." (Ask the question, "How many of you have heard of 360-degree feedback?" at your local Lions Club or Rotary Club, however, and you will find that it is not as widespread as we like to think.)

Although it is an extension of the attitude survey work on the HR scene since the 1960s, using 360-degree feedback to inform and evaluate leaders in organizations is a measure of how much organizations and leadership have changed over the last twenty years. Dunnette (1993) begins his overview of the articles making up a special 360-degree issue of *Human Resource Management* by recounting an experience of "some years ago" when he recommended that subordinate ratings be included in a performance appraisal process. The HR executive in his response to the proposal repeated one phrase over and over: "The power structure around here would never stand for it" (p. 373).

No longer. Operating in organizations where *how* a leader gets results can be almost as important as *getting* the results, where spans of control may literally span the globe, where both organizations and individuals struggle for even a slight competitive advantage, and where leadership development opportunities may supplement if not replace upward mobility as a career motivator, leaders see 360-degree feedback as a useful tool.

How is the 360-degree process used? Hollenbeck (1992) identified three models that companies were using. In the *better management* model, the focus of the process was on generally agreed-upon management or leadership practices that someone thinks would make the individual a better manager—universal truths usually defined by a standardized feedback instrument. (Van Velsor & Leslie, 1991, provide descriptive reviews for sixteen commonly used better leadership instruments.) A *job performance* model keys on current, job-related behaviors that will affect immediate or short-term job performance and ties the development plan directly to the individual's performance management plan. Companies using a *strategic leadership* model strive to change executive behaviors to fit a desired set of competencies fitting their vision of the future. The leadership competencies described at both Chase Manhattan and AT&T were developed as part of such strategic change efforts.

No matter what model is used, the issue arises as to whether the 360-degree data should be used for development (that is, private feedback) or for evaluation of the leader (that is, performance appraisal and succession planning). Similar to the old coach-versus-judge dilemma of performance appraisal, the issue centers on the appropriateness and validity of ratings, acceptance by the individual being rated, and the likelihood of actual change taking place. Although there is a view that unless executives are accountable for results (that is, are formally appraised on them) they aren't likely to change much, using 360 degrees for evaluation seems to require a special set of conditions (Timmreck & Bracken, 1995, discuss these issues and the experiences of a consortium of organizations).

Dalton and Hollenbeck (1996) weigh in on the development side. They describe the essential role of feedback in generating energy and providing direction for development and a set of necessary conditions for development feedback. They argue that although feedback is all around us, only occasionally does it help us to develop—when it is credible (provided by raters who are competent to give good feedback) and meaningful (in a form that makes sense to the executive), addresses potential (something that the person can do something about), is confidential and anonymous, and is timely (feedback loses credibility when it is old). Bracken (1996) discusses this in terms of who owns the data, the individual or the organization, and how that decision drives the 360-degree process.

The widespread use (fad?) of 360 degrees is not without its detractors. One criticism is simply the time and effort involved; the prospect of completing 360 rating forms for twenty-plus other executives has dampened the enthusiasm of many a line manager. With the maturation of the 360-degree process, however, considerable effort is going into technology, providing computerized, Internet or Intranet, and client or server data collection that can ease the burden of administration and reporting. Other concerns are these: little development actually takes place because the process doesn't have organizational support; the one-size-fits-all 360-degree process doesn't come at a time of change for the executive; without extensive follow-up, action plans don't get carried out; and the feedback isn't powerful enough to energize a person to change. A recent management book even questioned the premise of using observers, calling 360-degree feedback "a quasi-Maoist device" (Micklethwait & Wooldridge, 1996, p. 57).

Does 360-degree feedback work? Convincing research is not available. But perhaps that is asking the wrong question. Most people would argue that developmental change requires feedback that motivates change and points the direction. Whether that feedback is 360 degrees, a heart-to-heart talk with a mentor or boss, or some other experience, much depends on what happens after the feedback is given. As one of us was told by a participant after a 360-degree session, "We don't need to do 360 degrees, we need to do a 180."

Use of Executive Coaching

Executive coaching is "a practical, goal-focused form of personal, one-to-one learning for busy executives. It may be used to improve performance, to improve or develop executive behaviors, to work through organizational issues, to enhance a career, or to prevent derailment" (Hall, Otazo, & Hollenbeck, forthcoming). Most organizations also expect that personal learning will pay off in better organizational performance.

Like 360-degree feedback, coaching's rapid rise to the front ranks of leadership development methods reflects the new business realities. Coaching is a tempting all-purpose answer for the HR generalist who is asked, "What can we do with George?" or "What can you do for me?" An executive can't give a speech? Get a coach. An executive can't use the Internet? Get a coach. An executive runs roughshod over peers and direct reports? Get a coach. An executive is at the bottom of the pile on 360-degree results? Get a coach. An entire executive team wants further development on managing conflict? Get a coach for each executive (or for the whole team).

Executive coaching is a catchall development method because it appears to meet so many of the needs of the organization and the executive: it doesn't require much commitment or disruption and it provides individualized, targeted, flexible, just-in-time development for executives on the run.

Coaching conducted by executive coaches is different than the manager-as-coach process first written about by Mace (1958) and popularized in the late 1970s and early 1980s. Coaching is thriving as a "helping" activity far beyond the reaches of what most HR professionals imagine. The curious reader will find a visit to the Web site *(www.coachfederation.org)* of the International Coaching Federation an enlightening experience. But the literature on coaching is growing, following the practice—an article in *Fortune* (Smith, 1993); a special issue of the *Consulting Psychology Journal* (Kilburg, 1996); a Center for Creative Leadership report by Witherspoon and White (1996).

How are organizations using coaches? Most frequently coaching is a follow-on to 360-degree feedback. Recognizing that 360-degree feedback alone is unlikely to produce much change, coaches interpret 360-degree feedback reports and help executives generate development plans. Hall, Otazo, and Hollenbeck (forthcoming) described the coaching process at Avery Dennison: eight external coaches were given half-day training to prepare them to provide twelve hours of coaching to executives receiving 360-degree feedback. In the first meeting, the coach and the executive opened the feedback data and explored how to read it; subsequent meetings reviewed the feedback and planned and implemented development actions. After the twelve hours of coaching contracted and paid for by the corporate client, coaching continued at the discretion and on the departmental budget of the executive.

Coaching may also be applied to an entire group of executives. At Texas Commerce Bank (TCB), senior vice president Robert Gregory described to us the bank's use of executive coaches for its senior twenty-five executives. Each of the executives was assigned one of five external coaches for six coaching sessions over six months. Although the development theme began as conflict management, the coaching of each executive followed his or her own needs and desires. The TCB program illustrates an advantage of a coach for everyone. Coaching is not a secret when everyone has a coach; it can be discussed in the hallways and it provides a natural reason for discussing the "undiscussable" with other executives.

Plus, the coaching can be coordinated with other executive development activities. A disadvantage, however, is that inevitably some executives are more receptive to coaching at the time it is offered than are others, resulting in very different outcomes.

How are coaches selected? External coaches are usually selected from the card files of an HR person asked to find a coach. What criteria are used? Hollenbeck (1996) has suggested that source credibility, as defined by communications professionals, is good. Credibility includes being trustworthy (a sine qua non of coaching), having expertise (in coaching and in business), and being dynamic (having the personality to engage and convince the person being coached). So defined, credibility is very much dependent on the context and is defined quite differently for a coach asked to teach an executive to use the Internet than for one asked to help an executive deal with sensitive interpersonal issues.

The effectiveness of coaching tends to be evaluated by anecdotes rather than by research, and separating coaching from the other elements of the leadership development process makes evaluation difficult. A follow-up study by Edelstein and Armstrong (1993) of a coaching-based executive development process found that participants rated the process very valuable (3.95 out of 5.00) and consistently reported that they changed (4.07 out of 5.00). Hall, Otazo, and Hollenbeck (forthcoming) asked executives to rate the overall effectiveness of their coaching experiences and found the most frequent rating to be 4 (very satisfactory) on a 5-point scale. They concluded, and so will we, that "the positive image of coaching that is presented in the business media is supported by the experiences of the people we interviewed."

Use of Action Learning

Twenty years ago, the term *action learning* was associated almost exclusively with outdoor programs like Outward Bound. Today, use of the term has expanded considerably, and it is more often associated with programs whose content is business- and strategy-focused. Multidisciplinary teams are created in a development setting to address important organizational problems.

A typical action-learning program begins when an organization's senior executive group identifies a range of problems or strategic issues that need solving and chooses the people to attend the program. The program contains presentations by the senior executives, content modules relevant to the target problems, and team-building activities. Teams are created and assigned to (or choose) specific problems to work on during a time period, which may vary from a few days to six months. A second session is held at the end of that time to present problem solutions and recommendations to senior management, who then decide whether to implement them, and if so, what authority and resources the team will need to carry out the plan.

Almost any aspect of this basic paradigm may vary in a given program. Topics may be generated by the CEO or the teams themselves; participants may be handpicked by the CEO, human resources, or the succession planning process; participants may be a cross section of individuals, even including outsiders or intact business unit teams. Content and presenters may include consultants, university faculty, customers, or vendors; team building may be brief or extensive; the initial session may last a day or a week or two; the program may have multiple sessions or only one; if the problem is global the teams may travel to relevant countries; each team may have a sponsor or coach, or may be on its own. The finale may come in a presentation to peers, the sponsoring party, senior executives, or the training staff, and it may or may not involve a commitment to take action. If action does follow, it may be carried out by the same team, a subset of that team, a new team, or some combination.

The potential impact of the project and its visibility is strong motivation for the participants. There is, however, a difference between action learning's motivational power and the actual learning potential it carries. Teams that are left on their own, with little additional coaching or new input, are less likely to learn as much as those that have to master new skills, learn how to work as a team, and have some help. Indeed, action learning is not without its limitations.

Effective programs are difficult to produce and maintain. A poorly screened group in unfacilitated teams assigned "make-work" problems during a brief residential program who then present results to an uninvolved panel with no decision-making prerogative creates a breeding ground for cynicism rather than development.

Even well-designed teams working on significant problems but without learning support may view the task as just another important job assignment rather than an opportunity to develop new skills. With results rather than development paramount, team members may divide up the work according to already-demonstrated expertise and work independently on "piece parts" to come up with a solution.

Another approach to business-centered action learning focuses on individuals rather than on organizational issues. This design uses the group training experience to generate individual development plans, usually providing individual coaching during a follow-up period for carrying out the plan. Returning for a second training session, participants share their results with the training group. The strengths of this approach include that the problems are relevant to the individual and that one-on-one coaching and feedback are provided. Its limitations spring from the same source: individuals may not choose the most important areas to work on, there may be little accountability for results, and even if individuals change, the unchanged context to which they return may not support that change over time.

The more traditional form of action learning—based on contrived team challenges rather than on specific business problems—has evolved substantially over the last twenty years. These "outdoor" programs (which may not be specifically out of doors) use various kinds of mental and physical challenges as a vehicle for managers to focus on team process and personal development goals in a safe environment, theoretically allowing them to experiment, make mistakes, and receive honest feedback without risking their careers.

There is no doubt that these programs can have a powerful impact—as with the self-report ratings on coaching, people highly value these types of action-learning experiences (Conger, 1992). Whether that impact carries over into job performance depends on the training staff's ability to translate learning into its applications in relevant business situations. In a well-designed program, the challenges are sequenced so that the team can progressively improve and learning is self-directed (that is, the team analyzes its performance and sets its own performance goals for the next task). Effective facilitators are careful to preserve the participants' dignity and responsibility for their own learning, and they understand the business context well enough to help people make the connections between the here-and-now behavior and what happens "back home."

On-the-Job Experience

Two of the great strengths of business-centered action learning are that it captures elements of job relevance and that participants are playing for real stakes. That is even more true of experience on the job itself. Although almost any discussion of leadership development will quickly turn to programs, we have argued elsewhere (McCall, 1998) that the primary classroom for leadership is on-the-job experience. Despite the ready acknowledgment of its importance by most managers and executives, this primary source of development often is the least effectively used.

Use of job experience for development has a long history. Such phrases as "earning one's stripes" and "doing time" have long been used to describe organizational career progress. In their heyday, when long-term employment and steady progression were the norm, systematic rotation programs and career paths mapped the experiential path to the top. Today's organizations, emerging from the downsizing era and finding themselves short of needed leadership talent, have neither the time nor the stability to wait for such processes to produce results. In a trend unlikely to fade, organizations are attempting to accelerate development, with both good and ill effects. Although acceleration efforts have caused companies to look more closely at the assignments they provide to their high-potential managers and to become more efficient and effective in their use, the emphasis on speed has led to shortcuts that may cause talented people to derail, or even worse, may encourage moving poorly prepared people into senior roles.

Although much is known about the impact of job experiences on development (McCall, Lombardo, & Morrison, 1988; McCauley, 1986), such as which experiences have the most developmental clout and what lessons can be learned from them, most organizations still fail to use experience effectively. The most fundamental reason is the inherent conflict between maximum performance and maximum development (Yukl, 1994). The executive likely to get the best results—the one who has already mastered the skills required for effective performance in that job—is less likely to develop as much as someone for whom the job is a stretch.

Also, after putting people in challenging assignments, organizations often step back to "see how they do," assuming that learning will occur on its own. It is rare to find organizations that enhance such seat-of-the-pants learning by coordinating on-the-job experience with systematic use of developmental feedback, coaching, specific development goals, and rewards for development. With the premium solely on performance, the incumbent of even a potentially developmental job may get results without changing or acquiring significant new leadership skills.

Despite all of these problems, systematic use of on-the-job experience still holds the most promise as an approach to developing leadership talent. When combined with supportive goal setting, feedback, reward, and training practices, experience can be the most valuable teacher in the arsenal.

Technology

In-person attendance at development programs has become increasingly difficult for high-potential leaders (as well as high-performance faculty) in global organizations. Time pressures, time zones, and immense distances all threaten the practicality of classroom-based instruction. Enter technology. Interactive instruction via satellite from a studio on a university campus in Los Angeles can enable a professor to lead a case study discussion with a room full of managers in Frankfurt. The cycle for 360-degree feedback and development planning can be dramatically shortened—it's an impressive sight when thirty-five high-potential managers traipse down to the computer lab to custom-design their 360-degree instrument, collect their data on-line, analyze their feedback, identify development goals and corresponding development activities, and produce specific development plans. What required four to six weeks and numerous mailings ten years ago can, thanks to technology, be done in one sitting.

In addition to shorter cycle time, technology enables us to increase dramatically the richness of the learning situation. Traditional development vehicles like in-basket exercises and computer simulations have become much more complex and highly interactive. VCRs are so commonplace that most business cases now come with companion videos. Role-plays can now be put on CDs to present visual scenarios for participants' responses in a kind of video game that instantly leads to the next scene. Managers can face a tough subordinate's performance problems through their personal computers, choose a course of action, see the impact of their choice, respond again, and so on. The effectiveness of a given response can then be compared with expert choices.

The interactive case study is now a reality. One of the authors saw the power of such an approach in a Harvard classroom. In conjunction with a case on one airline's unusual hiring process, the instructor was able on the spot to choose any of ten job candidate interviews on a video disk and show it to discussion groups. After viewing the candidates, groups could make their decision and then watch the actual decision-making panel, again on disk, debate and decide.

And needless to say, the modern classroom makes the bridge of the *Enterprise* look as old-fashioned as the original Star Trek series' special effects. Computer consoles routinely connect everything with everything else, projecting images from CDs and videodiscs, playing videocassettes, and even dimming the lights. From their chairs, participants in state-of-the-art classrooms can see their opinions instantly tallied and projected on the screen. Professors can get instant evaluations.

As the software and hardware developments that have revolutionized business practices find their way into leadership development activities, opportunities for learning abound, as do questions. Can interactive technology replace face-to-face interaction? Can emotional intelligence be learned at a computer? Can all the important lessons of experience be learned through computer simulation? Impressive as it looks, does a computer-generated development plan replace careful thought and deep understanding with speed, color, and graphics? With no answers, these may be merely the musings of the old-fashioned teacher resisting change. Still, it is difficult to imagine executives describing technology-based experiences as the key developmental events in their leadership lives.

Emphasis on the Learner

With all the energy produced by the controversy over competency models and with all the excitement generated by new technologies, it is easy to let a discussion of development hover around content and method issues. But a third and critical part of this equation is the learner. Developmental opportunities, regardless of their content and method, are valuable assets with limited availability. Not everyone can have access to these opportunities, nor is everyone equally likely to benefit from them. Inevitably a selection decision must be made about who will be developed.

One aspect of the learner side of development involves how the chosen get chosen or, who will be the learners? Another, perhaps more subtle, aspect is the degree to which content and method are tailored to the individual learner, as opposed to exposing all of "the chosen" to the same learning experiences.

Which Leader Is Chosen?

The traditional approach to the "who" of leadership development has been to identify those with leadership potential through some systematic assessment procedure. Better companies use validated assessment center procedures or carefully selected and trained executive panels to perform a thorough review. The resulting high-potential pool is then managed by a corporate-level entity, helping to prevent talent hoarding by business units and reducing the difficulties of making cross-boundary assignments. Those in the pool are often dubbed *corporate assets* or *corporate property*.

The changing nature of the competitive environment, new organizational forms, globalization, and more sophisticated theories of leadership have all contributed to the emergence of new ideas about who should be developed. For example, new organizational forms are driving who gets development: programs involving as participants joint venture partners, customers, suppliers, unions, and even competitors are becoming more common as organizations become more virtual and see leadership as something that must cross fuzzy boundaries. Similarly, flatter, leaner organizations and the rise of team-based structures have broadened the leadership pool to include teams with no formal leaders, managers and executives along with their subordinates, and even multiple hierarchical levels. The underlying idea is, of course, leadership is a shared responsibility so leadership development should be shared also.

Globalization has changed the complexion of the high-potential pool; candidates now may come from anywhere in the world. As it turns out, cultural variety in the audience changes the nature of the process itself. One of us teaches two similar leadership-related courses in the MBA programs of a major university. One course is part of a two-year MBA program in which three-quarters are U.S. students and about one-quarter are international students. In the other, included in a one-year compressed international MBA, three-quarters of the students are from thirteen countries other than the United States. The different dynamics of the two classes requires that both content and method be changed to fit the groups. When the majority of participants are not North American, greater demands are placed on the development setting to recognize religious, cultural, and language differences that can interfere with learning. Indeed, the shift in learners has had valuable effects on the way development is being designed. Recognizing that learning to manage people with quite different perspectives has become core to leadership in many companies, increasingly we see programs designed on the basis of diverse cultural representation. In essence the participants are the content; instead of talking about working with people different from themselves, diverse participants in an action-learning approach actually have to learn to work with one another.

One Size Fits All?

Organizations often assume that all members of the high-potential group should have the same or similar experiences, and so they design lockstep programs or rotational assignments for the pool rather than for individuals. Even though the sequence of programs or events is often timed to coincide with presumably critical development transitions (for example, after taking a first managerial job) with content designed for the challenges faced at each level, the assumption is still that people in the same cohort have the same developmental needs. Organizations are learning, however, that development can be frustratingly individual and even gearing programs to generic transition points may not be tailoring enough. Some are taking individualization one step further by combining individual assessment with individual coaching to provide different development plans for each executive. Cost, of course, has been a major consideration in individual approaches, but the cost in salaries and bonuses of executives who fail plus the business losses incurred as a result of inadequate performance have grown so exorbitant (Michael Ovitz's exit cost Disney $90 million!) that even the expense of an individual coach can seem modest.

Yet another promising approach, prompted by increased emphasis on the learner and on-the-job learning, has been assessment of high-potential ability or openness to learning. A recent study of global executives identified eleven factors that distinguish between high-potential and solid-performing international managers and executives (Spreitzer, McCall, & Mahoney, 1997). These dimensions reflect two characteristics of potential: willingness to take (when offered) or to create (when bored) opportunities to learn new things; and necessary skills and willingness to create an effective learning situation once in those opportunities (for example, seeking out feedback, learning from mistakes, treating people in ways so that they are willing to help, and so on). This research resulted in a multirater assessment instrument to help leaders assess their readiness to learn (McCall, Spreitzer, & Mahoney, 1997) and in turn improve their own ability to use experience effectively for growth. This, of course, is the ultimate step in individualizing development.

Context and Conclusions

Leadership development happens one leader at a time and like leadership itself is always in a context. The context of the process extends from the potential leader's immediate manager and organization unit all the way to the global business arena. Development is a fragile part of that context, which may be development-friendly and supportive or development-hostile and destructive. Many of the development-friendly factors were implied in our review of the content, methods, and participants in leadership development. Hinrichs and Hollenbeck (1991) provide an extended list of supportive development factors at the organizational level, including open career channels, a human assets business strategy, and a performance focus throughout the organization.

The forces shaping context are, of course, inherently neutral—neither friendly nor hostile. What are some of these forces and what do they hold for the future context of leadership development in organizations?

Increased competition, whether global or local, is unlikely to go away, so there will be continued downward pressure on costs. Leadership development is vulnerable because we have yet to demonstrate convincingly its cost effectiveness.

Efforts to document the impact of development usually are restricted to an evaluation of specific practices (for example, 360-degree feedback) or training programs (for example, a leadership class). Little has changed over the years in the outcomes of such research—the "smiles test" shows high participant ratings but documented improvements in job performance, much less in organizational performance, are few and far between.

Programs are highly susceptible to fads and pundits, which sweep through and disappear with regularity. Small wonder that defending the leadership development budget can be difficult!

More optimistically, however,

Changing organizational forms (flatter hierarchies, high-involvement systems) will require more sophisticated leadership skills at both the top and the bottom of organizations (Lawler, 1992, 1996).

The increasing diversity of the workforce, resulting from both globalization and demographic changes, will make leadership more demanding and require better skills at leading the diversity (Puffer, 1996).

Increasing experimentation with and implementation of new organizational systems to promote learning and creativity (for example, Senge, 1990) and bold innovations in the use of organizational rewards to reinforce growth, such as skill-based pay that predicates pay increases on acquisition of new skills rather than on production (Ledford, 1995) will support development of new skills.

Advanced technology will make exposure to development opportunities more readily available to more people.

Increasing mutual dependence among corporations (for example, joint ventures, partnerships, and redefined supplier relationships) will create pressure for effective leadership and greater recognition that investing in leadership development is a best practice of successful corporations like General Electric and visible leaders like Jack Welch.

These are powerful and encouraging forces that bode well for leadership development in the future. But there is a dark side as well.

The same partnerships and organizational dependencies that call for better leadership have a temporary quality to them that may discourage long-term investment in development.

The changing psychological contract (Hall & Associates, 1996) between organizations and employees—even the Japanese are moving away from lifetime employment—provides an argument for not investing in individuals over time.

With fads based more on the communications skills of their purveyors than on substance, corporate development advocates may retire or themselves run into trouble and take their advocacy with them.

The same competitive pressures that demand better leadership also spawn the development of systems that define performance narrowly and produce short-term rewards.

Given the substantial nature of the forces and the fragile quality of leadership development, we leave to the futurists a description of alternative scenarios. We are, however, optimistic. Although the popularity of the term *leadership* itself will likely fade, the demands associated with leading complex organizations will not. We believe that people, having tasted more effective leadership, will come to expect it and even demand it. Organizations that do not cultivate leadership will falter. The view that leaders can be hired away from other corporations on an as-needed basis will prove shortsighted indeed.

We believe that the trend in leadership development will be toward more individualized approaches, tailored both to the growth needs of individual executives as determined by feedback and coaching methodologies and to the business needs of the organization. Business schools, unlikely to regain their monopolies of times past, will find new niches in design and delivery of these increasingly individualistic approaches.

Still, the action in leadership development will move inside corporations, supported by an array of service providers. Organizations will become more effective in using experience as a teacher and as their leaders become more committed to and better at coaching their executives will learn their way into better performance. Improvements in technology will support more effective use of on-the-job learning, just as it has revolutionized business practices.

The business imperative for leaders who can handle the complexity and change ahead is so compelling that efforts to develop leadership skills will continue unabated. Corporations that do not develop leadership as a competitive edge will not survive.

References

Advanced Management Assessment Center Staff Manual. (1982, June). AT&T Staffing and Development.

Bass, B. (1985). *Leadership and performance beyond expectations.* New York: Free Press.

Bennis, W., & Nanus, B. (1985). *Leaders: The strategies for taking charge.* New York: HarperCollins.

Bolt, J. (1989). *Executive development: A strategy for corporate competitiveness.* New York: HarperCollins.

Bongiorno, L. (1993, Oct. 25). The professor is in: More companies are bringing teachers to the office. *Business Week,* p. 105.

Bracken, D. W. (1996). Multisource (360 degree) feedback: Surveys for individual and organizational development. In A. I. Kraut (Ed.), *Organizational surveys* (pp. 117–143). San Francisco: Jossey-Bass.

Bray, D. W, Campbell, R. J., & Grant, D. L. (1974). *Formative years in business: A long-term study of managerial lives.* New York: Wiley.

Briscoe, J. (1996). *Competency-based approaches to selecting and developing executives: Current practices and suggestions for improvements.* Paper presented at the Executive Development Roundtable, Boston University School of Management, Boston.

Burns, J. M. (1978). *Leadership*. New York: HarperCollins.

Conger, J. (1992). *Learning to lead*. San Francisco: Jossey-Bass.

Covey, S. R. (1989). *The seven habits of highly effective people*. New York: Simon & Schuster.

Dalton, M. A., & Hollenbeck, G. P. (1996). *How to design an effective system for developing managers and executives*. Greensboro, NC: Center for Creative Leadership.

Deal, T. E., & Kennedy, A. A. (1982). *Corporate cultures*. Reading, MA: Addison-Wesley.

de Lisser, E. (1993, Sept. 10). Just for you: More corporations shun off-the-shelf courses in favor of custom-tailored ones. *Wall Street Journal*, p. R5.

Dunnette, M. D. (1993). My hammer or your hammer? *Human Resource Management, 32*(2–3), 373.

Edelstein, B. C., & Armstrong, D. J. (1993). A model for executive development. *Human Resource Planning, 16*(4), 51–64.

Hall, D. T., & Associates. (1996). *The career is dead—Long live the career: A relational approach to careers*. San Francisco: Jossey-Bass.

Hall, D. T., Otazo, K. L., & Hollenbeck, G. P. (forthcoming). Behind closed doors: What really happens in executive coaching. *Organization Dynamics*.

Hinrichs, J. R., & Hollenbeck, G. P. (1991). Leadership development. In K. N. Wexley (Ed.), *Developing human resources* (Vol. 5, pp. 221–258). Washington, DC: Bureau of National Affairs.

Hollenbeck, G. P. (1992). *360 degree feedback and developmental plans*. Paper presented at the Executive Development Roundtable, Boston University School of Management, Boston.

Hollenbeck, G. P. (1996). *An essay on issues in executive coaching*. Paper presented at the Executive Development Roundtable, Boston University School of Management, Boston.

Keeping track: Executive education at a glance. (1993, Sept. 10). *Wall Street Journal*, p. R3.

Kilburg, R. R. (Ed.). (1996). Executive coaching. *Consulting Psychology Journal: Practice and Research, 48*(2), 57–152.

Kotter, J. P. (1988). *The leadership factor*. New York: Free Press.

Kotter, J. P., & Heskett, J. L. (1992). *Corporate culture and performance*. New York: Free Press.

Kouzes, J. M., & Posner, B. Z. (1995). *The leadership challenge* (2nd ed.). San Francisco: Jossey-Bass.

Lawler, E. E., III. (1992). *The ultimate advantage: Creating the high-involvement organization*. San Francisco: Jossey-Bass.

Lawler, E. E., III. (1996). *From the ground up: Six principles for building the new logic corporation.* San Francisco: Jossey-Bass.

Ledford, G., Jr. (1995). Paying for the skills, knowledge, and competencies of knowledge workers. *Compensation and Benefits Review, 27*(4), 55–62.

Lepsinger, R., & Lucia, A. D. (1997). *The art and science of 360 degree feedback.* San Diego: Pfeiffer.

Mace, M. (1958). On-the-job coaching. In H. F. Merrill & E. Marting (Eds.), *Developing executive skills.* New York: AMACOM.

McCall, M. W., Jr. (1998). *High flyers: Developing the next generation of leaders.* Boston: Harvard Business School Press.

McCall, M. W., Jr., Lombardo, M. M., & Morrison, A. M. (1988) *The lessons of experience: How successful executives develop on the job.* San Francisco: New Lexington Press.

McCall, M. W., Jr., Spreitzer, G., & Mahoney, J. (1997). *Prospector.* Greensboro, NC: Center for Creative Leadership.

McCauley, C. (1986). *Developmental experiences in managerial work: A literature review* (Technical Report No. 26). Greensboro, NC: Center for Creative Leadership.

McGregor, D. (1967). *The professional manager.* New York: McGraw-Hill.

Micklethwait, J., & Wooldridge, A. (1996). *The witch doctors: Making sense of the management gurus.* New York: Times Books/Random House.

Peters, T., & Waterman, R. H. (1982). *In search of excellence.* New York: HarperCollins.

Puffer, S. M. (Ed.). (1996). *Management across cultures: Insights from fiction and practice.* Cambridge, MA: Blackwell.

Schaffer, G. (1994, Nov.). Competency-based managerial and leadership development. *Proceedings of the National Conference on Using Competency-Based Tools and Applications to Drive Organizational Performance,* Boston.

Schein, E. H. (1985). *Organizational culture and leadership.* San Francisco: Jossey-Bass.

Senge, P. M. (1990). *The fifth discipline: The art and practice of the learning organization.* New York: Doubleday.

Smith, L. (1993, Dec. 27). The executive's new coach. *Fortune,* pp. 126–134.

Sontag, L. (1996). *The evolution of competencies at Chase: Lessons learned.* Presentation to Boston University's Executive Development Roundtable, Spring Meeting, Boston.

Spencer, L. M., McClelland, D. M., & Spencer, S. M. (1990, Aug.). *Competency assessment methods: History and state of the art.* Paper presented at the annual conference of the American Psychological Association, Boston.

Spreitzer, G., McCall, M. W., Jr., & Mahoney, J. (1997). Early identification of international executive potential. *Journal of Applied Psychology, 82,* 6–29.

Stogdill, R. M. (1974). *Handbook of leadership: A survey of the literature.* New York: Free Press.

Tichy, N., & DeRose, C. (1995, Nov. 27). Roger Enrico's master class. *Fortune,* pp. 105–106.

Tichy, N., & Sherman, S. (1993). *Control your destiny or someone else will.* New York: Doubleday.

Timmreck, C. W., & Bracken, D. W. (1995, May). *Upward feedback in the trenches: Challenges and reality.* Paper presented at the Tenth Annual Conference of the Society for Industrial and Organizational Psychology, Orlando, FL.

Tornow, W. W. (1993, Summer–Fall). Introduction to special issue on 360 degree feedback. *Human Resource Management, 32*(2–3), 211–219.

Tornow, W. W., & London, M. (Eds.). (1998). *Maximizing the value of 360 degree feedback: A process for individual and organizational development.* San Francisco: Jossey-Bass.

Twenty leading b-schools offering the executive MBA. (1993, Oct. 25). *Business Week,* p. 107.

Van Velsor, E., & Leslie, J. B. (1991). *Feedback to managers: Volume II. A review and comparison of sixteen multirater feedback instruments.* Greensboro, NC: Center for Creative Leadership.

Whyte, D. (1994). *The heart aroused: Poetry and the preservation of the soul in corporate America.* New York: Doubleday.

Witherspoon, R., & White, R. P. (1996). Executive coaching: A continuum of roles. *Consulting Psychology Journal: Practice and Research, 48*(2), 124–133.

Wofford, C. (1993). What is meant by a competency? *Leadership & Organizational Development Journal, 14*(1), 29–36.

Yukl, G. (1994). *Leadership in organizations* (3rd ed.). Upper Saddle River, NJ: Prentice Hall.

Zaleznik, A. (1977). Managers and leaders: Are they different? *Harvard Business Review, 55*(3), 67–78.

CHAPTER 9

Building Room at the Top

Selecting Senior Executives Who Can Lead and Succeed in the New World of Work

Joseph L. Moses
Scott L. Eggebeen

This chapter is designed to broaden our perspective about selecting leadership talent in business environments that are continuing to evolve and change. We will examine how assumptions about the individual and the organization have changed, focusing on both the planning and implementation process used for senior-level staffing.

As other chapters in this book have noted, traditional assumptions behind the identification and nurturing of talent are being questioned as organizations, the business environment, and the leadership challenges faced have changed. Increased globalization, competitive pressures, technological advancement, and the information explosion represent some of the many changes that force companies to reexamine how they go about acquiring or building leadership talent.

What This Chapter Contains

This chapter is largely conceptual, because specific details have been effectively documented for many traditional approaches and may be located elsewhere. We will focus on long-term strategic processes rather than on filling specific positions immediately or finding just-in-time solutions. Effective executive selection and succession planning is most important not when an immediate selection needs to be made but rather when preparing for such an event.

Our discussion focuses on senior management and executive positions because we believe these are the most critical areas for a business as well as the least understood or addressed by current practitioners (Hollenbeck, 1994). Although many of the concepts we describe are also applicable to middle management, this chapter will target only general managers, vice presidents, senior vice presidents, and CEOs. Thus, our comments will apply principally to individuals who are the primary managers of large operating or service divisions within an organization. Much of the focus of management selection and succession planning has shifted to include external candidates, and our ideas are intended to apply to both internal and external talent.

Finally, it is our belief that executive selection and succession planning is based on a sophisticated type of behavioral profile matching. At any given time, it is heavily influenced by the notion of fit between the skills, management style, and personal characteristics of the individual and the situations and needs of the organization. Predicting the future fit for both individuals and organizations is a basic underpinning of the way in which we address our subject matter.

Changes in Assumptions

Before discussing either planning or selection practices, we must begin by examining changes in assumptions about individuals and organizations.

Do Managers Become Leaders?

The stable, hierarchical organizations of the past created a set of assumptions concerning career progress. High-potential candidates were expected to move across many functions. In effect, this model told managers not to worry about preparing for the future. The firm would tell them when the next rotation or transfer was imminent. They needed to worry little about developing a broad, balanced portfolio of skills, because the organization would choose and provide assignments as needed. Their job was simply to meet or exceed performance expectations, work aggressively as directed, make decisions in line with firm goals, and think of the organization's needs before their own.

In practice, many of these cross-functional transfers never actually materialized. Many managers simply advanced within the traditional career ladders of a particular function, having been denied the critical development experiences essential for success at expanded levels of responsibility.

Zaleznik (1978) was one of the first to distinguish among leadership acts by asking the defining question: Are managers and leaders different? A few years later, Gerstein and Reisman (1983) suggested that we needed to view leadership behavior in multiple contexts. More recently, Kotter (1990) broadened Zaleznik's approach by distinguishing between performance outcomes expected of managers and leaders. Locke (1991) provides an excellent introductory chapter summarizing these contemporary perspectives on leadership and management. These writers have caused organizations to question the implicit assumption that effective managers can be simply trained or developed to be leaders. In essence, managers were traditionally put in place to carry out initiatives directed from above. Their role was not to redefine process but rather to implement it effectively. Organizational vision, strategy, and initiative were viewed to be the domain of a select group of leaders at the top of the organization. These leaders were expected to be insightful and persuasive, to note trends and environmental changes affecting the direction of the organization. In contrast, managers were most often seen to be careful organizers and planners, detailed implementers, and efficient processors of instructions. These characteristics were viewed as quite different from those of leaders; thus, some began to question whether the differing skills and characteristics of the managers meant that different individuals might be necessary for the two roles, rather than assume, as previously, that the best manager could be molded into the best organizational leader. Traditional succession-planning, development, and high-potential processes have focused primarily on "growing" a class or cohort of managers into the next generation of leaders. Recent advancements, however, have challenged this thinking, and suggest that an individual's unique characteristics, skills, and abilities play a more significant role in determining the best potential leaders of an organization in the future.

Does One Size Fit All?

Traditional approaches to management selection and succession planning developed in large, stable organizations. They focused primarily on smooth transitions through long-term development and rotation patterns. Development primarily consisted of functional knowledge, which was attained through rotations through the various functions.

The structures themselves were hierarchical and despite short-term deviations were expected to be stable over time. Candidates fit into well-defined boxes on an organizational chart. These structures became confining for many organizations and did not allow for the flexibility necessary to survive in today's competitive environment.

This situation led to management selection and succession-planning exercises that focused on a candidate's direct work experience, summarized in massive annual paper-gathering initiatives that had less and less relevance to corporate success in the marketplace. Although significant effort went into collecting volumes of information on the experiences of key managers and leaders, these systems added little value when key executives were placed in entirely new situations (for example, joint ventures) as opposed to the stable positions in which their experience had been obtained. Thus, organizations tended actively to maintain information but not use it in making real choices. Bureaucratic, paper-driven succession-planning processes that did not directly influence major decisions often became the target of cost-cutting efforts. Rhodes (1988) even suggested that the rapid changes taking place in most major organizations doomed traditional succession-planning approaches to failure in the 1990s.

Other Factors to Be Considered

Three other factors need to be considered to implement planning and selection for relevant leadership behaviors. As individuals and organizations have begun to adapt to changes in shifting career and work expectations, few researchers or practitioners have investigated these other topics even though they significantly influence the behavior and expectations of senior-level leaders.

Cycle Time

Cycle time refers to the length of time needed from the development to the delivery of a product or service. Cycle time is a matter of both time and stability. Some industries (newspaper publishing, for example) have short cycle times but contain highly repetitive activities that can be planned for. Other industries (pharmaceuticals, oil and gas, aircraft manufacturing, or power transmission) have longer cycle times, whereas industries specializing in consumer products, information management, consulting, or entertainment all have relatively shorter cycle times.

Both organizational and leadership behavior vary as a function of cycle time in the industry. For example, industries with long cycle times tend to encourage reflective thinking, research, trials, and experimentation. Contrast these behaviors with that of organizations with much more rapid cycle times, where speed, responsiveness to change, urgency, and constant updates of competitor and market conditions dominate actions. Because of increased competition and competitiveness, even organizations with a traditionally long cycle time find themselves under significant pressure to shorten it. Thus, they may need leaders with additional ability and skill to deal effectively with change more rapidly.

Organizational Life Stages

In addition to the speed of product or service delivery, every product and organization goes through several life stages, from start-up to business expansions and turnarounds. In addition, many organizations face significant challenges as a result of mergers, reengineering, joint ventures, or entry into different settings such as international markets.

McCall, Lombardo, and Morrison (1988) were among the first to articulate how leadership behaviors vary in each of an organization's life stages. For example, successfully leading a start-up requires considerable skill in leading others through ambiguity, leading an expansion involves focusing on building relationships with new marketplaces, and leading a turnaround requires ability to rebuild and heal an organization. In contrast, skills stressed in leading a joint venture include the ability to manage conflicting operating agendas.

Cultural Change

Recognizing changes, or differences, in a firm's values or culture is often central to an organization's success as well. For example, currently popular concepts like teamwork, empowerment, and service quality are widely expressed values in many organizations. Specific leadership skills and behaviors are needed for teamwork, for example, in start-up organizations where leaders must build a team. Similarly, if a company is to move toward an empowered environment or a service-quality framework, a unique skill set in the senior leadership team is also required to support these interventions successfully.

Treating the organizational setting and its leadership challenges as a unidimensional system based on differing levels of hierarchical or functional responsibility does not reflect the divergence of leadership behaviors that exist or the skills needed to demonstrate potential for new environments.

Cycle time, life stage, and cultural conditions warrant examining not only hierarchical differences in responsibility but also the context in which leadership acts occur, their implications and outcomes. This requires an understanding of both current and future leadership expectations. It also requires frequent updates as the business setting, business values, or marketplace affect change.

We are currently at a critical juncture at which we can extract the best practices in executive succession planning and selection and modify them to adapt successfully to an ever-changing world. We begin by first examining succession planning itself.

Succession-Planning Processes

Succession-planning techniques have evolved significantly over the last decade. In its traditional context, succession planning has been thought of primarily as replacement planning. For example, Cowherd (1986) reflected on the realities of the 1980s by noting that the top five to twenty positions in a corporation were filled based on longevity, being in the right position at the right time, and luck. Greller and Nee (1989) identified implications of the demographics of the baby boom and baby bust generations for future staffing needs—such as the relative oversupply and undersupply of individuals capable of and interested in ascending into more senior positions—but their predictions seemed to be ignored during the reengineering frenzy of the late 1980s. Spoor (1993) pointed out that many companies were so distracted by the need to reengineer and downsize to survive that they allowed short-term pressures to override long-term growth issues and only now are realizing that it was a mistake to divert their attention.

Successfully emerging from difficult downsizing, cost reduction, and product and service redefinition cycles, many organizations are finding that they have not prepared the management and leadership talent to take the organization in the direction that the reengineered vision and strategy suggest. Curtis and Russell (1993) report that 70 percent of eighty-six U.S. Fortune 500 firms surveyed currently consider succession planning to be a top priority. Wallum (1993) points out that the most successful organizations are beginning to merge their career planning and development systems with succession planning to ensure that development efforts result in candidates with the desired skills and characteristics. In order to understand the shift in emphasis needed from replacement planning to a more flexible, "live," and actionable trade-off approach that represents a competitive advantage, we first review traditional practices.

Replacement-Planning Practices

Succession planning meant having talent in reserve. In other words, it was much like the minor league system in professional baseball. An organization needed a stable of talent in case major league players were injured, lost their skills, or retired. Thus, organizations took many years to train and develop junior managers, watching carefully to cull the most talented from the pool and move them forward. In a survey of fifteen large corporations reflecting practices used as recently as fifteen years ago, Carnazza (1982) reported that one of four strategies was generally used for succession planning: a "crown prince" was handpicked by the departing officer; a small slate of candidates was reviewed and compared; a pool of talent was identified and picked from as opportunities arose; or development processes were used by the organization to prepare "waves" of equivalently skilled and experienced managers and leaders.

Replacement-planning practices often commanded the most attention by practitioners. Often labeled *high-potential programs,* replacement-planning activities have been detailed elsewhere. For example, Drake (1993) profiled specific approaches at the Royal Bank of Canada, Merck, PepsiCo, Hershey Foods, and Kmart. Clark and Lyness (1991) illustrate the process used by Citicorp, whereas Kramer (1990) provided a painstakingly detailed account of the steps necessary in developing and implementing a traditional succession-planning system. The best scenario was often to have someone very similar move in to replace a departing manager so that the direction, pace, decision-making style, and fundamental assumptions of the unit would not change.

The Changing Paradigm

During the last decade, the limitations of these approaches have begun to get significant attention. Hall (1986) was one of the first to identify pitfalls in replacement planning, including these: lack of alignment with an organization's strategy; executives' selecting successors like themselves; and a focus on identifying candidates rather than developing talent. Similarly, Pinto (1992) presented an insightful explanation of key paradoxes that both challenged and plagued succession planning, such as promoting from within instead of bringing in new ideas from outside the organization, evaluating success in terms of "hit rate" based on previous experience instead of providing new challenges for managers, and focusing on individual achievement rather than emerging team-based structures. Finally, Bardwick (1991) and Tichy and Sherman (1995) both pointed out that the stability and relative calm that were the result of such approaches caused organizations and individual managers to miss key opportunities, competitive threats, or even customer demands in the marketplace.

The succession-planning paradigm based on finding internal replacements changed rapidly as market forces outpaced the literature and practice. A free-market economy approach has evolved as organizational loyalty began to change through significant downsizings and reorganizations. Faced with potential displacement, little chance for advancement, or limited development, highly skilled employees began to seek out opportunities outside the organization.

What has developed is actually a clearer, less secretive model that is more straightforward about the realities of potential opportunities. It is also perhaps a better arrangement for both the individual and the organization overall. The current environment is predicated on the assumption that organizations only need managers or executives for as long as they have opportunities that match the individual's skills and abilities. This closely parallels changes in the manager's intent to stay with an organization only as long as development and movement continues and increased career success is attainable within the system. As Buckner and Slavenski (1994) point out, traditional succession-planning approaches have too often failed to incorporate these needs and career interests of the executives themselves. Hall's description of the *protean career* (Hall & Associates, 1996), with the individual at the center of career development, suggests a similar movement occurring in career development practices as well.

Trade-Off Plans

The notion of the employee contract for life has shifted to the contract for assignment. The agreement is only for the current position. If the manager is successful and the organization has other needs, the contract can be renegotiated at the end of the current assignment. If not, the organization can help the manager find other opportunities elsewhere. Given a changing environment, succession-planning approaches need to operate more in terms of trade-off analysis than replacement planning. Much like a chess game, multiple moves can be made. It is the responsibility of the organization to figure out which of the possible combinations of pieces (managers) and positions together make for the best forward move to attain the overall objective.

At any given time, an organization will have differing critical leadership opportunities and demands. As we noted earlier, the requirements for start-ups and other phases of an organizational life cycle often have significant impact on the senior leadership team. Each of these requires different skills and leadership styles. Organizations can either build or buy this talent, using techniques discussed later in this chapter.

Still "Garbage in, Garbage out?"

Computer support systems and technology enhancements have also resulted in many changes in succession planning. The rapid increase in computer capabilities allows for succession planning to be conducted on a single microcomputer platform. Many vendors have emerged to service this need. For example, Brush and Nardoni (1992) describe a microcomputer-based approach that they claim increases the degree of security of confidential information, allows for extensive data (for example, ratings, experience summaries, development needs, and so on), minimizes the difficulties of growth and change over time, and provides charts, graphs, and tables quickly and easily.

At the same time, these programs have many limitations, primarily concerning the quality and relevance of the data put into the system. Many organizations have had difficulty computerizing their processes. Voluminous information can be meaningless if it is not easily accessible or cannot be easily manipulated for comparing and contrasting candidates. Furthermore, databases can become quickly out of date. Keeping data current proved to be too difficult for several companies. These firms have since replaced their data-intensive systems with smaller, contained, more "live" succession-planning processes.

The right data solution must present a good balance between the urge to keep every bit of information and the need for only current, critical decision-making information that can be accessed quickly and easily. Having accurate and relevant information often means input by the key decision maker, rather than reliance on an internal HR support system several steps removed from the decision maker. Software vendors have products designed primarily for this application and more can be expected soon. Although users report success with several different programs and approaches, the best have connections to selection and resume databases and are constantly updated by other current data sources.

Research Needs

Because there is a dearth of research in this area and because most organizations approach the subject of senior-level succession planning with such secrecy, little is known compared with entry-level and midlevel employee selection. Eastman (1995) and Rothwell (1994) provide some recent reviews of contemporary practices. Although the popular press highlights examples of successful high-level placements (for example, Gerstner at IBM), we more often hear about failures (for example, the departure of Michael Ovitz from the Walt Disney Corporation). These suggest the importance of improving the approach and the clear need for additional research and alternative methodologies. The question becomes this: How best does an organization test fit between an executive and its opportunities? One solution is by applying more rigorous selection techniques, discussed next.

Selection of Senior-Level Talent

As noted earlier, our focus in this chapter is on senior-level populations rather than lower-level selection systems. We have chosen to emphasize this target population for several reasons. First, during this decade a significant revival of interest in identifying and staffing talent for more senior populations has emerged. Second, many of the leading-edge techniques described can also be applied to lower-level populations; well-designed systems for senior-level talent often serve as a point of departure that sets or models examples of what can be done for other parts of the organization. And finally, one of the most common complaints about senior levels is their weak coaching and mentoring skills. By providing this audience with firsthand experience about themselves, they often become much more facile in identifying and coaching others.

We begin by defining executive performance, potential, and suitability, and then examine how relevant competencies are identified. This is followed by descriptions of potentially promising techniques.

Defining What We Are Measuring

Performance is a description of current work behavior in relation to work standards or mutually agreed-upon work objectives. Performance measures are outcome-based, either in terms of specified standards (for example, number of units produced, errors, customer complaints, increase in revenue, decrease in costs, and so on) or in comparison with a specific business objective (gaining *x* percent market share, successfully closing down a troubled plant, or gaining access to a new market).

Potential refers to the estimated likelihood of success in more complex, demanding, or unfamiliar assignments that are significantly different from activities faced in the current work setting. Potential reflects a guess, which can be improved on by relying on a number of well-developed and validated techniques to identify talent.

Suitability is a judgment of appropriateness for a more senior assignment that takes the individual's past performance, potential, and development actions into account. Judgments about suitability involve making comparisons to others in order to select best fit to target assignments.

Commonly observed errors in applying these terms occur either by confusing the distinction between adjacent terms—such as using performance measures as indicators of potential, or potential indicators as measures of suitability—or by applying the wrong standard of comparison. For example, suitability always implies a comparison with other available talent. Performance measurement may also require comparative measures at times, such as when normative data are used or some arbitrary cutoffs are applied (for example, top 10 percent of group). Judgments about potential, however, are individually based, predicting how effectively an individual can move to more complex assignments.

Determining Relevant Competencies

The word *competency* has become a popular one that is often used to describe the outcomes of a specific form of job analysis. Historically, the word has undergone several revisions as the literature and practice have evolved in more contemporary terms. The OSS Assessment Staff recommended that researchers "obtain from members of the organization a list of the attributes of personality which, in their opinion, contribute to success or failure in the performance of each role" (1948, p. 476). Further, they suggested that "these determinants will constitute the *variables* which, if possible, will be measured by the assessment procedures" (p. 477, emphasis added).

Hemphill (1959) used the term *executive dimensions* to describe the behaviors he first identified in his Executive Position Description Questionnaire. Bray, Campbell, and Grant (1974) describe the characteristics they assessed as *variables,* because they were the independent variables in the AT&T Management Progress Study. Campbell, Dunnette, Lawler, and Weick (1970) use the term *managerial job dimensions.* Byham (1970) described these as *dimensions,* which rapidly became a widely used commercial term during the 1980s. Boyatzis (1982) picked up on the term *competency* as previously defined by McClelland (1973), which seems to have become the term du jour.

Recently, Briscoe (1996) summarized a number of approaches to competency development. We have adapted his model for identifying senior-level competencies. Three approaches are popular today.

Superior Performance Approach

In this approach, data are obtained from superior performers through self-reflective interviews and are compared with data obtained from average performers. It should be noted that behaviors identified may not reflect emerging or future competency needs.

Value-Based Approach

This approach is based on normative and cultural values held by the organization. These often result from input of organizational development specialists rather than being based on empirical research. These competencies are difficult to define in behavioral terms. They often reflect values, such as "valuing diversity," rather than the implicit outcomes associated with the value itself, such as managing conflict, working across organizational boundaries, or acquiring relevant information from diverse informational sources.

Behaviorally Based Strategic Approach

This approach is based on anticipated future needs and strategic business objectives rather than driven from the past. This can be highly appropriate to many business settings undergoing rapid change. Speculation about future behaviors can be minimized by going to relevant subject matter experts (such as new product developers) to anticipate the behavioral changes that are likely to occur. The behaviorally based approach seems to be most effective in identifying what is really needed in the future. Although the behaviors identified can reflect many traditionally based competencies, the focus is to mirror the strategic direction for the firm, such as expanding into radically new markets, understanding skills needed to lead different elements of a product or organizational life cycle, realigning the firm through mergers or downsizing, or entering into new organizational relationships like joint ventures. To gather this kind of data, interviews, simulations, or focus groups with key experts (both the very senior leadership and selected SMEs) identify anticipated key behavioral situations.

Evaluating Senior-Level Talent

We will examine several techniques suited for identifying the talent pool for senior management. Many of these are well suited to entry-level and midlevel selection, but often the question raised is one of resources (such as the quality and knowledge base of the assessors or evaluators).

We do not wish to replicate a number of excellent studies or reviews of this topic (Sorcher, 1985; Hollenbeck, 1994). We will, however, review a number of techniques that are appropriate to these populations and, when staffed by assessors and evaluators with high organizational credibility, can be modified to lower-level groups.

One of the main challenges is to ensure the relevance of the judgments to future assignments. Many well-managed organizations, such as AT&T and IBM, relied on identification and succession-planning procedures that resulted in having the right kinds of leaders for the wrong times (Tunstall, 1985; Schlesinger, Dyer, Clough, & Landau, 1987; Mills, 1988).

In most organizations the competencies deemed key to succession planning and identification need to be regularly updated.

As the business environment changes, particularly in organizations producing products with short cycle times, we recommend updating and modifying competencies at least every three years. With a well-designed competency process that captures the future needs of the organization, the following techniques (in addition to selection interviews) represent some of the more contemporary identification tools that can be used to enhance succession-planning input for this population.

Group Evaluation Process

Developed by Sorcher (1985) and recently reviewed by Hollenbeck (1994), this technique melds performance appraisal data with future leadership expectations. Groups of executives work together to determine what they really know, what they need to know, and how to go about finding out critical information about a candidate. Key to this process is a highly qualified facilitator who challenges the data providers to give behavioral evidence, not just opinions. As a result, the process forces executives and other appraisers to examine the criteria they use and provide concrete on-the-job behavioral data in order to examine future implications. Hollenbeck (1994) notes that despite its use, very little data have been reported about the process. When led by a qualified professional capable of challenging senior-level input, this process can improve the quality of behavioral evidence that can be developed to make much better decisions than those generated by typical performance appraisal reviews.

360-Degree and Multiple Rater Feedback Systems

Tornow (1993) describes the practice of involving multiple raters, often including self-ratings, to provide data for feedback that is solicited from important others (superiors, peers, customers, and so on) and notes its increased popularity over the last fifteen years. Much has been written about this subject, but reviews by Van Velsor and Leslie (1991a, 1991b) and Tornow (1993), who edited a related special issue of *Human Resource Management,* are particularly helpful. Although the technique has become widespread, Moses, Hollenbeck, and Sorcher (1993) raise many questions about the enthusiastic, noncritical acceptance of this process, particularly for selection. They note that most 360-degree instruments are based on other people's observations (OPOs), which are often

incomplete descriptions of past performance. They propose instruments based on other people's expectations (OPEs), which reflect how others think about a person in a given situation. They
note that few instruments create a proper observer context for situational specificity, such as how people will respond in situations
that require them to encourage innovation in others, deal with the
conflict inherent in a joint venture, or respond to multinational
interests or constituencies.

Although multiple rater instruments have considerable popularity, they seem to be more valuable as a tool for individual development or cultural assessment than as an identification technique.
Nevertheless, some organizations have begun to use 360-degree
tools in such contexts as performance and promotion appraisal.
Although there is a great deal of descriptive literature, there is a
paucity of evidence that 360-degree tools provide predictive
information. Furthermore, little interrater agreement has been obtained among the various stakeholders completing the instruments. However, this technique has the capacity to be integrated
with other assessment devices and thereby serve as a source of "tri-
angulation" with other measures.

Personality Measures

In addition to Grant, Katkovsky, and Bray's review (1967) of projective techniques used in the AT&T Management Progress
Study, are Bentz's description (1987) of the use of tests in Sears's
selection process and Campbell and Van Velsor's review (1995) of
the personality measures applied in CCL's Leadership Development Program. Bernardin and Bownas's review (1985) of specific
personality-based assessment techniques used in organizations is
dated but highly descriptive. In recent years, advances in personality research (Barrick & Mount, 1991; Hough & Schneider, 1996)
and the development of new measures (Campbell, 1990; Hogan,
Hogan, & Roberts, 1996) have renewed appreciation for the potential value of these measures. Often administered as part of an
external individual assessment process, they provide additional information concerning a person's style that, when combined with a
firm understanding of expectations in the target job, can provide
additional insights. Again, we stress the usefulness of personality-
based techniques as part of a well-rounded assessment process
rather than as stand-alone instruments.

Individual Assessment Processes

Individual assessments are conducted either by independent consultants or by psychologists employed within an organization. Usually conducted by psychologists with varying amounts of expertise and professional credentials, the testing techniques range from a brief battery of pencil-and-paper personality tests to 360-degree instruments to extensive behavioral simulation.

Examples of job analysis research to support the assessment battery are rarely offered, and many of these assessments are sold based on the expertise of the assessor. Most employ some form of diagnostic interview or personality or intellectual measures. Despite their widespread use, there has been little systematic research on the topic. In an excellent review, Ryan and Sackett (1998) summarize both the literature on this topic and their own systematic research. The published literature is not very supportive, but Ryan and Sackett note that the evaluation of interpersonal skills, traditionally a focal point for individual assessment, may have particular relevance for judging effectiveness when working in teams or with diverse populations.

Senior-Level Assessment Centers

The assessment center method has been extensively described elsewhere (Moses & Byham, 1977; Thornton & Byham, 1982). For many years its widespread application was for entry level and mid-level selection. With the emergence of better understanding of managerial and executive development, in part stimulated by the developmental insights provided by McCall, Lombardo, and Morrison (1988), organizations have been using high-level assessment centers both for selection and for development.

A consistent theme in senior-level assessment centers is the use of third-party assessors who provide an independent, objective verification of strengths and development needs, which is then incorporated in the firm's succession-planning and development efforts. Several features of these programs distinguish them from assessment centers used with lower-level candidates. These usually include customized simulations based on an intensive competency analysis, such as the key behaviors expected in current and future leadership roles in the target organization; an external team of experienced professional assessors who have firsthand knowledge of the behaviors and style of the client's organization; a highly interactive and integrated assessment process that enables participants to relate to each other during an interactive in-basket exercise and other exercises; professional actors who simulate many of the key interpersonal issues faced by this group; and personalized coaching, offered on a case-by-case basis, to explore "derailment" indicators or provide targeted coaching for organizational and personal career transitions.

The use of this process is expected to grow, particularly as organizations reengineer or acquire new resources. Its advantages to the organization include minimal involvement in the mechanics of running assessment centers; high credibility among participants (many of whom become assessors for lower-level programs); and firsthand appreciation of coaching and development techniques that can be transferred back to the organization.

Considering Research Issues

As Hollenbeck (1994) noted, there is considerable interest in executive selection but little empirical data to verify its effectiveness. Part of the problem stems from our empirical validation models, which require fairly large samples and stable performance indicators—challenges that future researchers will need to address. A second issue concerns the secrecy generally associated with senior-level selection (and rejection) and later with success or failure, which prevent systematic research. We may need to look at alternative research approaches, for example, using public data such as annual reports. One approach that offers promise is relying on information in the public domain, as suggested by Van Maanen, Dabbs, and Faulkner (1982).

Some Key Questions

As practitioners who both research and apply executive selection and succession-planning practices in a wide array of settings, we recognize the difficulty of prescribing best practices in a highly evolving and dynamic field. Our view is that the relative success or failure of a program can be best understood if a series of questions are answered. We offer the following questions as both a checklist for practitioners and researchers to test the success of their efforts and a guide to their program development efforts.

- Do the competencies measured have clearly understood behavioral implications that reflect competitive advantages for the firm?
- Are these competencies clearly articulated to differentiate senior leadership actions from activities needed at other levels in the firm?
- Does the system effectively differentiate among key candidates on the expected behaviors in different types of situations (for example, start-up, expansion, turnaround, and so on)?
- Does the system provide observations about situations that require openness and directness but not political or position power (for example, dealing with conflict, ambiguity, or providing negative feedback to a peer or superior)?
- Is the system sufficiently flexible, and can it incorporate decision making about both internal and external candidates?
- Is the system useful for unanticipated crises and unexpected opportunities (for example, a potential rearrangement of executives even if not necessitated by a vacancy)?
- Is the system able to take into account the needs and makeup of the team in which the individual is most likely to operate?
- Can the system provide a meaningful framework for evaluating the "cultural fit" necessary to make for successful mergers and joint ventures (for example, the ability to evaluate preferred decision-making style of organizational leaders)?

If an organization can answer these questions in the affirmative, then it can be reasonably assured that its planning and selection efforts will be relevant to the success of the enterprise.

Implications

To suggest that the field has changed so much that we need to reevaluate all of our succession-planning and identification practices would be grossly misleading. Nevertheless, the lack of systemic research efforts and the difficulty in obtaining representative, realistic subjects in a highly evolving and competitive world makes it very easy for vendors to provide, and for practitioners to fall prey to, quick fixes.

We see a positive development in the increasing sophistication of many of our executive-level clients about the implications of behavior—not only theirs but also that of the leaders of potential alliances and vendors or governmental representatives. Just as we see professional jury consultants helping to develop legal strategy, we can expect parallel examples as organizations continue to change. For example, a number of our colleagues have participated in assessing the leadership capabilities of potential partners in joint ventures or other business alliances in parallel with other business experts evaluating the financial and marketplace consequences of these alliances. Others work concurrently with key decision makers to challenge and reexamine data concerning individual and organizational fit.

Moving from Background Profile to Behavior Matching

We have focused on many of the more effective practices in succession planning and executive selection. In reality, only a few organizations have superlative systems. It is far easier to identify those needing to change. In many poorly designed systems, the most common model used in both planning and selecting talent is background matching, similar to biodata approaches to selection. Usually a poorly defined, static list of education, experience, and training activities is matched against a poorly designed list of job criteria.

Of critical importance is to reexamine is the nature of *fit*. Organizations need more versatile managers and are finding fewer candidates available with the skills they need. In turn, talented executives in high demand are increasingly restricting the conditions under which they will take an assignment, specifically defining the terms of authority, decision-making latitude, and fiscal freedom that must be present to ensure the success of their own careers. Organizations must work within these new expectations and constraints and adjust the measure of fit to include not only past experience but also individual concerns and expectations.

Rather than relying on traditional past-experience models, a more effective approach would be to apply the best principles of future-oriented competency development with the best principles of behavioral identification to develop a *behavior matching profile*. Behavior matching requires a comprehensive analysis of both situations and individuals—not simply determining if people have gross disqualifiers that prevent them from succeeding but determining if they possess the requisite behavioral flexibility and adaptability to succeed. For this, decision makers need to identify the specific leadership acts expected in the business environment while evaluating the likelihood that a candidate can exhibit these desired behaviors. Behavior matching would address the needs of both the organization (Do we need to build or buy talent to respond to what will likely occur in our marketplace?) and the individual (How do I prepare myself to be most marketable for the future?).

We have stressed why behavior matching is preferable to traditional background matching as well as its suitability as a key mechanism to predict the fit between individuals and organizations in the future. This helps us better define the question, "Potential for what?"

Considering Challenges and Opportunities

Curtis and Russell (1993) point out that executive selection and succession-planning efforts have often not been successful in moving female and minority candidates forward. As businesses expand globally, this will become an increasingly important issue.

Self-guided team-based approaches are also taking hold in many organizations. Indeed, the whole notion of a management and executive hierarchy is being eroded to some degree. Large organizational systems are being replaced by a new form of flatter, flexible, interactive, less level-bound organizational architecture. Different skills and developmental experiences will be required to prepare leaders for enticing-and-persuading rather than command-and-control approaches to problem solving and decision making.

The potential of advanced information systems technology is emerging, with just-in-time information systems providing on-line resources for both applicants and organizations. To employ it, better ways to audit and inventory the talent within an industry, assess organizational cultural fit, and provide access to currently proprietary or private information on both individuals and organizations are needed. Similar to the stock market, executive selection and succession processes may evolve into an open system with critical comparative information available for all participants. The explosive growth of the executive search business points to the need for more sophisticated services and knowledge about the available talent pool and its relation to the current challenges of the organization. Inventorying available human talent to fit strategic challenges may one day be as practical as inventorying for just-in-time manufacturing processes.

Some Concluding Thoughts

The task of selecting the right leader for the right situation is often left to executive search firms, boards of directors, or other parties who do not have the tools or experience to differentiate among the varying characteristics necessary for executive success. As Hollenbeck (1994) aptly notes, the process is often carried out by novices. We need to broaden our perspective, from focusing on improving selection and planning techniques to ensuring that the data generated from these processes are appropriately applied.

We have suggested a number of actions that will result in more effective choices for an organization. Begin with a clear understanding and differentiation between performance, potential, and suitability. Have clearly defined and behaviorally based performance expectations. In this way, decision makers can focus on the critical skills and experiences needed in a target assignment, which in turn will enable them to focus on comparing a talent pool on the basis of key dimensions that will be essential in the leadership role to be filled. Finally, a long-term strategic process for harvesting executive-level talent will enable all parties to understand and prepare for a continuously changing and dynamic future rather than rely on static data driven from past experiences that may no longer be relevant.

References

Bardwick, J. M. (1991). *Danger in the comfort zone: From boardroom to mailroom—How to break the entitlement habit that's killing American business.* New York: AMACOM.

Barrick, M. R., & Mount, M. K. (1991). The Big Five personality dimensions and job performance: A meta-analysis. *Personnel Psychology, 44,* 1–26.

Bentz, V. J. (1987). *Explorations of scope and scale: The critical determinant of high-level executive effectiveness* (Technical Report No. 13). Greensboro, NC: Center for Creative Leadership.

Bernardin, H. J., & Bownas, D. A. (1985). *Personality assessment in organizations.* New York: Praeger.

Boyatzis, R. E. (1982). *The competent manager.* New York: Wiley.

Bray, D. W., Campbell, R. J., & Grant, D. L. (1974). *Formative years in business.* New York: Wiley.

Briscoe, J. (1996). *Competency-based approaches to selecting and developing executives: Current practices and suggestions for improvement.* Executive Development Roundtable, Boston University School of Management.

Brush, V. J., & Nardoni, R. (1992). Integrated data supports AT&T's succession planning. *Personnel Journal, 71*(9), 103–109.

Buckner, M., & Slavenski, L. (1994). Succession planning. In W. R. Tracey (Ed.), *Human resources management and development handbook* (pp. 561–575). New York: AMACOM.

Byham, W. C. (1970). Assessment center for spotting future managers. *Harvard Business Review, 48*(4), 150–160.

Campbell, D. (1990). *Campbell leadership index.* Minneapolis: National Computer Systems.

Campbell, D., & Van Velsor, E. (1995). *The use of personality measures in the leadership development program.* Greensboro, NC: Center for Creative Leadership.

Campbell, J. P., Dunnette, M. D., Lawler, E. F., & Weick, K. E. (1970). *Managerial behavior, performance, and effectiveness.* New York: McGraw-Hill.

Carnazza, J. P. (1982). *Succession/replacement planning: Programs and practices.* New York: Center for Research in Career Development, Columbia University.

Clark, L. A., & Lyness, K. S. (1991). Succession planning as a strategic activity at Citicorp. In L. W. Foster (Ed.), *Advances in applied business strategy* (pp. 205–224). Greenwich, CT: JAI Press.

Cowherd, D. M. (1986). On executive succession: A conversation with Lester B. Korn. *Human Resources Management, 25*(2), 335–347.

Curtis, L. B., & Russell, J. E. (1993). *A study of succession planning programs in Fortune 500 firms.* Paper presented at the Eighth Annual Conference of the Society for Industrial and Organizational Psychology, San Francisco.

Drake, S. (1993, May). Succession planning. *Human Resource Executive,* pp. 30–31.

Eastman, L. J. (1995). *Succession planning: An annotated bibliography and summary of commonly reported organizational practices.* Greensboro, NC: Center for Creative Leadership.

Gerstein, M. S., & Reisman, H. (1983, Winter). Strategic selection: Matching executives to business conditions. *Sloan Management Review*, pp. 33–49.

Grant, D. L., Katkovsky, W., & Bray, D. W. (1967). Contributions of projective techniques to the assessment of managerial potential. *Journal of Applied Psychology, 51*(3), 226–232.

Greller, M. M., & Nee, D. M. (1989). *From baby boom to baby bust.* Reading, MA: Addison-Wesley.

Hall, D. T. (1986). Dilemmas in linking succession planning to individual executive learning. *Human Resources Management, 25*(2), 235–265.

Hall, D. T., & Associates. (1996). *The career is dead: Long live the career: A relational approach to careers.* San Francisco: Jossey-Bass.

Hemphill, J. K. (1959). Job descriptions for executives. *Harvard Business Review, 37,* 55–67.

Hogan, R., Hogan, J., & Roberts, B. W. (1996). Personality measurement and employment decisions: Questions and answers. *American Psychologist, 51,* 469–477.

Hollenbeck, G. P. (1994). *CEO selection: A street-smart review.* Greensboro, NC: Center for Creative Leadership.

Hough, L. M., & Schneider, R. J. (1996). Personality traits, taxonomies, and applications in organizations. In K. R. Murphy (Ed.), *Individual differences and behavior in organizations* (pp. 31–88). San Francisco: Jossey-Bass.

Kotter, J. P. (1990). *A force for change: How leadership differs from management.* New York: Free Press.

Kramer, D. (1990). Executive succession and development systems: A practical approach. In M. London, E. B. Bassman, & J. P. Fernandez (Eds.), *Human resource forecasting and strategy development* (pp. 99–112). Westport, CT: Quorum/Greenwood.

Locke, E. A., & Associates. (1991). *The essence of leadership.* San Francisco: New Lexington Press.

McCall, M. W., Lombardo, M. M., & Morrison A. M. (1988). *The lessons of experience.* San Francisco: New Lexington Press.

McClelland, D. C. (1973). Testing for competence rather than intelligence. *American Psychologist, 28,* 1–14.

Mills, D. Q. (1988). *The IBM lesson: The profitable art of full employment.* New York: Random House.

Moses, J. L., & Byham, W. C. (1977). *Applying the assessment center method.* New York: Pergamon Press.

Moses, J. L., Hollenbeck, G. P., & Sorcher, M. (1993). Other people's expectations. *Human Resource Management, 32*(2–3), 283–297.

OSS Assessment Staff. (1948). *Assessment of men.* Austin, TX: Holt, Rinehart and Winston.

Pinto, P. R. (1992). *Succession planning: Paradigms, paradoxes, and paradise.* Paper presented at the annual conference of the Human Resource Planning Society, Fort Lauderdale, FL.

Rhodes, D. W. (1988). Succession planning: Overweight and underperforming. *Journal of Business Strategy, 9*(6), 62–64.

Rothwell, W. J. (1994). *Effective succession planning: Ensuring leadership continuity and building talent from within.* New York: AMACOM.

Ryan, A. M., & Sackett, P. R. (1998). Individual assessment: Research base. In J. P. Jeanneret & R. F. Silzer (Eds.), *Individual assessment* (pp. 54–87). San Francisco: Jossey-Bass.

Schlesinger, L. A., Dyer, D., Clough, T. M., & Landau, D. (1987). *Chronicles of corporate change: Management lessons from AT&T and its offspring.* San Francisco: New Lexington Press.

Sorcher, M. (1985). *Predicting executive success: What it takes to make it to senior management.* New York: Wiley.

Spoor, J. (1993, Dec.). Succession planning: Once a luxury, now an emerging issue. *HRFocus,* pp. 1–4.

Thornton, G. C., & Byham, W. C. (1982). *Assessment centers and managerial performance.* New York: Academic Press.

Tichy, N. M., & Sherman, S. (1995). *Control your destiny or someone else will.* New York: Doubleday.

Tornow, W. W. (1993). Introduction to special issue on 360-degree feedback. *Human Resource Management, 32*(2–3), 211–219.

Tunstall, W. B. (1985). *Disconnecting parties: Managing the Bell system breakup.* New York: McGraw-Hill.

Van Maanen, J., Dabbs, J. M., & Faulkner, R. R. (1982). *Varieties of qualitative research.* Thousand Oaks, CA: Sage.

Van Velsor, E., & Leslie, J. B. (1991a). *Feedback to managers: Vol. 1. A guide to rating multirater feedback instruments* (Report 149). Greensboro, NC: Center for Creative Leadership.

Van Velsor, E., & Leslie, J. B. (1991b). *Feedback to managers: Vol. 2. A review and comparison of sixteen multirater feedback instruments* (Report 150). Greensboro, NC: Center for Creative Leadership.

Wallum, P. (1993). A broader view of succession planning. *Personnel Management, 25*(9), 42–45.

Zaleznik, A. (1978). Managers and leaders: Are they different? *Harvard Business Review, 55*(5), 67–80.

CHAPTER 10

Worker Participation
Current Promise, Future Prospects

Katherine J. Klein
Virginia L. Smith-Major
R. Scott Ralls

In the past decade, the widely publicized efforts of businesses to compete in global markets by adopting Total Quality Management practices, organizing into self-directed work teams, and otherwise "empowering" workers have made *participation* a buzz word in the media. Yet worker participation is neither a new practice in the American workplace nor a new subject in the academic and popular business press. Early in the twentieth century, the Hawthorne studies piqued the interest of business scholars and practitioners' interest in worker participation. Later, in 1948, Coch and French published their classic study documenting the role of worker participation in reducing resistance to change. And in the decades to follow, Kurt Lewin, Chris Argyris, Edward Lawler, and others proclaimed the merits of participative management.

Then as now the primary goals of most worker participation programs were to increase productivity while improving employee satisfaction. But does worker participation actually help companies achieve these goals? Is worker participation the right solution for the businesses of today and tomorrow? Unfortunately, despite the long history of worker participation in America, the literature on worker participation contains few absolutes and many ambiguities.

There is, for example, no widely accepted, clearly articulated model to explain how, when, and why participation might enhance employee satisfaction and performance. There is not even a single widely accepted definition of worker participation. And although academic reviews of worker participation studies have proliferated in the last decade, these reviews have generated few definitive conclusions and considerable debate.

Our goals in this chapter are to clarify the nature and possible consequences of worker participation and to consider the future of worker participation in light of current and expected changes in the business environment. Our analysis highlights the variety and complexity of the forms and consequences of worker participation. Practitioners face a number of difficult choices in deciding whether and how to implement worker participation. To aid practitioners in making these choices, we consider several questions.

What is worker participation? We begin by reviewing the many definitions and dimensions of worker participation.

Is worker participation effective? In this section, we review research on the effects of worker participation.

How does participation work? We consider existing theoretical models of worker participation, extracting practical guidelines for the implementation of worker participation.

What is the future of worker participation? Worker participation programs have been popular for many years, but are they really here to stay? We explore changes in the world of work that may affect the prevalence and effectiveness of worker participation in the years to come.

What Is Worker Participation?

Worker participation is not one thing but many things to different people and different organizations. The terms *worker participation* and *employee involvement* are used, often interchangeably, to describe a variety of workplace practices. In writing about worker participation, some authors provide no definition of the term, as if the meaning is self-evident. Others offer a general definition. Wagner (1994, p. 312), for example, suggested that "participation is a process in which influence is shared among individuals who are otherwise hierarchical unequals." Wagner's definition captures what we, and many others, consider the essence of worker participation: the sharing of influence among hierarchical unequals. Yet Wagner's definition leaves the precise nature of influence-sharing unspecified. Some definitions of worker participation focus on formal programs. Miller and Pritchard (1992, p. 414) suggested that employee involvement refers to "systematic efforts to involve employees in problem-solving processes intended to improve efficiency and morale ... [including] employee involvement or participation programs such as quality circles, self-managing work teams, and problem-solving task forces." Other definitions describe employee involvement not as a formal program but as a set of diverse, interrelated organizational processes. For example, Lawler, Mohrman, and Ledford (1992) suggested that employee involvement encompasses four mutually reinforcing processes: sharing information with employees, increasing employees' knowledge, rewarding employee performance, and redistributing power.

In sum, scholars use the terms *worker participation* and *employee involvement* to refer to a great variety of programs, practices, and activities. To highlight the potential diversity of worker participation programs, practices, and activities, we describe eight dimensions along which worker participation may vary. These eight dimensions can be combined to yield 256 different forms of participation! And that's a very conservative calculation—based on the unrealistic assumption that worker participation may be high or low on each dimension but not moderate. In short, there are many, many forms that worker participation may take. The first step in determining which form of worker participation is most likely to be effective in a particular organization is simply to recognize the myriad possibilities available to the organization.

Amount of Influence

First, the amount of influence that employees have as a result of worker participation varies. At one extreme, employees may have full decision-making authority. At the other extreme, employees may only make suggestions; management retains all decision-making authority. Vroom and Yetton's depiction (1973) of five levels of participative decision making (from the most autocratic to the most participative) captures this dimension well.

Range of Issues

Second, the range of issues over which employees have influence varies in importance and impact. Employees may have influence over relatively minor issues—the upcoming employee party, for example. Or employees may have influence over issues of more but still limited importance and impact—for example, when and how they carry out specific assigned work tasks. Or employees may have influence over issues of considerable import for the entire organization—such as where to locate a new plant (for example, Semler, 1989).

Direct or Representative Worker Participation

Third, worker participation may be direct or representative. If worker participation is direct, individuals have opportunities to influence decision making directly, by attending total quality meetings, responding to their supervisors' requests for their input, and so on. If worker participation is representative, employees are represented by their elected or appointed fellow employees, who serve on formal decision-making bodies, such as the company board of directors.

Mandatory or Voluntary Worker Participation

Fourth, worker participation may be either mandatory or voluntary. That is, it may be required by top management; employees may be directed to join work teams or quality circles, for example. Or it may be optional; for instance, subordinates may choose to volunteer their views to their supervisors or to join quality circles.

Levels of Analysis

Fifth, worker participation may occur at different levels of analysis. It may typify the organization as a whole; that is, worker participation may be uniformly practiced across the managers and units of an organization. Alternatively, worker participation may be a unit-level phenomenon, varying between the units of an organization with high levels of worker participation characterizing some units and low levels of worker participation existing in others. Or worker participation may be a dyadic-level phenomenon, varying between supervisor-subordinate pairs. Thus, a supervisor may be highly participative in his or her interactions with one or more subordinates, but far less participative with others.

Intervention or Status Quo

Sixth, worker participation may constitute an intervention within an organization or it may be the status quo. That is, worker participation may represent a change in an organization—a deliberate act, usually on the part of one or more managers, to increase employee influence in decision making. Or it may simply constitute an ongoing, accepted practice within an organization. Worker participation may not be novel; it may be standard operating procedure.

Ongoing or Occasional Worker Participation

Worker participation may also be an ongoing workplace practice, woven into the fabric of everyday life in an organization, or a more occasional and thus peripheral or exceptional activity. Self-managing teams, for example, usually represent an ongoing, participative workplace practice. Conversely, quality circles—groups of employees that meet once a week or so—constitute occasional exercises in worker participation.

Isolated or Complementary Practices

Finally, worker participation may be a unidimensional, isolated workplace practice or instead constitute simply one element among a larger, multidimensional constellation of complementary workplace practices. In the former case, worker participation represents a relatively independent program or practice, largely incongruent with other human resource (HR) and management practices. In the latter case, employee influence in decision making is supported by an array of congruent HR and managerial practices—including, for example, employee training in group processes, group incentive systems, and employee involvement in the selection of new hires.

Together, these eight dimensions capture the tremendous variety of worker participation forms and suggest the complexity of both studying and implementing worker participation. Consider just three of the numerous possible forms of worker participation. First consider worker participation that is dyad-level, part of the organizational status quo, voluntary on the part of subordinate and supervisor, direct, of moderate influence over job-related issues, ongoing, and supported by complementary workplace practices. Worker participation of this sort is less a formal program than a job characteristic—job autonomy—and is, we suspect, a very common, if often overlooked, form of worker participation in the United States. Very different is worker participation that is organization-level, an intervention, mandated, representative, of moderate influence over corporate-level issues, occasional, and unidimensional. This kind of participation characterizes worker councils or worker representation on corporate boards of directors, committees, and similar groups, and it is more typical in Europe than in the United States.

Between these two extremes are worker participation teams. Such teams constitute a form of worker participation that is usually unit-level, an intervention, mandated by management, direct, and of relatively strong influence over job-related issues. And yet, this seemingly simple form itself encompasses distinctive forms of worker participation that are likely to have differing consequences. Worker participation teams may be occasional (as in the case of quality circles) or ongoing (as in the case of self-managing teams). Further, worker participation teams may constitute an isolated workplace practice or may be embedded in a supportive network of congruent workplace practices (for example, participation training). Surely, the experience and effects of a worker participation team that is an occasional practice out of character with the organization's other HR strategies, and those of a worker participation team that is ongoing and in character with the organization will differ dramatically.

And thus, we come again to the point with which we started this section: worker participation is not one thing, or even three things, but many things. Unfortunately, as we explain in the next section, participation scholars have often failed to differentiate between the various kinds of worker participation, leading to confusion about the effects of participation and the processes that may influence these effects. In illuminating the complexity of worker participation, we hope to clarify the choices managers may face in implementing worker participation and the steps that an organization may take to enhance the benefits of participation.

Is Worker Participation Effective? Potential Outcomes

For nearly two decades now, research on the effects of worker participation has been dominated not by original, primary research on the topic but by narrative reviews and meta-analyses of prior studies. (Meta-analysis is a statistical technique for summarizing the results of numerous studies of the same topic—here the effects of worker participation on employee satisfaction and performance—after controlling for each study's sample size, measurement quality, and so on.) At least five narrative reviews and meta-analyses have been published since 1979. Remarkably, each was published in a prestigious volume or journal, and each reviewed largely the same studies. Overall, these literature reviews suggest that worker participation has a moderate effect on employee satisfaction and morale and a somewhat more limited effect on productivity. We briefly review the reviews as follows.

Twenty years ago, Locke and Schweiger (1979) reviewed over fifty studies of the relationships between participation and satisfaction and between participation and productivity. They concluded that participation usually does not lead to greater productivity than more directive management approaches, but it does lead to higher employee satisfaction than more authoritarian or directive management practices.

To provide a more precise assessment of the participation literature, Miller and Monge (1986) used meta-analysis to estimate the exact relationship between participation and both satisfaction and productivity. They examined forty-seven studies and found a moderate correlation (.34) between participation and satisfaction and a weaker but still-positive correlation (.11) between participation and productivity. The authors noted, however, that the research setting affected the observed relationship; the results of laboratory studies of participation differed from the results of field studies of participation.

Wagner and Gooding's meta-analysis (1987) of participation studies highlighted the impact of percept-percept research designs on the research findings. Percept-percept studies obtain measures of both the predictor variable and the outcome variables from the same respondents, using the same questionnaire, at one point in time. In contrast, multisource studies use at least one objective measure or assigned condition, different respondents for measures of participation than for measures of the outcome variables, or a longitudinal break between the collection of data on both participation and outcome variables from the same respondents. Wagner and Gooding (1987) found that the correlation between participation and performance was significantly larger in percept-percept studies (.45) than in multisource studies (.11). The participation-satisfaction results showed a similar pattern.

Cotton and others (1988) argued that the effects of participation reflect the form of the participation program. Accordingly, they sorted the participation literature (ninety-one studies) into six forms. Using a traditional narrative literature review (not meta-analysis), Cotton and his colleagues concluded that formal and informal forms of worker participation in which employees had direct, long-term, and moderate influence were likely to be more effective in increasing satisfaction and performance than were short-term forms of participation and representative forms of participation.

Wagner (1994) conducted a meta-analysis of the studies Cotton and his colleagues had summarized in their review. Wagner questioned the conclusions of Cotton and colleagues, arguing for example that percept-percept bias explained the positive relationship between informal participation and satisfaction. Summarizing his results and the results of prior reviews and meta-analyses, Wagner concluded that, across studies and reviews, the participation-performance multisource correlation usually ranges from .15 to .25, whereas the participation-satisfaction multisource correlation usually ranges from .08 to .16.

Our review of these reviews leads us to three basic conclusions: First, existing research suggests that participation typically has a modest positive relationship with satisfaction and a somewhat weaker positive relationship with performance. Second, the reported effects of participation may vary as a function of the research setting (laboratory or field); the research methodology (percept-percept or multisource measures); and the nature of the participation (short-term or long-term, direct or indirect). And last, there have been enough reviews of research on worker participation! It's time for new, original, theory-based research on worker participation.

Existing research on participation paints a fairly positive but ultimately unsatisfying picture of the nature and consequences of worker participation. Yes, participation seems to have positive if modest effects. But what kind of participation program should companies establish? Should participation be direct or representative? Must participative practices be supported by complementary HR practices, and if so, what are these complementary practices? Existing empirical research is unsatisfying because it offers few if any answers to these questions. Existing theories do, however, offer a few tentative answers. We are reminded of Lewin's dictum (1951) that there is nothing so practical as a good theory. In the absence of research on the practical questions we have posed, we turn to good theory.

How Does Participation Work? Lessons from Theory

What can worker participation do for an organization, its managers, and employees? What should an organization do to achieve the intended benefits of participation? What should organizations watch out for? In this section, we turn to four theoretical models for preliminary answers to these and other questions. Like the proverbial blind men who each touch a different part of the elephant, each theory captures a different aspect of worker participation. Collectively, the theories underscore both the complexity and the possibilities of worker participation.

Need Satisfaction Models

Perhaps the most common explanation of the proposed benefits of worker participation is that worker participation leads to need satisfaction. McGregor (1960, pp. 130–131), for example, wrote: "Participation ... offers substantial opportunities for ego satisfaction for the subordinate and thus can affect motivation toward organizational objectives. ... The subordinate can discover the satisfaction that comes from tackling problems and finding successful solutions for them. ... Beyond this there is a greater sense of independence and of achieving some control over one's destiny. Finally, there are the satisfactions that come by way of recognition from peers and superiors for having made a worthwhile contribution to the solution of an organizational problem."

Although intuitively appealing, need satisfaction models of participation appear to rest on a number of assumptions that are not fully tenable. For example, need satisfaction models of the benefits of participation suggest, implicitly or explicitly, that participation enhances employee satisfaction, which in turn enhances employee performance. However, decades of research show at best a very weak direct relationship between satisfaction and performance (Ostroff, 1992). Further, need satisfaction models of the benefits of worker participation seem to be predicated on the assumption that worker participation is direct (not representative) and that employees' suggestions are accepted and implemented by management. Although the assumption of direct rather than representative worker participation is usually true in the United States, the assumption that managers routinely and regularly accept employee suggestions is challenged by reports that they often find employee suggestions for improvements at work too expensive, impractical, and threatening (Klein, 1984).

The invocation of need satisfaction models of individual attitudes and needs (for example, self-expression, control) suggests that they may best explain individual-level rather than group- or organizational-level processes. This feature is not a flaw in the model, but it does raise a red flag. If need satisfaction models are correct and worker participation enhances individual-level satisfaction and performance, group- and organizational-level performance may nevertheless go unchanged. In fact, individual performance gains often fail to yield gains in group and organizational performance (Schneider & Klein, 1994).

In sum, need satisfaction models of worker participation suggest the following lessons:

Worker participation can:	Increase employee satisfaction.
To achieve this goal:	Implement direct forms of worker participation.

But be careful: If worker participation is to
                                   increase employee satisfaction,
                                   managers must accept employ-
                                   ees' increased input.

Cognitive Models

Cognitive models of the effects of participation "propose that workers typically have more complete knowledge of their work than
management; hence if workers participate in decision making, decisions will be made with better pools of information" (Miller &
Monge, 1986, p. 730). Followers of the cognitive school (for example, Scully, Kirkpatrick, & Locke, 1995) thus suggest that participation "works" to the extent that it either allows managers to
make more informed decisions than they would make in the absence of employee input or allows employees to make decisions
themselves regarding issues over which they have critical, pertinent
information. Vroom and Yetton's normative model (1973) of managerial decision making elaborates these points in a decision tree
outlining the extent to which employees should be involved in
decision making given the characteristics of the employees, the decision, and the organization. Building on Vroom and Yetton's
model and research, Locke, Alavi, and Wagner (1997, p. 309) have
recently proposed that organizational decision making should be
guided by "the rule of requisite knowledge: assuming commitment
to the values and vision of the firm, whoever has (or has the capacity to readily get) the requisite knowledge relevant to a given
decision is either consulted or allowed to make the decision."

Cognitive models rest, of course, on the assumption that employees have information that managers lack—an assumption that
perhaps never held more true than today, as organizations grow
more and more decentralized, pushing critical responsibilities and
decisions down the chain of command to frontline workers (Locke,
Alavi, & Wagner, 1997). Yet cognitive models rest as well on the assumption that managers are open to employee influence and information, a somewhat more uncertain assumption, as we have
already noted.

Cognitive models suggest a strong link between participation
and group-level or organizational-level but not individual-level performance. These models suggest not that individuals will perform

better as a result of their participation in decision making but rather that organizations will make better decisions—and hence will perform better—if they allow workers to participate in decision making. In their purest form (uninfluenced by need satisfaction models) cognitive models do not suggest a link between participation and satisfaction.

In sum, cognitive models of worker participation suggest the following lessons:

Worker participation can:	Improve group and organizational performance.
To achieve this goal:	Involve employees in decision making if they are committed to the group's or organization's goals and have relevant knowledge that their managers lack.
But be careful:	Employees must have relevant knowledge and managers must accept their input.

Commitment Models

Commitment models of the effects of worker participation suggest that it increases employee support for organizational decisions. That is, employees are hypothesized to be more committed to decisions that they helped make than to decisions in which they had no input.

Commitment models usually take one of two forms. Some commitment models (for example, Kotter & Schlesinger, 1979) suggest that participative decision making allows employees to shape a proposed new organizational program or action to their liking. Other commitment models draw on psychological theories of cognitive dissonance, rationalization, and self-perception (for example, Festinger, 1957) to suggest that individuals become committed to a course of action when they participate in decision making and voice their support freely, publicly, and explicitly for that course of action.

In sum, commitment models suggest that worker participation provides a mechanism for overcoming resistance to change. Commitment models rest, of course, on the assumption that employees ultimately endorse (or at least accept) the organization's or unit's intended change of direction. These models seem most applicable to all forms of direct employee participation but may be less likely to apply to indirect, representative forms of participation. Further, the more influence employees are granted through their organization's participative decision-making practices, the more relevant commitment models become. Employees are, of course, more likely to be committed to decisions they have shaped fundamentally than to decisions over which they were only granted a nod of approval.

Thus, commitment models of worker participation suggest the following:

Worker participation can:	Overcome employee resistance to change.
To achieve this goal:	Offer employees direct and substantive involvement in planning organizational changes.
But be careful:	Participation may not foster commitment to a course of action that employees oppose fundamentally.

Contingency Models

Contingency models suggest that the beneficial effects of participation are dependent, or contingent, on characteristics of the employees, the participation program, or the larger organization. Early contingency models of participation highlighted the influence of employee characteristics—for example, employee "growth need strength" (Hackman & Oldham, 1975) and employee expertise (Vroom & Yetton, 1973)—in shaping the consequences of participation.

More recent commentators (for example, Ledford & Lawler, 1994; Lawler & Mohrman, 1991) have drawn on organizational systems theory (for example, Katz & Kahn, 1978) to suggest that the benefits of participative practices are contingent on the adopting organization's use of congruent HR and management policies and practices, such as goal setting, group incentives, gain sharing, and training. Ledford and Lawler (1994, p. 634), for example, asked rhetorically, "Why should we expect large effects from changes in participation that are not reinforced by appropriate rewards, communication practices, training, selection practices, and so on?" Implicitly or explicitly, authors of this new contingency school of participation effects note the many organizational forces that may counter the benefits of participation. These forces include managerial resistance to increases in employee influence, pay systems that reward individual rather than group contributions, and organizational pressures to produce a product quickly and efficiently.

Advocates of this perspective suggest that participation may indeed enhance employee satisfaction and organizational performance, as suggested by other theories of participation, but add the important caveat that such benefits cannot be realized in the absence of supportive organizational policies and practices.

Let us summarize:

Worker participation can:	Enhance employee satisfaction and organizational performance.
To achieve this goal:	Offer employees opportunities to participate in decision making.
But be careful:	Worker participation may only yield benefits to the organization if other HR and management practices and policies (for example, reward systems, selection practices, training opportunities) are congruent with worker participation.

Summary

Although the four theories we have outlined cannot answer all of the questions we have posed regarding the optimal structure and design of worker participation, they do suggest several practical guidelines for organizational decision makers to consider when questioning whether and how to increase worker participation in their organizations. First, manager buy-in is key. If organizational managers at every level accept neither the broad concept of worker participation nor many of employees' specific suggestions for change, an organization's worker participation effort is doomed to failure. But manager buy-in is far from automatic. Managers may well perceive that increased employee participation in decision making threatens their power. Building on commitment theories of worker participation, we propose that organizational leaders should involve managers at all levels in any decision to augment worker participation. Gaining managers' commitment to participation by involving them in planning for an increase in worker participation may be time consuming and difficult. But in the absence of such commitment, worker participation is very likely to fail.

Second, the theories suggest that to increase satisfaction and commitment to organizational change among employees, organizations should offer them opportunities to participate directly in decisions about matters that affect them. Indirect representation may not provide employees with the same sense of investment or control over decisions central to their work lives.

Third, the theories suggest that employees should participate in making decisions related to areas of their expertise. When they have relevant expertise, their participation in organizational decision making will enhance the quality of the organization's decisions. Further, managers are relatively likely to accept employee input on issues that employees know well. An obvious implication is that an organization may need to provide training—for example, in business processes and accounting, organizational strategy, and marketing—if employees are to participate effectively in making organizational and job-related decisions.

A fourth and related suggestion is that any worker participation effort should be supported by congruent HR policies. If an organization's goal is to create an involved, participative workforce, it ought to offer not only opportunities for worker participation but also extensive training regarding task-relevant skills as well as business processes and outcomes; rewards for innovation, initiative, and group performance; and opportunities for interaction and cross-fertilization among the members of the organization's diverse functions. When participation is well integrated into the fabric of an organization's policies, practices, and culture, participation will become an accepted norm. When it is an aberration—the exception to the norms of organizational culture—then participation is very likely to be a short-lived innovation.

Finally, the theories suggest that an organization may use worker participation not only to enhance employee satisfaction and performance but also to facilitate organizational change. The greater employee participation in planning change—regarding new computerized systems, new customer services, or new production strategies, for example—the more committed employees will be to the change and thus the more successful the change initiative is likely to be.

What Is the Fate of Worker Participation in the Next Century?

Will the twenty-first century bring even more employee participation in decision making? Although American business has grown increasingly participative over the course of the twentieth century, our speculative analysis of coming changes in the American economy and workplace suggests at best a slow increase in—and not an unfettered burgeoning of—worker participation. In the following paragraphs we describe current and future changes in the workplace that may influence the course of worker participation in the coming decades.

Responses to Change: Teams, the Flattened Organization

Prognosticators agree that to survive and thrive in the twenty-first century, businesses must produce a broader array of goods and services than they now produce and they must produce these goods and services at a faster pace, lower cost, and higher quality (Howard, 1995). Throughout most sectors of the American economy, the pressure to produce more, better, *and* (not *or*) cheaper goods and services is familiar. With increasing global competition and technological change, such pressure is likely not to decrease over time but to increase steadily.

A wealth of theory and research suggests that decentralized work structures and practices are most appropriate for uncertain and rapidly changing times. And, indeed, organizations are increasingly adopting such structures and practices. Thus, for example, they are relying more and more on teams, and the use of teams is expected to grow further in the coming decades. The decentralization and reduction of bureaucracy in organizations is also apparent in the flattening of organizations, another trend that is expected to continue.

These trends are highly compatible with worker participation. As organizations face increasing demands for quality, productivity, and flexibility, they are likely to turn more often to their employees for input. Furthermore, as organizations become more decentralized, these frontline employees will be more likely to have critical knowledge to pass along. Indeed, Locke, Alavi, and Wagner (1997, p. 306) comment, "In the future, more than ever, the organization that knows the most, knows it fastest, and can use it most readily will be in the best position to succeed at its chosen endeavor. Participation, if matched to knowledge contingencies, appears critical to the assumption of this position." In short, worker participation may be just what is needed to help twenty-first century organizations manage the ever-increasing pace and pressures of change.

Increasing Computerization

Other changes anticipated at the start of the twenty-first century are less clearly conducive to worker participation. Already pervasive, computerized technologies are expected to grow only more prevalent in manufacturing, office, and retail settings of the future. Studies of the effects of computerization on job characteristics paint an inconsistent picture. Some conclude that computerization increases centralization and deskills jobs; others conclude the opposite. The results of recent research thus defy technological determinism—the view that specific technologies have direct and uniform effects across organizational settings. Accordingly, many analysts (for example, Zuboff, 1988; Wall, Jackson, & Davids, 1992) now suggest that the impact of identical computerized systems may vary significantly from organization to organization as a function of managerial choice regarding how the technology is implemented and used.

Thus, although it is tempting to argue that new technologies spread access to information and facilitate communication across organizational locations and hierarchical levels, such effects are contingent on organizational choice and managerial culture. Within manufacturing plants, for example, computerized manufacturing resource planning systems may or may not be used to spread information about scheduling, production, inventory, and costs to employees throughout the plant. E-mail systems facilitate upward, downward, and horizontal communication throughout an organization—unless, of course, organizational norms dictate that e-mail be used solely for top-down pronouncements and horizontal exchanges and not for bottom-up suggestions.

When organizations use computerized systems not only to accomplish critical work tasks but also to facilitate communication and share information across employees at different hierarchical levels and at different locations, they increase their employees' readiness for worker participation. Thus, if an organization's goal is to increase worker participation, it must not overlook its computer applications. They can facilitate or inhibit information-sharing and interaction within an organization, and thereby facilitate or inhibit the maintenance and growth of worker participation in the organization as well.

Increasing Diversity

The diversity of the American workforce has increased tremendously in the past decades and is likely to increase still more in the coming decades. Nevertheless, most American businesses remain dominated, particularly at the upper levels of management, by white males. Given the strength and persistence of the "glass ceiling," white males appear likely to retain a majority hold on the ranks of upper management within most American businesses for decades to come. Considerable theory and research (for example, Kanter, 1977; Ibarra, 1992, 1993) suggest that within organizations dominated by white males, women and minorities often are somewhat "out of the loop"—left out, to some degree, of the informal networks through which white males share job-related information and social support.

Worker participation that is voluntary, informal, and direct is, as we noted early in the chapter, perhaps the most common form of worker participation in America. But this form of worker participation rests upon voluntary interaction of coworkers, subordinates, and supervisors. The conclusions of research and theory regarding racial and gender dynamics in organizations dominated by white males do not bode well for this form of worker participation. If employees in increasingly diverse organizations nevertheless retain work and friendship networks that are relatively homogeneous in gender, race, and ethnicity, then the practice and effectiveness of informal, voluntary worker participation may decline.

In sum, in the years to come, the increasing diversity of the American workplace is unlikely to foster—and may act as an inhibiting force against—a rise in voluntary, informal worker participation. Yet, intriguingly, within the increasingly diverse organizations of the early twenty-first century, mandatory, group-level, direct forms of worker participation such as teams may be extremely valuable for uniting a workforce divided by race, ethnicity, or gender. Thus, the good, if challenging, news is that an organization can increase positive interactions across diverse groups of employees and increase worker participation through the same interventions: interventions requiring or simply encouraging direct, group-level forms of worker participation. To succeed, such interventions must of course be backed by congruent HR practices and cultural norms.

Trends Toward Downsizing and Using Contingent Workers

In the past decade, the psychological contract linking employee to employer has changed dramatically. Downsizing has spread throughout American business, altering dramatically the confidence among employees that if they perform well, their jobs will be theirs to keep (Howard, 1995; Rousseau, 1995). Further, the use of contingent workers—independent contractors, part-time, seasonal, leased, temporary, and home-based workers—has become increasingly commonplace throughout American business (Pfeffer & Barron, 1988). Even skilled Americans can no longer be certain that they will be employed full-time, on-site, and on an ongoing basis in the future. Downsizing and contingent employment are expected to persist and increase in the next century.

These trends are not conducive, we believe, to worker participation. Cognitive models of worker participation, as noted earlier, suggest that worker participation is most effective and indeed only appropriate if employees have the knowledge necessary to make intelligent, informed decisions about organizational problems and opportunities. Contingent workers, however, have limited information and knowledge about the organization's goals, history, strategy, and culture to draw on in decision making. Further, when workers participate in decision making, volunteering suggestions to improve company performance, they are expressing their hopes for, trust in, and commitment to their company's future. Downsizing and contingent employment are antithetical to the development and expression of such hopes, trust, and commitment.

Conclusion

In this chapter, we have explored the complex reality behind the buzz word *participation*. Although participation in various guises has long been lauded in the popular business press, it remains a challenge for practitioners, researchers, and theoreticians. A central problem, of course, is the very inclusiveness of the term; participation encompasses numerous, distinctive forms. What form of participation will work best in a given organization? Unfortunately, the research literature provides few definitive conclusions. We know from the literature that participation usually yields modest but significant improvements in employee satisfaction and performance, but we must turn to theory for guidance in determining how to enhance the benefits. The theoretical literature offers numerous insights, highlighting the importance of offering employees—when feasible—opportunities for direct participation in substantive organizational decision making, of gaining management support and acceptance of worker participation, of matching participative decision making to employee expertise, and of reinforcing participative practices with congruent employee training, reward systems, and cultural norms.

Participation is not easily implemented. It is not a quick fix. But it can offer substantial organizational benefits. The new millennium will bring new challenges as well as new incentives for the implementation of worker participation. Buttressed by strong management support, congruent HR practices, computerized information systems designed to foster information sharing and communication, and policies encouraging long-term rather than contingent employment, worker participation may increase the performance and satisfaction of the skilled and diverse workforce of the twenty-first century.

References

Coch, L., & French, J.R.P., Jr. (1948). Overcoming resistance to change. *Human Relations, 1*(4), 512–532.

Cotton, J. L., and others. (1988). Employee participation: Diverse forms and different outcomes. *Academy of Management Journal, 13,* 8–22.

Festinger, L. (1957). *A theory of cognitive dissonance.* Stanford, CA: Stanford University Press.

Hackman, J. R., & Oldham, G. R. (1975). Development of the job diagnostic survey. *Journal of Applied Psychology, 60,* 159–170.

Howard, A. (1995). *The changing nature of work.* San Francisco: Jossey-Bass.

Ibarra, H. (1992). Homophily and differential returns: Sex differences in network structure and access in an advertising firm. *Administrative Science Quarterly, 37,* 422–447.

Ibarra, H. (1993). Personal networks of women and minorities in management: A conceptual framework. *Academy of Management Review, 18,* 56–87.

Kanter, R. M. (1977). *Men and women of the corporation.* New York: Basic Books.

Katz, D., & Kahn, R. L. (1978). *The social psychology of organizations* (2nd ed.). New York: Wiley.

Klein, J. A. (1984). Why supervisors resist employee involvement. *Harvard Business Review, 84*(5), 87–95.

Kotter, J. P., & Schlesinger, L. A. (1979). Choosing strategies for change. *Harvard Business Review, 57,* 106–114.

Lawler, E. E., III, & Mohrman, S. A. (1991). Quality circles: After the honeymoon. In B. M. Staw (Ed.), *Psychological dimensions of organizational behavior* (pp. 523–533). Old Tappan, NJ: Macmillan.

Lawler, E. E., III, Mohrman, S. A., & Ledford, G. E. (1992). *Employee involvement and Total Quality Management: Practices and results in Fortune 1000 companies.* San Francisco: Jossey-Bass.

Ledford, G. E., & Lawler, E. E., III. (1994). Research on employee participation: Beating a dead horse? *Academy of Management Review, 19,* 633–636.

Lewin, K. (1951). Problems of research in social psychology. In D. Cartwright (Ed.), *Field theory in social science* (pp. 155–169). New York: HarperCollins.

Locke, E. A., Alavi, M., & Wagner, J. A., III. (1997). Participation in decision making: An information exchange perspective. In G. R. Ferris (Ed.), *Research in personnel and human resources management.* (Vol. 15, pp. 293–331). Greenwich, CT: JAI Press.

Locke, E. A., & Schweiger, D. M. (1979). Participation in decision making: One more look. In B. M. Staw (Ed.), *Research in organizational behavior* (Vol. 1, pp. 265–339). Greenwich, CT: JAI Press.

McGregor, D. (1960). *The human side of enterprise.* New York: McGraw-Hill.

Miller, K. I., & Monge, P. R. (1986). Participation, satisfaction, and productivity: A meta-analytic review. *Academy of Management Journal, 29*(4), 727–753.

Miller, K. I., & Pritchard, F. N. (1992). Factors associated with workers' inclination to participate in an employee involvement program. *Group and Organization Management, 17*(4), 414–430.

Ostroff, C. (1992). The relationship between satisfaction, attitudes, and performance: An organizational level analysis. *Journal of Applied Psychology, 77,* 963–974.

Pfeffer, J., & Barron, J. N. (1988). Taking the workers back out: Recent trends in the structuring of employment. In B. M. Staw, (Ed.), *Research in organizational behavior* (Vol. 10, pp. 257–303) Greenwich, CT: JAI Press.

Rousseau, D. M. (1995). *Psychological contracts in organizations: Understanding written and unwritten agreements.* Thousand Oaks, CA: Sage.

Schneider, B., & Klein, K. J. (1994). What is enough? A systems perspective on individual-organizational performance linkages. In D. H. Harris (Ed.), *Organizational linkages: Understanding the productivity paradox* (pp. 81–103). Washington, DC: National Academy Press.

Scully, J. A., Kirkpatrick, S. A., & Locke, E. A. (1995). Locus of knowledge as a determinant of the effects of participation on performance, affect, and perceptions. *Organizational Behavior and Human Decision Processes, 61*(3), 276–288.

Semler, R. (1989). Managing without managers. *Harvard Business Review, 67*(5), 76–84.

Vroom, V. H., & Yetton, P. W. (1973). *Leadership and decision making.* Pittsburgh, PA: University of Pittsburgh Press.

Wagner, J. A., III. (1994). Participation's effects on performance and satisfaction: A reconsideration of research evidence. *Academy of Management Review, 19*(2), 312–330.

Wagner, J. A., III, & Gooding, R. Z. (1987). Shared influence and organizational behavior: A meta-analysis of situational variables expected to moderate participation-outcome relationships. *Academy of Management Journal, 30,* 524–541.

Wall, T. D., Jackson, P. R., & Davids, K. (1992). Operator work design and robotics system performance: A serendipitous field study. *Journal of Applied Psychology, 77,* 353–362.

Zuboff, S. (1988). *In the age of the smart machine: The future of work and power.* New York: Basic Books.

CHAPTER 11

Diversity
Lessons from Global Human Resource Practices

John R. Fulkerson
Michael F. Tucker

Given the substantial issues of diversity that all organizations are confronting today, the successful human resource (HR) practitioner needs a conceptual framework to deal with them in both global and single-country business environments. Diversity should be viewed not as a confounding factor but rather as a source of energy that drives change and growth. Rhinesmith (1993) points out that globalization has arrived and that "diversity—both domestic and international—will be the engine that drives the creative energy of the corporation of the twenty-first century. Successful HR managers will be those who are able to manage this diversity for the innovative and competitive edge of their corporation."

We believe that diversity can no longer be discussed only from a single-country perspective. Workforces in all countries are becoming more diverse, not just in gender, age, and race but also in culture. The workforce of any industrialized or developing nation will increasingly be a mix of domestic and international ethnicities. To deal with this challenge, the HR practitioner of tomorrow will have to understand the impact of cultural or global diversity, as well as of country-specific diversity, on the effectiveness of the organization and the workforce. A grounding in global diversity will allow the HR practitioner to address diversity issues from a broader perspective than that normally associated with a single country. It is important to remember that the diversity that exists within a country (for example, the United States) may be as great as the diversity between nations. With an examination of global diversity, it stands to reason that the emerging principles guiding HR actions will also be applicable within a country.

In order to think globally about single-country diversity the HR practitioner must understand several issues: the meaning and implications of global thinking for single-country applications; the transcending principles for enhancing diversity; globally derived models of thinking that foster diversity; the competencies HR practitioners require to be effective when working with global diversity issues; and the importance of grounding all HR initiatives in business relevance. This chapter discusses these topics in the following paragraphs.

Definitions: Diversity and Globality

If they understand the nature of diverse global HR practices, domestic HR practitioners will be better equipped to deal with a broader range of cultural mindsets and thus enhance an organization's ability to use diversity. Domestic or single-country diversity and global or cultural diversity are both based on the same fundamental principles; global diversity simply has the additional cross-cultural dimension. However, this "simple" additional dimension includes a range of entirely different mindsets that make HR practices more complex. Understanding this broader perspective can lead to more creative use of locally diverse ideas and practices. In business terms, this practice is referred to as *leveraging*. In this case, leveraging means that a little understanding of global or cultural diversity can lead to larger gains from local initiatives because broader and perhaps transcending principles are considered.

As organizations become more global, they need to develop appropriate HR practices that transcend national borders. Global HR practitioners are called on to address such issues as facilitating effective multinational (diverse) teams—for example, satisfying a top executive in China who is complaining that the expatriates sent on assignment to China are poorly selected and having great difficulty adapting to the culture—and developing HR practices, such as pay, to allow the equitable transfer of an individual from one country to another. Even the notion of accepting different approaches to diversity vary depending on the culture. Cultures may be more or less open to new ideas. For example, North Korea is a more closed society, the United States a more open society. The global challenge for HR today is to help organizations operate in a complex, culturally diverse environment. This chapter starts with its own bias: we suggest that if the best HR practices from many diverse cultures are combined, then a more global and perhaps more effective practice may emerge. Furthermore, such a practice would be more generalizable and perhaps more efficient from a business perspective.

When we use the term *global thinking,* we refer to thinking in terms of higher-order principles of behavior or HR practices. The term also generally refers to universal (that is, more widely applicable) principles and values. Thus, global diversity as a starting point means accepting different paths to a positive outcome. For example, some business products are the same regardless of the culture in which they are sold—a soft drink or a cell phone are basically the same whether they are found in Russia or Egypt. It can be argued that the actual production of products, goods, or services have globalized more rapidly than HR practices.

A second basic premise of this chapter is that successful diversity and globalization initiatives are driven by competent people supported by appropriate corporate practices. The key questions that the industrial-organizational or HR practitioner should ask are these: How well do HR systems help produce and support global practices that may be appropriately localized? How prepared and equipped is an organization's culture to support globalization, that is, to balance domestic and international practices? To what extent do issues of diversity help or hinder the development of both successful business and HR practices?

Bartlett and Ghoshal (1989) have proposed a conceptual framework for understanding globalization that they refer to as the *transnational solution.* This solution suggests that to compete effectively organizations have to develop global competitiveness, multinational flexibility, and worldwide learning capability. In HR terms, this means that the HR practitioner must focus on such actions as ensuring an adequate supply of diverse international talent, high levels of individual and idea mobility, and an organizational culture that embraces diversity of thought, rather than imposing an "HQ-centric" approach. The definition of *global* then must encompass and embrace diversity at its foundation. An effective organization must be open to ideas or ways of thinking that come from any source. In contrast, thinking of diversity in single-country terms may limit potential sources of best practices or ideas.

Transcending Principles

A broad set of principles regarding diversity has emerged that applies equally well to single-country or multicountry situations. This thinking is grounded in the belief that contributions of any individual regardless of age, gender, race, or ethnicity have value. For example, Thomas and Ely (1996) suggest that there are eight preconditions for making diversity more pervasive in any organization, whether domestic or global. These preconditions are described as follows:

1. "The leadership of an organization must understand that a diverse workforce will embody different perspectives and approaches to work, and it must truly value variety of opinion and insight." Global thinking means that a company is open to any new ideas. Diversity in the cross-cultural sense means that ideas stem from a richness of different mindsets and cultural backgrounds. For example, when ideas about how to reward and pay individuals from both collective and individualistic cultures are blended, the process can be educational for both cultures.

2. "The leadership of an organization must recognize both the learning opportunities and the challenges that the expression of different perspectives present for an organization." Global thinking recognizes that change must be embraced and constant. Accepting diversity of thought and action is the starting point for change and creativity.

3. "An organization's culture must create an expectation of high standards of performance from everyone." As this chapter points out, HR practices must be grounded in results and based on appropriate values. High standards can be expected across cultures but still account for cultural differences.

4. "An organization's culture must stimulate and value personal development." If diversity is to be a truly positive thing, the lessons

offered by diverse views must be shared. Effective personal development can then be tied to many different sources of experience.

5. "An organization's culture must encourage openness." Openness and flexibility are essential for personal as well as organizational growth. Openness translates into a willingness to accept new ideas, and diversity is a source of new ideas.

6. "An organization's culture must make workers feel valued." Global thinking demands that differences be valued and celebrated. If a worker feels valued on an individual level, then both the organization and the individual win. In other words, when this is the case individuals will feel free to act and be empowered to apply their diversity of thought and action.

7. "An organization must have a well-articulated and widely understood mission." Results and outcomes are an organization's reason for existence. To be accomplished, the mission must take full advantage of the diversity of thought available. If there is a clear mission, differences and diversity issues become secondary to the achievement of a common and shared mission.

8. "An organization must have a relatively egalitarian, nonbureaucratic structure." The structure must make it easy, not hard, for people to share ideas. Organizations that are resistant to change and diversity have heavy structures that make even simple new ideas difficult to execute or implement.

In a global organization, it is essential that the cross-cultural dimensions of behavior be sufficiently understood to leverage HR practices properly. Schuler, Fulkerson, and Dowling (1992) highlight five basic and very practical constraints that may affect the transportability of HR programs in global organizations. Although these constraints may not be quite as dramatic in a one-country setting, the principles of diversity at work globally also have implications for the one-country setting. Some examples of complicating HR and cross-cultural issues are as follows.

Global Versus Local Considerations

For the sake of globalization and efficiency, it does not make sense to have HR practices that are different in every country or location.

Still, many generally accepted practices found in U.S. businesses may not be universally applied in other cultures with different laws and customs. For example, the U.S. headquarters of an organization may decide that pay for performance and performance appraisal are useful tools as a matter of principle. But the specifics of how those principles may be applied in subsidiaries around the world is another matter. For example, the Asian approach to pay for performance may place more emphasis on group or team rewards than more individually driven U.S. methods. Likewise, appraisal, a concept based on individual performance and development, may be very difficult if not impossible to carry out in a highly socialist country where jobs are scarce and wages low. In the traditional socialist or communist systems, individual rewards and indeed the very concept of individual differences are traditionally not acceptable; one individual cannot really be that different from another and therefore cannot be rewarded differently.

A look at feedback practices provides another example. In the United States, feedback has become a centerpiece of performance improvement. A whole set of rules or understandings have grown up around how feedback is to be delivered. These rules include not making the feedback personal but rather focusing it on the behaviors; never giving negative feedback in front of others in order to protect the dignity of the individual; making specific recommendations about how to improve; and saying the right words to build the self-esteem of the individual receiving feedback. Such assumptions must be challenged to understand what elements may be inappropriate cross-culturally. For example, in Japan a salesforce had not met its performance quotas. This primarily collectivist society required that each salesman (there were no women in the group) who had not met the quota stand up in front of the entire salesforce, admit his culpability, point out his failings, and then publicly promise to do better. This seems counterintuitive for a collectivist society but is consistent with the cultural principle of shared accountability and responsibility to the group. It should be noted that in some cultures negative feedback, if delivered improperly, can cause an individual to lose face and feel humiliated. The point for the HR practitioner is that the relationship between diversity and HR practice specificity must be understood.

Different Circumstances and Acceptance
of the Notion of Diversity

The mind of a global executive is focused primarily on the profitability of the enterprise. Diversity issues, if considered, are looked at in financial and market-specific terms. Most global executives do not start their thinking process with a focus on the cross-cultural implications of their work. The HR practitioner's role is to ensure that diversity is fully appreciated and seen to be a practical issue. In other words, the HR practitioner must be able to show in practical terms that an effective global organization is one that leverages and actively solicits diverse cultural views.

The story of an HR planning meeting in Hong Kong between local Chinese management and a senior U.S. executive will serve to make the point. The U.S. executive did not have extensive international experience and was struggling to understand the concept of empowerment and the need to listen to local executives and fully understand their points of view. This particular executive, a U.S. citizen, had the benefit of having seen a few decisions go awry as the result of natural conflict between the hard-driving U.S. style and the more measured Chinese way. Through heavy exposure to Chinese culture, the executive had also begun to realize that there were patterns of behavior and business practice that were dissimilar to those of his country. HR's role was to provide both feedback and coaching on how to be more effective in the Chinese culture. The HR executive, also a U.S. national, was able to engage the senior executive, along with the local Chinese HR director, in a conversation on how meetings and process take place in Hong Kong. As a result, the senior executive began to understand the need to modify his behavior and ask lots of questions without revealing his personal points of view.

In one particularly interesting HR planning meeting, the local Chinese were discussing and debating the particular skills of an individual leading to a next job assignment. The conversation was studded with careful diplomatic phrases that would allow everyone to save face once a decision on a job placement was reached. The Chinese used such phrases as, "I know that you may have a different point of view, but I would like to respectfully ask you to consider the following," and "I don't see it the way you do, but perhaps that is because I have not had the same experiences with the individual that you have. Would you please share your thoughts with me fully?" Because he wished to have the Chinese team succeed and had newly found a willingness to listen more carefully, the U.S. executive was more patient with the process and discussion. He was able, in a relatively short period of time, to begin to accept and see cultural differences that were manifested in business transactions. In short, he was beginning to accept and internalize the appropriate behavior for the culture in which he was operating. At the end of this particular meeting, the executive was asked for an opinion and gave it, but in a Chinese way. Views were shared, but it was made clear that the decision of the Chinese team would be respected and that the ultimate decision would be left to the locals.

In sum, to improve the outcomes of HR interventions, the successful HR practitioner must be skilled and sufficiently grounded in the reality of business outcomes as well as the culture.

Volatility of the International Environment

There is great volatility in international HR. A political coup or a dramatic change in legal environments can produce the need to change both business practices and HR practices overnight. The lesson for the HR practitioner is that nothing is done until it is done and that things constantly change. For example, the delivery of a planned route sales training program in Eastern Europe was interrupted because of local political unrest. The HR lesson is not that an intervention is inappropriate but that the establishment of systems and processes requires a series of small steps taken over time. Any HR practitioner who aspires to work globally must not be thrown off stride when circumstances or business necessities change dramatically.

Separation by Time and Distance

One of the great frustrations for global, field-based executives is that international headquarters may not have a complete picture of what is happening locally. In other words, corporate policy making, measurement, and enforcement often do not take adequate account of local practices or circumstances. This is particularly true in developing markets where basic infrastructure, such as phone service, makes regular contact with policy makers difficult. For example, a decision driven by a U.S. headquarters to initiate performance management practices in a subsidiary unit in Italy did not fully recognize the militancy of a local union or its potential for delaying or even halting implementation of the new work rules. Headquarters staff needs to be more patient, and local HR personnel need to communicate their circumstances much more concisely. In particular, greater clarity is required on what outcomes are expected and greater patience is required to allow local operations to find the most effective way to achieve an end result.

Variable Levels of Market Maturity

HR practices must be tailored to the sophistication of the market and the employees working in those markets. A comparison of almost any practice common in the United States with one in a developing market such as India or Vietnam will show great differences. In developing markets, practices must be slimmed down and given greater sophistication only as the workforce and management become more adept. Merely starting up a production line for soft drinks is a Herculean chore for individuals who have had limited exposure to modern manufacturing technology.

A very important example of cultural specificity is in the area of business ethics and standards of conduct. The Conference Board, a research organization in New York City, estimates that at least 95 percent of the Fortune 500 companies now have codes of conduct, as opposed to approximately 84 percent of 250 major companies surveyed in 1991. This push for ethical standards has spread worldwide. Still, HR practitioners must be very careful in trying to apply standards that were developed in the United States, ethical or otherwise, to other cultures.

For example, an American company had developed standards for business conduct and planned to apply them to its business in Japan by means of a training program. The company did not fully consider how its standards would be interpreted by the Japanese and ultimately had to redesign the training program to fit the Japanese learning style. The American company had erroneously assumed that its specific standards of behavior would apply to all people in all situations. The American culture is characterized by principles and legal codes that are assumed to have broad application, but the Japanese are much more situational. They make a clear distinction between behavior that is appropriate within the group *(Uchi)* and that which is appropriate with those from outside *(Sato)*. The Japanese also distinguish between surface feelings and behavior *(Tatemae)* and true feelings *(Honne)*. The company had to reexamine the standards carefully and help Japanese employees interpret where, when, and with whom those standards would apply. The American experiential training model also had to be modified to fit more closely the Japanese didactic learning model in order for it to be effective with the Japanese.

Models for Framing Global Diversity

A full discussion of cross-cultural issues can stand alone, but for the purposes of this chapter a basic understanding of the link between diversity and business or HR practice is critical to making global diversity work locally. This section presents an example of the applied model for dealing with cross-cultural differences as defined by Trompenaars (1993). For a review of other models, readers may wish to consult Kluckhohn and Strodtbeck (1961), Hofstede and Bond (1988), Hofstede (1980, 1991), Hampden-Turner and Trompenaars (1993), House, Hanges, Agar, and Quintanilla (1995), and Wilson, Hoppe, and Sayles (1996). A thorough discussion of these cultural models is beyond the scope of this chapter; the Trompenaars model is selected because of our experience using it to design HR practices.

Trompenaars (1993) favors characterizing behavior and its diverse mindsets along seven key dimensions. Trompenaars's framework illustrates how different cultural groups view their individual worlds and illustrates how effective HR practitioners in a global enterprise must be aware of the impact a specific mindset may have on an HR initiative. Trompenaars's cultural dimensions or constructs and an example of HR relevance for each are summarized as follows.

Universalism versus particularism refers to the extent to which rules apply to everyone universally rather than being modified to apply to a particular situation. An HR example would be the extent to which a yearly salary increase is universally dictated by head-quarters versus an increase based on local-country conditions.

Individualism versus collectivism refers to the extent to which considerations of personal freedom are paramount or group thinking and action are valued over individual considerations. An HR example would be the extent to which a company encourages and rewards individuals for innovative ideas versus requiring teamwork and group rewards.

Neutral versus affective refers to the extent to which an individual maintains self-control or is spontaneous and emotional. An HR example would be the extent to which a leader is aloof versus being seen and heard at all levels of the organization.

Specific versus diffuse refers to the extent to which relationships are specific to a setting (for example, this is strictly a business discussion) or include all aspects of family or personal life (anything can be discussed at any time). An HR example would be asking only certain, legally acceptable questions in an interview rather than probing extensively for information about family connections and relationships.

Ascription versus achievement refers to the extent to which status depends on background or family rather than on personal accomplishments and drive. An HR example would be giving a promotion to one's family member instead of to a nonfamily member who is more personally qualified and experienced than the family member.

Internal versus external locus of control refers to the extent to which an individual believes in control of self and circumstances and that he or she can overcome any obstacle rather than be more controlled by the forces of nature or fate. An HR example would be an individual who is empowered and eager to take actions to improve a business situation as opposed to an individual who feels helpless and must wait for managerial approval before acting.

Past versus present versus future refers to the psychological orientation an individual has toward history and time. An HR example would be an individual who thinks almost exclusively in terms of how things were done in an organization rather than about what is needed right now or for the future.

Each of these dimensions helps explain how and why a particular HR practice may succeed or fail in a given culture. Without understanding these dimensions, it would be easy to overlook issues of diversity and simply assume that a practice will produce a desired outcome.

Wilson, Hoppe, and Sayles (1996) present a summary of how to translate cultural dimensions into HR actions and practices and make the point that all HR initiatives are grounded in three domains of human behavior: relating to others, accomplishing work, and responding to change. Most important, the successful HR practitioner must understand how diverse cultures operate within a particular dimension and then design interventions consistent with that particular mode of thinking or behaving.

Characteristics of Cross-Culturally Effective HR Practitioners

To be effective in the global business environment and understand the implications of diversity, HR professionals must help business managers develop a new set of competencies that go beyond the traditional planning, staffing, organizing, leading, and controlling competencies required for a domestic strategy. Global competencies have been specified by Rhinesmith (1993). These global competencies may be paraphrased to reflect a foundation of understanding that is also needed so that an HR professional can be effective in an environment with a diversity of people and of business circumstances. These global competencies are as follows:

1. *Managing the global business environment:* knowing how to develop and use multiple sources of information to monitor global trends, conditions, and resources that are important to the organization.

2. *Managing the competitive strategy:* knowing what the competition is doing (and will likely do) in key global markets well in advance in order to adjust organizational strategy.

3. *Managing organizational versatility:* ensuring that the organization does not have blockages in allocating resources quickly wherever and whenever they are needed.

4. *Managing multicultural teams and alliances:* bringing people together from different cultural backgrounds within the company, as well as in joint venture arrangements, and forging them into synergistic work groups.

5. *Managing change and chaos:* developing the ability to deal with unpredictable change as the norm and being able to thrive in a chaotic environment.

6. *Managing personal intercultural effectiveness:* being able to adapt one's own cultural-based style and behaviors to work effectively with people from other cultures.

For illustrative purposes, the last competency—managing personal intercultural effectiveness—will be examined thoroughly. Michael Tucker has conducted research over the past twenty years that has identified eleven specific attributes of people who can effectively manage personal intercultural effectiveness in globally diverse situations. (For further discussion readers may wish to review Tucker, Benson, & Blanchard, 1978; Hawes & Kealy, 1979; and Shell & Solomon, 1997.) These dimensions are measured by the Overseas Assignment Inventory (OAI), a test based on work by Tucker (personal communication, 1997). The OAI characterizes the attitudes and beliefs held by an individual toward living and working in other cultures. The dimensions measured by the OAI are discussed in the next sections.

Worldview Dimensions

Worldview dimensions include *open-mindedness,* or receptiveness to different beliefs and ideas without feeling as if personal ideas are being challenged or threatened, and *respect for other beliefs,* or the capacity to be nonjudgmental of other people's religious and political beliefs.

Approach to Situations

One's approach to situations includes *flexibility,* or the ability to consider new ideas and to realize there is more than one valid way to approach and solve a problem, and *patience,* or the capacity to remain patient when business protocol demands a seemingly roundabout decision-making process or way of doing business.

Also included are *sense of humor* (having a good sense of humor and the ability to bring humor into difficult or confusing situations to ease tensions and facilitate communication); *initiative* (this describes self-starters, who do not sit back and wait for things to happen or rely on someone else to take care of things); and *risk taking* (a willingness to take risks, meet challenges, and cope with change).

Social-Interpersonal Style

Social style includes *trust in people* (the capacity to build meaningful personal and professional relationships through mutual trust); *interpersonal interest* (sincere interest in, acceptance of, and concern for others); and *social adaptability* (the ability to socialize comfortably with new people in unfamiliar social situations and to accept and be accepted by new groups of friends and acquaintances).

Self-Direction

A characteristic that falls under this heading is *locus of control,* or the belief that the control of events and circumstances resides more with the individual rather than with external forces.

According to Tucker, individuals who consistently demonstrate these characteristics are able to achieve higher-quality intercultural relationships. With very little modification, the global dimensions measured by the OAI also apply to single-country situations. It would appear that an individual's ability to relate interculturally, work, or live in diverse circumstances is relatively independent of a particular cultural background. As Thomas and Ely (1996) suggest, diversity is being increasingly defined in terms that apply to individuals regardless of culture, race, or gender.

Business Relevance

The issues of diversity and culture and global organizations have become very popular as business activity has become increasingly more globalized. The uniqueness and inherently interesting nature of cultural differences have also produced a great deal of conventional wisdom about how different cultures or ethnic groups approach the accomplishment of business and organization objectives. For the HR practitioner who aspires to "think globally" and "improve locally," a thorough grounding in the specific competitive business practices and realities of an enterprise must be the starting point for the development of any global, cross-cultural, and diversely effective HR practices. All HR practices, global or domestic, must be grounded in and measured against a standard of how well or poorly these practices add value to an enterprise.

Thomas and Ely (1996) make a point of broadening the definition of diversity from a local doctrine to include the varied perspectives and approaches that members of all cultural groups bring to improving the effectiveness of an organization. They specify a paradigm for leveraging diversity that focuses first on producing business results and second on blending diverse ideas and approaches to produce a desired business result. Thomas and Ely's work makes a strong case that enhanced business outcomes are possible only if differences are given appropriate value. Although their work is based primarily in the United States, our own experience suggests that their principles are universal and apply equally well to the conditions necessary for diversity in any effective organization, whether global or local. Any business outcome–diversity paradigm demands that the HR practitioner think first about business outcomes and second about diversity.

Although this chapter cannot possibly describe all of the strategic and technical business constructs used by an executive to run a global business enterprise, it is essential that any HR practice be thoroughly grounded in the operating realities of an enterprise. The first questions that the practitioner of diverse global HR practices must ask are these: What is the key business objective of this organization? How will the HR practice I am initiating add value to the business? How will I make my actions both clearly understood and accepted by a cross-culturally diverse population of users? No discussion of global HR practices can proceed unless it is first grounded in the reality of the daily life of an organization and its workforce. Just as important, no initiative is likely to get under way unless the decision makers and executives of that organization understand and support it. Thus, the globalization of HR practices must start with the HR practitioner's ability to have a clear line of sight to the business's bottom line.

A Case Study: Diversity as a Business Imperative

An attempt to install a senior leadership training initiative based on 360-degree feedback met with stiff resistance from the senior executives of a global organization. A key part of this leadership initiative was to ensure synergies across borders, cultures, and markets. In other words, the initiative would harness diversity. However, the senior executives could not understand why so much time, energy, and funds were necessary. After all, the leadership training initiative was to be provided to general managers who were already more or less successful and currently running businesses around the world. Further, these general managers, from more than thirty different cultures, were thoroughly grounded in the vision and strategy of the business and such a leadership program would only unnecessarily take them away from their respective businesses. In addition, the leadership initiative was initially viewed by the senior executives as little more than a training program.

Eventually, the leadership program was successfully launched, but not before it was thoroughly grounded in the behaviors and outcomes that the senior executive team agreed were vital to the business. Some of the objections that had to be overcome were these: Who would have access to the 360 data and would it be used to ferret out weaknesses in managers and punish them? Wasn't all this just "soft" HR practice that was common sense and could be coached by the superiors of the general managers? Was there any real business purpose for this leadership training, and did the program even teach specific business-building skills required in very different markets with very different business propositions? What were the specific benefits that would be applied back "in-country?" Finally, what was the return on investment for the effort of bringing general managers, at no small expense, from all over the world for a full week of training? The question of diversity, it should be noted, was not a primary question.

To launch this initiative, the HR practitioners first had to present the concepts of international leadership in a way that was relevant to the business and allow the cross-cultural synergies to emerge as the program developed. Although very important, the cross-cultural dimensions of this initiative alone were not going to sell it to management. Only after the business relevance was made clear could both the benefits and importance of understanding and leveraging cross-cultural differences be woven into the sessions. To make this leadership initiative effective, the following steps and actions were taken to emphasize both positive business outcomes and enhanced use of diversity.

First, agreement was reached on the behaviors that would be taught in the program, for example, that empowerment and performance management have certain fundamental qualities regardless of where in the world they are applied. By working through the practices and behaviors to be emphasized by the general managers, cross-cultural issues were forced to the surface. Discussions on the nature and limits of empowerment provided a forum for examining differences between empowerment in Third World and First World countries as well as how relatively unskilled workers need to be trained before they can be empowered.

Second, the limits of confidentiality for the 360 data were specified, that is, the attending manager owned the data and could decide to share or not share them. This discussion opened up another healthy discussion on the role of performance feedback in various countries and how, for example, many Asians are uncomfortable with the typically direct feedback familiar to American executives. This, in turn, led to a discussion that helped Western executives understand the importance of "face" for Asians and how "face" could be preserved in performance management discussions.

Third, the general managers brought a live business issue to work on during the program to ensure heavy business content for the initiative. Discussing this requirement led to a discussion of how various disciplines such as marketing could and should be modified to meet the cultural differences existing in different markets.

Fourth, the program was designed also to ensure heavy sharing of best practices to help identify global synergies, which further grounded the program in business relevance. For example, a discussion of how to motivate workers led to a rich sharing of cultural differences that affect motivation and pay practices.

Finally, each general manager had to go home with a specific action plan that blended business and personal change commitments. All of the personal and business change initiatives were enriched because of the different cultural mindsets applied to each issue. Interestingly, a later suggestion to allow only managers from a given region (Europe) to have geographically limited sessions was summarily rejected because the global perspectives and views gained from a mixed program would be lost.

The main point that the case makes is that the process of developing a leadership initiative drove issues of diversity to the surface. The development process not only helped define future HR practices but also provided a forum for discussion of some previously ignored diversity issues such as performance management in a global organization. Interesting by-products of the leadership initiative were much stronger appreciation for and use of the diverse ideas that each culturally unique group brought to the program. The very act of getting culturally diverse general managers together produced a forum where different mindsets and best practices could be explored.

It is highly unlikely that a specific cross-cultural training initiative could have produced such benefits. The lesson that emerged was that the HR practitioner must know how to persuade and convince leadership that such initiatives serve both business and globalization (diversity). Almost paradoxically, however, this persuading and convincing must be done in the context of a conceptual framework that simultaneously understands and teaches the principles of diversity understanding to an executive population that does not naturally think in these terms. In sum, we believe that getting to the business relevance, in terms that a global businessperson can understand, must be the starting point for any cross-cultural or diversity-based HR action.

This case presents some key lessons for the global HR practitioner.

1. *Transcending principles of business and human behavior must be blended in a global and diverse environment.* The leadership initiative was consistent with a strategic business objective that required ideas from around the globe to be shared and leveraged. This sharing of ideas is a cornerstone for any organization aspiring to be truly global. In a global enterprise, brands, key processes, and best practices must have transportability across boundaries. In this case, this meant that best practices and live business issues had to be at the core of the leadership initiative. It also meant that the competencies and standards for effective global executive behavior had to be captured, described, and sold to the senior team as a way of thinking about how to run a global enterprise most effectively. The essential end prod-

ucts from this initiative were business improvements and the HR practices needed to drive a global, diverse enterprise.

2. *The diversity and cross-cultural nature of the general managers have to be blended with the stated vision of the organization.* In this case, even though all of the general managers had their own unique and specific ways of looking at organizational effectiveness, that diversity needed to be celebrated but also carefully linked to the vision of the organization to be one of best and fastest-growing consumer product companies in the world. The vision of the organization served as a rallying point because it transcended boundaries and country-specific practices. The notion of what constituted "best" was left to the individual general managers and individual countries as long as the resultant actions were philosophically consistent with the global organization's vision and values.

3. *Specific leadership competencies or behaviors, such as drive for results or respect for others, must ultimately be defined in country-specific terms.* The concept of executive optimism will be different in India than in America simply because Hindu philosophy is more fatalistic and does not value, as Americans do, the need to take control and change the world. Hindu philosophy certainly understands optimism but may stop short of driving a specific business activity to produce what is called, in American terms, an optimistic response. The leadership initiative allowed cultural differences to emerge, be discussed, and ultimately be better understood. Leadership competencies were part of the program, but only a limited attempt was made to tell the Indians, Chinese, and Argentines who participated how that concept should be manifested in their country. The higher-order principle of a competency, however, must transcend borders. For example, drive for results means that all actions must be taken with appropriate speed, whereas respect for others means that cultural differences must be valued and integrated into business activities.

In all cases, the examples presented here are grounded in business relevance. Understanding this business-relevant linkage is critical to the success of HR initiatives in a global enterprise. Before attempting to apply the wealth of cross-cultural wisdom and diversity principles, the effective HR practitioner must be sufficiently astute to sell complex cross-cultural issues in a way that is understandable to the business decision maker.

Summary of Lessons for Driving Global and Local Diversity

Fulkerson and Schuler (1992) provide a list of lessons that can help keep the design of cross-cultural HR practices aligned with the business they are intended to help while also ensuring that cultural or diversity differences do not present a barrier to effective implementation. These lessons are applicable to local diversity. In the context of this discussion, understanding global diversity can enrich practices associated with one-country issues.

Values Drive HR Actions

In a global work environment, transcending principles are needed to hold a complex and widespread organization together. These principles may first deal with broad-brush statements, such as "being the best consumer products company in the world," and then more specific objectives, such as being the gold standard for quality on a particular product. The point is that if global HR practices are first grounded in values and aspirations, then all diversity practices have a common starting point.

The Culture Needs to Be Founded on Business-Building Actions

A global culture needs HR practices and values that are first grounded in the work to be done. Aspirations alone, although motivating, are not a necessary and sufficient condition to direct a workforce. For a worker in Indonesia who is unlikely ever to visit or understand U.S. work practices fully, Indonesian HR practices must have meaning for the work life and aspirations of that worker. It is often easier to agree on the work that must be done than on cross-culturally acceptable practices in a more abstract sense.

Individuals Are Fundamentally the Same

Our experience suggests that most people in the world of work, no matter their culture or national origin, want to achieve. This means that the global HR practitioner starts by assuming that individuals fundamentally want to do the right thing on the job. Practices can be designed with the end game of providing people with the right tools, procedures, and intent to win in the marketplace; these transcend the singular issue of diversity. Treating people with fundamental respect and believing that they have intrinsic worth is fundamental to effective diversity practices.

Feedback and Listening Work

If there are generalities that fit across cultures, our experience is that careful consideration of what is occurring in a particular culture is best done by developing an understanding of the meaning a particular culture attaches to HR practices. This is best accomplished by carefully listening and offering feedback about what has been heard and then modifying one's understanding appropriately. Feedback and listening and a discussion of different mindsets allow the modification of practices that will lead to appropriate outcomes.

Cultural Differences May Occasionally Be Exaggerated

The leadership initiative example discussed earlier demonstrates that business practices may often be sufficiently powerful to carry an HR initiative. For example, if a production line must run in a certain way and at a certain speed, that very fact will guide and focus the behavior of those ensuring that line speed. Although culture is important in determining how the workforce will organize to achieve that line speed, it will have very little to do with the speed of the equipment. Start with what must be accomplished and then be ready for cultural consequences, but do not assume that cultural consequences come first.

Adler (1997) makes the point that effective cross-cultural HR practices mix business practices with the social scientist's knowledge of culture, values, attitudes, and behaviors as they play out across cultures. Just as an understanding of global or cross-cultural issues can be used as a tool to improve local diversity issues, the opposite is also true. The key operating principle is that differences—all differences—are valuable as sources of creative solutions to individual and organizational behavior issues. The challenge is to be well equipped and technically grounded but also prepared to act as an explorer or anthropologist who will constantly uncover and apply the appropriate dimensions of diversity to improve organizational behavior.

Finally, this chapter has focused primarily on the differences that exist between cultures and nations. In the minds of some HR practitioners, international differences have a larger variance than those within a single culture or nation. When we use these somewhat obvious and large international differences, it is easier to make a point about the importance of recognizing and working with diversity. The principles of working effectively with diversity within a single country (for example, the United States) are fundamentally the same as those that exist globally. Diversity is, indeed, not a confounding factor but rather a source or energy and ideas to drive individual as well as organizational change and growth.

References

Adler, N. J. (1997). *International dimensions of organization behavior.* Cincinnati: South-Western College Publishing.

Bartlett, C. A., & Ghoshal, S. (1989). *Managing across borders: The transnational solution.* Boston: Harvard Business School Press.

Fulkerson, J. R., & Schuler, R. S. (1992). Managing worldwide diversity at Pepsi-Cola International. In S. S. Jackson (Ed.), *Diversity in the workplace: Human resource initiatives* (pp. 248–276). New York: Guilford Press.

Hampden-Turner, C., & Trompenaars, A. (1993). *The seven cultures of capitalism.* New York: Doubleday.

Hawes, F., & Kealy, D. J. (1979, Sept.). *Canadians in development: An empirical study of adaptation and effectiveness on overseas assignment.* Ottawa: Canadian International Development Agency, Communications Branch, Briefing Centre.

Hofstede, G. (1980). *Culture's consequences: International differences in work-related values.* Thousand Oaks, CA: Sage.

Hofstede, G. (1991). *Culture and organizations: Software of the mind.* London: McGraw-Hill.

Hofstede, G., & Bond, M. H. (1988). The Confucius connection: From cultural roots to economic growth. *Organization Dynamics, 16*(4), 4–21.

House, R. J., Hanges, D., Agar, M., & Quintanilla, A. R. (1995). *GLOBE: The global leadership and organization behavior effectiveness research pro-*

gram. Philadelphia: Wharton School, Department of Management, University of Pennsylvania.

Kluckhohn, F. R., & Strodtbeck, F. L. (1961). *Variations in value orientations*. Westport, CT: Greenwood Press.

Rhinesmith, S. H. (1993). *A manager's guide to globalization*. Burr Ridge, IL: Irwin.

Schuler, R. S., Fulkerson, J. R., & Dowling, P. J. (1992). Strategic performance measurement and management in multinational corporations. *Human Resource Management, 30*(3), 365–39.

Shell, M. S., & Solomon, C. M. (1997). *Capitalizing on the global workforce: A strategic guide for expatriate management*. Burr Ridge, IL: Irwin.

Thomas, D. A., & Ely, R. J. (1996, Sept.–Oct.). Making differences matter: A new paradigm for managing diversity. *Harvard Business Review*, pp. 79–90.

Trompenaars, F. (1993). *Riding the waves of culture: Understanding cultural diversity in business*. London: Economist Books.

Tucker, M. F., Benson, P. G., & Blanchard, F. (1978, Aug.). *The measurement and prediction of overseas adjustment in the Navy*. U.S. Navy Contract #N00600-73-D-0708, Task Order 77/95/D.

Wilson, M. S., Hoppe, M. H., & Sayles, L. R. (1996). *Managing across cultures: A learning framework*. Greensboro, NC: Center for Creative Leadership.

PART 3

Perspectives on the Future and How to Get There

CHAPTER 12

Helping Organizations Change
Coping with Downsizing, Mergers, Reengineering, and Reorganizations
David M. Noer

Those of us attempting to understand and practice leadership, organizational psychology, and management today find ourselves the victims of an ancient Oriental curse: we are *really* "living in interesting times!" What is taking place is that we are experiencing first-hand the fundamental change in worldview that Kuhn (1980) described as a *paradigm shift*. It is a basic and irrevocable shift in the way people connect with their jobs, and it strikes right to the heart of our theory and practice. What has been called the *new paradigm* or the *new employment contract,* or may be more plainly described as the *new reality,* makes us uneasy at best and at times troubles us deeply. This is because many of our core beliefs and values concerning such things as loyalty, motivation, and commitment were shaped in the old reality and require some reshaping in order to be relevant in the new world. As our beliefs have been reshaped, we have come to understand that four concepts are important to the researcher and practitioner alike:

- Motivation and commitment are not irrevocably bound to lifetime employment, organizational loyalty, and fitting in.

- It is possible—often essential for individual and organizational survival—for people to do excellent work in the service of others without being guaranteed lifetime employment and without placing all of their social, emotional, or financial eggs in the organizational basket.
- Organizational commitment and productivity are not diminished by loyalty to one's self, work team, or profession.
- The management process is very different in a workforce unencumbered by fear, false expectations of promotions, or the distractions of organizational politics and attempts to impress the boss.

The Route to Relevance

Our practice and theory are grounded in some experiential and academic "commandments." For many of us these commandments were formulated in the old reality, which was based on such things as long-term employment relationships; loyalty, which meant placing a premium on fitting in and conforming; norms against actively seeking other employment; boss-subordinate relationships that were stable and hierarchical; and organizational systems that rewarded tenure. Although these commandments may have been appropriate in the old reality, they require reexamination in the new paradigm. Here are two examples of the difficulties that may arise when the old reality remains unexamined:

Turnover Myopia

I recently worked with the top marketing group of a large technology-based organization. The Friday before the marketing vice president and his direct reports went on a weekend retreat, one of the executives "caught" a young, high-potential employee making a copy of his resume on the departmental photocopy machine. The entire first morning of the retreat was taken up with an angry discussion that centered on the disloyalty of the young employee. After all the organization had done for him, how could he look for another job, let alone do it on company time and the company's copy machine?

At the time of the retreat, this company was in the midst of a significant downsizing. The marketing vice president was struggling with how to reduce his head count. As a matter of fact, this was to have been the primary topic of the retreat. The marketing department had a history of hiring bright MBA graduates, and it had recruited what turned out to be more than could be assimilated in the past few years. In reality, the department had far more high-potential employees than it could afford. The question was asked, "If you have too many high-potential employees and need to reduce your head count, what is wrong with this person copying his resume on the company machine? After all, you have no shortage of people to do his job. Maybe you ought to encourage others to do the same thing. That way you won't have to force anyone out if they get lucky and find a better job!"

This line of questioning moved the group to an intense and emotional discussion of their norms of loyalty and commitment. It turned out that most of the executives on the retreat had started as new-grad MBAs and worked their way up the ranks. When they were coming up in the organization it would have been unthinkable to look openly for another job. It was this cultural imprint that caused them to react so emotionally to the resume-copying incident. At the end of the session the group concluded, with much pain, that the rules had indeed changed and that the earlier commandments on organizational loyalty didn't apply to the new reality.

Not all executive groups have such a straightforward opportunity to reflect on the current relevance of their early organizational commandments. Even for this group of enlightened and relatively open executives, the process was not easy. The pain is, however, definitely worth the gain. For unless leaders make the necessary against-the-grain efforts to examine the validity of their old reality organizational commandments, they will not provide relevant leadership for their organizations' futures.

Flawed Perspective, Activity Trap

The person I shall call Larry is a seasoned industrial-organizational (I/O) psychologist. When I met him he was working for the human resources vice president of a regional financial services organization. Larry had cut his organizational teeth on test validity and employee attitude surveys in a very stable public utility. He was recruited into the financial services organization to work on something he saw as an exciting change of focus: a performance management system that would link career development, performance appraisal, and compensation. When I met him he had been in this new position for nearly two years. During that time, the organization had gone through a wrenching merger and a downsizing and was currently involved in a decentralization process that would result in still more people reductions.

The organization was in turmoil; people were confused, angry, frustrated, and anxious about their future—a classic condition that I call *layoff survivor sickness*. Larry, too, was frustrated and angry. His project was derailed and he couldn't seem to get it moving again. The harder he worked on the performance management system, the more it seemed to unravel. He felt isolated and useless. I had been brought in to help deal with the demoralized workforce, but the human resources vice president asked me also to spend some time with Larry and try to "get him focused again." I knew Larry to be a competent professional from our past association, and after a couple of long sessions we began to make some startlingly illuminating discoveries from Larry's perspective. He was so narrowly focused on developing what he called a "world-class performance management system" that he neglected the very changed internal environment. In the traumatic post-merger-and-layoff environment, a performance management system, world-class or not, was simply not an organizational priority. But because Larry had moved directly from graduate school into his former very stable organizational environment, he had made some invalid assumptions when designing his new system:

- He had assumed a relatively stable boss-subordinate pairing, but most of the employees—particularly those in management roles—had a number of bosses in a very short period of time.
- He had assumed a one-on-one, hierarchical boss-subordinate relationship, but what was becoming clear was that in the new, flat, dynamic organization, most managers and professionals spent more time with their work teams, peers, and task forces

than with their bosses. Many supervisors had limited contact with those who in theory reported to them.

- He had assumed a predictable, long-term career path with promotions based on measurable and objective competencies, but in his organization's new environment, career paths were short-term and task-focused and competencies were ad hoc, situational, and fluid.

Larry was the victim of two things: his own flawed perspective and an activity trap. His flawed perspective was a function of his commandments. His training and experience emphasized stable relationships between boss and subordinate; hierarchical, one-on-one relationships between supervisor and employee; predictable and objective competencies; and long-term career paths. Although these were often the core of old paradigm structures, they are not the stuff of new reality organizations. Larry's activity trap was that he was so focused on his project that he lost site of the organization's changed priorities, the most important of which was the need to focus on dealing with the survivor symptoms of the workforce. Fortunately, Larry is now working on a performance management system that fits into the new reality and also has the promise of truly being world-class. He is also experiencing a newly discovered job satisfaction because he is using his considerable analytical and conceptual talents to help his organization develop systems to deal with the new reality.

A Prescription for Practitioners

We are well into the paradigm shift when it comes to the relationship between people and organizations. Like it or not, we are all temporary employees. Even with their return to profitability, organizations cannot afford to make a commitment to take care of an employee over a forty-year career, so it is a bad bargain for individuals to put all their social and psychological eggs into one organizational basket. Nowhere can the practitioner—whether formally trained as an I/O psychologist or operating from a line management position—make a more profound difference than by helping individuals and organizations work through this basic change in the nature of the connection between employee and organization. Although many of us are painfully aware both personally and organizationally of this new reality, we often tend to ground our work and frame our practice in the old paradigm. Much of our frustration is the result of responding to the stress of the new paradigm by working harder on solutions and perspectives that are artifacts of the old.

There are five things that practitioners can do now:

1. Move from spending energy helping organizations "take people out" to spending energy dealing with those people who remain. Facilitate grieving, offer transition management, and above all, help both individuals and organizations accept and accommodate the new reality.

2. Help organizational leaders move from outdated theories and beliefs, which equate long-term loyalty with motivation and paternalism, to enlightened management practices. Help them discover new theories and beliefs that equate quality work with customer focus, enlightened self-interest, freedom, and autonomy.

3. Examine your interventions, strategies, normative assumptions, and theories to determine if they are relevant to the new reality or grounded in the soil of the old paradigm. If they don't fit, throw them out or revise them. Yesterday's technology will not solve today's problems.

4. Be a missionary of hope. When people break organizational codependency by putting their self-esteem into what they do and not necessarily into where they work, there is a powerful freeing of energy and spirit. Paradoxically, this is reflected in increased feelings of job security and organizational productivity. This is good news and we need to understand and communicate this positive side of the new reality!

5. Be a reflective and not a reactive practitioner. The new paradigm is frightening and still unclear. We all need to tell one another what is happening. Do action research. Write and publicize your interventions and theories. Make presentations. Spread the word. What works and what doesn't?

Some Definitions and Observations

Based on field research that led to the books *Healing the Wounds* (1993) and *Breaking Free* (1996), I have developed a theory and a model for intervention. Like all models, it attempts to abstract reality and is certainly not as complex or dynamic as is the real world in all its infinite variety. Although it is a work in progress, the model has formed the basis for interventions in over a hundred organizations around the world. It offers an action-taking frame of reference for both the line manager and the I/O psychologist. However, before describing my Pyramid Intervention Model, I will outline some key definitions and offer some observations.

Layoff Survivor Sickness

I coined the term *layoff survivor sickness* to describe the set of symptoms people experience when they remain in organizations after involuntary reductions of others. As is the case with other classic survivor symptoms, the root cause is a deep sense of violation. The symptoms include four feeling clusters: fear, insecurity, and uncertainty; frustration, resentment, and anger; sadness, depression and guilt; and injustice, betrayal, and distrust.

Survivors cope in ways that are neither personally healthy nor organizationally productive. The two primary coping mechanisms are aversion to risk taking and reduced productivity. Thus, organizations with survivor sickness are working at a handicap, often attempting to compete in the global economy with workforces made up of wounded employees who are risk-averse and not as productive as they could be. Furthermore, without planned interventions the symptoms do not seem to go away; they often appear to intensify over time.

Organizational Codependency

The term *codependence* was first used to describe the unhealthy relationship of a significant other to an alcoholic (Beattie, 1987). The significant other enjoys a positive self-image only when the alcoholic stays dry. The codependent's self-esteem is contingent on someone else's addiction. The idea has now been expanded to cover many other forms of addiction, and codependency is considered by some to be an underlying, primary disease in itself (Schaef, 1986).

It is not healthy to make our self-esteem or sense of relevance contingent on the behavior of any individual or organization. The theory of codependency provides a clear lens through which to visualize the unhealthy dependence that is the underlying cause of layoff survivor sickness. To the extent that we index our self-esteem to remaining employed by a single organization, we are organizationally codependent. A key question I often ask my clients is this: "If who you are is where you work, what's at threat if your job's at threat?" The answer is a great deal more than a paycheck: self-esteem and sense of relevance and purpose!

Here are five observations in regard to organizational codependency that will be of interest to the practitioner:

1. The conscious fostering of organizational codependency has been a cornerstone of human resource strategy for the past fifty years. Organizations have had benefit plans, status symbols, group purchasing programs, social clubs, compensation systems, promotional patterns, and many more implicit and explicit policies and cultural norms that have resulted in binding employees to organizations for more than just a paycheck.

2. Organizations have done such a good job in fostering a dependent relationship at the emotional and social level that many employees react to a threat to their employment relationship with a feeling of violation.

3. The way for people to develop personal immunity to organizational codependency is to refuse to put all their social and emotional eggs in the organizational basket. They need to define themselves by their work, not where they currently happen to do that work. They should not put a taproot into the organization for their self-esteem but rather develop a diffuse root system in family, community, profession, and a place of spiritual nourishment.

4. Many organizational leaders who were raised under the old reality have difficulty letting go of three basic management tenets grounded in a codependent strategy: they equate dependence with commitment, motivation with loyalty, and paternalism with leadership.

5. Organizational codependency is systematically reinforced by organizational norms and myths carried over from the old reality. Organizational cultures that tolerate an internal focus on entitlement (Bardwick, 1991) do not fit the new reality. Employees are conditioned into a codependent relationship not only by their

employer but also by powerful outside institutions, such as family and school. It requires an act of courage on the part of the individual and faith on the part of the organizational system to break codependency and form a new, more productive relationship.

Old and New Realities

The old reality or *old paradigm* are labels for a pattern of beliefs that held that a person who performed properly and complied with the organizational culture could count on remaining with one organization until voluntary departure or retirement. The reciprocal organizational belief was that the individual was required to make a total commitment. In response to this commitment and dependence, the organization accepted the obligation to provide a lifetime career.

In the new reality or the new psychological contract, there is no long-term job security; we are all temporary employees. Organizations have no obligation to plan lifetime careers and employees have no obligation to trust blindly that their organizations will take care of them.

It is important for the practitioner not to collude with the organizational propensity to want to turn back the clock. The change is irrevocable. We must find interventions that deal with it as opposed to developing programs that are geared to getting things "back to normal." What is taking place is a fundamental redefinition of the connection between employee and employer. Efforts to tell employees that "if you just make these cuts" or "just get with the new program" (quality, reengineering, customer alignment, and so on) we will finally get through it and things will return to the way they were—these efforts communicate the wrong ideas. In fact, the nature of the change is that despite the most well-intentioned, well-designed, and badly needed improvement programs, things will never return to the way they were.

A Model for Intervention

The four-level Pyramid Intervention Model pictured in Figure 12.1 was developed to provide a frame of reference for action taking. We will now discuss the levels.

Figure 12.1. The Pyramid Intervention Model.

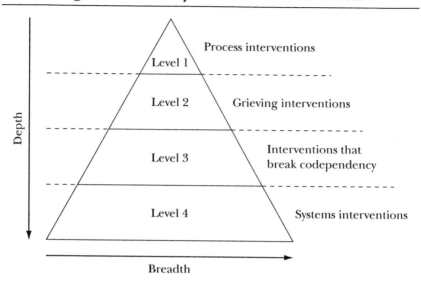

Level 1: Process Interventions

Level 1 interventions deal with the way reductions take place, the process of laying people off. These interventions do not provide a cure for survivors or help organizations develop systems that are in alignment with the new reality. However, they are tactically important. They keep survivors from sinking too deeply into depression and guilt, help them stay afloat until other, more permanent interventions can be applied to pull them out. Although Level 1 interventions are only the tip of the iceberg, they are important and do affect the recovery of those who remain (Brockner, 1992; Davy & Tansik, 1986) Survivors' involvement in the decision-making process, their level of attachment to those who leave, and their perception of the fairness of layoffs have all been documented as important process factors.

Level 2: Grieving Interventions

Level 2 interventions focus on helping survivors deal with their feelings and emotions and are critical to the catharsis necessary for letting go and moving forward. These interventions help release repressed feelings. Even when the best Level 1 processes are enacted, survivors feel violated. Because many organizations have norms against employees' even admitting the presence of survivor emotions, let alone sharing and dealing with them, these interventions must tease out these repressed feelings. The bad news is that repressed anger and other emotions are widespread; the good news is that when properly facilitated they come out and employees can move on. Helping employees externalize their feelings and facilitating their moving forward with their lives and work is fertile ground for external and internal interventionists.

Level 3: Codependency-Breaking Interventions

Level 3 interventions (often individual acts of courage), involve recapturing individual self-esteem and disconnecting it from organizational membership. Organizational codependency is seductive. It is the outcome of nearly a century of organizational strategies designed to tie employees in for the long term. The link happens at many levels and it is easy for employees to develop a dependency relationship, to define who they are by where they work. Interventions that help employees develop a diffuse root system are necessary—rather than a taproot through which their self-esteem and feelings of relevance are only nourished by the organizational soil.

Interventions are also necessary to help organizations with the detachment process. Breaking organizational codependency is essentially an individual effort. The individual detaches from the organizational system as a culture. Organizations too need to detach, let go, and discover their core purposes. Organizational struggles mirror those of individuals, and it is difficult for organizations to detach from their paternalism. Moving away from employee control and toward true employee empowerment means letting go of a very old attitude. Searching for a new purpose and vision in the face of global competition and world economic parity involves the pain of creating a new identity. But for both individuals and organizations the gain is well worth the pain. The payoff is survival and relevance in the new paradigm. Codependency-breaking interventions represent a new and powerful arena for the practitioner.

Level 4: Systems Interventions

Level 4 interventions are processes, policies, and organizational cultures that accommodate the new reality. They allow individuals the autonomy to put their spirit into their work, and they free organizations to serve customers without becoming paralyzed by internal issues of status and control. In the years after World War II—when the United States enjoyed a clear competitive advantage over other countries, which seemed unlikely to become threats for many years—a distinct relationship was forged, built on several implicit assumptions that were shared by employer and employee. The employment relationship should be long-term and organizations should develop strategies and processes to tie employees in over a career; the reward for good performance was promotion; career paths were predictable and long; employees should trust that organizations would take care of them and employers had a mandate to be paternalistic; loyal employees did not look for jobs outside the organization. Changing these and many other basic, often implicit assumptions is more fertile ground for the change agent and practitioner.

The four-level pyramid is a stage model intended to convey the increasing depth and breadth of each successive intervention. Although the model generally holds true, I have also found that what happens in organizations is always different from what any models or theories describe. For example, Level 1 interventions sometimes lead directly to Level 4 systems changes; the act of breaking codependency (Level 3) can stimulate grieving (Level 2). But regardless of the sequence, the model provides a frame of reference for interventions that work in the new reality. However, two conditions are necessary if the interventions are to be relevant in the new paradigm.

First, the practitioner must have the courage to go against the grain of previous experience and education and confront old paradigm beliefs about the nature of loyalty, commitment, and motivation. A practitioner can't be relevant to the needs of the new reality while operating from an old belief system.

Second, those seeking to be useful to organizations struggling with new paradigm issues need the courage and spirit of experimentation necessary to discard old tools and intervention strategies and seek new, often unproved and intuitive strategies and tools.

Application Examples

The Pyramid Intervention Model formed the basis for a four-day public training program offered by the Center for Creative Leadership from 1993 to 1997 and is currently delivered as a custom program for individual organizations. Versions of the model have been used by a large number of consultants and trainers and have been incorporated into many internal training programs. In April 1995, an invitation-only conference entitled "Best Practices in Leading Downsized Organizations" was held for practitioners, researchers, and trainers who either were using the model or were familiar with it. Ninety-six people attended the conference. What follows are excepts from presentations made by six representative organizations included in the conference proceedings (Noer & Bunker, 1995). These stories offer a look at ways in which the model has been used in real-world practice as well as the lessons these organizations reported learning.

A Regional Telephone Company

Experience: "Working with senior management (corporate officers) became a strategic priority. After they were exposed to the model there was an increased awareness for the need to break the survivor syndrome and the old psychological contract."

"As a part of the layoff process we incorporated modules that allow for venting and emotional release in all training courses. We brought in consultants to talk with senior managers about the impact of the layoffs on the remaining employees. Then, to work on breaking the codependency mindset, we originally brought in a prominent external speaker. The result was that our culture was not ready for his philosophies."

"The CEO was instrumental in driving a change in culture because he knew that even though business strategies were coming together, the culture/people side was not. The cultural transformation under way is part of their work at the fourth level of the model."

Lessons learned: "There is no one answer or one right way. Explore, explore, explore alternatives!" "Senior management's attention will come when the business problems are severe enough." "Layoffs cannot be done as a project with a start and an end; they must be done as an ongoing change process for the entire organization."

The Canadian Federal Government

Experience: "The approach we had been using had neglected the behavioral side of change strategy—the need for layoff survivors to acknowledge and deal with strong emotions of grief, anger, and fear. Our strategy was to work with the top leaders in key departments first in order to let them make their own safe, personal transition. My thesis was that the leaders have to do it first, before others can. My other goals were to develop leadership skills for transition, create a cross-government support network, and cause a debate about the 'new deal'—the new employment contract—in the Canadian public service."

"Seven programs based on the model have now been conducted. Most of the executive leadership cadre in the government will have gone through the program. The change is noticeable. There are already 190 executives in the network. Participants say it gives them a sense that they are not the only ones suffering trauma."

Lessons learned: "Lessons learned so far are that ... networking is not as easy as it looks ... and that any effort like this should offer hope, safety, peace, and energy."

A Large Division of a Pharmaceutical Corporation

Experience: "We served as the primary team for planning and implementing the downsizing and restructuring effort."

Lessons learned: "The transition model that I found to be most useful does not presuppose a nice, clear, linear, sequential process. ... You cannot communicate too much. Once is never enough. The key messages need to be simple, few, and often repeated."

A Major Aerospace Corporation

Experience: "Something basic was missing. Somehow the company had to find a way to help the people. The improving numbers weren't doing it. Then, after I read the book [*Healing the Wounds* (Noer, 1993)] I decided to do something different. As one of the top executives, I decided to take my direct reports off-site and try to be real. This allowed us to talk about our feelings of insecurity, violation, and anger in a safe environment. For the first time we were free. Everything had changed. We were free to take charge of ourselves. Pleasing the boss was no longer the primary game."

Lessons learned: "Company power bases have changed dramatically in recent times and managers are laying low until they figure out what the new power base is. The people are the new, emerging power base."

A Major Government Contractor

Experience: "Since 1989, restructuring and downsizing have been almost continuous—thirty-five hundred employees have been cut from the company's workforce and a number of facilities have been closed. The different elements of the first three levels of the model (doing it right, grieving, and breaking codependency) can be seen in different parts of the organization. Flexibility, adaptability, and continuous improvement are now being demanded of the workforce."

Lessons learned: "The paradigm for career development is still being worked on and no victories are as yet being claimed."

A Large Telecommunications Corporation

Experience: "We have a one-day workshop for all managers of managers based on the Pyramid Model. The objectives are to (a) increase leadership understanding of 'survivor' management strategies; (b) promote understanding and tolerance of 'loss reactions'; and (c) introduce the concept of a new psychological contract. Some people leave the workshop uncomfortable with the formidable challenge. Reviews have been mixed."

Lessons learned: "We underestimated the extent to which downsizing would lead to anger, fear, and mistrust." "There is no painless way to downsize." "People issues associated with downsizing are secondary to core business issues." "There is a lack of measures to assess the training and communication interventions."

Application Observations

The following five observations are based on my personal experience and understanding of how others are using the Pyramid Intervention Model.

A Focus Beyond Level 1 Interventions

In the mid-eighties to the early nineties, many organizations focused on administrative processes that dealt with the way in which reductions were handled. Although these process interventions are important to survivor recovery (Brockner, 1992), deeper and more systematic interventions are necessary. In many organizations today the level of awareness and dialogue involves issues such as the centrality of postreduction leadership and vision (Marks, 1994), the importance of variables such as self-esteem and self-identity (Brockner, 1992), and the need to be clear about the changing psychological contract (De Meuse & Tornow, 1990). In many cases this movement toward deeper levels of intervention appears to be caused by the practical reality of attempting to deal with workers who are demoralized and organizations that are not reaping the productivity gains promised by downsizing (Cascio, 1993).

A Significant Increase in Level 2 Interventions

The core of many of the interventions described in the previous section focus on dealing with survivors' feelings and emotions. This trend continues. Organizations are beginning to deal with survivor feelings such as anger, frustration, and anxiety through a variety of processes. Examples include venting sessions, individual counseling, team-building sessions focused on externalizing emotional blockages to team performance, and line manager training in basic helping skills. The so-called soft side is coming out as organizational leaders realize that feelings and emotions are the currency of the realm when dealing with wounded employees.

A Continuing Struggle with Level 3 Interventions

Although many organizations have developed communication themes that emphasize employee autonomy, the provisional nature of the employment contract, and the importance of being "self-employed" within a large organization, these messages are often transmitted in an environment of doubt and confusion. The old assumptions of loyalty, commitment, and motivation remain deeply entrenched in many organizations. I have found that this is often a generational issue, with younger professional employees comfortable with the new reality and able to tie their self-esteem to what they do rather than to where they work; those in midcareer, particularly middle managers, often seeming conflicted and confused; and top managers seeming to have the most difficult time dropping the assumptions of the past. Because of this uncertainty, Level 3 work is fertile ground for both research and practice. The implementation of the Pyramid Model is taking place sequentially, and the current action seems to be moving to Level 3.

Continuing Gaps Between Espoused Strategy and Support Systems

Despite organizational strategies that call for a flexible, diverse, and situational workforce, many benefit, compensation, and status systems remain grounded in tenure and conformity, with an internal focus. In my opinion, these Level 4 issues will remain unresolved until the Level 3 issues currently being worked on are taken care of.

Intervention Movement from Staff to Line Manager

In the early eighties, most of the interest in dealing with layoff survivors came from staff functions, primarily human resources or employee communications. They were seeking ways to get line managers to understand the issues and were looking for processes to get their attention. However, in the past five years, the energy seems to have shifted to line managers themselves. This appears to be a result of the pragmatic understanding that treating lay-off survivor sickness can have a positive impact on organizational performance.

Trends and Prescriptions

One way of conceptualizing the environment for interventions is to visualize the movement from the old reality to the new reality, focusing on four particular paths.

From Long-Term to Situational Employment Relationships

Organizations operating under the old contract assumed that employees would be there "over the long haul." They therefore developed strategies that rewarded tenure and kept employees tied in over the length of a career. This strategy does not match the new reality. What are needed are strategies and interventions that are more compatible with the new reality, such as the following.

Deemphasize or Discard Inappropriate Trinkets
Tie bars, cuff links, bracelets, wall plaques, and other public symbols that celebrate tenure all give the wrong message when an organization is looking for flexible, situational relationships. One organization tells the tale of a well-liked production supervisor who received her ten-year bracelet on a Monday and was terminated on a Friday!

Celebrate Achievement
Catch people doing things right and find a way to reinforce the achievement publicly. There is nothing wrong with trinkets, awards such as dinners or theater tickets, or simply a pat on the back. It isn't the awards themselves but rather what they are intended to celebrate that is the issue. The new contract bonds employees and organizations around goal achievement and excellent customer service and production, not around remaining employed. Thus practitioners need to develop systems that reward achievement, not tenure.

Celebrate Departures

Under the new contract, leaving is a cause for celebration, not lament! If the goal is a just-in-time workforce, then there will be a continuing flux of arrivals and departures. Leaving is a planned event, a celebration of achievement and past contributions. The departure ritual should be more than just a quiet departmental lunch; it should be an organizationally sanctioned rite of passage.

Eliminate Distinctions Between Classes of Employees

In some organizations today it is impossible to determine from their activities whether a person is a temp, a part-time worker, a contract employee, or a full-time employee. Artificial distinctions in terms of pay, benefits, and status of these classifications don't fit the new reality. Although there are some legal requirements—which are themselves artifacts of the old reality—differences, particularly those of status, should be minimized if not eliminated. In the final analysis we are all temps, and artificial distinctions based on how temporary we are do not fit the necessary flexibility of the new reality.

From Motivation by Promotion to Motivation by Participation

Promotion was the currency of the realm in the old paradigm. But the currency in the new reality is made up of job enrichment, the philosophy of quality, and techniques such as self-directed work teams.

Job Enrichment

Job enrichment is an old idea (Herzberg, 1968) whose time has come. Job enrichment does not mean adding the duties of departed employees to those who remain. It involves eliminating nonessential tasks and investing employees' energy in relevant, useful, achievable work. This is a central concept in the reengineering process (Hammer & Champy, 1993). The opportunity to do quality work in an enriched environment replaces promotion as a motivating factor in the new paradigm and points the way toward a number of relevant interventions for the practitioner.

The Philosophy of Quality

What the quality philosophy is all about when separated from its techniques is relevant work that serves others and is performed by empowered people. This is the essence of the new employment contract! This shining theme runs through the basic philosophies (as distinct from the often distracting techniques) of all the quality gurus. Whether you are a Crosbyite, a follower of Deming, or choose the way that Feigenbaum, Ishikawa, or Juran conceptualize quality, the central idea is the same: empowered people, linked together by good work, in the service of others.

Self-Directed Work Teams

Semiautonomous, task-focused, self-directed work teams are an example of a technique that fits the new reality. Organizations with team-based cultures (Shank, 1997) will have a competitive edge. Again, it is necessary to separate technique from essence to gain perspective. The advantage of self-directed work teams is that managers move to a helping, facilitating, and coaching role while empowered teams bond around good work, unfettered by the hierarchical and bureaucracy constraints of the old paradigm.

From Paternalistic to Empowering Leadership

Most organizations do not like to think of themselves as paternalistic, but the reality is that they take a great deal of pride in taking care of "their" employees. But employees who are "taken care of" become dependent, and in the new reality such dependence is hazardous to both their health and their productivity. An exciting and liberating part of the new contract is the opportunity for all employees to develop the skills and perspectives to take care of themselves, increase their self-esteem, and move beyond the constraints of a codependent organizational relationship. Here are three areas in which practitioners can help organizations.

Don't Condition Employees to Be Dependent

If you expect employees to be responsible adults they will behave that way. Just as with teenage children, employees need guidance and limits but most of all they need trust and independence. At some point parents need to let go. Just as it is not healthy for families to create unnecessary dependence, it is not in the best interest of organizations to attempt to overcontrol employees.

Resist the Temptation of Detailed, Long-Term Career Planning
Establishing inflexible, long-term career paths are an artifact of the old paradigm. Task and skill planning, not career planning, are the stuff of the new reality. In the past, organizations responded to employee requests for maps to get to the top with detailed, often elaborately prepared professional advice about what tickets needed to be punched. In the new reality, organizations are flat, growth is not hierarchical, systems are temporary, and careers are short-term and situational. Detailed career planning makes no sense when organizations can neither guarantee employment continuity nor forecast which of many rapidly evolving skills will be needed over a thirty-year career.

From Lifetime Enlistment to In-and-Out Careers

Two basic tenets in the old contract for the individual were "I am grateful for my job" and "I will plan a career within the organization." The reciprocal organizational strategies were "We will take care of our employees" and "We will promote only from within." Two new paradigm realities are that organizations can't keep their end of that agreement and that the outcome of adherence to a rigid internal promotional policy is a narrow and skill-deficient workforce. The new paradigm demands organizational flexibility, employee choice, and nontraditional career paths that often lead outside the organization and sometimes back in again. Here are some ideas.

Eliminate Penalties and Barriers to Returning
Some organizations still won't rehire employees who have left or, if they do, will penalize them through pay and benefit practices. In-and-out career paths are a central part of the new reality, and benefits and support services should not discriminate between those who have remained and those who have returned.

Develop Processes to Stimulate Leaving

One model is a mandatory career review at fixed time increments, for example, every five years. This review is a time when employees can assess their life and career options in a safe and objective manner. The result may be a decision to "reenlist" in the same job, explore other options within the organization, or leave. Regardless of the mechanics, such a system will only work if it is not seen as a setup by the employee and the outcomes are accepted by the organization.

Tell the Truth Up Front

The unvarnished truth is that organizations can't guarantee employees that if they do a good job they can count on continued employment until they retire or choose to leave on their own. New employees can be offered the opportunity for learning, challenging work, and a safe and clean work environment. Anything beyond that is conjecture.

Helping create the organizational systems that support the new reality is not an easy task for the practitioner. Even though these systems and processes fit the new world and help provide structural immunity for the ravages of layoff survivor sickness, they are often a hard sell to entrenched organizational leaders whose values and perspectives were formed in the old reality. Nevertheless, there is no more important task for the interventionist than to help organizational leaders explore the link between new reality systems and organizational productivity, profitability, and long-term survival.

The Power of Applied Human Spirit

The centrality of the human spirit in holding organizations together is not new, it is just that until recently it felt somehow unscientific or unprofessional for the practitioner to talk about it. It goes back a long way. It is the *Y* that is contrasted with the control-oriented *X* in Douglas McGregor's classic theory (1960). It is the *esprit* of the *esprit de corps*. It is what we seek when we look for something greater than ourselves in the twelfth step of dealing with an addiction. It is the *joy* in Connelly's *work-joy* (1984).

In the old reality, human spirit was often undervalued, suppressed, or ignored. It couldn't be precisely measured, manipulated, or contained in an organizational chart. *Spirit* was a word that was not safe for the I/O psychologist to use in the workplace.

Why Human Spirit Needs to Come Out of the Organizational Closet

There are three reasons why practitioners can no longer afford to ignore and devalue human spirit:

1. The most valuable employees are those who choose to be in an organization, not those who are forced to be there. Pay and benefits are not enough. What will attract this type of person is meaningful work in the service of others. Meaningful work is work that captures the human spirit.

2. When people are working at their best and investing their spirit in their work, they are vastly more productive and creative. Organizations desperately need this applied human spirit as a competitive advantage.

3. When organizations create a culture that nurtures human spirit, management moves out of the grim, unrewarding grind of attempting to motivate people whose work does not engage them and into the delightful task of coaching liberated employees who are self-motivated and internally directed. Leading the liberated puts the manager's time to much better use than attempting to motivate the dispirited.

How to Measure Human Spirit

In a discussion between two colleagues, one a psychologist schooled in what has sometimes been called "prairie empiricism" and the other an organization development practitioner with training and orientation in the more holistic and intuitive aspects of organizational theory and practice, the empiricist postulated that anything that couldn't be measured couldn't be studied. The organization development practitioner responded that anything that could be reduced to measurement would be too trivial to merit study! The basic ingredient of the new glue—the human spirit—would appeal to both of them and has application through a wide variety of practitioner's lenses.

When people are truly connected to their work through their human spirit, it is reflected through measurement tools such as productivity indexes, attitude surveys, and the most basic of all: sustained improvement to the bottom line. You can also feel it. We have all been in organizations where we can tell that people are "tuned in" and "turned on" but have not "dropped out," as that expression from the sixties put it. In fact, they seem to have "dropped in!"

Organizations that engage at the level of human spirit do not tolerate sideline sitters. Connecting at this level is not a spectator sport. An outside observer can, indeed, feel it. "It" is a creative, vibrant, and vigorous workplace. Practitioners can work in both the objective and subjective realms. Or, as is increasingly the case, they can deal with measurement and intervention in both.

How Practitioners Can Ease Human Spirit Out of the Closet

To psychotherapist Carl Rogers, the key to establishing a helping relationship is unconditional positive regard: there is a kernel of hope and goodness inside everyone that will grow with enough encouragement and support (Rogers, 1961). The way to kindle human spirit in organizations is to emulate Rogers. Two old paradigm managerial orientations that get in the way are excessive control and a judgmental attitude. It isn't that organizations don't need some control or that exercising prudent judgment isn't important. It's that for the new glue to work its magic, leaders need to have a very light hand on the controls.

Here are three ideas for practitioners.

*Eliminate Policies, Processes, and Cultural
Commandments That Block Human Spirit*
Examples include excess controls, narrow job descriptions, inflexible performance measurement systems, organizational climates that instill risk aversion and fear of failure, rigid barriers to job entry based on artificial standards, and false status distinctions such as those between managerial and professional job categories.

Stimulate Voice and Choice

There is great power in participation, and if organizational leaders are serious about leveraging human spirit as a competitive advantage, very little risk. How work gets done, who does the work, performance standards, and processes that allow employee development and training—all are opportunities for participation.

Be Developmentally Optimistic

Organizations can no longer guarantee long-term employment, but they can offer employees the opportunity to learn and develop. It goes beyond job-related skills training. If an employee's interest and spirit leads to an area where the rules say she isn't qualified, the wise organization will take a developmental risk. Human spirit has an amazing ability to overcome barriers and developmental optimism is a tangible manifestation of unconditional positive regard.

How to Nurture Human Spirit

Human spirit is a fragile commodity. The key to maintaining it is constant attention to the basics. It is similar to tending a garden: the flowers will grow and blossom only if the gardener pulls the weeds, nourishes the soil, and waters it.

Practitioners in the new reality need to continue to work at eliminating barriers (the equivalent of weeding), fostering participation (nourishing the soil), and maintaining a developmentally optimistic climate (watering the garden).

Final Thoughts

Helping organizations make the transition to the new reality is neither a gentle nor a spectator sport. Practitioners must develop the skills and competencies that will facilitate both their and their client's transition from the certain and comfortable old to the relevant but uncertain new. Interventionists must create meaning in a time of profound change. They must stimulate an environment where organizational leaders take the risk of discarding cultural systems that have served them well for nearly a century in exchange for others that often require a leap of faith. All stakeholders in the system—I/O psychologists, managers, and nonmanagerial employees—must master new or neglected competencies such as transition facilitation, visioning, value congruence, empowerment, self-understanding, and process wisdom.

External interventionists as well as organizational leaders need to embark on a process of continuous self-improvement. No one has yet designed a core curriculum to teach leaders the functional skills necessary to manage a complex business and in addition be authentic, congruent, self-aware, process-wise, and other-centered in the midst of major cultural change. The skills needed by those who attempt to intervene are no less challenging. In addition to technical skills they need to develop intrapersonal understanding (self-awareness); interpersonal competence (helping and empathy); and a particular variety of continuous self-improvement (honing one's own mind and feelings as the primary instrument of intervention).

The benefits are immense. Practitioners have the opportunity to help organizations form structures and processes that shed the limitations of the old, control-oriented culture. The payoff for the individual is relevance and work that is in harmony with their human spirit. The payoff for the organization is global competitiveness and survival.

References
Bardwick, J. M. (1991). *Danger in the comfort zone: From boardroom to mailroom—How to break the entitlement habit that's killing American business.* New York: AMACOM.

Beattie, M. (1987). *Codependent no more: How to stop controlling others and start caring for yourself.* San Francisco: HarperCollins.

Brockner, J. (1992, Winter). Managing the effects of layoffs on others. *California Management Review,* pp. 9–27.

Cascio, W. F. (1993). Downsizing: What do we know? What have we learned? *Academy of Management Executive, 7,* 95–104.

Connelly, S. (1984). *Work spirit: Recapturing the vitality of work.* Unpublished doctoral dissertation, George Washington University, Washington DC.

Davy, J. A., & Tansik, D. (1986). *Procedural justice and layoff survival: Preliminary evidence for the effects of voice and choice and survivors' attitudes and behavior.* Unpublished manuscript, Arizona State University, Tempe.

De Meuse, K. P., & Tornow, W. W. (1990). The tie that binds has become very, very, frayed! *Human Resource Planning, 13,* 202–213.

Hammer, M., & Champy, J. (1993). *Reengineering the corporation: A manifesto for business revolution.* New York: HarperCollins.

Herzberg, F. (1968, Jan.–Feb.). One more time: How do you motivate employees? *Harvard Business Review, 46*(1).

Kuhn, T. S. (1980). *The structure of scientific revolutions* (2nd ed.). Pacific Grove, CA: Brooks/Cole.

Marks, M. L. (1994). *From turmoil to triumph: New life after mergers, acquisitions, and downsizing.* San Francisco: New Lexington Press.

McGregor, D. (1960). *The human side of enterprise.* New York: McGraw-Hill.

Noer, D. M. (1993). *Healing the wounds: Overcoming the trauma of layoffs and revitalizing downsized organizations.* San Francisco: Jossey-Bass.

Noer, D. M. (1996). *Breaking free: A prescription for personal and organizational change.* San Francisco: Jossey-Bass.

Noer, D. M., & Dunker, K. A. (Eds.). (1995, Apr. 5–7). *Best practices in leading downsized organizations: Proceedings of a conference.* Greensboro, NC: Center for Creative Leadership.

Rogers, C. (1961). *On becoming a person: A therapist's view of psychotherapy.* Boston: Houghton Mifflin.

Schaef, A. W. (1986). *Codependence: Misunderstood, mistreated.* San Francisco: HarperCollins.

Shank, J. H. (1997). *Team-based organizations: Developing a successful team environment.* Burr Ridge, IL: Irwin.

CHAPTER 13

Organization Surveys
Coming of Age for a New Era
Allen I. Kraut
Lise M. Saari

Employee opinion surveys have changed gradually but dramatically in recent decades. Some of the changes were allowed by enhanced computer technologies, and still more changes were the result of mature use of such surveys. By far, though, the major driver of the changes has been a shift in the *strategic purpose* of such surveys. Going beyond mere assessment of employee attitudes, surveys nowadays are likely to focus on organizational change and its impacts, a result of the push for greater organizational competitiveness. In consequence, these surveys are notably different from their predecessors.

The central aim of this chapter is to describe and explain the new look and function of surveys, and what they mean for the organizations that use them. We think this can be done best by looking at the following topics: purposes of surveys; shifts in content; use of models in survey research; use of surveys to predict organizational performance; use of surveys to provide research links to outcomes; data collection technology; data reporting; census and sample surveys; people surveyed; special topic surveys; oversurvey-

Note: The authors acknowledge with thanks the helpful comments of Angela Lynch, Maria Park, and Paul Yost on an earlier draft of this chapter.

ing; need for new skills among survey researchers; and action and follow-through.

Purposes of Surveys

The earliest ancestors of today's organizational surveys date back to the 1930s (Viteles, 1953). Since then, surveys have gradually increased in popularity until some three-quarters of all medium-sized and large companies report using them today (Kraut, 1996). In the early days, the clear purpose of surveys was to measure employee "morale," whereas the underlying intent was often to avoid unionization activities (Higgs & Ashworth, 1996). Indeed, some studies have shown that dissatisfied employees are far more likely to unionize and vote in favor of unions (Hamner & Smith, 1978; Getman, Goldberg, & Herman, 1976).

In the 1950s and 1960s, the emphasis was still on measuring employee job satisfaction, often in the hope that higher job satisfaction would lead to greater productivity. As several reviews have noted, though, studies have found this assumed relationship between job satisfaction and individual performance to be a weak one that is neither simple nor straightforward (Iaffaldano & Muchinsky, 1985; Petty, McGhee, & Cavender, 1984).

In some cases, especially in the 1970s, the search for meaningful correlates of employee satisfaction moved to more easily measured and visible criteria, such as absenteeism and turnover. Indeed, a strong case was made for lower satisfaction leading to higher absenteeism and turnover, and these relationships are now well established and accepted (Porter & Steers, 1973).

During the 1980s and 1990s, driven by intense global competition, many firms undertook dramatic changes in the way they operated. These changes were often evidenced in downsizing, closing or moving plants and other work facilities, and mergers and acquisitions. In an attempt to become more efficient, effective, and competitive, they also tried to do business differently. Although such innovations sometimes appear to be a parade of "fads of the month," there is no doubt that changes like Total Quality Management, process reengineering, focusing on customer service, and other efforts to change corporate culture to line it up with new values, visions, missions, and goals were usually quite earnest attempts to improve organizational functioning. One thing was clear: the need for change was inevitable.

A profound shift in the use of surveys could be noted as a result of these change initiatives. Surveys were now being used to drive and measure organizational change. No longer did we see an exclusive emphasis on employee opinions and attitudes; now we were getting reports from employees on the extent to which they understood and supported the organizational changes being attempted. Moreover, the employees were now the sensors reporting how well these changes were going and the observers of how well their managers and coworkers actually upheld the changes intended by top executives. (In some surveys, respondents actually were asked if their managers modeled the desired behavior, that is, whether they "walked the talk.")

The role of surveys had bifurcated. The older and still-present mode was to assess employee opinions and attitudes. The newer and potentially more powerful role was to drive and measure organizational change. (See Nadler, 1996, for a fuller discussion of these two roles.) Surveys that are built to foster change will include items directly related to the desired changes. In this way they educate and remind all employees, including management, about these efforts to change. The survey data also measure the amount of change seen by members in the organization, and how this varies by job level and in different organizational units.

Shifts in Survey Content

The data from calibrations in this newer type of survey can be highly motivating in an organization, creating energy and direction for the issues being measured (Nadler, 1977). Surveys have always had a motivational effect, but this role becomes patently obvious when the underlying issues are organizational change. As a result of the shifts in focus, survey content has changed dramatically to include new items dealing with issues such as corporate vision, customer service, and quality.

Consider the following example. A major division of a petrochemical company had recently embarked on a new quality program. In the year after the program began, the division conducted its first survey of all employees. Items in the questionnaire were organized into ten sections, each headed with one of the principles of the new quality program, such as responsiveness to the customer and continuous improvement. Many traditional items, such as those dealing with pay and benefits, or promotions, were simply omitted. Newer concepts such as team effectiveness became prominent.

In other surveys, even items that cover traditional issues may have their wording changed in ways that have a powerful if sometimes subtle impact. For example, the topic of training has often been covered by the following item, drawn from the Mayflower Group consortium's list of original core items, developed in the early 1970s (R. H. Johnson, 1996): "How satisfied are you with the training you received for your present job?" (Answers range from "very satisfied" to "very dissatisfied.") By comparison, a question added to Mayflower's core items in 1995 and now used by a number of companies has a different emphasis: "I have received the training I need to do a quality job." (Answers range from "strongly agree" to "strongly disagree.")

The implications are clear. Firms like this are no longer interested merely in the employee's *satisfaction* with training but rather with the impact of such training on ability to *perform*. The earlier question implies that employees should be satisfied with training; the later item asks about training as needed to perform a job. This change in emphasis is part of a process sometimes described as a move away from an "entitlement mentality" to an "earning mentality" (Bardwick, 1991). Ironically, based on our experience, it is usually the employees themselves who most welcome anything that helps them do a better job.

Some companies have dropped so-called traditional items—like those on pay, benefits, promotions, and employment security—from their surveys. They may be doing this for fear of insulting people by asking about job security in a time of layoffs, or there may be deliberate symbolism in not asking about compensation because the desired emphasis is on customer service or product quality.

This emphasis on measuring employee views on topics directly related to organizational change and the strategic needs of the business (for example, customer service or quality) has been a positive trend in many corporations and has helped surveys align with business imperatives. At the same time, totally eliminating all other survey items deemed to be traditional may need to be done with caution.

Even research that focuses on the need for strategic survey items finds that some of the traditional items are correlates of important organizational outcomes, such as customer service measures. For example, employee views on career advancement and development are related to customer views of service (Schneider & Bowen, 1985; Schneider, Ashworth, Higgs, & Carr, 1996). Also, when low unemployment rates make the retention of talented professionals more critical than in an era of downsizing, questions about intentions to remain with a company take on renewed importance.

Indeed, recently some of these traditional topics have been reintroduced. This is because companies are obtaining feedback from various sources (such as line managers and exit interviews of employees who leave the company) that these topics relate to critical organizational outcomes, such as the retention of key performers. These traditional items may be rewritten to reflect the new focus of the organization, as in the previously noted training question that now emphasizes training to do a quality job. In other cases, the topic may be reintroduced and expanded upon to gain greater understanding. An example of this is the reintroduction of workload questions on some surveys, with the addition of related questions on work-life balance.

Use of Models

Survey practitioners in recent years have made active use of conceptual models to guide their work. Such models are important because they are powerful aids, in several ways (Wiley, 1996). A model can

- Influence the choice of items that are put into a survey
- Lay out and test causal relationships—between initial management actions and the resulting employee perceptions and reports, for example
- Display and test the links that employee perceptions and observations have to vital outcomes like customer service or quality production

- Organize the data simply, so that reports to management take form in a connected, meaningful way, and are not just a rambling array of survey items

The use of conceptual models to guide survey work has increased greatly in recent years, as has the variety of models available to practitioners. It was not always so. In decades past, most surveys seemed to be barely disciplined collections of items covering a vast variety of topics. What passed as "models" for organizing items seemed to be primarily lists of topics, or labels, that survey researchers thought were important to tap (Burke, 1994). Much of this may have come about because many of the early surveys were initiated by researchers trying to understand job satisfaction.

In the late 1970s, job satisfaction took on a new mantle—"quality of work life"—and with that shift came more attention to organizational (rather than individual) variables, a broader view of what employee perceptions should be measured, and the emergence of a definitive model. The open systems view of Katz and Kahn (1978) was further developed by Nadler and Tushman (1983), specifically for use in effecting organizational change and in using the surveys that could help such efforts.

Other models currently available come in many varieties, ranging from simple to complex, homegrown to highly professional, and research-based to models based on practice and experience. (Of the pragmatic models, many are grounded in useful research, although not of a caliber that would appear in a professional journal.) Naturally, some models are better for some purposes than others. It may be useful to illustrate this point with two erudite, well supported models.

Use of Surveys to Predict Organizational Performance

A useful and straightforward model dubbed the Linkage Research Model has recently been offered by Jack Wiley (1996), based on research carried out by himself and others (for example, see Schneider & Bowen, 1985). As shown in Figure 13.1, leadership practices such as quality emphasis and employee training are believed to be linked (in a causal fashion) to employee results such

Figure 13.1. The Linkage Research Model.

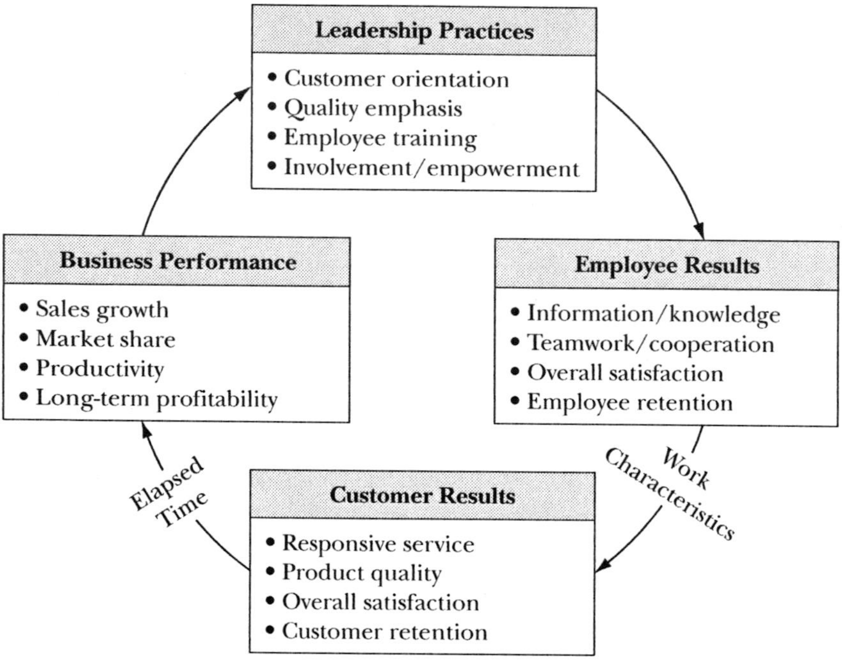

Source: Wiley, 1996. Used by permission of Jossey-Bass Publishers.

as better information and job knowledge. This in turn affects customer results (like satisfaction and retention) and, ultimately, business performance (like market share and profitability). Furthermore, it is assumed that, by way of feedback, better business performance reinforces good leadership practices.

Such models can be extremely helpful. On a conceptual level, models can be clear and understandable. On a practical level, they help us formulate and use questions that tap the important issues. After data are collected, degrees of favorability can be interpreted in terms of the effect of one variable or another. Despite its apparent simplicity, with just four "boxes," this model is far more sophisticated than many earlier versions. For example, it introduces the notion of time passing before one set of behaviors has the linked effect on the next set of behaviors, as reflected in the causal arrows. It also allows for different relationships, depending on the nature of the work being done.

A similar, widely publicized model now attracting management attention appeared first in the *Harvard Business Review* (Heskett and others, 1994) and then in the form of a book with the inviting title *The Service Profit Chain: How Leading Companies Link Profit and Growth to Loyalty, Satisfaction, and Value* (Heskett, Sasser, & Schlesinger, 1997). As shown in Figure 13.2, the model shows that a firm's internal system—the operating strategy and service delivery system—leads to the customer's experience—satisfaction and loyalty—which in turn leads to revenue growth and profitability. It can easily be seen that organizational surveys could provide measures of many of the key aspects of the internal system, such as employee capability, perceptions of reward and recognition, decision-making latitude. In fact, the authors support their model with many convincing anecdotes and stories about leading firms that use surveys as part of a strategy to achieve superior results.

Sears, a longtime user of organizational surveys, employs a model similar to the one shown in the figure (Rucci, Kirn, & Quinn, 1998). Indeed, several firms use their own highly simplified and customized models to communicate to management the key concepts and relationships being measured in their surveys and as an aid in communicating survey results. A *Fortune* magazine interview with Anthony Rucci, the Sears executive then responsible for human resources (himself a highly regarded industrial-organizational psychologist), shows the extraordinary impact of these relationships when they are systematically measured and examined: "Now we know that if a store increases its employee-satisfaction score by five measuring units this quarter, the following quarter its customer-satisfaction scores will go up by two units. And its revenue the following quarter will beat our stores' national average by 0.5 percent. It's not guesswork or theory anymore. We have built an empirical model that says unless you have a trained, literate, motivated, competent workforce and give them decision-making authority, you don't get satisfied customers no matter how good the merchandise is. The right workforce creates customer satisfaction, and that produces superior financial performance" ("Bringing Sears," 1997).

Figure 13.2. The Service Profit Chain.

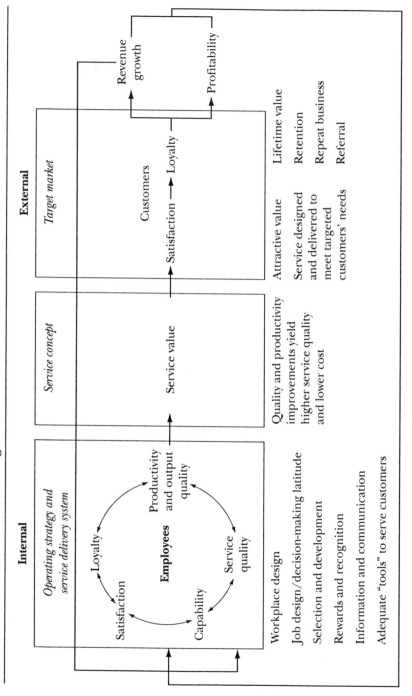

These findings have an extraordinary meaning, namely, survey data are very likely to be *leading indicators* of organizational performance! The reports given by survey respondents can forecast an organization's effectiveness in terms of productivity, quality, and customer satisfaction before it shows up in the typical financial measures. Rather than duplicating what is already being reported, survey data may precede and foretell shifts in these traditional measures—in time to make corrections.

A related concept in management thinking that coincides with these newer ideas about measurement of employee views, is the notion of the *balanced scorecard* popularized by Kaplan and Norton (1992). In brief, this concept states that management must go beyond the narrow financial measures of the past and collect data on customer attitudes and employee perceptions. All three sets of data are important and provide a "balanced" view of organizational effectiveness. The employee data are seen to provide a useful measure of the organization's ability to learn, grow, and innovate. In other words, the data show how well the firm can improve. Thus, we again see surveys being used as a measure to help us understand the capabilities of the organization to perform well in the future!

Use of Surveys to Provide Research Links to Outcomes

Surveys have often been the basis for research linking attitudes and various employee behaviors and outcomes. As noted earlier, studies have demonstrated the relationship between employee attitudes and turnover (for example, Carsten & Spector, 1987; Ostroff, 1992; Tett & Meyer, 1993), attendance (for example, Smith, 1977), unionization (Hamner & Smith, 1978), and organizational commitment (Tett & Meyer, 1993). Less support has been found for a direct link between employee attitudes and individual performance (for example, see reviews by Iaffaldano & Muchinsky, 1985; Petty, McGhee, & Cavender, 1984).

Recently, as we saw in the previous discussion of models, more research has been aimed at significant organizational outcomes. For example, Ryan, Schmit, & Johnson (1996) found significant positive relationships between employee attitudes (about teamwork, workload, supervision, and training, for example) and branch productivity measures in an automobile finance company. (But they note that "messy" data make some of the cause-and-effect links murky.) As the focus on competitiveness and customers continues, there has been increased interest in the link between employee views and customer satisfaction and retention. One of the strongest relationships found is that employee perceptions of service climate are significantly related to customer perceptions of service (Schneider, White, & Paul, 1998).

Surprisingly, at a time when many companies are downplaying career advancement, a consistent theme in several studies is that attitudes about company policies on employee career growth and development are positively related to customer service (Jones, 1992; Schneider & Bowen, 1985; Schneider, Ashworth, Higgs, & Carr, 1996). Somewhat weaker but still-significant relationships to customer measures have also been found in employees' views of their firm's human resource (HR) practices (Schneider & Bowen, 1985). Hansen and Wernerfelt (1989) also found that employee attitudes on HR practices and their views about whether there was an emphasis on goal accomplishment predicted firm performance.

A difficulty with drawing conclusions from the diverse studies in this research domain is that they do not necessarily use the same employee attitude measures or the same organizational outcome measures. An item that may be significant in one study may not even have been asked in another, so results are not comparable or cumulative. Likewise, there may be imprecision in the definition as well as the measurement of the constructs, available longitudinal data, and sample size. In addition, the importance of employee attitudes and good customer service may vary by the nature of the business, the competition, and other features of the firm. Nevertheless, it can be concluded that employee attitudes are related to important organizational outcomes, especially customer measures.

Data Collection Technology

Technological changes that allow for new ways of working have provided new opportunities for administering surveys. More and more we see surveys done through computers, e-mail, Web sites, centralized on-line systems, and even by telephone. These technologies are developing at a rapid pace; exactly how they will develop and be used in survey administration cannot be predicted precisely.

With the advent of e-mail, as well as the Internet and the Intranet (that is, a company's own internal Internet), electronic survey opportunities have developed rapidly. As companies move to conducting their business electronically and provide computer access for all employees, the notion of universally conducting surveys on-line becomes a reality and, for global companies, may be the only option for conducting a survey with reasonable turnaround time. Current emphasis is primarily on Web-based (Internet- or Intranet-accessed) and e-mail–based surveys, with a variety of companies exploring these techniques for on-line administration.

These new technologies offer both opportunities and challenges. A 1997 survey of the Mayflower Group companies (L. M. Saari, personal communication, 1998) found that although paper and pencil was still the most common survey method, electronic surveys came in a close second, with estimates that 85 percent of employees would have access to them by the year 2000. Important reasons reported for using electronic surveys include greater speed of data collection and reporting time, greater ease of administration, ability to customize surveys, and ultimately, reduction in survey administration costs.

However, there are concerns with electronic surveys, including the following:

- *Worries about confidentiality* may be solely a matter of respondent perceptions, or they can be real if anonymity is not built into the system.
- *Computer accessibility issues* arise if employees don't have computer access or do not have the needed "system" for access. In both of these instances, there is the potential to lower response rates and thus undermine the value of the data. (Accessibility may even send unintentional messages about the perceived value of any employees who have limited access to computers.)
- *Issues of data representativeness and accuracy* arise because some electronic survey designs do not ensure "one employee, one survey" (for example, the survey can be taken multiple times by the same respondent).

- *Technological glitches* (for example, "the system going down" while the survey is being administered) are another issue.
- *Initial investment costs* (development time and costs) for running on-line surveys are higher than a paper survey, but many companies are moving toward having an infrastructure (that is, computer access for all employees) that justifies the initial investment. With the rapidly growing, widespread use of networked computers, costs may soon be a moot point.

Some noncomputer-based technological methods that are also used are telephone self-administration and paper-and-pencil surveys with fax return. Telephone self-administration methods are useful because almost everyone has phone access, but such surveys may be restricted to less than fifty items (Macey, Lenz, & Barbera, 1997). Fax return methods still require a paper survey but reduce mail-back time and cost (which can be useful when surveys are administered globally). With this type of survey, fax accessibility may be an issue; one study showed a lower return rate for nonmanagers, presumably because they had less access to fax machines than did managers (Nilan & Paul, 1997).

Corporations may use all of these methods as part of a suite of methods for administering surveys. As various technological approaches for surveying have been developed, many companies have started using them; therefore, organizations nowadays may employ multiple survey data collection methods within their company. However, the results obtained from various methods may not be interchangeable. Kraut, Oltrogge, and Block (1998) found answers to telephone interviewers were far more favorable than answers to a paper-and-pencil survey. Although Yost and Homer (1998) are typical of several researchers who found little difference in responses to electronic and paper-and-pencil surveys, they noted that less favorable responses tend to come from employee groups who have less access to on-line technology. Data obtained via different methods cannot be blithely (or blindly) compared.

Data Reporting

Just as improvements in technology now allow for collecting survey data electronically, on-line methods are also being used to provide survey results directly to managers or work groups and teams. A variety of companies (Allstate, Duke Power, IBM, Xerox, and 3M among them) now provide survey results via on-line systems (Fuller, 1997). The benefits of these approaches are that they save turnaround time in providing results, decrease the need for centralized printing (although they provide for printing locally), and may eliminate the need to "reinput" the results for presentations. In addition, some of these reporting systems provide users with greater understanding by allowing for query of results (trending results, or comparing with broader organizations or external norms, or comparing by job category).

As with on-line survey data collection, there are challenges with these electronic reporting tools. Significant issues include development costs and technical challenges (such as different, incompatible computer systems within a company). Other decisions that companies must contend with are the type of access and by whom—managers only? team members?—and the need to ensure that any opportunities to "cut" the data by demographic information do not break anonymity.

Companies like Xerox have combined their on-line reporting of survey results with on-line information on how to conduct feedback sessions and take action. In addition, some companies (Boeing, Duke Power, Ford, IBM, Pacific Bell) are starting to use internal Web sites to report on companywide results and actions. It is likely that technological developments will continue to allow for greater ease and quicker turnaround in reporting results.

A particularly interesting development now occurring is the use of so-called text-mining tools to do content analysis of write-in comments. Such responses to open-ended questions are often a valuable and untapped source of information on key and emerging issues (Wagner & Spencer, 1996).

Ideally, the essential purpose of this high technology is to provide clearer data more rapidly. The reports must make it easier to understand and act on the data. So presentation of results needs to be simple, to the point, and easy to comprehend. We can reasonably predict that the next step will be the development of some sort of "expert systems" that identify the major problems and offer a series of potential actions for the work group and manager to take in response to the findings. (At this writing, a very limited number of companies are already experimenting with such expert systems, "coaching" managers on-line.)

Census and Sample Surveys

The increased ease of collecting survey data has challenged the ability of many firms to absorb and use the findings quickly. Ironically, the use of methods to respond rapidly and process data faster has raised employee and management expectations for quick follow-through. It has also forced management to think through who needs particular information and at what levels action should be expected. In turn, this has influenced the number and sampling of respondents.

A recent benchmarking study (Kraut Associates, 1998) highlights current practices. Interviews with twenty large companies that were believed to be effective users of organizational surveys found that almost all (85 percent) did census surveys of all employees, 60 percent did sample surveys, and *70 percent did both*. It is the use of both types of surveys by so many that seems most remarkable. The intent and use of these survey modes is also illuminating.

For most companies, the census surveys are used for work group issues. These issues are the sorts of things that can be acted upon by lower levels of management and work groups, like understanding of unit goals, availability of tools, necessary information, training, and local management behavior. Naturally, everyone in that unit needs to be invited to take part in the survey for the results to be meaningful, to create ownership of the results at the local level, and to lay the groundwork for follow-through.

Reports of the findings are furnished to each work group with some minimum number of participants, usually from five to ten employees. The work group's data often are provided to the next higher level of management and also "rolled-up" to provide reports for higher-level units as well. Actions are usually expected to take place at similar levels of management.

Over time, many large companies have come to realize that for other issues only a statistically meaningful sample is needed to provide useful data. These issues are primarily companywide (or business unitwide or countrywide), rather than local. Examples might include perceptions about the firm's strategic direction, or understanding and acceptance of a chief executive's messages. Survey items might also include those that can be acted on most easily at a corporate rather than a local level, such as employee benefits, pay, and employment security. Sample surveys enable companies to remove such questions from the census that goes to all employees. Bolstering this approach, lower-level managers have often complained that they cannot respond to such issues. Ideally, all the items in a census survey are ones that unit managers feel are under their control.

Sample surveys can also be used to ask items that are used for comparison with external norms or consortium data. In addition, sample surveys can cover topics of current interest, such as understanding and support for corporate vision statements, diversity issues, or recent mergers. (Such topics may also merit surveys of their own, as noted in a following section.)

People Surveyed

The question of whom to survey will continue to become more difficult to answer as organizational membership takes on new forms. For example, most firms employ many more part-time and contract employees than they did in the past. They also employ joint venture employees and depend on key supplier and alliance companies. All of these "noncore" employees may be central to the organization's success and thus quite legitimately included in an organization's surveys.

Another subset of employees of interest are those who work in matrix organizations, with more than one "boss." Like matrix organizations, global firms are quite complex. They mix survey data analyses by product, functions or departments, and skill groups, with geographical splits (country and region). The decisions about whom to include in a survey and where to send the results often follow a sense of responsibility and ownership for dealing with the results, but there is not always agreement among the different potential "owners." This was not usually an issue in traditional, hierarchical organizations.

It should also be expected that surveys of customers as well as of employees will continue in their own right, but there will be greater integration of the two as organizations attempt to understand better the relationship between these two constituencies.

Special Topic Surveys

The success of organizational surveys and their capability to collect meaningful data have led to their use for many topics of special interest to organizations. Some examples of such surveys from recent years reflect issues that today's organizations and their members face.

- Merger surveys have been carried out as part of major mergers (for example, Chase Manhattan and Chemical Bank; Union Pacific and Southern Pacific Railroad). These surveys focus on issues related to the success of the merger and may be conducted as a series of surveys during the merger transition.
- Diversity surveys have been carried out as workforce demographics have changed. Some of these began around the time of the Workforce 2000 report, which gained widespread attention in U.S. corporations regarding the upcoming changes in workforce demographics. As a result of these surveys, many corporations embarked on or intensified their diversity initiatives (Allstate, Xerox, and IBM to name a few). These same companies actively use special topic surveys to assess the progress of their diversity initiatives.
- Work-life balance surveys are another current special topic survey in some companies. These surveys developed in response to the changing workforce demographics (for example, with more women in the workforce, issues of child care and work-life balance became more apparent). These surveys may cover a range of topics, from child care and elder care to general work-life balance issues. Some organizations, which are downsizing in a competitive global arena, are also tracking the impact these reductions have had on organizational members' workload and ability to balance work and family responsibilities.

Additional special topic themes in recent years include benefits programs (for example, flexible benefits, feedback on programs), HR services, communications, ethics, and teamwork (Higgs & Ashworth, 1996). With the increased ease of obtaining employee feedback, thanks to technology, such surveys will likely be part of the landscape in organizations of the future, as long as new issues evolve for companies and employees.

Oversurveying

With more than one type of survey going on, care must be taken to avoid "oversurveying" employees. Among the twenty companies in the benchmarking study noted earlier, the practice among almost half was to survey annually, among the other half to survey every two years. This was true for both census and sample surveys, with several firms reporting that the two types were alternated. In fact, some report that they use the sample surveys in part to follow up issues raised in the census surveys, and vice versa.

Anecdotal evidence suggests that the perception of oversurveying is most likely when participants don't see any action taken in response to their input. Sometimes this perception is quite accurate; at other times, action may have been taken but not communicated or connected to the survey so that participants can understand that something has indeed been done. For most companies, both taking action and communicating it are major challenges in the overall survey process. (A related issue is the proliferation of surveys by many different staffs and departments in a company, which may not be coordinated or even known to one another. Some firms have set up a "registry" through which various surveys must be coordinated.)

Need for New Skills Among Survey Researchers

A currently popular idea is that HR management is a strategic partner of line management. The same sort of thinking directly affects the role and activities of survey researchers. In order for surveys to be credible and seen as valuable, they must be aligned with the organization's strategic objectives. Their content, timing, and language must have strong and obvious ties to the organization's goals and objectives, whether they be cost savings, customer satisfaction, or innovation. This requirement puts special demands on those doing surveys, demands that may not have been made just a decade or two ago (Kraut, 1996a).

Most of the earlier expectations remain, however. The people doing surveys are still expected to have a sound methodology, understand statistics and sampling, and be skillful in analyzing and reporting data. They are required to be astute wordsmiths when putting together questionnaires and communicating the findings. And they ought to be familiar with current practices among other companies and able to use new technologies for collecting and communicating information.

The newer demands, we believe, center on two themes. The first centers on understanding the "business" of their organizations. Survey researchers must really comprehend how their organizations function, their core competencies, strategic objectives, and plans. This comprehension should be obvious to the executives with whom they interact.

A special case of expertise bridging business knowledge and organization development skills shows up in international companies or those that operate in a global environment. This global expertise includes awareness of and sensitivity to the cultures and local practices of various countries as they may affect survey content and processes (S. R. Johnson, 1996). One example of this is understanding that some U.S.-based concepts, such as empowerment, coaching, job challenge, and organizational climate, may not exist as constructs in some other cultures—and may not even be translatable. In addition, the process of survey feedback meetings, wherein a manager asks for employees' ideas for action, may need to be adapted for other cultures, so as to account for differences in the way people relate to their managers (Hofstede, 1997).

The second theme centers on having organization development skills. Generally, organization development skills are less apparent and more important to making good use of survey data. Those responsible for doing surveys must be capable of developing and using the organizational "energy" to conduct and apply surveys. They must be skillful at involving top management and getting support at all levels. They need to excel in designing and facilitating feedback and action processes; otherwise, they wind up acting and being seen merely as a service bureau for data collection. If key individuals in the survey process lack these skills, it will condemn surveys to be exercises generating inaction and resulting in cynicism.

Action and Follow-Through

Based on our observations and experience, as well as the laments of many colleagues who conduct surveys, the Achilles heel in the organizational survey process is the failure to take meaningful, visible action in response to the findings. Employees are very sensitive to this issue, as surveys invariably raise the expectation that something will be done with the findings. We have heard employees in many focus groups complain bitterly that nothing was done with the results of prior surveys. It is also an interesting paradox that the managers who most need to take action because of poor survey results are usually the least able or willing to do so. (This inertia may account for their getting poor results in the first place!)

There are probably several reasons for inaction in dealing with survey results. One may be a feeling of awkwardness about reporting the findings to participants. But in reality a great deal is known about how to communicate survey results effectively and hold manager-employee feedback meetings (Hinrichs, 1996). Furthermore, training can be conducted that vastly improves managers' skills in holding good meetings.

Another view on who has responsibility for taking action is based on the modern notion that work groups themselves are the ones to use and take action on survey data. Self-managing teams are a clear example where the group, rather than the manager alone, bears the responsibility to respond.

However, just reporting data is not the same as taking action. An important reason for inaction is often a sense of being overwhelmed by the amount of data (as well as the adrenaline it seems to stimulate). This can be combated if surveys are kept relatively short, but more so if managers are urged to prioritize issues and focus on just the two or three most important ones. The few best issues to work on may also be chosen based on which can be solved quickly, certainly, and with fewer resources. Of course, we cannot ignore the reality that another significant reason for inaction is the lack of any meaningful consequence for it. Often, higher organizational priorities are put on the manager's or business's "core" or measured activities, displacing attention from the survey findings.

A common complaint among managers is that the data don't tell them what to do. This remark often reveals a crucial, often unspoken, philosophical assumption—that managers should be able to analyze such data to gain the true meaning without discussing the data with the respondents. In fact, that is rarely possible. Survey data often reveal problems or successes without pointing to solutions. For example, how do you respond to feelings of low "overall satisfaction?" By first discussing the reasons people feel that way!

It is far better to see survey data as creating a platform on which to hold meaningful dialogues—to analyze and solve problems. Effective survey users recognize the data to be just one part of a problem-solving process. If questions are asked about topical initiatives, then apt managerial actions may be more obvious and forthcoming.

Perhaps the most important stimulus for action is a clear expectation by top management for action, backed up by a disciplined process of communication, review, and follow-up to see that appropriate action is really taken. This can be achieved if top management is involved in the survey process and has a real stake in the topics being covered.

When survey items tap into management's strategic business issues, management generally gets involved. And in such cases, the survey data may lead to understanding and strategic decision making as part of the information base that executives use to run the business (along with financial data). Actions taken in this manner are usually not visible to employees but are still quite important.

To be successful, survey researchers must have the organizational skills to engage management at all levels and create the processes for really using the survey results. In today's organizations, we may even find this action role played by self-directed or cross-functional teams.

How to do this has sometimes led to strong debates. In some organizations, survey results for a particular unit are still treated as if they are "owned" by the unit manager or work team. That is, they are seen as a sort of developmental input to the manager and team and are not reported to the manager's superior. It is hard to imagine that other serious business information, such as budget data, would be treated the same way. Restricting the availability of survey data to just that unit seems a doomed practice—properly so, we think. (Nevertheless, we recognize that this is a complex issue, and automatic sharing of data with superiors may be hazardous and dysfunctional in some cases—such as brand-new survey programs or multisource (360-degree) feedback.)

In other organizations, survey data affect managers' pay. Survey results can directly affect a portion of incentive income or, indirectly, feed into a performance appraisal. This is a controversial issue. Some observers worry that such consequences lead to deliberate manipulation of survey results (by "buttering up" employees or even cajoling or threatening them to give good reports). Although these concerns are reasonable, a good case can be made for rewarding managers for favorable survey results, just as they are rewarded for other desired business outcomes. To avoid misuse, a good understanding of survey measurement issues must be exercised.

Comparisons between units within a company is also a debated practice. There is a fear that this may lead to undesirable internal competition. However, internal comparisons to other units coping with similar conditions (as well as to prior survey results) seems a valid practice to many survey researchers. Desirable actions can be stimulated if intracompany comparisons are used to identify "best" (or at least "better") practices for others to consider or adopt. Meetings and dialogue have to take place to make this sharing happen. In addition, such best practices sharing can fight lethargy and help to reinforce managers who have achieved positive results.

Conclusion

For years, many organizations have proclaimed that employees are their most important resource. Often this has been mere rhetoric, but recent research shows that the employee views captured in organizational surveys do have a powerful impact on business performance. If companies sincerely believe that employees are a key resource, this will show up in many HR practices, such as selection, training, and recognition. Most of these are or can be measured by organizational surveys, making this technique a most valuable device to sense and stimulate appropriate management behaviors.

A changed business environment, the result of intense global competition, heightened customer expectations, and rapid changes in technology, has put a premium on farsighted and well-executed business strategies. The same dynamics are causing organizational surveys to align with those business strategies. Both the topics in surveys and the use of the data have gone beyond measuring morale to helping achieve the business strategies.

These more recent goals for the role of surveys are facilitated by electronic technology and improved computing, which allow more and better focused surveys. At the same time, they put a higher premium on the skills of the survey researchers to conduct sound surveys as well as to mobilize organizational resources and energy to make effective use of the survey data. Those survey practitioners who can rise to this challenge and adapt as they move forward will greatly help their organizations to succeed.

References

Bardwick, J. M. (1991). *Danger in the comfort zone: From boardroom to mail-room—How to break the entitlement habit that's killing American business.* New York: AMACOM.

Bringing Sears into the new world. (1997, Oct. 13). *Fortune,* p. 184.

Burke, W. W. (1994). Diagnostic models for organizational change. In A. Howard & Associates (Eds.), *Diagnosis for organizational change.* New York: Guilford Press.

Carsten, J. M., & Spector, P. E. (1987). Unemployment, job satisfaction, and employee turnover: A meta-analytic test of the Muchinsky model. *Journal of Applied Psychology, 73,* 374–381.

Fuller, W. L. (1997, Apr.). Spreading the word through wide area networked data access tools. In K. Paul (Chair), *Survey techniques at work.* Paper presented at the Twelfth Annual Conference of the Society for Industrial and Organizational Psychology, St. Louis, MO.

Getman, J. G., Goldberg, S. B., & Herman, J. B. (1976). *Union representation elections: Law and reality.* New York: Russell Sage Foundation.

Hamner, W. C., & Smith, F. J. (1978). Work attitudes as predictors of unionization activity. *Journal of Applied Psychology, 63*(4), 415–421.

Hansen, G. S., & Wernerfelt, B. (1989). Determinants of firm performance: The relative importance of economic and organizational factors. *Strategic Management Journal, 10,* 399–411.

Heskett, J. L., Sasser, W. E., & Schlesinger, L. A. (1997). *The service profit chain: How leading companies link profit and growth to loyalty, satisfaction, and value.* New York: Free Press.

Heskett, J. L., and others. (1994, Mar.–Apr.). Putting the service profit chain to work. *Harvard Business Review,* pp. 164–174.

Higgs, A. C., & Ashworth, S. D. (1996). Organizational surveys: Tools for assessment and research. In A. I. Kraut (Ed.), *Organizational surveys: Tools for assessment and change.* San Francisco: Jossey-Bass.

Hinrichs, J. R. (1996). Feedback, action planning, and follow-through. In A. I. Kraut (Ed.), *Organizational surveys: Tools for assessment and change.* San Francisco: Jossey-Bass.

Hofstede, G. H. (1997). *Cultures and organizations: Software of the mind.* New York: McGraw-Hill.

Iaffaldano, M. T., & Muchinsky, P. M. (1985). Job satisfaction and job performance: A meta-analysis. *Psychological Bulletin, 97,* 251–273.

Johnson, R. H. (1996). Life in the consortium: The Mayflower Group. In A. I. Kraut (Ed.), *Organizational surveys: Tools for assessment and change.* San Francisco: Jossey-Bass.

Johnson, S. R. (1996). The multinational opinion survey. In A. I. Kraut (Ed.), *Organizational surveys: Tools for assessment and change.* San Francisco: Jossey-Bass.

Jones, J. W. (1992, May). *Relationship between bank employee attitudes and customers' ratings of service.* Paper presented at the Seventh Annual Conference of the Society for Industrial and Organizational Psychology, Montreal, Quebec.

Kaplan, R. S., & Norton, D. P. (1992, Jan.–Feb.). The balanced scorecard: Measures that drive performance. *Harvard Business Review,* pp. 71–79.

Katz, D., & Kahn, R. L. (1978). *The social psychology of organizations* (2nd ed.). New York: Wiley.

Kraut, A. I. (1996a). Introduction and overview of organizational surveys. In A. I. Kraut (Ed.) *Organizational surveys: Tools for assessment and change.* San Francisco: Jossey-Bass.

Kraut, A. I. (1996b, Apr.). *What I have learned about organizational surveys, so far.* Distinguished Professional Contributions Award presentation at the Eleventh Annual Conference of the Society for Industrial and Organizational Psychology, San Diego, CA.

Kraut, A. I., Oltrogge, C. G., & Block, C. J. (1998, Apr.). *Written versus telephone surveys of employees: Are the data really comparable?* Paper presented at the Thirteenth Annual Conference of the Society for Industrial and Organizational Psychology, Dallas.

Kraut Associates. (1998, Feb.). *A benchmarking study of survey procedures in premier companies.* (Proprietary research from Kraut Associates.)

Macey, W. H., Lenz, A. H., & Barbera, K. M. (1997, Apr.). Survey data captured by phone: Implications of presentation method on nonresponse and response favorability. In K. Paul (Chair), *Survey techniques at work.* Paper presented at the Twelfth Annual Conference of the Society for Industrial and Organizational Psychology, St. Louis, MO.

Nadler, D. A. (1996). Setting expectations and reporting results: Conversations with top management. In A. I. Kraut (Ed.), *Organizational surveys: Tools for assessment and change.* San Francisco: Jossey-Bass.

Nadler, D. A. (1997). *Feedback and organization development: Using data-based methods.* Reading, MA: Addison-Wesley.

Nadler, D. A., & Tushman, M. L. (1983). A general diagnostic model for organizational behavior. In J. R. Hackman, E. E. Lawler, & L. W. Porter (Eds.), *Perspectives on organizational behavior.* New York: McGraw-Hill.

Nilan, K. J., & Paul, K. (1997, Apr.). Fax versus paper: Two survey methods—One result? In K. Paul (Chair), *Survey techniques at work.* Paper presented at the Twelfth Annual Conference of the Society for Industrial and Organizational Psychology, St. Louis, MO.

Ostroff, C. (1992). The relationship between satisfaction, attitudes, and performance: An organizational level of analysis. *Journal of Applied Psychology, 77*(6), 963–974.

Petty, M. M., McGhee, G. W., & Cavender, J. W. (1984). A meta-analysis of the relationships between individual job satisfaction and individual performance. *Academy of Management Review, 9,* 712–721.

Porter, L. W., & Steers, R. M. (1973). Organizational, work, and personal factors in employee turnover and absenteeism. *Psychological Bulletin, 80,* 151–176.

Rucci, A. J., Kirn, S. P., & Quinn, R. T. (1998, Jan.–Feb.). The employee-customer-profit chain and Sears. *Harvard Business Review,* pp. 82–97.

Ryan, A. M., Schmit, M. J., & Johnson, R. (1996). Attitudes and effectiveness: Examining relations at an organizational level. *Personnel Psychology, 49,* 853–882.

Schneider, B., Ashworth, S. D., Higgs, A. C., & Carr, L. (1996). Design, validity, and use of strategically focused employee attitude surveys. *Personnel Psychology, 49,* 695–705.

Schneider, B., & Bowen, D. E. (1985). Employee and customer perceptions of service in banks: Replications and extension. *Journal of Applied Psychology, 70,* 423–433.

Schneider, B., White, S. S., & Paul, M. C. (1998). Linking service climate and customer perceptions of service quality: Test of a casual model. *Journal of Applied Psychology, 83,* 150–163.

Smith, F. J. (1977). Work attitudes as predictors of attendance on a specific day. *Journal of Applied Psychology, 62*(1), 16–19.

Tett, R. P., & Meyer, J. P. (1993). Job satisfaction, organizational commitment, turnover intention, and turnover: Path analyses based on meta-analytical findings. *Personnel Psychology, 46,* 259–293.

Viteles, M. S. (1953). *Motivations and morale in industry.* New York: Norton.

Wagner, D. B., & Spencer, J. L. (1996). The role of surveys in transforming culture: Data, knowledge, and action. In A. I. Kraut (Ed.), *Organizational surveys: Tools for assessment and change.* San Francisco: Jossey-Bass.

Wiley, J. W. (1996). Linking survey results to customer satisfaction and business performance. In A. I. Kraut (Ed.), *Organizational surveys: Tools for assessment and change.* San Francisco: Jossey-Bass.

Yost, P. R., & Homer, L. E. (1998, Apr.). *Electronic versus paper surveys: Does the medium affect the response?* Paper presented at the Thirteenth Annual Conference of the Society for Industrial and Organizational Psychology, Dallas.

CHAPTER 14

Is the Sky Really Falling?
A View of the Future
Benjamin Schneider

When Allen Kraut and Abe Korman originally asked me to write the concluding chapter of this volume, it seemed to me that they were concerned that I/O psychology as a discipline and HRM as management practice were not adapting effectively to the changing nature of work and work organizations. I sensed this also in some writings at that time, especially a series of fascinating articles in *TIP (The Industrial-Organizational Psychologist)* by Karen May (1995). In addition, I had been asked by the Society for Industrial and Organizational Psychology to conduct a workshop on how well we were adapting to the changes occurring to us and around us, and again there was the implication that we were not doing well. Finally, both the popular press (for example, Uchitelle & Kleinfeld, 1996) and professional business publications like *Business Week* (for example, "The Pain of Downsizing," 1994) were full of articles about the intended and unintended consequences of downsizing

Note: I appreciate the efforts of the authors of the other chapters in this book very much. They presented thoughtful insights around which I could develop the themes of my own chapter. The present version of this chapter was significantly improved based on comments provided by Allen Kraut and Abraham Korman. My chapter was prepared with the financial assistance of the Army Research Institute for the Behavioral and Social Sciences. I am completely responsible for the content of the chapter; nothing in this chapter should be construed to represent positions of the U.S. Army or the Department of Defense.

and restructuring, frequently emphasizing the consequences for both the people who had been "rightsized" and the people remaining in organizations. They seemed to be saying that the pace of life and the pace of technological change in the way we work and in the global nature of economic life are overwhelming and that we have not done a good job in keeping up with these changes—much less staying in front of them.

I had two thoughts at the time I was asked to do this chapter and the workshop: First, the sky is not falling at all for I/O or HRM because we are adaptable and flexible and always have been; indeed, this is a wonderful time for us and for the field. And second, change is the nature of the world and every generation wonders if it can possibly cope.

In the paragraphs that follow I will first deal with the issue of the continuity of change, and then I will review the current very interesting collection of chapters, each of which documents well my belief that we *are* coping, and effectively, with the ongoing changes in the world of work. Not that there aren't things we could do better and not that there aren't things we may need to attend to that we are not attending to now—but nevertheless, I/O and HRM are becoming increasingly important players in contemporary business (Ulrich, 1996).

On the Ubiquitousness of Change

My grandmother came to the United States in the wave of Eastern European immigration of the late 1800s. She left Russia alone at age eighteen for the trip to Ellis Island and traveled here in steerage aboard one of the early steamships of the day. When she arrived in the United States there were no telephones, electricity was just being widely used, horses still were the main means of both personal and mass transportation, and indoor plumbing existed primarily for the upper classes. Nevertheless, what she found in the United States was light-years ahead of what she had left behind in Russia—where bread was still communally baked, *pogroms* were a constant threat to life, and an existence beyond peasantry was rarely possible. Before my grandmother died, she saw a man land on the moon, traveled by jet from Brooklyn to Florida, conversed by telephone many times per day, had running hot water whenever she wanted it, and watched wrestling matches on television while cursing the bad guys with great gusto.

The point is that change is not new and should not be news. Each generation experiences change in its lifetime and each generation believes it is party to the greatest, most difficult, and most rapid change ever, change requiring heroic efforts in order to cope and succeed. I suggest that this is the personal psychology—the narcissism—of change. The narcissism of change and the stress change produces in us do not provide the frame of reference necessary to appreciate the idea that one's own experience is no more nor less than previous generations' experience of change. In essence, then, my argument is that change is ubiquitous and the change we experience as "the greatest ever" is no greater *in the way it is experienced* than the change preceding generations of at least the last two hundred years in the United States and other Western societies also experienced. Today, we look back and say that the changes they experienced were not as great as ours—but that is not the way they experienced it.

Consider, for example, the issue of the global nature of contemporary work organizations. Is this something new? Of course not. In the silk route connecting China, Rome, and the Middle East since the first century B.C.E. we can see how deeply interconnected different cultures were, both in work and in quality of life. People knew many languages and were capable of exchange in many currencies as well as in barter systems involving other objects of value—silk, wool, silver, gold, and so forth. Consider next the issue of diversity in the workplace. When the huge influx of immigrants arrived from Eastern Europe, Ireland, and Italy in the late 1800s, diversity in the workplace was a given. Recall too that the Army Beta test for enlistments and inductions in World War I was one of the first attempts to design a culture-fair examination.

Issues of work and family life are not new either. As Kanter (1977) documents, the *disconnect* between work and family is what is new because, before the industrial revolution work was a family affair. Speaking of the industrial revolution, it takes tremendous *chutzpah* on our part to believe that the changes we are experiencing today are somehow more startling to our system or happening more quickly to us than those experienced by the millions of people who moved from farm to factory, from fresh air to polluted air, from the closeness of the family at work to the separation of husband and wife and parents from children, during it (Kanter, 1977).

What *is* new is the involvement of I/O psychologists and HRM as part of the mix for coping with change and facilitating the integration of people into the changing work organization. What is truly laudatory is that I/O psychologists and their research and practice and HRM practitioners have effectively coped with these continual changes since the profession began in the early 1900s. Dealing with change is not new for people and it is not new for us.

Consider this quotation about the demands on executives: "An uncomfortable feeling of uncertainty besets the men who sit behind the executive desks in high offices of organizations in our society. The delightful unambiguity of the past has been shattered by the imprecise and transitory present and the unpredictable future. The executives in the centers of communication networks receive information, weigh possibilities, and make decisions about problems and events which make the activities of their predecessors seem earth-creeping in comparison."

This was not written today but forty years ago by Gene Jennings (1962, p. 1). Jennings devoted his career to helping executives of the day deal with the stresses caused by the ambiguity and uncertainty they experienced, not unlike in what has become an increasingly active component of the I/O portfolio—executive coaching (Hollenbeck & McCall, Chapter Eight of this volume).

And how about the "new" impact of technology? "One of the clear and present pressures [for attention to human issues in the workplace] arises from the technological character of American industry. We have today in America an industrial machine of vast productive potential, but one which is primarily built on technological change. Our national genius has been for introducing new methods, machines, and processes to speed and improve production and to make it less expensive" (Haire, 1956, pp. 1–2).

Perhaps Robert Frost (1914) best captured the theme I wish to suggest here: "Most of the change we think we see in life is due to truths being in and out of favor." I will return to this theme periodically in what follows.

The Need to Examine Where
We Are and What We Do

The Frost quote is not meant to suggest a lessened need for continual examination of the status of the field in the face of the demands placed on it in practice. I am certainly not arguing that the chapters in the present volume are not useful. In fact, they constitute a necessary audit of where we are when faced with the DELTA demands placed on us (Kraut & Korman, Chapter One). The chapters in this volume offer invariably interesting perspectives on important facets of the field that will serve us as well in the future as Viteles's perspective (1932) on industrial psychology did into the 1950s. It is useful from my vantage point to note that in both Viteles and the present volume the influence of the zeitgeist on the topics covered is obvious. Viteles had numerous chapters on fatigue and monotony, two issues associated with the advent of the then-new world of manufacturing industries. In the present case, the issues of information technology and the new employment contract dominate the chapters. Given the influence of the current zeitgeist on the issues that dominate our efforts, the one guarantee we can make is that the topics of concern will be different in the next volume of articles dealing with the changing nature of work. The good news is that we have been an extraordinarily adaptable and flexible bunch, neither wavering from the principles by which we demonstrate our effectiveness nor shrinking from the new demands the environment presents.

The mere existence of the present volume, combined with other recent publications (for example, Cascio, 1995; Howard, 1995; Rousseau, 1997), is a sign of vitality and a willingness to confront ourselves when faced with change. Our willingness simultaneously to try new applications of our theories and models and also demand evidence that what we are doing has validity has served us well and helped us avoid succumbing to the seduction of success. As Miller (1990) has shown, success can be the progenitor of demise when people persist in doing what yielded success in the first place. Miller shows that many organizations experience a plateau in their growth because they continue to pursue, with ever-increasing refinement, that which made them successful in the first place. He describes Procter & Gamble as a company that went from being a salesman to a drifter, losing its way; he writes of Texas Instruments as a company that went from being a craftsman to a tinkerer. In both cases, malaise in growth is a function of the failure to adapt to changes occurring around the organization. In I/O and HRM we *sense and respond* to the zeitgeist rather than allow it simply to overwhelm (see Noe, Hollenbeck, Gerhart, & Wright, 1997, Chapter One, for an incisive discussion of HRM adapting to change). John Stuart Mill made the point well: "History shows that great economic and social forces flow like a tide over communities only half-conscious of that which is befalling them. Wise statesmen foresee what time is thus bringing and try to shape institutions and model men's thoughts and purposes in accordance with the change that is silently coming on." I/O psychologists and HRM professionals have been such a breed.

A Framework for Exploring the Change That Is Coming Not-So-Silently

Figure 14.1 offers one way in which to visualize the connectedness of environmental turbulence and the issues of interest to I/O psychologists. It begins with the issues identified so neatly by Kraut and Korman (in Chapter One of this volume) with the DELTA label: demographic changes, economic changes, legal changes, technological changes, and changes in attitudes and values. As Kraut and Korman noted, these changes have repercussions on the issues salient to I/O psychology. Next, the figure presents some consequences of the turbulence in the larger environment—the kind of work that people perform, where it is performed, and the nature of the relationships at work—between workers and between workers and the larger organization. These changes in turn suggest a number of consequences for I/O and HRM. For example, if the nature of work relationships changes with the advent of teams and the flattening of hierarchies, what do we know about teams and hierarchies and how should we respond? And if technology changes the nature of work, how should we study what workers do and the knowledge, skills, abilities, and other attributes (KSAOs) required to do it? How shall we recruit and select workers for what the authors here refer to as the "new reality?" And what kinds of leadership and management experiences are required to lead effectively

**Figure 14.1. Environmental Turbulence and
Issues of Interest to Industrial-Organizational
Psychology and Human Resource Management.**

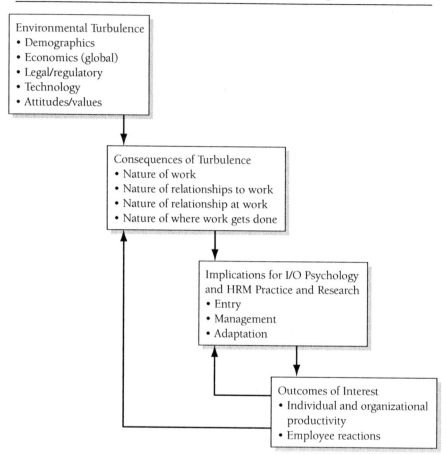

the people in and the organizations of the present and future? Finally, the figure presents the kinds of outcomes or criteria that have been of interest to us—employee reactions like job satisfaction and other attitudes, and individual and organizational productivity. In the following paragraphs, I will use Figure 14.1 as a frame of reference for a discussion of the issues raised in the chapters of this book. As I proceed, I will present some conclusions by way of two metathemes that stood out for me as I had the pleasure of reading and considering the insights here.

Issues of Environmental Turbulence

DELTA is good! Kraut and Korman's acronym captures well the issues that one reads about in contemporary treatments of changes affecting modern U.S. organizations and the people in them (Cascio, 1995; Dunnette, 1998; Katzell & Austin, 1992; Noe and others, 1997; Rousseau, 1997; Ulrich, 1996). Each of the other chapters in this volume reiterates the DELTA themes, or close relations thereof, attributing the changes observed in organizations to these environmental and social forces, with subsequent changes in the focus of our own work and how we as scholars and practitioners carry it out. As I read over the descriptions of these changes, I was struck by the fact that all of those noted are external to psychology, I/O psychology, and HRM.

Within I/O psychology itself, the most significant change I observe is the introduction and exploration of meta-analysis and, specifically, validity generalization (for example, Hunter & Schmidt, 1990). I am not the only one to see the advent of meta-analytic techniques as of central importance to I/O psychology. Dunnette (1998, p. 138) notes, "This [meta-analysis] clearly is one of the major methodological advances made over the last twenty years in industrial and organizational psychology." Issues of the transportability of validity have vexed I/O psychology since early times (Guion, 1998), and documentation of the stability of validity across settings is a dramatic accomplishment with considerable potential power. This is true because if validity is transportable across settings, it may also be transportable across the kinds of DELTA forces that form the context for this book. Does the new reality change validity? Perhaps not, and if so that is of considerable import.

Within psychology itself, changes have been important for issues related to understanding people at work. I think here of what might be called the "cognitive revolution" in psychology, as new conceptual and methodological approaches emerging in cognitive science have considerable relevance for such diverse topics as motivation (the resource allocation model; Kanfer, 1990), attitudes (the social cognition construct and measurement; Brief, 1998), and performance appraisal (the information processing models; Murphy & Cleveland, 1991). Also important have been advancements in understanding behavior as a correlate of familial and genetic heritability. Job satisfaction and other attitudes appear to be at least as much a product of the durability of personality over time (Staw, Bell, & Clausen, 1986) as of situational influences, suggesting a dispositional component to these attitudes. Such findings obviously have implications for personnel selection (for example, hire happy people and they will be happy employees, and perhaps, deliver superior service). Of course, personality itself has been rediscovered in psychology in the form of the five-factor model, perhaps legitimizing it for use in research and practice (see Hough & Schneider, 1996). I say "perhaps legitimizing" because despite the misinterpretation of Stogdill's review (1948) and the seemingly negative review of Guion and Gottier (1965), personality has been alive and well in practice, especially for the selection of managers and executives (for example, Bentz, 1992).

In light of the contemporary importance placed on dispositional and personality issues, it is interesting to realize that Viteles (1932) dealt with the subject of job satisfaction as worker maladjustment—something attributable to the worker and not to the workplace. It is also interesting in this light to reflect on the chapters by Korman (Chapter Two) and Callahan and Greenhaus (Chapter Seven) in this volume, both of which observe a move from the *organizational* career to the *self-managed* career as a function of the new employment contract.

Thus, the first metatheme I identify in these two chapters and others (for example, Rothstein, Chapter Four, and Noer, Chapter Twelve) is that of *the individual*—individual efficacy, individual responsibility, and indeed individual initiative (Frese, Kring, Soose, & Zempel, 1996)—that is again alive and well when we think about people in the workplace. If one looks into the genesis of the functionalist school of psychology out of which I/O and modern HRM grew, the current emphasis on individual initiative is not surprising. What is surprising is that the era of what Noer calls "codependence" (which lasted, say, from 1960 to 1985) has come to such a dramatic and screeching halt. Noer argues that what might be called the *human relations movement* in HRM actually created a situation in which the implicit contract between organization and employee was based on mutual codependence—organizations provided security for employees and employees provided loyalty to the organization. In his view, codependency is dead, and both the individual and organizations must face up to the new reality.

But is codependency really dead? The authors of the present chapters seem to me to have what might be called "large-organization envy." The chapters are written from the perspective of what happens in the companies of *Fortune*—the Fortune 500 or maybe the Fortune 2000—but to my mind not in the realm of *Inc.*, where most people work. Large companies certainly went through dramatic downsizing in the ten years between 1985 and 1995, with its accompanying trauma (Korman, Chapter Two; Noer, Chapter Twelve), but during the same period the unemployment rate in the United States dropped to new lows (nationally 4.5 percent in 1998). How can this be? The answer is that most people (perhaps as many as 80 percent) work in small and medium-size companies (under five hundred people) and the number of such companies is growing (National Alliance of Business, 1996). These are companies that I/O researchers and practitioners rarely if ever enter—such firms either can't pay for the I/O practitioner or the samples are too small! And still, HRM is required in small companies too (see May, 1997).

In fact, we probably know very little about the typical employment relationship of workers in the United States because we do not consult with the companies they work for and we do not study them. I suspect that codependence and the old psychological employment contract, among other practices, is alive and well in most companies today—and not just in smaller companies. When Malden Mills (the factory that makes Polartec, a synthetic fleece used in outdoor clothing for companies the likes of Lands' End) burned down in Maine last year, the owner continued to pay his workers while the factory was rebuilt. Codependency with customers is also alive and well—and growing. In marketing the concept is called *relationship marketing*, connoting the desire to build long-term loyalty and commitment from customers; these constructs are isomorphic with the idea of organizational commitment so well studied by organizational researchers (see, for example, Christopher, Payne, & Ballantyne, 1991). I must say I was very pleased to see the emphasis that this volume places on customers—it seemed customers were everywhere, as they should be (Schneider & Bowen, 1995).

These cautions about too quickly concluding that the "new reality" and the "new employment contract" are in fact the dominant reality for most people and most organizations do not diminish my belief that there is indeed a new reality and a new contract for a significant portion of the work population and work organizations. In fact, identifying these issues, even if the identification is for a relatively smaller number of organizations and workers than many authors presume, can be very useful. It can be very useful because the chances are good that the larger and more sophisticated organizations are experiencing these trends first and that other firms will soon follow. What the authors in the present volume have accomplished for us is to outline what the *leading edge of change might be,* helping us to avoid the somnambulant method of dealing with the coming change that Mill described.

Let me summarize what I said in this section. I presented a metatheme I picked up in the chapters of this volume regarding the idea that people are "back" as a central causative agent in the management of their careers, work life, and work attitudes. No longer is the organization to be counted on to supply the womb-to-tomb golden handcuffs that were characteristic of the "fat times" of the post–World War II period, roughly 1960 to 1985, dominated by the baby boomers. I offered a caution on this metatheme, however, on the assumption that these changes are universal. The changes to date may for the most part apply only to larger organizations, not the smaller ones (with less than five hundred employees) in which most people work. I support such a conclusion and urge researchers to begin to study the issues raised under DELTA in smaller companies. Such an effort would require creating one or more consortia of smaller companies, with perhaps different university settings being responsible for different regions of the country but sharing methodological approaches (Abraham Korman, personal communication, September 11, 1998).

But there are other contingencies, for the most part correlates of company size, that may also be important with regard to the universality of the new reality and the need for individual employees to take control, such as the following: Most companies are not directly involved in the global economy (most are small to medium-size service businesses); most companies have not and never will encounter the legal issues regarding age, gender, and racial discrimination that occupy many of us; the nature of employment relationships has remained very stable over time and, I predict, will continue to remain so in the future (Uchitelle & Kleinfeld, 1996). I have stated these as absolutes, as if I am creating dichotomies between large and small companies. Actually, all of these differences exist on a continuum, because surely there are small companies that have global involvement if only because they make products for larger companies that are directly involved in global markets. And surely there are small and medium-size companies that have legal issues related to HRM practices. That is not the point; the point I wish to make is that there is good reason to suspect that DELTA is generally more accurate as a description of environmental turbulence in larger than smaller organizations.

Consequences of the Turbulence

The second box in Figure 14.1 focuses on some of the consequences associated with turbulence in the world of work. Although they may not be universal, the changes exist: there have been changes in the nature of work, where it is performed, with whom it is performed, and the relationship between work and worker. These issues are presented well in Sanchez and Levine's chapter (Chapter Three) on job analysis. Their exposition of the issues is very evenhanded, not throwing out the job-analysis baby with the new-reality-of-the-workplace bathwater. Particularly useful was their isolation of the contrasts between *the job* as perhaps conceptualized in the old edition of the *Dictionary of Occupational Titles* and *work* as it is currently designed. Sanchez and Levine appear to tell us that we must certainly adapt the technology of job analysis to changes in information technology, hierarchy, and employment relationships, but that a focus on work and an understanding of the KSAOs required to perform work effectively is still necessary. Whether it is a temporary, contract, or part-time worker who is hired, issues of competency and conscientiousness will still remain salient (Rothstein, Chapter Four). They also describe well the recent efforts to conceptualize performance at work broadly. Here I refer specifically to issues of what has been called *citizenship behavior* or *contextual performance* as important facets of total job performance (for example, Borman & Motowidlo, 1997).

Sanchez and Levine's chapter stands in some contrast to others who have written about the death of the job and the subsequent loss of identity for I/O psychologists (see Pearlman in Church, 1996, pp. 58–59). In this light, a quotation from Michelle Crosby of Aon, formerly HRStrategies (Church, 1996, p. 57) is informative: "Certainly jobs have been evolving and changing dramatically at many levels, in many organizations, and in many industries. Technological advances, job redesign, organizational restructuring, empowerment, teaming, and a host of other changes have impacted the jobs individuals perform. However, in most instances, people still have jobs."

One way in which many jobs have changed is that work is done more and more frequently in teams. Gibson and Kirkman (Chapter Five) do a very helpful job of identifying the boundary conditions in which teams appear to be effective. I think this list (for example, high task interdependence, high degree of cooperation and coordination required) is useful because teams are (a) not always required and (b) not always easy to implement. On this latter issue, the authors' detailing the organizational requirements for teams to be effective is also helpful; just setting up teams and expecting them to be functional and effective is simply not going to work. Teams must be trained to function as a team, for example.

As the nature of work and the nature of the relationship between worker and organization evolve, one of the forces leading to these changes—information technology—can also be used as a tactic for coping with the changes. Although Sanchez and Levine note several of these uses of technology for work analysis, Rothstein provides a real service in elaborating the many ways in which potential employees and potential employers may attract and recruit each other. Testing on the Web, specifying employee requirements for a match via the Web—who knows how else the Web may be used? Clearly, traveling to conduct an interview is inefficient given televiewing capabilities, which can also permit on-line taping for reliability checks in ratings. Assessment centers are obviously in the works when distance learning permits a coach in Walla Walla, Washington, to help a manager in London (Hollenbeck & McCall, Chapter Eight).

While I was reading Rothstein's chapter, it occurred to me that the new alliances made possible through the Web are merely more efficient ways of handling the job and employee matching that was characteristic of the early 1900s. Immigration waves to the United

States yielded all manner of self-help groups and the establishment of job placement services targeted on common ethnic/religious/racial identity. There were both formal (for example, Jewish Social Services) and informal (the local parish priest) matchmakers to help employers and employees find one another. The Talent Alliance, then, takes a well-developed tactic for matching work and workers and puts it on the Web, making it available to the broadest interests possible.

Another consequence of the turbulence has been the way in which work is organized. Two effects have been an increased use of teams, as noted earlier (Gibson & Kirkman, Chapter Five), and a concomitant increased focus on worker participation and empowerment (Klein, Smith-Major, & Ralls, Chapter Ten). Clear in the Gibson and Kirkman chapter is an emphasis on deliverables and accountability. But this theme is not associated just with the Gibson and Kirkman chapter. I see accountability for the attainment of organizational goals almost everywhere! For example, Banks and May (Chapter Six) emphasize that performance management systems must be linked to organizational goals and requirements from the individual on up at all levels of the organization. Similarly, Hollenbeck and McCall (Chapter Eight) focus on leadership development for anyone who can move the organization forward. In their chapter, these authors continually use phrases like "move the business forward," "move the organization forward," "drive for results," "continuous focus on results"—a far cry indeed from the take-whatever-you-would-like-to-take-and-we-will-pay management and leadership development models of the 1960s. Also, in the chapter on diversity (with the emphasis on cross-cultural and global diversity rather than within-organization gender or racial diversity), Fulkerson and Tucker (Chapter Eleven) also come down in favor of results—results *and values* to be sure, but results, nevertheless. I just received a flyer from the International Quality and Productivity Center for a conference entitled "Transforming the Recruiting and Staffing Function into a Value-Added Business Partner." Recruitment and staffing as a business partner? Yes, in the new reality.

Perhaps most interestingly, that old standby of the humanistic organization and codependency—the employee attitude survey—also emerges with an organizational performance bent. Kraut and

Saari (Chapter Thirteen) address such issues as the design of surveys to assess strategy implementation, the analysis of surveys as leading indicators of organizational performance, and the use of surveys to assess immediate issues of concern to management— how the merger or acquisition is playing out among employees, how the new training programs are being received, for example. Bottom line, they say, employee surveys in the new era will be aligned to corporate objectives in terms of content, timing, and language— a far cry from survey items focused on whether one's supervisor (does anyone these days have a "supervisor?") is friendly. It is fair to note that Kraut and Saari attempt to retain such "old-fashioned" topics as work and life balance and career development, but these definitely take a backseat to surveys that target organizational performance issues directly.

But if we have known since Brayfield and Crockett (1955) that individual employee attitudes are at best modestly related to performance, how can Kraut and Saari promote this perspective? Times have changed and we now know that individual employee attitudes are related to contextual performance in the form of organizational citizenship behaviors (for example, Organ & Ryan, 1995) and that individual employee attitude data *in the aggregate* are related to important organizational outcomes (for example, Schneider, White, & Paul, 1998). On this latter conclusion, Kraut and Saari do not elaborate on the fact that they have jumped the level of analysis on the reader from the individual to the aggregate and that it is these aggregated, business-focused, attitude survey data that are related, for example, to customer satisfaction (Schneider, Ashworth, Higgs, & Carr, 1996) and high school performance effectiveness (Ostroff, 1992).

The second metatheme I identify in the chapters, then, is the focus on *organizational performance,* the attainment of organizational objectives, and in general, the alignment of HR systems with the goals of the organization. Whether it is diversity, employee surveys, leadership and management development, or more usual processes for targeting outcomes like performance management, the chapters strongly emphasize the bottom line or assumed reasons for the bottom line.

In contrast, less emphasis than I would have suspected is placed on the issue of *where* work will be done. A potpourri of facts follows. Estimates vary depending on when the survey was taken, but as much as 10 percent of workers now work continuously or mostly from home; in 1950, 32 percent of all employees worked in manufacturing whereas by 1990 it was 17 percent; IBM cut the cost of supporting four hundred thousand square feet of office space by providing employees with laptops and having them telecommute. It would seem that *where* people work will have considerable consequences for how they are hired, compensated, trained, supervised, and so forth. If people are working alone in their homes what happens to teamwork? If people are working alone in their homes what happens to performance management? In other words, in addition to the questions raised by many of the authors about the changing nature of the employment contract regarding work *in organizations,* there are other interesting issues to be raised when the work is being done *in the home* rather than in the organization.

Indeed, there is a hint in the chapters by Kraut and Korman (Chapter One), Korman (Chapter Two), and Rothstein (Chapter Four) that what we now know as the *employing organization* may be a less viable concept than it has been. When workers move from organization to organization at their own initiative or during restructuring, when they are on contract, or when they work at home and may have never even been to "the company," then what is the meaning of "the organization?" For me this question is closely allied to the personal initiative theme I raised earlier. The organizational career may be dead, but the personal career is not (Arthur & Rousseau, 1996; Hall, 1996). As Tim Hall (1997, p. 61) recently put it: "[The career] resides more within the individual today than within an organization, but the career is alive and well."

Implications for I/O Practice and Research

I will cluster the implications of the changes just reviewed into three categories: *issues of entry, issues of management,* and *issues of adaptation.* As I discuss each of these, I will note when the two meta-themes identified earlier seem relevant.

Issues of Entry

By the term issues of entry, I refer to recruitment and training in particular as well as to organizational socialization—for both employees and management. Sanchez and Levine (Chapter Three) list many of the individual attributes that are going to be required in a world where personal initiative and a focus on organizational outcomes are part of the new reality. For example, they note that in a work world of teams, interpersonal competence and sensitivity to cultural differences will be required, and in a work world where personal initiative will be required, people will require emotional stability. Rothstein (Chapter Four) makes the interesting observation that the entry-level requirements for new workers who will be full-time and permanent (the "core employees") may be quite different than for those hired as temporary or contract workers. The latter, filling much more specific and perhaps temporary needs, will have to possess specific *task* skills whereas the permanent workers may have to possess more *work* skills (using Sanchez and Levine's distinction). Rothstein also identifies the need to develop measures of interpersonal and team competencies and to adapt effectively to changing environments.

Managerial and executive selection does not escape these requirements, according to Moses and Eggebeen (Chapter Nine). They emphasize the idea that the most significant attribute executives require is to keep their eyes on the future. But the authors add the very important contingency notion that this future may differ for organizations in different life stages, cultures, and life cycles of production—and, I would add, in different industries and in different market segments within industries.

I/O and HRM research and practice sorely need to take account of these kinds of contingencies if we are going to be a partner in organizational performance. There is no right kind of training program, performance management system, or executive selection system; the "right" system is what fits the requirements of a specific organization at a specific life stage and in a particular context. The trouble is that this is a moving target, requiring constant monitoring and continual change.

After the people are recruited and hired, they must be trained and socialized. The chapter on leadership development by Hollenbeck and McCall (Chapter Eight) is very up-to-date in what seems to be happening in organizations today and also appropriately skeptical about whether any of it is working. It seemed as if each of the topics the authors mention—360-degree feedback, coaching—was followed by a statement such as "evidence is sparse" or "no hard evidence." People seem to like these educational and development opportunities but, as Kirkpatrick (1959, 1960) showed many years ago, positive reactions may not be reflected in learning. Is it possible that I/O and HRM have become *only* practice and not research when it comes to managers and executives? If this is the case, it would not be in keeping with the hard-nosed image we portray to the business world and requires serious soul searching. Bottom line, if we are to demonstrate that we are making a contribution then it would be wise to demonstrate it in the hiring, socialization, and development of the highest-level people in the organization—and their successors. It may be time, for example, for people doing individual assessment to join forces with some researchers and document the validity we believe exists in these processes. Or perhaps an institution like the Center for Creative Leadership might capture the work it has accomplished on 360-degree feedback and put it in a research mode to estimate the effects on organizational performance for companies. Such multi-organizational research, by Mark Huselid (1995) for example, has begun to reveal the very significant impact that human resource practices can have on organizational performance. It would seem a ripe time also to show how these more individually focused efforts, such as executive selection and management development, affect organizational performance as well (Schneider, Smith, & Sipe, forthcoming).

The training of nonmanagers did not receive very much attention in the current volume, although it might be a crucial issue for future organizations, following from the predicted pace of technological changes, the predicted increase in diversity in the workplace, and the predicted increased movement of workers from one organization to another. This latter subject raises another topic not explicitly considered in a chapter of this volume—new employee socialization. As employees move from organization to organization, by what procedures do we help them "learn the ropes?" Louis (1990) has documented the various agents of socialization in organizations, including what might be called *self-socialization*, which the authors of the present chapters apparently expected would occur. But what if self-socialization is not effective alone and what if it fails to capture the essence of the organizational goals that apply to the new setting, what then can organizations do to promote appropriate socialization? Formal training, if it exists, may be one vehicle for teaching local attitudes and values, but research on the importance of early adjustment and fit for later satisfaction, commitment, and performance (O'Reilly, Chatman, & Caldwell, 1991) suggests that socialization issues must be carefully explored in the new reality. For if socialization of new employees is not managed explicitly, that does not mean it fails to happen. As with sex, it is better to manage knowledge acquisition than just let it happen!

The DELTA forces outlined by Kraut and Korman certainly have many implications for the training of new employees, too many to discuss in depth here. Suffice it to say that training in self-management principles (Korman, Chapter Two; Callahan & Greenhaus, Chapter Seven), adapting to new settings (Rothstein, Chapter Four), and working in teams (Gibson & Kirkman, Chapter Five) with diverse others (Fulkerson and Tucker, Chapter Eleven) look to be very important topics over and above the more immediate task-based training that has been traditional. And in keeping with the second major theme I identified, it appears that all of these must be designed to focus on organizational goals. Bowen, Ledford, and Nathan (1991) have written about the need to recruit and hire *for the organization,* not just the job. Their logic is that with the broadening of jobs into work, with increased movement within organizations, and with decentralization and flattening of hierarchies, a focus on the contributions that individuals can make to the total organization rather than to just one job is required. The idea, then, would be to tie down the strategy of the organization and the goals to be achieved and then select people who empathize with them and have the skills and competencies to contribute to those goals.

For example, I have designed both assessment exercises and interviews for hiring workers for *all* jobs in a bank that focused on service quality as a strategic goal. The empirically based reasons for the focus on all jobs were these: data revealed that management behavior was central to the creation of a service climate, which was, in turn, related to customer perceptions of service quality; and results from statistical analyses also revealed that the degree to which employees reported they received the *internal* help (service) they needed to do their work was significantly and directly related to the service quality customers said they received (Schneider &

others, 1998). How entry processes are managed at all levels of the organization are critical for access to the people who will have the initiative required in the new reality and for the accomplishment of organizational goals.

Issues of Management

The second set of implications for I/O and HRM concerns the broad topic of management. Here I refer to the issues of managing and leading at all levels of the organization. If we accept that there is a new reality, then the new management and the new leadership fit well with the idea expressed in the earlier quotation from Gene Jennings. The buzzing complexity and ever-evolving nature of the job of management and leadership in the organization of the future is almost overwhelming. Just as one example, consider the "simple" issues raised by Moses and Eggebeen (Chapter Nine) with regard to the life stage of the organization and then add such issues as the culture in which the organization functions (Fulkerson and Tucker, Chapter Eleven) and the requirement to assess constantly the state of the organization with regard to changing superior-subordinate relationships, the presence of temporary and contract workers (Rothstein, Chapter Four), and mergers and acquisitions (Noer, Chapter Twelve), and we gain some understanding about the anxiety about which Korman (Chapter Two) writes so passionately.

Fortunately, Noer (Chapter Twelve) provides a checklist of ways by which such management anxiety might be reduced. Attention to the five factors he mentions could well be an antidote to, at a minimum, not knowing what if anything one can do! As practitioners, we can adopt the role of "reality tester" for management and leadership and inform them of ways in which the organization might effectively struggle with the ambiguity caused by actions seen as necessary to remain competitive. In the following list, I first note Noer's suggestions and then add my own commentary.

Focus on Those Who Remain After Downsizing
Researchers and many practitioners have been consumed by the anxiety of those who have been laid off; those who stay have been abandoned. Yet if organizations are going to be successful, we know

for sure that the act of carrying out downsizing is not going to do it for them; it is what *else* they do that will matter (Cascio, 1993; Whetten & Cameron, 1990). Organizations must ensure that they have the vision not of cost-cutting but of performance enhancement to accompany the downsizing. This will be revealed by what they do in the way of training, performance management for those who remain, and learning from those who remain about how to improve. Klein, Smith-Major, and Ralls (Chapter Ten) provide an insightful list of conditionals about the appropriateness of participation, and they would, I am sure, agree with the research literature that says participation works when those who participate have the knowledge required for effective performance. The key is to focus HR practices on what it takes to be effective.

Let Go of Outdated Theories About Motivation

In 1957, Chris Argyris published the first of a series of books that later appeared in the 1960s (for example, Katz & Kahn, 1963; Likert, 1961; McGregor, 1960), all espousing the de-infantilization of employees. Their new model proposed the following: treat employees like adults, not like children, and they will behave like adults. It is now forty or so years later and we have, I hope, seen the light. And the light we see is expressed well in the metatheme concerning individual initiative that I identified earlier. Were I an I/O psychologist, I would design a new measure (probably an assessment center set of exercises) for the selection of executives and managers that tapped into their inclinations to treat people as adults, not children. My hypothesis is that such a measure would explain a meaningful amount of variance in the later performance of the organization. Theories take a long time to die and the theory that we need to protect workers from the harsh realities of life must be replaced by one that offers them partnership in that harsh reality.

Discard or Adapt Old Technologies
Not Relevant for the New Reality

Job analysis, performance appraisal and management, leadership development, employee attitude surveys, recruitment and selection, and grappling with diversity—these are just some of the new and adapted techniques outlined in the present volume. I feel most fortunate to have these chapters as a standing checklist of the issues I need to assess in every organization with which I work. That kind of checklist should prove useful to every HRM manager.

One of the books I already use as a checklist when working in organizations is *Reframing Organizations: Artistry, Choice, and Leadership,* by Bolman and Deal (1997). This book presents five different frames or lenses through which organizations can be viewed as human systems. For example, three of the frames are the political frame, the symbolic frame, and the human resource frame. Because I have these different lenses through which to see organizations, I gain a fuller appreciation of the diverse ways in which they are simultaneously functioning for the people in them. In the future, I will use this volume in the same way, because it reveals the varieties of tactics by which HRM systems in organizations may help cope with the changes that are coming on. Now I need a similar elaboration of the political and the symbolic frames!

Be an Optimist

In graduate school we are all taught to be so critical that we tend to carry this critical stance into the organizations with which or in which we work. We are great at identifying what is wrong, what needs fixing, and so forth. In the new reality, we must learn to acknowledge the positive, that which works and that which has permitted organizations to survive. A number of years ago I realized that my organizational diagnoses of existing companies read as if the organization just has to be a failure. It was this realization that changed my stance. I now believe that organizations survive because of what the people who work in them do, that identifying what they do well is the key to the future.

Spread the Word on What Works

Well, we are surely trying to do that here!

Noer's view (Chapter Twelve) is optimistic, grounded in the idea that what is good and done well needs to be applauded and appreciated; it is a model of change that is psychologically uplifting and that deserves increased adoption by us as we increasingly take on the role of change agent in organizations. However, as I have said throughout this commentary, it is crucial that we not focus overly on the individual and the individual role and initiative to the exclusion of the demands for the organization to grow and prosper. Thus, the second metatheme I raised concerned the importance of focusing HRM on organizational goals. Management in particular determines what the goals of the organization actually are through its behavior. Mission statements and advertising are words but behavior is communication, and as McGregor (1960) noted many years ago, behavior determines the climate of the organization in which and to which people respond. In the example reported earlier for service quality, what managers do determines the message employees receive about what *they* should do. I now think of the climate or culture of the organization as what employees believe management believes—and they develop this idea based on what management *does*. How HRM carries out its role— what it emphasizes in recruitment, selection, and training, where the emphases are in performance management and reward systems, how the issues of "core employees" and contract workers are handled, how much and over what issues participation is encouraged and attended to, and what issues are the foci of employee attitude surveys—these will truly communicate the message of the strategic focus of the organization and the goals that matter (Schneider, Gunnarson, & Niles-Jolly, 1994).

Issues of Adaptation

By adaptation, I mean the acts of coping and adjusting. It will take adaptation to accept and work in the new paradigm. Everything we do will have to be examined for its contemporary relevance. As is probably obvious by now, I believe that we have been very good at adapting over time and that we continue to be. Maybe it is in our genes, but I/O psychologists and the folks who go into HRM appear to be a breed who require proof before accepting something yet are always willing to try something new to see if it actually works! I guess it must be the curiosity factor that permits us to be willing to try new things—and not require a decade of philosophical musings before being willing to try it. Andrew Pettigrew (1990), a sociologist by training, has observed that I/O psychologists in particular are not comfortable wringing their hands about definitional issues; they go out and measure to see what is there.

Dealing with the two metathemes I have identified will take some adaptation on our part. We like our structure, we like our association with management, and we believe in job satisfaction so much that it is the most studied topic in the field, so it will be difficult to let go of the paternalistic model we have regarding employees. It will be less difficult for us to adapt to a focus on organizational goals, but this will not be as easy as it would seem at first blush. Let me explain.

We have been a very individually focused field, as would be expected of a field that focuses on people. The problem is that most managers think about their *organization* and care about individuals for the most part only insofar as those individuals perform in the aggregate to facilitate organizational performance. In both research and practice, though, our level of analysis for theory and data has remained the individual. I suggest that we add to our research whenever possible organizational performance as a relevant outcome (Huselid, 1995).

In sum and with regard to the issue of implications for I/O psychology, I see three meta-issues that will require attention in the new reality: entry processes, management practices, and adaptation needs. Each chapter in this volume raises issues that must be taken into consideration and procedures for taking action that are relevant in dealing with these challenges.

Outcome Focus

The last box in Figure 14.1 addresses outcomes of interest associated with the DELTA forces and HRM practices: individual and organizational performance and employee reactions. I have already devoted several pages to the issue of individual and organizational outcomes of interest in the discussion of my two metathemes. In other words, the individual criterion of interest in future research and practice must be the degree to which individuals are recruited, hired, socialized, and trained to demonstrate personal initiative. In a work world less inclined to take care of (that is, infantilize) employees, individual employees will have to be adults and take control of their futures.

Several chapters in this volume make this point more clearly than I have seen it made before and they serve as sobering reminders of the changes with which we now live. As noted earlier, I have some questions about the universality of the new paradigm for the present time and wonder if—when the majority of the organizations reach the new paradigm—those currently there will be on to something still newer. If it is whitewater that characterizes contemporary work, then there will be new rapids to shoot requiring still new adaptations. When I wrote this chapter (in fall 1998), for example, Japan was in economic turmoil, Northwest Airlines pilots were on strike, the Russian economy (or what was left of it) was in disarray, and the Dow-Jones was down five hundred points for the week. What are the long-term effects for I/O?

Probably anxiety. Perhaps Korman (Chapter Two) is correct, and the employee reaction that will be of most concern to us in the future will be anxiety. But at the same time, I think employees are the silver lining for organizations. I am absolutely convinced (which probably means I'm wrong!) that were it not for the people on the shop floor (or its equivalent) most organizations would have already failed. Poor strategy, inappropriate attention to costs versus revenues, concern for production capacity rather than production quality, a focus on internal standards for judging effectiveness rather than a focus on quality and customer satisfaction, a failure to capitalize on employee knowledge to facilitate long-term organizational learning—these are just some of the ills I have seen. The paradox is that I see them in some of the most successful companies in the country. That is when I began to ask, "How can this be?" And I find individual employees who deliver contextual performance, sneak around their bosses to make things work and do things right, violate rules and guidelines to serve customers, and, indeed, have managers and team leaders who tell them to do this!

Recently Podsakoff and MacKenzie (1997) demonstrated that contextual performance [organizational citizenship behavior (OCB)] is very much linked to organizational performance, and this finding may serve as a strong foundation on which to establish further the link between human resource practices and organizational performance. We know that we can predict OCB at entry (Borman & Motowidlo, 1997) and that employees who have more positive attitudes in the workplace demonstrate higher levels of OCBs (Penner, Midili, & Kegelmeyer, 1997) and deliver superior performance to customers as diverse as R&D clients (Vanderheyden, 1998) and bank customers (Schneider and others, 1998). If I were in HRM in a business setting I would surely focus on creating HRM practices and policies to promote the display of OCBs!

One last item in Figure 14.1 deserves some attention—that is, the two feedback arrows from the outcomes to the implications for I/O and HRM research and practice and to the consequences of turbulence. The outcomes on which we focus become the goals of the organization, and these should affect how work is organized and how and where it is accomplished as well as the foci of entry, management, and adaptation systems and procedures. The choice of outcomes on which to focus cannot be an end; such a focus has consequences that must be made explicit for the way the whole HRM process works. Although we can have little control over the DELTA forces, we can certainly influence the responses to them through the goals we choose and the systems we establish to accomplish them.

Conclusion

HRM in the workplace is part of a larger system. This chapter makes it sound as if it stands alone and the other chapters in this volume have taken a similar angle, but this is obviously an over-simplification of the way the world works. Schneider and Bowen (1995, p. 5) referred to this perspective on HRM as falling into the "human resources trap." By this they meant that HRM seems to take on the burden for everything in the organization because people do everything in organizations and HRM is responsible for people. In some abstract sense this is true, but marketing, operations, production, finance, legal—not to discount general line management—must be integrated with and partner to what happens in the organization. The modern organization is evolving into an interdependent set of functions because the silos got too high and the walls supporting them too thick. Although we will most likely have silos again sometime in the future, it is certainly time that HRM and research focus on the interrelationships across functions in organizations if we are to gain a more complete understanding of what makes for organizational effectiveness.

I find the high level of involvement of I/O and HRM in this venture to be both liberating and challenging. This is true because it is critical for our society that work organizations continue to be successful and effective. The two themes that stood out for me in this volume—the individual as causative agent and an emphasis on organizational goal accomplishment—make me feel the future of our field is both challenging and bright. The sky is not falling at all—it is opening up.

References

Argyris, C. (1957). *Personality and organization.* New York: HarperCollins.

Arthur, M. B., & Rousseau, D. M. (Eds.). (1996). *The boundaryless career: A new employment principle for a new organizational era.* San Francisco: Jossey-Bass.

Bentz, V. J. (1992). Contextual issues in predicting high-level performance: Contextual richness as a criterion consideration in personality research with executives. In K. E. Clark & M. B. Clark (Eds.), *Measures of leadership.* West Orange, NJ: Leadership Library of America.

Bolman, L. G., & Deal, T. E. (1997). *Reframing organizations: Artistry, choice, and leadership* (2nd ed.). San Francisco: Jossey-Bass.

Borman, W. C., & Motowidlo, S. J. (1997). Task performance and contextual performance: The meaning for personnel selection research. *Human Performance, 10,* 99–110.

Bowen, D. E., Ledford, G. E., Jr., & Nathan, B.E. (1991). Hiring for the organization, not the job. *Academy of Management Executive, 5,* 35–51.

Brayfield, A. H., & Crockett, W. H. (1955). Employee attitudes and employee performance. *Psychological Bulletin, 52,* 396–424.

Brief, A. P. (1998). *Attitudes in and around organizations.* Thousand Oaks, CA: Sage.

Cascio, W. F. (1993). Downsizing: What do we know? What have we learned? *Academy of Management Executive, 7,* 95–104.

Cascio, W. F. (1995). Whither industrial and organizational psychology in a changing world. *American Psychologist, 50,* 928–939.

Christopher, M., Payne, A., & Ballantyne, D. (1991). *RM: Bringing quality, customer service, and marketing together.* Oxford, UK: Butterworth-Heinemann.

Church, A. H. (1996). From both sides now: The changing of the job. *The Industrial-Organizational Psychologist, 33,* 52–62.

Dunnette, M. D. (1998). Emerging trends and vexing issues in industrial and organizational psychology. *Applied Psychology: An International Review, 47,* 129–153.

Frese, M., Kring, W., Soose, A., & Zempel, J. (1996). Personal initiative at work: Differences between East and West Germany. *Academy of Management Journal, 39,* 37–63.

Frost, R. (1914). The black cottage. In R. Frost & E. C. Lathem (Eds.), *The poetry of Robert Frost.* New York: Holt.

Guion, R. M. (1998). *Assessment, measurement, and prediction for personnel decisions.* Hillsdale, NJ: Erlbaum.

Guion, R. M., & Gottier, R. F. (1965). Validity of personality measures in personnel selection. *Personnel Psychology, 18,* 135–164.

Haire, M. (1956). *Psychological foundations of management.* New York: McGraw-Hill.

Hall, D. T. (Ed.) (1996). *The career is dead—Long live the career.* San Francisco: Jossey-Bass.

Hall, D. T. (1997). Special challenges of careers in the 21st century. *Academy of Management Executive 1997, 11,* 60–61.

Hough, L. M., & Schneider, R. J. (1996). Personality traits, taxonomies, and applications in organizations. In K. R. Murphy (Ed.), *Individual differences and behavior in organizations* (pp. 31–88). San Francisco: Jossey-Bass.

Howard, A. (Ed.). (1995). *The changing nature of work.* San Francisco: Jossey-Bass.

Hunter, J. E., & Schmidt, F. L. (1990). *Methods of meta-analysis: Correcting error and bias in research findings.* Thousand Oaks, CA: Sage.

Huselid, M. A. (1995). The impact of human resources management practices on turnover, productivity, and corporate financial performance. *Academy of Management Journal, 38,* 635–672.

Jennings, E. E. (1962). *The executive.* New York: HarperCollins.

Kanfer, R. (1990). Motivation theory and industrial and organizational psychology. In M. D. Dunnette & L. M. Hough (Eds.), *Handbook of Industrial and Organizational Psychology* (2nd ed.) (pp. 75–170). Palo Alto, CA: Consulting Psychologists Press.

Kanter, R. M. (1977). *Work and family in the United States: A critical review and agenda for research and productivity.* New York: Russel Sage Foundation.

Katz, D., & Kahn, R. L. (1963). *The social psychology of organizations.* New York: Wiley.

Katzell, R. A., & Austin, J. T. (1992). From then to now: The development of industrial-organizational psychology in the United States. *Journal of Applied Psychology, 77,* 803–835.

Kirkpatrick, D. L. (1959). Techniques for evaluating training programs. *Journal of the American Society of Training Directors, 13,* 3–9, 21–26.

Kirkpatrick, D. L. (1960). Techniques for evaluating training programs. *Journal of the American Society of Training Directors, 14,* 13–18, 28–32.

Likert, R. (1961). *New patterns of management.* New York: McGraw-Hill.

Louis, M. R. (1990). Acculturation in the workplace: Newcomers as lay ethnographers. In B. Schneider (Ed.), *Organizational climate and culture* (pp. 85–129). San Francisco: Jossey-Bass.

May, K. E. (1995). Work in the 21st century: Implications for I/O psychologists. *The Industrial-Organizational Psychologist, 33*(2), 27–28.

First of a series of articles. [See also her articles in *The Industrial-Organizational Psychologist,* 1995 to 1997, *33*(3), *33*(4), *34*(1), *34*(2), *34*(4), *35*(1), *35*(3).]

May, K. E. (1997). Work in the 21st century: Understanding the needs of small businesses. *The Industrial-Organizational Psychologist, 35*(1), 94–98.

McGregor, D. M. (1960). *The human side of enterprise.* New York: McGraw-Hill.

Miller, D. (1990). *The Icarus paradox.* New York: HarperCollins.

Murphy, K. R., & Cleveland, J. N. (1991). *Performance appraisal: An organizational perspective.* Needham Heights, MA: Allyn & Bacon.

National Alliance of Business. (1997). *Workforce development trends.* New York: Author.

Noe, R. A., Hollenbeck, J. R., Gerhart, B., Wright, P. M. (1997). *Human resource management: Gaining a competitive advantage* (2nd ed.). Burr Ridge, IL: Irwin.

O'Reilly, C., III, Chatman, J., & Caldwell, D. F. (1991). People and organizational culture: A profile comparison approach to assessing person-organization fit. *Academy of Management Journal, 34,* 487–516.

Organ, D. W., & Ryan, K. (1995). A meta-analytic review of attitudinal and dispositional predictors of organizational citizenship behavior. *Personnel Psychology, 48,* 775–802.

Ostroff, C. (1992). The relationship between satisfaction, attitudes, and performance: An organizational level analysis. *Journal of Applied Psychology, 77,* 963–974.

The pain of downsizing: What it's really like to live through the struggle to remake a company. (1994, May 9). *Business Week,* pp. 60–70.

Penner, L. A., Midili, A. R., & Kegelmeyer, J. (1997). Beyond job attitudes: A personality and social psychology perspective on the causes of organizational citizenship behavior. *Human Performance, 10,* 111–132.

Pettigrew, A. M. (1990). Conclusion: Organizational climate and culture: Two constructs in search of a role. In B. Schneider (Ed.), *Organizational climate and culture* (pp. 413–432). San Francisco: Jossey-Bass.

Podsakoff, P. M., & MacKenzie, S. B. (1997). Impact of organizational citizenship behavior on organizational performance review and suggestions for future research. *Human Performance, 10,* 133–152.

Rousseau, D. M. (1997). Organizational behavior in a new organizational era. *Annual Review of Psychology, 48,* 515–546.

Schneider, B., Ashworth, S., Higgs, A. C., & Carr, L. (1996). Design, validity, and use of strategically focused employee attitude surveys. *Personnel Psychology, 49,* 695–705.

Schneider, B., & Bowen, D. E. (1995). *Winning the service game.* Boston: Harvard Business School Press.

Schneider, B., Gunnarson, S. K., & Niles-Jolly, K. (1994). Creating the climate and culture of success. *Organizational Dynamics, 23,* 17–29.

Schneider, B., Smith, D. B., & Sipe, W. (forthcoming). Personnel selection psychology: Multilevel considerations. In K. J. Klein, & S.W.J. Kozlowski (Eds.), *Multilevel theory, research, and methods in organizations.* San Francisco: Jossey-Bass.

Schneider, B., White, S. S., & Paul, M. C. (1998). Linking service climate to customer perceptions of service quality: Test of a causal model. *Journal of Applied Psychology, 83,* 150–163.

Staw, B. M., Bell, N. E., & Clausen, J. A. (1986). The dispositional approach to job attitudes: A lifetime longitudinal test. *Administrative Science Quarterly, 31,* 56–77.

Stogdill, R. M. (1948). Personal factors associated with leadership. *Journal of Psychology, 25,* 35–71.

Uchitelle, L., & Kleinfield, N. R. (1996, Mar. 3). On the battlefields of business, millions of casualties. *New York Times,* pp. 1, 26, 28–29. [First of seven articles on downsizing in America.]

Ulrich, D. (1996). *Human resource champions: The next agenda for adding value and delivering results.* Boston: Harvard Business School Press.

Vanderheyden, K. (1998). *The influence of human resources practices and interdepartmental connectedness on the effectiveness of the customer orientation of the R&D department.* Belgium: University of Gent, DeVlerick School of Management.

Viteles, M. S. (1932). *Industrial psychology.* New York: Norton.

Whetten, D. A., & Cameron, K. S. (1990). Organizational level productivity initiatives: The case of downsizing. In D. H. Harris (Ed.), *Organizational linkages: Understanding the productivity paradox.* Washington, DC: National Academy of Sciences.

Name Index

Subject Index

A

Ability to learn: competency in, 131; measuring, 80

Abilities, common core of, 72–73, 79

Accountability: to customers, 48; and environmental turbulence, 341; and teams, 98–99

Action learning, for leadership development, 186–189

Adaptability: assessing, 81–82; to change, 332–333; issues of, 350–351

Administration, and performance management, 138

Allstate, and surveys, 315, 318

American Red Cross, and teams, 98

Antidiscrimination laws, extensions of, 12–13

AON Consulting, and employment processing, 84

Army Beta, 330

Assessment: automated, 77–78; individual, 217; performance, 122–124

Assessment centers: and distance learning, 340; senior-level, 217–218

Assessment Solutions, Inc. (ASI): and employment processing, 84; and interactive simulating, 78–79

Assumptions: changing, in human resource management, 19–20, 28–30; in executive selection, 202–204; in leadership development, 173–174; in performance assessment, 124; and teams, 95–99

AT&T: and career development, 164; and deregulation, 13; downsizing at, 26; and executive selection, 214; and labor pool, 35, 86; and leadership development, 175–176, 183; Management Progress Study at, 213, 216; and teams, 93

Attitudes: change in, 4, 17–19, 154; surveys of, 311–312

Automated Prescreening Process, 77

Avery Dennison, coaching at, 185

B

Baby boom, 6

Baby bust, 6–8

Balanced scorecard, and surveys, 311

Behavior: changes in, 154; cultural dimensions of, 258–259; and executive selection, 214, 220–221

Bell South, downsizing at, 27

Benchmarking, and teams, 110

Benefits: to domestic partners, 18; in labor pool associations, 35, 37

Boeing: downsizing at, 27; and leadership development, 180; and surveys, 315

Boston University, and leadership development, 180

Business problems, and leadership development, 177–178

Business relevance, and global diversity, 262–267

Business schools, for leadership development, 179–181

Business strategy, and performance management, 136

Printed in the United States
34110LVS00002B/299

9 780787 940126

Philosophical

Interrogations

Philosophical

Interrogations:

Interrogations of

Martin Buber,

John Wild,

Jean Wahl,

Brand Blanshard,

Paul Weiss,

Charles Hartshorne,

Paul Tillich

Edited, with an Introduction,
by Sydney and Beatrice Rome

Holt, Rinehart and Winston

New York   Chicago   San Francisco

Library of Congress Catalog Card Number: 63-22050

First Edition

Designer: Ernst Reichl
87554-0114
Printed in the United States of America

Acknowledgments

Tribute is accorded in our Introduction to Paul Weiss, John Irving, Richard Barber, Maurice Friedman, Robert Champigny, Henry Veatch, Newton Stallknecht, Louis Mink, Ellen Haring, William Alston, and William Reese. We here acknowledge their respective contributions with deep gratitude.

We wish also to acknowledge and thank Ingrid Stadler for translating the queries of Metzger; Robert Rosthal for translating Levinas' question; Paul E. Pfuetze for translating the questions initially put to Martin Buber in German; and Elizabeth Zorb for assisting Professor Pfuetze.

We are, finally, beholden to Arthur A. Cohen for his assistance and guidance in bringing this volume to fruition, and, of course, to our querists and to our principal authors, without whose patience and endurance this volume could not have been realized.

Contents

Philosophical

Interrogations

Introduction

I. GENESIS OF THE WORK

These *Philosophical Interrogations* grew out of a proposal made to us some seven years ago. Professor Paul Weiss, founder and editor of the *Review of Metaphysics,* suggested that we assume direction over a project already under way but even then in danger of overwhelming its participants. Weiss had the daring idea of opening the pages of the *Review* to a continuing series of living interrogations. Major contemporary philosophers would be invited to expose their thought to open queries by their professional colleagues. Weiss was convinced that knowledgeable philosophers, aware of the lures and opportunities, as well as of the pitfalls and dangers, that perennially confront the creative philosophic mind, would eagerly come forward to question, even challenge, the directions in which their leaders were going.

Stirred by Weiss's enthusiasm and fully convinced that this would be a pioneering effort and that it would make a vital contribution to the philosophic community, we agreed to supervise the task. We felt that, despite our century's proliferation of conferences, symposia, itinerant lecturing, and endless informal table talk, rarely does a philosopher have the opportunity for a direct confrontation by his colleagues and peers and for a formal, deliberate, and serious response to them. True, in the seventeenth century, such a living interchange of ideas took place between Descartes and a few of his distinguished contemporaries through the devoted auspices of Father Mersenne. But this form of communication has since fallen into desuetude. We perceived in Weiss's proposal an opportunity to revive such vital philosophic discourse.

We found that under the earlier guidance of Richard Barber and the

3

counsel of John Irving, part of the project was well under way. But much more had to be done. How much more we should have, but did not then fully appreciate. Invitations were addressed to a number of major figures in philosophy, both in this country and abroad. We were gratified over the warm interest and the large number of acceptances. Indeed, at once this proved embarrassing to us. More eminent scholars accepted than we could immediately handle.

In order to launch the continuing series of interrogations and to obtain concrete, practical results, we gave initial consideration to those philosophers whose interests and writings would be especially congenial with the existing nuclear participants, as well as to the readers of the *Review of Metaphysics*. No doubt our selection also reflected a personal bias. At that time, as at the present, our philosophical research focused on the phenomenological and existential analysis of large-scale social structures. We were constructing philosophical foundations for a theoretico-empirical science of such structures. We were concerned with the logic of hierarchy and the dialectic of social conflict and participation, with the nature, process, and authenticity of social decision and choice, with the laws of symbolic coding and intentional address in social communication, and with the concatenations of social interactions. This research, known as the Leviathan Research Studies, has developed in two directions simultaneously—the formulation of abstract, formal, quantitative, computerized models, and laboratory experimentation with large groups of live decision-makers who act in symbiotic relation with dynamic computer simulation. Our work has in no small measure been affected by the authors chosen for the initial interrogations.

Our selection of authors also depended on our finding professional philosophers to serve as editorial colleagues and to conduct the interrogations of the individual principal authors. The task we were attempting to impose on our prospective editorial colleagues was a delicate and challenging one. Some colleagues we found able but unwilling, others willing but unable, to devote the intellectual as well as physical effort required to seek out suitable querists, maintain the relevancy and searching quality of the queries, guarantee genuine communication from query to author's reply, and organize an entire individual interrogation. One colleague, indeed, who conducted a most interesting and spirited interrogation, now amiably but resolutely wishes to be disassociated from final responsibility for the interrogation associated with his name. He is Professor Henry Veatch, and the previous sentence attests the delicacy of the task that he and six other colleagues undertook to perform. Between the time when Veatch first solicited queries and the time when his author, Wild, prepared replies, Wild, who has always been a seeker in philosophy, had developed fundamental doubts concerning his former realistic beliefs and had shifted toward phenomenology and existentialism.

To prepare their respective interrogations, co-ordinators were given genuine autonomy and freedom. They were encouraged to exercise independent judgment concerning the selection of querists, the arrangement of materials, the mode of presentation, and the editing of queries and replies, subject to the approval of the principal author. We adopted and followed this policy because we sought not to impose any single prescriptive formula uniformly over all the interrogations. We are deeply convinced that each major philosophic effort is, or aspires toward, an organic unity, and therefore merits unique treatment. We hold, furthermore, that excellence can most surely be evoked from a center of personal enthusiasm, and this we tried to inspire in our editorial colleagues. Too, since the style is the man, we often permitted or even encouraged the sacrifice of a nicety or smoothness of English expression for the sake of greater immediacy and contact with the author's lived and fluid response.

This editorial creed was also extended to the matter of translation. With one author, Buber, we found that every effort to compress his sense of dialogue into a standard sentence structure, or into conventional forms of expression, tended to transform his eloquence into something commonplace. We understand and acknowledge the strength of Friedman's rendition. A frequently roughhewn, but exact, literalness preserves Buber's gaunt build-up and massive simplicity. One cannot separate Buber's style from his thought; he is independent of the laws of grammatical construction. His style is shocking—it is the shock of an existential encounter; it demands an intimate dialogic engagement with Buber, the man. Champigny's liberal translation of Wahl, on the other hand, nicely captures the subtlety and fluency of Wahl's thought. It has been said that the next best thing to an existential awakening is to meet Wahl. But with Wahl, although the encounter is as intense as it is with Buber, it is an embrace, a delicate confluence.

Notwithstanding the foregoing editorial latitude, we did demand clear communication from querist to author. We insisted that the author understand the question. On some occasions, nevertheless, we allowed an author to understand only too well—to reformulate the query so that his philosophical convictions might result in a more fruitful response. But we allowed exceptions even to this rule, for sometimes it is philosophic wisdom to know when no answer is possible.

We also reserved and exercised the right of final editorial review. Upon us fell the unlovely burden to discipline, restructure, cajole, prod —in short, to decide *no* and to provoke *redo*. When an editorial colleague was unwilling to subject his author to severe philosophical criticism, this task reverted to us. Upon occasions, we even presumed to assert that an author's initial draft was not doing justice to his own philosophy. Our insistent demands elicited extensive revisions and modifications in several of the interrogations. And one interrogation even failed completely to meet our standards and had to be undertaken anew from the beginning. But this oppressive role had its rewarding moments. We treasure a letter from one of our authors in which he writes: "You have read my rejoinders with real care, and your queries have been the toughest of the lot. I feel that you have really been following me." Some of the interrogations, on the other hand, are being published with few or no revisions.

Thus a long period of painstaking and often feverish activity followed the efforts to launch the entire series of interrogations. From the outset, there were endless disappointments and frustrations. For reasons of health, heavy lecture engagements, or teaching or publishing obligations, colleagues were unable to meet commitments. Philosophers, moreover, are notoriously mobile and peripatetic, and global communication, even by air mail, is a slow and lengthy process. Once manuscripts were drafted, even the task of obtaining suitable translations from the French and the German was itself no minor hurdle to overcome. That all these and other labors were finally encompassed is owing entirely to the dedicated, zealous, and unstinting generosity of our seven editorial colleagues—Friedman, Veatch, Stallknecht, Mink, Haring, Alston, and Reese—and of our seven principal authors.

Decision had been taken that at least four or five interrogations be fully completed before their serial publication might begin in the *Review of Metaphysics*. When at last a number of finished interrogations lay before us for final review, we were impressed with their excellence, scope, broad appeal, contemporaneity, and solidary relevance to our age. We came to feel that the result of an undertaking of this magnitude was worthy of an audience even broader than the unusually ample and wide-ranging readership of the *Review of Metaphysics*. Encouraged by Paul Weiss, we decided to prepare a selected set of Interrogations for publication in book form as the first volume of a projected series. This first volume, then, includes the interrogations of seven principal figures: Martin Buber, John Wild, Jean Wahl, Brand Blanshard, Paul Weiss, Charles Hartshorne, and Paul Tillich.

II. NATURE OF THE WORK

An international company of more than a hundred querists focus a rich and varied body of criticism on the philosophic thought of these seven individuals. The querists are distinguished scholars whose interests range over social, political and moral issues, psychiatry, phenomenology, art, logic, cosmology, theology. Among these interrogators are jurists, diplomats, political analysts, administrators, doctors and psychiatrists, clergymen, editors, social scientists, critics, linguists, historians, and, of course, educators, theologians, and philosophers. They were selected by their peers, our seven editorial colleagues, because of their intimate knowledge of and their long-standing concern with the contributions and writings of the principal authors. Concerned and knowledgeable, they unhesitatingly subjected the seven authors to a bombardment of questions, probes, observations, disagreements, commentaries, and even spirited eulogies:

Is Buber's "I-Thou" engagement possible? Under what conditions? Is it open to all, even idiots and children? In meeting with other persons, can we always transform the "I-It" attitude of distance and de-

tachment into an I-Thou attitude of total engagement? Does our assurance of God depend only on such a dialogic encounter with the
Eternal Thou? Can Buber really dispense with a systematic metaphysics to ground his faith?

Does not John Wild advocate an ethics of such untrammeled freedom
that it leads to social anarchy? Does he not make way for even the
most horrible and inhuman choices, provided that they are made permanently and authentically, with the full integrity of personal being?
In short, how about an authentic monster or a society of lonely au-
thentics?

To Wahl: If metaphysics is the foundation of poetry, and poetry of
metaphysics, must there not be some ground common to the two? Is
it prelinguistic? In what sense can a painter's or a poet's work be called
true? What is the distinction between *vérité sentie* and the truth of
propositions? Why does Wahl find it meaningful to speak of the philosophy of existence?

Why does Blanshard even deny that existence is meaningful? Would
he be willing to substitute "coherence with experience," as a test of
truth, for simple coherence? Is Blanshard's appeal to coherence in line
with actual scientific practice? Is not the understanding of the contingent as contingent truly understanding? What are his doubts about
extensional logic? Does Blanshard's way of thinking not endanger the
self?

As for Weiss, does he really believe that metaphysicians describe or
explain anything? Is there any sense in which they solve problems?
Why is Weiss so sure that there are just four modes of being? Are these
modes abstractions or themselves real, concrete beings? How does the
fundamental proposition of his metaphysics differ from the Hegelian
thesis that makes pure being identical with pure nothingness?

Is it true that in Hartshorne's philosophy nothing is what it is, but
always some other thing? How does he defend his view that process is
the irreducible mode of reality? That it can be quantized? How can I
be held morally accountable if I do not endure through time, if I am
no more than a succession of absolutely self-identical, particular events
or occasions? What can it mean to say that the world transcends God?

How does Tillich answer a process philosopher, like Hartshorne, on
the nature of being and becoming? Under what conditions would he

grant that Christian faith could be falsified or falsifiable? How do symbols participate in what they symbolize? If Tillich now says that the present period of man is a holy vacuum, a wait for a new reality, is he thereby relinquishing his earlier demand for a socialistic reorganization of society? Can Tillich admit that God actually participates in the agony and tragedy of human life?

The questions are often polemical, barbed, blunt, and they provoke equally animated replies. One critic of this book has called one of the questions almost tactless, and at the same time credits its pointed attack with having elicited a priceless response. The intellectual excitement is further enhanced by the presence of five of our editorial colleagues as querists and of five of the principal authors in the added role of interrogators, questioning one another.

This drama of question and answer yields a haunting quality of openness and creativity. Friedman notes how peculiarly appropriate this form of discourse is to Buber's philosophy of dialogue: "Dialogical 'truth' takes the form of question and answer much more readily than of simple statement, of dynamic interchange between persons much more than of substantive or dialectical contents of a single consciousness." The other authors too, by opening themselves to the challenging clash of query and response, achieve, in varying degree, a sense of philosophy being sought, made, and expressed.

No more than in their hitherto published writings do the seven philosophers exhibit a unanimity of philosophic thought. Indeed, there is pronounced diversity. Buber denies the need of a systematic metaphysics: "I have dared to believe . . . I have no metaphysics on which to establish my faith, I have created none for myself, I do not desire any, I need none, I am not capable of one." Tillich, in contrast, insists upon systematic thinking: "The systematic thinker—and I cannot deny that this is my natural inclination— . . . has the advantage of envisaging his field as a whole and, consequently, the relations of every problem with every other problem. . . . I believe that the *telos,* the inner aim of all thinking, is the system, the unity in which every statement is under the critical control of every other statement."

Again, Buber refuses to call his central insight, his dialogical reality, a philosophy of existence. Wahl, whose world of becoming is at once continuous and discontinuous, renounces the epithet existentialism and seems to favor a philosophy of existence. Tillich, maintaining that existentialism does not answer its own questions concerning finitude, loneliness, guilt, emptiness, assimilates its responses to his own special tradition of Christianity. Wild, moving away from classical, naïve, objective realism, lives in a rich, ambiguous, relational *Lebenswelt* in which there are no uninterpreted phenomena; all objects, although independent and real, are relative to a subjective attitude without which they cannot be understood. Blanshard, with his permanent, all-embracive, internally self-coherent unity, turns an Eleatic back both to existentialism and to the philosophy of existence. Hartshorne also stands outside the entire debate, preoccupied with lifting an Ionic torch to a fluid, creative process that emerges in quantized events. And Weiss, denouncing a modern tendency to insist on limited perspectives in philosophy, proclaims: "It is neither possible nor profitable to give an account of being *qua* being, for there is no such being. . . . The universe is the interlocked totality of four distinct kinds of being, each of which is a unity and a plurality, referring to and being referred to by all the others."

Despite the diversity of philosophic visions and despite Hartshorne's plaintive cry in replying to a query of Paul Weiss—"Alas for the forlorn hope of understanding between philosophers!"—there are bounds of profound agreement and communality. Life for Tillich is an inner witnessing and encounter; for Buber, too, it is a personal adventure, the risk of faith without security or objective criteria. Buber's audacity to believe—his dialogic encounter with his addressed God—is not too distant from Tillich's explanation concerning how to achieve cognition of the factual historicity of Jesus: what guarantees the event is not scholarly historical research concerning Jesus' existence and activities; rather, by faith is the event guaranteed. Again, Wild's concern with man's integral ecstatic being and authentic living is very near to Wahl's aesthetic devotion to *vérité sentie,* to felt truth and the immediate encounter of objective existence, to his demand for living in accordance with freedom. And Weiss, bent on formulating an impersonal, cosmic story, deliberately attempts to reconcile all discontinuities, paradoxes, apparent contradictions, unintelligibles, in a single, all-encompassing whole.

Above all, the seven authors and the majority of querists are united by what they believe it is important for philosophers to do. They are concerned far more with substantive than with methodological results. They have withstood every assault by positivists and behaviorists to cancel them out or to deny them the right to enter the universe of meaning. They are innovators and moderns who speak for and to our own times, yet are endowed with the philosophical wisdom and maturity to cherish and nourish our century's historical intellectual roots. Collectively, they show the remarkable vigor and vitality of genuine philosophy in our century.

SYDNEY C. ROME

BEATRICE K. ROME

Interrogation of

Martin Buber

Conducted by Maurice S. Friedman

Martin Buber, Israeli philosopher and theologian, is Professor Emeritus of Social Philosophy at the Hebrew University in Jerusalem. He was born in Vienna in 1878 and was educated at the Universities of Vienna, Berlin, Leipzig, Zürich. In 1901, in Vienna, he was editor of *Die Welt*. He is co-founder of *Jüdischer Verlag* and was founder and editor of *Der Jude*. From 1923 to 1933, he served as Professor of Comparative Religion at Frankfurt. He left Germany in 1938, having been Director of the College of Jewish Studies in Frankfurt. He holds honorary degrees from the Universities of Aberdeen, Paris and Jerusalem, and from the New School in New York. Among his extensive writings are: *Moses, Between Man and Man, Tales of the Hasidim, The Prophetic Faith, Paths in Utopia, Two Types of Faith, Eclipse of God, Israel and Palestine, Images of Good and Evil, For the Sake of Heaven, The Legend of Baal-Shem, Pointing the Way, I and Thou, Hasidism and Modern Man, Origin and Meaning of Hasidism, Begegnung,* and *Logos. The Philosophy of Martin Buber*, edited by Paul A. Schilpp and Maurice S. Friedman, is forthcoming.

PREFACE BY
MAURICE S. FRIEDMAN

Buber's own philosophy of dialogue makes this Interrogation particularly appropriate. Dialogical "truth" takes the form of question and answer much more readily than of simple statement, of dynamic interchange between persons much more than of substantive or dialectical contents of a single consciousness. What is more, Professor Buber has indicated that much of his thought remains unexpressed because he has not been asked to develop it.[1]

A word may be in order, therefore, about the relation of "dialogue," as Buber understands it, to this Interrogation. When I invited the noted psychoanalyst Ludwig Binswanger to contribute, he wrote that no questions occurred to him, precisely because he was too close to Buber for them to arise, and suggested that I quote him to that effect: "I have for decades been in so close personal and scientific contact with him and find his work, as far as it falls within my competence, so conclusive, so clear and consistent, that almost no doubt remains about which I must ask him for fuller particulars." Lewis Mumford, on the other hand, replied that he disagreed with Buber's thought until he met the man, showing that if dialogue is hampered by insufficient distance, it is also made impossible by too great distance.

All of the questions and answers in this Interrogation justify themselves as clarifications—those that proceed from misunderstanding serve this function just as much as those that do not. Some, however, add to dialectic clarification of thought an unmistakable achievement of dialogue that itself demonstrates the relation between dialogue and dialectic about which so many of the interrogators have asked. Some of

[1] The short questions of this Interrogation, together with Martin Buber's answers, form, as a result, an invaluable supplement to the longer essays and *responsa* of the forthcoming *Philosophy of Martin Buber* in *The Library of Living Philosophers* which, in cooperation with Professor Schilpp, I have had the honor of editing.

these dialogues are continuations of personal dialogues of long standing, like those with Hugo Bergmann and Eugen Rosenstock-Huessy;
one is directly taken from a "trialogue" of correspondence between
Reinhold Niebuhr and me, and Martin Buber and me, itself based on
earlier spoken dialogue between the three of us, again, two at a time.
Some, like that between William Ernest Hocking and Buber, as both
men indicate, attain the height of dialogue without the two ever having
met.

   In addition to dialectic and dialogue, this Interrogation offers in
small compass a systematic examination of Buber's thought in most of
its major aspects. This systematic organization grew out of the questions themselves. When I had assembled the questions of the interrogators, the present outline suggested itself to me as the best way in
which Professor Buber might respond and in which question and answer together might be presented to the reader.

I. THE PHILOSOPHY OF DIALOGUE
A. Philosophy in General

   Walter Kaufmann: My questions are concerned with the relation
of your thought to traditional philosophy as we know it from the
works of Plato, Aristotle, Descartes, Spinoza, Hume, and Kant, to give
a few examples. Most people would surely agree that it makes sense
to ask about Kierkegaard's relation to philosophy of this sort—perhaps
also about Nietzsche's relation to it, or Heidegger's. The answer, of
course, will be different in each case. I am assuming that this question
makes sense when asked about you; and to facilitate an answer, I shall
suggest a few specific subquestions.

   1. A large part of traditional philosophy was concerned with the
analysis of concepts, though this was not the only concern of any great
philosopher. Do you attach less value to such analysis than the traditional philosophers named above?

   2. Do you feel that your central intentions are closer to those of Amos
than to those of Aristotle? Closer to Lao-tzu's than to Hume's? Closer
to Hermann Hesse's than to G. E. Moore's?

   3. Is it more important to you to bear witness of an experience and
to exhort men than to clarify concepts or to develop speculative the-

ories? If so, of what traditional philosophers would you say the same?

4. Are you at all apprehensive that your main concerns might be buried under the weight of appreciations that are too academic and, in one sense of that word, too philosophical?

Buber: The nature, strictly speaking, of the relationship of my thought to "traditional philosophy" seems to me more a theme for my critics than for me. But through answering your subquestions, I believe I can, at any rate, give a few hints.

1. An ever-renewed analysis of basic concepts appears to me, too, a central task of thought because it is the presupposition for an ever-renewed confrontation with reality. Concepts, the grandiose instrument of human orientation, must repeatedly be "clarified"; a final validity can never be accorded them, although each of the great explanations claims for itself the character of final validity, and clearly must claim it. But in all genuine philosophy, analysis is only a gateway, nothing more. To be sure, the great philosophers who have conducted these analyses have held them to be more important than I do, doubtless because they held philosophizing to be more important. I *must* philosophize; there is no other way to my goal, but my goal itself cannot be grasped philosophically.

2. Certainly my "central intentions" are closer to those of Amos than to those of Aristotle, much closer. But for Amos a concept such as "righteousness" is, in fact, nothing at all other than the condensation into words of a command that is to be fulfilled in a given situation; as a concept it does not concern him. And when I have to philosophize (and I must, indeed, do so, as I said), I must learn from Aristotle and not from Amos. It is otherwise with the distinction between Lao-tzu and Hume. Lao-tzu ushers me, far more deeply than Hume, into the problematics of conceptuality; he discloses to me, as Hume does not, the abyss beneath the concepts; he helps me do what Hume will not and cannot do—see through the indispensable logicizing of reality. Note well, I am no disciple of Lao-tzu; I see the reality of being entirely otherwise than he. Indeed, it is at times much easier for me to "accord the right" to Hume than to him. But his speaking and his silence are instructive to me even today for the rational intercourse with that which is beyond concepts.

3. To bear witness to an experience is my basic intention, but I am not primarily concerned with exhorting men; rather, with showing that experience to be one accessible to all in some measure, in some form. In this I do not feel myself far either from the Platonic dialogues or from Descartes' *Discours de la Méthode*.

4. My main concerns could just as easily be buried under the weight of appreciations that are too philosophical as under those that are too historical (in the sense of the history of religions) and even too literary. There are many methods of evading the vision and practice of the life of dialogue through theoretical discussions of the dialogical principle.

Rollo May: To what extent is Buber an existentialist? He is often referred to under that appellation, and his thought has obvious similarities with the philosophy of modern crisis called existentialism, but he frowns on the title. Specifically, what is his relation to Kierkegaard and Heidegger, as well as to the broader cultural movement of existentialism?

Buber: I cannot, of course, be particularly pleased when, instead of paying attention to what I directly have to say, a questioner furnishes me with the label of an "ism" and then wants to know concerning it. But if those be called existentialists who transpose human existence itself into the center of rational contemplation, then one could call me that. Only one thing must not remain unnoticed: everything else may be discussed purely speculatively, but not our own existence. The genuine existentialist must himself "exist." An existentialism that contents itself with theory is a contradiction; existence is not one philosophical theme among others. Here witness is made.

B. Ontology

Helmut Kuhn: 1. Should we not try to broaden the concept of community as based upon the I-Thou relationship into the idea of an all-embracing ontological community?

2. Is it not true that the meeting (*Begegnung*)—that meeting of minds which unseals the depths of personality—takes place within a fixed order and under an unbending law which we know, however imperfectly, as the law of love?

3. A question about the antithesis which opposes the fellow man (the Thou) of whom we have a living awareness to the object as a rationally defined fixity: Shall we not be more true to the facts if we replace this dichotomy by a hierarchically diversified concept of "object"?

EXPLANATION: Martin Buber's thought has always impressed me by its great simplicity and integrity. It is alive and, like all living things, it is essentially and emphatically one. So, in trying to interrogate him (which costs me no special effort, since as a fairly diligent reader of his books I have merely to indulge in a habit of mine), I find only one question to put to him. The three questions as formulated above differ from each other only superficially. On closer inspection they turn out to be no more than three different aspects of a single query.

In modern times, a narrow concept of object, modeled on the object of physical science, has exercised a tyrannical dominion over thinking minds. In opposing this dogmatism Martin Buber has restored to its true status the human person as revealed through his communion with other persons. Heeding his great lesson seems to me imperative for all of us. Yet I wonder whether he has fully developed the implications of his master thesis. The person concretely envisaged has to be located in a space defined by three dimensions: the God-man relationship, the inter-human relationship, and the man-world relationship. So far this last dimension has been neglected by Buber, and as a result Buber's concrete living man lacks his proper habitat and his subhuman companions. In Buber's admirable recent address on the problem of art (*Der Mensch und sein Gebild*) he speaks about an ancient lime tree in accents that show how alien from his mind is the "acosmic" type of thought. Yet under the influence of Kant he refers to the thing-in-itself as an x, and his mighty tree, instead of being rooted in real earth of this our world, seems to belong to the "as if" world of the *Critique of Judgment*. The lack of an adequate comprehension of the world has for its counter-part a somewhat oversimplified epistemology. Buber, it seems to me, has not yet fully freed himself from that false alternative which con-temporary existentialism has inherited from Kierkegaard. With him the subjective (though interpersonal) truth is still opposed to the objec-tive truth, the latter being committed to the tender mercies of the phys-icist, and the world in which we live is interpreted in an instrumentalist fashion reminiscent of Heidegger's *Zeug-Welt*. This, in short, is the critical meaning of my questions: Martin Buber, it seems to me, has entered the domain of *philosophia perennis* without as yet taking full possession of his kingdom.

Buber: 1. By community I understand a connection of men who are so joined in their life with something apportioned to them in common or something which they have apportioned to themselves in common that they are, just thereby, joined with one another in their life. The first and the second unity are not meant as continually actual, but as of such a nature that no essential hindrance stands in the way of its transition from time to time from a vital latency to an actuality.

With this presupposed, the present constitution of the human race and, over and above that, that which manifests itself in the present as "historically" surveyable, does not seem to me to authorize the idea of an all-embracing ontological community.

It would be otherwise if the ontological conception of an idea might be consummated independently of the actualities known or knowable by us. It is a part of my strongest concern, however, to contest this.

But for me this idea is, in fact, connected in its innermost base with the faith accorded us that the human race is given, by creation, the task of becoming a community and that, according to the promise, the achievement of this goal of creation is eschatologically true.

2. Meetings stand—as I have repeatedly indicated—under freedom and under grace, therefore not under an "unbending law." A fixed order of meetings is, in any case, neither in our hands nor accessible to them. When we truly say "Thou," we do not experience "order" and "law," but liberation and blessing in one; shall our thinking really disregard this experience?

What love is I can know; what a law of love is I cannot know, not even imperfectly. The biblical commands of love of God and man are not unfolded in the form of law; the disclosing of their meaning was left to the recurringly loving heart alone.

3. This question touches on the foundation of what I have to say. For were the "dichotomy" replaced by a "hierarchic" diversity, then the decisive distinction between I-Thou and I-It would be dissolved by degrees.

Certainly there is a graduated structure of I-It relationships where stage by stage the distance from the I-Thou relation becomes greater, and this graduated structure is, by its nature, to a certain extent survey-able. But its highest stage is unmistakably set in contrast to the realm of the I-Thou relation, since even there an objectification prevails for which there is no room in this relation. A being to whom I really say "Thou" is not for me in this moment my object, about whom I observe this and that or whom I put to this or that use, but my partner who stands over against me in his own right and existence and yet is related to me in his life. I can adequately contemplate this being as "a rationally defined fixity" when I again see it as It. When we do not resolutely effect the distinction between the two attitudes, we further, even if very much against our wills, the tendency which has grown so strong in our time to "manipulate" the existing being.

Kuhn rightly objects that the relationship of the human person to nature has not been sufficiently dealt with by me. There remains here, as in many of the border areas between the two attitudes, something of basic importance to be done that is not granted me to do myself. But I may hope that it will be done without surrendering the uncondition-ality of the distinction.

Kuhn also rightly sees that I have not fully liberated myself from Kant. That I have not been able to do so probably lies in the fact that no one has yet been able to explain to me what, for example, the hard-ness in the bark of a lime tree means independently of my perception of the hardness. I simply do not succeed in understanding the existing lime tree as the sum of my perceptions of it. Even the otherwise-useful symbols of the physicist are incapable of helping me here. Now then, the lime tree that became known to me only in elaboration through my perceptions, the lime tree that *is,* that, although it became known to me, yet remains unknown—this I mean when I say *x.*

F. H. Heinemann: 1. What is the precise philosophical meaning of the dialogical principle? Is it to be understood as *either* (*a*) an ontolog-ical principle ("pointing to a neglected reality"), or (*b*) an existential category (*Kategorie der Existenz*), or (*c*) a category of a philosophy of life (*um neuen Grund für menschliches Lebenkönnen zu legen*), or (*d*) are all these meanings and functions implied in it?

2. Your philosophy has been called "dialogical philosophy." Would

you accept this? (*a*) Do you hold that the dialogical principle could be the basis of a philosophy in the same manner as, for instance, the axioms "Being is," "God is," and *"Cogito, ergo sum"* were the first principles of Greek, medieval, and modern philosophy respectively? (*b*) If yes, would you regard it as the basis of (1) a system of philosophy or (2) of a manner of philosophizing? (*c*) In other words, would you regard your principle, in Kant's terminology, as (1) constitutive or (2) regulative?

3. What is, in your opinion, the relation of the dialogical philosophy to the philosophy of existence? Would you regard yourself as a philosopher of existence, and if so, in what sense?

4. I believe I have shown in my book on existentialism (especially in the second English, German, and Spanish editions) that the principle of existence is insufficient as a basis of a comprehensive and systematic philosophy, and that it has in fact been given up by all the leading existentialists.

You have certainly not given up the dialogical principle, and it has proved most fruitful in many fields, from anthropology and the study of prehistory to theology. It would be of great interest to philosophers if you could show that the dialogical principle differs in this respect from the principle of existence.

Buber: 1. The dialogical principle is an ontological one because it is concerned with a basic relationship between man and being; hence with the being of man, since this is grounded in his relationship to being. This principle is to be regarded as existential only insofar as it is necessarily realized in the sphere of existence of the person. It is not, on the other hand, to be understood as a category of a "philosophy of life" (*Lebensphilosophie*); what is cited of this nature, to suggest that it is such, does not belong to it itself, but merely to the motivation behind its presentation.

2. As I have explained in full in my *responsa* in the volume of the *Library of Living Philosophers* dedicated to my philosophy, to join a basic experience, which became evident to me as a basic experience of man, with its proper sphere of thought, I had to go the only way suitable to that purpose, the philosophical. It has not been my intention to give a basis of philosophy in the sense indicated by Heinemann and

cannot be, although I cannot foresee what may yet come out of it in other hands. I call my philosophy "dialogical philosophy" not without a certain irony, because basically it cannot be pursued otherwise than dialogically, but the writings dealing with it have been cast into the, for the most part, quite undialogically constituted human world of this hour—and must be cast there.

3/4. "Philosophy of existence" appears to me an imprecise and unsteady concept. I have never included myself in such, but feel myself as standing perhaps between an existential thinking in Kierkegaard's sense and something entirely different, something which is still out of sight.

The dialogical principle presupposes existence, to be sure, but not a self-contained principle of existence. It is rather, as it seems to me, summoned to call in question every self-sufficient principle of existence in that it posits in ontological unconditionality the essential presence of the other as the other. I welcome every philosophy of existence that leaves open the door leading to otherness; but I know none that opens it far enough.

Emmanuel Levinas: Certain formulations of Buber with respect to the I-Thou relation, such as "Ich werde am Du; Ich werdend spreche Ich Du" or "Es gibt kein Ich an sich, sondern nur das Ich des Grundworts *Ich Du* und das Ich des Grundworts Ich-Es," [2] imply that the terms "I" and "Thou" have neither meaning nor independent existence apart from the relation into which they enter. The interval itself, the "betweenness," so to speak, of that relation is, according to Buber, the concept of the foundation and ultimate structure of being. The important question that must be raised in this context, therefore, is whether the concept of Relation is capable of defining this original structure.

The substantiality and independent reality of the self, upheld by a respectable philosophical tradition in the past, have been rejected by the philosophical thought of the present day. Edmund Husserl's theory of intentionality and Martin Heidegger's *In-der-Welt Sein* or *Miteinandersein* are a repudiation of the independently existing self. The self, once separated from that which transcends it, whether this be the world or the existence of the other, is reduced to the status of a thing. However,

[2] "Ich und Du," *Dialogisches Leben* (Zürich: Gregor Muller Verlag, 1947), pp. 16, 23.

Buber does not attempt merely to posit the I in a relation, for the Thou is also posited as the absolutely other: the I-Thou is a relation in which one of the terms remains absolute. This apparent contradiction between the absolute and the relative is overcome in the case of social relations and is indicative of the logical originality of the relation which can be traced back to the main themes of the *Parmenides* and to the later thought of Plato.

Is Buber fully aware of the original nature of this relation, however? If the I derives its *ipseity* from its confrontation with the Thou, and if, moreover, that relation is reciprocal, as Buber affirms, then the I and Thou are related, as are the terms in any relation, that is, as objects, united by the same act which separates them, each definable in terms of the other. The two terms, then, are correlated and constitute a totality from which they cannot be separated. If the terms are related in this way, we must infer that it is logically impossible for them not mutually to define one another, because a term which was absolutely *sui generis* would destroy the relation. For, we may ask, is not its identity defined by the Other according to the dialectic of the Sophist, since the Same is itself Other by being related to the Other? Ipseity, or the living self, however, would seem to imply a radical break with this dialectic, for ipseity is not the result of ascribing a unique predicate which is foreign to the relation. It is determined as an I quite apart from any objective relation whatever, that is, the I, or living self, is a Same which does not participate in the Other even in the sense of excluding it. To affirm this is not to be guilty of the major error of modern thought, namely, reification. For the isolation of the I implies neither solitude nor society and requires a category wholly alien to that of things, namely, happiness. Ipseity resides in the very egoism of the self, in the jubilation and exaltation of a happiness which removes it to a level above that which prosaically is.

In any event, since the *Ich-Werden* is not the contrary of the *Du-Sprachen,* the Thou may reveal itself as the absolutely other, but it does so in a relation which does not imply reciprocity. Asymmetry of relation is the rule in this case, for it is only in virtue of this that the otherness of the Thou may be distinguished from the purely formal kind of otherness ordinarily possessed by a term because of its position in a relation. Despite the appropriateness of the examples cited in "Dialogue" (*Between Man and Man*), Buber is not able to qualify the relation properly, and he merely reiterates the formal nature of the relation. However, asymmetry when recognized presages an ethics, that is, it discloses a dimension of height, a recognition of the other as a master to be served. For in a sense, ethics is but the privilege possessed by the other *qua* other.

On the basis of the above we may inquire first whether the I-Thou relation can be extended beyond the ethical realm to include nature, insofar at least as it is mediated by art; and second, whether the third person, *he* and *she* (*Er und Sie*), can in turn be relegated to the realm of the It (*Es*). For the Thou whom I address is already committed with respect to a third person who in effect is not absent from the dialogue.

In what medium does the meeting of the I and Thou take place? How does this *Zwischen* or betweenness where it takes place, the "shock" (*Geschehen*) or "trust" which defines that meeting, encroach on the consciousness that is aware of it? How can this unusual relation of the I-Thou be reflected in our conscious awareness when the latter is essentially awareness of an object, without at the same time leading us to suspect that it involves but a moment of consciousness? It is not psychologism but objectivism to which the analysis of consciousness invariably leads; that must be avoided, but Buber does not even raise this problem. It must of course be recognized that Buber's thesis consists not in defending the view that the other is first known and then subsequently recognized as Thou but, inversely, that the primary relation is the recognition of the other as Thou and that the latter can then be objectified. However, the recognition of the other is not a *knowledge* of the other similar in kind to other bits of knowledge and differing only in its content. It must be shown that such recognition is not identifiable with a state of conscious awareness since it transcends consciousness. If the concept is not revised, therefore, the I-Thou relation is jeopardized, for it is assimilated to a moment of conscious awareness.

These objections or, better, questions, stem from a reflection on Heidegger and on certain passages of the *Phaedrus* where the problem of the absolutely other is encountered, and it is in the desire for the Other that a definition of metaphysics itself has been sought. Buber's descriptions are essential to that metaphysics, and in formulating these objections or questions we deny ourselves the ridiculous position of him who wishes to "improve upon" the work of a creative spirit. My objections to the latter may be summarized in the following manner:

1. Is it not the case that the reciprocity of the I-Thou relation compromises rather than promotes the originality of the I for whom separation is essential? Is not the absolute distance of the Thou or Other thereby compromised?

2. Should the other be posited as Thou? "He," "she," and "they" cannot be construed as Itness (*Das Es*). For in the encounter with the Thou they are present and "participate" in the dialogue as "the voice of your brother's blood that cries to me from the ground."

3. Are we not compelled to substitute for the reciprocity of the I-Thou relation a structure which is more fundamental and which excludes reciprocity, that is, one which involves an asymmetry or difference of level and which thereby implies a real distancing? The metaphysician is always oriented toward the Other and is incapable of meeting himself in the same way that he meets the other. Even when he philosophizes on the I-Thou relation, he perceives the Other, so that a totality is never encompassed. Dialogue, in effect, signifies the ontological impossibility of a totality.

4. The I-Thou relation cannot be characterized in purely formal terms as a contact without either content or a principle. The asymmetrical nature of the I-Thou relation implies the realization of an ethics which is distinguished by the inequality of the I and the Thou, and the latter creates an original dimension of ideality and height.

5. Consciousness, the realm of our inner processes of thought, is not subjected to any analysis by Buber. Such analysis, however, is indispensable if a *synousia,* or social communion, as distinct from a mere union, is to be considered as a philosophical question. For the Western philosophical tradition this relation to what is outside is synonymous with religion. In spite of its many windings and turnings, the path of philosophy from Socrates to Heidegger follows the itinerary to which Plotinus referred when he affirmed: "When the soul begins again to mount, it comes not to something alien, but to its very self; thus detached, it is in nothing but itself." [3]

[3] *Enneads,* VI, 9, 11.

Buber: I have never designated the between as "the concept of the foundation and ultimate structure of being" ("le concept de base et la structure ultime de l'Être"), nor have I ever understood it thus; I have only pointed out that we cannot do without this category for a full comprehension and presentation of what passes between two men when they stand in dialogue with each other.

My critic mistakenly identifies this concept of the between, which belongs to the sphere of the I-Thou relation, with the essentially different concept of *Urdistanz* (primal distance), which provides the anthropological presupposition for the origination of the duality of the "primary words," of which the I-Thou relation is one (cf. my "Distance and Relation"[4]): I-It signifies the lived persistence in the primal distance, I-Thou the movement from it to relation, which at times, to be sure, establishes itself only as overcoming the given distance between two beings.

Since Levinas, in the first place, accepts a signification for the two concepts which they do not have in the context of my thought and, in the second, equates with each of them other concepts belonging to totally different spheres of this thought, he makes a direct answer to his questions impossible for me. I must therefore content myself with making a few clarifying comments on his objections so far as that fundamental misunderstanding allows.

1. It is not true that I "unceasingly affirm" (*affirme sans cesse*) the reciprocity of the relation. On the contrary, I have always had to talk about it with great reservations and qualifications, which I recently summarized in my Postscript to the second edition of *I and Thou*.[5]

2. I cannot concede that the I and the Thou offer themselves to each other "as objects" in the relation. Becoming an object is, in fact, precisely what most strongly characterizes the I-It relationship in its opposition to the I-Thou relation.

3. No matter how all-embracing the relation of two beings to each other may be, it does not in any sense mean their "unification." If I posit a "correlation," it still in no way follows from that, that a "totality" exists. Hermann Cohen speaks in his posthumous work of the "cor-

[4] Trans. Ronald Gregor Smith, *Psychiatry*, XX, No. 2 (May, 1957), 97–104.
[5] Trans. Ronald Gregor Smith (New York: Charles Scribner's Sons, 1958), pp. 123–137.

relation" existing between God and man; with what kind of totality can that be equated?

4. The importance of the indications concerning ipseity I readily acknowledge. Between the I that in a given moment detaches itself from the other existing being and the I that in another given moment turns to the other existing being, there exists, incontestably, a special kind of continuity that is preserved despite all discontinuities; and it is this which one customarily designates as self-consciousness. But I do not see that this fact justifies the acceptance of an isolated I that stands over against neither a Thou nor an It and is not even comprehended in the transition from the one to the other relationship to being. Levinas assigns the ipseity its place in the "happiness" of the human person at being an I. To me it seems that this self-identification involves at the same time the deepest suffering of which we are capable. The polarity of these feelings points us back to a deep duality of which the pronominal concept on which I have founded my philosophy perhaps merely makes manifest the foreground that we can grasp.

5. The "asymmetry" is only one of the possibilities of the I-Thou relation, not its rule, just as mutuality in all its gradations cannot be regarded as the rule. Understood in utter seriousness, the asymmetry that wishes to limit the relation to the relationship to a higher would make it completely one-sided: love would either be unreciprocated by its nature or each of the two lovers must miss the reality of the other.

Even as the foundation of an ethic, I cannot acknowledge "asymmetry." I live "ethically" when I confirm and further my Thou in the right of his existence and the goal of his becoming, in all his otherness. I am not ethically bidden to regard and treat him as superior to me through his otherness. I find, by the way, that our relationship to the domestic animals with whom we live, and even that to the plants in our gardens, is properly included as the lowest floor of the ethical building. The Hasidim even see it as beginning with the implements of work. And shall there not perhaps be an ethic for the relationship to oneself?

6. That the acknowledgment of the other as my Thou does not originate in a mere act of consciousness belongs to those elements of my thought whose actuality I can neither prove nor wish to be able to

prove. I offer the philosophical expression of an experience to those who know this experience as their own or are ready to expose themselves to it. More than this I cannot do; but I venture to believe that in this "not" I am faithful to my task.

Walter Blumenfeld: By what justification does Buber see the dialogue as decisive in man, since there are enough other methods of differentiation as, for example, symbolic expression, knowledge, science, art, and religion, which in any case do not cover all examples of the genus *Homo.* Is that preference not merely the expression of a personal evaluation and therefore in a certain sense arbitrary?

Buber: I am of the opinion that an attentive reader of my book *Eclipse of God* will find the foundation demanded by Blumenfeld

C. Human Life

Perry LeFevre: Can you point to some of the kinds of factors in the lives of individuals which make it more or less likely, which make it easier or more difficult for them to enter into dialogue? In other words, what do you believe accounts for the fact that some individuals seem more capable of dialogue than others?

Buber: This is a field into which I can venture only with difficulty. But one thing seems certain to me: There are men who allow as little as possible what befalls them in life to be dependent on something other than themselves; and there are men whom, in a deep sense, it suits that the other, until now unknown, unforeseen, shall enter into their lives. The counterstriving of the first type of man is to be understood thus: All risk that his own plans, projects, attempts, undertakings entail is, in fact, by its nature nothing at all compared with that to which one exposes oneself through the genuine contact with otherness. The aims of the first kind of man—let us call him the self-withholding man—often ripen faster and more easily than those of the man whom we can designate as exposing himself; however, the easily and quickly ripening aims often prove to be worm-eaten. With a simplification unavoidable here, I might say that these men not seldom become famous—they have success—but no sphere of existence seems to me so thoroughly penetrated by deception and self-deception as that which the man of heedless heart books as a success.

Friedrich Thieberger: The insight toward which Buber led us is this: Only after we inwardly grasp the Thou within the It of men or events or things which confront us do we enter into a real relationship with them, and only then do we have a share in true reality.

My question is concerned with the origin of such a comprehension and awareness, that is, the starting point of the transformation of the It into a Thou. There is doubtless no method which can be made to serve the will here. The conditions vary from case to case and become incalculable and vast. Suddenly one sees the Thou in a flash and is seized and gripped by it. Nevertheless, there is a difference between the very first phase of the illumined I-Thou relation and all subsequent ones.

Buber himself once said that a poet has entered into his own innermost being through one of his works and that he, the poet, will continue to dwell there notwithstanding that which he might create later. The earliest phase is something that overpowers the individual and sets him afire; the later phases conserve the new view, deepen and broaden it. Only the illuminating breakthrough that opens the senses in a flash —the spontaneous, the unique—characterizes the origin.

Another characterizing distinction between the original phase and all later ones is the consciousness of a personal upheaval, of the inner transformation of the I. The later phases merely follow the new but already indicated way; they bring the I and the Thou into a kind of balance.

A third distinction between the original and all later phases is the encounter of ages: the encounter of the past that is still experienced as something quite different with a newborn present; on the other hand, all subsequent phases are characterized by an assurance, shielded from the storms of time, and a trust in all the future potentialities of the I-Thou relationship.

All these are not distinctions of a similar kind of process, but rather of qualitative differences. What we consider to be the first phase is probably connected with the I-Thou relationship as its first cause, but is not to be equated with it. Should not one, therefore, separate the

"original phase" from the later ones, that is, place it before the phenomenon of the "deeply stirred," the "awakening," and attempt to comprehend it as a particular kind of human reality?

Buber: It frequently happens, indeed, that the I-Thou relation
begins with an "illumination," an "awakening." But I am in no case
inclined to understand this manifestation as the rule. I cannot do this
because I already find this relation—as I have maintained from the beginning—in the life of the small child, as in that of the so-called primitive man, in a directly natural form; and I also understand the meaning
of most spiritual forms in their connection with the natural.

I acknowledge, therefore, the significance of "being seized," but I
can see in it no necessary presupposition for the origin of an I-Thou
relation.

D. Time and Historicity of Man

Eugen Rosenstock-Huessy: The real gulf or gap between Buber's
and my way of thinking is our approach to the historicity of man.

To me, any word spoken makes sense only if testifying to the spiritual coexistence of three or *more* generations of men. To speak means
to live backward before one's own birth and forward beyond one's own
death.

To be named establishes one into a time sequence with at least two
epochal and decisive breaks: the death of the person who named me
and the death of myself, the career of a name which is meant to survive any physical destruction.

Pluri-aged is my thought; single-aged is Buber's. This also happens
to be the distinction between socialism (with its as yet liberal, i.e., single-
aged conception of the social order) and communism (with its religionlike pluri-aged approach to the reproduction of the social order and
within the social order).

Buber as well as myself is perfectly aware of this dividing line between these two approaches. To me, no individual and no individual
generation seems capable of making any experience of history. *Man,
the individual,* cannot do more than realize the experience of his five
senses. *Sense,* common sense, is not the travesty of the democratic super-
stition, that is, the identity of perception for fifty or a thousand indi-

viduals at the same time. It is the power of a dynasty of generations—at least three or four—to pool their energies around one and the same experience and for making one and the same experience. For instance, the Constitution of the United States of America is that incorporating tool through which that nation is made *at all* capable of registering certain domestic experiences over one hundred and fifty years! In foreign affairs, the United States has not created any such incorporating "spine"; hence Americans are unable to develop common sense in this area: they are incapacitated for making *any* experiences in history: *vide* the ruin of World War I "experiences." These many experiences of 1918 never became an experience of the United States!

This diversity of approach lies behind all my other points against Martin Buber. For instance, *Ich* (I) and *Du* (Thou) to me are fictitious abbreviations for the real pluri-aged, named, "nationalized" and century-bound real person. To me, pronouns are *omissions*. To Buber, they suffice. If you look into my *Zurück in das Wagnis der Sprache,* you may find ample proof for my thesis that pronouns are neither here nor there. You are Mr. Friedman and Maurice Friedman long before you are I or Thou. This, today, goes unrecognized. Liberalism and humanism have perverted the relations of names, nouns, pronouns. Buber had no reason to fight this centennial [6] tradition. Hence, his reconnoitering into the I and Thou was not felt to be ruinous for the whole humanistic and naturalistic traditions about man—as being "naturally himself." To me this is nonsense.

For me, *time* is indivisibly three in one: Future, Past, and, as their victor, Present are only *simultaneously* given. They are trinitarian, prismatic aspects of one and the same whole: Time. Time is given to real man (not to the abstraction called "physicist") as one in three: (1) the Times I enfold myself; (2) the Times which have preceded my con-

---

[6] In a communication to the general editors of this volume, who questioned this usage of "centennial," Rosenstock-Huessy explained that he is challenging a hundred years of academic tradition down to Hitler as naïvely atomistic and egocentric. "I" and "Thou" is proper for Buber, he insists, because Buber simply extends, but never changes, the views of academic agnostics who remain within the unchallenged Greek tradition. Rosenstock-Huessy declares: "My whole approach is the reverse of Buber's. I do *not* enlarge on the academic premises; I contradict them. Obviously, this seems preposterous." Only a hundred years hence, he adds, it might become clear why such a frontal attack could not be avoided.

sciousness; (3) the Times which follow after I am dead. Buber, on the other hand, accepts the phenomenon of time in its reduction to an inarticulate, logically indefensible, present.

Hence, our soil for speech differs fundamentally. Mine is at least three-dimensional in time; his is at best one-dimensional, but in truth *none*-dimensional.

Buber: In the central part of his formulation of his questions regarding the historicity of man and the contemporaneity of the generations, Rosenstock-Huessy gives a striking presentation of the difference between what is important to him in man and what is important to me. In the last sentences, where he speaks of the pronoun and of the "dimensions," he makes his criticism more pointed and loses thereby the ground under his feet.

The historical nature of man is the aspect of reality about which we have been basically and emphatically instructed in the epoch of thought beginning with Hegel and ending with Heidegger. I account it a great merit on the part of Rosenstock-Huessy that he has concretized this teaching in so living a way, as no other thinker before him has done: in his pointing to the generations living in contemporaneity with one another—a pointing out which I was especially happy to invite him to make in print when, more than three decades ago, I began to edit the periodical *Die Kreatur.* As a focusing of attention to the one side, just in its concreteness, it was and is welcome to me; but if he exhibits it as the most important and decisive reality in man, then I am compelled to hold him to be not less misleading than that whole teaching of our epoch—an epoch that has presented to us the cup that we have sipped until we have now reached the dregs.

Certainly man is an "historical" being, which, to be sure, means for the description of a Patagonian something other than for that of a Chinese or even of an American. Certainly memory and promise are mingled in language, and both extend immeasurably beyond the birth and death of the speaker. But even here, in the realm of language, we can remark that with this perception of the "historical" we are still far from having come sufficiently close to the reality of man, indeed, that thereby we have not at all obtained a glimpse of the most characteristic fact, the open mystery of the person. In the actually spoken word the eternally new event is not the said but the saying; and the saying stands in the present, the personal present that must at times let itself be represented in the said through the purely evocative word.

When I say "person," I point to the underivable. Were we endowed with a perfect historical knowledge, nonetheless we could not explain the essential constitution of a single person. I may not conceal the fact that by the words "essential constitution" I point to this person's having been created, to the fact of facts that, in the Jewish tradition, has been clothed in the saying that three work on the origin of every human child: father, mother, and God; this same fact that is proclaimed to me by each newborn child to whose cradle I step, through his traits, gestures, sounds that never yet have been. And, God be thanked, I too am there, as the father, the grandfather, the great-grandfather, or perhaps only as a guest, gazing ever more deeply into the mystery. Human existence, even the most silent, is speech; and speech, whether intentionally or unintentionally, directly or indirectly, along with gaining ground and forcibly penetrating, along with sucking and tasting, along with advancing over untried ways, is always address. What addresses you, not in the said but in the saying, is the underivable person, the now living new creature. The person becomes known in the I-Thou relation.

Of course, the personal pronouns are also neither here nor there; they stand only for the relation that cannot be expressed in any other way. Rosenstock-Huessy's opinion, influenced by grammatical teaching, that they stand for a name or even for a proper name, appears to me an error having serious consequences. Whether I say, "Eugen has written a 'sociology' in which such-and-such things are spoken about," or, "You Eugen, what were you calling to mind when you wrote so-and-so in your 'sociology'?"—that is the vital distinction. The pronoun "He" does, indeed, stand for a name, but the pronoun "Thou" only in the case of the first "You" in the latter sentence.

And to go back to the theme of the generations, but still only incidentally: Out of his valuation of the proper name—which I regard simply as an indispensable and unsatisfactory symbol of personal uniqueness—there follows for Rosenstock-Huessy the so-to-speak biographical equation of two deaths: the death of him who named me, and my own. That is an Old Testament manner of thinking to which I cannot adhere; it is, at any rate, already relinquished by the Gospels, where the giving of the name is no longer an important biographical act and changes of name are no longer undertaken by God or the people, but by the person. Since then much else has changed. But I myself am deeply opposed to him who, in such a manner, sets as legitimate, next to one's own death, the remembered death of the man who has given him his name (who could, e.g., have been the superintendent of an orphanage); next to my death there is place for no other aside from that of the man with whom I have exchanged the most genuine Thou of my life.

My thought is not "single-aged." But my faith is. I believe in the hour, in the life of individuals, and in the life of the human race, where the historical bursts open and the present reveals itself. I believe in this hour because I know it. I know that it opens men to each other and establishes community between them. This, my faith, hence this experience of faith, this knowledge of faith, and this hope of faith you call a "single-aged socialism" and select as its opposite a communism whose approach is not only pluri-aged, but even religionlike. Are you thinking of the historical manifestation of our time on the banner of which, the most massive of all times, that term is written, that movement which has been frequently described by objective observers as religionlike? In any case, let one last thing be said: My innermost heart is indeed with those (in the near or remote future) who, driven into high despair by the pseudo realization of this religionlike world program, by this planetary centralism of power that will quite possibly invert everything, will summon with their last strength the single-aged and all-aged present, the presence between men.

E. Philosophical Anthropology

Walter Blumenfeld: 1. Is "the" human being of Buber the real human being or a rare, if ever realized, ideal, the "authentic" and especially the mature, normal person? Buber's teaching can hardly be applied to the mentally ill, to small children, and to idiots. Is not his "man" only a potentially and in no case a universally prevalent being?

2. Is there a dialogue with things and with God in the same sense as with persons? Surely there can be no discussions with them, even if one grants that one can be "addressed" by God and by things. Furthermore,

a conversation does not always develop between persons, however present good will may be: for example, in the case of unhappy, unrequited love, it remains a one-sided attempt. And how are those cases to be regarded in which good will is lacking? Do such individuals cease to be human beings?

Buber: 1. I believe that I have made sufficiently clear that that which concerns me does not belong to an upper story of human nature. I have shown in detail how the I-Thou relation establishes itself, naturally as it were, in the small child as in "primitive" man. As for the so-called idiots, I have many times perceived how the soul of such a man extends its arms—and thrusts into emptiness. On the other hand, I have, not at all seldom, learned to know persons of a high spiritual grade whose basic nature was to withhold themselves from others even if they let this one and that one come near them. No, I mean no "spiritual elite," and yes, I mean man as man. Hindrances everywhere place themselves in the way, from without and from within; it is heart-will and grace in one that help us mature and awake men to overcome them and grant us meeting.

What is of importance? That the spirit execute in a spiritual manner the projects that nature lays before it.

2. So far as I am able to formulate it, I have given the answer to this question in the Postscript to the new edition of *I and Thou*.[7]

That man can "discuss" with God can be learned ever anew from the Book of Job; he who undertakes such must bear in mind the one crushing answer that Job receives, an answer that allows no reply. That one cannot discuss with things, simply as such, is self-evident, since he who does not hear cannot rejoin. In any case, it can be reported here, as the repartee of reality, what befell me several times in my youth: I wanted to fix an object, to compel it, as it were, in order to find through so doing that it was "only" my conception; but it refuted me through the dumb force of its being.

F. I-Thou Relation with Nature

Malcolm L. Diamond: There is a common misunderstanding of the philosophy of I and Thou which presents the I-Thou attitude as

[7] Trans. Ronald Gregor Smith (New York: Charles Scribner's Sons, 1958).

one proper to man's relation with other men and the I-It attitude as proper to man's experience of things. *I and Thou* insists that the I-Thou attitude is as appropriate to man's relations with things, ideas, and works of art as it is to man's relation to other men. It is the quality of relatedness, not the object of the relation, that determines whether an I-Thou or an I-It attitude is to prevail. Therefore, it would seem that all beings are of equal worth as Thou's, and that within the framework of the philosophy of I and Thou there would be no basis of evaluation between different I-Thou meetings or between different Thou's. If this is the case, the exploiting of children in a sweatshop would be no more reprehensible than the exploiting of a forest. Is this a fair picture of the consequences which follow from the emphasis upon the quality of man's relation with all beings in lieu of traditional moral concern with the nature of the objects to which man relates, as well as with the quality of the relation? If so, is there any basis within the philosophy of I and Thou for affirming the humanistic distinctions which value a child above a tree?

Buber: Here I must again refer to the Postscript to *I and Thou:* there are several different grades of the capacity for mutuality. But I am by no means of the opinion that from this alone a "basis of evaluation" can be established. To this end, rather, our whole knowledge about the world must co-operate, a knowledge that is ever again renewed through the I-Thou relation, but is not borne by it.

G. I-Thou and I-It

Maurice Nédoncelle: What place would Professor Buber give to the impersonal in the evolution and elevation of dialogue?

Buber: The essential significance of the impersonal for the "evolution and elevation of dialogue" seems to me to lie in the fact that it is at times common to two men and yet not common to them. That of which the other and I speak, that of which the other and I think, both describing it with the same word, indeed, what we perceive at the same time as this particular thing, is problematic just herein: we mean the same and not the same; we see the same and not the same; the word with which we designate it has for both of us the same and not the same significance. Thus the impersonal ever again involves a tension between the partners in dialogue. But the tension is fruitful; more precisely, it can be fruitful in that between what this "impersonal" is for you and what it is for me a fusion can take place, which is only possible in dialogue. That over which we have "come to an understanding" is then not in the least more pallid than what existed before on the one side and on the other; it can even be stronger, clearer, more definite. The difference that at times again exists after the dialogue is in any case different from that which existed before.

On this theme there is still much to say; here I must content myself with what I have just said.

Malcolm L. Diamond: 1. According to the philosophy of I and Thou, man in his meetings with other beings must assume either the I-It attitude of distance and detachment or the I-Thou attitude of engagement and relation. As I understand it, a pure I-Thou meeting would be one in which the total self was engaged, so that all the material channeled from the I-It attitude of detachment would be transformed into the I-Thou mode of relatedness and engagement. Is such a pure I-Thou meeting possible? If so, is it a rare phenomenon analogous to mystical experience or a comparatively frequent occurrence?

2. In an I-Thou meeting one is seized by the power of exclusiveness. The whole man is absorbed into the relation which exists between himself and his Thou, so that all else exists in the light of the relation. Would it therefore be correct to say that if a person becomes aware of being involved in an I-Thou relation, this would itself be a sign that the element of detachment characteristic of the I-It attitude has entered into and vitiated the I-Thou relation? If so, how is consciousness of an I-Thou relation possible? Is it possible only in retrospect?

Buber: 1. I speak very reluctantly of perfection as of something empirically verifiable. Since the perfect I-Thou relation in general makes no statement concerning itself, I do not know how frequent or how rare it is. But I am not at all concerned about perfection, either here or in general. I am concerned that the I-Thou relation be realized where it can be realized, and I cannot declare where it cannot be realized. I am concerned that the life of man be determined and formed by it. For I believe that it can transform the human world, not into something perfect, but perhaps into something very much more human, according to the created meaning of man, than exists today.

2. One must be careful about the double meaning of the concept "consciousness." If what is understood by it is that one becomes conscious of an object, an It, then naturally the I-Thou relation must from time to time come to an end with this becoming conscious—for the present. But the interhuman I-Thou relation does not belong to the unconscious, even in its most exclusive form, although its roots, of course, are sunk in the "unconscious," that is, in the ground of being of the person. The consciousness of the I-Thou relation is a highly intensive one; but it is a direct, an elementary consciousness. It does not make itself an object; it does not detach itself from itself; its knowing about itself is given it with its being.

David Baumgardt: Has the life of dialogue a supremacy also over the intensity of the scientist's impersonal exploration of, and submersion in, the It of inorganic matter?

I fully agree with what you say in *Zwiesprache.*[8] Even in the *Betrieb* of huge industrial plants, a far-reaching *Durchdrungensein von Vitaler Dialogik* (being soaked in vital dialogic) is possible and needed; and the worker may *seine Beziehung zur Maschine als eine dialogische empfinden* (experience his relation to the machine as one of dialogue). Moreover, as the philosophies of nature in the early European Renaissance and modern romanticism show, everything inorganic can be *angesprochen* (addressed) in this way.

But would you not agree that it may be no less of a profound attitude to abandon age-old vagueness of the dialogue in favor of a precise impersonal description of inorganic matter by means of exact mathematical formulas? For any kind of dialogue in this direction would do no justice to what is to be explored in this field; and it would even undermine and destroy the profoundly impersonal devotion of the scientist to his "object of investigation." Is there not the grave danger of human

[8] Pp. 96 ff. Cf. *Between Man and Man* (Boston: Beacon Press, paperback, 1958), pp. 36 ff.

vanity in expecting "personal" or even emotional response, in whatever sense, from the nature of dead matter which was wisely created not in the way of living personalities?

Does it not follow from these two basic experiences—the *amor fati* and the reverence for the impersonal character and the mathematical structure of natural processes—that it is not the life of dialogue which makes the difference between true and minor value but exclusively the *how* of saying Thou or It?

Buber: I do not speak of a general supremacy of the life of dialogue, but rather of its especial importance for the personal existence of man. The series of meetings that a man has taken part in is more important for this personal existence than his total possession of impersonal scientific knowledge, no matter how highly this too is to be prized. It is the former that builds up the core of the person. That holds also for the life of the investigator, even for his life as an investigator. What an "original" investigator discovers, what he "finds," he discovers and finds in his contacts with the unique: in the vision of a familiar and yet in-this-moment surprising natural phenomenon, in the "penetration" into a text granted to the genuine philologist from which the intention of the author shines forth to him, in the visions of the great historian that show him long-past events in their interconnection in which not only his presentation of the happening, but also his interpretation of the epoch has its origin. Certainly, an I-Thou relation in the full sense of the term does not, for the most part, prevail here, but the essential is there: a person and what he stands over against, which in this hour is, to begin with, only presence, not yet object, the contact of the unique with the unique, still prior to all transposition into the general. What the investigator has relinquished when he proceeds to this transposition is no "age-old vagueness," but the act of standing before concrete reality. Certainly, he must from time to time radically relinquish it in order to attain general insights or even exact formulae, but at the beginning of the way he is ever again led by the genius of meetings until it can deliver him to the reliable spirit of objectification.

That it is not by any words of mine that "human vanity" may be summoned to its expectation of a "personal or even emotional response from the nature of dead matter" I have ever again, and even ever more strongly, stressed.

Peter A. Bertocci: The underlying ambiguity which for me casts a deep shadow over almost every problem touched in Buber's thought seems to center in two incompatible modes of being, process and relation, which this "brink" philosophy would "somehow" bring together. First, and so far as I can see, the dominating one in Buber's thought: the part-whole relationship. To be sure, this is a very dynamic conception of part-whole as opposed to Spinoza's essentially logical substance-mode relation [9] and is closer to Hegel's experiential dynamism of the *Phenomenology of the Mind.* But the part-whole model of metaphysical relationship, when it escapes a rigid logicism, falls into a spatializing interpretation of metaphysical relationships, which deduces what seems to me to be the essentially *non-spatial interaction* involved in all personal experience. Thus the fundamental relation of I-Thou is conceived of in such words as *meeting, participation, inclusive, exclusive, entering.* While absorption in God is explicitly denied, we are told to "include the whole world in the *Thou,* to give the world its due and its truth, to include nothing *beside* God but everything *in* him." [10] Thus, curiously enough, we find ourselves using terms to describe an I-Thou relation which fit, I would say, It relations but never personal relations.

For is it not true to experience to say that the distinguishing characteristic of persons is that they are dynamic-unities-in-striving-and-purpose? [11] But purposes do not "meet" or "participate," and when they "include" and "exclude" they do so because their growth-of-meaning, their creativity, their directive goals are distinctive. The unity of purposes, human and divine, then must be conceived in admittedly difficult, unpicturable, nonspatial terms: but the analogy must be closer to that of husband and wife and children, each coming closer in a directive, controlling purpose and in action at different levels. *Interaction* is not the flow of energy from one to another *within* a common medium. It perhaps can be better conceived in terms of stimulated-

---

[9] Cf. *I and Thou,* pp. 78–79.
[10] *Ibid.,* p. 79. Italics added.
[11] *Ibid.,* p. 89.

evoked growth of common meanings, which are possible to individuated I's because such commonness is potentially present in their *created* being. There is much in Buber's exposition [12] which is consistent with this conception of interpersonal unity as a growth in purposeful community, but his thinking at all explanatory levels seems to be closer to the unity of an organic whole rather than to the growing unity (or disunity) of created-creative purposes with their Creative Purposer.

EXPLANATION (REQUESTED BY BUBER): Why do I say that the tension in Buber's system for me centers in the "spatializing" of the relations? I mean by spatializing not separation but inclusion; that is why I speak of part-whole, and "organic unity." I am, I hope, sufficiently aware of Buber's attempt to resist only ultimate unity in which all cows are black, and of his concern to keep a unity in which plurality will be meaningful and individuality productive. But my point is that the metaphysical relation which is to keep unity and productive individuality does not seem to me to be explicit, and, so far as I can make out, succumbs to "part-whole" to be intelligible. Even if Buber uses spatializing terms as metaphors, why such metaphorical terms as suggest fusion and overlapping? Why the frequent use of (spatializing) terms like "grasp," "embrace," "participate" to express both the epistemological and the metaphysical relation between I-Thou and knower-known? Buber, I take it, does not want a Spinozistic type of logical inclusion of minds "in" substance; but like Spinoza, I take it, he rejects *creatio ex nihilo,* which conception historically has attempted to protect the freedom and relative ontological independence especially of finite persons. *Creatio* would suggest, I suspect, too much "externality" for him. But granted that on *any* view the relation of the finite to the Ground is mysterious, I find that his language and description over and over again suggest "inner" unity and even fusion (participation).

Similarly, to protect the integrity of the knowing experience, he would avoid the possible skepticism of epistemological dualism (in which the object known and the knower are never one). "Immediacy" is emphasized in the sense of "grasp" and "embrace." But it seems to me that the guarantee of knowledge which such description (metaphoric or not) hopes to provide flounders when error appears on the scene.

[12] *Ibid.,* p. 82.

In a word, then, the attempt to anchor plurality in unity, to guarantee knowledge by "grasping," always stands in danger of losing significant plurality, adequate autonomy.

Perhaps I fear this too much, and will find myself collapsing into the chaos of ontological plurality. But as a (relative) pluralistic personalist, I resist every conception of relation in which autonomy delegated to finite persons seems to be jeopardized. Thus I conceive the relative autonomy of created persons to make impossible ontological unity, fusion, participation, or embrace, and urge that unity be the moral unity of Purposer and purposers. Thus, I would say, finite persons are created and re-creatively sustained by the cosmic Purposer whose aim is to persuade, with unending love and care, finite purposers to cooperate in developing a realm of creative persons.

Perhaps this suggests the concern behind my question. I am asking for a description of ontological and knowledge relationships which adequately protects the individuality that Buber, I believe, wishes to protect.

TO BE MORE SPECIFIC: There is no explanation in Buber of why man with his "sense of Thou, which cannot be satiated till he finds the endless Thou" can, in fact, become so alienated from the Thou. A doctrine of real yes-and-no freedom, of relatively independent individuality, might help here. Indeed, such seems to be necessary in the devolution of Thou to It; otherwise, why is It thinking and action so pervasive? Yet if man is responsible for turning Thou to It, to transform Thou to It must it not also be *his* (created) capacity, rather than Thou *in* Him, which can turn from It-thinking and acting to Thou. (This seems to be affirmed in *I and Thou*.[13])

Buber: Bertocci's objections appear to me to rest in great part on a deep misunderstanding of some of my basic concepts. But that he finds in my thought the idea of an evident all-embracing "unity of an organic whole" or of a "part-whole relationship" I cannot even explain to myself in this way. This completely erroneous conception of my philosophy must have formed itself very early in Bertocci's thinking and then he has apparently understood, that is, misunderstood, this-and-that concept as a confirmation of it.

[13] P. 94.

I have, since I matured to independent thought, never sought to explain man as a "part" of God. All that I have thought and said of the relation between man and God proceeds from the fixed presupposition that man, the human person, stands over against God from birth till death (my thinking about man does not extend further); nothing that befalls us in our lives, and nothing that happens through us, can attenuate this primal fact of standing over against. Therefore, since I wrote *I and Thou*, I have ever again designated the conception of a *unio mystica* as a mistaken interpretation of the unification of the person himself. Therefore, too, I have treated pantheism, where I have had to deal with it, as a speculative oversimplification.

The words "to include . . . everything in him" can then only be misunderstood as pantheism if one does not pay sufficient attention to the context; they correspond to the phrase that stands shortly before, "to see everything in the Thou." What concerns me fundamentally is that our relation to our fellow man and our relation to God belong together, that their basic character, that of a reciprocal I-Thou relation, joins them to each other; practically speaking, that in reality there does not exist a special sphere of "religion" and a special sphere of "ethics."

Although I say and mean that reality exists only where there is mutual action,[14] yet I can in no way accept the characterization of the person as a "dynamic-unity-in-striving-and-purpose." It does not do justice to the most essential in the person, the connection of full uniqueness and full capacity for relation. And now Bertocci continues thus: "But purposes do not 'meet' or 'participate' "—now, instead of persons, only "purposes" are being talked of. But real persons really meet each other, not merely in space, but also, for example, when they think of each other at the same time, therefore in pure time. "To participate," however, is only seemingly a "spatial" concept; in reality, "to participate in each other" is so much a category of spiritual existence that the primal metaphysical ground of the expression is no longer even perceptible. And only by means of their difference, by means of the uniqueness of this man and the uniqueness of that one, can men participate in one another.

But now Bertocci misses in my thought a "doctrine of real yes-and-no

[14] *I and Thou*, p. 89.

freedom." I am, on the contrary, of the opinion that just such a doctrine is to be found in the second part of *I and Thou*.[15]

II. THEORY OF KNOWLEDGE

A. In General

William Ernest Hocking: LOCUS OF THE QUESTION: The real as given in experience rather than pure reason; immediacy *vs.* concept; prophet *vs.* philosopher; yet dialectic as the *conscience* of realization.

QUESTION: Calling the experienced presence of the Real (as in the togetherness of dialogue) "realization," in arriving at realization, is dialectic operative? In spreading realization, is dialectic useless? In winning universal assent to realization as "truth," is dialectic a broken reed? Although we properly distinguish realization of the Real, as in the immediate experience of togetherness in "meeting," from any process of conceptual thought or any result thereof, may not conceptual reasoning—let us say dialectic—be present in that realization, as it were in solution? And may not that dialectic be a potent aid in giving currency to the experience itself?

EXPLANATION: The question itself can have meaning only within a "meeting" between Buber, as respondent, and myself, Hocking, as questioner, involving not only propositional assent but mutual understanding-through-experience of the inseparable union of I-am and Thou-art. From my side, this meeting exists, even *in absentia*. I agree that the type of truth here involved must be discovered, not proved; and aided if at all by the prophet rather than by the philosopher—dialectic cannot alone bring it about.

Yet speaking as I must from my own experience, I testify that when first this "realization" arrived—a very definite experience—it followed a period of wrestling and anxiety due to perplexities over internal contradictions of thought in which the subjective necessities stemming from Descartes and Kant contended with objective necessities I could not banish—the Real must be in some sense *other;* and the resolution

[15] Pp. 57–61.

through what appeared to be a dialectical discernment was definitely relevant to the joy of realization: dialectic was the midwife of vision.

And the conceptual structure of truth seems to remain within the experience itself as, let me say, its cognitive good faith, always of the ultimate truth of meeting itself; a vision, not an argument, followed an agonizing turmoil of thought (involving a tearing away from Husserl, who was not then concerned with "intersubjectivity"), and this turmoil, having its dialectical sense of inner contradiction, was far from irrelevant to the joy of vision.

How relevant? To most students, Descartes' experience comes at some time with a certain revealing force—there is something the doubter cannot doubt; a touch of dialectical reason "stabs us broad awake" to our own immediacy—reason the midwife of vision! But in time, the subjective vision rankles: even the Kantian *Ich-denke* is somehow false. Reject it out of hand: seize normal objectivity by force! One tries it, and knows the inner *Zwiespalt!* At last one notes that there is a reason in the case: Descartes was inconsistent; like the Buddha, his action belied his thoughts; he *published* his thought, confessing thereby that his private vision is in his own conviction Everyman's vision. Descartes must be "stabbed broad awake": his "I-exist" reveals "Thou-art." The dialectic is thus operative, as a conscience within the struggle, unwilling simply to fall back on the immediacy of intuition: realization contains in solution the structure of the thought that sets it free. The ghost of the philosopher lives *within* the soul of the prophet, and sanctions his appeal. Sometimes the two speak with one voice.

If this is the case, would it not follow that "System"—of which my colleagues Gabriel Marcel and Buber are both more than chary, I might say suspicious—may be defended as not inconsistent with the life of realization and relation, and further, as its integrity, its inner coherence?

Buber: Professor Hocking's questions give me the welcome opportunity to elucidate an important point more fully.

He rightly distinguishes between "arriving at realization" and "spreading realization." I must distinguish between them far more sharply. According to my experience, conceptual thinking can, to be sure, play a part in the first of the two, but it is not essential for it. For the second, I too hold it to be essential.

The experience from which I have proceeded and ever again proceed is simply this, that one meets another. Another, that does not mean, for example, a "dog," an "English sheep dog," one that is to be described thus-and-thus, but this particular animal, which a child once, about to run by him, looked in the eyes and remained standing, they both remained standing while the child laid his hand on the head of the dog and called him by a name that he had just invented or found. When later at home he sought to make clear to himself what had been special about the animal, he managed without concepts; he only needed them when he had to relate the occurrence to his best friend.

But now Hocking leads me in an entirely other direction: on the heights of the conceptual turmoil that he once went through, and as I make this present to myself, I feel myself standing in a genuine dialogue. That the dialectical rules here is not, indeed, to be doubted. But the question arises as to what was it then that called forth the decisive turning. Was this too of a dialectical nature or was it not rather something that broke through the conceptual framework as a real event, something of which only the consequence was the "vision"? Was it not a direct dialogical reality that brought the transformation? This was my own experience: I must, according to my own way, answer Yes to every analogous question.

It is otherwise with the stretch of the road leading beyond the vision. In order to insert what is thus experienced into my thought on being at the place that belongs to it and then, in order to communicate it to others who have not stood with me in a common experience, I am now, according to my understanding, directed to conceptuality, dialectic, reason. To come to an understanding with myself and with others over the truth of something I have thought can naturally take place only in the realm of "dialectic."

Does not, however, the deep and fearful problematic of the idea of truth open up? Can the truth attain its authenticity otherwise than when it steps out of the realm of concepts into that of meeting? What the dialectic must name "truth" is not something that one possesses; it is a preparation and a practice.

Perry LeFevre: Professor Buber, in your writings you have emphasized the interrelationship between the world of I-It and I-Thou; the I-It world is necessary to the I-Thou world; the I-Thou world is continually falling into, or returning to, the I-It. The important thing is which relationship dominates the life of the individual, of the group, of society. How do you then conceive the relationship of objective knowledge (especially from psychology, psychotherapy, education, etc.) to the world of I-Thou? Can knowledge of the processes of human growth and development, of the processes of therapy and education contribute to our individual and social movement into the achievement of dialogue? Do you believe that any normative generalizations can be derived from these objective studies of the person?

Buber: I have often indicated how much I prize science, so-called "objective knowledge." Without it there is no orientation in the world of "things" or of "phenomena," hence no orienting connection with the space-time sphere in which we have to pass our individualized life on earth. Without the splendid condensations, reductions, generalizations, symbolizations that science turns out, the handing down of a "given" order from generation to generation would be impossible. On it, on its current "position," man's current world-images are built. More than that, the remarkable basic knowledge of mathematics has a relation— one that remains ever mysterious to me—to being itself; and from this arises an incomparably compact body of reliable knowledge on which the triumph of the inherited knowledge of the human race from Euclid to Einstein is founded.

I honor science, the astonishing sphere of the sciences with its always expanding borders behind which the twilight horizon ever further recedes. But when I am asked what is its contribution to the work of a man who executes faithfully his office in the service of life, for the work of a true therapist, for the work of a true educator, then I stand in an entirely different perspective. Rather, I have exchanged all perspectives for the heart-point of life; and then, to stay with the examples already chosen, I can only regard science as a help: psychology as a help for the therapist, pedagogy as a help for the educator; both, in the hands of a man without a true vocation, manifoldly deceptive and misleading; both, in the hands of one who is truly called to his task, useful and regulative. Modern psychology is an especially instructive example. Its province, as is well known, is divided into several, in good part mutually contradictory, "schools" and methods. No school, in my judgment, can claim the predicate of truth for its manner of dream interpretation. Every genuine therapist can heal with any of the methods that have been developed; every psychotherapist can destroy with any of them. What matters and what is inseparable from the being and becoming of the person—the right relation to the Thou—will be furthered in their work whenever they reach toward the events of the research. Science always stands ready to serve the server; it is up to him to make the right, cautious, reserved, knowing use of it.

Beyond this, thus outside the responsibility practiced by a responsible man with all its Yes and No, "normative" generalizations that are made in the name of science have no real meaning for me.

Maurice Nédoncelle: Does not the passage from Him to Thou in religious philosophy risk leading us to the void or to illusion? I have read *Eclipse of God* with admiration; but I had, perhaps incorrectly, the impression that the author was not sufficiently attentive to the danger that I have just indicated; and I asked myself whether philosophy, insofar as it is such, is able to be an invocation or an interpellation.

Buber: The passage from Him to Thou is not "dangerous" for philosophy, it is impossible. I myself feel obliged, when I philosophize, to avoid "invocation," but justified in pointing to its meaning.

Kurt H. Wolff: What is the locus of reason in cognition, both of the Thou and the It (although it may not be proper to apply "cognition" to the former)? This raises the question of the relation between ecstasy, enchantment, the unique, on the one hand, and philosophizing, theorizing, the general, on the other. While the unique is related to the I-Thou, and the general to the I-It relation, these relationships are not identities; hence a third question, about the nature of these relationships. Do not answers to these questions, at least to begin with, have to take the form of "Man is such that," "The world is such that," and "The relation between man and world is such that"?

Buber: Just in that way, with a sentence about the relation between man and the world, I once began my first book on the dialogical principle, *I and Thou,* characterizing this relation as "twofold." Only I would not willingly speak of ecstasy "on the one hand"; it is easy to forget in so doing that it is not a matter of the exceptional hours, but of the everyday (cf. the chapter "A Conversion" in "Dialogue," *Between Man and Man*).

E. la B. Cherbonnier: While it would require pages to express my own indebtedness to Martin Buber, my principal criticism can be exhausted in a single sentence: Is his philosophy in fact open to criticism at all? The hallmark of philosophic discourse, as distinct from bare assertion or arbitrary insistence, is corrigibility. That is, the philosopher acknowledges a criterion by which his mistakes, if any, might be detected. Professor Buber's writings, however, not only appear to lack such a criterion, but indeed to preclude it.

Every objective criticism of his philosophy would belong, by definition, to the realm of I-It. But no I-It statement could ever impinge upon an I-Thou statement, either to refute or to confirm it. The philosopher is thus provided with a built-in immunity to criticism. He can, at his pleasure, disqualify any objection simply by placing his own statements under the sign of I-Thou. Maurice Friedman's brilliant exposition of Professor Buber's position apparently acknowledges this; it speaks of "the logical impossibility of criticizing I-Thou knowing on the basis of any system of I-It." [16] Perhaps this explains the tendency of Professor Buber's apologists to dismiss the critic, not with refutation, but by declaring that he has failed to understand.

In this respect, I-Thou dialogue appears inferior to Socratic dialogue. The Socratic philosopher is corrigible. When he contradicts himself, he acknowledges that he has fallen into error. I personally am convinced that Professor Buber's writings contain the rudiments of a philosophy which, with intensity and relevance undiminished, could satisfy a rigorous Socratic examiner. Professor Buber himself, however, repudiates consistency and embraces paradox as the appropriate vehicle for "existential truth." My question therefore is: How might his philosophy

---

[16] Maurice S. Friedman, *Martin Buber: The Life of Dialogue* (New York: Harper Torchbooks, 1960), p. 168.

be corrected, should it contain any errors? Specifically, how does one determine which paradoxes are true and which are not? Unless these questions can be answered, would not the "narrow ridge" of "holy insecurity" broaden, in practice, into a boundless plain with unlimited room for maneuver? Would not I-Thou statements then begin to resemble statements *ex cathedra?*

Buber: My answers to my critics in this Interrogation and my fuller (more detailed, comprehensive) answers to them in the volume of *The Library of Living Philosophers* devoted to me seem to me to remove all force from the suspicion of a claim to speak *ex cathedra*. Inner contradictions are no less possible here than in a Socratic philosophy, and with him who seriously seeks to point out to me such a contradiction, I go seriously into it. In no way, therefore, do I reject consistency. But where I am compelled to point to "paradoxes," there are none that are meant as being beyond possible experience; rather a silent understanding is again and again established between me and those of my readers who are ready without holding back to make their own the experiences that I mean.

William H. Poteat: 1. First of all, I should like to ask about philosophical method. In the philosophic climate powerfully influenced by the Vienna Circle, the early Russell and Wittgenstein, then the later Wittgenstein, and now by the Oxonian "ordinary language" analysis, it might occur to one to wonder whether what you have done in your distinguished career—and I will take the hardest case, for example, *I and Thou*—is philosophy at all. I might say that philosophy is a highly technical analysis of the logical syntax of language or a kind of therapy for an irresponsible and pretentious use of language or, at most, a seeing where before there has been either a not-seeing or a mis-seeing, a seeing, however, whose only instrument is argument. But what is *I and Thou?* A poem, like Rilke's *Duino Elegies?* A prayer, like Augustine's *Confessions?* A series of apothegms, like La Rochefoucauld's or like Wittgenstein's *Tractatus?* Or is it that what you are doing is such that any inquiry concerning "method" must take place in a purely analogical way? That is, "method" is an *I-It* concept.

2. You say: "The primary word *I-Thou* can only be spoken with the

whole being. The primary word *I-It* can never be spoken with the whole being." What am I to understand by "whole being"? To use an idiom quite different from your own: "What is the logical status of the concept "whole being"?

We cannot fill it out by multiplying propositions about what I do, think, say, feel, etc. ("[Human life] does not exist in virtue of activities alone which have some *thing* for their object.") We cannot distinguish "whole" from "partial" by pointing to "inner" against "outer." ("Inner things or outer things, what are they but things and things!") "Whole being" seems to mean a nonobject—something "outside" the subject-object structure of *all* language, which is to say, "outside" the world and hence unutterable. Must we not, then, remembering Wittgenstein's aphorism, remain silent?

Buber: 1. I think that I have already answered this question sufficiently. I point, I believe, to what has not yet been sufficiently "seen" and, of course, as it seems to me, through the kind of "argument" requisite for it.

2. "With the whole being" can be described most simply thus: I enter into the act or event which is in question with all the available forces of my soul without conflict, without even latent much less perceptible conflict. A surmounted conflict can create a condition accessible to the decisive self-awareness that can no longer, to be sure, be compared to vacillating, but perhaps—if one may use such an image—to a vibrating of the edges of the soul. "Wholeness" is not yet there, but a transformation of the total condition can now, as it were, take place from which it follows. Note well, the resistance must certainly not be presupposed in any given situation; there are souls that have long since overcome analogous resistances and now are already capable of meeting as a whole the situation that accosts them; indeed, there are souls of whom we do not know that the battle within them has ever been fought through, yet whose wholeness nonetheless in an unforeseen situation begins forthwith to shine like the sun.

Jacob B. Agus: In your exaltation of the I-Thou relationship, do you not consign reason to the subordinate role of manipulation in the realm of I-It, failing to recognize the objectivity of reason as a supreme value category, coeval with love and supplementing its impetus?

EXPLANATION: Your discovery of the I-Thou relationship was a magnificent contribution toward the understanding of the fullness of human nature, especially its paradoxical quality, the I discovering itself by yielding itself in devotion to a Thou. This perception of a dimension of being and value served as an excellent corrective to the way of thinking, common to scientism and philosophical idealism, in which the personality of the individual was completely dissolved.

Do you not, however, overlook the fact that, in the process of searching for truth, human reasoning constitutes in effect a rigid and austere surrender of the self to the majesty of being? Already the ancients distinguished between utilitarian thinking, in which reason is simply a manipulative instrument, and philosophical thinking, in which reason constitutes man's worship of the objective and the universal.

A one-sided worship of love may be as false as a one-sided worship of reason.

Buber: Since I am not authorized to philosophize by any metaphysical essences, neither of "ideas" nor of "substance" nor even of the "world reason," but must as a thinker concern myself alone with man and his relations to everything, so reason as an object of my thought is important for me only insofar as it dwells in man as a property or function. In such a manner, therefore, regarded from the viewpoint of philosophical anthropology, reason seems to me to take different attitudes in different times and circumstances. Either it knows itself as belonging as a part to the total being of the human person, and is active in full co-operation with the other properties and functions, and can in just this sense have a significant, yes even a leading, share in the intercourse of this person with other persons. Or it claims for itself the supremacy to which all the other faculties of man have to subordinate themselves. If it makes such a claim, then it appears to me presumptuous and dubious. To take the example lying nearest to hand, the "corrective" office of reason is incontestable, and it can be summoned at any moment to set right an "error" in my sense perception—more precisely, its incongruity with what is common to my fellow men; but it cannot replace the smallest perception of something particular and unique with its gigantic structure of general concepts, cannot by means of it contend in the grasping of what here and now confronts me.

Peter A. Bertocci: 1. In the epistemological relation, epistemic dualism of a Kantian sort is both accepted (in It) and rejected in Thou-I; epistemic confidence is won by insisting ultimately on the unity and solidarity of knower-known relation. But no account seems to be forthcoming of how epistemic error, which means that man can have "in mind" what is not objectively there, is possible on this view.

2. Inferential knowledge of other minds, divine or human, is rejected once more in favor of unity and direct presence. But, again, how is error in knowledge of other minds even possible on this view?

3. Granted that there are many experiences whose psychological certitude may indeed suggest epistemological monism, should not the fact of error force us to reconstruct our view of what is involved in such relations: Perhaps the underlying conception of knowledge which we should distrust is that of knowledge as a kind of infallible relation. What I wish were possible, at any rate, is less of a *declarative* tone in this total perspective, and more an expository-explanatory one in which the grounds for weaknesses and errors of other views became more articulate. By what criterion does one judge the "apprehensible" as opposed to the "comprehensible"? [17]

Buber: 1. As I have repeatedly stated, I know no criterion for the "objective existence" of what becomes present to me in the I-Thou relation; indeed, to me none is conceivable. I have never concealed the fact that he who wishes to live securely would do better to stay far from the way which I have indicated. So far as I have a philosophy, it treats man as a being to whom it is given to make present what stands over against him and to exist without guarantees.

2. In the true I-Thou relation there is no knowledge of objective facts, hence also none that in the state of the I-It relationship can be compared with any of these data that it has yielded and corrected as an "error." That is implicit in the sentence that the world is twofold for man. But in the I-It relationship we do, indeed, elaborate much that we have received in the I-Thou relation and that, manifoldly broken up,

[17] *I and Thou,* p. 94.

persists in our memory; here "errors" are possible because in this state one has the possibility, even though a limited one, of "objectively" establishing and comparing what has passed and passes in the minds of others.

The concept of knowledge of the divine mind is for me, moreover, pure contradiction. God gives us signs for the establishing of our relation to him, but he still does not make himself into an object for our observation. In the language of the prophets of Israel, the "knowledge of God" properly means intercourse with him.

3. An epistemological monism is entirely alien to my thought; I have always fought the attempt to establish any such in our time. A knowledge, in the sense of an objective given and what can be discussed accordingly, a knowledge in this sense that would be "infallible," is for me, in the human world, a *non-ens*.

For the rest, I have the impression that Professor Bertocci has only read a little of my works; most of what I have written in this province after *I and Thou* seems to me precisely to possess "an expository-explanatory" character.

Maurice S. Friedman: 1. To discover the implications of the I-Thou philosophy for epistemology, is it not necessary to distinguish between two types of "I-It" knowledge: that which, as word, symbol, image points back directly to the unique reciprocal knowing of particular I-Thou relationships and that which, because it takes the form of abstract and general categories, can no longer point back to the concrete and the unique, but can only take its place?

EXPLANATION: In "Religion and Philosophy" (*Eclipse of God*) you speak of the symbol which points back to the immediate relation with God yet always eventually swells itself up and blocks the road to God. In my chapter on your theory of knowledge in *Martin Buber: The Life of Dialogue,* I have similarly distinguished between I-It, or subject-object, knowledge which points back to the I-Thou relation from which it derives, and that which blocks the return to I-Thou by posing as reality itself.

The "word" may be identified with subject-object, or I-It, knowledge while it remains indirect and symbolic, but it is itself the channel and expression of I-Thou knowing when it is taken up into real dialogue.

Subject-object, or I-It, knowledge is ultimately nothing other than the socially objectivized and elaborated product of the real meeting which takes place between man and his Thou in the realms of nature, social relations, and art. As such, it provides those ordered categories of thought which are, together with dialogue, primal necessities of human existence. But as such also, it may be, like the indirect and objective "word," the symbol of true dialogue. *It is only when the symbolical character of subject-object knowledge is forgotten or remains undiscovered . . . that this "knowledge" ceases to point back* toward the reality of direct dialogical knowing and becomes instead an obstruction to it.[18]

It now seems to me that the italicized part of this statement is true only of one kind of I-It knowledge: that which retains a symbolic, or pointing, connection with the I-Thou meeting from which it derives. Such I-It knowledge may or may not point back. It is a first level of abstraction and objectification which may lead us again to the concrete or may itself serve as material for still further abstraction from the symbol to the general concept. Once this second step of abstraction and objectification is accomplished, it cannot lead back to the particular I-Thou meeting even though it originally derive from what you have called "true scientific confrontation." An operationalist description of interpersonal relationships from the standpoint of a behaviorist observer, for example, though it is based on the observation of relationships many of which were genuinely I-Thou, can never point back to the concreteness and uniqueness of an I-Thou relationship in the way a poem or novel could, because it extracted only the general categories through which these relationships could be compared.

2. If the above distinction is valid, what then is the relationship between this second type of I-It knowledge and I-Thou knowing? Is it correct to say that it derives indirectly from I-Thou knowing by a double process of abstraction? Or must one say that here an independent order of reason and objectification enters in and that the alternation between I-Thou knowing and I-It knowledge is not after all a sufficiently comprehensive approach to understand either the rational categories of logic, on the one hand, or the empirically-based generalization of scientific method, on the other?

---

[18] Friedman, *Martin Buber: The Life of Dialogue* (New York: Harper Torchbooks, 1960), p. 166. Italics added.

EXPLANATION: In *Martin Buber: The Life of Dialogue* I speak of "the symbolic function and the dependent and mediate reality of the I-It relation."

What takes place in the present is ordered through the abstracting function I-It into the world of categories—of space and time, cause and effect. We usually think of these categories as reality itself, but they are actually merely the symbolic representations of what has become.[19]

Does the reasoning that lies behind this statement, that which sees the dialectical interrelation between I-Thou and I-It, itself derive from I-Thou knowing? Are the categories of which it speaks only social objectifications or do they have some objective logic of their own that is not adequately explained by speaking of them as secondary derivatives of I-Thou knowing?

Buber: 1. Certainly there exist various stages of the I-It state, according to how far these are alienated from the I-Thou relation and relinquish the pointing back to it. But I am not inclined to replace these stages by two types different from each other by their nature. On the one side, there is no abstraction so ethereal that a great living man could not conjure it with its secret primal name and draw it back down to the earth of bodily meetings. On the other side, however, just in our time the crassest absence of relation has begun to find a consistent "empty" expression in novel and in drama. It may be harder to oppose to it the genuine might of human meeting than to the behaviorist defective description.

2. Since a "world" in which we find our way and whose coherent knowledge we transmit from generation to generation can exist only on the basis of the I-It relationship, I cannot hold its logical foundations to be secondary derivations. These foundations that bear human thought are not to be derived either from the one or from the other of the two "basic worlds," that is, the two human world-aspects that I distinguish. I am not empowered to formulate a metaphysical thesis that would lead beyond the duality of these aspects. But how the two aspects again and again have co-operated and co-operate in the human construction and reconstruction of a "world" accessible to human thought, I have at-

[19] P. 168.

tempted to indicate by the category of "we," in "What Is Common to All." [20]

Paul E. Pfuetze: What are the criteria by which we can distinguish the true I-Thou relation from the alienated world of I-It?

EXPLANATION: Your "narrow rocky ridge" stands between the abyss of irrational subjectivism, on one side, and the abyss of abstract rationalism, on the other. On the central ridge is the concrete, spontaneous meeting with the particular Thou, which in awareness and response we try to experience from the other side.

Are there, then, no clearer principles of guidance, no more objective norms for determining the true world of Thou, more reliable criteria for judging what aspects of experience we shall choose as the true Thou of the self?

Is there no way to distinguish true from false, the true I-Thou relation from the alienated world of I-It?

How shall we combine intense personal commitment and venture with a measure of critical detachment?

Or is insecurity and uncertainty the inherent and inevitable predicament of finite human existence?

Must we live always by faith, trust, venture, and unfathomable risk —never by truth in which we can have some confidence?

Buber: I would have to be untrue to my basic experience, which is an experience of faith, if I should seek to establish such "objective" criteria. I do indeed mean an "insecurity," insofar as criteria are concerned, but I mean—I say it once again—a holy insecurity.

B. In Psychology and Psychotherapy

Walter Blumenfeld: Can it be maintained that Buber's method differs essentially from psychological introspection and retrospection?

Buber: I do not know exactly what is understood here by "my method." My few occasional remarks on the task of the anthropologist are hardly sufficient to be discussed as a method. Yet I shall gladly

[20] Trans. Maurice S. Friedman, *Review of Metaphysics*, Vol. XI, No. 3 (March, 1958).

make a little more precise the essential difference between the psychological methods and the anthropological.

For this purpose I shall only just touch on the specific problematic of so-called introspection. A few modern psychologists have indeed recognized that so-called self-observation exercises transforming influence upon the psychic process comparable to that which the physicist has posited for the observations of electrons. Therefore the retrospective method that works with the more or less reliable events of an unarbitrary memory is the more useful of the two. An anthropologist who is aware of his task and his way will employ no method analogous to "introspection."

Far more important, however, is the fundamental difference between the psychological and the anthropological methods and, in particular, that between psychological and anthropological "retrospection."

Psychological methods may, by their nature, be called reductive, anthropological integrative. The first have set the knowledge of "psychic phenomena" as their task. But how far are these given to us in our self-experience as an isolated self-contained kind of phenomenon? In our factual life, at least in our factual waking life, are not psychic phenomena for the most part closely bound up with those of other kinds? The psychologist shrinks the remembered event to its psychic side; the anthropologist, who is concerned with the whole body-soul man, renews in reflection the memory of what happened to him in a certain life-context, "from within" and "from without" at the same time, in the closest union of inner and outer. And this is still not enough: his reflection also grasps the remembered share of other men in the common situations, grasps the remembered relation from the one side and from the other. In such integrative making-present of human existence, his knowledge of what man and only man is becomes ever more complete.

Maurice S. Friedman: Since guilt manifests itself to our awareness as a feeling, how is one to distinguish between that guilt-feeling that accompanies existential guilt and that which accompanies neurotic guilt?

EXPLANATION: In "Guilt and Guilt Feelings" [21] you point to

[21] Trans. Maurice S. Friedman, *Psychiatry,* Vol. XX, No. 2 (May, 1957), pp. 114–129.

the fact that psychoanalytic theory has neglected the existence of real, or "existential," guilt—"guilt that a person has taken on himself as a person in a personal situation," guilt that "occurs when someone injures an order of the human world whose foundations he knows and recognizes as those of his own existence and of all common human existence." This distinction between "existential guilt" and neurotic guilt derived from a distorted self-relationship rests in turn on the distinction between the "interhuman"—the sphere of direct, mutual relations between men—and the merely psychic, including the psychic effect of indirect, nonmutual interpersonal relationships. Your protest against reducing all guilt to neurotic guilt is an essential part, therefore, of the larger protest against psychologizing the dialogue between man and man and reducing the interhuman to the psychic.

The therapist who recognizes the validity of this protest will overcome the tendency he may have had to reduce all guilt to guilt feelings. But as a therapist, he must still deal with sickness, and that means with many manifestations of guilt feelings that may have no base in existential guilt or that may be the product of an inextricable mingling of genuine existential and "groundless" neurotic guilt. How is the therapist, who knows the event in which the guilt arose only through the report and the eyes of the patient plus his own inferences and surmisings, to distinguish in practice between that guilt feeling or element within a guilt feeling that is existentially based and that which is neurotically based? Or for that matter how is any person in his self-knowledge to make such a distinction? This is not a question of specifics for specific situations, but of the nature and source of the criteria whereby one distinguishes between real and seeming I-Thou relationships and between real and seeming violations and denials of I-Thou relations.

Buber: In this province too I have no objective, universally applicable criteria to offer, with the exception of one that I have indicated in "Guilt and Guilt Feelings": that the neurotic guilt feelings have their essential place in the "unconscious"; the relationship of man to an existential guilt, in contrast, has its essential place in memory. But the proper distinction cannot be described in terms which have general validity; the genuine therapist who relates to his patients as a partner, again and again makes this distinction, though naturally not always;

but the pseudo therapist, for whom the patient is an object of investigation and manipulation, customarily misses it, at times in a quite artistic manner.

I can only point ever again to the necessity of the distinction; how it is to be made I cannot teach in a general way. I even incline to assume that others also are not capable of doing so. It depends, I believe, crucially upon the doctor, crucially upon the human person.

III. EDUCATION

Robert Assagioli: Your essay on "Hasidism and Modern Man" contains in my opinion an important and most timely message. How can present-day humanity, and particularly modern youth, be induced or helped to the rediscovery and the recognition of the "Sacred"? In what ways and by what means—expressed in terms understandable and acceptable by modern man—do you think that (also apart from the message of Hasidism) the *totalité lesée de l'homme* (the injured wholeness of man) can be re-established?

Buber: This question is especially important, but in this general form hardly adequate to be answered. I know no generally applicable methods that merely need to be set forth in order to effect a transformation. I do not believe that a How, formulable as a principle, exists here. Only the personal involvement of the educating man can help, the man who himself knows the holy and who knows how; in this our time, persons of the most varied kinds suffer the often unavowed, indeed, on occasion, vigorously denied, pain over the unholiness of their lives. I say personal involvement; therefore, not an already existing teaching that lies to hand and needs only to be transmitted to those who suffer in this manner in order that they may learn that the holy exists and what the holy is; furthermore, that it is just this which the sufferer misses, and finally what he has to do to attain it. No, what can help is the simple personal life, the educator's own life, in which the everyday and its actions are hallowed, a life that is so lived that he who suffers from the unholiness can, and finally even will, participate in it. I have known no one whom I might call a saint, but many whose everyday performances, without being meant to be holy actions, work exactly such.

But what is meant here by holy? Now, quite simply this, that the one who lives in contact with this man feels against his will, against his *Weltanschauung:* That is genuine to the roots; that is not a shoot from an alien stem; its roots reach into that sphere from whose inaccessibility I suffer in the overlucid hours of midnight. And at first unwillingly, then also willingly, the man thus affected in contact is himself drawn into connection with that sphere. It is indeed a matter of "hallowing"; it is a matter, hence, of the *humanly* holy; and what is to be understood by that, in my view, does not admit of any definition and any method that can be taught; one learns to know it in doing something spontaneously, otherwise than one is accustomed to do, at first only "more really," that is, "putting more of oneself into it," then with more intention, more meaning, finally opening oneself to the sphere from which the meaning of our existence comes to us.

The crisis that has come over the human world has its origin in the dehallowing of existence. It appears, at times, as if the crisis would assume the sinister tempo of "world history." Is there not reason to despair that education could overtake it, or at all obviate it? True education is never in vain, even if the hour makes it appear so. Whether it manifests itself before or in or after the threatening catastrophe—the fate of man will depend on whether the rehallowing of existence takes place.

Heinz-Joachim Heydorn: How is it possible to liberate the relationship of the individual to himself from its distorted state, without at the same time destroying his relationship with his total environment, and while maintaining this relationship as meaningful?

EXPLANATION: In the address on "The Education of Character" delivered in Tel Aviv in 1939, we find the following:

In order to enter into a personal relationship with the absolute, it is first necessary to become a person again, to rescue one's real personal self from the fiery jaws of the collectivism which devours all self-hood. The longing to do this is hidden in the pain that the individual suffers through his distorted relation to his own real self. Again and again he deadens the pain with a subtle poison and thus suppresses the longing as well. To keep this pain alive and to awaken the longing—this is the first task of everyone who regrets the obscuring of eternity. This is also the primary task of the genuine educator in our time.[22]

There exists without doubt, among members of the younger generation, an awareness that their lives lack a deeper fulfillment. Along with a characteristic realism, one often finds a vague and floundering search for an "image," in which the longing of humanity is revealed in the strangest and most varied disguises. But if this longing, as it still remains evident today, is to lead to a rediscovery of the self, then it must be supported by the expectation that a meaningful relationship *can* be established between one's own self and reality. The young person, however, feels himself to a large extent the object of a reality which he does not comprehend or, worse yet, which he comprehends just enough to make use of its inner fragility. He lacks the courage to make a new beginning with his own existence; freedom loses its meaning in the face of reality; and he finds himself a fatalist, abandoned to his fate. No amount of theoretical analysis will relieve him from this consciousness of his own incapacity when confronted with reality. The danger exists that the dark mounting pain, when once it becomes a conscious one, can turn upon itself with destructive power and abandon the individual to the unillumined awareness of his own isolation.

Buber: I speak expressly of the *first* task of the educator because the awakening of pain and of longing is the indispensable presupposition. But I do, indeed, say ever again that one can only become a genuine person through a genuine relation to the real, through genuine saying of Thou. To further, to strengthen, to encourage the readiness and openness to this relation in the young cannot be separated in time from that "first" task; here there must again and again be decided, according to the individual and the situation, what is bidden in this and that hour. Certainly the young person today feels himself largely the object of reality; but how can one help him break this spell? Why, only through guiding him—it goes without saying, in an unemotional, unromantic, unsentimental manner—toward coming into a genuine contact with the reality *accessible* to him. But, you say, he lacks the courage. How does one educate for courage? Through nourishing trust. How does one nourish trust? Through one's own trustworthiness.

[22] *Between Man and Man* (Boston: Beacon Press paperback, 1958), pp. 110 ff.

Robert M. Hutchins: I have spent all my life as an administrator. That means that I have been primarily concerned with the management and direction of institutions. *Émile* is very little good to me because the hero did not go to school. My question has been, What is possible in educational institutions, granting the inevitable handicaps of numbers, organization, finance, etc.? Moreover, I have been required to face the fact that the great teacher—Buber, for example—is a rarity. What are the best guides for ordinary teachers dealing with ordinary pupils?

The question is therefore not merely, What is man, but, What is the *special* role of educational institutions with regard to man? Have they the same role as that of the family and the church? How can American educational institutions best play the role that should be assigned to them?

For example, I am as much against a one-sided intellectualism as Buber is. I believe that man is not a centaur and that human reason is to be understood only in connection with human nonreason. These statements are not a guide to the American educational administrator because they do not tell him what aspects of man are the special obligation or object of the educational system. No doctrine has promoted the disintegration of American education as much as that of the "whole man": it has been used to justify the inclusion of the most frivolous trivialities in the course of study.

There is grave danger in too literal and immediate an interpretation of Buber's insistence on "our present situation" and "our hour." If it is Buber who is defining the situation and naming the hour, one can with confidence select educational material in the light of his decision. But the whole view of American education that we must adjust the student to his environment—which I regard as radically erroneous—can be justified by an interpretation of Buber's language, of which he would be the last to approve. Only in a Buberian sense do we know what the situation of our pupils will be or understand the exigencies of the hour. In a literal, narrow sense, we do not know what economic, political, social situation they will confront, or what time it will be. Since we do not know the situation or the hour, we should try to help them to learn how to deal with any situation and with any time.

"A truly reciprocal conversation in which both sides are full partners" suggests a situation that would be wholly unreal in the vast majority of cases. Those cases are those from kindergarten up in which the assumption of full partnership would be an elaborate fake, where the pupil was immature and his experiences and opinions, no matter what his age, were of the most infantile kind. If what is meant here is that the pupil and teacher are full partners in the search for truth, I heartily agree; but if the implication is that a man of great experience and profound wisdom must act as though pupils who are *ex hypothesi* of little experience and small wisdom had the same experience and wisdom as himself, and if he must allow them to act on the same assumption, then I must protest.

A great teacher, like Socrates or Buber, can start with anything and move by ordered stages to the most tremendous issues. The ordinary teacher who begins with triviality is almost certain to end there. The virtue of great books is that they are the thoughts of great men about great issues, most of which are so fundamental that they are issues of our present situation and our hour in any definition of those terms. We must bring our own concrete reality to our reading, of course. We need to bring these ideas to our concrete reality.

Buber: 1. Dr. Hutchins rightly sees a great danger in an all-too-literal interpretation of my view that the decisive pedagogical task is to educate men so that when they are grown they will be equal to the historical situation that then confronts them. Every all-too-literal interpretation of a truth is dangerous. What is important is not formally to fix the true, but to preserve it in its living context.

That the educational task consists of adjusting the student to his environment I too regard as a fateful error. We must not adjust ourselves to the changing situations, but we have to take our stand toward them and master them.

Naturally we cannot foresee the situation before which our pupils will one day stand, and consequently we cannot prepare our pupils for it. But we can and should teach our pupils what a situation means for the mature and courageous man; in other words, we can and should teach them the right relationship between idea and situation, namely, that the idea receives its reality from situations in which it has to authenticate itself.

We live in a time when, less than in any earlier time, men dare to look in the face the situation into which they have fallen. From this comes the frightening lack of leadership in our days. The fathers have imparted principles to the generation ruling today, but not the capacity of the soul to let the principle-true praxis be determined by the situations. This must change if the coming generations are to trust themselves to undertake the salvation of the human race.

This must change, that is: education must change; and that means above all: the educator must change. We must begin with the education of the educator. More exactly: the leading men of the teachers colleges must be chosen most carefully; they must be men who know the connection of idea and situation both conceptually and practically; and from the community of these men one of the highest professions of the land must be formed.

2. That there can be no question here of a full partnership I have already stated and offered specific reasons for in my "Education" [23] and recently again in my Postscript to the second edition of *I and Thou*.[24] I have indicated that and why an inclusive reciprocity between teacher and pupil neither should nor can exist. The good teacher knows the soul of his pupils; the pupils would cease to be pupils if they knew the soul of their teacher. The teacher is obliged to *mean* the person of the pupil in its highest possibilities and, so far as it is up to him, to develop it; it would be absurd to conceive anything analogous from the side of the pupil. The educational relationship that is desirable is, to be sure, founded on trust on both sides; but the trust is basically different on each side: the pupil has in relation to the right teacher the trust that he is what he is; the teacher has in relation to the right pupil the trust that he will become what he will become. It would also be contrary to all pedagogical sense, as Hutchins says, if the teacher acted as if he were not far superior to the pupil in experience.

But from all this it is not to be inferred that no real dialogue is possible between the educator and his charge. Hutchins' acknowledgment of the fact "that the pupil and the teacher are full partners in the search for truth" does not satisfy me. However much the teacher is superior to the pupil in experience, there is, nonetheless, something that the former can learn from the latter: this is the personal experiences that

[23] *Between Man and Man* (Boston: Beacon Press paperback, 1958), pp. 83–103.
[24] *I and Thou* (New York: Charles Scribner's Sons, 1958), pp. 123–137.

the pupil has had and that he communicates directly or indirectly. Every teacher who has ears and a heart will willingly listen to such reports, which are irreplaceable because they are grounded in individuals; and he will incorporate them in his manifold world-and-life-experience; but he will also help the pupil to advance confidently from the individual experience that he has now had to an organic knowledge of the world and life. Such an interchange, although it cannot be a full one, I call, in spite of all, a dialogical one.

I esteem highly the educational value for the growing man of reading "great" books; it once did much for me. But it cannot replace the dialogue, for the highest work of the spirit, no matter how high it exalts its reader, cannot offer him what the simple human meeting between teacher and pupil again and again can give: the helping immediacy. It educates the pupil because he is here meant as he whom he is created to become.

3. I know of very few men in history to whom I stand in such a relation of both trust and veneration as Socrates. But when it is a matter of using "Socratic questions" as an educational method, I am against it. I agree, indeed—with some qualifications—to the statement of Confucius that in order to clarify human realities one must clarify concepts and names, but I am of the opinion that such clarification should be united with a criticism of the function of concepts and names. Confucius overvalued the significance for the life of man of designations in comparison with proper names; Socrates overvalued the significance of abstract general concepts in comparison with concrete individual experiences. General concepts are the most important stays and supports, but Socrates treated them as if they were more important than bones—that they are not. Stronger, however, than this basic objection is my criticism of a pedagogical application of the Socratic method. Socrates conducts his dialogue by posing questions and proving the answers that he received untenable; these are not real questions; they are moves in a sublime dialectical game that has a goal, the goal of revealing a not-knowing. But when the teacher whom I mean (apart from the questions he must ask in examinations) enters into a dialogue with his pupil and in this connection directs a question to him, he asks, as the simple man who is not inclined to dialectic asks: because he wants to know something: that, namely, which this young person be-

fore him, and precisely he, knows to report on the subject under discussion: a small individual experience, a nuance of experience that is perhaps barely conceptually comprehensible, nothing further, and that is enough. The teacher will awaken in the pupil the need to communicate of himself and the capacity thereto and in this way bring him to greater clarity of existence. But he also learns, himself, through teaching thus; he learns, ever anew, to know concretely the becoming of the human creature that takes place in experiences; he learns what no man ever learns completely, the particular, the individual, the unique. No, certainly no full partnership; but still a characteristic kind of reciprocity, still a real dialogue.

But now you will object, dear Dr. Hutchins, that there are too few good teachers, and you will be right: there are far too few. What follows from that? Why, just this, that our most pressing task is to educate educators, is it not so?

IV. SOCIAL PHILOSOPHY

Arthur A. Cohen: In your discussions of Hasidism it is clear that the directness and immediacy of meeting are founded upon the fact of community. It would appear that you do not consider Hasidism a merely dead fact in man's spiritual history. Can this fact be re-created, that is to say, is the order of Hasidic existence a real possibility or only an ideal, but implausible, possibility for modern man?

Buber: It is not correct to say that in my presentation of Hasidism the immediacy of meeting is "founded upon the fact of community." Rather, in my view, it is the other way round: the community is founded upon the immediacy of relation. The Hasidic communal group, like all genuine community, consists of men who have a common, immediate relation to a living center, and just by virtue of this common center have an immediate relation to one another. In the midst of the Hasidic community stands the *zaddik,* whose function it is to help the Hasidim, as persons and as a totality, to authenticate their relation to God in the hallowing of life and just from this starting point to live as brothers with one another. That is a great historical example

of a communal reality which can arise to this or that extent, in this or
that form, at different times and at different places. Why should that be
implausible for modern man? He need only become radically wearied
with the meaninglessness of his existence and acquire an intractable,
bold desire to win again a life that has meaning. The beginning in this
direction I have recently discussed in the essay "Hasidism and Modern
Man" (1957).[25]

Kurt H. Wolff: 1. What is the relation between I-Thou and I-It if
Thou is a civilization and It is that civilization transformed into an
object of assessment? How can "every civilization . . . be hallowed"?[26]
Assuming that the answer is: By relating It back to Thou, what is the
sociological cogency of doing this? What, in other words, is the relation
between spirit and world?

2. Another instance of the relevance of the last question is that of the
significance of the I-Thou philosophy at this time. What are the safeguards, if any, against the use of this philosophy as an instrument of
political reaction; against its being seized upon as an injunction to
withdraw into one's private garden? How does this philosophy escape
such a danger of "ideologization"—the twin danger, perhaps, of the
"politicization" of our time (cf. "Abstract and Concrete," *Pointing the
Way*)?

Buber: 1. The first question is not wholly clear to me: I cannot
imagine that I address civilization as "Thou"; I cannot conceive anything at all real thereby. On the other hand, my own statement that
every civilization "can be hallowed" may not be formulated clearly
enough. I do not mean thereby that one can hallow any civilization
as a whole; rather, I mean thereby that it is possible for man in every
civilization, whatever it is, to hallow life, lived life. What the "sociological cogency" of that is I do not know; indeed, I doubt very much
that anything of the sort exists. But I do certainly believe that when
men who hallow their lives live with one another, this can also have,
among others, the most real and significant "sociological" consequences.

[25] Cf. *Hasidism and Modern Man,* Vol. I of *Hasidism and the Way of Man,* ed. and
trans. by Maurice S. Friedman (New York: Horizon Press, 1958).
[26] Buber, *At the Turning* (New York: Farrar, Straus and Company, 1952), pp. 21 f.

But if the question is now posed in a metaphysical instead of a socio-logical framework, as the question of the relation between spirit and world, then by way of an answer I know only to refer to the fact that there are many different kinds of relation. What concerns me in an especial, and for me decisive, way is the spirit that enters into the human world, that wills to "realize itself" in it. It is clearly the case that the world resists this will far more than yields to it; but it also seems to be true that the longing of the world to become the body of the spirit is secretly becoming ever greater. It appears, too, that the world masks its resistance as yielding, with the intention, of course, of overcoming its longing through seeming satisfaction of it.

2. Against the danger that the I-Thou philosophy will be used as "an instrument of political reaction" there is, so far as I know, no safeguard other than that all its true friends fight this misuse; the weapons for this fight they will find within themselves. As a small example of this I cite what is said against "withdrawal into one's private garden" in my essay of 1919, "What Is to Be Done," in *Pointing the Way*.[27]

"Ideologization" is, indeed, the worst thing that can befall the I-Thou philosophy. My friend, the Benedictine Father Caesarius Lauer, pointed out in 1951 [28] that the easiest manner of evading the demand of the dialogic is to accept it as discussable but unbinding theory. I can only repeat in opposition to this what I wrote in 1923 and Father Caesarius quotes: "The way is there in order that one may walk on it."

Heinz-Joachim Heydorn: 1. In the last analysis, does not all hope for the future depend upon a renewed "community" (*koinonia*), arising as an earnest of what is to come, as the harbinger, so to speak, of a new power through which history is anticipated? How is such a power possible without hope for the meaning of history?

EXPLANATION: In the address entitled "Hope for This Hour" given in Carnegie Hall, New York City, in 1952, it was said:

The Hope for this hour depends upon the renewal of dialogical immediacy between men. But let us look beyond the pressing need, the anxiety and care of this hour. Let us see this need in connection with the great human

[27] *Pointing the Way: Collected Essays,* ed. and trans. by Maurice S. Friedman (New York: Harper Torchbooks, 1963), pp. 108 ff.

[28] Cf. Maurice S. Friedman, *Martin Buber: The Life of Dialogue,* pp. 271 ff.

way. Then we shall recognize that immediacy is injured not only between man and man, but also between the being called man and the source of his existence. At its core the conflict between mistrust and trust of man conceals the conflict between mistrust and trust of eternity. If our mouths succeed in genuinely saying "thou," then, after long silence and stammering, we shall have addressed our eternal "Thou" anew. Reconciliation leads towards reconciliation.[29]

Complete reconciliation of man with creation is an idea which we are apt to associate with the end of human history, in which our destiny is expected truly to fulfill itself. But is not hope for a relative reconciliation with history necessary if the meeting between man and man is to grow into community? Surely in every genuine meeting the deeper reality of our existence is present. "Community," however, if it desires to be real community in this world and for the sake of this world, requires faith in a new revelation in human history in which the Eternal becomes more visible. I would not here exclude those communities which rely exclusively upon their trust in the activity of God alone. Only this faith lends strength to a community to start on its way and develop the power of its activity, while dialogue can become a conversation in the desert, a kind of final confirmation that the True and the Eternal continue to exist without manifest revelation—like a stream which for ages seeks its way below the surface. Active community with others is community under the image of the future. For the present, we live on the mass graves of visions of the past.

2. The question as to whether man will have a place in the society of the future, in the sense of a spiritual understanding of his own nature, undoubtedly depends to a large extent on the question of whether this society will succeed in developing a rich inner diversity. What are the existing objective prerequisites for this?

EXPLANATION: In *Paths in Utopia* we read: "An organic commonwealth—and only such commonwealths can join together to form a shapely and articulated race of men—will never build itself up out of individuals but only out of small and ever smaller communities: a nation is a community to the degree that it is a community of communities."[30]

[29] *Pointing the Way,* pp. 228 f.
[30] *Paths in Utopia,* trans. by R. F. C. Hull (London: Routledge & Kegan Paul, 1949), p. 136.

The faith of our fathers during the past century was to a great extent a faith in history, in the fulfilling principle which history discloses through its own activity. Today on the European continent, except in the Communist lands, this faith has broken down completely and has been replaced by its exact opposite. However, enough of this awareness of history remains so that we cannot pose any problem without immediately connecting it with the question concerning the meaning of history, that is, concerning the objective possibilities which are held in store by history. The idea of progressing beyond a capitalistic society to dwell in the new community and to live for the day when this present society will be overthrown has led to the formation of the modern communes. These communal associations have, however, all too often and to a large extent adapted themselves to the economic structure of their surroundings and thus have lost their original character. They do not now represent an historically potential power. At the same time that traditional forms that belong to the past are dying—a process that has been going on uninterruptedly since the beginning of modern times—man has hardly ever succeeded for long periods of time in preserving new forms in their original meaning. The reality of industrial society, its unifying and rationalizing power which results in the isolation of the individual, has proved to be stronger. In spite of occasional and noteworthy exceptions, the general drift in the development of society is toward a weakening of the interior diversity of our forms and ways of life.

In his *Das Problem des Menschen*,[31] Martin Buber rightly calls the spirit an "event," but this event depends at the same time upon the existence of objective conditions which must be evident in the reality of society itself and which the spirit helps to make visible.

3. To what extent is the agreement of way and goal conceivable within the possibilities of historical existence?

EXPLANATION: In the address "Education and World-View," delivered in 1935 at the *Freun Jüdischen Lehrhaus* in Frankfurt am Main, it is stated:

How far the future community will correspond to the desired image depends essentially upon the life-attitude of present-day persons—not only of those who lead but of each individual in the ranks. The goal does not

[31] "What Is Man?" trans. by Ronald Gregor Smith, *Between Man and Man* (Boston: Beacon Press paperback, 1958), pp. 118–205.

stand fast and wait. He who takes a road that in its nature does not already represent the nature of the goal will miss the goal, no matter how fixedly he holds it in sight. The goal that he reaches will resemble the road by which he has reached it.[32]

Certainly these sentences contain a decisive insight. However, the will to realize the future in the present is limited by the deep opposition between image and reality, which opposition we may well diminish but which we can never totally remove. In our decisions, wherever we carry responsibility, we cannot avoid the painful realization that there is no action which is without guilt, without failure toward the goal and thereby also toward our neighbors. Does not the greatness of the human potentiality lie rather in the constant striving toward this agreement of way and goal, in the midst of and in spite of contradictions which we inevitably meet whenever we assume responsibility?

Buber: 1. I too hope in history (as I have clearly stated in the concluding section of "Prophecy, Apocalyptic, and the Historical Hour," *Pointing the Way*[33]). And that means: I too hope in the growth of "community" in society, in the growing capacity of society to contain community. But this growth is naturally not at all conceivable otherwise than in intimate union with a transformation of men and their relations to one another, and this union not otherwise than as a reciprocal influencing. One must not lose sight of the fact that "society" very easily insinuates itself into the attempt at a realization of "community." I have observed that here in the land of Israel, in the not unproblematic development of the *kibbutzim,* and, in fact, in two manifestations: as a result of the economic principle, the growing subjection to the market, which had as its consequence the fact that in times of crisis the *kibbutzim* could not arouse the courage and energy needed for taking the initiative in the reduction in price of the products; and, as a result of the political principle, the cleavage of unified fellowships into party groups fighting one another, which has repeatedly led to the self-destruction of communities. What can be hoped for in the face of such dangers? Just for those men in whose hearts genuine relation and the striving for its taking effect are so strong that they dare to take their

[32] *Pointing the Way,* p. 105.
[33] Pp. 203 ff.

stand against the alleged necessity, the economic or the political. Here as everywhere—in this direction goes my bold hope—will the inner battle, the battle of the spirit, ultimately be the decisive one.

That this hope is deeply connected with trust in God—however one may call him—is clear. But I by no means identify this trust with a "trust in the exclusive activity of God"; I do not believe in *such* an activity, I contest it, I number it among those "visions of the past" to whose "mass graves" Heydorn points. I believe that man is created as a partner of God; which means that I believe in a co-working of the deed of mortal man and the grace of eternity incomprehensible to the human mind.

2. The argument is incontestable on the plane of argumentation; how could it be contested that the spirit has no starting-point for its working outside the currently given reality! Nonetheless, I dare to believe in the implausible. Where the spirit begins may be foreseen; what it attains to from that point cannot be foreseen. Whatever may be inferred from history until now, it cannot be inferred how mighty the spirit can become, perhaps at the time of an elevation of man in his uttermost crisis to the great will to remain man.

3. I said that from the soul. But I have not talked of all that whereby the man who is underway, on the right road taken by him, time after time loses his way; rather I have said and can only repeat it: "He who takes a road . . ."

Walter Goldstein: Since our first exchange of letters in 1942, Professor Buber has known that for a long time this present train of thought has been disturbing me greatly. There are many kinds and conceptions of socialism. But in actuality only one; for effective socialism on earth has until now been unable to do without Marxism, that is, without historical materialism. The various types differ from one another only in degree, which to be sure does not amount, as in Russia, to 100 per cent. I know of only one statement in a letter from Martin Buber to me which is completely unequivocal and clear. Everything else of his about socialism which I have read leaves the door open to historical materialism. I therefore ask Professor Buber once more: Can there be in any form at all a rival material kingdom beside the not-to-be-doubted Kingdom of God?

Buber: I can hardly imagine a rejection of Marxism still clearer than I have expressed in my books *Between Man and Man* ("What Is Man?") and *Paths in Utopia.* Of course, I reject Marxism just because it is unsocialistic. And what is powerful in a given historical time I can in no case acknowledge as "valid."

Paul E. Pfuetze: Professor Buber, many of your friends as well as your critics have said that they find a strain of romanticism in your social philosophy. I too have thought that there is a certain perfectionism, even utopianism, in your understanding of man and society, which expresses itself, for example, in your optimistic faith in the Israeli *kibbutzim* and in a failure to deal realistically with the dynamics of large-scale social and political movements.

This criticism strikes home to me personally because your position here is so close to my own; and in the past I too have been charged with the same perfectionism. So I raise this issue with you, seeking some reassurance and answer to my own problem.

My most serious reservations arise at the point of asking whether and how the intensity of I-Thou attitudes and "we-feeling" can be maintained in any but primary groups whose size permits face-to-face relations?

How adapt the I-Thou theory to the practice of great industrial aggregates, of cities like Detroit, New York, or Essen, of highly industrialized nations like England or Germany?

How can the small decentralized organic groups, based upon an ethic of primary group attitudes and loyalties, maintain the I-Thou relation without becoming sectarian and separatist?

I believe that the small sectarian group is always an answer for the few. I would encourage the wider spread of small, functional, autonomous groups of all sorts as both desirable and possible. But does the spread of such communities, even the larger confederacy of such small organic communities, constitute an adequate total social strategy for the renewal of community?

Have recent historical events or your own experiences in Israel done anything to change either your general social philosophy or your faith in the decentralized co-operative settlements as the solution for the social problem?

Buber: I by no means see in "decentralized co-operative settlements" "the solution for the social problem." I explicitly call them "experiments," and even the federative unification of "the most diverse social forms existing side by side" I see only as *"aiming* at the new organic whole." [34] Even the *kibbutzim* I discuss merely as "an experiment that did not fail," [35] and I have not concealed my critical attitude toward its development (cf. also my answer to Professor Wolff, in this same section, pp. 69, 70). I am of the opinion that the co-operative experiment, developed, can make a fundamental contribution to a restructuring of society; nothing more, but also nothing less.

My socialism is not a perfectionist but a meliorist one; what is decisive is what shall be and remain the *direction* of the always renewed melioration, ever adapting itself to the new historical conditions. The direction is determined for me by a single goal, but by a double motive in its attainment: a negative motive, the reduction of the political in favor of the social principle, of "government" in favor of "administration" so far as it is admissible under the current historical conditions; [36] a positive one, the increasing unfolding of the forces of community within society. Many kinds of things can contribute to this unfolding outside of the communal experiments, things of such different nature as, for example, a more organic ordering of the choice of political representatives, the fostering of neighborliness, even in the streets of New York, the fostering of comradeship, even in the factories of Detroit, etc. Utopian? Thus the road to a new topicality is always regarded, before this road has been seriously taken. Romantic? I am used to this reproach; to the answer that I made to it more than a quarter of a century ago in the third part of "Dialogue" (*Between Man and Man*), I have today hardly more to add than this: that by the "community," the unfolding of whose forces I desire, I understand nothing that has already found its form in some past time; and that, when I talk about realization, I think of certain conditions that will presumably be given for it.

Jacob B. Agus: What is your view at present of the nature of romantic nationalism?

[34] *Paths in Utopia,* pp. 58 ff.; p. 79.
[35] *Ibid.,* pp. 139 ff.
[36] Cf. "Society and the State" in *Pointing the Way,* pp. 161 ff., and also "The Validity and Limitation of the Political Principle," *ibid.,* pp. 208 ff.

EXPLANATION: In your early writings and addresses, you expounded a profound conception of Jewish romantic nationalism. Specifically, in your series of lectures published under the heading *Reden über das Judentum* ("Talks on Judaism"), you speak of a person's true self as being contained in the history and aspirations of his people. "The past of his folk is his own personal memory, the future of his folk is his personal task. The way of his folk teaches him to understand his own self and to will his own self." [37] Your philosophy of Zionism was at that time a reflection of your conception of the organic unity of a people. You discovered in the "national soul" of the Jew "unique" tendencies—such as are calculated to save the world. In general, you asserted the primacy of the people as against the individual, maintaining that "only the one truly bound to his people can answer with his whole being." [38]

Three great events of our generation may have led you to modify your views on this subject:

1. The development of demonic Nazism out of the seeds of romantic nationalism in Germany. Evidently, the "voice of the blood" cannot be trusted.

2. The emergence of the State of Israel, proving in its brief career its similarity to all other nations, its unwillingness and incapacity to rise above immediate, narrow, national gains.

3. The demonstration in recent decades that the soul of democracy is respect for the sanctity of the individual and the universality of the divine law. These ideas are the basic foundations of Anglo-Saxon democracy, where the individual is viewed as primary. Democracy in Germany was wiped away by the very idealization of the concepts of "folk" and "state," which loom so large in the thought of German political philosophers. In view of our recent experience with both these systems of political thought, do you still assert the primacy of the "folk"?

Buber: This question surprises me, for it is formulated as if I had not long since answered it in print.

My all too simple treatment of the national problem in my "Talks on Judaism" of 1909–1914 I have already corrected with all requisite clarity

[37] *Reden über das Judentum* (Frankfurt am Main:Rütten & Loening, 1911), Lecture 1.
[38] *Cheruth* (Vienna:R. Löwit Verlag, 1919), p. 8.

in my talk on "Nationalism" [39] in 1921, thus quite a long while before the historical evolution of Nazism, on the one side, and of the State of Israel, on the other, to which Agus points. At that time, during the Zionist Congress of 1921, I pointed out that "the spirit of nationalism is fruitful just so long as it does not make the nation an end in itself."

But already in those early "Talks on Judaism" the *core* was not romantic. Essentially, it only modernized the fundamental biblical concepts of "seed" and "land" (Gen. 12:7). It was important at that time to state that in order to be able to develop fully what was intended in it, a community needs biological and territorial continuity. This development is by no means produced by this continuity; and it is just not possible without it.

To the monstrous abuse of these two fundamental concepts by National Socialism, I have again, with all requisite clarity, made a reply, in the midst of Hitler's Germany, in a public speech of 1936 on "The Power of the Spirit." [40] Again, it is sufficient here to quote a sentence from it: "Blood and soil are hallowed in the promise made to Abraham, because they are bound up with the command to be a blessing" (Gen. 12:2).

But as for the State of Israel, the hour for a verdict on it has by no means arrived. He who lives here senses how in the hearts of a growing segment of the young is ever more strongly fought out the battle between the two kinds of nationalism, the opposition between which I pointed out in that speech of 1921.

Reinhold Niebuhr: [41]   I am afraid that I must completely disagree with Buber on his attitude toward political problems. In every respect he seems to think that there can be an ideal dialogic relationship if one could only "restructure society." As a matter of fact, all these personal relations exist in transcendence over the basic structure of society, which is partly organic and partly an artifact. It is an artifact insofar as the

[39] *Israel and the World: Essays in a Time of Crisis* (New York: Schocken Books, 1963), pp. 214 ff.

[40] *Israel and the World*, pp. 173 ff.

[41] This statement is taken with Professor Niebuhr's permission from a letter he wrote June 22, 1956, in reply to a letter of mine concerning his criticism of Buber's social philosophy. Professor Buber's reply also comes from letters to me in July and November, 1956 (Friedman).

justice, particularly in modern technical society, depends upon artfully constructed equilibria of power. If one leaves out the structure of the nation or other group and considers the relation of groups to each other, the East-West conflict, for instance, one realizes that there is a tremendous chance of influencing the relation by moral and religious factors. For instance, the mitigation of fanaticism and self-righteousness, the recognition of the humanity of the other side, and so forth. And yet all these relations are not personal but collective. This is a dialogue, as it were, between America and Russia.

With all my appreciation of, and devotion to, Professor Buber, I think it is slightly ironic that he should have such a rigorous personal, not to say individualistic, interpretation of human relations, when I have always regarded Hebrew thought superior to Christian thought because it had the norm of justice rather than the norm of love, or rather it had the two norms of justice and love, while Christian thought always tended to be perfectionist in terms of the love doctrine.

Buber: I am very far from thinking that "there can be an ideal dialogic relationship if one could only 'restructure society.'" I never thought an ideal dialogic relationship possible in our world as it is. I am a meliorist and not an idealist, and so I want only as much dialogic element as can be realized in human life here and now.

The real strength of "collective relations" depends on the strength of the personal relations involved in them. A "dialogue between America and Russia" cannot lead to a real understanding (which goes beyond the "understanding" expressed in pacts and manifestos), except through persons here learning to see in their mind's eye persons there, and vice versa; that is, really meeting the others.

I have no doubt whatever concerning the influence of "moral and religious factors." But what seems to me of most importance is that their decisive action is done by them not in the form of "principles," but of elements of interpersonal relations.

There is no "norm of love" at all. The commandment of love cannot command other than to be ready to love and willing to act lovingly "with all thy soul." But there is indeed a norm of justice. I have spoken of it at length in *At the Turning,* in the Amos chapter of *The Prophetic Faith,* and in several chapters of *Moses.* But man tends to accept and to realize this norm only in general and abstract laws (*nota bene:* Torah does not mean law, but instruction!) and without justice in personal relations, justice becomes poisonous.

As to Niebuhr's statement on the "transcendence" of personal relations, it is obviously a part of the truth. But what he calls the basic structure of society is historically and even prehistorically (as I think in opposition to the prevailing opinion of ethnologists) based on personal relations, and where it subdues them it becomes wrong. As to modern technical society, of course it depends upon "artfully constructed equilibria of power," but what depends on them is its order and not its justice. If Niebuhr cannot concede this, then obviously we shall have to distinguish carefully between two very different kinds of "justice," and I for myself am harassed by the thought that the concept of justice must be split in two, bearing even different names. I cannot see the God-willed reality of justice anywhere other than in "being just," and this means of course: being just as far as it is possible here and now, under the "artful" conditions of actual society. So in my opinion it is not the justice that depends upon them, but ever again the realizable "how much" of it. Sometimes, striving to be just, I go on in the dark, till my head meets the wall and aches, and then I know: Here is (now) the wall, and I cannot go further. But I could not know it beforehand or otherwise.

V. PHILOSOPHY OF RELIGION

A. General

Friedrich Thieberger: The "awakening" is no mere psychological process; it seizes the whole man, as well as his thinking and the decision of his will. That also holds true for the I-Thou relationship. Therefore Buber can speak of an interhuman reality, particularly when the "Thou" that confronts me is seized by a similar relationship to my "I."

Now here the question arises: What if the "Thou" to which I am raised from the I-It into the I-Thou relation is not a visible living creature or a concrete object or event that accosts me, but an idea or a mental image formed in imagination, of which we have innumerable examples in personal, artistic, or political life? In that case, does not the *dialogue* become in fact a *monologue* into which one can enter so dramatically that even from the idea or the image one seems to hear an answer or reply from the "Thou"?

To be clear on this point seems to me particularly important, because in the realm of religious experience above all others, one should not counterfeit a reality which transcends the transformed "I" and think to discern in the idea a superhuman being, a "Thou," which exists independently of me. Here we would have confronting us nothing but the repetition of the ontological proof of God on another plane. For it would only be saying "Thou" to an idea or figment of the imagination, unless the belief in the existence of a higher being stems from quite another source.

Buber: That one can turn with passionate devotion to a fantasy image that one regards as God we know from the lives of individuals and from that of the human race. How often too is he who genuinely believes in God driven beyond the indispensable anthropomorphism that even dwells in prayer to "make an image"! It is very easy to understand how Freud, steeped in the psychologism of his age, saw in religion in general such an illusion. But how can we avoid calling a pure "fantasy image" by the name of God? An objective criterion that could be employed for a comparison, so to speak, naturally does not exist. However, Thieberger adds: "Unless the belief in the existence of a higher being stems from quite another source." If by this is simply meant that eternally indeterminable primal source from which all genuine faith comes, then question-and-answer has already reached its end. But perhaps this is meant still otherwise, namely, so that it is, despite all, to be known from something whether the Thou of my language of faith rightly exists. From something—from what then? Does Thieberger perhaps mean a no longer religious, in the narrow sense, but perhaps "ethical" content of what I sense as addressed to me by God? But then Abraham—who in the decisive moment certainly did not, as many imagine, feel sufficiently reassured through the promise—would indeed have had to become suspicious as to whether he did not mistakenly imagine a Moloch image talking to him, which had passed over from the folk fantasy into his own! There is, in fact, no other "source" that can be discovered than the simple experience of a leading of God through good fortune and bad; not without reason does the speech about the beginning of the way "that I shall show you" recur here, in the final trial. But there is one inward "source," even a double source, that has become well known just to us latecomers. That is, first of all, the wholeness of the soul: I know only—to repeat ever again the same thing—that we can speak the true Thou only with the whole soul, where the stubborn contradiction no longer lurks in the corners. And there is, after that, the unity of life: life as the service of an idol, however it is called, disintegrates hour by hour, success by success; life as the service of God collects itself ever again in all stillness, even in the shallows of disappointments and in the depths of failures.

Maurice S. Friedman: Does the relation to the Eternal Thou include not only the temporal I-Thou relation, but the I-It relation too?

EXPLANATION: In *I and Thou* you speak of the meeting with the temporal Thou as at the same time a meeting with the Eternal Thou: "In each process of becoming that is present to us, . . . in each *Thou* we address the eternal Thou," "the *Thou* in which the parallel lines of relations meet." But you also speak of the relation to the Eternal Thou as summons and sending and of the primal twofold movement of "estrangement from" and "turning toward" the primal Source.

Every real relation in the world is consummated in the interchange of actual and potential being, but in pure relation—in the relation of man to God—potential is still actual being. . . . By virtue of this great privilege of pure relation there exists the unbroken world of Thou which binds up the isolated moments of relation in a life of world solidarity.[42]

Does this not mean that we relate to the actual and present Eternal Thou even when the temporal Thou has again become only past and potential, that is, when it has again become It? Is it not through a *continuing* relation with the Eternal Thou that we are able ever again to find the Thou, either with the person who was Thou for us but is now It, or with some other whom we have never before met as Thou? If we know the unique value of another only in the I-Thou relationship, is it not the potentiality of his being, or again being a Thou for us, that

[42] *I and Thou,* p. 100.

ultimately prevents our treating the man whom we do not know as Thou purely as a dispensable It? And does not his "potential Thou" rest not only on the "actual Thou" of remembered I-Thou relationships, but on the "actual Thou" of Present Reality—the relation to the Eternal Thou "in which potential is still actual being"? Is it not our trust in the Eternal Thou that gives actuality and continuity to our discontinuous and often merely potential relations to the human Thou?

Buber: I perceive in this question, from words of mine which have been quoted here, that I have already come close to the limit of what is accessible to our experience. I hesitate to go a step further with words the full responsibility for which I cannot bear. *In our experience* our relation to God does *not* include our I-It relations. What is the case beyond our experience, thus, so to speak, from the side of God, no longer belongs to what can be discussed. Perhaps I have here and there, swayed by the duty of the heart that bids me point out what I have to point out, already said too much.

Paul E. Pfuetze: Is not a metaphysics necessary for a religious thinker and do you not have an implicit one, even if not an explicit and systematic one? Must we not put forth some sort of argument for the reality of God if faith is not to be an incommunicable mystery or psychic event? Does a "philosophy of religion" serve any useful function, or is it only "grace" which operates here? Is the only assurance of God to be found in the concrete particular I-Thou relation with the Eternal Thou?

EXPLANATION: I have been critical of what I thought was the lack of any clear, systematic metaphysical formulation of your thought. You deny that you have a metaphysics. You describe your standpoint as being on the "narrow ridge" to indicate that there is no certainty of expressible knowledge about God or the Absolute; and that it is presumptuous of man to think that he can have an adequate idea of God or the Absolute.

These are reasons which I respect and largely share. Yet I am one of those who think it is impossible for philosophers to side-step metaphysics. Furthermore, it has seemed to me that you have implicit metaphysical assumptions throughout—certainly theistic, and probably realistic, personalistic, and holistic. In my judgment, your philosophy would gain, would be firmed up, by a more clearly developed metaphysics.

You regard "metaphysics" as necessarily putting the absolute idea in some form in place of God—and this you refuse to do. This would be a kind of idolatry. Yet you seem to have no such difficulty with "ontology," which I would regard as a part of metaphysics. For myself, metaphysics is our attempt to deal with the structure and substance of the ultimately real. There are different *kinds* of metaphysics, but they all deal with the fundamental questions, with first principles about the real and the whole. We cannot help thinking about the most general features of reality, about the frame and principles and destiny of our lives. You, too, have basic convictions about the ground and content of the world in which to place your understanding of natural and human events. Actually, it seems to me that you claim a good deal: Your willingness to reify "the between," the ontal character of "relations"; your conviction that God is Person or meets us as Person in more than an analogical sense; your unshakeable Jewish faith in the reality of God —all these, I should say, have a metaphysical or ontological quality.

Buber: "Some sort of argument for the reality of God"? No, I know no cogent proof of God's existence. If one were to exist, there would no longer be any difference between belief and unbelief; the risk of faith would no longer exist. I have dared to believe—not on the basis of arguments, and I cannot bolster my faith with arguments. I have no metaphysics on which to establish my faith, I have created none for myself, I do not desire any, I need none, I am not capable of one. When I say that something has for me an ontological significance, I mean thereby to state that it is not a purely psychological event, although it encompasses such an event, or rather phenomenalizes itself "inwardly" into such a one. If I say that my faith-relation has an ontic character, what is said thereby is that it is not to be reduced to a psychic process, that it happens between my body-soul person and God. In saying that, I give my faith-experience the conceptual expression necessary for its being understood, but I posit no metaphysical thesis. Certainly I am not concerned about the communication of the individual, but about the common clarification of the common, of what has become and what is becoming common; I build no towers, I erect bridges; but their columns are not sunk into "isms" and their arches are not fitted together by means of "isms."

B. Creation

William H. Poteat: Assuming that there are two primary words which man speaks, "I-Thou" and "I-It"; assuming further that the former expresses a *religious* posture and that the latter does not; and granting that any "thing" in the world which may be addressed as an It may also be encountered as a Thou; it must follow that, the world being "twofold, in accordance with [man's] twofold attitude," no It, as It, can ever be the bearer of the divine, no being the incarnation of Being. If this is so, how can we ever say that the world is God's creature? (Cf. *"How* the world is, is completely indifferent for what is higher. God does not reveal himself *in* the world." L. Wittgenstein, *Tractatus,*[43])

Buber: I do not say that the world is twofold, rather, the world is twofold *to man.* I do not thereby say anything concerning anything existing independently of man. Moreover, in the biblical creation story God creates the things through the fact that he *calls* them out of their not-yet-being into being; in the third person, to be sure, but the grammatical form is not decisive here for what is meant: clearly God does not dispose here over something with which he otherwise has nothing to do; he really turns to what shall come into being, the light, the water, the earth; and it is only the completion of this turning, when he finally says to man who has come into being, "you." Wittgenstein is right: God does not reveal himself in the world; he is wrong: God addresses the world thus existing, thus created as his own.

Maurice S. Friedman: Is God loved *only* through the creature and never apart from him?

EXPLANATION: In "The Question to the Single One" you write:

God wants us to come to him by means of the Reginas he has created and not by renunciation of them. . . . The real God lets no shorter line

---

[43] *Tractatus Logico-Philosophicus* (London: Routledge & Kegan Paul, 1922, 1933), VI, 432.

reach him than each man's longest, which is the line embracing the world that is accessible to this man. For he, the real God, is the creator, and all beings stand before him in relation to one another in his creation. . . .[44]

Granted that one cannot love God by turning away from creation and the creatures, does one never love God without this love being at the same time the love of a creature or creatures? Prayer and devotional literature of all religions speak tirelessly of a direct relation to God, a turning toward, and praying to, him which does not seem to come necessarily through the relation to any creature, even though it does not exclude such relation.

Buber: When I speak of the exclusion of the world from the relation to God, I do not speak of the *hour* of man, but of his *life*. I regard it as unqualifiedly legitimate when a man again and again, in an hour of religious fervor, adoring and praying, enters into a direct, "world-free" relation to God; and my heart understands as well the Byzantine composer of hymns who speaks as "the alone to the Alone," as also that Hasidic rabbi who, feeling himself a stranger on earth, asks God, who is also, indeed, a stranger on earth, to grant him, just for that reason, his friendship. But a "life with God" erected on the rejection of the living is no life with God. Often we hear of animals who have been loved by holy hermits, but I would not be able to regard anyone as holy who in the desert ceased to love the men whom he had left.

C. The God Who Becomes

Arthur A. Cohen: In *I and Thou* you reject the concept of the "God who becomes" as "turgid and presumptuous talk."[45] Nevertheless it would appear from your view of revelation that such a view of becoming in God is unavoidable. If God's self-disclosures are never normative or apodictic, but depend for meaning only on the situation and moment in which God and man meet, then in some sense God is never the same. From the point of view of man (although perhaps not from God's point of view) God does change, for the simple fact that he is encountered ever anew and must be encountered ever anew for genuine meeting to occur.

[44] *Between Man and Man*, p. 52.
[45] P. 82.

Buber: Here a misunderstanding clearly holds sway.

The teaching of the God who becomes that I have indicated sets the divine at the end of the world process, as its event and its fulfillment. I can, of course, only perceive a trace of God's eternity, but it suffices to show me how foolish it is to wish to lodge him in time, namely at its end. According to my insight of faith, God is before as well as after time; he encompasses time and he manifests himself in it. When he manifests himself in it, when he "reveals himself," he gives a norm to men, that is, he shows them the direction to right living. When men, in their need for interpretation and supplementation, make out of the holy norms "laws," that is in particular, specifications of forbidden actions, then my faith compels me at times to prostrate myself and ask for illumination as to what I must do in a given situation, and what I must not do in it; I must, not seldom, refuse to follow the traditional, because my faith prevents me from acknowledging that God wants this of me. And that means, that God changes himself, or even, that he is a "God who becomes"!

Peter A. Bertocci: To say, "What turgid and presumptuous talk that is about the 'God who becomes,'" and yet never to explain how God can be otherwise *to some extent* if man is to have any effect on him, is a good instance of being declarative but not illuminating. More basically, any relation which is a real relation, as opposed to a logical one, must *relate*, that is, a difference must be made to both terms in the relation. I never discover what it is that man does to God—even in the passage referred to above. For what does God need man?

Buber: Here, too, what the content of the teaching is that is under discussion—and for which the Nietzschean "superman" represents a generally known example—is not at all taken into consideration. Instead of a God who is conceived of as becoming and who in some indeterminate future will have become, Bertocci speaks of the effect of man on God that necessarily means a change in God. But is it really so incomprehensible that our concepts shatter when they are applied to God, and that we nonetheless must use them in order to talk about our relation to him? Because I point to the effect that the pure relation exercises on man, may it for that reason be demanded of me that, in order to be "illuminating," I discuss its effect on God, something about which I know nothing and can know nothing? Or shall I, when I experience myself as addressed and addressing, and when such experience also is made known to me by others, keep silent about this fact because it is only possible to speak "declaratively" of it?

D. God as Person

Helen Wodehouse: In Professor Buber's own view, does God have a special and separate center of consciousness, as a Person apart? When Martin Buber writes that God wishes to redeem us [46] and that "everything desires to become a sacrament," [47] is he speaking literally in the first case and metaphorically in the second? Or is he in *both* statements using a legitimate metaphorical extension of much the same kind?

Buber: What it means to me to speak of God as a person, more exactly, as a being that is also personal, I have tried to explain in the Postscript to the second edition of *I and Thou*. However, I must repeat here that no concept can be applied to God without a transformation taking place in it, and that it is the task of him who thus applies the concept to characterize and explain this transformation so far as possible. To ascribe to God a "special and separate center of consciousness" means to say at once too much and too little. I have sought to guard myself against such simplifications through designating God as the absolute Person.

I beg that my interpretation of Hasidic teaching not be confused with my own thought; I can by no means in my own thinking take responsibility for Hasidic ideas, although my thinking is indebted to them and bound up with them. But when, in my interpretation of Hasidic teaching, I say of God that he "wishes to redeem us," then that is, in this context, meant literally; and when I say in the same interpretation that "everything desires to become a sacrament," then that is of course not fully, but still in good part meant literally; since, in fact, according to this teaching, divine sparks, stemming from a precosmic primal catastrophe, hide in the beings and things—sparks that long for redemption by man, namely, through man relating to these

[46] *Hasidism*, trans. by Greta Hart (New York: Philosophical Library, 1948), pp. 95–116.
[47] *Ibid.*, p. 144.

beings in holiness and using these things in holiness. In my own thinking, I would not be able to talk of a wish of God's or even of a desire
of things in such a manner; and yet the reality that is ultimately meant
by the former and that which is meant by the latter have their place in
my more cautious thought.

Frank B. Dilley: Does not knowledge of God in relationship to
him, knowledge of God as a person, also imply that knowledge of the
nature of God which Martin Buber has insisted is outside the province
of man? If we know God as the "Absolute Person," the "Eternal
Thou," the Creator who created men to love and be loved by him, do
we not already know a good deal about his nature?

EXPLANATION: Martin Buber claims that his use of the words
"absolute" and "eternal" speak only of the relation between man and
God and not of God. No symbols about God are possible, Buber holds.
God in himself can only be addressed, not expressed. All that can be
stated, Maurice Friedman points out in his discussion of Buber's symbolism,[48] are symbols of the relation which holds between man and
God, symbols which point to that kind of relation.

Yet in his interpretation of Hasidism, Buber speaks of "the limitless
original Godhead" and of "the God Who has not entered the world,
the Unlimited, the bearer of limitless light, the Godhead, the pure
Being, Who is at work" and goes on to describe this God as working
"as a person." Again, "it is at one and the same time the complete unity
and the limitless person. . . . 'Esse est Deus' says Eckhart, and that
can also be said here, but here Being includes Person . . . in the paradoxical sense, the limitless, the Absolute person." Buber speaks of "an
absolute person, faced by nothing" who becomes "one faced by a recipient"[49] even when he is as yet unrelated, before creation, making
Buber also fall under Friedman's strictures in defense of him, since he
too seems to misconceive of personality, as Friedman claims Buber's
critics have done, "as an objective description of a being taken for himself rather than as something that only exists in relation."[50] Buber
seems to see that some structure of personality exists *before* creation

[48] *Martin Buber: The Life of Dialogue,* Chap. 24.
[49] *Hasidism, passim.*
[50] *Martin Buber: The Life of Dialogue,* p. 226.

and persists *between* moments of relation, that is, that God can be spoken *of* as a Person apart from a concrete I-Thou relation. This is apart from the consideration that only a Person can *choose* to become related, so that if God wills to come into relation, he must be a Person.

Buber further says about God:

The Godhead as a perfect unity, God before and after creation, is at the same time the ruling God. For even He is the kind One, Who created the world to actualise His kindness; He is the great lover, Who has placed man in the world that He might be able to love him,—but there is no perfect love without reciprocity, and He, the original God, longs thereafter that man should love Him.[51]

Elsewhere Buber writes: "The Eternal *Thou* can by its nature not become *It:* for by its nature it cannot be established in measure and bounds," and Buber speaks of "the existence of a Being who, though in Himself unlimited and unconditioned, lets other beings, limited and conditioned indeed, exist outside Himself." [52]

For one to whom any knowledge of God as he is in himself is impossible, Buber is able to say much about his nature. He is limitless, pure Being, the absolute person, perfect unity, the ruling God, the kind One, the great lover who longs that men should love him, who cannot be established in measure and bounds *by his nature,* who is unconditioned. Almost all these terms are appropriate to personality. That the personal realm is the source of the most fitting symbols for God again points to a personal nature of God. God has revealed to man his nature as well as his will. To deny this is to deny God's word about himself.

Buber: A more exact clarification of what I mean and what I do not mean is evidently desired. Let us make the matter more precise, therefore. But one thing must be stated in advance: My interpretation of Hasidic teaching is not, to repeat, to be understood as a presentation of my own theology or philosophy.

Hasidism has exercised a great personal influence on me; much in it has deeply affected my own thinking, and I have felt myself called ever again to point to its value for the life of man. But there is also not a little in Hasidism that I am, to be sure, obliged to interpret within the

---

[51] *Hasidism,* p. 157.
[52] *I and Thou,* p. 112; *Eclipse of God* (New York: Harper & Row, 1952), p. 126.

framework of my presentation of it, but that I cannot in the least make my own, in particular the Kabbalistic ideas, taken over and developed by Hasidism, of the emanations of God and their relationship to one another. These are essentially Gnostic ideas, and I have ever again most decisively opposed Gnosis, which presumes to know, so to speak, the inner history of God. Hasidic theology always comes into contact with my own at those points where the relation between God and the world is concerned, as it manifests itself to us in our own experience of the relation between him and us.

That I proceed just from the relation between God and man, when I speak of God as the absolute Person and the eternal Thou, I have stated many times, most explicitly in the concluding chapter of the Postscript to the second edition of *I and Thou*. But I believe that I have already indicated sufficiently in *I and Thou* itself that one cannot comprehend a Thou outside of the relation to an I that says Thou and a person beyond his relations to other existing beings. If there existed no I in the world, it would make no sense to call God the eternal Thou; and I have said after due reflection that, in order to enter into relation with the existing beings that he calls into being, God has put on himself "the servant's garment of the person."

E. Revelation

David Baumgardt: If, as you emphasized again at Columbia University (Spring 1957), man in the dialogue with God must adhere to him unconditionally, even if God's ordinances appear to us immoral, is there still any fundamental gulf between the pagan *amor fati* and the Jewish *emunah* (trust) to the personal God? And can one, as you do in "Spinoza, Sabbatai Zevi, and the Baal-Shem," reject Spinoza's "*monologic amor dei intellectualis*" as a *glorreiches Verdorren* (glorious withering) of the soul in *monologischer Verselbständigung* (monological self-sufficiency)?

Buber: What I have said and mean is the following, which is, for the believing man, properly self-evident: when he becomes aware that God demands something of him, then he must just do it, if necessary involving himself in it with all his strength. In other words, the positing of an "ethical" criterion that is to be consulted as to whether one shall fulfill God's will, of which one has become aware, is pure contradiction: he who really believes in God cannot acknowledge any other court above his. He who deduces the question from a situation so simply incomparable to ours as that of Abraham, construes it; the believing man of our world can confidently subordinate his ethics to his religiousness because he knows that it is God who shows him the right way, and that means just: because he trusts God. But what then does this trust have in common with the *amor fati?* When someone not merely receives what befalls him from a "blind" fate, but accepts it, affirms it, "loves" it, and when someone seeks to follow with trust a divine being who knows and instructs him, what has the one in common with the other? I do not at all and in any sense feel myself an object in the hands of God. I stand over against one who holds the world in his hands; nonetheless I stand with my own meaning and will. My father Job (no Israelite, it seems, and yet my father) protests and trusts in one; we come to feel that he loves God, whom he charges with injustice, but that to love his own fate remains alien to him to the end, and God encourages him not to love it. He stands in an unsurpassably awesome dialogue; but God does not deny himself to him as a partner in dialogue.

And the *"amor dei intellectualis"?* Spinoza characterizes it as *pars infinitis amoris, quo deus se ipsum amat.* This concept of "a part" I reject basically. I stand over against God because I have been set by him in my own being in the most real sense, that is, I have been "created." Because I stand over against him, I can love him. Besides, the idea that a being loves himself stems from a dislocation of the concept of love. "Egoism" is not self-love but a lack of love. To ascribe to God love of himself is to use an illegitimate metaphor.

Norman Kelman: In your William Alanson White Memorial Lecture on "Guilt and Guilt Feelings" you define existential guilt as follows: "Existential guilt occurs when someone injures an order of the human world whose foundations he knows and recognizes as those of his own existence and of all common human existence." You also, in that lecture, speak of it as "guilt that a person has taken on himself as a person and in a personal situation. . . ." [53]

[53] *Psychiatry,* Vol. XX, No. 2 (May, 1957), p. 117.

When Abraham is asked to sacrifice Isaac (Gen. 22), is he not also in such a personal situation? Is he not also tempted by God, and does he not make a decision to obey, a decision that entails an action that would "injure an order of the human world"? In the brief dialogue with Isaac, there seems to be no indication that Abraham is involved in guilt, nor does there appear to be the tension or the problem that modern man is involved in when confronting this account, or a concrete situation. It appears that Abraham behaved in the way he did and not otherwise since there was no otherwise for him. (It was God's command, you have said, and without this Abraham's response meant nothing.) But for most, there is an otherwise, thus posing a problem, a conflict, a tension. To act as did Abraham would seem to involve a person in the existential guilt you speak of. To fail to heed God's command would be to sin.

Buber: I believe that I have answered this question in my book *Eclipse of God* in the chapter entitled "On the Suspension of the Ethical." Kierkegaard did wrong to quote the biblical narrative of the temptation of Abraham in order to make understandable his renunciation of his fiancée as a sacrifice desired by God; he knew no way out, as we see from his diaries, in the highly complicated motivation of this action. "A divine protest opposed it," he says; but since he also says explicitly that a man only learns that God demands a sacrifice of him, but not also which sacrifice, then, with the word "protest," the sphere of the experience of faith is already overstepped, especially as we read with astonishment in another place in his diaries: "Had I had faith, then I would have remained with her." Had not God perhaps—so I venture to ask—actually demanded of him the sacrifice of his "melancholy," his renunciation of it—and that would mean just the opposite of his renunciation of Regina.

From the narrative of the temptation of Abraham nothing is to be concluded *in abstracto* as to what one of us must do if God's voice demands of him tomorrow to become existentially guilty toward a fellow man. Such stories, in their terrible uniqueness, are placed at the beginning of the instruction ("Torah"): something representative is concealed in the narrated event, but it itself is not reported for imitation; never again has a man of faith heard the like from God; and since then, it is just faith that helps us distinguish from one another the voice of God and the Moloch voices of the idols of the age.

Jacob B. Agus: Does not the conception of a "hiding God" rob human initiative of decisive significance and deny to all human valuations any permanent import?

Explanation: The conception of a "hiding God" is designed to solve the problem of evil. If God is truly alive, he is capable of giving guidance and withholding it, evoking love from man or leaving humanity to its own devices. In a real sense, this conception is mythological, countering the trend from God as Life to God as Ideal, which was begun by Abraham, extended and deepened by the exponents of rationalistic religion in the three concurrent streams of scholasticism, and then evolved into the modern forms of philosophical idealism. The "hiding God" lives in time and beyond good and evil.

Hence, we may ask, is not human initiative robbed of intrinsic importance? Who can tell whether at any moment God is "near," or whether he is floating in the vastnesses of space? What becomes of the biblical assurance, "And if he cries to me, I will hear, for I am compassionate"? (Exod. 22:27)

Does not this conception too set up a mysterious, unknown being as the ground of all our valuations? Since our knowledge of right and wrong is ultimately a response to a being whose essence is indetermination and variation, how can we be certain of our judgments? Is not the logical conclusion of such a conception to do precisely as the philosophers of primitive paganism had done, namely, to separate morality from the character of the gods and ground it in the insights of humanity itself? When, in Judaism, morality and the divine being were reunited, human insights and human judgments were given cosmic endorsement, banishing the fantasies of mythology. Does not the vision of a "hiding God," one who is removed from all that is humanly conceivable, also project the possibility of many gods and of the entire phantasmagoria of mythological thought?

Buber: What I say is, first of all, enormously exaggerated, and then what is thus exaggerated is attacked. I have never said that God is "removed from all that is humanly conceivable"; what I have said ever again is this, that we know God in his relation to us, not apart from it.

The conception of a God "who hides himself" is not "mythological" but biblical. The prophets proclaim time and again to the insubordinate of Israel that God will hide his face from them, and in the hour of the great world crisis the peoples who turn themselves to him call to him (Isa. 45:15): "Verily, thou art a God who hides himself, O God of Israel, liberator." In the darkness of the crisis they had experienced his hiddenness; now in the radiance of the redeeming hour they perceive his helpful self-revelation. And what then is "revelation" in general other than the coming forth out of a (greater or lesser) hiddenness?

The conception of a "hiding God" as I use it is by no means "designed to solve the problem of evil." Nowhere have I indicated anything of the sort; I have never sought the origin of evil anywhere else than in the primal freedom of man. In the Bible, the hiddenness of God is not a cause of evil, it is his answer to it. But an answer that is not powerless over against man: when he turns back to God, then he can again share God's revealed nearness.

To ascribe to me the view that God's essence is indetermination means to stand what I say on its head. But I do, indeed, believe that God manifests himself ever again in different forms, all of which, of course, point to his all-subduing unity.

Paul E. Pfuetze: Professor Buber, will you clarify your doctrine of revelation, both as to the divine initiative and the human appropriation of it? I know you remain close to the dialogue and interpret revelation in terms of the dialogue as an address by God to man.

But how do you know whether and when the revelation is actually from God and not from the Devil or from within oneself?

How do you know when any *mitzvah* in your life is really a command from God?

And a related question: How do you derive the specific law or moral imperative from revelation? How do you *know* the will of God? And when the alleged address by God to particular individuals is interpreted and fulfilled in such widely divergent ways, how do you or can you reach any confident agreement as to what is *mitzvah* in the community?

Is the *Existenz*-thinker, trying to communicate his insights out of his particular I-Thou relation, reduced to sheer autobiographical utterance?

Where are the objective criteria and methods by which one can communicate his insight or revelation to others so as to evoke a similar experience, to reach agreement with the others in the community?

Buber: I repeat once more that I know no "objective criteria" and no "methods" in the relation to God. He who asks me concerning such misunderstands my intention. The question "How do you know?" is answered of itself in the personal experience of the believing man and in the genuine living-together of men who have analogous experiences; rather, there it is not asked. I give no guarantees, I have no security to offer. But I also demand of no one that he believe. I communicate my own experience of faith, just as well as I can, and I appeal to the experiences of faith of those whom I address. To those who have none, or imagine they have none, I recommend only that they do not armor their souls with preconceived opinions. I turn to those readers who either know from their own experience that of which I speak or are ready to learn it from their own experience. The others I must leave unsatisfied, and content myself with that.

VI. THE BIBLE
AND BIBLICAL JUDAISM

A. The Bible

Friedrich Thieberger: The differentiation between tent and temple in the development of religious faith is presented by Buber in his book *The Prophetic Faith (Der Glaube der Propheten)* as though the tent were a tangible symbol of God accompanying the people in all their wanderings and in all the events of life, that is, as the king of the people who alone led them, while the temple, as an immovable fixed residence, had, by its enclosed, isolating walls, "reduced" the God-relationship of the people to the level of pure cult. Only in the temple was the sacrificial service of the priest permitted; all else in life was removed from this temple-sphere, which alone was thought to have direct access to God, or made subservient to a representative of God, namely the King. According to this view, the temple might well be regarded as a decisive diminution of the mighty Israelite conception of the Kingdom of God who reigns in all spheres of existence directly and exclusively.

Now my question is this: Is this "reduction" not merely a historical phenomenon which does not at all affect the religious concept of the temple? With the erection of the temple, all other places of sacrifice, dedicated to the one and only God, were to be abolished; the sacrificial ritual and all the magic that was connected with it were to be confined to the temple area; the practice of oracles was to cease completely. Does this not signify a purification of the concept of God, an intensification of the inner relationship to Him? This was indeed a tremendous transformation that the people, to be sure, were not equal to. And this failure was welcomed by the kings, for it gave them a free hand in public life. Only then was the right atmosphere created for the prophets with their spiritual demands, which were directed not against the temple, but against its misinterpretation. Solomon's temple created a grave crisis which, viewed historically, led for a long time to a "reduction" of the exclusive dominion of God. But does it not have a place in the development of religious thinking which is higher than that of the tangible tent, continuously wandering from place to place?

Buber: Certainly this reduction is a "historical" manifestation, but it is not "merely" a historical one. The development of a religion, unfortunately, does not in fact consist of a series of genuine conceptions of faith; ever again there stand opposite each other a genuine conception of faith and its adversary which likewise is represented "religiously," namely, in the development of cult and of creed; and, all too often, the historical form, which belongs indeed to "religion" as well, is determined by the adversary. Very soon it is joined by an exegesis, a theology, an apologetic. Are the priests, against whom Jeremiah turns because of their teaching that the temple offers objective security, to be stricken from the history of religion? I see in this pseudo security of "religious possession," of the intentionless sacrifice, the intentionless fulfillment of command, in all *opus operatum*—I see the arch enemy of religion that rises against it from within. Is the magic really curtailed, as Thieberger says, through the fact that it is centralized in a "narrow temple enclosure" to which all the people shall make a pilgrimage three times a year? Certainly, a religious idea is contained in the innovation of a fixed center and of the rhythmically regulated streaming of the people to it; but it is coupled historically with its contradiction, because no new form of divine leadership was associated with the end of the tent—in other words, because after Moses there were no prophetic men who were leaders of the people, and because between Moses and Solomon there might still persist, to be sure, isolated, politically authorized admonishers in the court; but from Solomon on, "prophecy" degenerated into official soothsayers and more or less suspect outsiders, which last we call "the prophets of Israel."

Karl Thieme: 1. Do you consider your published biblical studies (beginning with *Die Schrift und ihrer Verdeutschung* and the translation of the Bible itself from the Hebrew into German, and including *The Prophetic Faith* as well as *Das Sehertum*) the quintessence of your life work and your discovery of the "key-word style" of the Bible as your most fruitful contribution to its interpretation?

To me, your repetition of symbolic words and word-stems respectively to point up related meanings in the Scriptures (as you practiced it, for example, in "Abraham der Seher" (Abraham the Seer) and I did, following your example, in "Die Komposition des Buches Genesis" [54] and in "Nimrod Kusch und Babel" [55]) seems to have proved itself a key to the understanding of the biblical kerygma to such an extent that one can only hope that the scholars of the Old and of the New Testaments will not continue to ignore the fact that here is revealed "the secret of form of biblical narrative," as Franz Rosenzweig first pointed out in the essay of that same title which he dedicated to you on February 8, 1928.[56]

2. Would you deem it possible to recognize, at least historically (quite apart from the possibility of following it today), the *Law* as the foundation stone of the existence of the Jews (and, *cum grano salis,* of Christians also): The Law to which the proclamation of the prophets was added from time to time as an indispensable corrective and as an actualization according to the situation, yet without being able to supplant it; so that Ezra does have the inestimable importance for the factual

---

[54] *Schweiz Kirchenzeitung,* January 11, 1945.

[55] *Historisches Jahrbuch,* LXXIV (1955).

[56] Cf. "Babel," *International Journal of Translation* IX, 1 (Special Issue, Translation of Sacred Texts).

survival of the Jewish people and of our whole Judeo-Christian civilization that is ascribed to him by tradition (and today, for example, by H. H. Schaeder in his *Esra der Schrieber*)?

As you know, and as my currently continuing debate with Martin Noth's *Collected Studies on the Old Testament* for the *Una Sancta* [57] develops more at length, I hold the revealed Law to be the most important common concern of both Jews and Catholic Christians in contrast with Protestants (with of course some not unimportant exceptions). I realize that you yourself side with the Protestants in this matter; and your incisive argument with Rosenzweig on this point, through the appeal he openly directed to you in "Die Bauleute" (1923), continues to occupy my thoughts. I should like to ask you, however, whether you could not acknowledge the Law as something which we cannot possibly conceive of as historically *nonexistent,* and without which there would not be any Jews on earth today?

3. Is your blunt antithesis of "Prophecy and Apocalyptic" really your last word on this subject? Was I mistaken when I thought I was detecting a higher appreciation of Apocalyptic in *Zwei Glaubensweisen,* [58] to the effect that, in times when a people enslaved by totalitarianism "can no longer be saved by earthly means," God can then from heaven vouchsafe their redemption by means of apocalyptic phophecy (insofar as they have adhered to his Torah)?

4. How would you characterize Franz Rosenzweig's contribution: (*a*) in your collaboration in the translation of the Bible, and (*b*) in the discovery of the "key-word style" and other exegetical devices?

Buber: If I myself should designate something as the "central portion of my life work," then it could not be anything individual, but only the one basic insight that has led me not only to the study of the Bible, as to the study of Hasidism, but also to an independent philosophical presentation: that the I-Thou relation to God and the I-Thou relation to one's fellow man are at bottom related to each other. This being related to each other is—if I may retain the expression—the central portion of the dialogical reality that has ever more disclosed itself

---

[57] *Rundbriefe,* 1957.
[58] *Zwei Glaubenweisen* (Zürich:Manesse Verlag, 1950), pp. 114 f.; *Two Types of Faith,* trans. by Norman P. Goldhawk (New York: Macmillan & Co., 1952).

to me. All my work on the Bible has ultimately served this insight, and within it also that reference to the repetition-forms in biblical writings to which Thieme has called special attention. They are eminently dialogical forms: the speech of God in the Hebrew Bible proceeds from the fact that man hears and understands the word not merely according to its "what," its content, but, in its innermost context, according to its "how." That means: Speech is here no robe that one can exchange for another; it is the unique and irreplaceable gesture itself. The repetition in its biblical form is the gesture with which the word explains itself. To man too, for his true intercourse with his fellow man, the dialogical forms, the unity of "what" and "how," the self-interpretation of the word is given and delivered.

2. I cannot desist from pointing out that *Torah* in its original biblical meaning does not mean "law," that is, an objectivum detachable from its giver, but the instruction of an instructor in the right path of life, the teaching of a teacher about the true way, and indeed such that in the perception of the perceiver the instruction cannot be separated from the instructor, the teaching from the teacher. Certainly, in part already early, many individual "directions," of a ritual and general nature, have also been designated by this word, and in biblical and postbiblical times the concept has become ever more completely independent until the Septuagint could take it as self-evident that it should be rendered by "law." But the binding of memory to the verbal dynamic in the root-depths of the noun—the inner might that through the mouth of narrators, prophets, and psalmists praises God as he who "instructs" Israel "in its ways"—has not come loose in any religiously living age.

It is, in fact, the living Torah, the instruction of the living God, that has preserved Judaism. But as in many other religions, so here too there has prevailed a highly consequential dialectic between the objectively defined law, from time to time extended by the "pen of the scribe," and the group listening to the eternal voice of the revealer, those who "turn" to him. From the prophets to the Hasidim, no one has wanted to "replace" the Torah; what matters ever again is that the command be fulfilled with the undivided intention of the loving soul as one commanded by the commander.

3. The antithesis between the prophets and the apocalyptic writers is not that of "redemption from the side of earth" and "redemption from

the side of heaven." No prophet has ever proclaimed a redemption that proceeds from the earth; each has glorified God as the redeemer; but the prophets have demanded of man his share in the preparation for redemption: the active readiness of the whole existence, hence just that which they designate as the "turning," turning to God, and what later the Greek translator of the traditional sermons of the Baptist, Jesus, and the Apostles rendered in weakened form as *metanoia,* repentance. What sunders me from the apocalyptists is not, say, that the call to *metanoia* disappears from their mouths, but that it, so to speak, fundamentally disappears from them. God continues to call to man, God always calls to man; but men wish to know nothing of it.

4. About Franz Rosenzweig's share in our translation of the Bible I have faithfully reported in the essay written in 1930, "Aus den Anfängen unserer Schriftübertragung," and reprinted in the book *Die Schrift und ihre Verdeutschung,*[59] which contains both our contributions to the problems raised by the work. The question about the discovery of the "leading-word (*Leitwort*) style" Rosenzweig himself has answered in the essay cited by Thieme, "Das Formgeheimnis der biblischen Erzählungen." What I have to add to it is found in my aforementioned essay.[60]

B. The Biblical View of History

Ewald Wasmuth: 1. The first question asks about the relationship or the distinction between the dialogical and the dialectical principles, and more specifically about the meaning of the two principles, respectively, in history.

2. The warrant for this question is confirmed by the fact that there are statements in your writings which appear to be indebted not to the dialogical principle, but rather to the dialectical principle or, more correctly, to the apocalyptic principle as you understand it; which, however, you have rejected and the dubiousness of which you have convincingly pointed out. The statements, however, which give me the right to pose this question are by no means incidental ones, but assertions which are so decisive for the interpretation of history and of man

---

[59] Martin Buber and Franz Rosenzweig, *Die Schrift und ihre Verdeutschung* (Berlin: Schocken Verlag, 1936), pp. 316–329.

[60] *Die Schrift und ihre Verdeutschung:* Rosenzweig, p. 242; Buber, pp. 323 f.

that obviously there remains something that cannot be explained by the system of the dialogical principle. The result is that both act as thesis and antithesis which are to be somehow resolved in the synthesis.

EXPLANATION: The first question needs no explanation since it is explained by the second question (above) and the third question (below, p. 103). May I try to make the second question clear by quoting a few sentences from your work. In your book *Das Problem des Menschen* you say:

> In the history of the human spirit, I distinguish between the epochs of habitation and the epochs of homelessness. In the former, man lives in the world as in a house, as in a home; in the latter man lives in the world as in an open field, and at times does not even have four pegs with which to set up a tent. In the former epoch anthropological thought exists only as part of cosmological thought. In the latter, anthropological thought gains depth and, with it, independence.[61]

This alternation you deduce, at least as far as our present homelessness is concerned, from the invasion of the cosmos by the Infinite, as man used to and still does interpret it.

This thesis is convincing. It corresponds to the experiences of modern man and finds its confirmation in history. Upon examination, however, this alternation points toward something like a "cosmological law," that is to say, toward a law of the sort that apocalyptists presuppose. And in this company, as you have elsewhere shown, one must include, among modern philosophers, Hegel, Marx, Nietzsche, Heidegger, and others. The law is not consistent with the "tidings of the prophets" and the alternatives proclaimed by them. Of these two teachings, however, you have said: "The first, i.e., the teaching of the alternatives, derives from the hour of greatest strength and productivity of the oriental spirit; the second, i.e., the apocalyptic, stems from the decline of its cultures and religions."

Neither the alternations of the epochs nor the hours of productivity or of the decline of cultures can be traced back to the principle of alternatives, to the dialogical principle. Nevertheless, both statements are convincing. They are in our estimation correct. One can hardly doubt

[61] *Between Man and Man*, p. 126.

that. But as soon as one attempts to understand them, one must admit that they more readily coincide with the dialectic than with the dialogical principle—in any case, with that principle from which the apocalyptists derive their authority.

3. With this I come to my third question, which has to do with your interpretation of good and evil. You equate evil with decisionlessness, that is, you understand or define it in the way zero defines the magnitude of the finite numbers in arithmetic. Decisionlessness is the absolute nothing over against the good. There are only degrees of good and, strictly speaking, no degrees of evil, since it can have no reality in and of itself. This "nothingness" of moral good corresponds to the position of zero in arithmetic, that position of the zero to which Pascal alluded when he said in Fragment 72 (*Pensées*) that he knew people who could not comprehend that zero minus four was zero; which, incidentally, led Pascal's worthy editor, Havet, to remark, in the middle of the last century, that Pascal must have been in error in this statement since zero minus four was actually *minus four*. That is now valid in algebra and thus also for us today, "and we cannot believe anything else," just as +4 and —4 correspond to the right and left branches of the Cartesian system of co-ordinates, so that both differ merely by their sign, both having equal reality. That, however, is the presupposition of all modern science, in which negative quantities are quite as real as positive quantities. It follows from this that this science belongs basically to the Zoroastrian and Manichaean world-view, which has been magnificently confirmed in this science and perhaps explains why these natural sciences have come into collision with the biblical Judeo-Christian tradition.

Although I wholeheartedly agree with what you say about good and evil, it does seem to me as though decisionlessness as such does not fully suffice, but that evil has degrees just as good does, that there is a dialogue with the opposite of good. This, however, in my opinion, appears as dialectic which in and of itself could be only logical, not existential. But in spite of that—and probably undoubtedly—the process is the historical potential out of which derive the alternations of "being at home" and "homelessness."

However, I did not wish to give my answer to this question but to learn yours.

Buber: The question that looms behind those formulated by Wasmüth is so abysmal that I cannot try to deal with it adequately here, not even in some measure. I must content myself with a brief reply to the individually formulated questions.

If by dialectic is here understood the connection of processes that, according to immanent laws, take place in history between antithetical primal powers of many forms, then I cannot acknowledge its reality; I can glimpse here only the admirable attempt of human thought not merely to order historically and categorically the confusing fullness of historical happening, but also to ground it metaphysically and according to principle. Certainly I see opposing forces struggle with each other in every hour, in the historical sphere as well as in the biographical; but I do not find in history a simple comprehensible necessity like that of the fate of individual death in biography. History is, indeed, in essence nothing else than what happens just now in the human world; and thus I am oppressed, day after day, at how the fate of the generations now living depends on the decisions, the decisionlessnesses, and the seeming decisions of persons and groups. The "unmasking" thought of modern man has succeeded in grandiose manner in discovering "behind" history the stratagem of world-reason or the compulsion of economic-technical transformations; but to me the "historical" reality that penetrates to me calls into question all this kind of analysis as to what lies behind history.

Wasmüth refers to the fact that, according to my own presentation, the present epoch of "homelessness" has proceeded out of the Copernican invasion of the infinite. But this invasion has had the effect that it had only because man has merely opposed to it the Kantian antinomy of the infinity and finiteness of space and time; so far he has not opposed to it a greater image of God than the traditional one, a greater one *and yet one that can still be addressed,* the image of a God who out of his eternity has set in being this infinite-finite, space-time world, who embraces and rules over it with his eternity. But to seek to explain by a historical dialectic why man has not done this, could not do this, would be to explain the question—away.

The abyss that opens behind the question of the dialectic is the mystery of the relationship between God's "omnipotence" and the actual freedom of man. As Wasmüth knows indeed, it cannot be replaced by any theory of history and it cannot be re-expressed by any. But the apocalyptic also injures the mystery because in its perspective only God, but not also man really exists.

I have neither the intention nor the capacity to derive the alternation of epochs from the dialogical principle. But does not history teach us that, in times of the fruitfulness of culture, a grand and direct intercourse between man and man shines and radiates, and that in times of decadence it is extinguished?

To the problem of evil: In "Images of Good and Evil" [62] I have pointed out that evil proper is the affirmation and strengthening of one's own decisionlessness against the God who demands decision, hence a Yes and No at the same time. But the Yes in it is in no way a Yes of decision. One does not decide for Baal, one falls to him; in other words, one does not decide for the Having (Baal is the "possessor" who grants the Having) against the Being, one is swallowed by the Having. And where does "a dialogical relation to evil" show itself here? Adolf Hitler, the Baalish man, is precisely the exemplary living being with whom a dialogue is no longer possible. But where the life-ground of one called "evil" is still accessible to the address, we are obliged, when we come into a common situation with him, to turn dialogically to just this life-ground, in which the neglected decision putrefies, not, of course, as a preacher: *"Abyssus abyssum clamat."* Here too I see no "dialectic."

C. The Ontic Status of the Mythical Image

Samuel Hugo Bergman: My question to Martin Buber has to do with his view of the ontic status of the mythical image, such as the one about the speaking ass of Balaam or the divinely guiding cloud which, according to the biblical report, descended in the desert upon the tent of presence (Num. 9:15, etc.).

As far as I can see, only the following points of view are possible regarding the reality of the mythical world:

1. The naïvely pious attitude.

2. The transformation of the myths into psychic realities, such as we find in the work of Jung.

3. The view that there is no other reality outside our own, that there-

---

[62] *Good and Evil* (New York: Charles Scribner's Sons, 1953), pp. 63–143.

fore the myths can be rationally explained and must therefore be traced back to the familiar reality of our senses. I find an example of this view in Buber himself when, in the book *Moses,* he substitutes for the dying of the first-born "a pestilence, a children's epidemic," [63] ostensibly in conscious contrast to what the Scripture itself tells: it speaks only of the death of the *first born* in the land of Egypt.

4. The view that the mythical world is a reality *sui generis,* as real as the world of our senses but, to be sure, able to be experienced only by means of some special sense organs which contemporary man either no longer possesses or does not yet possess. This may be the approximate position of Rudolf Steiner or that of Leopold Ziegler who speaks of the mythical world's having an oscillating center between the two extremes of an ideal image and an actual reality. One might ask in this connection whether these two worlds, the mythical and the sensuous-objective one, could meet at some point in time or space (as, for example, Jesus the Christ was born in Bethlehem in the reign of Pontius Pilate)?

Is Buber willing to identify himself with one of these points of view or does he permit the use of various points of view, now one, now another, and if so, which?

A further question arises here, concerning the meaning and the possibility of a *demythologized* religion? Is such a religion desirable or at all possible? Is religion at all possible for man once he has been driven out of the Paradise of his mythical world and has "seen through" the myths as such?

Buber: I cannot identify my conception of the mythical image with any of the standpoints cited by Bergman. This can easily be made clear through the two examples cited by him.

To believe "naïvely" that at a certain hour in a certain place an ass spoke is not given to me. But the view that such a speaking is, to be sure, "real," but present-day man does not possess the organs to perceive it does not seem to me to differ so very much from that belief, except for the fact that for the former there exists only the one great biblical exception, whereas the latter view is ready to understand the speaking of asses as a rather frequent exception, only "no longer or not yet" grasped by our organs of consciousness. But to see therein a "psychic reality,"

[63] (Oxford and London: East and West Library, 1946), p. 68.

whether a symbol in the Freudian or an archetype in the Jungian sense, would probably be far from my thoughts, even if I were a psychotherapist and a patient told me a dream in which a speaking ass appeared. But the fourth standpoint, too, which Bergman seems inclined to ascribe to me, that of a "rationalistic" explanation, I cannot make my own: a mythical image may, to be sure, be induced by a real historical event, but the image itself is not thereby explained for me. To stay with the death of the first born cited by Bergman: this image may have been induced by an event of a general nature, but it probably would not have arisen if the first narrator had not been permeated by the statement of God, "My first born is Israel."

But I also do not know at all how I am to rationalize the narrative of the speaking ass. Rather, I am inclined to accept the fact that underlying this narrative is a real, to be sure in no way "supernatural," but still quite particular, indeed certainly unique occurrence; more exactly, an experience that either could not find its expression otherwise than in a mythical image or, even in the experience itself, had been tinged in some measure and in some manner with the character of this imagery. In order to be rightly understood, I must say something in explanation: in my view, a saying like that of Balaam cannot arise if there has not been a man who experienced something analogous to that of which the saga tells in mythical images. What I mean is this: A man who practices the calling of soothsayer was once seized by the genuine might of prophecy. He now no longer produces for the curious magic reflections of a would-be future, but proclaims what is given to him, things revealed, past, present, and coming in one, and admonishes his hearers about the actual situation in which they have to authenticate themselves. The soothsayer-nature in him resists this, no matter how gently (the biblical text hardly indicates wherein the resistance consists); then a divine messenger confronts him on the way as "Satan," as the hinderer. Balaam does not notice it, but the natural being, his trusted animal on which he rides, seems to notice something of the sort, for it refuses to go further. It is this experience of his, of nature refusing to take part in his resistance against God, that is presented in the mythical image of the speaking ass; I can devise no other that would be so adequate to what is meant, but just mythically adequate, not rationally. The mythical image is no allegory; what is involved here is not something abstract that has been carried over into the sphere of sensory perception; it is bodily experience that has engendered the image. In whom? One may answer: in the narrator of the saga—but had it not perhaps already entered into the heart of the magician himself in the hour when that something had befallen him: when nature denied him its service and when he felt that denial, to be sure, only with the limbs in contact with the animal, but as if it sounded in his ears? The mythical image expresses something that cannot be expressed otherwise than in such language.

The character of the mythical image manifests itself still more precisely in the other example.

A band of people attains its decisive relationship to God in its belief that it is led on its wandering by him. Natural manifestations that it encounters are included in this belief: while the band follows a shining cloud, it is powerfully permeated by trust in the divine leading. It *sees* in the cloud the messenger of God; it will tell of it, and its narration will be a myth of experience. I am not in the least inclined to accept the idea that earlier men "through special organs of consciousness" were in a position to perceive a divine cloud as reality *sui generis;* but, on the other hand, the fact that men found their binding with God through the faith-experience of being led by him and that they perceived natural occurrences in this context of meaning is for me by no means merely a "psychic reality."

D. Judaism and Christianity

Maurice Nédoncelle: Does Professor Buber still maintain the opposition that he established some years ago between the *emuna* of the Jews and the *pistis* of the Christians? Does he hold that the notion of the chosen people suffices for the obedience of the believing Israelite and is absent from the Pauline faith (except in the form of a society of converts)?

Buber: I have never been of the view (as I have emphasized in the Foreword to *Two Types of Faith*) that an *"emuna* of the Jews" and a *"pistis* of the Christians" stand in opposition to each other. What I meant and mean is that the first was developed in an especial manner in ancient Israel, the second in an especial manner in Pauline Christianity.

It is wholly alien to me to accept the notion of the chosen people as "sufficient for the obedience of the believing Israelite." I have described the relationship of Israel to God only as the *origin,* not as the essence of the relation of the believing Jew to God. The great trust, as for example it is expressed with unconditional clarity in Psalm 73, is a *personal* trust of the person as such; it was and is for me the decisive one, except that it has grown and ever again grows on the ground of that experience and hope of Israel. But thereby an exclusiveness is by no means expressed: I have come to know in the course of my life a succession of Christians who had an ideal relationship of trust that could not be injured through any failure, through any misfortune. But this trust did not originate in the faith that something was thus and not otherwise: the faith served them, as it were, only as an aid to comprehension. I experienced this most strongly several years ago in conversation with the leading personality of an important Christian sect. It was one of those conversations that is conducted between two men without holding back and reserve. We spoke of the readiness, common to both of us, to be overtaken by what one customarily designates as eschatological happenings, in an entirely unexpected manner contradicting all previous conceptions. Suddenly I heard the words: "If God should then demand it of me, I am ready, even to give up . . ." Where I have here placed three periods, the center of the Christian dogma was stated. Even now, while I write this, I feel the emotion of that moment.

As for Paul, I do not in the least mean that the concept of the chosen people is lacking in him. What I mean is that he has *fundamentally changed* this concept. I have, it seems to me, expressed this with sufficient clarity in the eighth chapter of *Two Types of Faith.*

Arthur A. Cohen: If you will excuse a direct question, what do you consider the two or three primary problems to which serious Jewish theologians ought to address themselves in our time?

Buber: I do not need to excuse "direct questions"; I prefer them. But I do not feel myself theologian enough to answer this question—at least in so general a form. I myself have dealt only with theological problems when I had to, that is, when they bore down on me as imperatively actual, when they burned in my heart. My advice goes in this same direction.

VII. EVIL

William Ernest Hocking: LOCUS OF THE QUESTION: The nature and destiny of evil.

QUESTION: Agreeing that wherever there is a "relative" there is an absolute to which the relative is relative, then if, as against Vedanta, evil is relatively real and not illusion, must there not be an absolute evil toward which our attitude must be "fight, eject, destroy"? In brief, absolute rejection?

EXPLANATION: In the actual world, good and evil are *objectively* present, and the acceptance of the given world-and-life cognate with the love of God implies the absorption within a greater "good" of both good and evil. If both good and evil are *within* us, we may still accept the polarity as good, in the spirit of the *Mishnah,* whereby we love and serve God with both our good and our evil impulses, the latter as potential good. But if we give vent to evil impulse, with *prior self-forgiveness,* in view of God's promise of redemption, this prospective demand on God to honor the proposed *fait accompli,* as banking on God's future forgiveness—is this not evil absolute? Is this not unforgivable?

Buber: First of all, speaking quite generally, I am not at all of the opinion "that wherever there is a 'relative' there is an absolute to which the relative is relative." We become acquainted day after day with all degrees of relative stupidity; shall we conclude from that that there exists an absolute stupidity?

An absolute evil, however, would mean that there is a power opposing the divine that cannot be derived from God. A modern Manichaeanism of this kind, however, is not what Hocking means.

What Hocking means is rather "radical" evil as it enters into the reality of life. That something of the sort exists I have explicitly pointed out in the final chapter of my book *Good and Evil*,[64] and, in fact, it exists in what I call the "second stage" of a definite individual life-reality, the stage, namely, in which the man who has abandoned himself to directionlessness and decisionlessness affirms this proclivity of his just as his own, and presumes to want to remain in it as in the basic attitude proper to him. But since it is always a question of the stage or stages of an individual life-way, I prefer to speak of it not as a "radical evil" (as, for example, Kant does) but rather as an evil that radicalizes itself. Note well, we always remain in the sphere of the facts of individual existence, in the sphere of individuals. Certainly we must often fight this evil, especially when it joins with its like and unites with all kinds of wretched mixed forms and then entrenches collectively upon human history. But when we have "destroyed" it, have we then really helped the good to victory over the evil? Is not the true fight against the demons of a wholly different kind? Must we lead the "bad" man to his unredeemedness? Does there not exist ever again what is almost incomprehensible, the possibility that we can help the man who has apparently completely succumbed to that arrogant self-affirmation to find the way out? Certainly there have been many in this our time who would not have believed themselves capable of wanting to save some son of this time [65] before themselves. And nonetheless, I confess that I can hold no one to be "absolutely" unredeemable.

The saying that there is no forgiveness, which Hocking has taken over from the Jewish tradition and applied to him who says, "I will sin and then I shall repent," does in fact touch the most serious injury of the relation between divinity and humanity. But is it impossible that, in a later hour, the insight into the fact that he cannot be forgiven may seize hold of the man who has spoken and acted thus, like a heart-purifying lightning flash? What can transpire between the real God and a real man is of so paradoxical a nature that no saying, be it ever so "true," is equal to it. Something, the idea of which is unforgivable, may be resolved in paradox. And we—shall we, if this is so, hide from ourselves the possibility that we too could be called on in certain circumstances to forgo "absolute rejection"?

[64] *Ibid.,* pp. 133–143.
[65] "Such as Goebbels," Professor Buber offers as an example in a letter to me. (Friedman.)

Yes, evil radicalizes itself—and it is granted us to co-operate in its deradicalization.

Kurt H. Wolff: 1. What is the locus of evil? Within the I-Thou relation, how is one to discriminate between good and evil: for instance, how does one know when to acquiesce in the demand of the other, when to resist it; how does one know when one acts as the "single one," rather than as the pseudo "single one"?

2. Whatever answer this question receives, one implication of the answer would appear that reason is relevant to it. The statement, "Evil cannot be done with the whole soul; good can only be done with the whole soul," [66] suggests that in doing evil, one part of the soul is excluded, and this part I cannot identify as other than reason; and this is why evil cannot be done with the whole soul.

Buber: 1. I know a "locus of evil" only within the concrete individual life-reality, and here I know it, as I have said, as the willed direction and decisionlessness. Therefore, I have naturally not set up an objective criterion that tells one in the manifold situations "how one does know," and I cannot do so. One must quite often, indeed, struggle hard in a given situation, without having an adequate criterion to hand, until one knows and takes the right direction here and now. But in a life in which the good is more and more realized, the strength of finding often grows. The more complete an I-Thou relation is, so much the more one knows what the other really needs in order to become what he was created to be. And he who has become a genuine "single one," he receives confirmation—even though he never has a share in blank security—but from other sources, certainly, than from reflection on whether he is genuine or not genuine.

2. That it is "reason" that opposes in me the evil that I do seems to me an inadmissible simplification. When I think about doing an injury to my neighbor who has vexed me, and I succeed in sensing somewhere in a corner of my being the injury that I want to do, or when I want to deceive my partner in an action and a little drop of lying substance corrodes the rim of my own heart, and I nonetheless do the evil, although "not with the whole soul," what role has "reason"

[66] *Good and Evil*, p. 130.

played in the event? It was not at all, in fact, a thinking that took place there; it was only that gentle protest of the soul to which we so often are accustomed to pay no attention.

Walter Goldstein: 1. First of all I pose the question regarding the nature of evil in Buber's works. Allow me to add that I do not mean the *phenomena* of evil. The fact that they are represented in Buber's work *For the Sake of Heaven* in great enough detail, I think I have sufficiently pointed out in my writings. Besides, I share Buber's opinion that man is not born in sin, and is able to free himself from it without assistance from outside. On the other hand, however, it would be quite impossible to deny that evil *as such* does exist on earth. Thus I do not wholly agree with Buber that man in general is neither good nor bad. Possibly this type of person constitutes the overwhelming majority, but I have met in my life a number of conspicuously good people and, unfortunately, a yet greater number of bad people who *consciously willed* the evil and the bad. It appears to me that Buber treats of evil adequately in its *manifestation,* but he does not deal exhaustively with evil *as such.* Let me add, by way of suggestion, what I have already told Buber: I am aware that he rejects the isolation of evil in order not to permit even the slightest trace of a satanic rival divinity to emerge.

2. This problem of evil again and again plays a disturbing role for me in my thinking through his system of the dialogue. I am also reasonably certain that all the lines of genuine meeting intersect in the eternal Thou. Yet these meetings form only a very small percentage of all earthly meetings. Let us suppose that the lines of the numerous indifferent meetings likewise intersect in the eternal Thou. What then of *the* meetings with men which aim fundamentally at extracting evil from this meeting and leaving nothing undone to give the meeting a painful aspect? That there are such meetings, unfortunately not too rare, can likewise not be denied. It is, however, difficult to accept the thought that the lines of all of these meetings also intersect in the eternal Thou, since in this case attributes would have to be ascribed to the Almighty which are all too earthy. No principle of "loving more" was able to save Hasidism from premature decline, and it collapsed not as the result of opposition from without, but rather from within, as was decisively shown in *For the Sake of Heaven.* No Jew of our generation needs to

be told that there are people—indeed masses of people—for whom the principle of "loving more" broke down in complete failure. On the other hand, since I am equally convinced of the invalidity of the opposite principle ("hating more")—for he who conquers by the sword has always inevitably perished by the sword—I am unable to determine the role of evil in the meetings of men, and I ask Professor Buber to say a word on this point.

Buber: 1. I do not know evil "as such," but only as a condition and attitude in the life of individuals. As condition, I have characterized it probably most clearly as "the convulsive shirking of direction" ("The Question to the Single One," *Between Man and Man*), as attitude probably most clearly as the self-affirmation of those who remain in directionlessness.[67] If the good that I mean is already in its origin the direction of the human being to God, then it is still certainly clear that no one of us is simply evil, for none is denied by his nature taking the direction. It is also certainly clear that none of us by his nature is simply good, for it is accorded to none by his nature to become free from all the impulses of the passion revolving in itself. The individual experiences both in the depths of his self-awareness. It seems to me in the same way to be at variance with the hidden reality to hold the other to be simply bad and oneself to be simply good. Man is—to this I hold fast— "in an eminent sense good-and-evil"; he is fundamentally twofold, and he is empirically capable of attaining to unification, that is, he is capable time after time of lending his passion the direction to the truth, to God; wholly one, wholly good is no mortal being.

2. Here a misunderstanding prevails. By "meeting" in the pregnant sense in which I use the word, I understand an occurrence of the genuine I-Thou relation in which the one partner affirms and confirms the other as this unique person. That the lines of these relations intersect in the eternal Thou is grounded in the fact that the man who says Thou ultimately means his eternal Thou.

The innumerable cases in which the men who encounter one another intend and do to one another incalculable evil is indeed an incontestable basic fact of existence. I know nothing else to oppose to it than the

[67] *Good and Evil,* pp. 133–143.

warning renewed time after time that the man who makes the other from a Thou into an It thereby destroys his own life at its core.

Paul E. Pfuetze: If the I-Thou relation, man with man, is the real way of things, why is it such a task to "socialize" people? Why is it so difficult for man to live in the world of Thou, so easy to slip into the world of It?

EXPLANATION: I know that you have no simplicist notion that the achievement of the divine intention is easy or inevitable. You have never identified historical process or change with inevitable progress. You are well aware of conflict and tragedy and moral evil, and of man's indecision and rebellion against God. Yet I have always sensed in your writings a certain romanticism about human nature, a perhaps unwarranted optimism about man. And I keep looking for some satisfactory answer to the following kinds of questions:

Why is it that, even at his best, man feels an inordinate tug of self-interest?

If man as "social individual" is actually in harmony with the law of life, how shall we account for the constant rupturing of the fabric of human community?

Why is evil, sin, self-will so powerful?

How are we to deal with man's destructive and stubborn self-preference and with the evil corporate structures into which his sin is built in society?

Buber: I have never said, so far as I know, that the I-Thou relation is "the real way of things." I have ever again said that it is one of the two basic attitudes of man, one of the two possibilities of existence. That in the present human world the other is the more frequent, the more powerful I have never concealed, nor have I even neglected to explain why the man of our time is so very much inclined to treat all existing beings as It, as the object of his observation and his use. Yet I hold the statement that "even at his best, man feels an inordinate tug of self-interest," to be inexact. Certainly, every living being, including man, experiences his life in its relationship to himself; each is naturally concerned with the preservation of its existence, the betterment of its lot, striving after advantage and all kinds of pleasures, and I have no criticism of this basic biological fact; I would not dream of removing man from it. But that in the lived day of man, day after day, self-interest is always operative, in no way accords with many men whom I observe in my environs and of whose inwardness I can perceive something. I see how they concern themselves, each in his own way, the one noisily or awkwardly, the other goodnaturedly and at times even tenderly, with their environs—family, comrades, passers-by—with open spirit for what takes place, and, not at all seldom, ready with participation, information, and help. In all this the relationship to oneself is a self-understood, undetachable constituent, but not an important factor. I sometimes watch boys playing. What really concerns the individual is just the game itself, and that means, of course, before all, his share in it; but I see such a boy, not at all infrequently, also really concern himself about another, about the other's share, his fortune and misfortune, and at times I see such a young heart, as it were, fly across to where the other stands, with the wish that he could help there where, according to the rules of the game, no help at all is possible.

I will certainly not deny that the earth abounds with so-called self-seeking, in lower and higher varieties. But that seems to me to mean nothing else than that the biological self-relatedness in man, with its so strongly developed ego-drive, easily becomes a "mania," thus takes on a basically pathological form. Self-seeking is not something given man by nature, but the event of a twisting through which the biological presupposition of the individual life-reality, the self-relatedness, is made into goal and intention and thereby becomes more or less pathologized.

In this connection there should not remain unmentioned the interesting fact that an entirely different development, to another end, so to speak, can also take place in self-relatedness. This is especially true with men of strongly differentiated intellectuality, if they have a special talent for reflecting in a perceptive manner on their own share in the events of their lives, and particularly on the psychic side of this share. Thus arises the so-called egotism. This kind of reflexion often begins in modern man at the moment of the event itself, perhaps at the moment of an action, as a result of which the spontaneous character of the action can be injured or even destroyed.

That man "is actually in harmony with the law of life" I have never asserted; indeed, I have rather advocated the opposite view, since I have tirelessly pointed to the fact that the I-Thou relation between men is ever again interrupted by an I-It relationship.

To pronounce me a romantic optimist is very easy because, despite all adverse experiences, I have always clung to the messianic belief in the redemption of the world by God with the participation of the world. But it is quite false; for I have never and nowhere asserted that man can overcome his disharmony, the inner conflict of human existence through his own fullness of power, through his own "good will." I am a realistic meliorist; for I mean and say that human life approaches its fulfillment, its redemption in the measure that the I-Thou relation becomes strong in it, the relation in which man, without surrendering his self-relatedness, has to do with the other not as with his object, but as with his partner.

If one prefers to think that God does not exist, then man must be regarded as the most dangerous experiment of nature, but still as one in whose success he himself has a share.

Interrogation of

John Wild

Conducted by Henry B. Veatch

John Wild is Professor of Philosophy at Yale University. Born in Chicago in 1902, he studied at Chicago and Harvard Universities. He taught in the Harvard Philosophy Department between 1927 and 1954, when he joined the staff of the Harvard Divinity School. From 1960 to 1963 he served as Chairman of the Department of Philosophy at Northwestern University. Wild has served as visiting professor at the Universities of Chicago, Honolulu and Washington and was Powell Lecturer at Indiana University. Twice recipient of a Guggenheim fellowship, he holds the honorary degree of L.H.D. from Ripon College. He was president of the Association for Realistic Philosophy from 1947 to 1950, of the Metaphysical Society of America in 1953, and of the Eastern Division of the American Philosophical Association in 1960. Since 1947 he has been a member of the editorial board of *Philosophy and Phenomenological Research* and, since 1951, of *Philosophy East and West*. His writings include: *George Berkeley, Plato's Theory of Man, Introduction to Realistic Philosophy, Plato's Modern Enemies and the Theory of Natural Law, The Challenge of Existentialism, Human Freedom and the Social Order,* and *Existence and the World of Freedom,* and he has edited a volume of Spinoza and *The Return to Reason.*

I. HISTORY OF PHILOSOPHY

Vianney Décarie: What is the task of the history of philosophy, as John Wild conceives it? [1] Should not the study of philosophers include textual criticism, historico-doctrinal setting, etc.?

Wild: Two conceptions of historical research may be distinguished in philosophy: one, the antiquarian approach which sets itself the task of penetrating to a past thinker exactly as he was in his own setting, and another which recognizes its own historical perspective and tries to carry on a living dialogue with some thought of the past from its own point of view. This latter aim I tried to follow in my book. As the years have gone by, I have come now to feel even more strongly that this was more proper.

The antiquarian approach, as I called it, wants the real Plato, as he was in himself, not a later reconstruction. But where, after Plato himself, has this real Plato ever emerged? In the works of Aristotle? In the Middle Ages? Or in modern times? In the commentaries of A. E. Taylor perhaps? Or in those of Leon Robin? They cannot all be true, the antiquarian says, for they are very different. So he must choose one, his own perhaps, as the real Plato, and condemn the rest as false or distorted. I do not care for these exclusive claims, and I find the heated controversies to which they lead uninstructive. I cannot help but feel that a fallacy has been committed. Trouble lies, I think, in a too substantial conception of the individual human thinker. Plato was not an isolated substance, but a communicating agent who spoke to many persons including Aristotle, stirring them to living dialogue, and who by his writings stirred many more throughout history to further reflections and questions. Why then should we make an arbitrary cleavage between all this and the real Plato? Did he not initiate this ever expanding flow of thought and meaning?

[1] *Plato's Theory of Man* (Cambridge: Harvard University Press, 1948), p. 1.

Yes, but other men, not Plato, carried it on. We must not confuse the two.

I am afraid that the answer to this interjection is that every real dialogue is precisely a fusion—a confusion—of the two. It is not wholly mine or yet wholly yours, but a living tissue between, which belongs to both of us. The being of a thinker includes his thought, and his thought is communicated to other minds where it expands and grows.

Where then does the thought of Plato end and that of the others begin?

This question is not to be correctly answered in a cut-and-dried manner. The real Plato, in his essential being, is to be found in the history of Platonic criticism and commentary. Certainly these critics cannot be understood without him, and he, or at least what is best in his reflections, is not to be understood without them. Facts about Plato, like the date of his death, can be readily memorized and repeated. But the thoughts of Plato are not facts of this sort. They are meanings which must be understood. And meanings cannot be understood without being set in a new horizon, which brings me to a second error in antiquarianism.

This is the neglect of its own historicity. How strange that historians should be so unhistorical! The different interpreters of Plato have lived in different ages, and have shared with their contemporaries certain common interests and problems. Hence they have raised new questions and developed new meanings. Furthermore, each of those living in a given time has his own mode of approach. I have been in Europe these last months and have been reading a number of different commentaries on Descartes written by living authors. These authors are well informed and thoroughly acquainted with all the relevant facts. But it is striking not only how these interpretations differ from that of a past period, say that of Octave Hamelin, but also how they differ from one another. A commentator may think that he is recapturing the real Descartes as he was, but what is actually written down is something of the commentator's own, a selection, an evaluation, the result of a dialogue. Why should he try to reduce himself to zero or to pretend that he is not himself in history?

Because he must be objective, and because the intrusion of subjective features is bad.

But Descartes was not an object, and knew that he was not. The commentator himself is also an existing subject. He cannot be Descartes. He can try to find in Descartes something that is significant for himself, for his own time, and also for the future. This is the task of the true commentator. But a certain false objectivism now weakens the disciplines of man. It is a primary responsibility of philosophy, in my opinion, to correct this objectivism.

Does this mean that no mistakes can be made, that anything attributed to a past author is actually there? By no means! Every dialogue is threatened by misunderstandings. Some may be corrected by textual criticism, factual study of the time, etc. In a dialogue the speaker's words must be clearly audible, and one must know who he is. But then the real work must begin, to understand the meaning, to assimilate it into a different world, and to respond. This is threatened by more basic errors such as misunderstanding, missing the point, confusion, and lack of clarity. No technical rules or factual procedures can protect us against these. Insight is required. Textual criticism and factual study are, of course, necessary. But they play a subordinate and instrumental role.

II. ETHICS

Brand Blanshard: My first question is: How can values be intelligibly ascribed to nonliving things? The second is: How are natural tendencies to be identified? These questions need a little amplification.

John Wild holds to an ethics of natural law. According to this theory, goodness is "the completion of existence," the fulfillment of natural tendencies; "whenever we find goodness, we find some capacity or tendency in the act of realization." This view seems to me plausible if the tendencies referred to are those of sentient beings. Why do we call the experience of knowledge or of beauty good? G. E. Moore and W. D. Ross would call this an idle question; these things are self-evidently good, and that ends the matter. Wild would disagree. He would say that they are good because they satisfy universal human wants, and would add that their fulfilling or satisfying these wants is what we mean by their goodness. His case for this view is strong. But, like Thomas Aquinas and others in the realist tradition, he carries it too far.

For he holds not only that all goodness is the realization of natural tendency, but that the realization of natural tendency is as such good. "The world is dynamic," he says, "and moving toward completion. There are natural norms embedded in the structure of all material existence," and anything is held to achieve goodness so far as it realizes these norms. He seems even to hold that existence as such is good in the sense that it is better for anything to be than not to be.

It is intelligible to say of human nature that it achieves goodness in the pursuit of ends. It is plausible to say this also of animal life, and possible to say it even of the sunflower that "tends" toward the sun, if one is willing to stretch sentient existence that far. But to say it of stocks and stones? I suspect a false analogy. The tendency of waves to "make toward the pebbled shore" is not a tendency at all in the sense in which the swimmer tends to the shore. The swimmer is, or may be, striving for an end; but in the movement of the waves there is nothing of this whatever, so far as we can see—nothing beyond bare mechanical causality. If the waves, in thus fulfilling the law of their nature, are achieving goodness, then goodness is to be found everywhere, and has lost all distinctive or useful meaning. It is good that a boulder in pre-human times should roll down hill, since it is thus fulfilling a natural tendency. This is to carry a strong empirical case to unverifiable speculative extremes. Even so hardy a realist as G. E. Moore had to admit in the end that in a world without experience there would be no value. I think our metaphysical realists should do the same.

Suppose they did: there would still remain our second problem. If you equate goodness with the fulfillment of natural tendency, and find in some men natural tendencies to be sadistic or jealous, do you not have to call their fulfillment good? Wild is of course aware of this difficulty. His way of meeting it, I understand, is to cut off some tendencies as abnormal or unnatural, and to confine goodness to the realization of the normal and natural ones. But how are you to tell which are normal? If you say, "Those whose realization would be better," you are moving in a circle, since you are defining better by normal and normal by better. If you say, "Those that are common to the species," you are still in difficulty. For there seem to be some tendencies common to the race, for example, tendencies to jealousy and hatred, whose realization is bad, and tendencies not thus common whose realization is good, such as that of the musical genius (if his impulse is held to be common) with a novel and unique gift.

In his theory of goodness, Wild is moving in a direction in which I should like to follow him. I should be grateful if he would clear up these difficulties for me.

Lon L. Fuller: (1) Is the notion of a tendential quality in inanimate nature an essential part of any theory of natural law? (2) Some who adhere to the natural-law point of view use such phrases as "according to natural law," or "the natural law teaches us" so-and-so. Others, including myself, would no more use phrases of this sort than we would say such things as "according to the truth," or "a full view of reality teaches us." In other words, some seem to think of natural law as a body of doctrine (they would say *"the* natural law"), while others think of it as a point of view or a method of thinking. What is your opinion with reference to this difference in conceptions of the meaning of natural law?

Wild: In his first question, Professor Fuller asks about "tendential quality in inorganic nature." Natural law, as I understand it, names a kind of moral thinking that attempts to avoid relativism without hypostatizing values in a special realm divorced from concrete existence. This commits it to the view that human existence at any rate involves certain normative factors. In Plato, Aristotle, and Aquinas these "natural norms" were identified with dynamic forms or tendential qualities necessary or essential to man. The realization of these essential needs is good, their frustration bad. Since there certainly have been thinkers who defended such a view without raising questions about inanimate nature, I must answer No to his first question. But I must introduce a qualification. If this question is raised, I do not see how anyone defending such a natural or existential ethics can fail to recognize analogous tendencies in inanimate nature and how he can with consistency then deny them any normative character. In my opinion, such natural norms are implied by any coherent theory of natural law. I suspect that Professor Fuller is expressing a profound doubt concerning this implication. If this is part of his question, I shall deal with it in answering Professor Blanshard, who has expressed this same doubt.

I do not care for either of the extreme views which Professor Fuller suggests in his second question. On the one hand, I certainly share his distrust of any view which claims to have access to the natural law as a complete body of moral doctrine. I believe that human freedom penetrates more deeply into human existence than classical thought ever recognized and that it affects even the essence of man, which is not fixed for all time, but is transformed in human history. I cannot believe, for example, that the basic needs of man in a closed tribal society are the same as in an open society where individual thought and decision are possible. Even now we have no final and inclusive list of the essential needs of man, and who knows what transformations lie ahead? Man is essentially unfinished. Hence I doubt if any definitive version of moral doctrine will ever be formulated.

But on the other hand, I have difficulty in understanding what Professor Fuller can mean by "a method of thinking" with no definite content, and how he can have any confidence in it if, after two thousand years, it has produced no defensible results at all. I am impressed by the constantly recurring attempts to formulate moral laws and bills of rights. None of these is complete. All are subject to question. Many of them, nevertheless, agree in certain significant respects. From the time of Plato down to the recent United Nations declaration, nonrelativistic moral theorists have generally agreed that the human child has a basic need or right to education. It is hard for me to doubt that this is so. I wonder if Professor Fuller doubts it. Such a principle is very abstract and leaves room for infinite flexibility. But it is not empty, and yet it seems to hold for all mankind without exception.

I am not particularly attached to the term "natural," which may have outlived its usefulness. I would rather speak of existential principles. But whatever we wish to call a nonrelativistic ethical view based on human ontology, I believe that such a view should be thought of both as embodying a certain minimal content and also as a method ever seeking for further refinement and development.

Professor Blanshard holds that in extending goodness beyond sentient experience, realistic moral theory has fallen into an "unverifiable speculative extreme" which deprives goodness of "all distinctive or useful meaning." It is, of course, only our own conscious values that we know directly from the inside and with which the discipline of ethics is concerned. An ontology of value, therefore, which identifies it with ways of existing not restricted to man does lead to conclusions which cannot be confirmed by subjective reports. We cannot ask a star to tell us about its values. But is it true that there are no unconscious human values and disvalues which can be judged from the outside?

Many aspects of our moral experience would seem to point toward a negative answer. We recognize a moral significance in acts that are nonreflective and spontaneous. Thus we condemn in the child, and even more in the adult, acts of egoism or cruelty which are performed as a matter of habit without reflection. Similarly, we admire acts of generosity and sacrifice all the more insofar as they are done as a matter of course without calculation or effort. This lack of reflection gives us a sense that the act really belongs to the person, and wells up from the depths of his being. Has not psychoanalysis taught us how we give ourselves away by unconscious mistakes and slips of the tongue? Unconscious automatic activities of this kind not only reveal, they also bear important intrinsic values of their own which make an essential contribution to our purposive acts. In the light of our present-day knowledge of psychosomatic integration, is it plausible to make a sharp separation between the conscious and unconscious levels of what we call our "higher" activities? It is true that we are now prejudiced in favor of consciousness and rational control. Hence, we ignore the semiconscious values of bodily functioning except in moments of crisis when we miss them and they suddenly leap into view.

Let us suppose that Professor Blanshard has a favorite pianist who is playing a piece in a manner justly appreciated as magnificent. Here is a high intrinsic value in an act that is, of course, not exclusively automatic. Nevertheless, many semiconscious and unconscious factors are making their contributions. Take the detailed movements and pressures of the fingers which are running off automatically! The artist is not conscious of them. But suppose suddenly a mistake is made. Then the value borne by an automatic act will leap into view. Such a mistake can ruin the whole performance. Such automatic values are also poignantly revealed when a musician suffers serious injury to a finger or hand. They are not mere neutral instruments. This is a rationalistic prejudice. They bear a value of their own, as we can see perhaps more clearly if we think of the real pain suffered by those who finally break with their family, their nation, or their religion. The loss of conscious values they are prepared to accept. But the loss is always more severe because of those factors of long-established habit which have become so familiar as to be no longer noticed. Nevertheless, the values borne by these automatic acts are by no means unimportant, and once lost, they are poignantly perceived.

Must we not conclude that both conscious and unconscious factors play essential roles in the purposive acts of embodied men? But if the orderly and unconscious functioning of the human body can bear value, why should we reject the idea that the unconscious orderly functioning of bodies in nature, apart from man, can also bear a minimum value? That human existence is good is, I think, a postulate underlying all ethical theory. Unless the notion of existence is wholly equivocal, is it unreasonable to believe that any act of existing, in its act, has some minimal intrinsic value? There is no time here to argue the complex question of analogy. All I can say is that in my opinion the term "existence" is not wholly equivocal.

Professor Blanshard is repelled by the idea that "existence" is good which leads to this conclusion. But is not existence included within the object of all moral endeavor? Suppose I could have all the values under heaven on the sole condition that they would not exist? Would I be any better? Of course, existence alone is not enough, for existence may be evil. This brings me now to Professor Blanshard's second question concerning the analysis of goodness, which certainly has its difficulties.

He wants to know how the ontological realist identifies certain tendencies as "abnormal or unnatural." I myself find these terms, which I have used in the past, less and less satisfactory because the first (normal) suggests something that everyone does, and the second (natural) a fixed set of properties which needs only to be actualized. Hence, the term authentic is perhaps preferable. I am impressed by the way we use the terms "real" and "really" in this connection. What I am striving for is really to be myself, not a confused, diluted, or second-rate version. The moral ideal for man as such is to be authentically human. This I now believe is the best way of expressing the key conception of an ontological ethics, which of course takes us back to the key question: What is man? The only way I can find out which tendencies should be expressed and which repressed is to gain a more adequate conception of who and what I really am.

Classical thought made some progress in analyzing certain tendencies and *the kinds of act* required for their realization. These analyses lie at the root of what is called *moral law* and *natural law* today. But man is more than *what he is* and *what he does*. He is also the concrete act of existing, not merely as it can be objectively observed from the outside, but as it is lived subjectively from the inside. This subjective existence and its necessary conditions were slurred over by the objective methods of traditional thought and were not clearly focused until modern times. For example, it has now been shown that man is not an isolated substance but rather a being who is open to the world without which he cannot exist at all. It has also been shown that he cannot be separated from those future possibilities which belong to his being, and that his concern for this being is always expressed in some mode of choice which affects not only himself and his associates, but the structure of his world.

As Professor Blanshard suggests, this personal existence is constantly thrown into situations in history which are novel and confronts individual problems not met by the abstract generalizations of traditional ethics. But in the light of its new understanding of the conditions of human existence, modern thought has been able to reveal certain ways of acting (not properties or *kinds of act*) which seem to belong to human existence as such, though in fact they are usually ignored and evaded. Any failure to act in these ways is to this degree a failure to embrace the only existence to which he has access. Hence, he should act in these ways no matter where he is or what he does. These are open obligations capable of embracing an indefinite range of factual determinations and, therefore, applying to any existing person in any historical situation.

Thus it may be claimed on the basis of such an analysis that whatever an individual's peculiar circumstances may be, he should take account of his integral being and that of the world in which he lives, should listen to his conscience, should act freely as the result of a permanent choice, should maintain the temporal integrity of his being by the repetition of such choices, but always in such a way as to be open to further being. These recommendations are concerned not so much with *kinds of act* as with *ways of acting,* not so much with essence as with existence. Hence, they suggest a number of questions, two of which, at least, now require a brief comment.

First of all, will not such an ethics of freedom lead to a social anarchy in which "authentic" individuals achieve only further loneliness and isolation? Those who press this question are confusing freedom with an arbitrary preference which fails to face the whole dynamic world and is enclosed within itself. Freedom, however, is aware of the ambiguity of existence and is open to further being, as we have said. Hence, it is ready for genuine communication with others whose worlds are radically different. Such communication, which penetrates to the free roots of our personal being, is the only way that leads through the wastes of isolation. Those who doubt its existence should consider the history of Western philosophy where the spirit of freedom has expressed itself not only in world views which are radically divergent, but in disciplined modes of communication between them which constitute the very history itself. A free society cannot exist without free individuals, and mutual understanding and respect are its necessary conditions.

In the second place, it may be asked whether such freedom is not too unrestricted? Does it not make way for any choice, even the most horrible and inhuman, provided that it is made permanently with the full integrity of personal being? How about an authentic monster? Questions of this sort forget the finiteness of human existence, which is limited always by suffering, physical and social dependence, conflict, guilt, chance, and death. These limits cannot be adequately understood as determinate properties of the human organism which require fixed kinds of action for a natural realization. They are indeterminate negations surrounding the whole human world and each human act with a margin of ambiguity and nothingness. They can never be eliminated by any kind of action. Whatever we do, they must still remain. Nevertheless, these boundaries of our existence can be revealed as they are, faced with courage, and to some degree pressed back by the authentic exercise of freedom in the sense we are suggesting. The inhuman monster is not merely one who commits an act of a certain kind. His condition is far more serious. He is, rather, one who ignores and evades these limits, carrying death and destruction within himself and spreading them throughout the human world wherever he goes.

This, of course, is only a bare sketch. But it may serve to suggest what I mean by the distinction between authentic and unauthentic action. In my opinion, the traditional ethics of natural law must move in this direction if it is to be of any help to living men today.

III. EPISTEMOLOGY

Francis H. Parker: In his insistence upon the primacy of empirical data,[2] which results in a preservation of the general outlines of the world of common sense, does John Wild institute and utilize adequate critical and intellectual safeguards against the possibility of fraudulent data? This is my sole general question, but I shall try to exemplify it through the following three interrelated, more specific critical questions, each question corresponding to one of what are still "the three basic doctrines of realistic philosophy"[3] according to Wild.

I. D O C T R I N E 2.   Wild's belief that there are nonmutual relations, relations lacking converses, seems to be entailed by his epistemological realism,[4] which in turn preserves our ordinary view of the nature of knowledge. But is the notion of nonmutual relations, or Wild's use of the notion, intellectually defensible? If xRy is a nonmutual relational complex, then not only is x related to y, but it is also true that y, the term of relatum, has the property of being the term of xR. But this is a relational property and therefore founds a converse relation: yRx. Hence, the relation xRy is not nonmutual. Wild's reply is that the converse relation, yRx, is not a real relation but only a logical one,[5] that y itself is not really related to x, for if it were, y would depend upon the cognition of it, and this would abandon the epistemological realism of common sense in favor of epistemological idealism. But does not this reply also forfeit epistemological realism, though now in favor

[2] E.g., *The Return to Reason*, ed. by John Wild (Chicago: Henry Regnery Co., 1953), p. 37.

[3] *Introduction to Realistic Philosophy* (New York: Harper & Row, 1948), p. 6.

[4] *Ibid.*, p. 350.

[5] *Ibid.*

of a radical epistemological dualism? For if it is not really y itself which is related to x, then it is not really y itself which is the term, or relatum of xR. If this be so, however, then the cognitive relation, xR, does not really terminate in y itself, but only in a mental counterpart of y, in which case it does not seem true to say that "real existence can be known by the human mind." [6] In short: If the converse of a cognitive relation is real we have epistemological idealism, and if it is merely mental we have complete epistemological dualism, which would seem inevitably to turn into epistemological idealism. Has Wild rejected George Berkeley's epistemological idealism only by being insufficiently critical?

2. DOCTRINE 1. Is not Wild's view that any predicamental relation is an accident of a substance [7] incompatible with his ontological pluralism,[8] which in turn preserves our ordinary view of the world? For if any predicamental relation, R, is an accident of a substance, x, then, since R essentially or analytically involves a term, y, Ry is also an accident of x. But if Ry is an accident of x, then, analytically, y also is an accident (or a part of an accident) of x. Since every finite thing is related to every other finite thing (at least by relations of similarity or dissimilarity [9]), then is not each finite thing an accident of every other finite thing, so that nature is one substance? In any event, does not the present argument, plus the argument in Question 1, plus Wild's assertion of God's omniscience [10] imply that God is the only substance, that every finite thing is an accident or mode of God? In short, has Wild rejected Spinoza's monism only by being insufficiently critical?

3. DOCTRINE 3. Can then such knowledge, either dualistically or idealistically conceived, of such a monistic world be "the only reliable guide to human conduct," [11] the basis of a natural-law ethic? Furthermore, can there be such a thing as human conduct, if by "human" we mean, in part, "free," for is not the element of indeterminacy which Wild finds present in freedom [12] incompatible with his belief in the

[6] *Introduction to Realistic Philosophy*, p. 6.

[7] *Ibid.*, p. 347.

[8] E.g., *ibid.*, p. 316.

[9] *Ibid.*, p. 347.

[10] E.g., *ibid.*, pp. 377–381.

[11] *Introduction to Realistic Philosophy*, *ibid.*, p. 6.

[12] E.g., *ibid.*, p. 382.

natural universality of causality? [13] Or, if this indeterminacy is subsumed under material causation,[14] on what grounds can freedom be
declared to be the prerogative peculiarly, or even preponderantly, of
human beings? [15] Or if this indeterminacy is subsumed under "the possible intellect," [16] how is action to be distinguished from thought, will
from intellect? Finally, can there be such a thing as conduct if every
possibility is an actual property of God, as the argument in Question 2
above indicates? In short, has Wild rejected Spinoza's ethic of resigna-
tion only by being insufficiently critical?

It is a fact (to adapt Etienne Gilson's statement [17]) that between ourselves and the Greco-Medieval tradition not only existentialism but also
modern philosophy and science have intervened, and have profoundly
modified the conditions under which philosophy has to work. Is it
therefore possible any longer to maintain so easily that the structure of
reality is given in immediate experience?

Wild: Professor Parker has raised three specific questions of an
epistemological nature and also a very general question at the beginning and end of his interrogation. I shall begin by dealing with his
three specific questions.

1. There are two aspects of the argument presented here which I
cannot accept. The first is an underlying assumption which leads Parker
to view the mind as a thing (x) and knowledge as a relation (categorical) of this thing to another thing (y). I have never defended a view
of this kind. The mind is not a thing having relations to other things,
but a mode of indeterminate being which is in itself relational. In such
relational acts, as I have called them (transcendental relations as they
were called in the tradition), the foundation (x) cannot be distinguished from the relation (R). Hence they should not be symbolized
as xRy, but rather as Ry, the act itself (x) merging with the relation
(R). Power or potency has a structure of this type. My capacity to read
this book is not something in me which has a real relation to the book.

[13] E.g., *ibid.*, p. 314.

[14] E.g., *ibid.*, p. 315.

[15] E.g., *ibid.*, p. 40.

[16] *Ibid.*, pp. 460–461.

[17] *The Spirit of Mediaeval Philosophy*, trans. by A. H. C. Downes (New York: Charles
Scribner's Sons, 1936), p. 5.

It is rather a phase of my being which is in itself relational. In the same way, my act of awareness itself relates me to its object.

When I examine such acts, I find that they are nonmutual. No change has ever been observed in any object as a result of its being known or thought about. Thus, I can ask my friend if he experienced any change when I glanced at him while he was meditating. Of course, his knowing that I glanced at him means a change in him, though not in the glance. Evidence of this sort, and there is much of it, seems to indicate that the knowing relation is nonmutual. My knowing this pencil is really related to the pencil, but the pencil is not really related to me. I cannot see that Parker offers any evidence to dispute this claim. His sentence, "For if it is not really y itself which is related to x . . ." (cf. p. 132), is an unsupported assertion on his part which I reject for the reasons given.

2. I cannot accept this argument for several reasons, two of which I shall briefly mention. First, the foundation and the term of a categorical relation, like similarity, must be distinct. Nothing is similar to itself. It is true that we speak of the *whole* relation xRy; however, this is never a substantial whole, but a *sui generis* relational whole which cannot require that the term be the same as the foundation. If this were true, there could not be any relations of similarity and dissimilarity. Hence, in his third sentence under (2) he equivocates with the term "part," confusing a relational part with a substantial part (p. 132). Second, as I explained in (1), I do not agree that in knowing an entity, God turns this entity into one of his own modes or accidents (p. 134).

3. I cannot here answer all the questions addressed to me under (3), but will restrict myself to two: (*a*) in my opinion, the knowledge (?) of a monistic world such as that of Spinoza cannot be a reliable guide to human conduct; (*b*) freedom is peculiar to man, since subhuman entities, while they possess indeterminacy, nevertheless lack other factors, such as insight and choice, which are essential to any free act.

At the beginning and end of his interrogation, Parker raises a more basic question on which I should like to comment. I have maintained that the everyday world of common sense and common language is the peculiar object of philosophical study. Here we find great ranges of qualitative data and structures, like that of the world itself, with which no science is concerned. This is the peculiar province of philosophy. But Parker wonders whether the structure of reality is given "so easily," and whether I have taken adequate precautions against "the possibility of fraudulent data." The implication is that there are other more reliable data to which the philosopher should turn. What are these data?

I suppose that he must mean the "data" of the special sciences gained with the aid of instruments where an effort is made to abstract from the personal interests and point of view of an observer. For the purpose of impersonal calculation to gain control over subhuman objects this is, no doubt, legitimate. From this point of view, the subjectively saturated phenomena of the *Lebenswelt* may be properly referred to as biased, sloppy, and even fraudulent. But such statements are relative to a certain purpose. For the artist who wishes to reveal personal life as it is lived, such data are relevant, and for the philosopher who wishes to understand human existence in the world, they may be even more important. From this point of view, in fact, the "objective" data of science are partial and derived, and any attempt to use them as the exclusive basis for an interpretation of man as he lives must be judged as biased, inexact, and fraudulent.

The term "datum" suggests a bare fact which is simply presented to a neutral observer. But the *Lebenswelt* is pervaded by subjective factors and saturated with value. In this primordial horizon, objective data, like those of science, are not found. Here there are no uninterpreted data, all objects being relative to a subjective attitude without which they cannot be understood. Hence, the term "phenomenon" is preferable to "datum" or "given." If we are to understand ourselves as we exist, even if we are to understand science as it arises and in its ultimate frame, these subjective-objective phenomena must be accurately described and analyzed exactly as they are manifested. The bent stick under water may not be in the abstract space of the physicist. Hence, from his point of view, it is unreal. But it is not unreal in the rich ambiguous space of the *Lebenswelt* in which we live. Therefore, this space also, and its contents, must be described and analyzed if we are to understand the world in which we really exist. No phenomenon can be ignored by the really radical empiricist or phenomenologist.

This task of describing the human life-world has been neglected in the West since the time of Plato, who called it a cave of fleeting shadows, and now faces serious difficulties and possible aberrations, which are apparent to any careful reader of the recent phenomenological literature. In the first place, it is necessary for the phenomenological investigator to recapture the act as it is lived from the inside, not objectifying it, but at the same time revealing its structure with clarity and penetration. This is not easy, as we can see from the difficulties with which Edmund Husserl so persistently struggled and never completely overcame. Second, in this vast field of lived experience, the investigator must be able to distinguish sharply, as Martin Heidegger has not always done, between what is of universal significance and what is only particular and autobiographical. Third, he must beware of accepting an arbitrary frame, like that of objectivism, which leads him to consider only those fragmentary phenomena which fit into this frame, and then to ignore the rest. Finally, he must avoid the error of supposing that this analysis of the *Lebenswelt* is the only function to be performed by philosophy, and that it must provide him with an answer to all philosophical questions. These last mistakes, with several others, are found in the work of Jean-Paul Sartre.

Nevertheless, in spite of these errors, the long-neglected task of describing the human *Lebenswelt* has now been inaugurated by the British linguistic analysts and the Continental phenomenologists, and lasting results have already been achieved. In this connection, we may mention Sartre's critique of objectivist psychology, Husserl's perspectival analysis of perception, Maurice Merleau-Ponty's account of the lived body as against the objective body in his *Phenomenologie de la Perception,* and Heidegger's description of human space, human time, death, conscience, and history in *Sein und Zeit.* As these investigations proceed, we may hope for further light on the nature and origin of science, on authentic human existence, and on ultimate questions of what Aristotle called first philosophy. To pursue this research further into the world of ordinary language in which we actually live, with no pragmatic abstraction or oversimplification is, in my opinion, the most important task of the philosopher at the present time.

Herbert Spiegelberg: 1. How does your "direct realism" differ from (*a*) "naïve" realism, (*b*) American neo-realism, (*c*) Max Scheler's phenomenological realism?

EXPLANATION: (*a*) Your reference to "uncritical naïve realism of common sense in its crudest manifestations" [18] hints at modifications of common-sense philosophy which I would like to see spelled out. (*b*) Your unequivocal rejection of dualistic realism would make a clarification of your position in regard to the original new realism particularly pertinent. (Do you share Francis Parker's criticism of neorealism in *The Return to Reason?* [19]) (*c*) Scheler's realism would seem to be more congenial to your position than the pronounced epistemological dualism of Nicolai Hartmann, who seems to meet with your approval.[20]

2. In what sense do you call existence an indubitable datum of experience?

E X P L A N A T I O N : Apparently there are for you such items as hallucinated data.[21] According to your formulation in *The Return to Reason* [22] these would have to share in the pervasive indubitable character of existence. But is it not necessary to distinguish between the phenomenal character of existence, which indubitably belongs even to hallucinated objects, and the actual existence, which they essentially lack? Hence, does not existence in the second sense remain dubitable in principle, while it is indubitable in the first sense?

3. Can a realistic phenomenology dispense entirely with the suspension of judgment characteristic of a neutralistic phenomenology?

E X P L A N A T I O N : Granting that existence is a pervasive and indubitable character of the given, should phenomenology accept it at its face value? Even "direct realism" admits that existence differs from essence by presenting "special difficulties in apprehending it," and apparently by being less clearly and distinctly given than the latter.[23] Besides, if existence implies anything like independence of the experiencer, it contains a transcendent reference that can never be completely veri-

[18] *Philosophy and Phenomenological Research*, XIV, 2, Dec. 1953, "An Examination of Critical Realism with Special Reference to Mr. C. D. Broad's Theory of Sense," p. 144.
[19] Op. cit., p. 162.
[20] *The Challenge of Existentialism* (Bloomington: Indiana University Press, 1959), p. 223.
[21] *Philosophy and Phenomenological Research*, I, 1, Sept. 1940, "The Concept of *The Given* in Contemporary Philosophy—Its Origin and Limitations," p. 82.
[22] Op. cit., p. 41.
[23] *The Return to Reason*, p. 41.

fied, and that for essential reasons. This would seem to suggest at least a precautionary and preliminary suspension of the question of existential validity, as it is implied even in Charles S. Peirce's phenomenology of Firstness. Such a neutralistic stage of phenomenology would, of course, not preclude a final decision for realism on phenomenological grounds, let alone commit us to phenomenological idealism.

4. What are the precise implications of the time lag in sense perception for the epistemology of direct realism?

EXPLANATION: In *Introduction to Realistic Philosophy*[24] you refer to the need and possibility of "understanding and correction by rational apprehension." What form would such a correction assume? How would it differ from a dualistic inference which distinguishes between the now given galaxy, which may no longer exist, and the now existing galaxy, which cannot yet be given?

Wild: Professor Spiegelberg has raised some very important phenomenological questions. To answer them adequately would require not only far-ranging knowledge and great insight, but prolonged discussion as well. Perhaps in the space at my disposal I can indicate the direction which I believe such answers would take.

1*a*. The naïve realism of common sense is primarily concerned with things and takes their presence in experience for granted as though it made no difference whatsoever. Hence, it is uncritical in confusing presence with what is present and world with things in the world. Since writing the lines you quote, phenomenology has taught me to become more critical of this naïve realism which constantly forgets that things are revealed in a finite world horizon in relation to a corporeal, personal center. I am now much clearer on this point. I myself, the personal center, exist together with my relations. It is not just things, but things in this relational context which make up experience. I hold, precisely as a phenomenologist, that this relational context can be directly revealed as it is with no noetic distortion.

This revealing power is not exclusively objective. Every man has at least a dim unthematic awareness in his basic purposes and intentions. When asked about these ultimate meanings which lie at the center of his world, he can explain his meanings to some degree. As he pursues

[24] Op. cit., pp. 432 f.

these purposes, there is a similar awareness *in* his acts that enables him to know not only what he is doing in the very act as he does it, but also the so-called object, not in isolation, but precisely in relation to his intention. Phenomenology is the attempt to intensify and to explore this consciousness that lives *in* our acts from their first intentional sources to their last termini. Insofar as it succeeds, it reveals neither a purely inner realm of introspection nor a purely objective universe, but a more primordial world of intentional structures which are subjective as well as objective, both together in one.

The things and persons with whom we are dealing in this *Lebenswelt* are, of course, not created by us, but are independent. First of all, however, we know them not as they are "in themselves," but as they are in the world, in relation to our intentions, as opposing us, or helpful and friendly. What then are they "in themselves," apart from us and our human meanings?

In suggesting an answer to this question, I see no reason to doubt the claim of objective science to give us a structural knowledge of this sort. If you want to know what things are like apart from man, and even with man so far as he is seeking simply to master them, then go to science! It can tell you. This claim is justified. But if it is then supposed that this is the world as it really is, and that in terms of this perspective, man and his whole life-world can be explained as a sort of subjective illusion, *this claim* is totally unjustified. Man and his life-world are also very real. In fact, this is the richer and more ultimate horizon out of which science develops as an abstract perspective.

Our human revealing power does not create things or alter them. This, I believe, was Kant's mistake. It makes them present to us precisely as they are in relation to ourselves. When used in a special way, this revealing power may also give us some knowledge of what they are apart from us. Such a position cannot be properly identified either with what has traditionally been called idealism or with realism. As against idealism, it holds that things are completely independent of us. Against realism, it holds that ultimate meanings are due to us. Nevertheless, insofar as it holds that these independent things and the intentions that give them their human meaning can be revealed to us exactly as they are, this position is appropriately called *direct realism,* and in this respect, indeed, it resembles common sense. But it also recognizes that what we know primordially in this way are not just things, but things whose meaning is in part revealed. In this respect, as in many others, it is very unlike the pragmatic realism of common sense.

1b. Dualistic realism, as I understand it, recognizes the act of knowing, but separates its direct object (essence or sense datum) from the existent entity. I cannot accept this view because: (a) I see no evidence for such a separation, and (b) I do not see how, on the basis of such a separation, the knowledge of one (the sense datum) would enable me to know the other, that is, the existent entity.

The new realism, as I understand it, resembles naïve realism in slurring over the noetic act. Rightly supposing that we can know the existing entity, it makes no distinction between the thing and the thing-as-revealed-by-finite-knowledge. Thus every object of awareness tends to gain the status of an independent existing thing, and all being is reduced to the objective, as witness the susceptibility of several of the neo-realists to an objective behaviorism. Both of these conclusions seem wrong to me on phenomenological grounds.

First, all objects of awareness have some mode of existence, but they do not exist as independent things in realms of their own. Many of them are partial aspects of things seen in perspective, as the top of the table now before me, which is certainly not a thing. Many of them are relational, as dreams, which cannot be understood apart from the person dreaming. Others, like numbers and geometrical space, are abstractions which cannot exist in themselves, apart from the act of abstracting. Second, to reduce being to the objective fails to take account of human existence as lived from within, including its noetic aspects. This existence is violently reduced and distorted when approached from the standpoint of categories which apply only to objective things. I am in substantial agreement with the criticism of Parker in *The Return to Reason*.

I am therefore led to a position between these two extremes. With the neo-realists, I agree that it is the existent that is directly known. But I disagree with them in holding that this existent is never known completely and in separation, but always partially, in perspective, and in relation to the knower. With the critical realists, I agree that to know an entity is not to be that entity and that there is an important difference between being and being known. But I disagree with them in not wishing to separate the two into diverse things (the entity, on the one hand, and the sense datum, on the other). The object known is distinct from the existent in the sense that it is not completely but partially or relationally identical with it. This position is what I mean by direct realism.

1c. I value Scheler's work very highly and have learned a great deal from him, especially in connection with his theory of levels and his studies of feeling. As a working phenomenologist, I believe that his attitude is essentially realistic. But he was sometimes led to hypostatize abstractions in a neo-realist manner which I believe is unsound. Thus, I cannot agree with his sharp separation of fact from value and his restriction of reason to the former and of feeling to the latter. In my book I was approving certain ideas of Nicolai Hartmann's in the philosophy of nature, not his general epistemology.

2. I believe that the sheer fact of our being in the world is prior to perception and judgment and, therefore, in a sense indubitable. I agree with Husserl that the living presence of an existent entity in this world horizon is also indubitable. But it is inexhaustibly rich in structure and can be perceived only in partial perspectives. These perspectives as such are really existent. But since they are always incomplete, any judgment as to what the whole thing is may be in error. Such a judgment also exists, but it exists as a real intention that cannot be fulfilled. Its object has no independent existence. The latter exists only relatively as the object of an intention. Such intentional existence is distinct and can be distinguished from independent existence. To confuse the two is an error which can be corrected only by empirical investigation. Such corrections are often made. If this were not so, the terms "error" and "illusion" could have no meaning for us.

Recent studies have shown that the traditional objectivist and so-called empirical theories of hallucination are wholly inadequate to the facts. This is no mere matter of placing isolated objects of imagination and judgment in the world as though they were independent. Here the whole world pattern has crumbled into a mass of debris. The hallucinated person does not see or hear or judge in the normal sense of these words. He himself often makes this distinction, saying that the voices he hears are only whispers or that they are like the radio. He makes use of these sensory fields and of his natural being in the world in order to fabricate in front of these a construction of his own which agrees with a warped intention of his being.[25]

3. The phenomenological *epoche* may partially suspend the ordinary judgments and attitudes that govern our daily life, such as affirmation, desiring, and hoping for this or that. It does this in order to understand the whole phenomenon, say hoping for x in its intentional entirety. But it cannot suspend a judgment of existence, since such an intentional phenomenon is always existent. I cannot agree with your statement about the unverifiability of transcendent references. Internal references are no more easily verified than external ones. Human existence is ecstatic, not locked up within a private substance.

4. This question requires an extended answer. I will have to be content with this suggestion concerning the example you give. The naïve realist, I suppose, might say that at night he sees a galaxy with the naked eye, which is of course absurd. So the dualist suggests that what he sees is definitely not a galaxy or anything external, but a mind-dependent datum of some kind. The direct realist, on the other hand, is prepared to recognize the ambiguities of sense perception. He points out that what we really see at night is neither a galaxy nor a nongalactic sense datum, but rather a small point of light coming from a distance which might emanate from an indefinite number of things. Scientific study, involving many probabilities and inferences, tells us that this light comes from a galaxy now no longer existent. This I should say is the rational determination and interpretation of a perceptual experience that is in itself ambiguous.

IV. MAN AND METAPHYSICS

Hermann Wein: What is your opinion about the term "new metaphysics"?

EXPLANATION: A series of dialogues have constituted the dramatic history of occidental thinking. The primordial metaphysics, for example, of Parmenides, Pythagoras, and Plato is about as old as the primordial "antimetaphysics" of Democritus, Protagoras, etc. Meta-

---

[25] For a discerning interpretation of recent literature on this complex topic, cf. Merleau-Ponty, *Phenomenologie de la Perception* (Paris: Gallimard, 1945), pp. 385–397.

physics preserved its importance on the European continent up to Descartes, Spinoza, Leibniz, and the systems of German idealism, with Hegel's universal system as its last high peak. In contrast, the traditional line of "antimetaphysics" was constantly interrupted by the influence and authority of metaphysics in alliance with religion. Yet, we see the *membra disjecta* of that line: the ancient atomists, sophists, skeptics, the nominalists of the Middle Ages, the later atomists, as Pierre Gassendi, the British empiricists, the early materialists, and the originators of positivism in France, etc.

Finally, the nineteenth century, that of Marx, Nietzsche, the monists, and of Mach and Avenarius, saw an antimetaphysical explosion that resulted from the successful alliance of antimetaphysical thinking with the quickly developing sciences.

In Europe, after World War I, the term "new metaphysics" was coined. Whatever the exact meaning of this term may be—if there be one!—it finds its illustrations in Europe in the extensive *opera* of Alfred North Whitehead and Nicolai Hartmann, compiled between the two world wars.

Wild: I agree that we are now living in a period of intellectual crisis, in which we are witnessing the breakdown of traditional conceptions originating with Plato and the initial formulation of radically novel conceptions. But I would analyze the reasons for this breakdown and the nature of the new metaphysics it is eliciting in a somewhat different way.

You are right in calling attention to the antimetaphysical schools of thought, which were first repressed, but suddenly exploded into prominence in the nineteenth century in alliance with the rapidly expanding natural sciences. Since metaphysics of some sort is an inescapable necessity, it has now become clear that this antimetaphysics rests on basic conceptions of a naturalistic and objectivistic kind which fail to do justice to the concrete life-world from which science itself originates. The philosophy of German idealism has failed to withstand realistic criticism and other objections connected with the development of modern sciences. And while the classical and medieval tradition of realistic philosophy is still alive and developing, it shares with naturalism an objective point of view which has so far prevented it from taking account of nonobjective phenomena in the life-world and which has exposed it to certain basic objections raised by modern thinkers. Although exposition of these criticisms is not appropriate here, I can briefly state what I believe to be the most important. My comments fall under five heads.

1. Since the time of Plato, the finitude of man has been nominally recognized. But it has also been held that human reason can escape from these limitations to some degree. For example, human reason has claimed to gain an absolute and overarching knowledge of the existence of a transcendent being, of its properties, and of the universe as a whole. As you suggest, this claim has been constantly supported and influenced by Western religion. It is amazing how closely the Western conceptions of God, presumably worked out by pure reason, resemble the God of Christian revelation.

This notion of a pure reason capable of absolute knowledge has not been able to withstand criticism. Its claims have been shown not only to be exaggerated, but to threaten the integrity of philosophy and the freedom of man. Many thinkers have contributed to this critique. But the name of Kant is of peculiar importance in this connection.

2. Another related idea, also found in Plato, is the claim that the reason of man has access to changeless truth (eternal verities), which exists in a realm of its own apart from human time and history.

This claim also has been shown to be without foundation. Many modern thinkers have contributed to this criticism and to that sense of a pervasive human historicity which it has elicited. But the idea that truth itself has a history was first systematically developed by Hegel. In this respect, his thought was radically revolutionary and still lives, though in many other respects it was bound to tradition, as you have pointed out in your book *Realdialektik*.

3. While the name of Plato cannot be mentioned in this connection, and while there have been other noteworthy exceptions, the tradition on the whole has been governed by an essentialist mode of thought which conceives of being as an object there before one. This has led it to pay insufficient attention to the act of existing and to whole ranges of experience long named but not analyzed by the obscure epithet "subjective."

This objectivist trend, closely related to the ethos of modern science, has now been clearly focused and subjected to a devastating criticism by many modern writers, of whom Kierkegaard is certainly for us the most important.

4. The tradition has thought of cosmic structure as finally fixed and capable of being formulated in a closed system of thought. Human freedom was then conceived as the adjustment to an external universe essentially fixed and finished.

This idea also has broken under disciplined criticism. It has been shown not only that creative spontaneity and freedom play a far more basic role in human existence than our tradition recognized, but that they have something to do with the structure of the world in which we live. The thought of William James and his attack on the block universe must certainly be mentioned in this connection.

5. Finally, our Western tradition has been characterized by a neglect of basic notions which it has itself regarded as fundamental. Thus things that are present have been carefully analyzed, but presence itself neglected. Concepts and things which have meaning are clearly focused, but meaning itself has never been adequately understood. The most glaring instance of this sort is being itself, correctly recognized by the tradition as the most basic concept on which all others depend. Aristotle, indeed, defined philosophy first as the study of being as such. In spite of this, we find in traditional metaphysics a great web of theory devoted to beings and their different kinds. But beyond a persistent tendency to identify being with present objects, the theory of being as such is almost nonexistent.

It is to Heidegger that we now owe the most precise and cogent formulation of this criticism.

A negative criticism is not really telling unless it is able to indicate not only that a mistake has been made, but how this mistake may be rectified. The critics I have mentioned, and there are many others, have actually done this to some degree. Thus, Kant made important suggestions as to how a genuine metaphysics of finitude might be possible. Hegel showed how the idea of a truth developing in history can be made intelligible. Kierkegaard not only attacked the essentialism which mars this formulation, but shed some light on the regions of subjective existence which essentialism neglects. James attacked the block universe; but he also felt his way into the atmosphere of a truly open world.

Heidegger has revealed the substitution of beings for being in traditional metaphysics. He has also been able to make a few suggestions, though fragile and obscure, as to how this defect may be corrected.

The realistic tradition is perhaps less foreign to these suggestions than any other historical alternative. Whether or not it is open to such a development is a question which I shall consider in my answer to Professor William Barrett. In any case, it will lead to a metaphysics which has never as yet been fully formulated and therefore deserves to be called new. This metaphysics will recognize the radical finitude of man, the historicity of truth, the experience of personal existence, the openness of the human world, and the radical need for light on being.

George P. Klubertanz S.J.: 1. Granted that the method of discovering the primitive evidence of philosophy (especially metaphysics) is a phenomenological one, can we show that this method involves no postulates or presuppositions?

2. In addition to the phenomenological method of discovering primitive evidence and principles in philosophy, do we not also need a method of going from these evidences to conclusions such as the existence of God? Is this method the same in all the "parts" of philosophy, or are there distinct methods in metaphysics, in the philosophy of nature, and in ethics?

3. What is the relation between the existentialist analysis of freedom and the traditional ones? In other words, is this contemporary analysis primarily ethical, or natural, or does it constitute a new area distinct from all the others?

4. Is the natural law entirely and completely determined in some kind of objective order which is always there to be discovered, but perhaps because of human weakness is not discovered until circumstances call for it? Or is the natural law the practical judgments of right reason in concrete (and varying) circumstances, and therefore not entirely determined and unchangeable?

Wild: My answer to this must depend on what Father Klubertanz means by presupposition. If he means clear, thematic propositions incapable of further modification and development, my answer will be Yes. If, however, he means vague and unthematic meanings susceptible to modification in the light of an examination of the evidence, my answer will be No. For example, every human being has a vague, unthematic preconception of being. Without this, we could not understand what we mean by "a being," and the difference between a being and nothing. Preconceptions of this kind are unavoidable. Under the influence of Greek thought, however, Western philosophy has generally accepted the notion of being as equivalent to objective being, something there, on hand, before the eyes of a neutral observer. What cannot be observed in this way, out there, does not exist at all. This notion of being as objective presence before the eyes, thematized by Aristotle, has dominated the whole history of Western thought. Such a thematic preconception can be avoided, and the time has now come when it must be avoided if philosophy is to survive.

2. Of course, there are the methods of logical inference. But this is a formal answer that only touches the surface. The basis of such an inference is always a meaning or a connection of A to B. Knowledge progresses only by the discovery of such connections, or the completion of them when they are perceived in a partial form. Thus Charles Darwin saw a connection between the unconscious "purpose" in nature and the struggle for existence. From this, many inferences could be drawn which could then be checked by observation.

I think that there are important differences between natural sciences (including the philosophy of nature) and the human disciplines (including ethics). Science starts with atomic facts that are intrinsically meaningless, though often connected with other facts. To see this connection requires a large element of constructive invention. Hence, the method of science is hypothetico-deductive. The human sciences start with human beings, who are not only factual but also intrinsically meaningful, that is, originally related to meaning as such. These disciplines advance by the discovery and completion of meanings already present in their objects. Hence their methods must be more receptive and descriptive. The method of metaphysics must be even more purely phenomenological, for it is concerned with the clarification of basic structures, like meaning itself, which are already dimly understood but almost impossible to grasp thematically. This is no doubt why so little light has been shed on meaning in the past history of Western metaphysics.

3. The term "existentialist" is, of course, ambiguous at the present time. But existentialist analyses of human freedom do possess certain traits in common which distinguish them from classical analyses, say that of Thomas Aquinas, who considers it in connection with a faculty, the will, after his examination of the rational essence. One gathers that freedom is an attribute(?)—or quality(?)—which attaches itself to the will, a property of the fixed human substance already there. This analysis abstracts from the fact of human existing, and the role that is played by freedom in this concrete act. One might call it an essentialist analysis, which attempts to abstract freedom from its exercise. The existentialist, if we are to use this term, would object that freedom is not properly understood as an attribute or quality or property, or indeed anything in the abstract order of essence, but rather as an existential, a way of existing, in the concrete order of existence. When examined in this context, it is far more fundamental than any classical analysis, including that of Thomas Aquinas, would seem to suggest. Thus it is seen to be "essential" to human existence as a whole, and necessarily connected with the exercise of human thought, human feeling, and the actual world in which man lives. There are other differences, but this I think is the most basic one.

4. As I have tried to explain in my answer to Professor Fuller, it is the latter alternative that I would accept.

Y. P. Mei: 1. John Wild's concept of being is a catch-all concept, but it is set in absolute opposition to nonbeing. "Only nothingness lies beyond its absolute universal scope. Hence, the opposition between being and non-being is the most absolute and unqualified of all oppositions."[26] In Eastern thought, being and nonbeing are regarded by a number of important schools not so much in terms of opposition as in terms of continuity or, perhaps, levels. Indian expressions such as *"neti, neti"* and *nirvana,* and Chinese concepts of *wu* (nonbeing) and *wu-chi* (nonultimate) do not refer to a realm excluded from being so much as to one that transcends being, and is actually more inclusive, one of ultra-ultimate existence, one might say. Existentialist Heidegger's senti-

---

[26] "Certain Basic Concepts of Western Realism and Their Relation to Oriental Thought," *Essays in East-West Philosophy,* ed. by Charles A. Moore (Honolulu: University of Hawaii Press, 1951), p. 253.

ments are probably not too far removed from this. Will Wild want to give the being-nonbeing relationship a second thought, or will he want to stand by the statement quoted above? If the latter, then one important gap between East and West will remain as wide as ever, and what will Wild say to this Eastern emphasis on nonbeing?

A related question would be whether Wild's being can ever be completely divested of all the modes of existence.

2. This question has to do with the position of man. Among the Eastern philosophies, Confucianism distinguishes itself for its persistent theme of the centrality and dignity of man. Man is elevated above things and kept from being swallowed up by some deity. I am not sure just what is the place of man in Wild's ontology and whether sufficient status is given to him.

Wild: 1. I still believe that there is an unqualified opposition between being and absolute nothingness which our Western tradition has called contradiction. Both of these notions, however, are opposed to those determinate things with which Western metaphysics has been almost exclusively concerned in its long history. Being as such is also no-thing and stands over against determinate entities, though it cannot be thought without them. In this respect, it resembles what we call "awareness," which is distinct from any of its objects and is yet identified with all of them. Hence it has been easy, on the one hand, to follow James in denying the existence of consciousness and reducing it to nothingness and, on the other, to follow the idealists in thinking of it as a great container identified with things. As a matter of fact, it is neither.

Hence one finds in the West a constant tendency, clearly expressed in the first movement of Hegel's *Logic,* to identify being with nothing. That which really exists is always a specific entity. Being as such is a sheer abstraction, namely, nothing. Western metaphysics, therefore, has focused its attention on the different modes or kinds of being. But being itself has been neglected. This neglect has been clearly recognized by Heidegger and others, and the time has now come when Western thought must once again wrestle seriously with the problem of being *as such*. In this obscure and arduous enterprise, I believe that we may have much to learn from oriental thought where, as you suggest, though negative terms were used to indicate the sense in which being transcends beings, this primordial notion was never identified with absolute nothingness.

You ask whether being "can ever be completely divested of all the modes of existence." This question, I believe, can be affirmatively answered and I wish I knew the answer. As a matter of fact, I have only one small suggestion to make concerning a possible mode of approach through the study of what we call awareness. There are at least five reasons which indicate that consciousness is closely related to being as such.

a) Like being, awareness is so intimately bound up with determinate entities or objects—yes, even identified with them—that it is impossible for us to separate it from them or to think of it apart from them.

b) And yet, like being, it is not reducible to them, and can be clearly distinguished as in itself indeterminate and evidently transcending any one of its so-called objects or any set of such objects. Hence, like being, it has often been identified with nothing. As a matter of fact, it is similarly like nothing in being distinct from any specific determination. Nevertheless, it is not sheer nothingness, for this is certainly not aware of anything.

c) The idealists have tried to identify being with awareness and to think of this entity as a whole containing specific objects as parts inside itself. This simple identification is surely wrong. But neither is being a whole made up of beings. If we examine these negative assertions more carefully, we shall discover that they are both true for similar reasons. Any whole, no matter how complex, made up of determinate beings and relations, would itself be a determinate being, not being itself, which would still transcend any such composite entity. Similarly, any totality of objects no matter how complex would be a determinate object, not awareness as such, which would still transcend any such composite object. This would seem to indicate a marked similarity in the two structures.

d) To use Heidegger's terms, both being and awareness are *ecstatic*. Thus being is found "in" a given entity. But it stands out of these limits, bringing this entity into action which relates it to other entities, and these to others, etc. Consciousness seems to be ecstatic in a similar way. It is found "in" the conscious agent but it reaches out beyond these limits, uniting this agent with other objects and these with others, etc.

e) Finally, in the higher levels of awareness we come to understand a given entity only by relating it to being, the ultimate meaning—meaning itself. This meaning is found in determinate facts or objects. It attaches to them, but it cannot be identified with them. The fact of Napoleon's death is not the same as the meaning of this fact, just as this particular being is not the same as its being. Thus meaning would seem to coincide with being. But it also seems to coincide with consciousness, for without awareness of some kind there is no meaning.

Of course, the idealistic identification of being with awareness must be avoided. But these considerations would seem to indicate a very close relation between the two. Is being the same as presence, not that which is present, but presence itself? Is it a global presence in us and around us? If so, how are these two related to each other? And how are they related to the beings they reveal? I do not know the answers to these questions. Perhaps the East can help us here. If so, I hope that Professor Mei may tell us how.

2. In his second question, Y. P. Mei asks about "the centrality and dignity of man." So far as we know, inorganic entities are not conscious at all. The highest form of animal awareness is determined by each shifting situation, and cannot free itself from immediately felt drives and impulses. His possession of arbitrary symbols enables man to say No to a given situation, to gain a distance from it, and what we call an objective view of himself and the world. This symbolic distance lies at the root of that freedom which distinguishes him from all other finite entities known to us. I believe that this difference is so great that it can be adequately expressed only by saying that man exists in a different way.

We may perhaps focus this difference more clearly if we think of the peculiar phenomenon we have been referring to as awareness, that awareness which to some degree dwells in our human acts. This awareness involves both a spatial as well as a temporal transcendence. Thus at a given juncture of my act, I say that "I am here," but this "here" is determined only in relation to a "there" beyond me where my act is already projected. Human existence can never be circumscribed within any fixed boundaries. Wherever it goes, it carries a spatial field around it where its action may be projected. The same is true of time, for this existence can never be squeezed into a momentary now. At any given moment it is stretched out into the past that it has been, and ahead of itself toward the future where its action is directed. We may generalize this by saying that free existence always transcends its given determinations. As soon as it is *x*, it is already *not-x*. This self-transcendence appears very clearly in what we call the human imagination. No matter what is presented to him, man can always imagine it to be otherwise. He becomes what he is only by being other than what he is. This dialectic is a necessary phase of human life. We can phrase it by saying that man is always open to more than what he is, always specifically and factually determined but ever open to being.

As to the "centrality" of man, I am not so sure. He certainly plays a central role in the divergent worlds which are constituted by different human cultures. I still believe, however, that human philosophy can help us to find a more worthy "center" and to free us from an anthropocentrism which is to some extent inevitable. But perhaps this can be fully achieved only with the aid of religion. I would, however, strenuously object to any religion which jeopardizes human freedom and "swallows it up" in some deity.

Gerd Brand: 1. Philosophy, whatever else it is, is an explanation or an attempted explanation. We always can and in fact we do judge the achievements of this explanation. This reveals a rather extraordinary situation. Indeed, if we judge the explanation, we must already know about the *explicandum,* and this knowledge is such that the explanation itself is measured by it. From this arises a question of many aspects. Why must we explain at all, and what is explanation if the point of arrival is measured by the point of departure which, in a way, we never leave? What is this "knowledge" of the *explicandum* asking to be explained and at the same time being the measure of the final explanation? What is this fundamental relationship between us and the reality to be explained? (Has it not, in a way which remains to be determined, the character of a "circle"?) What are the real terms of this relationship? And what is the criterion of explanation?

2. Existentialism and phenomenology treat questions such as situationality, choice, chance, struggle, failure, anxiety, suffering, guilt, death, human time, etc. Another discipline with an approach to reality differ-

ent from that of philosophy treats problems bearing the same names, that is, psychoanalysis. The new philosophy promoted by John Wild is to go on with an ever deeper examination of these questions. What is or will be the relationship between psychoanalysis, psychology, and the new philosophy, and how will this relationship affect these different disciplines in themselves?

Wild: 1. In connection with Dr. Brand's first question, I shall organize my comments around two themes he suggests, explanation and the circular nature of knowledge, which I do not find it easy to reconcile, as I see that he does not. The ideal of explanation is deeply ingrained in our Western tradition and has come to us from the Greeks. Individual events are to be explained in terms of causes or principles which already have within them that which is explained and more. Thus the scientific law (referring to a tendency in nature) contains within it those determinate aspects of the particular event which fall under it. Given the tendency in nature, the event must be so-and-so. Given the law, these aspects of the event can be deduced. The perfectly intelligible universe would be one in which everything that happens is already contained within a first cause or principle that is self-explanatory, containing its own reason within itself. Such a universe we may say is closed. Everything, so to speak, has happened already. The perfect explanation would be a finished system from which everything could be strictly deduced unilaterally from the theory to the fact, with no circular reasoning.

Three things in particular need to be noticed about this ideal: (*a*) its nonphenomenological tendency to pass over the given fact to some cause beyond it, for every cause is distinct from its effect and the first cause is of course not given in experience; (*b*) its critique of circular reasoning as vicious; and (*c*) its closed or systematic character. The aim of philosophy as you express it in your first sentence is to arrive at such a systematic explanation of the universe. Of course, this ideal has never been realized, but it has exerted a tremendous influence on our intellectual history, on science and on philosophy as well. Now, however, each of its three phases is faced with serious difficulties.

The coming of phenomenology has revealed serious difficulties in this theory and has opened up new possibilities. Time after time it has been shown, especially in the field of anthropology, that certain explanatory theories, of sense data, of conditioned response, of hedonistic motivation, etc., were wholly incapable of accounting for the given facts which turned out to mean something else quite different when subjected to careful scrutiny. It is true that an explanatory theory involves one kind of meaning, but it restricts our vision and closes our minds to the possibilities of new meanings which may be elicited from the facts. The phenomenological method, in turning to the things themselves with an open mind, has shown us that such meanings may be elicited, often with results that are surprising to the highest degree. It is now clear, at least in the field of human phenomena, that it is not safe to devise explanatory theories before such investigations have been made. Things no doubt can be explained and then manipulated by their extrinsic causes. But in the case of free persons, it is more important to understand than to explain.

But even if we should work out an explanatory theory which did justice to human phenomena, we would necessarily be judging the former in terms of the latter and thus arguing in a circle, as you point out. As a matter of fact, all human understanding proceeds in this circular manner. This is because what we understand is meaning of some kind, and meaning as such is inclusive. No matter how rudimentary and partial a view of the world may be, it is a world of meaning with open horizons in which some place for anything may be found. Nothing presented to us can be wholly meaningless. Hence, all understanding moves in a circle from what is already dimly and confusedly seen to the same thing seen more sharply or comprehensively. Explanation is one mode of understanding that applies to certain areas but not to others, as mystery, for example.

Even scientific explanation moves in a circle, as is now well known. First, certain facts are understood in a nonexplanatory manner. Then the meaning of these facts is explored by the formulation of an explanatory hypothesis. From this hypothesis other conjectured facts are deduced. If the traditional ideal were sound, the matter should end there. But it does not. The confirmation of the theory will now depend on these conjectured facts. If they occur, it will be confirmed. But no explanation in the traditional sense can be confirmed by one of its own necessary consequences. This is arguing in a circle, a vicious circle, for the explanation depends on what it is already supposed to explain. But though it may be called vicious, this is certainly the method of science, a constant development of meaning from fact and fact from meaning, each depending on the other. This circular movement, which is in different forms characteristic of all reflection, casts a grave doubt on the traditional theory of explanation.

As we have noted, the universe that corresponds to the traditional theory of explanation is closed. The happening of something is merely the replacing of it outside its causes (*extra causas*). But since everything (and more) was already in its causes, nothing really new ever happens. The type of mind that regards explanation as the only kind of meaning constantly tends to absolutize what it already knows. When confronted with something strange, it turns away to look for some available cause rather than dwelling on the thing itself. It thinks of philosophy as the elimination of wonder, and equates understanding with the absence of mystery. As against this type of procedure, the new phenomenological empiricism has once again revived the conception of an open universe whose being is historical. This type of mind would rather deepen the significance of a single real phenomenon than explain a million figments. It recognizes the inexhaustible richness of the concrete and the infinite fertility of new perspectives of meaning. It is not afraid of wonder, and is ready to seek for meaning in mystery.

So in response to your first question, I would rather think of philosophy as the search for meaning than for explanation. This search is always circular, for a meaning cannot be deepened and refined unless the original starting point is held in mind. Finally, no criterion can be given other than that revealing power which belongs to the being of man.

2. The task of philosophical anthropology is to clarify by phenomenological analysis the meaning of those existential structures such as being-in-the-world, anxiety, death, and historicity, which belong to the human person as such and which are, therefore, presupposed by the psychological disciplines you mention as well as by the other sciences of man. As to just who is disturbed and as to the exact psychosomatic conditions involved, these are matters for the psychiatrist and analyst to decide. But the relation of sickness of that kind to the human being as such and the general norms that the practitioner should have in mind in his

healing procedure lie beyond the province of so specialized a discipline. The responsible study of these prior questions requires a different phenomenological approach in which some progress has now been made. Insofar as this kind of philosophical discipline can be developed, it will mean that the psychiatrist, instead of having to draw his basic conceptions from objective constructions and vague ideas found in literature and religion, can fall back on the clearly articulated results of phenomenological investigation. One may find a penetrating account of the aid which such an analysis can give the practicing psychiatrist in an article by Ludwig Binswanger, *Der Mensch in der Psychiatrie.*[27] This relation, of course, is reciprocal. The philosophical anthropologist can also be aided by investigations in the special human sciences. The study of man must be a co-operative task. But to accomplish anything of value, the philosopher must maintain the autonomy of his own phenomenological approach.

William Barrett: 1. Why do you hold that though existentialism has changed the traditional view of man, it seems to have left the meaning of being where it was with Aristotle and Thomas Aquinas?

If, as you say, the view of man that we find in Aristotle's *Nichomachean Ethics* or in Thomas' *Tractatus de Homine* (in the *Summa Theologica*) seems to us today abstract and, so to speak, geometrical, would not this also apply to their conception of being itself?

MORE EXACTLY: Is it possible to conceive the being of man in a radically new way (at least for philosophers) without conceiving of being in a radically different way?

2. Can you reconcile the ontology of *Sein und Zeit* with your own realism?

Wild: 1. I believe that recent anthropological studies, largely stimulated by the thought of Kierkegaard, have shed some light on vast regions of lived experience hitherto ignored by the tradition as "subjective" and have developed an ontological perspective on human existence which is radically new. You seem to think that man is very close to being as such, and that therefore this must have resulted in a radically different view of being. In my answer, I shall suggest two points.

[27] *Schizophrenie* (Pfullingen: Verlag Günther Neske, 1957).

First of all, it is perfectly possible to examine particular beings and modes of being, even human being, with only a vague, implicit impression of being as such. In my opinion, this is essentially true of the classical realistic tradition. It has presented us with detailed analyses of particular beings, kinds of being, and modes of being, including man, but has never clearly focused being as such, which is not a being (even a divine being), not any set of beings or any conceptual abstraction, even an analogous one. Second, the question about being has been raised again in our time, especially by Heidegger. But so far as I know, he has not as yet given us (certainly not in *Sein und Zeit*) any coherent and articulate answer. The new conception of man, about which you speak, may imply a new conception of being. But as yet this has not come to light. It is perfectly possible to develop a new kind of anthropology which is closer to concrete existence and human historicity without explicitly working out a new conception of being. This, I think, is what has happened.

If this is true, I see no reason for denying that the notion of being implicit in the realistic tradition might be developed in such a way as to bring it into harmony with a similar development of the notion of being implicit in *Sein und Zeit*. But if it takes place, this development will involve certain definite changes in basic conceptions drawn from classical ontology. For one thing, being as such must be clearly focused, and must be identified neither with a being, nor with any set of beings, nor with any mode of logical abstraction, nor with any combination of these. For another, the priority of existence to essence must be taken very seriously and developed along the line already suggested by Professor Étienne Gilson and his students. Finally, as I shall indicate more fully in my answer to Professor Paul Tillich, the whole conception of a fixed essence, especially in the case of man, will have to be abandoned. Whether changes as radical as these can still be thought of as falling within the tradition will depend, of course, on how one defines this term.

2. Since there is no fully developed ontology in *Sein und Zeit,* I shall interpret this question as asking whether the view of man which is worked out here can be reconciled with realism. If the definition of realism suggested in the platform[28] of the Association for Realistic

[28] Published as the appendix in *The Return to Reason.*

Philosophy is accepted, an affirmative answer can, I think, be given. Man is surrounded by beings whose existence is completely independent of him. These beings can also be revealed, at least in part, as they are. Furthermore, the structure of human existence points to the possibility of an ethics with real content. But any modern view of man which is similar to this will differ markedly from classical anthropology, say that of Thomas Aquinas, in at least two vital respects.

In the first place, the Thomistic analysis regards man from a purely external point of view as an object of a peculiar kind, with a changeless essence and various attributes and properties. No effort is made to analyze him, so to speak, from the inside, in terms of his lived existence. As you say, such a merely external analysis is bound to strike us today as rigid, geometric, and radically one-sided. In the second place, the Thomistic distinction between a self-enclosed substance and accidents does not do justice to what we may call existential structure, and arbitrarily cuts man off from his life-field or world. Thus from this point of view, freedom is perhaps a necessary property, but not essential to man. I do not believe that an existence which showed no signs of freedom could be recognized as human. The Thomist has to say that a basic choice, which determines the whole way of life for a person, is only an accident of his substance. Few of us would want to maintain that the way of life of an existing person is an accident without which he could be essentially himself. Finally, in Aquinas' *Tractatus de Homine* in the *Summa Theologica,* nothing whatsoever is said about the human world, and one certainly gets the impression that the human substance can be understood apart from any world. This also is some kind of accident. But it is now very clear that a man without a world is a hopelessly barren abstraction. If realism is defined in terms of such an essentialist conception, then of course no analysis in terms of lived existence can be realistic.

Charles Hartshorne: Consider the following argument:

p: God knows that the world exists.

q: The world exists.

q^*: q is contingent.

r: p entails q.

   s: ((*p* entails *q*) and (*q* is contingent)) entails (*p* is contingent).
   r, q*, s: Inference, *modus ponens: p* is contingent.
   t: That which a contingent proposition affirms, and its contradictory denies, cannot be in something which is in all respects necessary. Therefore, since *p* is contingent, knowledge *that* the world
   exists cannot be in God, if God is an, in all respects, necessary
   being.

My question is what step, if any, in the above do you reject?
   1. Where is the knowledge, if not in God?
   2. Is the remark of Thomas Aquinas that since the world exists,
necessarily (it follows that) it exists, to the point; seeing that in *this*
sense any proposition whatever is necessarily true, so that the remark
would save the "necessity" of the divine knowing only in the trivial
sense in which anything, however contingent, can be called necessary
(the sense that *p* entails *p*)?
   3. Is it relevant to say that knowledge and its objects should not be
assumed to be alike in all respects, seeing that the argument given
above makes no such assumption? For instance, it permits knowledge
(say, ours) of the necessary (say, God's existence) to be contingent
(if *p* is contingent and *q* necessary, that *p* entails *q* is no contradiction;
indeed, any proposition entails a necessary proposition [C. I. Lewis]).
   Concerning divine knowledge, the argument assumes only that this
knowledge cannot err; hence, God knows that *p* is true, entails its truth.
Is this open to denial?
   4. What can the referent of "God knows that the world exists" and
of "God knows that the world does not exist" (which he *would* know,
if it did not) have in common that could be necessary (i.e., unaffected
by the contingent alternative) beyond this: God knowing the tautology,
"The world exists or does not exist"? And is this what anyone ever
meant by omniscience?
   5. My solution, of course, is to admit the contingency of *p* and of
that in God which it asserts without giving up the necessity of the
proposition asserting that God exists *qua* infallible. From *this* proposition, *q* does not follow, for had the world not existed, God would have
known infallibly that it did not. But this solution only works provided
God's knowing that the world exists can be outside God *qua* necessary,

yet in him *qua* contingent. Have you any solution which, like this one, avoids the contradiction of viewing God as wholly necessary, yet as having something which a contingent proposition alone can assert, and also avoids the at least apparent absurdity of supposing that God "has" knowledge that the world exists, and yet this knowledge is not in him?

Wild: I have no formal fault to find with the logic of this argument. My difficulties are concerned with the underlying ontological meanings which this kind of logical "exactitude" does nothing whatsoever to clarify. If Professor Hartshorne had explained more exactly what he means ontologically by the terms "necessary" and "contingent," he might have helped me. But using these terms as he does, with the meanings they ordinarily have in a *logical* context, I find this argument unconvincing.

He seems to be regarding a contingent proposition as one which can be denied without contradiction; a necessary proposition as one whose denial is contradictory. As thus defined, the two terms are themselves contradictory and absolutely exclusive. There is no way in which the same proposition can be both necessary and contingent. It must fall either into one category or into the other. This assumption underlies the whole argument. There is no escape through the horns of this dilemma, no concept like freedom, for example, which might lead us beyond the necessary and the contingent to being which is in a sense both and in a sense neither. So Professor Hartshorne confronts God himself with this dilemma. Is God necessary or is he contingent? To say that God is all one or all the other is one-sided and reductive. So Professor Hartshorne concludes that God is a little bit of both, something in him (existence) being necessary and something else (his knowledge of the world) being contingent (cf. 5, p. 159). This splits God up into parts that are not only different (which is bad enough), but absolutely contradictory. Is this really the one God, or two contradictory gods tacked together? Furthermore, how is this extreme duality, one part of which is contingent and the other necessary, reconcilable with Professor Hartshorne's statement (3) that "God's existence," presumably the whole of it, is "necessary"?

I suggest that we need to reflect more seriously on the ontological (not the logical) meaning of "necessary" and "contingent." If we do, we may discover, I think, that an existing entity (not a proposition) as a whole may be both in a sense contingent and in a sense necessary with no contradiction. There is certainly a sense, for example, in which I might not have been as I am, for contingent choices played a role in my whole origin and development. But, as Thomas Aquinas points out, there is also a sense in which my whole existence as I now am is *hypothetically necessary,* as the tradition calls it. This is far from the logical and trivial sense in which *p* entails *p* (cf. Professor Hartshorne's remarks under 2, p. 159). It is an essential phase of my being, the sheer facticity of my being thrown into the world just as I am, and about which I can do nothing, though of course I also know that I might have been otherwise, and indeed might not have been at all. This, of course, is not absolute necessity (with which we are never confronted), but it is a way of not being able to be otherwise, and hence a mode of necessity that constantly affects our being and our awareness.

I mention this only to show that ontological contingency and necessity are by no means as unambiguous and exclusively opposed as Professor Hartshorne's logical approach would seem to suggest. I am not suggesting that God is plagued by our contingent facticity; or that he is confronted by such a dilemma as that between an ideal necessity, on the one hand, and an ideal contingency, on the other. But if God is not, then I think it is meaningful to ask if there is any human experience which can give us some indication of the way in which he is beyond this alternative. I think that the experience of what we call freedom does provide us with such an indication. At its ordinary levels it provides us, of course, with clear examples of what we call contingency. But let us not be content with these. Let us take an example of saintly freedom at its highest level—St. Francis, let us say, assisting the lepers with a real risk to his bodily health. This act was certainly chosen by him. Therefore, it was free. At the same time, those who have studied his personal existence are left with the impression, as they read this account, that it could not have been otherwise. Therefore, it was genuinely free in the most authentic sense of this term, and yet at the same time also necessary, given the man as he was.

This, I believe, can give us an important clue as to how we should think of the free creative acts of God. They transcend our categories of necessity and contingency. These acts are both necessary and yet contingent and, therefore, not precisely one *or* the other. We are faced with a real transcendence which looms above our finite categories. This is what I miss in Professor Hartshorne's analysis. We will never gain wisdom by running the concept of God through a calculating machine. It is insight we need here, not formal calculations based on what we already know. We do not know enough.

V. PHILOSOPHY AND THE CONTEMPORARY WORLD

P. T. Raju: 1. Is there a point of view from which logical empiricism and existentialism can be reconciled and synthesized? What is it?

2. What important elements of truth does Professor Wild find which are emphasized in Indian philosophy, but not emphasized in Western philosophy? Does Professor Wild think that they can be incorporated into Western thought? If he does, how can they be incorporated?

Wild: 1. The term "existentialism" suggests a closed system of thought. Hence other names like "phenomenology" and the "philosophy of existence" are less inaccurate. I see little hope of any reconciliation between this open mode of philosophizing and logical empiricism. From such an objective, analytic logic we cannot gain any light on the concrete data of experience, now known to be subjective and relational in character. The very phrase "logical empiricism" is now an incompatibility. Indeed, in the Anglo-Saxon countries this movement has begun to break down through internal criticism, and also through an awakening of interest in the rich shades of meaning and global perspectives of ordinary language, bitterly attacked not long ago as a swamp of chaos and confusion. It is, of course, a mistake to set up ordinary language as an ultimate standard of insight. It is often both confused and superficial. But it is far less abstract than the most perfect of artificial languages. Any careful attention to our ordinary modes of speech is bound to lead us toward the global structures of the *Lebenswelt*. I should not be surprised, therefore, in the near future to see an alliance between this mode of linguistic analysis and phenomenological research.

2. With respect to Professor Raju's last question, there are three "important elements of truth" which, in my opinion, are emphasized in Indian philosophy but not in the West and which I believe can be incorporated in Western thought.

The first and most basic is that close attention to the inner life of the human person which is a marked feature of Indian thought. In contrast to this, the dominant traditions in the West, from classical times to modern behaviorism, have been objectively focused. Attention was directed from the very beginning to objects brought before the mind rather than to the mind itself and to its sources in lived feeling. Even man himself was considered primarily as an objective substance and studied in the same way as physical things. This objectivist thought has given us a remarkable control over external nature, which culminated in the revolutionary technological developments of recent times. But it has shed little light on the inner existence of man, which does not fit into this objective picture of things and is dismissed as a whimsical and chaotic factor by the scientific mind.

While we now exercise a far-reaching control over subhuman forces of nature, we have developed no comparable disciplines for controlling ourselves. At the present time we are like little children playing with the switches of a vast generative plant still intact with masses of unleased energy. As our technology has advanced at an even more rapid rate, together with the modes of understanding that go with it, our understanding of ourselves has deteriorated, and we wander about like displaced persons in a world of machines and gadgets from which all that is essentially human is more and more conspicuously absent. Through the work of Kierkegaard and others we have now achieved some insight into personal existence and its essential structures, an insight which stands in desperate need of further development and refinement. In this I believe that we may be greatly aided by the thought of India, which has pursued a very different course, and by the marvelous techniques of self-control, meditation, and prayer which have emerged from this age-long study.

A second "element" is the strong emphasis on that global awareness which is always found to some degree in personal existence, and which is a characteristic feature of Indian philosophy. In the West this has been diluted by the analytic tendencies (noted in 2, above) which have distracted attention from being to beings, and which at an early stage divided philosophy into different subordinate disciplines such as logic, ethics, and epistemology. It is a primary function of philosophy to elicit and to nourish such global understanding, which was once provided by myth. But in following the example of the sciences, philosophy has now largely abandoned this essential task. Many "departments" have aestheticians, logicians, and ethicists. But there are few philosophers. I believe that a closer contact with Indian thought may help us to recapture this capacity to raise far-reaching questions and to consider far-reaching answers, which is a marked feature of personal existence at its highest levels.

The third "element" is derived from the second. It is that gracious tolerance, as it is sometimes called, that amazing capacity to understand and often to assimilate seemingly opposed and even contradictory points of view, which always strikes Westerners when they first come into contact with Indian thought. In India this is no doubt due to a glimpsing of being and its vast scope and richness, from which we have much to learn, though if we ever arrive at such openness in the West, it will probably take a different form. We may win it rather through glimpses of transcendence and of the limitations of human thought. But, however we may develop, I am sure that only good can come from further contacts with the thought of this Eastern culture so very different from our own, and from the very basic questions which such contacts are bound to raise.

Takehiko Kojima: 1. You have tried to describe phenomenologically the concrete subjective-objective existence which can shed light on itself only in paradoxes. Your description of a person as he really is, against essentialism (Hume), abstract intellectualism (Descartes), and abstract objectivism (Hegel, Marx), makes possible your "radical empiricism" of personal ethics as a practical awareness. I agree with your attitude, but when I reflect that the term "empiricism" has fulfilled its role in naturalism, objectivism, essentialism, and contemporary technology, I cannot understand how this term fits into your theory.

2. I was deeply moved by your statement: "Freedom does not lie in abandoning ourselves to the ceaseless flux of the ever new. It lies rather in standing firm, in holding to the real future that has been trans-

mitted to us by living traditions, and realizing them, so far as we are able, in the new situation facing us. Here also is an existential norm." [29]

There is, however, one question I would like to ask: What is your tradition? And what is that which transcends the tradition?

Wild: 1. Dr. Kojima raises a point about empiricism, and wonders how I can reconcile the use of this term with an ontological approach that discovers modes of existence in man. Are not nothingness and the mediation of reflection necessary? It is true that existence is not passively received by any perceptive organs, as the seal of the signet is received by wax. To believe that sensations and sense data are received in this way is a mistake still made by many so-called empiricists. But this does not imply that meanings are created *ex nihilo* by the human mind. They are discovered and revealed. Thus I believe that being-in-the-world, anxiety, human historicity, and other existential structures can be found in his own lived experience by any person who will devote the requisite time and attention to this matter. These structures are in fact part of what it means to be human, and everyone without exception has already a dim understanding of this. To discover beings as they are, that is, as they exist, without any admixture of prejudice or arbitrary construction, is part of the original intention of empiricism, though this intention has become sadly confused with forms of dogmatism in the history of this school. Nevertheless, I believe that we should not abandon the original meanings of words to artificial interpretations of "schools" without a struggle.

2. Finally, after quoting a comment of mine on the importance of tradition as constituting the essential continuity of history, Dr. Kojima asks me point blank what my tradition is, and how it can be transcended. A fair question! Speaking roughly, for lack of space, I should like to say first of all that my tradition is now complex and confused. I hope that he will note that in the passage he quotes, I speak of tradition in the plural (traditions). I believe that this is the situation of anyone now not living in a primitive society. He is encompassed not by one but by many traditions soliciting his favor. A basic current in our Western culture is the union of Christianity with Greek thought achieved in the Middle Ages. I have spent a large part of my life studying the classics

[29] *The Challenge of Existentialism,* p.261

of this tradition by which all of us in the West have been influenced. And I do not regret this study. But there is a germinal core of freedom in this tradition which elicits independent thought. My own reflections have led me to believe that this great system is no longer defensible as it stands, and requires basic alterations in the light of truths revealed by other living movements, like phenomenology, which originated in modern times.

For the first time in our history, we in the West are beginning to gain some accurate knowledge of Eastern ways of thinking, which are completely independent of our own. I attended the East-West Philosophers' Conference in Honolulu in 1949, and it opened my mind to many perspectives. I believe that through friendly and disciplined interchanges of this kind, the individual may be freed from many defects in the thought which has nurtured him and may be opened to the perception of new truth. One unexpected feature of this conference impressed me very much. It was the minds of those with the deepest understanding of their own traditions who seemed most capable of grasping supposedly alien modes of thought. Wherever we are, we shall never transcend our traditions by trying to run away from them, but only by exploring their depths. This is my answer to your last question.

Paul Tillich: 1. How would you relate your existentialist position to the necessity of every philosophy to deal with "essences"? In other words: What is the essentialist framework within which your existentialism would have a function?

2. How do you solve the problem: Faith and rational intuition? In other words: Is the Christian existentialism which you suggest a product of faith or of intuitive reason and, if of both, how do they work together?

Wild: 1. Recent thought has at last succeeded in throwing some light on the human act of existing, but has left the factor of structure, or essence, in darkest shadow. I agree with you that this is a serious defect, and that the problem of essence cannot be avoided by any serious philosophy. The distinction comes originally from classical thought, but I am no longer satisfied with this way of dealing with the matter, primarily for two reasons. First, I do not believe that essence can be so sharply separated from existence as the traditional doctrine of pure possibility would imply. I see no evidence for such pure possibilities or essences. They are reified abstractions. Without existence there can be no essence. Even to be conceived, an act of thought is required. Second, I do not believe that existence is rightly viewed as the realization of an antecedent possibility, already there, so to speak. This is a kind of essentialism which fails to do justice to a creative, productive factor which is present in man and even in nature. Hence I am led toward the following conclusions.

Existence is an act which we express by means of verbs (not nouns), opposed to nothing and therefore subject to degree. It is dynamic and necessarily ecstatic or reaching out to what is *structurally different* from itself. As over against this, in ourselves and in all the finite beings known to us, there is *another structural factor* (essence) which can be *distinguished,* but never separated, from existence. This factor is an inactive structure which we express by means of nouns, is opposed not to nothing but to other essences, is not subject to degree, is in itself changeless and self-enclosed. How are the two related?

Instead of regarding essence as a prior guiding factor which is then realized (or not) by an act, I believe it is more fruitful to regard structure as the limit of an act from which it is only modally distinct (as the end-point of a line belongs to the line), and from which it can be separated only by an act of thought. Essence will then not be prior to existence, for apart from existence it is nothing, as a point apart from all extension. In fact, existence will be prior to essence in the sense that it can *be* apart from any given limit. Of course, this needs to be developed in further detail. But one consequence is important. Such a conception will make it possible to avoid the unfortunate dogma of a fixed, closed essence which has plagued traditional thought on this subject since the time of Aristotle. It will no longer be necessary to think of the human essence, for example, as locked within the body, squeezed into a momentary present, and closed to growth and decline. This essence will follow its act of existing in being projected into a world with past and future dimensions, and in being open to development and decay. An act of existing requires some limit, but is in constant tension with the limit it has. As a given limit is transcended, the essence also grows; as it is missed, the essence also declines. This conception of a growing essence will be far more in keeping with the known facts about the evolutionary novelties of nature and the creativity of man.

2. Turning now to your second question, I have already expressed my dislike of the term "existentialism," but since some phrase is necessary, a Christian philosophy of existence perhaps will do. Having spent some time in the study of medieval philosophy, I certainly believe that both faith and intuitive reason must make essential contributions to any defensible philosophy of this kind. The theologian would like to be completely independent of philosophy. But as you are fond of pointing out, he cannot proceed without using such terms as unity, truth, freedom, time, and history, which refer to everyday experience and are subject to philosophic description and analysis. When he tries to deal with them in his own way without any reference to an "alien" discipline, he falls precisely into such subjection, usually to philosophical assumptions current in his time. Such meanings cannot be clarified without philosophy.

On the other hand, the philosopher, in trying to understand the basic elements of human experience, is eventually confronted with the phenomenon of the sacred, which he must deal with in some way, either positively or negatively. Those who have tried to deny it have been forced to set up spurious substitutes, like the individual person or the human state, and have thus ended in monstrous and evident forms of idolatry. Those, on the other hand, who have accepted it and have tried to interpret it in wholly "rational" terms, have constructed pseudo-religious absolutes which embody their own ideals of rationality and which lack evidential support and all persuasive power.

Against such objective absolutes, the criticism of theologians who respect the word of revelation have a deadly telling force. Each discipline seems to need the other and yet to be all-inclusive and independent. Is a Christian philosophy really possible?

It is possible, I think, but only under certain conditions which require a constant tension. Christianity, of course, is not a theory, but a way of life involving theory. The formulation of a truly Christian philosophy, therefore, presupposes not only some understanding of biblical revelation, but also a firsthand understanding of the almost impossible task, as Kierkegaard put it, of trying to exist as a Christian, not one day only but seven days in the week. Anyone in such a position will soon be confronted with philosophical problems, and will be under an obligation to grapple with them, for the renewing of the confused and fallen intelligence is a constant New Testament theme. But this intelligence, though confused and fallen, is autonomous and free. Hence it cannot be renewed by direct external authority, but only by a guiding spirit which is not afraid to enter into its own confusions and to deal with them honestly by its own proper methods. In other words, such a philosophy must be not only truly and existentially Christian, but truly philosophical as well, and freedom lies at the root of all philosophy.

As our Western history clearly shows, any such attempt must face great risks. On the one hand, it may produce something religiously respectable only at the cost of arbitrary philosophical choices which are blind to many facts of life. Or on the other, it may produce something philosophically respectable at the cost of religious mystery and existence. Or, as is more likely, it may produce a "synthesis" which is sound and acceptable neither to critical reason nor to personal faith. A Christian philosophy must be both. I wish I knew more about what it would be like.

If it were ever formulated, such a philosophy would really respect the freedom of human understanding and stay within its proper limits. It would assume no responsibility for harmonizing with any specific content of revelation, but would be open to a Christian interpretation. Such a philosophy would have to be realistic and close to the concrete. It could be neither materialistic nor idealistic, both of these views, and especially the latter, having now been shown to be wholly inconsistent with the implications of Christian faith. Such a point of view would be humble, hesitant, and open, ever raising problems and ever seeking. It would be utterly different from theology and even separate from it. In my opinion, such a philosophy has never yet been formulated. But the present time is ripe.

Charles Malik: These are the questions I wish to submit to John Wild:

1. How would he relate, in his own life, the life of the mind with a life of active religious faith? However this relation is actually achieved in his own life, how would he theoretically work it out for the modern world?

2. Is modern existentialism really autonomous with respect to the Christian tradition?

3. How is Western (including American) responsible thought meeting the Communist challenge, both on the side of theory and the side of action? What reform would Wild suggest to enable this thought to cope more adequately with this challenge?

4. If Aristotle is the most important ground on which the responsible thinking of the East as represented in Islam met with that of the West, may not the realistic philosophy to which Wild seems to be especially devoted, and which grounds itself for the most part upon Aristotle, serve as a modern rallying ground for the responsible thinking of the Middle East and the West? How would Wild transform the Association for Realistic Philosophy so as to enable it to serve this end?

5. What are the main structural lines for the development of a modern *summa* on the basis of realistic thinking and comprising all grades and modes of being as revealed to modern existence?

These matters are very much on my mind and I think they are also on the mind of John Wild. I believe a co-operative effort to grapple with them is of the utmost importance to the sanity and peace of thought and life in the present world.

Wild: 1. Charles Malik asks how "the life of the mind" can be related to "a life of active religious faith." This question of course implies that they have fallen apart. I believe that he is rightly calling our attention to a most serious split in Western culture which affects us individually as well as in our common life. An unmistakable symptom of this strange divorce is the anti-intellectualism of our time which has had to be recognized as an independent political force in recent American history. But the scorn of the man of action for the arm-chair theorist is certainly reciprocated by the scorn of the theorist for the blind practitioner. Hence this opposition tends to intensify itself, philosophic thought on issues of vital importance becoming ever more artificial as action becomes less rational and coherent.

Any effective struggle against this conflict must depend upon an understanding of its nature and its sources. It is due primarily to a rational "scientific" mode of reflection which has dominated Western history since it freed itself from the rich but rigid mythological structure that first governed its life and still governs the action of primitive prehistorical communities. Mythical thought is close to the immediate data of experience and ready with a wide interpretation which is in touch with all the basic needs of man. It is bound up with a common style of action which is repeated with almost no change from generation to generation. It is aware of a divine transcendence to which everything is related. The common life is in fact an endlessly repeated liturgy. In this mythical world man feels at home. It is not an objective system, but a total world in which essentially human feelings and impulses are not missing. Hence the sense of relief and exhilaration experienced by sophisticated moderns when they are introduced to still-surviving forms of folklore and folk music. This mythical understanding, which is native to man, and which will exist as long as man exists, is opposed neither to action nor to religious feeling. But it has little place for the careful study of objective evidence, is filled with incoherence and contradiction, and is incapable of change. Hence it could not withstand the rational criticism which inaugurated our Western history in the islands of Ionia.

This history is guided by a radically different form of consciousness in a different human world. The objective alone is real, the subjective being discarded as an accidental and disruptive factor. These objects can be clearly apprehended only by a detached reason which is altogether uncommitted, and gazes at them from a distance. This is also true of action which can be adequately understood only as an object at a distance by a cold, impartial gaze. Such objective understanding is in fact the necessary condition for sound action, which otherwise will become subjective and uncontrolled. It is such an interpretation of the act of understanding that is responsible for the present gap between theory and action and for the widespread mistrust of the intellect. The inner springs of action cannot be objectified. Hence if the "subjective" is to be ignored, action also will be ignored or reduced to something not itself. The same is true of religion, for the living God is not an objective thing whose properties can be deduced and analyzed from a distance of this kind. Our distance is too great. When we look in this way, there is nothing at all to gaze at. Hence it is not surprising that Western philosophy has either reduced God to itself (as in Hegel) or denied him altogether (as in scientific positivism). From a Christian point of view, there is not much difference except that the latter is perhaps preferable because of its clarity and honesty.

This objective thought has ended the rule of myth, and has freed Western man from the endless repetitions of primitive society bringing history into being. It has brought forth modern technology and given us an amazing control over the things of nature, revolutionizing the world of human existence. But in this world of interchangeable things and functions, there is less and less place for what is individual, free, and essentially human. This is the real meaning, I think, of that divorce between the life of a detached objective mind and the life of faith and action which underlies Dr. Malik's question. How can the two be brought together?

This is in fact the question of our time, and for a complete and coherent answer, prophetic vision is required. I have no such vision; only a few suggestions. To destroy our technology would be the same as suicide. We do not wish to abandon reason, for there is certainly truth in its claims, and any relapse into the irrational will only take us to a lower region. What we need is a real shift of perspective without losing what we have already learned. Reason and science are not false, but they reveal to us only a single dimension of the world, not the world itself. The personal and historical existence of man is also real, and there are ways in which it can be felt and known and cultivated, though not by objective reason and science.

The methods of phenomenology are now beginning to explore these long-neglected regions in a disciplined way, and to bring some minimal understanding of them within the reach of all. We can hope that this widening of perspectives beyond the narrow range of what we call rational thought may lead to a deeper appreciation of the meaning of personal existence and the values which support it. These are being threatened today all over the world, not so much by external enemies and objective forces as by ideas and dogmatisms that chain our inner thoughts. If personal existence is to be maintained in the midst of the vast apparatus of modern life, the struggle against these ideological powers must be carried on in every walk of life, in teaching and all the professions, in business and in politics. In all these regions of the contemporary world, we can try to avoid shibboleths and slogans, and to understand and to support that which is essentially human. Wherever we may be, in living our lives from day to day, we may keep our eyes and ears open for the expression of human existence, and hold ourselves in readiness to listen and give aid. Unless this happens, freedom will die.

Any serious attempt to maintain one's personal existence brings one before the transcendent. Of all the great world religions, Christianity is most closely involved with time, history, anxiety, death, and freedom, the basic categories of personal existence. Hence, the churches could give crucial support in this struggle to decide whether personal existence is to survive in the mass societies of tomorrow. They cannot do this, however, until they have recaptured a deeper sense of the distinctive character of religious mystery, and have been purified of that rationalism which in the West has diluted the brute data of sacred history by weaving them into a network of timeless doctrine, and has interpreted faith as a set of propositions to be believed rather than as a care for existence.

2. If Charles Malik is thinking of *historical* autonomy, then my answer to this question is No. The modern existentialists (and here I must again protest against this epithet) owe their guiding insights to thinkers like Pascal and Kierkegaard. Hence it is a fair historical inference to hold that without the Christian tradition, they could not have appeared when they did. But I do not think that he means this. If he means *systematic* autonomy, then my answer is Yes. It is certainly possible for non-Christian thinkers to describe and to analyze structures of personal existence. Plato did this, and many non-Western thinkers as well. It is also possible to use an analysis of personal existence as the basic approach to an entire philosophy which is either non-Christian, like that of Karl Jaspers and Martin Heidegger, or radically anti-Christian, like that of Jean-Paul Sartre. Many of the basic existentialist themes such as human finitude, being-in-the-world, anxiety, death, and freedom are found in the New Testament, though placed in a different context. In this sense, one can say that it is impossible to be a Christian without recognizing many of the structures which modern phenomenologists have described in a secular context. But it is perfectly possible to recognize these structures, and even to build a whole philosophy upon them without being a Christian. I think it is fair to say, however, that a serious study of them corrects many fallacies of tradi-

tional anthropology in ways which harmonize very closely with concrete insights of Christian thought. Such a study is therefore an excellent philosophical introduction to biblical anthropology, and probably to the Christian faith in general.

3. Since I believe that Communist thought is presenting the Western world with an ideological challenge which can be adequately dealt with only through ideas, I shall restrict myself to the theoretical side of this question. Communist thought, of course, is not a mere agglomeration of ideas, but a great systematic structure based on a dialectical ontology derived from Hegel. No understanding or intelligent criticism of it is possible without an ontology. Many thinkers in America and England have been too distracted by problems of logic and language to consider seriously this basic philosophical discipline. Hence, one reform that is certainly required, before this challenge can be adequately met, is a serious concern with ontological questions which must first be considered before any sound ethics or social philosophy can be formulated. But those of us who are concerned with such questions suffer from an abysmal lack of information concerning contemporary Russian thought. Several accurate and comprehensive surveys have appeared in Europe, but nothing very thorough or precise as yet in English. This is a serious handicap to American philosophy, for without communication there can be no understanding. I have tried several times to interest Foundations in overcoming this difficulty, but so far linguistic difficulties have stood in the way.

In Europe, things are much better. Ontology is very much alive and Heidegger, as you know, has developed a most cogent critique of traditional Western metaphysics, including that of Hegel. Philosophers are well informed not only about the basic Marxist texts, but also about current Russian thought. A vigorous discussion is under way, and clear-cut issues have been formulated. The deepest and most telling criticisms have arisen from neo-Thomist and from existentialist sources, but each suffers from serious defects. The Thomist critique is weakened by traditional rationalist assumptions like that of a timeless truth remote from history. In order to defend such a view against the profound Hegelian conception of a truth that grows in history, something more is required than reference to the authority of Aquinas. The force

of philosophic arguments is often blunted by their admixture with religious "reasons" of a very different order.

We have already referred to Heidegger's incisive criticism of Western ontology, which is indeed profound and far-reaching. But as yet,
we have no coherent sketch of what might take its place. Damaging
attacks on Marxist social theory and its exaltation of the collective have
been developed from existential sources. These are no doubt the most
forceful attacks that have yet been formulated in the West. But these
also will remain unfinished until they can be connected with a social
philosophy which not only takes account of human existential freedom,
but of necessary social structure as well. So far, the radical individualism of existentialist thought has stood in the way of any such formulation. The West badly needs a philosophical critique of communism
based on existential foundations relevant to the modern world, but
based also on a coherent and intelligible social philosophy of genuine
originality and depth. Such a critique must take account of those
principles of natural law which underlie the recent United Nations
Declaration of Human Rights.

4. The Platform of our Association holds that there are certain truths
in the tradition of classical Greek thought, especially in Aristotle, which
must still be recognized by any sound philosophy. That all existence is
individual, that we have access to truth through feeling (*aisthesis*) as
well as through understanding, that a human being is his body, and
that practical reflection is quite distinct from theoretical are such truths.
But this Platform does not state that all or even most of the truth is to be
found in Aristotle. He disagreed with Plato in sharply distinguishing
logic from ontology, and therefore denied that our human reason could
grasp reality in its full richness. This rational thinking is abstract, and
gives us a certain limited perspective on things. As we have noted, other
modes of approach are also possible, though Aristotle never worked
them out with sufficient care, and he remains, in spite of his basic
critique of Plato, a moderate toned-down rationalist. In modern times,
these other approaches have been taken seriously.

In the light of these inquiries, it is now clear that Aristotelian philosophy is subject to several basic criticisms, of which we may mention
the following.

First, it is one-sidedly essentialistic in emphasizing the formal structure of things and in neglecting their existence. Second, its category of substance fails to do justice to certain distinctive traits of human existence such as, for example, human temporality and personality. Third, its doctrine of active reason is not active enough, and fails to take account of the new meanings that are developed in human history. Finally, in the fourth place, it ends in a closed universe in which everything is already actualized and can only repeat itself in endless cycles, a view which fits neither what we know of the real efficacy of inorganic nature nor what we know of the creative factors of human history.

To me the term "realism" has always implied an Aristotelian sense of the inexhaustible richness of being which transcends all our genera and species, and a radical empiricism which is ever ready for new modes of approach. Hence I hope that realistic philosophy will develop along the lines suggested by these criticisms. Such a philosophy would have to abandon the conception of an eternal truth already fixed and finished apart from human history. It would concern itself rather with a human truth to which we have access through the trials and exigencies of real existence in the world. It would have to study the conditions under which such truth develops and grows in human history, and would be constantly ready for the emergence of new meanings. Such a philosophy, it seems to me, would be better fitted to serve as a rallying ground for responsible reflection in the West and in the East than any fixed rationalism of the Western past.

5. The intellectualistic philosophy of the West has ignored the *Lebenswelt,* to use Husserl's term. From the time of Plato it has regarded this concrete world in which we actually exist as a confused mass of shadows, and has abstracted from it and from its subjective conditions to focus attention on particular objects which could be clearly conceived. For the first time in our history, the *Lebenswelt* has been recently discovered by formal philosophy and subjected to a disciplined and impartial scrutiny. This is the most interesting and indeed revolutionary feature of contemporary thought. Two important facts have emerged from this study. The first is the global character of this world phenomenon, its inclusive scope and range. It is from this primordial *Lebenswelt* that all the special sciences take their origin, and it is only in the light of this origin that they can be properly understood. The second is

the fact that this world, while inexhaustibly rich and often confused, is nevertheless not a mere jumble of fleeting shadows, as Plato supposed, but possesses a global structure centered in the human person to which both traditional realism and idealism have remained blind. The study of this structure of the concrete *Lebenswelt* has given rise to a new type of empiricism, more radical than any achieved before, which now goes by the name "phenomenology." This discipline is not content to describe and to analyze objects of a certain type. It is also interested in the relation of such objects to certain attitudes or intentions which reach out to them and make them possible. It is not only concerned with the description of these attitudes taken one by one, but also with their relations to one another in the global structure of the *Lebenswelt*. Any realistic philosophy which can hope to do justice to modern knowledge must recognize this bipolar nature of experience and pay serious attention to its global structures.

In addition to this basic and never-ending task of description, there are certain all-pervasive factors such as temporality, being, meaning, truth, and value which are presupposed by all the special sciences and which, therefore, require a distinctive philosophical consideration. This roughly corresponds to what Aristotle called first philosophy, though it is now clear that he did not carry this discipline very far and that some of his tentative answers are open to serious question.

Four different kinds of phenomena are found in the *Lebenswelt*, each of which is now the object of a distinct mode of scientific investigation: man himself, the realm of nature, other men and the realm of human culture, and, finally, the transcendent. In each of these regions, however, foundational questions arise which involve first philosophy and the *Lebenswelt* as a whole and which cannot be settled by science alone. In the case of man himself, it has been shown that there are vast regions of lived experience hitherto dismissed by objective reason as "subjective" which are absolutely essential to man and which can be described and understood by a disciplined phenomenology. Hence, in addition to psychology and what is now called anthropology, a philosophical anthropology which studies the total existence of man in his *Lebenswelt* is required. Some real light has been shed on these matters, and the further development and refinement of this discipline is of the first importance.

I shall not here elaborate the many problems and mysteries with which the philosophy of nature, the philosophy of culture, and the philosophy of religion are concerned. I shall make only one further remark concerning the last, namely that special precautions must here be taken against that strong temptation, so predominant in Western history, of reducing religion to a set of rational doctrines or even to a theory about itself. But it has now been shown that the distinction, phenomenon vs. intention of the phenomenon, and the deep self-consciousness, which are essential aspects of modern phenomenological research, can enable us to avoid such reductionism. A method which has some respect for the thing itself (i.e., the phenomenon) can gain some understanding of what is radically transcendent.

Such is my conception of a philosophy which might do justice to "all the grades and modes of being as revealed to modern existence." I do not think, however, that the term *summa* should be used. This suggests a closed system of thought in which all the basic questions have been given an eternally valid and definitive answer. We are too aware of our human finitude and historicity to accept any such grandiose claims. The Greek conception of a timeless truth, which received its highly qualified but final expression in the thought of Hegel, will have to go. The only truth to which we have any access is a human truth that lives and grows in history. We no longer expect a human philosopher to bring this history to a close. We expect him to give us insight into the world in which we live. This does not imply an abandonment of the whole notion of truth for a relativism in which everything now true will soon become false. What it implies is rather the infinite richness of being, the finitude of the human mind, and the lasting fertility of a genuine insight which breeds further insights and different perspectives in which it is seen in an ever new light. Before man appeared, there was no human truth or falsity. His life is a constant struggle with this meaningless waste of darkness. In bringing his flickering light and shadow into this waste, he has access not to timeless but to lasting truth. Such truth is worthy of final sacrifice on the part of the human philosopher.

Interrogation of

Jean Wahl

Conducted by Newton P. Stallknecht

Jean Wahl has been professor at Besançon, Nancy, Lyon, Paris, Chicago, Smith, and Mount Holyoke. He was born in 1888 at Marseilles. He was educated at the Lycées Janson-de-Sailly and Louis-le-Grand, the École Normale Supérieure, and the Faculté des Lettres at Paris. Wahl edited *Écrivains et poétes des États Unis d'Amérique*. His many works include *Études Kierkegaardiennes, Études sur le Parménide de Platon, Existence humaine et transcendance, L'idée d'être chez Heidegger, 1848 1948, cent années de l'histoire de l'idée d'existence, Ordre, désordre, lumière, La Pensée de Heidegger et la poésie de Holderlin, La Pensée de l'existence, The Philosopher's Way, Poèmes, Poèmes de Traherne, Poésie, pensée, perception, Les Problèmes de l'ontologie contemporaine: Nicolai Hartmann, La Théorie de la vérité dans la philosophie de Jaspers, Traité de métaphysique, La logique de Hegel comme phénoménologie.*

Frederick Charles Copleston,
 S.J.
Meyer Schapiro
Wilfrid Desan
F. H. Heinemann
Robert Champigny
Milic Capek

Albert William Levi
Vladimir Jankélévitch
Newton P. Stallknecht
Herbert Lamm
James Collins
Philip Merlan

Frederick Charles Copleston, S.J.: You have written, Professor Wahl, of the relation between poetry and metaphysics. In *Existence Humaine et Transcendance* you have said that "le fond de la poésie sera toujours métaphysique, et il est fort possible que le fond de la métaphysique soit également toujours poésie." Does it not seem that there must be a ground common to metaphysics and to certain types of poetry? For poetry, as articulate expression, can hardly be related to metaphysics simply as immediacy to mediation. If you agree with this, could you elucidate the nature of the common ground? Is it a pre-linguistic experience?

Wahl: I agree that the relation between poetry and metaphysics cannot be treated as a relation between immediacy and mediation. On the other hand, it cannot properly be said that there is a common ground to poetry and metaphysics. All depends on what is meant by "ground" and by "common." All the more so as we are in the field of the individual: We cannot speak of metaphysics in general, of poetry in general, but of this particular metaphysics, of this particular poetry. It must also be noted that the metaphysician will always have the ambition to take a general view of reality, which will not be the case for the poet.

We have reached a moment when several among the most important philosophers have the feeling that owing to the peculiar evolution of Western thought, certain essential features of reality have been left aside. It is our business to turn toward them and show their importance, their significance.

It is a fact that the philosopher, whether he be Alfred North Whitehead or Martin Heidegger, looks for the expression of a deep vision in the poets. It is also a fact that since the time of Arthur Rimbaud, the poet has conceived of himself as a *voyant*. Thus there is a set of facts which tends to corroborate our suggestions.

I should like to add that not every philosophy naturally culminates in poetry. It is not evident, for example, how the philosophy of John Locke or of David Hume would culminate in poetry. But it is not the same for the philosophy of George Berkeley. The proof of it is that one finds in some metaphysical poets a sort of fulfillment of this philosophy.

Father Copleston asks me whether there is a foundation common to metaphysics and to poetry, or more exactly to a certain type of metaphysics and to a certain type of poetry. But I believe that it would be necessary to avoid the idea of a common foundation, all the more so since here, each time, matter and form are closely related. Perhaps I am a bit at fault here in this sense, that I said it is very possible that the foundation of metaphysics is always poetry.

Father Copleston completes his interrogation by asking me whether there is a "prelinguistic" experience. But there again, we must say that there is such a unity between the form and foundation that it is very difficult to separate language and thought in poetry and even in philosophy; that if we are tempted to affirm that there is initially a prelinguistic experience, we must not do so except with great caution. Often with the poet, at the beginning of his construction of a poem, there is a rhythm, as Paul Valéry has noted. Sometimes with the metaphysician, as Henri Bergson has noted, there is what he calls a dynamic schema. But it is not by returning to this schema or to this rhythm that we shall find the true unity between poetry and philosophy. These are, says Heidegger, two summits, and the voices of those who are near to these summits respond to one another, but as if at a distance. It is neither in their origin nor in their end that we shall discover their unity. It is in a sort of inspiration which animates that which is between the middle and the end and which constitutes the essence of the work. The metaphysical spirit bloweth where it listeth; the field of metaphysical experience extends where one wishes to see it extended. Some names come to mind: Wordsworth, Shelley, Keats; before them, Blake; before him, Traherne; also Hopkins; in addition, Nerval, Mallarmé, Claudel, or again, Rilke; still others: Whitman, or perhaps Emily Brontë, Emily Dickinson.

Meyer Schapiro: Professor Wahl in his philosophical writings has often referred to art as providing insight or a view of the world parallel to that of the philosophers. Although the artist's view is not presented discursively, Wahl seems to imply that the painter's or poet's work is in some sense "true." I would like to hear his opinion on the nature of truth in art, its difference from "truth" in philosophy and science. Is the truth of art connected with the artistic quality of the work of art, or is it independent of that quality? Is the judgment of art relative to the judgment of its content, the latter's "truth" and range? Does the "truth" of art with a religious content presuppose or entail our judgment of the "truth" of the religious content? Since great individual artists present different outlooks, are they all "true"? Do they differ only in referring to different experiences or aspects of the world? Is art submitted to a criterion of "truth" that also holds in other domains, for instance, philosophy, science, common-sense knowledge?

Wahl: Professor Schapiro has asked me a question about truth in art which will allow me to continue the dialogue with Professor Copleston.

I have to admit that the truth of a work of art is related to its artistic value. Reflecting on this, I am led to recognize that the idea of truth in this case is different from the idea of the truth of a proposition. What I mean by truth in the work of art is rather what I would ordinarily mean by "reality."

But in order to see what this reality is, we have to make a distinction between the explicit project of the artist, which can be the exposition of a particular religious idea, and his implicit project, which can be something both more general and more profound. With some caution, we might on this point take advantage of the ideas of psychologists and try to grasp the latent content beyond the manifest content.

In order to go further, we would have to meditate about the unity and multiplicity of truth (or perhaps reality) and about its relativity. Every great artist brings with him an irreducible vision of reality. Is it possible to find identities between these irreducible visions? This requires an effort which takes us beyond the reach of understanding.

In any case it takes us beyond the application of a logical criterion. Such a poet as Rimbaud helps us to grasp a wild and magic aspect of reality. Is it the same aspect or not which appears in Vincent van Gogh? To such questions we cannot and must not give an answer. In a sense, there are as many visions of the world as there are great artists. And each vision, as we said, is irreducible. But, within the soul of the spectator that we are, there are communications between these visions.

There are many senses of the word "truth." There is no problem of the essence of truth in general. If one insists on starting from theoretical truth, the truth of a work of art will not be spoken of except by analogy. This truth of art will probably come, as Meyer Schapiro suggests, from the significance and the amplitude of the work of art. Why do we speak of truth in this case? The reason is that there is there a deepening of that which is before us and in us.

Professor Schapiro is entirely right in posing the question: Is it the case that the truth of an art which has a religious content presupposes or implicates a judgment on our part which would assert the truth of this religious content? If it is evident that without having strictly religious sentiments, he who looks at a work of art can participate in it, assimilate the primitively religious content by placing it, so to speak, in immanence, he can also, for a brief instant, relive the religious sentiments which have animated the creator.

This perhaps permits a reply to the following question: Since great artists have had different visions of the world, are they all true? There again, we are led to refer back to what I said of the different senses of the word "truth," of the very idea of truth. Then, as it has occurred to recent physicists, there can be in us and in works of art, complementarities.

Moreover, the world of one artist never coincides with the world of another, even if profound relations exist between them. This is what we would say, for example, of Rimbaud and van Gogh, as I have suggested.

The last part of Professor Schapiro's question bears upon the comparison between the truth of a work of art and the truth, on the other hand, of philosophy, of science, and of common sense. But even these last three truths are not similar. The truth of a work of art coincides more with the truth of philosophy than with that of science. When the comparison is with philosophy, we are led back to the preceding question, that of Father Copleston; when the comparison is with common sense, the poet may well claim, with Keats for example, his role and his value.

It matters little, from the point of view of art, that a pictorial work resembles its model, unless it is specified that what really serves as a model is, if not the form, as Montaigne declares, at least a form of the human condition. But it is even more complicated in the case of a great portrait: the artist portrays himself even more than he portrays his model. A great portrait is a communication between two persons and finally that something which surpasses even this communication. This something we can call "truth," if we wish, but noting well that it is something more profound than that which is signified by truth understood as communication.

Wilfrid Desan: Upon several occasions in his book, *Vers la fin de l'Ontologie,* Professor Jean Wahl asserts his personal view that since truth belongs to the proposition only, the traditional definition of truth as *adequatio intellectus rei* should be kept. As a result he believes that Heidegger's insistence upon placing truth not in the proposition, but in that-which-is and in its power to impose itself upon the human mind is wrong.[1] A similar view is proposed in the *Traité de Métaphysique.*[2]

Apropos of Professor Wahl's position, two remarks must be made. First, it appears that he constantly refers to Heidegger's more recent interpretation of *alētheia,* where the accent is laid upon the active overtness coming from the thing itself instead of upon the discovery coming from the mind. The latter interpretation, however, has not been dropped, as far as I know, although it is more typical of previous publications. On the other hand—and this is my second remark—in the *Traité de Métaphysique,* Professor Wahl expounds what he calls *la vérité sentie,* which can be defined, I believe, as an affective awareness of the real. He further claims, not without peril for a judicative expression, that a concession to its *relative* character has to be made.[3]

My question is whether Professor Wahl can consistently deny Heidegger's definition of truth under the pretext that the latter belongs

[1] Wahl, *Vers la fin de l'Ontologie* (Paris: Société d'Édition d'Enseignement Supérieur, 1956), pp. 41, 219, 226.

[2] Paris: Payot, 1953, p. 127.

[3] *Ibid.,* p. 482.

to the proposition only, when he himself proposes *la vérité sentie* as a necessary completion of the classical definition.

Wahl: I remember meeting Whitehead in Boston and telling him that I saw two or three inconsistencies in what he had written. He answered, "Philosophers have been too consistent." So, if I cannot justify myself in the eyes of Professor Desan, I shall at least have a consolation.

There is no doubt a difficulty there, since, on the one hand, I maintain the idea of truth as adequacy of judgment and, on the other hand, I grant what I call *la vérité sentie*. But I am not sure there is a contradiction. What I called *la vérité sentie* is something altogether different from *la vérité* as it is expressed in propositions.

I feel the need to affirm that truth, as a pure philosophical concept, belongs to the proposition, but I also feel the need to affirm that through the experiences of art, through feeling, we reach something real, which justifies, in my opinion, the use of the word *vérité* within the expression *vérité sentie*.

Desan declares that I affirm my personal conception that since truth belongs to the proposition, the traditional definition of truth as adequacy of intellect and of thing should be preserved. I should like to make here two reservations: the view that he attributes to me is not a personal view; it is basically the view of all philosophers (except Heidegger) and in particular of Plato and of Aristotle. It is true that sometimes with this view another is mixed which tends to make of truth a property of the real which is true in the same fashion as it is good and as it is One. But we can put aside this second more metaphysical view; there remains then this idea that the domain of truth is the proposition.

To this traditional conception I have opposed, as Heidegger himself has opposed, a conception, founded in part upon the etymology of the word truth (*alētheia*) which has been discussed by Hellenists of merit (I am thinking in particular of Eduard Fränkel). If I have mentioned as especially Heideggerian this conception of truth as disclosure (*vérité ouverture*), it is because the first conception, that of truth coming from the mind, is not particular to Heidegger, is not specific of Heidegger.

As for my expression "felt truth" (*vérité sentie*), if one wishes to admit a truth which is something other than the truth of propositions, it is necessary to designate by a word, here the word "felt," that one separates oneself from the classical theory. It is a kind of enlargement of the idea of truth. Whereas Heidegger thinks that truth as disclosure is first and that the conception of the truth of propositions constitutes a kind of fall in the history of philosophy, I think that this second conception, far from being a fall, is a permanent achievement of Plato and Aristotle; but in certain cases, we feel the need of enlarging this conception. Felt truth, such as I conceive it, is second, whereas for Heidegger truth as disclosure is first.

I have come upon some lines of mine which can serve to indicate the difficulty before which I find myself here: "We opposed," I said in 1950, in speaking of the idea of truth, "that which one might call a felt truth and an intellectual truth, and we were led to condemn the idea of a felt truth if it is true that truth must remain in the sphere of judgment. But the distinction, useless or harmful in the domain of truth, appears on the contrary useful in that of cause and of substance, as in that of being." [4] Thus at that moment I condemned the idea of felt truth which I have subsequently tried to reintegrate. I have added these lines so that one can realize the difficulty which the problem so well enunciated by Desan represents.

F. H. Heinemann: Why dialectic?

YOU HAVE WRITTEN: "La dialectique doit être elle-même dialectisée." But should it not rather be transcended?

You further sketched the way of your metaphysics as leading from a primitive, pre-predicative unity of perception to a transcendent unity which is hardly visible and difficult to express in words, but toward which the mind moves. And you deem a dialectic necessary in order to connect these poles. (These remarks would seem to be reminiscent of Hegel's way in his *Phenomenology of Mind,* though of course with important qualifications.) Similar to these remarks at the Brussels Congress, you say in your *Traité de Métaphysique:* "La Philosophie

[4] Cf. Wahl et al., *Cinquante années de Découvertes* (Paris: Éditions du Seuil, 1950), p. 90.

va de la réalité par la dialectique à l'extase." (This would seem to be rather Platonic-Neoplatonic.) My questions are:

1. Do you preserve the dialectic merely because of the role it played in Plato's, Hegel's, and Kierkegaard's philosophies? In each of these cases, however, it arose from inner necessity. The Hegelians as well as the Marxists regard the dialectic almost as a law of reality.

2. If you deny this ontological status, if you regard reality as non-dialectical, what is the justification for introducing it?

3. If you regard it as necessary, how could it be precisely defined?

Wahl: If I preserve the idea of dialectic, it is not only because of the role it played in some great philosophies. I agree that in these very philosophies it arose from something real. The question is: Is this "something real" a law of reality as a whole, or is it only a law of the mind? In order to answer this question, the first thing would be to define dialectic. If one defines it in the way of the Hegelians and the Marxists, as a succession of contraries, I do not think it is a law of reality. If, on the other hand, we define dialectic as a regulated becoming, it may be a law of reality. Here I am faced with a dilemma arising from two tendencies in my mind:

The one, toward a dialectical account of mind; the other, toward a nondialectical vision of reality (in the narrower sense of "dialectic").

Conceived in this way, as a succession of contraries, dialectic may not have any ontological status as regards reality as a whole, but I find it already there, in my mind, and as a method it has the merit of bringing fundamental tensions into focus and thus can serve as a revealing pattern insofar as the life of thought is concerned.

The formula that I have employed: "Dialectic must itself be dialectical" ("La dialectique doit être elle-même dialectisée") means the same thing basically as what F. H. Heinemann says: "Dialectic must be transcended." The difference between the two formulae is that the one which I have proposed appears to me to supply a justification, from the point of view of dialectic itself, to that *Aufhebung* (transcendence) of dialectic.

Plato and Hegel have had the merit of noting an essential process of the human spirit. Reality in Hegel is constituted by spirit. It was therefore normal that he conceived of dialectic seized in the spirit "almost as a law of reality." Let us note this word "almost," employed by Heinemann. The question of the use of the word "dialectic" is transformed from then on into the question of idealism. And moreover we must raise the question of the definition itself of dialectic. There can be non-Hegelian dialectics, as those of Pierre Joseph Proudhon and of Søren Kierkegaard. It appears evident to me that reality does not proceed by thesis, antithesis, synthesis, as the Hegelians insist. The question remains whether it does proceed by a kind of law of contradiction, as Hegel says; for the Hegelian dialectic presupposes in a general manner this law of contradiction, and in a more precise manner that which we may call the mechanism of thesis, antithesis, synthesis. But the very idea of contradiction can raise doubts. And if two great philosophers, Heraclitus and Hegel, have said that reality proceeds by a sequence or even by a simultaneity of contradictions, we can recall that another great mind, Leibniz, has seen in contradictions simply extremes which communicate one with the other by all kinds of gradations.

There is something a bit obscure in the interrogation expressed by Professor Heinemann. Let us reread these three sentences: The first: "Do you preserve the dialectic merely because of the role it played in Plato's, Hegel's, and Kierkegaard's philosophies?" The second: "In each of these cases, however, it arose from inner necessity." The third: "The Hegelians as well as the Marxists regard the dialectic almost as a law of reality." The second sentence affirms an internal necessity which would be the source of the dialectic; the third tells us, it seems to me, that it appears as an external necessity; the first insinuates or rather suggests that in my thought it is simply the conservation of a sort of tradition. But not one of the three ideas is elaborated; perhaps it was not the place in this dialogue, which I should call almost non-Platonic, to elaborate it.

Today there is a great deal of discussion concerning whether dialectic is a fact of mind and a necessity of mind or a fact of nature and a necessity of nature. If it is a fact and necessity of mind, I do not feel the need of justifying the use that I have made of it, since there would be a separation between reality, where there is no dialectic, and the mind, where there is dialectic. But perhaps, again, we fall back upon the problems of realism and idealism: in what way can we apprehend reality without the mind?

Robert Champigny: With reference to your *Étude sur le Parménide* and your *Études Kierkegaardiennes,* let me put the following question. In what context do you yourself consider the notions of the One and of the Unique? From an existentialist point of view, is it not true that an assertion of the One as more than a mere conceptual instrument involves an illegitimate expansion of a concept which is based only on our experience of our own existence insofar as this existence involves something unique? Would you accept as valid an attempt to reconcile, from a religious point of view, our experience of the Unique and our concept of the One by asserting the existence of a deity? More specifically, do you consider an attempt to derive the foundations of our existential unity from the unity of God to be free of contradiction?

Wahl: I feel as diffident as you concerning the abstract notion of the One. In an existentialist perspective, existential unity, or uniqueness, stands as an original datum and is not to be derived from any metaphysical principle.

I do not see why, from the fact that the concept of unity is based on our experience of our own existence, one would call it illegitimate.

I appreciate the Kantian aspects of the query by Robert Champigny. But precisely for this reason, I do not see in the necessity of reconciling our experience of the unique and our concept of the One a reason for affirming the existence of a divinity.

Milic Capek: In his essay on Whitehead, Professor Wahl, after restating concisely and accurately the main themes of Whitehead's philosophy of organism, raises two critical questions. The first one queries the separation of events; the second one challenges Whitehead's distinction between possibility and actuality. To quote Professor Wahl directly:

. . . nous nous retrouverions devant l'unique événement qui est le passage de la nature. Pour un empirisme radical, il n'y a pas un réel qui se détacherait parmi une pluralité de possibles, et qui lui-même serait fait d'une pluralité de réels. Il y a une seule réalité, sans bifurcation.[5]

It is clear that it is the sense of the *continuity of reality* which moves Wahl to distrust any division, separation, fragmentation, or compartmentalization of reality. The separation of successive events and the distinction between the realm of possibles and the actual events belong, according to Wahl, to such category of fictitious divisions. This distrust of any conceptual act, which arbitrarily separates reality into artificially created components, has a strong Bergsonian tinge. Bergson's insistence on the dynamic continuity of successive phases of any process is sufficiently known. But even Professor Wahl's doubt concerning the distinction between potentiality and actuality may be found in Bergson, both in his first and in his last books. Possibility antecedent to its own actualization is, according to Bergson, a mere retrospective fiction; only *after* a certain event has taken place do we project the possibility of its own actualization into the past *preceding* the event itself. Thus we claim that the character of Hamlet was possible before it was created by Shakespeare; but the very idea of the possibility of Hamlet could not have emerged before seeing a real Hamlet on the scene. Thus, according to Bergson, with whom Professor Wahl apparently agrees, we are in this case victims of *retrospective illusion;* in reality, there is a single process in which novelties are continuously emerging and there is no need to believe with Whitehead that each particular novelty was pre-existing from eternity in a diaphanous state of potentiality, awaiting, so to speak, the moment of its full-blooded realization.

It seems to me, however, that such radical rejection of the concept of possibility is contrary to the principles of radical empiricism and in its last implications would be fatal to any process philosophy, including that to which Professor Wahl seems to adhere. For in eliminating any distinction between the successive events or, in other words, in eliminating any bifurcation between actuality and possibility, we abolish the distinction between the actuality of the present and the potentiality of the future. All successive stages of the process would merge into

---

[5] *Vers le concret,* "La philosophie speculative de Whitehead" (Paris: J. Vrin, 1932), p. 219.

a single actuality. Thus the very character of temporality would disappear. Spinoza's simultaneous denial of possibility and contingency is characteristic of any philosophy insisting on the timelessness of the ultimate reality. Who else but Bergson criticized more effectively the fictitious fusion of the past, present, and the future into one timeless formula *à la* Laplace? Moreover, contrary to his own explicit denials of possibility, Bergson reintroduced it into his own system. Already in his first book he recognizes the pre-existence of the future in consciousness in the form of *tendency* or *possibility not yet realized*. Similarly, in his later works, "pure recollection" (*le souvenir pur*) is by its own nature *virtual* and as such precedes an actualized recollection (*le souvenir image*); also "the dynamic schema" (*le schéma dynamique*) in intellectual and artistic creation *precedes* the result of the creative effort itself. It was only logical that Vladimir Jankélévitch should conclude his book about Bergson with an excellent analysis of the notion of possibility; he showed at the same time that the Bergsonian potentiality (*virtualité*) is something concretely experienced and as such is compatible with radical empiricism.

Perhaps Professor Wahl has already answered my question to my satisfaction in the same book when he wrote in his essay about William James: "Cette idée des *parts to come,* c'est déjà tout l'essentiel de l'empirisme temporaliste, de cette conception ou il y a de l' 'à part' et de l' 'à venir.' " [6] But what else is this *à part* and *à venir* except another term for the experienced "openness of the future," that is, its potentiality? William James saw this clearly in his early essay *Dilemma of Determinism* in 1884. Thus it seems to me that the difference between Professors Wahl and Whitehead is largely semantic; Whitehead's idea of the "realm of possibilities," once it is freed of the inadequate Platonic terminology with its misleading static connotations, is hardly distinguishable from the dynamic potentialities of James, Bergson, Wahl, and Jankélévitch.

Wahl: I think we must separate the two questions, eliminating the distinction between the successive events and eliminating the bifurcation between actuality and possibility.

The difficulties with which I am faced in the first case are not the

[6] *Vers le concret*, p. 60.

same as those with which I am faced in the second, the latter being somewhat greater. I am not convinced that eliminating the distinction between the successive events abolishes the distinction between present and future. It merges all successive stages into one single event (which is the world) but not necessarily into one single present (*actualité*). It would not cause the very character of temporality to disappear, as Professor Capek seems to think. As regards the second question, Professor Capek kindly suggests that I have perhaps answered his question in the Jamesian idea of *parts to come,* but he asks me whether this is not the idea of potentiality in another form. I prefer the idea of the openness of the future, which he also mentions, to the idea of potentiality, which for me raises so many questions. However, if one succeeds in freeing the idea of potentiality of all its static connotations, as he suggests, I can accept it as an idea of dynamic possibility.

Professor Capek raises the difficult question, as the very terms show it, of reality and possibility. He observes that contrary to his refusal, at first explicit, of the idea of possibility, Bergson has reintroduced it into his own system. And, on this point, we can only render homage to the keenness of Capek's critical knowledge of Bergson. He indicates correctly that Jankélévitch admits a possibility in Bergsonian thought, and I believe that I can do no better than to repeat with him that it is necessary to distinguish a conceptual possibility and a felt possibility.

Professor Capek greatly and justly admires Whitehead, and he says that "once it is freed of the inadequate Platonic terminology" the theory of Whitehead would no longer be distinguished from the dynamic potentialities that he finds in James, Bergson, and Jankélévitch, as in me. I do not ask for more. The question remains to determine what is left of the theory of Whitehead, once it has been delivered from its "inadequate Platonic terminology." It is possible that what remains may be a thought quite analogous to that of the other philosophers cited. But it is also possible that thus transformed, it is no longer the very thought of Whitehead; and Capek is certainly aware of this difficulty.

Albert William Levi: You have suggested that continuity and discontinuity may both be significantly predicated of becoming and therefore presumably in a theory of time. This suggests the conclusion that you view the Whiteheadian epochal theory of time and the Aristotelian continuous time as subcontraries rather than as contraries.

Do you consider that *time* is a pragmatic concept rather than a qualitative matrix of reality?

Wahl: Professor Levi notes very justly that for me becoming is at once continuous and discontinuous; perhaps it might be even more appropriate to say that neither the continuous nor the discontinuous can be applied completely to becoming. But my remark on this point can be taken as a continuation of the reflection that Professor Levi proposes to us.

He asks me then whether time is a pragmatic concept rather than a qualitative matrix of reality. And I shall reply without hesitation that it is a pragmatic concept. Let us say with Berkeley that it is a general idea; and in this sense we can say that there is nothing which is "time." Without doubt it is quite difficult to comprehend that one admits a temporal character of the real and that one does not admit "time." And it is difficult to comprehend that one admits that there are events which succeed one another, without admitting the idea of time which would however be implicated in the ideas of "before" and "after" (not to speak of the idea of "at the same time as" questioned today by physicists). It is difficult, but nevertheless it is with this task that I find myself faced.

Vladimir Jankélévitch: How does Professor Wahl reconcile his deep concern for Bergsonism with (1) his insistence on the idea of the density of matter, and (2) his defense of realism?

Wahl: 1. I do not feel there is a contradiction. Bergson himself, in certain passages, has agreed that there is an original spatiality different from our mathematical space in the same way that duration, according to him, is different from time. In the second place, there is a sort of Bergsonian realism, which asserts itself for instance at the beginning of *Matière et Mémoire*. In the third place, cannot the concrete be said to have a certain density, since it is characterized by the condensation of rhythms of duration?

2. Professor Jankélévitch has also asked me about the possibility of

introducing the idea of existence into a philosophy of the Bergsonian type.

This question can hardly be answered except by fact; and the fact is that the human mind, insofar as one can speak of the human mind, has turned from Bergsonism to the philosophies of existence: In a movement both of complementation and antithesis, it has turned from Bergsonian continuity to the affirmation of certain discontinuities, from Bergsonian optimism to a philosophy of anxiety.

But it must be noted that Bergsonian continuity was not such that it did not imply certain discontinuities and that Bergsonian optimism was not unmitigated. Which explains to some extent the dialectic to which we alluded.

In the philosophy of Jankélévitch himself, we find a passage from the idea of Bergsonian continuity to the affirmation of certain discontinuities. This same idea of discontinuity (or is it another?) we find in the thought of Gaston Bachelard.

For me the ideas of continuity and of discontinuity each have multiple aspects, and the relations among them are also multiple. Let us say, for example, that the discontinuity conceived by Bachelard is not identical with that conceived by Charles Bernard Renouvier, nor is it that which is conceived by Jankélévitch.

Newton P. Stallknecht: Professor Wahl has subjected the notion of freedom to an analysis that undermines its validity as a concept.

The intellectual affirmation of freedom is essentially a negation—a negation of necessity. But what is necessity? It is in its turn a negation—the negation of possibility. The necessary is what cannot be, as Aristotle has said. And what is the possible? The possible, at least the possible as theoretically conceived, is in its turn a negative idea. The concept of possibility implies that in a particular case what has taken place "might not have taken place."

. . . Freedom is the conceived negation of the conceived negation of a conceived negation. If, therefore, we really eliminate the last negation (possibility), the second (necessity) is thereby canceled, and so is the first. Thus, the last card of this house of cards, freedom, or rather the concept of freedom, vanishes.[7]

[7] *The Philosopher's Way* (New York: Oxford University Press, 1948), pp. 132–133; *Traité de Métaphysique*, p. 540.

On the other hand, Professor Wahl recognizes that we enjoy an experience or a sense of freedom. My question then is this: May there not be a concept or "theory" of freedom or, shall we say, a responsible way of talking about the experience of freedom? Certainly we would hesitate to renounce all discussion of the subject. Perhaps such a theory would provide a positive notion of freedom rather than a series of "conceived negations."

Wahl: If someone could shape and formulate a nonconceptual idea of freedom, I would be with him. But it always seems to me very difficult to reason—or even to speak—about freedom. The only thing one can do is to act according to freedom; and the only thing that can be said is that one should act according to freedom. Beyond this, it seems to me impossible to speak of freedom except in a negative way.

The entire discussion turns about the question of what should be understood by Professor Stallknecht's words, "an experience or a sense of freedom" and "concept or 'theory' of freedom." I tend to deny the possibility of a theory of freedom, of a concept of freedom. I believe I find myself thus in accord with certain passages, at least, of James and of Bergson. The concept of freedom can serve only to indicate something which is beyond every concept. By itself, it implies the idea of possibility. We return to one of the questions formerly posed; the possible posed in the concept is a sort of retrospective abstraction. It is on the contrary toward a lived possibility that we must turn; and of that we can hardly speak.

Herbert Lamm: 1. In view of Heidegger's rejection, in a communication to you, of "existentialism" as an appropriate characterization of his philosophy, and a similar disavowal by Karl Jaspers, do you still find it meaningful to speak of "existentialism" as a philosophy?

2. It has become fashionable to classify all "nonexistentialist" philosophies as "essentialisms"; what is your view of such a classification of philosophy?

Wahl: 1. I believe it is preferable to employ the phrase "philosophy of existence" rather than the word "existentialism" to characterize the philosophy of Jaspers. As for the philosophy of Heidegger, it presents itself more and more, and wants to present itself more and more, as a philosophy of being. One therefore hesitates, in the case of Jaspers particularly, between the words "existential philosophy" and "philosophy of existence." In the case of Heidegger, neither of the phrases is appropriate, despite the place that he gives to *Dasein*. If one wishes to employ the word "existentialism," it is to the philosophy of what one might call the School of Paris, that is to say, to Jean-Paul Sartre, Simone de Beauvoir, Merleau-Ponty, that it would be fitting to apply it. At the same time, it would be necessary to take account of the differences between the two masters of this school, Sartre and Merleau-Ponty, well indicated in the article that Sartre has devoted to Merleau-Ponty, in *Les Temps Modernes*.[8]

2. This classification is far too crude and simple: What of Kant? What of Descartes? What of James?—to mention only a few names. This classification, among other things, implies the acceptance of an opposition between existence and essence, an opposition which, in my opinion, should be revised.

It seems to me that it is inexact to style as essentialism all philosophies which are not philosophies of existence. Conceptions such as that of Léon Brunschvicg or that of Ernst Cassirer cannot absolutely be said to be essentialist. It is the same with the different forms of pragmatism.

It is a superficial characterization even of the philosophy of Plato to call it essentialism.

Ultimately one would be led to say that essentialism is a verbal creation made by existentialists, in particular by Sartre.

James Collins: The present quickening of philosophical interest in Kierkegaard was largely pioneered by Jean Wahl, whose *Études Kierkegaardiennes* brought out the philosophical relevance of this religious thinker. Chapter 5 of his book is entitled "La lutte contre toute philosophie" ("The Battle Against All Philosophy"), and advances the thesis that Kierkegaard's polemic against Hegelianism is also a rejection of all philosophy. This position is reaffirmed in Wahl's *Les Philosophies de l'existence*,[9] where the paradox is noted that nevertheless Kierkegaard is a major source of the philosophies of existence. Wahl's argu-

---

[8] "Merleau-Ponty Vivant," *Les Temps Modernes,* Numéro Spécial: Maurice Merleau-Ponty, Vol. XVII, No. 184–185, pp. 304–376.

[9] Paris: A. Colin, 1954, p. 27.

ment is that Kierkegaard attributes to philosophy as such the same traits which he attacks in Hegelianism: immanentism, generality, and idealism. Hence his intention is to eliminate all philosophy.

Yet there are other considerations which may require a revision of this conclusion. Wahl himself seems to feel this need when he remarks that if Kierkegaard was a philosopher it was in spite of himself. This indicates the presence of a complex situation, all factors of which have to be included in the final interpretation of Kierkegaard's attitude toward philosophy. For instance, he is willing to accept philosophies of essence and abstract thought, in the degree that they accept a principle of self-limitation and do not claim to include every real element within their scope. There is a legitimate place for an immanent analysis and a general description as long as they make no pretence to be exhaustive of being. Furthermore, Kierkegaard offers at least two portraits of Socrates. The latter is sometimes regarded as the prototype of every Hegelian systematist, insofar as he finds a purely immanent way back to eternity. But the Kierkegaardian Socrates also appears as the prototype of the existential thinker, insofar as he accentuates individual existence, personal responsibility, and the committed pursuit of an open truth. The operative principle here is that there can be (prescinding from almost overwhelming cultural conditions to the contrary) an existential type of philosophy, provided that there is no assertion of a comprehensive speculative grasp of the existent.

My question is, then, whether some nuances should not be introduced into the view that Kierkegaard is opposed to all philosophy.

Wahl: The relation between Kierkegaard and philosophy is certainly complex. We may construe his attack against Hegelianism as intended against all philosophy. Yet he favors certain attitudes which may be called philosophical. Our concept of philosophy should be wide enough to include such thinking existents as Kierkegaard or Pascal.

Philip Merlan: You assume a parallelism to exist between Marx's and Kierkegaard's criticisms of Hegel. I consider any such interpretation to be in error. Marx agrees with Hegel (and Kant) that it is entirely proper to sacrifice man (or men) to save mankind (for which it makes no difference whether it is represented by past, present, or *only future generations*). And indeed it is impossible to see how else any political action imposing hardships on individuals against their private will could be justified. Kierkegaard, however, would find the idea of saving mankind entirely ridiculous, as it is only man (or men) who can be saved or lost, but never mankind. Therefore, as you yourself observed, there is for Kierkegaard no such thing as history in any significant sense of the word. How, then, can we assume that there is any similarity between Marx's and Kierkegaard's attitudes toward Hegel?

Wahl: Of course, for Kierkegaard, mankind exists only in individuals. On the other hand, we cannot think that, for Marx, mankind could exist independently of individuals. Moreover, there is in Kierkegaard an idea of mankind (redeemed mankind) which transcends all individuals, insofar as it is identical with one pre-eminent individual, namely, Jesus Christ.

I agree that for Kierkegaard there is no such thing as History in any significant sense of the word. Nevertheless, the historian of philosophy can detect some common features in Marx's and Kierkegaard's opposition to Hegelian idealism, although these may be only negative features.

Philip Merlan: I assume that the essential difference between existentialism and "academic" philosophy can be boiled down to the formula: Academic philosophy is interested in verity and the ascertaining of it, whereas existentialism is interested in veracity and the appropriation of verity. *Or:* Academic philosophy is interested in possessing truth, existentialism in being true.

What, then, will be the lasting impact of existentialism on academic philosophy? Or will there be none? Or should we prepare ourselves for a permanent split between the two?

Wahl: The appropriation of verity would have no meaning without veracity. Kierkegaard is right when he insists on the inadequacy of a purely objective concept of truth, or verity. But this does not mean, I think, that one should not be interested in the ascertaining of truth. What is important in Kierkegaard is the appeal he makes to the inner possession of truth.

Besides, what are we to understand by "academic philosophy"? What is interesting in the new trend of philosophy is the desire to do away with something too academic. But Plato was not "academic" in the pejorative sense of the word. There should be no permanent split between academic philosophy and existentialism. Such a split, if it were possible, would leave existentialism without a content and academic philosophy without real life.

Interrogation of

Brand Blanshard

Conducted by Louis O. Mink

Brand Blanshard was born at Fredericksburg, Ohio, in 1892. He is now Professor of Philosophy at Yale University. He studied at Michigan, Columbia, Oxford and Harvard. He was a Rhodes scholar and a Guggenheim fellow. Blanshard has taught at the University of Michigan and Swarthmore College. From 1942 to 1944 he was president of the American Philosophical Association, Eastern Division. His many honors include: Senior Award, American Council of Learned Societies; Honorary Fellow, Merton College, Oxford; Corresponding Fellow, British Academy; Gifford Lecturer, St. Andrews; Carus Lecturer, American Philosophical Association; Hertz Lecturer, British Academy; Adamson Lecturer, Manchester University; Howison Lecturer, California; Noble, Dudleian and Whitehead Lecturers, Harvard; Machette Lecturer, Wesleyan University and Brooklyn College; Fellow, Center for Advanced Studies, Wesleyan University; Visiting Professor, University of Minnesota; and honorary doctorates from St. Andrews, Swarthmore, Oberlin, Colby, Trinity, New Concord, and Simpson. He is co-author of *Philosophy in American Education* and *Preface to Philosophy*. He is editor of *Education in an Age of Science*. His works include: *The Nature of Thought, Reason and Goodness, Reason and Analysis,* and *On Philosophical Style.*

I. COHERENCE
AND CORRESPONDENCE

Truth is the approximation of thought to reality. It is thought on its way home. Its measure is the distance thought has travelled . . . toward that intelligible system which unites its ultimate object with its ultimate end. Hence at any given time the degree of truth in our experience as a whole is the degree of system it has achieved. The degree of truth of a particular proposition is to be judged in the first instance by its coherence with experience as a whole, ultimately by its coherence with that further whole, all-comprehensive and fully articulated, in which thought can come to rest. . . .

Fully coherent knowledge would be knowledge in which every judgment entailed, and was entailed by, the rest of the system. . . . No proposition would be arbitrary, every proposition would be entailed by the others jointly and even singly, no proposition would stand outside the system. The integration would be so complete that no part could be seen for what it was without seeing its relation to the whole, and the whole itself could be understood only through the contribution of every part.[1]

A. C. Ewing: What would be Blanshard's reaction to the proposal to substitute for "coherence" as the test of truth "coherence with experience"? Even granting that we cannot separate what is given from our interpretation of it, it is surely equally true that we cannot have interpretation without some experience to interpret, and must not the truth of interpretation depend at least as much on its conformity with the nature of what is interpreted as on its internal coherence and its coherence with other well-established judgments? Further, can we really say that we believe in the truth of judgments of memory pri-

[1] Blanshard, *The Nature of Thought* (London: G. Allen and Unwin Ltd., 1939), II, 264–266.

marily because they cohere? Do we not, in many cases, see them immediately to be true without having first to determine their coherence with anything? These considerations suggest that the criterion of truth should be not coherence alone but coherence as organizing and connecting immediate cognitions. It is true that immediate cognitions could not be *formulated* without a more or less coherent system of concepts; but that is not the same thing as to say that once formulated, the only *evidence for their truth* is coherence with other propositions.

Richard B. Brandt: In holding that "the coherence of judgments within a system is . . . our only test of any truth or fact," Blanshard is, I suggest, setting forth an imperative like this: "Believe all and only the propositions in the set S, in preference to all and only the propositions in S′, if and only if S is a more coherent system than S′, providing however that S contains at least the vast majority of the propositions which seem to express your present experience and your recollections of the past." (Blanshard could not quite accept the final clause, but I wish that he would suggest a reformulation which would make it reasonably acceptable to him.) What is his justification for this view?

Perhaps he has discovered fatal objections to all other possible proposals. But has he refuted, at least by implication, all proposals of imperatives to attribute certainty or antecedent probability to propositions which seem to describe present experiences or recollections?

Blanshard also argues that the coherence principle is the one we actually do follow in reflective moments, whatever we may say about it. But what would Blanshard say to such facts as these, which raise the question whether the intuitive convictions of responsible scientists can be shown to be in agreement with the coherence principle: (1) The widespread reliance on truth-table testing for analyticity does not seem like an appeal to coherence. (2) Is it an appeal to coherence if a scientist thinks a generalization more firmly established by evidence drawn from various fields, rather than by homogeneous instances? (3) Is it appeal to coherence that makes scientists shy away from *ad hoc* hypotheses? (4) Is it an appeal to coherence when scientists prefer the simpler of two theories if the two give results equally in agreement with experimental facts?

Charles Hartshorne: Blanshard has argued that the ideal of knowledge is a system in which all relations are grasped as necessary. But is understanding exclusively the grasp of necessities, or is it not rather the insight into both necessities as such and contingencies as such? Is not the significance of *"p* is necessary, given *q"* dependent upon its being *false* that *p* is necessary given anything whatever, and is not the significance of *"r* is necessary unconditionally" due to its being false that all things are necessary unconditionally? In short, is not all understanding the distinguishing of the necessary and the non-necessary, rather than the effort to collapse this distinction into a mere appearance?

Adolf Grünbaum: In *An Analysis of Knowledge and Valuation,*[2] C. I. Lewis argues that "every empirical supposition, being a contingent statement, is contained in some self-consistent system which is as comprehensive as you please," because whether we start with an empirical belief or statement *p* or its contradictory, one or other of every pair of further empirical statements can be conjoined with *p* to form a self-consistent set, or in the same way with *not p.* Hence no empirical truth can be determined by the criterion of consistency alone. What reply would Blanshard make to this objection?

Stephan Körner: What does Blanshard mean by "entailment"? He objects to Lewis' account of entailment as strict implication on the ground, among other things, that while *p* strictly implies *q* whenever *p* is logically impossible, *p* does not in this case also entail *q.* Thus he clearly holds that *p* entails *q* only if *p* and *not-q* are jointly but not separately impossible. His partial definition of "entailment" therefore seems to be the following: Whatever else may be meant by stating that a conjunction of antecedent members entails a consequent member, no subconjunction of the conjunction of the antecedent members and the negated consequent member is impossible or, which comes to the same thing, no subconjunction of the antecedent members entails the consequent member. (For the sake of brevity I am using "subconjunction" in a sense in which every member of a conjunction is a subconjunction of it.)

The difficulty which has prompted my question can now be stated

[2] La Salle, Ill.: Open Court Publishing Company, 1947, pp. 338–343.

with tolerable precision: The definition of coherence and the partial definition of entailment are incompatible.

Assume that the fully coherent system consists of the propositions $p_1, p_2 \ldots p_n, q$. According to the definition of coherence, every proposition of the system is entailed by the rest. This means, for example, that

$$(1) \qquad (p_1 \text{ and } p_2 \ldots \text{ and } p_n) \text{ entails } q.$$

According to the same definition, every proposition of the system is even singly entailed by any other. For example,

$$(2) \qquad p_1 \text{ entails } q.$$

But according to the partial definition of entailment, (1) cannot be correct unless no subconjunction of (1) entails q. It cannot be correct, for example, unless

$$(3) \qquad p_1 \text{ does } not \text{ entail } q.$$

The propositions (2) and (3) are straight contradictories.

The root of the antinomy lies, as I believe, in Blanshard's attempt to reconcile two, as it were, incommensurable concepts, the absolute idealists' elusive conception of coherence and the comparatively simple notion of entailment. If, he argues, we recognize that entailment is a wholly intensional relation between propositions, then coherence can be defined in terms of entailment. But the intensionality of entailment does not permit such definition. Blanshard implies that a proposition is *altered* in becoming part of a system or by the system's being enlarged. When we speak of the *same* proposition within and outside a system of propositions, we are on this view misrepresenting as identity what is at best similarity. But if coherence alters the propositions which it relates while entailment does not, the former cannot be definable in terms of the latter.

Blanshard: A. C. Ewing and Richard B. Brandt make some acute criticisms of coherence as the test of truth. Both think that coherence by itself is not enough. They do not offer the objection so often made against the theory, that a system may be large and logically well knit without being true—for example, some fantastic system of geometry —for they know that defenders of coherence have insisted that the only system providing a warrant of truth is one that includes actual experience. But they are inclined to say that such a qualification surrenders the case for coherence. When one says that the system must include actual experience, is not this really saying that some judgments of perception and memory are true independently of the system? Start with such judgments, and you can build a system around them, but unless you can start with *some* proposition known intuitively to be true, the whole system seems to hang in the air. The mere coherence of judgment A with judgment B will not increase its likelihood unless B is known to be true already. And that means that B's truth must be known on other grounds.

Ewing has argued persuasively for this view in his Hertz lecture on "Reason and Intuition." He agrees that coherence has an important role in the testing of truth, but holds that its office is to develop and organize our intuitions rather than to set itself up in their place as the exclusive authority. He asks whether I should not be ready to go along with this and accept as the test of truth not coherence simply, but "coherence with experience."

Yes, I should. This does seem to me to be the test we actually use. The only question is how it should be interpreted. Would the acceptance of it commit one to the correspondence theory of truth for those perceptual judgments which are presumably meant here by "experience"?

Suppose we say, "The table in the next room is round"; how should we test this judgment? No doubt by going to the door and looking. If our judgment "corresponds" with the given fact, we regard it as verified and true; if not, as false. To this the defender of coherence replies that when one talks of given fact, one is talking loosely. Presumably "given" means given in sense. But one cannot sense a fact, for a fact is of the form "that S is P," and what is of this form can be grasped by nothing simpler than judgment. This judgment need not be explicit or expressed; it may be of the lowly type that is commonly present in perception; but it must be the apprehension of at least two terms in relation. In the case in question, what verifies the statement of fact is the perceptual judgment that I make when I open the door and look. But then what verifies the perceptual judgment itself? Is it not the correspondence I discover between the judged roundness of the table and its actually sensed roundness? To which the reply is, as before, that a judgment of fact can be verified only by the sort of apprehension that can present us with a fact, and that this must be a further judgment. And an agreement between judgments is best described not as correspondence, but as coherence.

This is the line I took in *The Nature of Thought*. The most effective criticisms of it seem to me to be two: (1) that facts may after all be given, and (2) that, whether they are or not, at least particular data are given, and that these by themselves may serve to verify judgments. Let us consider these criticisms.

CAN FACTS BE GIVEN? "A is to the left of B." "A came before B." "This is darker than that." "This is a shade of red." These are all statements of fact, in which a relation is alleged between two terms. But is it not possible that the facts to which they refer, and which would serve to verify them, should actually be given, as the correspondence theory holds? If this means given in sense, it still seems to me very questionable. Take the last case above: "This is a shade of red." The relation apprehended here is that of genus and species, and to suppose that we could see or hear or otherwise sense a relation of this kind seems clearly mistaken; some form of apprehension that involves intelligence is at work. "This is darker than that." When we say this, the items compared are both before us, but the activity of comparing them and of placing them higher and lower on a scale is more than a process of sensing. "A came before B." When we grasp this fact, do we sense the passage of time? Kant thought not; at least we seemed to apprehend it in a very different way from that in which we are aware of colors and sounds, a way that he called "pure perception"; and the distinction is surely well taken. "A is to the left of B." Do we have here a sensible fact? We do seem to have a fact that is as clearly imposed upon us, and in that sense given, as any color, sound, or pain. But is the spatial relation *sensed,* as the items that form its terms are sensed? Once more, I think not. In all these cases the relation involved in the fact eludes apprehension by sense; in all of them the fact can be expressed by nothing short of a proposition or judgment. Thus if we seek to verify any of the four judgments above, we must do so by another judgment.

ONE MAY REPLY: "What is important about the fact referred

to is not that it is sensed, but that it is given. You have admitted that relations of genus and species, of time and space, are forced upon you, and if you call the apprehension of them judgments, there is at least nothing in these judgments that is uncertain or speculative; facts may be as truly given to intelligence as colors are to vision. And the innocent thesis that the correspondence theory maintains is that what renders such judgments true is their correspondence to these nonsensorily given facts."

I must agree that this is a reasonable way of putting the matter and if to accept it is to accept correspondence, I suppose I am an adherent of that theory. Whether the verification in these cases is by coherence or correspondence would seem to be a matter of words. Should the support given to a judgment by another and perceptual judgment, or, if you will, by a complex nonsensory intuition, be called by the one name or the other? It does not seem important. Still, the advocate of correspondence may say that we are really conceding his case, since coherence now means not coherence within a system, but coherence with given facts of experience. I can only reply that to me it means both. Coherence with fact can stand alone only if the fact as given is stable, in the sense of ultimate and incorrigible; for only then do we have a fixed object with which our judgment may be compared. But no such objects are fixed, and no such facts are incorrigible. For a fact to be given means that it is given to a mind in a context of other experiences; this context is in process of change, and this change does not leave the given unaffected. Could one reasonably say, for example, that the fact reported by "this shade is a color" would be absolutely the same as it presented itself, first, to one of the lower animals, then to a man whose experience of color was confined to red, and finally to a man who experienced a normal range of colors? I very much doubt it. A mind is not put together like a mosaic of hard, exclusive pieces. The pieces themselves change their character, some more, some less, with changes in the whole. Coherence with experience gives a good starting point. But it must be supplemented and corrected by coherence with a wider experience.

Do Sense Data Verify? The second main criticism of coherence as the test was that in some cases sense data by themselves serve, naked and unashamed, as tests of truth. And when that which actually confirms is a simple, unanalyzable sensory datum, it is idle to say that the test is still coherence within a system of judgments. Suppose I say that in exactly five minutes from now I shall see a bright flash, and I do in fact see it. My prediction has turned out true. Is it not clear that that which verified it was the occurrence of the flash, and that the relation between the prediction and the event was one of correspondence with a sheer brute datum?

Here again, the position seems to me very nearly correct. Nearly correct? But why not completely correct? For this reason: It seems to assume a pure sensory datum as that to which the judgment corresponds. Its defender would probably admit that so far as the datum is not pure, that is, so far as it is a construct molded by the relations or interpretations imposed on it by the perceiving mind, the language of coherence is still plausible, whereas if this ideal molding can be excluded and a pure sensum attained, correspondence is the more appropriate description. And the reason I am not content with correspondence by itself is that, however closely we approach the pure given, we never do in fact reach it. Even when we take correspondence at its best, as in the case of the bright flash, this still seems to be true. The flash that is taken as verifying the judgment has obviously been worked over by what can only be described as thought; its recognition as a flash and as bright puts it in a framework of concepts; it is placed at a particular point in an extended setting of space and time; it is grasped as something that fulfills a prediction, and probably also as produced by a particular kind of cause; its character as experienced may be so bound up with its affective setting—of apprehension, placidity, or terror—that it would lose its identity apart from this. As A. E. Taylor says:

It seems plain on reflection that merely to say "green" with significance is to perform an act of comparison and recognition; interpretation has already begun before we proceed to the implication "here, not there; now, not then." If there ever was a time, as we may fairly doubt, in our own past history when we were purely receptive, the time must have passed before we could so much as name things, and to recapture the condition must be beyond the power of "articulate-speaking men." [3]

[3] *The Faith of a Moralist* (London: Macmillan & Co., Ltd., 1930), II, 217.

The conclusion would appear to be that the correspondence theory is correct so far as the reference in judgment is to a pure given datum, but that in practice we never get either the datum or the reference. What we do get are approximations in various degrees to both. But in saying that the datum is thus an ideal limit rather than an isolable item of experience, I do not want to be taken as belittling its importance. If it is hard to capture in its purity, it is still harder to dispense with. Indeed, escape from it would mean the abandonment of any anchorage not only for common sense, but also for speculative thought, the dancing of an "unearthly ballet of bloodless categories." I trust that all this will make reasonably clear what I mean by saying that the coherence I accept must include Ewing's "coherence with experience."

WHAT SYSTEM IS USED AS THE TEST? I hope this will help, also, to meet a difficulty of Grünbaum's. He asks what I should say about the criticism of coherence as a test of truth offered by C. I. Lewis in *An Analysis of Knowledge and Valuation*.[4] Lewis' main contention is substantially the same as Ewing's, namely, that the system used as the test must not hang in the air, but must at some point rest on experience. But he offers another argument that calls for comment.

As I understand it, it runs as follows: Every empirical statement is contingent or non-necessary; its contradictory is conceivable. Very well; take any consistent set of empirical statements, for example, "the table is brown," "stones are heavy," "water is wet." Of each of these statements the contradictory is conceivable, and these contradictories, like the originals, will be consistent among themselves. This set of statements can be extended just as far as the original set of statements. The two sets or systems, then, will be equally extensive and equally consistent. Hence if mere consistency within a system were all that is required to warrant truth, you could warrant the truth of any empirical statement whatever, or of its contradictory, with equal readiness. By itself the appeal to coherence is thus worthless in distinguishing truth from falsity.

My comments on this are as follows: (1) I agree with Lewis that the

4 Pp. 338 ff.

system taken as the test cannot be any system taken at random; there must be coherence with experience in the sense explained above. But further, (2) coherence does not mean for me consistency merely, but also mutual entailment, and in this respect the two systems are not parallel. For some empirical statements entail others, while there is no parallel entailment between their contradictories. That this table is brown entails that it is extended; that it is not brown does not entail that it is not extended. I admit that with our present knowledge we can seldom see necessity linking empirical propositions, but I am inclined to think it is there whether we see it or not, and that it must be included within the meaning of coherence. And its presence is more readily discernible in System 1 than in System 2. (3) I take it that according to Lewis, empirical facts and propositions are not only contingent in themselves, but are contingently related; the fact that a billiard ball is moving with a certain velocity when it strikes another is not connected necessarily with that other's motion. Rightly or wrongly, I dissent from this view. All empirical facts are in the end necessitated, I think, by the remaining empirical facts. This view is far more readily acceptable if necessity is seen as implicit in causality. In the first of two systems contemplated above, there is room for causality; in the second, it is virtually excluded. Between the first billiard ball's striking the other with a certain velocity and the other's moving away, it makes sense to say that there is a causal relation; between the first's *not* having a certain velocity and the other's *not* moving away, the assertion of causality would be absurd; a thing's not having a certain property can cause nothing. Thus the systems are again not equivalent from the point of view of coherence as I conceive it. (4) The system that at any time I should use as a test of truth would of course include *a priori* as well as empirical statements, and if the proposed alternative system were to parallel it, it would have to include also the contradictories of these *a priori* statements. But it could not do this. For among the statements that would have to be denied is the law of contradiction, and I suppose it is obvious that if you include within your system the contradictory of this law, you cannot have a system at all. Thus a system consisting of the contradictories of *all* statements composing the present body of knowledge is impossible. (5) It is sometimes suggested that there might be more than one system which included all facts, and therefore that the notion of a single all-inclusive system is arbitrary. On the contrary, it is so far from arbitrary that its alternative—the notion of two or more all-inclusive systems—is unthinkable. For let us suppose that A and B are two systems, each inclusive of all facts, and exclusive of each other. If they are to be thus exclusive, there is one fact at least that will fall outside each of them: the fact that A is all-inclusive will not be included in B, and the fact that B is all-inclusive will not be included in A. But to say that either is all-inclusive while there is some fact lying outside it is self-contradictory. A plurality of all-inclusive systems is impossible.

A DIFFICULTY ABOUT ENTAILMENT. Stephan Körner raises a technical difficulty about the consistency of my view of coherence with my view of entailment. In discussing coherence I went so far as to suggest that if the ideal of understanding were achieved, every truth would be seen to entail every other, in the sense that if that other were denied, our initial truth could not be what it was. Körner thinks that in my account of entailment I deny this. I seem to do so in the course of a criticism of C. I. Lewis' account of strict implication. According to that theory, p implies q if it is impossible that p should be true along with the falsity of q; and Lewis so interprets this that p will imply q not only if this conjunction is impossible, but also if either of the conjoined propositions taken singly is impossible. On this interpretation, "$2 + 2 = 5$" implies "Keats wrote 'Endymion,'" and "Keats wrote 'Endymion'" implies that "$2 + 2 = 4$." I was not content with this. I held that, to make sense, the impossibility must attach not to the propositions taken singly, but to the conjunction of p's truth with q's falsity. Now, says Körner, let us apply this to coherence. In my account I say that every true proposition will be entailed by the rest of the system or, in symbols, $p_1, p_2 \ldots p_n$ will entail q; and this means that the conjunction of $p_1, p_2 \ldots p_n$ cannot be combined with the falsity of q. So far, all is clear sailing. Now where does my inconsistency come in? It comes in, according to Körner, at this point: When I say that $p_1, p_2 \ldots p_n$ entail q only if their conjunction is impossible along with the denial of q, I must mean also that no *sub*conjunction of $p_1, p_2 \ldots p_n$ is impossible along with this denial. But that means that no such subconjunction can entail q. Hence p alone could not entail q. Hence what I said about a single proposition's entailing the rest cannot be true. I have therefore contradicted myself.

The force of this argument depends entirely on the step about sub-conjunctions. Körner takes my view to be: "No subconjunction of the conjunction of the antecedent members and the negated consequent member is impossible." So far as I know, this view is neither stated nor implied in anything I have written. There is nothing in the statement "p_1, p_2, p_3 are jointly incompatible with $-q$" to com-mit me to "p taken singly *is* compatible with $-q$," and I am puz-zled why Körner should suppose I hold the latter. Of course one could conceivably reason as follows: Blanshard, in criticizing Lewis, held that what was essential for (p_1, p_2, p_3)'s entailing q was the im-possibility of this conjunction in conjunction with $-q$. And because he insisted that for entailment the second kind of conjunction must enter into the account, he must similarly insist that the first should do so. I do not attribute this to Körner, but I am at a loss to see how other-wise the ascription to me came to be made. The kind of reasoning on which the charge about subconjunctions is based, if one may put it in a parallel case, runs like this: If I hold that Washington's being dutiful, just, and honest implies that he strove to tell the truth, I can-not hold that his being dutiful by itself implies this. I fail to see why not.

COHERENCE AND SCIENTIFIC PRACTICE. Richard B. Brandt wonders whether the appeal to coherence is in line with actual scientific practice, and cites cases in which it apparently is not. He points out, for example, that when certain persons want to test whether a statement is analytically true, they resort to a truth table, and that this is a far cry from the appeal to coherence. So it is. But what this case reveals as remote from actual practice is not, I suggest, the coherence theory, but conventional symbolic logic. Take an instance. Some street-corner philosopher alleges that the evolution theory implies that all men are mortal. Is this an analytic statement or not? The logician brought up on Whitehead and Russell's *Principia Mathematica* says that statements of implication are by definition analytic, so all he needs to do is to test the statement against the ordinary truth table for impli-cation. According to this table, there are four possible truth values for the combination of p and q, namely, p and q both true, p and q false, *p* false and *q* true, or *p* true and *q* false; and *p* will imply *q* if any of the first three conditions holds. If now we ask whether the statement to be tested fits any of these conditions, the answer is that it does; it fits the first, for both the theory of evolution and the mortality of men are supposedly true. The first therefore implies, and implies analytically, the second. Perhaps this is not the sort of example Brandt had in mind, for I can only think he would agree with me that it is very remote from the way in which the scientific mind works. It is obvious that the scientist does not test whether one statement "implies" another by any such procedure, still less whether it does so "analytically," for unless he could determine the implications of a hypothesis in advance of knowing whether it was true, he would not know where to look for confirmation. And of course the truth-table procedure leaves the whole business of whether propositions are true or false to be determined otherwise; its interest is solely in deciding whether, when this *has* been determined, the resulting truth values fit into a prearranged set of pigeon-holes. I do not think, therefore, that it has anything to tell us about how truth and falsity, or even implication and analyticity, are actually determined.

Brandt points out, furthermore, that a scientist considers his generalization more firmly established if it is supported by evidence from various fields and not merely by a set of homogeneous instances, and asks whether this has anything to do with an appeal to coherence. I think it does. Consider again the theory of evolution. It is conceivable that the only evidence for this theory should have been foetal recapitulation, repeated in every known case of animal and man. The actual evidence is of course vastly wider; the implications of the theory are found to be actually realized in geological strata, in the remains of "missing links," in the presence of vestigial organs, in endless homologies of bodily structure, and in countless facts about the geographical distribution of species. The convergence of such evidence from diverse fields is taken to strengthen the hypothesis enormously. Why? Because the wider the diversity of fields, the less probable it is that this consilience is due to chance; if a single hypothesis will account for all these apparently unrelated facts, it is regarded as almost certainly true. But this is just what one would expect if the test of coherence were being used. It must be remembered that the coherence theory has two

factors, interdependence and comprehensiveness. Given two explanatory theories that cover the same ground, the one to be preferred is the
one whose parts are more closely knit; given two such theories whose
facts are equally closely knit, that one is to be preferred which is more
comprehensive. If a theory orders consistently the facts of foetal recapitulation, that is certainly a mark in its favor. If it orders consistently the vastly larger range of facts mentioned above, that is a
very much stronger mark in its favor. What coherence proposes biology
applies.

OCCAM'S RAZOR. This suggests my comment on Brandt's other
two cases. "Is it appeal to coherence that makes scientists shy away from
ad hoc hypotheses?" And again, "Is it an appeal to coherence when
scientists prefer the simpler of two theories?" Both these cases seem
to me to supply evidence *for* coherence as the test actually used by
science. Both suggest that in the practice of the scientist, the sort of
theory that more fully satisfies his logical instinct is the one accepted
as true. And what best satisfies his logical instinct in any given case
is the theory that most economically covers the evidence, that is, the
simplest theory that will do justice to all the facts. Suppose a family of
five is found murdered, and all the evidence regarding action and motive comports with a certain person's being guilty. Suppose someone
comes forward with a rival hypothesis that there were five distinct
murderers who, acting independently, happened to select different
victims from the same family on the same evening. This hypothesis is
entirely possible, but no one would accept it if the simpler theory covered the facts equally well.

Why not? What is the ground of Occam's razor? I once put that
question to Bertrand Russell, and his answer, if I remember rightly,
was that there was no ground, that what it represents is simply an ultimate human preference. And unless "preference" means nonrational
preference, I can accept that answer. There is at work in us a theoretical
impulse and what will satisfy that impulse is what we mean by "rational." It is not satisfied with any explanation in which there are
superfluities, for it wants the closest unity of theory consistent with
the diversity of fact. Why should it want this? It is pointless to ask
that, since the question is itself only a reassertion of this want and can
be answered only by an acceptance of the ideal it calls in question. What

we have in Occam's razor is one rule of formation of the system demanded by the theoretic impulse. Its acceptance is the ground for—if indeed it is not identical with—the rejection of *ad hoc* hypotheses. The trouble with *ad hoc* hypotheses is that they are adventitious; they do not grow out of the system in which the *explicandum* is embedded. Cardinal Newman notes that on certain occasions there is a lift of the spirit without evident cause, and offers as a hypothesis that this is due to the action of a guardian angel. The psychologist would regard this as an *ad hoc* hypothesis because it does not grow out of the laws which extended observation seems to have shown to govern the mind; it complicates matters by introducing a rival cause from outside the system of those laws. Such a cause may actually exist and be at work. But to drag it in before the possibilities of a natural explanation have been explored is needlessly to replace one system by two. Against that, coherence and Occam's razor both protest, and on the same ground. Both assume that the preference of the rational impulse will also be the preference of nature.

MAY NOT UNDERSTANDING BE OF CONTINGENCIES? Charles Hartshorne thinks that I conceive the process of understanding too exclusively in terms of necessity. He would grant that where necessity is reasonably to be looked for, as in geometry, understanding naturally appeals to it. But sometimes it is not to be looked for, and in such cases the understanding of the contingent as contingent is as truly understanding as that which proceeds through necessity. So far as we can see, there is no necessity whatever in the occurrence of toothache upon the occurrence of a certain change in a dental nerve. But to see such mere conjunction for what it is, Hartshorne would presumably say, is itself a process of understanding, and to work out a one-to-one correlation between a series of nervous conditions and a series of experiences is a further and very valuable process of understanding, whether necessity enters in or not.

Our difference here may be a matter of words. Where a relation we are trying to understand is one of mere sequence, like that of nervous and mental change, and we have no idea why one should follow the other, I should prefer to say that we do not understand it, no matter how regularly the two go together. To understand means, for me, to see *why* something holds, and hence an unlimited series of mere conjunctions, however confident it made our predictions, would still not give us the insight we want. But of course the term understanding is often given to his grasp of the law conjoining two events, and no one can object to such usage so long as it is clear and consistent.

But Hartshorne, I think, is making a further point. If everything is in the end connected necessarily with everything else, why explain at all? Would not any explanation pulled out of the air at random do as well as any other? Why demonstrate, with pain and effort, that B follows from A if it really follows equally from anything else one might mention?

This is an interesting objection, though the answer does not seem difficult. I incline, as Hartshorne suspects, to think that every truth is connected necessarily with every other, and also that no event of past or future could be changed without entailing change in every other. It follows that for an all-seeing eye there must be a limitless number of considerations on which the truth of any given proposition depends. If little George has a cold, it is because he got his feet wet, but it is also because his father met his mother under certain specific conditions ten years ago, and because they and the world they lived in had certain determinate constitutions. But granting this, it does not follow that explanation by the remote is as good for our purposes as explanation by the near and obvious. Strictly speaking, neither gives understanding in such a case because neither gives us necessity. But our preference in explanation turns on utility as well as on insight. If we know something about the connection of colds with wet feet, we can do something to prevent their recurrence, whereas if we were to wait till we had mastered all the conditions, both near and remote, we should have to defer action indefinitely. Even in the sphere of admitted necessity some explanations are preferred to others. A cube has recondite properties peculiar to itself, and hence in theory one could as well start from any of these properties by way of explaining the presence of any other. But no one does explain in that way. If one knows that something is a cube, one starts with that and goes to the result as directly as possible; one does not start with some out-of-the-way property, show that this entails being a cube, and only then go on to the result. In short, even if all things and truths are connected, they are not connected with equal immediacy; and our minds being what they are, we shall always prefer the shorter route to the longer.

II. INTERNAL RELATIONS

We hold that the ultimate object of thought . . . is an all-inclusive system in which everything is related to everything else. . . . Put more formally, the theory is this: (1) that every term, i.e., every possible object of thought, is what it is in virtue of relations to what is other than itself: (2) that its nature is affected thus not by some of its relations only, but in differing degrees by all of them, no matter how external they may seem; (3) that in consequence of (2) and of the further obvious fact that everything is related in *some* way to everything else, no knowledge will reveal completely the nature of any term until it has exhausted that term's relations to everything else.[5]

Francis V. Raab: Must necessity be always logical in character? Could not the intelligibility of the world be maintained on the view that the causal relation is a necessary but not a *logically* necessary one? And could not the complete intelligibility of the world be maintained even on the view that every event is causally related to some other event but not to *every* other event?

Ernest Nagel: Both in his statement of the theory of internal relations and his discussion of it, Blanshard uses the phrase "the nature of a term." What are we to understand by this expression? Blanshard's rejection of the false or abstract universal in favor of the true or concrete universal suggests that for him the nature of a concrete thing or individual is the *total* set of attributes, relations, and relational properties which it possesses, and only on such an interpretation of this expression do his arguments for the doctrine of internal relations fail to illustrate the fallacy of *non sequitur.* But if the nature of a thing is equated with the thing itself, how can the following consequences be avoided? In the first place, the nature of a thing, like the thing itself, would be something that is in principle indefinable and

[5] Blanshard, *The Nature of Thought,* II, 452–453.

could not therefore be made the basis for bringing into systematic order any of the characters which the thing displays. In the second place, every statement which mentions the nature of an individual would express no more than a trivial analytic proposition. And in the third place, since discursive thought would be inherently inadequate to the task of discovering the natures of things, the goal of understanding the natures of things could not be a pertinent ideal for human reason.[6]

One of Blanshard's main arguments for saying that causality may involve logical necessity is that in the process of logical inference the relation of necessity that links premise with conclusion is itself a factor in producing the conclusion. This argument is unimpressive for the following reasons: (1) One thought often causes another where there is no trace of implication between the propositions to which they are addressed, and we often entertain propositions with a view to deducing conclusions from them, but fail to do so, even when these conclusions are entailed by the premises. (2) The argument confuses the thought of a necessary relation with the necessity of a thought; it confounds the nontemporal relation of entailment with the temporal process of inference. (3) The serious consequences for the life of reason that Blanshard thinks would follow a denial of his thesis are illusory. For a man who, seeing that a conclusion follows from his premises, accepts it for that reason has all the rationality required, even if necessity had no part in generating that conclusion.[7]

Paul F. Schmidt: I think Blanshard would agree that the following characteristics are necessary to a system of deductive logic: (1) There are certain patterns of inference such as *modus ponens* and the syllogism in Barbara. (2) The so-called laws of thought are necessary general principles to which all propositions must conform. (3) Certain concepts like validity, consistency, and negation are applicable generally to propositions. But then the theory of internal relations seems to leave him with the following difficulties: (1) The meaning of basic concepts like validity must necessarily vary, since the terms or propositions which they relate are different. (2) Patterns of inference must similarly vary. (3) The laws of thought are not applicable in the

---

[6] Cf. Ernest Nagel, *Sovereign Reason* (Glencoe, Ill.: The Free Press, 1954), pp. 271–277.
[7] Cf. *Sovereign Reason*, pp. 287–290.

same way to every proposition, but vary in their meaning, depending on the specific propositions to which they are applied, that is, related. In general, principles and concepts which stand at the base of the philosophic enterprise cannot on the theory of internal relations be understood in exactly the same way with reference to different propositions. But if the meaning and nature of these basic concepts and principles change, how can a system of logic be constructed in terms of which we can evaluate philosophic claims?

Francis V. Raab: Blanshard nowhere explains how coherence between lesser systems within the "all-inclusive" system is possible. Would the proposition "orange is brighter than red" logically entail a proposition in physics? Would the proposition "useless pain is bad" entail the above proposition? If not, then reality might not be a whole in the sense of every part being internally related to every other.

Blanshard: Raab has given much thought to the nature of necessity, and he asks why I lay so much stress on necessity of the logical type. If we know that one event follows with causal necessity from another, is not that enough? And if we saw the causal connection of each event with all others, should we not have as complete an understanding of the world as anyone could desire? Now if a necessary cause is merely a *sine qua non,* a cause without which the effect never in fact occurs, I do not think it does give us all we desire. On the other hand, if it means something without which the effect *could* not occur, we must ask the meaning of this "could not." If it means only "could not consistently with actual law," we are back again where we started, since for science actual laws are merely descriptive. If it means more than that, what more? Is it suggested that "could not occur" means "would be prevented from occurring" or "constrained not to occur"? But preventing and constraining are forms of causing, and the question is what cause generally means. Raab, I think, would agree that causation involves a *must.* And my contention is that no must provides us a stopping place except the must that satisfies our desire for intelligibility. For of all the musts of hammers and billiard balls, we can quite intelligibly ask, as David Hume showed, *why* the nail must sink or the ball roll. When we ask that question, we are asking for insight into why an event of a certain nature should give rise to an event of another nature. Our answer, to be satisfactory, must connect those natures by some intelligible link. Such a link would be in my sense logical. Causal necessity either reduces to what is broadly logical necessity or it is not necessity at all.

To hold, as I incline to do, that every thing and event is related logically to every other implies that each is internally connected with every other. This doctrine of internal relations has come under fire. The most serious objection to it is that it is destructive of logic itself.

DOUBTS ABOUT EXTENSIONAL LOGIC. I should be moved by this objection if I had greater confidence in the sort of logic that is offered as an alternative. But I must confess to a large measure of skepticism about recent logic, by which I mean the logic of *Principia Mathematica* and of the numberless works that have been based on it. This logic has so little to do with the end men set before themselves in the actual work of thinking as to have become something of an incubus in philosophy. It has become an instrument for foisting a special kind of metaphysic on students who assume that they are studying a philosophically neutral discipline. It achieves this result by supplying them a language, supposed to be of all languages the most precise and adequate, in which the things that rationalist metaphysicians want to say are ruled out as inexpressible. When such persons say that what is red is colored or extended, or that space is infinitely divisible, they are presumably wanting to say that there is something in the *nature* of red or of space that involves or entails these characters. What they are noting is that the characters of the world are not all indifferent to each other, that some of them are so bound up with others that you can pass in thought from one to another over a bridge of evident necessity.

In *Principia* and other extensional logics, you cannot say that sort of thing. All you can say is that one attribute appears *along with* another or is *associated* with it. If you want to say "red is a color," you do so in exactly the same formula in which you say that all New York policemen were wearing blue uniforms on Thursday $(x) \cdot (\phi x)$, "for all x's, x is ϕ." Of course you can say $(x) \cdot \phi x \supset \psi x,$ but you find that this symbolism too is so devised as to cut you off from any expression of necessary connection between characters. For all it means is

that you never in fact find a case of ϕx that is not also a case of ψx;
and this misses the point you want to make, which is not that one
character accompanies another, but that it necessitates that other. This
kind of logic is thus a gigantic *petitio,* used—as a rule of course unconsciously—to outlaw the sort of thought with which rationalist philosophy has always been specially concerned.

The difference between the two ways of thinking is fundamental.
Extensional logic is a logic of coincidence; certain attributes go together; one class falls within or without another; certain propositions
happen to be jointly true. The rationalist way of thinking is an *intensional* way; it says that A-ness *as such* entails B-ness. I am not of course
saying that extensional thinking is invalid; both types are valid. If all
men are in fact mortal, it follows that Parisians, being men, will be
mortal; if there is something in the constitution of man that entails
his eventually dying, as Aristotle seems to have thought, then it follows equally that Parisians must die, whether one has exhausted the
class of men in one's enumeration or not. Now it is this second kind of
thinking that chiefly interests the man who would understand, not
the sort of calculation of class inclusions which extensional logic is concerned with, and which, given the data, can best be done by IBM
machines, on which our symbolic logicians are being increasingly
drafted as consultants. Hume, and Ludwig Wittgenstein following
Hume, say that no thing or event necessitates any other. When I hold
the contrary of that proposition, I am obviously not differing on a
point of detail; I am challenging the adequacy of extensionalist logic
to embody our actual thought. The grounds for this challenge appear
more fully in the first volume of my Gifford Lectures.[8] Meanwhile,
when I say that things and events are internally related, I am saying
that if we understood them fully, we should see that they are thus
connected through their *natures,* or *characters.*

An extended criticism of this view has been offered by Ernest Nagel
in an essay on "Sovereign Reason," to which more than one of my
commentators refer. It is a patient study by a competent logician of
my theory of internal relations, and is regarded by some who have
not read my book—and probably by some who have—as a decisive
disproof. I do not share this view, though I appreciate the careful and

[8] *Reason and Goodness* (London: Allen & Unwin, Ltd., 1961).

courteous attention Nagel has given to my theory, and would recommend the reader to study his article in full.[9] It appeared in the Kallen *Festschrift, Freedom and Experience,* and has been reprinted in his own volume *Sovereign Reason,* and again in A. C. Ewing's recent *The Idealist Tradition.*[10] I cannot attempt to deal here with all his strictures. But regarding two of the most important of these I have been expressly asked for comment by Brandt and Grünbaum, and with Nagel's permission, Louis O. Mink has briefly stated them above. These are, first, that my argument turns on an obscurity as to the "nature" of a term, and second, that I am wrong in thinking necessity a causal factor in inference.

TERMS AND THEIR "NATURES." I hold that terms are related through their natures to other terms. What do I mean, Ernest Nagel asks, by their "nature"? It is a fair question. But Nagel develops it in what seems to me an odd way. He offers four meanings among which he evidently thinks my choice must lie. He then points out that on the first three of these my argument is a *non sequitur;* only on the fourth, he says, would it escape this fallacy. On the same page, however, on which he says this, he offers evidence from me that it *is* the fourth which I accept. The natural inference would therefore be that my case is free from this fallacy. Yet he writes as if his argument had proved what, on the evidence offered, it could not prove. Let us look into this further; and let us consider first the meanings among which we are asked to choose.

The four meanings are substantially as follows: (1) By the "nature" of a term we may mean its definition in the traditional logical sense, as when we say that the nature of man, taken as a kind, is to be a rational animal. (2) We may mean a property, or a set of these, in the sense of what follows from the essence, but is not part of it. Thus if we recognize Socrates as a man, we may say that it is his nature to be mortal, since this follows from his humanity, but not to

[9] Nagel, *Sovereign Reason, and Other Studies in the Philosophy of Science* (Glencoe, Ill.: The Free Press, 1954).

[10] *Freedom and Experience,* ed. Sidney Hook and Milton R. Konvitz (Ithaca, N.Y.: Cornell University Press, 1947); *The Idealist Tradition: From Berkeley to Blanshard* (Glencoe, The Free Press, 1957).

be snub-nosed. (3) We may mean a set of attributes selected either for their utility or because we can derive from them in a systematic way many other attributes of the thing to which we ascribe them. Thus, we could classify Socrates in a hundred ways, but we prefer to say that he is by nature a man rather than snub-nosed or barrel-chested because we can deduce far more about him from the first way of conceiving him than from the others. (4) Finally, we may take the nature of Socrates to include his "total set of characters." There are a number of points in Nagel's discussion of these meanings which seem to me curious, such as his suggestion [11] that the mortality of Socrates logically follows from his humanity, an entailment I should certainly not claim to see. But I will pass this over because I am concerned only with the main thrust of the argument.

Regarding these four meanings, Nagel says that if I adopt any one of the first three, my argument for internal relations will be a *non sequitur*. What he appears to mean by this is that all these "essences" or "natures" are arbitrary abstractions from a complex, and that if I take them as giving the nature of the object, I fail to show in detail how we can pass from these nuclear attributes to the others.

May I first lift a wan eyebrow about this argument? To suppose that once these elementary distinctions be brought to light, a position regarding internal relations held by such logicians as Francis Herbert Bradley, H. W. B. Joseph, Bernard Bosanquet, J. M. E. McTaggart, and Alfred North Whitehead will forthwith fall apart shows a curious estimate of their logical competence. They were not unaware of the difficulties of defining individuals; indeed it is to them one must go if one wants the most searching and illuminating study of our knowledge of the individual. I do not think the foregoing argument touches even my own more modest case. I had supposed that I had repudiated emphatically all three of these types of "nature" as adequate to the object. In my discussion of "The Thing and Its Architecture," I stressed the nonlogical and practical factors that lie behind our present division of the world into things. In discussing the abstract universal, I went to extreme lengths in my polemic against setting up abstract characters as exhaustive of a thing's nature. When I am offered views about

[11] *Sovereign Reason,* p. 273.

the nature of a term which I have disavowed at length, and am told that if these are what I mean, I am involved in *non sequiturs,* I merely plead "not guilty" to the protasis.

THE "NATURE" OF AN INDIVIDUAL. Second, what *is* my "cryptic notion of the nature of an individual thing" which so puzzles Nagel? Let me spell it out as simply as I can. I hold that any attempt to abstract certain characters of Socrates, or any set of these characters, and to identify his nature with them, will fall short of what he is, and hence that nothing less than his "total set of characters," to use Nagel's term, will cover that nature. I hold that some of these characters—for example, being rational—are more important in immediately determining further characters of his nature than others are—for example, his snub-nosedness. But I hold also that one is not justified in excluding his snub-nosedness from his nature, nor his being an Athenian, nor his being married to Xantippe. Are there *any* of his characteristics or relations that you can leave out as totally irrelevant to his nature? I hold there are not. They are all relevant, though in different degrees, to making him what he is.

If this view is impenetrably "cryptic," what is the alternative to it? Nagel seems to me stronger in attack than in construction, but I think one can see fairly clearly what view he would urge on us instead. He holds, as do I, that the attributes of the individual are inexhaustible, and therefore that the abstractions we make in thinking fall short of his actual nature. He holds, again as I do, that in order to deal with it in thought, such abstractions are a necessity. On what principle, then, would he have us select them? He answers: "It is quite clear that just what characters are included in an individual, and just where the boundaries of an individual are drawn, depend on decisions as to the use of language. These decisions, though motivated by considerations of practical utility, are *logically arbitrary.*" [12] This seems to me an abandonment of the problem rather than a solution of it. There *are* individuals, Nagel would say, and these individuals are infinitely complex; but any attempt to say what belongs to them essentially is misguided; nothing is really more essential than anything else. Hence we must fall back on ordinary usage and accept as forming the essence whatever qualities it may be convenient to group together. Why this

[12] *Sovereign Reason,* p. 275, italics in text.

conversion of a problem of philosophy into one of linguistic convenience? Not primarily because the individual is inexhaustible; that view Nagel and I have in common. Apparently it is because the individual is "taken to include an inexhaustible set of *logically independent* characters."[13] Where characters are thus independent, none of them would provide better keys to the nature in question than any other. So any selection is bound to be arbitrary, and we may as well let ordinary usage prescribe our choice.

I do not think this view is either consistent with Nagel's own account or plausible in itself. As to the last point, he admits that many of the characters of an individual are *not* logically independent of each other, for example, "that many other characters possessed by Socrates, such as the ability to see and hear, to experience joy and sorrow, to resent injury, to remember and reflect, are logical consequences of his being a man";[14] it even "follows" from his being a man that he is mortal. This is carrying the claim to logical insight much farther than I would venture to carry it myself. If, from certain characters of an individual, masses of further characters logically follow, and from certain others none follow at all, why is it arbitrary to take the former as more essential? Suppose that it suited the linguistic convenience of some newly discovered Swiftian race to classify creatures by their noses and to take as the essential characteristic of Socrates his being a snub-nosed entity, would they have as much right to claim that they had caught his real nature as if they had seen in him a rational being? To this question Nagel's answer, so far as I can judge, is both Yes and No. If the nature of a thing is really to be settled arbitrarily or by logistic convenience, his answer is Yes. But in admitting that some characters give us a far more massive grasp of a thing's nature than others, his answer is No. Both can hardly be right. For my own part, I hold the latter view. The suggestion that Socrates is a congeries of externally related characters among which none is more revealing of his real nature than any other seems to me supported neither by common sense nor by critical reflection.

Having admitted that we are not as hopeless as Nagel thinks we are in finding the nature of an individual, I hasten to repeat that we shall

[13] *Sovereign Reason,* p. 275, italics in text.
[14] *Ibid.,* p. 274.

never grasp the whole of its nature until we grasp the total set of its characters. This is the fourth of Nagel's alternatives regarding the "nature" of a thing and, as I have said, it is the view I accept. Nagel finds it hard to believe that I do accept it, and offers a series of objections, all of which have been dealt with—I should have thought effectively—by earlier rationalist thinkers.

OBJECTIONS TO MY VIEW OF THE NATURE OF THE INDIVIDUAL. "In the first place," Nagel writes on this view, "the nature of a thing, like the thing itself, would be something that is in principle undefinable and could not therefore be made the basis for bringing into systematic order any of the characters which the thing displays." I agree that it is undefinable. But the second part of the statement does not follow from the first. It does not follow that because we cannot work into a definition *all* the qualities of an object, we cannot get any of them, or that those we can get will not enable us to order *some* of the remaining qualities. If we know that Socrates' humanity or rationality is essential to him, we can surely go some distance in ordering his other qualities as consequences, which Nagel indeed admits. It is true that if we knew all the qualities of Socrates and their relations, we should hardly talk about a "basis" from which the remainder might be derived in order—but only because we should have the order already, and there would be no remainder to derive.

"In the second place," says Nagel, "every statement which mentions the nature of an individual would express no more than a trivial analytical proposition." In a sense this too is true; indeed it is itself a trivial analytical proposition. If we had before us the full nature of a thing as described above, any statement about a part of that nature would be a statement of part of our meaning. But I hope it is obvious that I lay no claim to such complete knowledge. If the system seems to have point, it is probably because of an unconscious shift of meaning from what might be to what is. It *would* be paradoxical to say that a statement about the snub-nosedness of Socrates, made at our present level of knowledge, is analytic; I cannot see that it is at all paradoxical to say that if made with complete knowledge it would be so. Such force as the objection has comes from transposing the paradox illicitly from the second statement to the first.

"In the third place," writes Nagel, "since discursive thought would be inherently inadequate to the task of discovering the natures of things, the goal of understanding the natures of things could not be a pertinent ideal for human reason." Again I do not think the conclusion follows. Reason, to be sure, is inadequate in the sense that it would have to exhaust an infinity of characters and relations before it achieved the full understanding that it seeks, and hence it will presumably always fall short of its goal. But is such understanding therefore not a "pertinent ideal" at all? Take a parallel case. No one, I suppose, will ever achieve moral perfection. Are we to say, then, that because our present powers are "inherently inadequate" to achieve such perfection, it is not even a goal at which to aim? Certainly most moralists would not say so. An ideal is not impertinent, even though unattainable, so long as it supplies a direction for endeavor and a measure for advance. And in our effort toward understanding, the rationalist ideal supplies both.

Fourth, Nagel says that on my view "there will be only one individual, which will coincide with the conjectural 'totality' of all things, events, and relations," a consequence which, he says, is "practically undesirable, for reasons too obvious to need mention." [15] That there is only one individual who answers fully to the ideal of individuality is not, of course, an awkward inadvertence of my theory, but a thesis explicitly advocated—an old and not unrespectable thesis, by the way, shared by Spinoza, Hegel, and Whitehead. Whether it is "practically undesirable" I cannot say without knowing more particularly what this means; but I should not suppose that even if it were, its being thus "undesirable" would entail its being untrue.

ARE THE CHARACTERS OF AN INDIVIDUAL INTERNALLY RELATED? I cannot think that these difficulties, despite the weight Nagel attaches to them, give the main point of difference between us about the "natures" of things. Indeed on two main matters, as has been already suggested, we seem to agree. We agree that the concrete individual is inexhaustible in its characteristics, and therefore that any selection we may make from them will do less than justice to the individual's nature. The main issue between us is whether with fuller knowledge of these characteristics we should find them linked together by bonds of necessity. I think we should; Nagel thinks we should not.

[15] *Sovereign Reason*, p. 275.

I do not pretend, of course, to be able to show this interlinking in detail; that sort of insight would come, if at all, at the end of the trail, not at the beginning. All one can do is to show that there is no good reason for believing at the outset that the search is doomed.

Nagel appears to think that its doom can be read in ordinary scientific judgments. He offers us a typical instance: "If to be a metal is taken to be the nature of a concrete thing, this nature *may* entail the fact that the thing is malleable; but this nature will not, by itself, determine the specific degree of malleability exhibited by the thing, nor will it determine the specific shapes the thing may assume at different times." [16] If this is designed to show that we do not at present see how the other characters of the thing entail its degree of malleability and its shape, the point is freely conceded. If it is designed to show that further knowledge could not hope to find such entailment, it is not impressive. To know fully what being a metal means would involve, I suppose, a knowledge of the atomic structure of metals; to know fully this particular species of metal would involve knowing the special modification of that structure which distinguished it from other species of the genus. The belief that there is some intelligible connection between this specific atomic structure and a certain degree of malleability is surely no wild assumption; indeed it is the sort of assumption that justifies our continued attempt to understand, and it is quite rightly retained until shown to be hopeless. And it is not shown to be hopeless merely by present ignorance.

But what about the shape possessed by this lump of metal? Is not that entirely contingent in relation to the rest of its characters? Again, I see no reason for thinking so. The shape is determined by pressures from within and without; these pressures will have different results as the patterns and tensions of the atomic structures vary; given similar outer pressures, a lump of metal will not take the same shape as one of dough or rubber. This much is plain enough, even on the level of high abstraction. Will the picture change as we move downward toward the concrete? It seems to me gratuitous pessimism to say so. We have every reason to believe that in the degree to which we approach a complete knowledge of the interacting individuals, we shall see that there is nothing at all accidental in their assuming the shapes

[16] *Sovereign Reason*, p. 276.

they have. It may be objected that the necessity here referred to is causal, not logical. But I hold, and have argued at length, that causality involves logical necessity. And in any case, such an objection could not be made by Ernest Nagel; for we have just seen him admitting that the nature of a piece of metal may "entail the fact that the thing is malleable," and malleability is a causal property. To say that it is entailed is to say that if a thing possessing metallic character is acted upon in a certain way, it must react causally in a certain way. If the fact that it will so react may be entailed, so may the fact of its assuming a certain shape.

NECESSITY AS A CAUSAL FACTOR IN INFERENCE. I have now dealt with the first of Nagel's criticisms on which my commentators asked me to remark, the criticism that my case for internal relations rested upon obscurity as to the "natures" of things. I come next to the second criticism, which concerns my attempt to show that necessity may be at work in causation. In this attempt I call attention to what happens in the process of inference itself. I try to show that in that process the necessity linking premises with conclusions is itself a causal factor determining the course of the movement. This is the point to which my critics take exception.

It will be well to put my case again briefly, since I can hardly suppose that if anyone has done me the honor of reading *The Nature of Thought,* he will remember this particular discussion. I took in illustration the old case of the abbé and the squire. "Ladies," says the abbé, "do you know that my first penitent was a murderer?" "Ladies," says the squire, entering shortly afterward, "do you know that I was the abbé's first penitent?" An interesting conclusion, which hardly needs statement, leaped into the ladies' minds. Suppose one undertook to explain causally why this particular conclusion, rather than some quite different one, appeared. I held in my book that no explanation would be complete that failed to take into account the fact of the premises' entailing the conclusion. "What we hold," I wrote, "is that when one passes in reasoning from ground to consequent, the fact that the ground entails the consequent is one of the conditions determining the appearance of this consequent rather than something else in the thinker's mind." [17]

[17] Blanshard, *The Nature of Thought,* II, 496.

There is nothing at first glance novel or challenging in such a view. Indeed it seems pretty clearly the view of common sense. If the ladies were asked why the thought of the squire's being a murderer had come into their minds, they would no doubt have said something like this: "Because what we had just been told implied it." Nevertheless, this view of the role of necessity in inference has been the target of many attacks in recent years. Why? Because, innocent as it seems, it contains a high-explosive charge. If it is true, it shows that a merely naturalistic account of the thought process, explaining that process wholly by changes in the brain, cannot be adequate. I can only say that the criticisms made of my view seem to me to have failed conspicuously and that this failure does raise serious questions about naturalism. Nagel's particular attack is the best I know. It will repay us to examine it closely.

Some of his difficulties seem to rest on a misapprehension of the case he is criticizing, so let us first get this clear. I do not maintain that the relation of ground to consequent is ever a *sufficient* condition of inference. The actual process of thought is influenced by innumerable factors—by emotions, casual associations, suppressed and explicit desires, the state of the brain, general freshness or fatigue. To explain fully the complex state of consciousness which we call the acceptance of a conclusion, all these factors would have to be taken into account, and not logical entailment only. Nor do I hold that the entailment of a proposition by a premise is even a *necessary* condition for the appearance of that proposition. A belief may be accepted because it is suggested by one's newspaper, not because it has been deduced from grounds. To be sure, I agree with Bernard Bosanquet that even here the belief is never purely arbitrary; reason is imperfectly at work in its appearance; for example, if the belief is accepted on the authority of the newspaper, there is an implicit inference that moves in accordance with a principle, though that principle is not necessary. Still it is obvious that a man may accept a proposition in Euclid without having derived it by valid deduction. I do not hold, then, that the entailment of a consequent by its ground is either a sufficient or a necessary condition of the occurrence of the state of mind which we call the acceptance of that consequent. What I do hold is that on some occasions— how rare or frequent is in principle indifferent—the logical relation between ground and consequent does serve, and can be directly seen to serve, as one of the conditions leading to the result.

ALLEGED EXCEPTIONS TO THE THESIS THAT NECESSITY WORKS IN INFERENCE. To this thesis Nagel offers three types of objection. First come some examples alleged as exceptions to the thesis. What are they?

It is not an unfamiliar fact that at least in some cases when a man thinks of a premise he subsequently thinks of a proposition which, though he believes it to be the logical consequence of the premise, is in fact not a valid consequence at all. If we admit that in such cases the thought of the premise is a cause (or part of the cause) of the thought of the conclusion, we must also admit that thoughts may be causally related, though the propositions to which these thoughts are addressed do not stand to each other in the relation of logical entailment.[18]

Let us put this in an illustration. One discovers (1) that Jones is a Marxist. One finds oneself shortly believing (2) that Jones is morally untrustworthy. The belief in (1) may be a part cause of the belief in (2). But (1) clearly does not entail (2). Hence one belief may contribute causally to the occurrence of another when the object of the first does not entail the object of the second.

I do not think that such cases offer, on analysis, any inconsistency with my view. The act of accepting a belief is of course a complex psychophysical event. Let us symbolize the acceptance of proposition (1) by $A_{1,2,3 \ldots n}$, and the acceptance of (2) by $B_{1,2,3 \ldots n}$. The direction of awareness to (1) is only one part of the complex whole $A_{1,2,3 \ldots n}$, and its direction to (2) only part of $B_{1,2,3 \ldots n}$. When we say that the first of these complex wholes causes or partially causes the second, we are not committing ourselves to the view that what causes the particular component in $B_{1,2,3 \ldots n}$ consisting of the direction of attention to (2) is the entailment of (2) by (1). Of course that direction of attention is an event which has a cause; that cause lay in part among the complex set of antecedents $A_{1,2,3 \ldots n}$, and I should hold that whatever caused it would be seen, with sufficient knowledge, to cause it necessarily. But this is not to hold that the cause must be identified with the entailment of the accepted proposition by its logical

[18] *Sovereign Reason*, p. 287.

ground. In the case before us, one has presumably been determined to respond disapprovingly to anyone considered a Marxist, and the belief that Jones is a Marxist has called this disposition into play regarding him. Nagel appears to think that if I admit the direction of attention upon (2) to be sometimes caused by factors other than (1)'s entailment of (2), I cannot admit that in other cases it *is* partially caused by this. So far as I can see, the two admissions are quite consistent.

Second, Nagel writes:

It is also well known that men often entertain propositions with a view to deducing conclusions from them but nevertheless fail to do so, even though various conclusions may in fact be entailed by the premises. Evidently the presence of the implicative relation between propositions, therefore, is not a *sufficient* condition for the causal determination of a thought about a conclusion by a thought about the premises.[19]

If anyone has actually held that the mere implication of (2) by (1) is itself a sufficient condition of our thinking of (2) when (1) has been presented, I do not know who he is. The suggestion that once we think of the initial propositions of Euclid, the whole thirteen books must unroll themselves because they are implied by these propositions is absurd, I agree, and Nagel's example disposes of it. But this straw man does not appear in anything I have written.

He has another case to offer. "It sometimes happens . . . that each of two men will think of a premise and also come to think of a conclusion implied by it, where one of the thinkers perceives the logical connection between the propositions while the other, luckily hitting upon the conclusion, does not obtain it by following the chain of logical implication."[20] Since in the latter case the conclusion appeared without the help of the ground-consequent connection, this could have had no part in producing it in the former case. It is surprising to find this argument offered by an accomplished logician, who must be well aware of the pitfalls in the Method of Difference. Consider a parallel example. John and James both come down with the flu. John was in a state of extreme fatigue; James was not. Because James got the flu

[19] *Sovereign Reason*, p. 288, italics in text.
[20] *Sovereign Reason*, p. 288.

without being fatigued, we conclude that fatigue can have nothing to do with the flu in John's case or in any other. Plainly there is something wrong here. It is true that fatigue cannot be *the* cause of the flu, in the sense of being even a necessary condition, for the flu may occur without it; but it does not follow that in the complex of conditions that produces it in other cases, fatigue can play no part. It is the same with entailment in thinking. A theorem may be accepted by a schoolboy who has no notion how to deduce it. But it does not follow, and it is indeed an extreme paradox that, in the thought of the geometer, logical entailment plays no part in the work of deducing it.

THE RELATION OF IMPLICATION TO INFERENCE. Why is it that Nagel accepts this paradox? His answer forms his second general criticism of my view on this point. To hold that entailment plays such a part in the process of inference, he says, "is to confound the nontemporal logical relation of entailment or implication with the temporal process of inference that recognizes or discovers such implicative relations."[21] Entailment links timeless propositions, not events; causality links events, not timeless propositions. I may, by an act or process that is in time, apprehend a timeless necessity linking two propositions; this timeless necessity is the implication; my act or process of apprehending it is the inference. To suppose that the necessity enters into the causal process and helps to determine what will emerge in it is to mix two different universes of discourse, to confound implication, which is a static linkage, with inference, which is a temporal passage.

A little reflection will show, I think, that this neat compartmentalizing of the two orders will not hold. My introduction of logic into the world of fact and change is not exactly wanton; nature herself is the guilty party. The multiplication table is timeless; clothespins are not; but it is true nevertheless that five clothespins added to seven make twelve clothespins; these objects, though empirical and transient, are ordered by a system that is timeless. Even if you can have a logic without ontology, which I disbelieve, you cannot have an ontology without logic. And just as logical relations hold among existents, so also they affect the course of events. Nagel seems at times to have adopted the curious view of George Santayana that "essences" are vestal virgins, without issue in anything that happens. This is a position refuted hourly

[21] *Sovereign Reason*, p. 289.

in ordinary life. At one o'clock, for example, Nagel is listening to music; at two o'clock he is thinking about logic. Does he seriously hold that the character and relation of the objects engaging his attention make no difference to his responses? When he feels stirred by the music and puzzled by the complexities of the logic, are these effects to be explained without any reference to the subject matter engrossing him? If he says Yes, this very response, I should have thought, would convict him of inconsistency; if he says No, he is admitting that the relations of logic may, for all their timelessness, make a difference in the flux of events.

"THE INITIATIVE OF THE ETERNAL." It is an old mistake, often repeated, that the causal conditions of events must all be themselves events. They can perfectly well be timeless logical relations. The banks of a stream can direct its flow, even while themselves remaining unchanged, and we may recognize their causal influence without dissolving them into the stream. If we recognize similarly that when a geometer develops the consequences of a theorem, the implications holding in his subject matter affect the course of his thinking, we may do so without the least confusion between the logical necessity linking the theorems, on the one hand, and the psychological sequence of his thoughts, on the other. In logic the conclusion does not follow the premise, though it follows *from* it; in inference the apprehension of the conclusion does normally follow the apprehension of the premise. When we hold that what follows in logic may help to determine what follows in fact, we are not forgetting the obvious difference between these two "follows." With this difference in full view, we still hold that to deny that one affects the other is to deny plain fact. Suppose a man who is competent at figures is set to do an easy sum, and Nagel is offered $64,000 if he can guess what will come into the man's mind at the end of three minutes; what evidence would he think most helpful? Clearly it would be the figures that must be added, and what they add up to. Knowing this, Nagel would consider it far more probable that the man would think of the correct figure than of an incorrect one, or of the Battle of Hastings. The ground for this confidence is in part the sense that the logical relations in his subject matter will influence the course of the man's thinking.

It may be replied that what actually determines this result is some existent state or disposition—the man's intelligence, or his determination to follow the argument, or his habit of thinking correctly. All such explanations will be found, I think, to admit inadvertently what they ostensibly deny. The man's "intelligence" in this context *means* his power to see and to be influenced by logical connections; his determination to follow the argument could be effective only if there were a framework of argument to guide his views; if he has formed correct habits, it is because good habits have been selected, and bad rejected, under the influence of logical requirements. Thus when the constraint of logic on inference is denied, and replaced by psychical causes, those causes will be found, if plausible at all, to include this very constraint under disguise. This is true, I suspect, even of Nagel's favored alternative. He apparently holds that when a man reaches the right conclusion in such cases, it is owing to "the happy working of his own body." [22] It cannot be owing to that exclusively, however, since Nagel has admitted a page or two earlier that "the *thought* [my italics] of one proposition may be the cause [or part of the cause] of the thought of a second"; so when Nagel's body produced the notion that Newton's *Principia* was produced entirely by Newton's body, it can hardly have been working at its happiest. But even if we were to admit this explanation, we should still find in it the same *petitio,* only now buried a little more deeply. For what does "happy working" mean when applied to logical inference? It can only mean the kind of working that hews to the line of necessity, and hence is presumably influenced by it.

Readers of Nagel's criticism will almost certainly receive the impression that I am arguing for a view that is queer and paradoxical. It is, on the contrary, the view not only of common sense, but of the psychologists who have most carefully studied the matter, and of the main tradition of Western philosophy. Common sense would think it absurd to say of a debater who offered a closely reasoned case that this case was not "governed" by the relevance of the considerations offered. And if it is said that he did not introduce certain considerations because they were relevant, but because he saw they were relevant, the obvious answer is that he could not see them to be relevant unless they were so, and only their being so made it possible for

[22] *Sovereign Reason,* p. 290.

him to see them to be so. Again, among psychologists the only school
that has made a careful study of the relation between necessity and
inference is the school of *Gestalt*, and its conclusion is notorious that
our thinking is influenced by requiredness in the subject matter. Suppose one is asked, "2 is to 4 as 4 is to what?" or "A man is to a woman
as a stallion is to a what?" To say that when one goes on to complete
the series, the relations linking the concepts make no difference to
what comes to mind seems merely eccentric. Of course attempts have
been made to show that our thinking in these cases and indeed in all
others is a matter of association due to "conditioning." I will not stop
over this contention. One need only refer, by way of refutation, to
Socrates' interview with the slave boy in the *Meno*. And as Nagel well
knows, there is an old and respectable tradition which, on this issue,
is on Socrates' side.

LOGIC AND REASONABLENESS. There is another aspect of
my position which Nagel views unhappily. I hold that unless necessary connections in the subject matter could influence our thinking,
the attempt to be rational in thought and practice would be a hopeless one. We could never believe that the force of the evidence had anything to do with our reaching of conclusions. We could never assume
that when we argued with another, the strength of our logic would
have any tendency to produce in his mind the conclusion we were
urging. Indeed we could not even argue consistently for our inability
to be influenced by logic, since in doing so we should be assuming that
others might be moved by the logic of our case to the acceptance of
our conclusion, and this assumption would deny the conclusion itself.

It will be well to examine attentively Ernest Nagel's reply:

Why is it impossible to be moved by reasons if the *temporal passage*
from premise to conclusion in a valid inference does not involve a relation
of logical necessity? A man who first notes a premise *A*, and then perceives
that *A* logically implies *B*, *is* moved by reasons when he accepts *B* on the
evidence of the premise—even if the causal sequence, the thought of *A*, the
perception of the connection between *A* and *B*, the assertion of *B*, is a
logically contingent one. Such a thinker might not assert *B* did he not
perceive the connection between *A* and *B*; and his *perception* of this connection is doubtless one of the factors which causally determine his thought

and acceptance of *B*. But is there any reason for maintaining that if the connection between this factor and the effect attributed to it is a logically contingent one, its manifest operation is illusory? [23]

There seem to me serious confusions here, which I will try briefly to point out. Note the remark, "his *perception* of this connection is doubtless one of the factors which causally determine his thought and acceptance of B." Clearly, you cannot perceive the connection of A and B without an awareness of B. But this awareness of B is here the event to be explained. In attributing its appearance to the perception of the connection between A and B, Nagel is therefore explaining the awareness of B by saying that we were aware of it already. He seems not to realize that the evident erroneousness of this reasoning, exposed by Francis H. Bradley in 1883, was one of the reasons that rendered such an account as I have offered necessary. It is because the thought of A tends so strongly to produce the thought of B, even when their connection has *not* been perceived, and even when the ideas of them have never in the past been associated, that we must hold this connection to exercise some direction upon our reasoning.

While denying that necessary connections ever do exert this influence, Nagel thinks it still possible to admit that we are "moved by reasons." "A man who first notes a premise A, and then perceives that A logically implies B, *is* moved by reasons when he accepts B on the evidence of the premise. . . ." This is true. But should it not be more guardedly stated? Nagel can hardly mean that reasons in the sense of logical grounds or entailments move our acceptance, for that, I suppose, is what he is denying. What he must mean is that our *perception* that A entails B leads causally to our accepting B. The question, then, is whether A's entailment of B enters into *that* causal process. And surely it does. The causal influence of a perception obviously varies with what it is a perception *of*. Substitute for the perception that A entails B the perception that A is the contrary, or the subcontrary, or the contradictory of B, and the perception will have no tendency to produce acceptance. The relation perceived may, then, determine differentially whether the perception leads to acceptance or to something else. This is what Nagel presumably means in admitting that

[23] *Sovereign Reason*, p. 290, italics in text.

we are moved by reasons. But how can he admit it without abandoning his point that logical relations do not enter into the causation of beliefs?

TWO TYPES OF RATIONALITY.   The habit of accepting propositions because one's premises are seen to entail them is of course an important kind of rationality; and though I do not think that Nagel can accept it consistently with his own premises, it is pleasant to find agreement about its possibility. Nagel would hold, however, that even if he were to admit the influence on our belief of seen entailment, this would not commit him to the very different kind of rationality involved in the influence on mental process of entailments that are at the moment unseen. He thinks that the former kind is all we need in order to keep our respect for human nature, and our greater respect for reasonable than for unreasonable men.

I agree that this kind of reasonableness is most desirable—the kind, that is, which unflinchingly accepts what the argument leads to. But I also think the other kind important—the kind that follows where the argument leads. The one without the other gives us a miracle or a monstrosity. Nagel's rational man is one whose thinking is at every step determined by what (relatively to logic) is pure contingency; this purely contingent process leads with gratifying frequency to conclusions entailed by premises; and when they do turn up, they are embraced with a glad cry. It is hard to understand how we could reach these happy conclusions so often, and be so little surprised at the unearned bounty, if the fact that they are entailed by our premises makes no difference to our success in reaching them.

The rational man, as I view him, does not always stumble and grope in darkness till he arrives at conclusions by luck, and then for the first time exhibit his rationality by accepting them. Necessity aids in the process and not only at the end. I do not mean anything so absurd as that logic always rules our thinking, for then of course we should never think illogically. I mean that all men sometimes, and some men often, do think logically, and that it is incredible that they should succeed in this as much as they do if their thinking is never affected by the necessities that engage them. Apparently in Nagel's view all inferential processes are equally contingent. This I cannot believe. The suggestion that Socrates' thought at its best was as wholly contingent as Xantippe's at its worst, that necessity had no more to do with Spinoza's thinking in the *Ethics* than with that of his barber in idle chatter, seems to me to make the success of such thinkers virtually miraculous. Men at their best are blunderingly and brokenly rational: admitted. But neither in thought nor in action are we altogether puppets, pulled about by strings of contingency. At times we are picked up, so to speak, by the logic of our case, and carried whither it leads. I do not want to exaggerate man's reasonableness, and Nagel will agree that there is little enough temptation in these days to do so. But neither do I care to see such modicum of it as we possess belittled or denied. And it does seem to me undeniable fact that sometimes, looking back at the path of our thought as we conclude a syllogism or a geometrical proof, we can see that the relations holding in what we were thinking of did to some extent channel our thinking, not determining it exclusively, but influencing its direction and its course. That is all I have maintained. I still think it true.

INTERNAL RELATIONS AND IDENTITY. Paul F. Schmidt, in an acute criticism, has put his finger on a point of ultimate difficulty for anyone who holds to an internal-relations theory. He thinks that such a doctrine strikes at the validity not only of science, but also of logic, as this is commonly conceived. If terms depend on their relations, then universals themselves will change from context to context. But both logic and natural science depend on terms maintaining their identity intact through every context. When the biologist speaks of an organism, for example, he assumes that the term retains the same sense as he passes from plant to animal. Scientists assume that a law is the same, however diverse the matter in which it is exemplified. And unless the laws and patterns of logic, such as the principle of the syllogism and the law of contradiction, were identical in all contexts, logic would cease to be logic, since it *is* precisely the invariant frame to which all experience does and must conform.

If my view did involve this airy dismissal of the most secure of our intellectual achievements, it would have small chance of convincing anybody. But it is less arrogant, I hope, and less desperate. The way of thinking that moves through identities is indispensable, I agree, and one could not even attack such thinking without using it at every step. What I suggest is that this independence of universals from their context is not always of the same degree and that absolute irrelevance to their context is probably a degree that is never achieved.

Consider what is implied by the principle of identity itself. This is often put in symbols as "A is A." Bradley posed a dilemma about this which still seems to me effective: If the two A's really mean the same thing, then it is not a statement at all, for nothing is being said. On the other hand, if the second A is different from the first, then as a statement of pure identity it is false. He concludes that if you are to have the same, *mere* sameness will fail to give it, for the same *means* the same through difference. You may, for example, say that the character of being an organism preserves its identity in the amoeba and Socrates because their differences in respect to head, heart, and hands are irrelevant to this common organic character. But then this organic character is *not* the same if you abstract from the differences altogether, for "same" means "same as against diversity of context," and sameness without diversity is self-contradiction. The identity that abstracts wholly from differences is not even identity.

DEGREES OF IDENTITY. But the question, it will be said, is not to be solved by such dialectics. For that question is not whether identity is independent of difference as such, but whether it is independent of the special characters with which in its various instances it happens to appear. Given the set of attributes that make anything an organism, this nucleus of attributes is surely not different in Socrates from what it is in the amoeba merely because in the first it is associated with a head, heart, and hands, and in the second it is not. I question this. Though "organism" applies to both, I doubt whether any set of nuclear characters answering to the term and absolutely identical in both can be found in them. One can of course suggest an abstract definition, such as "a whole whose parts are reciprocally ends and means," but this concept is realized in far fuller measure in Socrates than in the amoeba, and the difference seems to me to infect the concept itself; Socrates is more of an organism than the amoeba is: he is not merely the amoebic essence with a set of accretions added from without. To hold in this case to a diamond-hard pellet of nuclear meaning which remains unaffected by its mode of embodiment is contrary at once to fact and to thought.

A. C. Ewing has somewhere suggested that "relevance" of relations would have been a better phrase than "internality," and would have saved much confusion. I agree. To say that relations are internal to a term suggests that they are all built into its meaning, and equally so, while relevance is admitted to be a matter of degree. It is this fact of degree that I would stress. I should suggest that in the case just discussed, the degree of relevance of context to nucleus falls somewhere between two extremes, represented, let us say, by the concept of religion at one extreme and the principle of syllogism at the other. Religion takes its character so largely from the individual and social setting in which it appears that it may well be the same in no two minds. On the other hand, tradition holds that the principle of syllogism is the same absolutely in all of its manifestations, and hence is wholly indifferent to its contexts. I agree that we find here an approximation to such indifference. Even here, however, I think it is approximation only. Irrelevance complete and absolute we never find. Let us look at the case more closely.

B a r b a r a . If the principle of syllogism is to be identical throughout, we must first know what it is. And it is not without significance that there is a wide disagreement as to what it is. There is disagreement even about so simple and firm a structure as Barbara. Is it the *nota notae* rule that gives the principle of reasoning in Barbara? Or is it the *dictum de omni et nullo*? Or is it $[(p \supset q) . (q \supset r)] \supset (p \supset r)$? It is pretty clear that none of these will do. Perhaps the best suggestion is Kant's as amended by H. W. G. Joseph: "Whatever satisfies the condition of a rule falls under the rule." But what does "rule" stand for? The major premise is sometimes a statement of necessary connection between characters, sometimes a statement of class inclusion, sometimes even a statement about a single individual. One could not understand the full meaning of "rule" unless one grasped it as involving these alternative possibilities. Suppose that for the sake of definiteness we confine ourselves to the first only, and refuse to recognize as Barbara any argument in which M-P is not necessary. We should still not have reached the sheer identity we are looking for. For necessity itself is not quite the same as one passes from one subject matter to another. Is it the same, for example, in the following? All triangles inscribed in semicircles are right-angled; all intense pain is intrinsically evil; in a series of colors arranged in order of likeness, orange will fall between red and yellow. Each of these seems to me a necessary proposition. But I cannot think that the necessity which links their terms is an isolable filament, precisely the same in each and unaffected by the characters of the terms it unites. If this is correct, Barbara itself is no bare identity.

The answer, then, to the criticism that my view of internality would make an end to logic and science seems to me clear enough. Far from condemning logical analysis, I hold that it is the only way in which understanding can be achieved. It is only by isolating characters in thought and trying to see how they are related to others that we could make any headway in this task; and to isolate a character is to treat it as an abstract universal preserving its identity through diverse contexts. But we must also recognize the fact that when we try thus to isolate it, we find it resisting us in varying degrees. Some identities, like the structure of Barbara, are affected relatively little by their diversities of embodiment, and no doubt for practical purposes it is better to regard them as abstract identical universals and have done with it. In others, like "organism," the extraction of an invariant kernel is less practicable; while in still others, like "middle C," if we were to strip the concept of its relations, we should have nothing recognizable left. Would my critics deny all this? I can hardly suppose they would deny that differences in degree of relevance do exist. What they would presumably maintain is that in some cases we get mere and pure conjunction, in which there is no degree of relevance whatever. I understand this position, and realize that it is more generally accepted than my own. But it involves a more sweeping negation than seems to me justified by present knowledge.

Is Irrelevance Ever Total? Francis V. Raab, however, is ready to cite actual cases of this thorough irrelevance. He takes propositions rather than terms as his units. "Would the proposition 'orange is brighter than red,'" he asks, "logically entail a proposition in physics?" This is the sort of definite challenge that I like. Let us ask, then, what precisely it is that this proposition asserts. It may be asserting about either of two things, about our actual sense data, or about the two colors as concepts or universals. Consider the first. What is asserted is that our sense data of orange are in fact brighter than those of red. Now will Raab agree to the following statements: first, that a proposition A is relevant to another, B, if B's denial entails A's falsity; second, that we have the sense data of orange and red only when our brains are in a certain state; third, that our brains are in that state only when they are stimulated by the impingement on nerve-ends of light waves of a certain form and frequency, or by some equivalent cause? If we are together so far, let us now suppose it denied that such stimulation ever occurs. This is a proposition in physics. If it is true, should we have any right to assert that the colors and brightness would still be what they are? I think not. The proposition in physics *is* therefore relevant to the proposition about the colors.

It might be replied that to deny a cause is to deny an antecedent, not a consequent. The answer is, first, that I have supposed the conditions to be "necessary" ones, but second that in any case an antecedent need not be irrelevant, even though its denial will not yield a conclusion. It may be further replied that the entailment here is causal, not logical. Again the answer is twofold. First, on my view causality involves logical necessity. Second, even in ordinary scientific language entailment is involved in reasoning of this sort. The proposition that one kind of sense datum is produced by one kind of cerebral change has never been adequately verified, but it logically follows from the more general proposition that *every* psychical event may be correlated with some kind or other of cerebral change; and this latter proposition, though only an induction of high generality not known to be necessary, is a law of crucial importance to science. And the falsity of an assertion as to the relation of sense data and brain states, assuming that assertion to be well attested, would reflect itself back by a simple logical process on this great generalization itself. Neither physics nor psychophysics would be the same.

But suppose Raab's proposition is read in its second sense. It is then not a statement about sense data, but a statement that one of two colors, taken in abstraction from their occurrence in experience or nature, and considered simply as characters, is self-evidently brighter than the other. How could this statement have any possible connection with physics? It is perhaps fair to point out that if this *is* the meaning, the question is unintentionally begged. To take something in abstraction is to take it out of relation, and one cannot prove that it is unrelated by stipulating this unrelatedness at the outset. When the question at issue is whether the truth of this proposition is bound up with truths about nature, one can hardly begin by explicitly cutting its connections with nature, though this procedure is often resorted to in all innocence by critics of internal relations. But I do not propose to press this because there are other ways of reaching our end. As it appears in actual thought, the proposition expresses an insight and indeed a necessary insight, between the degrees of brightness of two colors. The assertion is made on the warrant of a self-evidencing ideal inspection. Suppose we denied it; what should we be committed to? I am concerned now with implications not about nature, but about our knowledge of nature. Would not the denial of such an insight commit us to a denial of all insights possessing a similar warrant? There are numberless judgments in physics in which the comparative intensities of heat, light, loudness, and hardness rest on judgments of this same kind, and to question them in one case would require us in consistency to question them all along the line. The epistemological implications of a given statement are as necessary as its ontological ones; and if so, it is plain that the denial of our initial judgment would jeopardize many of the judgments actually made in physics.

III. THE RELATION OF
THOUGHT TO ITS OBJECT

Thought in its essence is an attempt to attain, in the sense of achieving identity with, a special end of its own. The relation between idea and object must be conceived teleologically, as the relation of that which is partially realized to the same thing more fully realized. When we say that an idea is *of* an object, we are saying that the idea is a purpose which the object alone would fulfil, that it is a potentiality which this object alone would actualize, a content informed by an impulse to become this object.[24]

Peter A. Bertocci: The essence of Blanshard's critique of epistemological dualism is that unless idea is identical with object known, skepticism must result. Dualism places a gaping chasm *horizontally* between the mind and the object known, and this should logically undermine

---

[24] Blanshard, *The Nature of Thought,* I, 473.

epistemic confidence. But what occurs in his theory is that a *horizontal* gap is replaced by a *longitudinal* gap, the gap now being between the partial realization of potentiality and its fruition in reality. If the existence of a gap between the idea and the known involves skepticism, what difference does it make whether the gap is horizontal or longitudinal? If the knowledge we have is a fragmentary realization of the full object, on what grounds can we have confidence that the whole is continuous with the fragment or that "for us every advance brings us closer to it"?

Moreover, Blanshard proceeds to eliminate the temporal connotation which such terms as "purpose" and "fulfillment" ordinarily carry, and substitutes for real growth in the knowing process the uncovering of logical relations already "there" in the thinker's mind. There results a dissociation of rational process from conative activity. But does not this idea play fast and loose with the conative factors in knowledge? Must not the destiny of the idea take account of the activity of the knower in such a way that his knowing process consists neither in simply laying bare what is already there nor in constituting what is there?

G. Watts Cunningham: In his attempt to establish the doctrine of ontological monism, Blanshard rests his case primarily on the contention that the ultimate end of thought is precisely such an all-inclusive system as the doctrine describes. But does not his conception of the relation between idea and object seem to warrant this conclusion only because it is open to two interpretations, one of which is tenable but does not support the conclusion, the other of which supports the conclusion but is not sound? On the first interpretation, the structure of the object is logically prior to the "actualization" of the idea. But this is no warrant for asserting that the object must be an all-inclusive system. If the object happens to be that sort of system, then in the end only that sort of system will satisfy the demand for intelligibility; if it happens not to be that sort of system, there is no reason to conclude that it is unintelligible. But Blanshard often seems to interpret the relation between idea and object as one between "thought as such" and an "ideal object"; and the weight of his argument is given by such reference to the "ideal object." On the first interpretation "thought as such" is mere verbiage. Is it not a flat self-contradiction to determine important ontological features of "the immanent end of thought" merely by appealing to thought's "satisfaction" before the eventuality of its "actualization"?

A. C. Ewing: According to Blanshard, we *mean* A when our idea is purposively directed toward identity with A, and we *know* A insofar as this purpose is fulfilled. However, if we had attained this identity with A, but were not in the least conscious that we had attained it, would it be knowledge? And, if it would not be, must not Blanshard add the adjective "known" to "identity" in the definition of knowledge —and thus be guilty of a vicious circle?

James Collins: Has not Blanshard failed to distinguish clearly between truth and wisdom, between accurate knowledge and exhaustive knowledge? The inadequacy of the counterpart theory of the relation between thought and reality need not lead to acceptance of the total-merger theory. Granted that the drive of the human intellect is to become the other and to assimilate the real, it may do this in such a way that the irreducible otherness and existential integrity of the thing known are respected. The truths and knowledges of human cognition are regulated minimally by the mind's intentional conformity with experienced reality. The ideal of wisdom or the total unity of ordered knowledge functions as a maximal limit and goal.

Theodore M. Greene: In Blanshard's account of the relation of the idea to its object, he is careful to preserve the distinction between thought and things while insisting on their connection, and he thinks this is possible only by regarding the relation as that of something partially realized to the same thing fully realized. But does not this only apparently serve to avoid the "confounding of thought with reality" because of the ambiguity of "realize," meaning, on the one hand, "apprehension of" and, on the other hand, "identification with"? Moreover, if the end is already in some sense realized, what account can Blanshard give of the connection between reason and the creative imagination?

Blanshard: The foregoing criticisms of my view of the relation of thought to its object are nonetheless searching because offered by writers with some sympathy for my position. I was driven to this view not by its initial plausibility, but by the failure of its alternatives. If you say with realists that what we immediately apprehend is the object as it is in nature, you run into the old and insuperable difficulties about error. If, with dualists, you take the representative view, you never *know* at all, for you can never check the correspondence of idea and object. Our knowledge of nature seems to require that the object itself be present in experience, not merely some surrogate for it, and yet that the object should fall beyond thought, as something to which this must conform. It seemed to me that the notion of thought as the partial realization of its object supplied what was needed. To use Josiah Royce's terms, the internal meaning of the idea was its content as actually apprehended; the external meaning was that to which this content must conform if knowledge were to be complete. The revision of the internal meaning into conformity with the external meaning I conceived as progress toward a rational system, the movement of thought toward a whole at once coherent and all-embracing.

THE INTELLIGIBILITY OF THE WORLD A POSTULATE, NOT A CONCLUSION. Peter A. Bertocci, James Collins, and G. Watts Cunningham all feel that at this point I leap too readily to the rainbow's end. How do I know, asks Bertocci, that the progress of my thought, or of the race's thought, must move in the direction prescribed? How can I be sure in advance that if reflection were pressed to the limit, it would arrive at an intelligible system rather than at some blank wall?

I cannot. I do not profess to know this or to be able to prove it. If there is any way of demonstrating that the world is intelligible, I wish someone would point it out. It may be, for all we know, that the pilgrimage of thought will end in just such an ignominious collision with a blank wall, or if not, that our conception of the ideal will itself profoundly alter as we go forward. The position of the intelligible whole in my own groping thought about it is not that of a demonstrated conclusion, but that of a postulate, a postulate which, nevertheless, is the natural one for the philosopher to accept. For implicit in all his thinking from the very first appearance of judgment is the attempt to find connections; to find these is what understanding essentially is; and thought as the attempt to understand would reach its goal only if this demand for interconnection were carried through to the end.

My critics remind me that to assume on the strength of an ideal that nature must be so obliging as to give us what we ask is wishful thinking. So it would be if I used the "must." But I do not. What I do say is that if you launch yourself on the task of understanding, the right procedure is to assume your task to be possible until you have reason to think it impossible, not to assume defeat at the outset. Again, I agree with Bertocci that the course of intellectual advance may take turns now unpredictable which may affect our notion of the end itself. But we cannot foresee what those turns will be. The sensible way of advance is to continue while we may in the path that has meant progress in the past, the path of what Bosanquet used to call increasing logical stability. What he meant by this, of course, was more coherence with more inclusiveness.

Collins draws an interesting distinction between truth and wisdom, and thinks I confound them. Knowledge may be accurate without being exhaustive; it may achieve truth about a point of detail without grasping all its connections. I admit that such knowledge is possible; indeed most of our knowledge is of this kind. But I should hold that the two characters condition each other, that a knowledge which is not complete is not completely accurate. It may be said that a man may have a perfectly accurate knowledge of the relation of two species of beetle even though he knows nothing about the place of beetles in the animal kingdom. I cannot agree. His more minute conceptions will be affected inevitably by his wider ones. Here we stumble again into the thorny thicket of internal relations; but I will not go into that further, since Collins can no doubt conjecture the path I should take.

DOES THOUGHT AIM AT ABSORPTION IN ITS OBJECT? A. C. Ewing and Theodore M. Greene, as well as James Collins, think me mistaken in placing the goal of thought in identification with its object. Suppose we are trying to know A; "If we had attained this identity with A, but were not in the least conscious that we had attained it, . . . would it be knowledge?" Ewing asks. Well, I still incline to think that our aim in thought is not simply to stand outside the object and direct a beam of attention on it, but to embrace it in our experience. We do not properly know a shade of scarlet until the shade itself is among our sense data; we cannot fully know Romeo's feeling for Juliet without feeling it ourselves. But if we did achieve a feeling exactly Romeo's in quality, would that in itself be a knowing of his passion? Clearly not. Romeo's passion is not knowledge, and neither is its repetition in ourselves. The identity that is the goal of knowledge is not the mere experience of something, but the experience of it in all its relations; and such knowing of Romeo's passion is, as Hegel intimated, a richer experience than Romeo's own, which is relatively an abstraction. If we ask, regarding such knowledge, whether we might achieve it without awareness that we were doing so, I must answer No. A mind that experienced Euclid's system as a whole would *ipso facto* be knowing it; the apprehension of his theorems in connection is what we *mean* by knowing them; and so again here. The question, then, whether it would be knowledge if we achieved identification with the object without knowing it, could hardly arise. We are brought here to the verge of a difficulty that has troubled mystically minded rationalists from Plotinus through Spinoza to Bradley, whether the merging of thought with its object would not mean the disappearance of thought as such. My own answer, for what it is worth, would be: If thought means idea, in the sense of a reference to something beyond and as yet unattained, it would by definition disappear when there was no beyond to refer to; if it means the experience or apprehension of characters in relation, I see no reason why merger should mean extinction.

IV. THE SELF AND INDIVIDUALITY

So long as one remains within a limited field of relations one is always confronted with a theoretic possibility (and nothing more is required) that this complex should be repeated, and just so long as one is tarrying within the land of universals. If this domain is to be escaped, it can only be by carrying the widening circles of relations on all their planes to completeness. When that completeness has been achieved, then, and only then, will one have attained particularity. But surely this conclusion is disastrous for those who believe in particulars in the ordinary sense. For all that we commonly call particulars, pots and pans, mountains and rivers, are now seen to be universals. The only true particular is the absolute.[25]

[25] Blanshard, *The Nature of Thought,* I, 639.

Theodore M. Greene: The more closely thought is identified with its object, the more inevitable will be the final fusion of the individual with reality as a whole. Given Blanshard's view that reality is an all-inclusive system, together with his view that the terms of this system are exhausted in their relations to other terms, what becomes of the individual, and of his autonomy and value?

James Collins: In Blanshard's view, what happens to the dependence of thinking upon individual finite existents? A forecast is made that the finite individual will dissolve and that the concrete reality of complete determination will be found only within the total complexus of relations. But this conclusion cannot be reached with the help of the doctrine of the internality of all relations. For this doctrine is the consequence of an attempt to define the individual entirely apart from a consideration of existence as the source of its unity and intelligibility. The finite individual as an existent is lost from sight, and its mental operations are transformed into logically determinate instances of the general process of thought as such. But is not the latter an abstraction made from observation of the workings of finite, individual minds? And by converting the general logic of systematic thinking into an ontological entity, are not the experiential point of departure and the real dependence of thinking upon the finite existent left in the shadows?

Peter A. Bertocci: In Blanshard's conception of mind and its "dimensions," he treats mind as a process in which there is a "co-working of dispositions," some of them unconscious, which are "factors in a purposive whole," and in which there is "co-operation between the conscious and non-conscious sides of our nature." It may be that we are misled by the metaphysical and dramatic forms of expression. But is the mental life in danger of losing the metaphysical unity which justifies the use of the singular term "mind"? If conscious and unconscious factors co-operate, what is the metaphysical unity which keeps them together, and how shall it be described? Unless there be such can we have a theory of mind "at the start" from which advance is possible?

Blanshard: Theodore M. Greene, James Collins, and Peter A. Bertocci suggest, though on differing grounds, that my way of thinking endangers the self. Greene points out that if terms are dissolved away into their relations, the self must share this fate. Collins protests that to resolve the individual into universals is to neglect the all-important fact of his existence. Bertocci asks what it is, in my theory, that unifies the thoughts and impulses of an individual into a single mind. These are pointed questions. Let me try to indicate my lines of answer.

I agree with Greene that it will not do to resolve terms away into their relations. If such a process is fatal to the terms, which then disappear into the relations, it is equally fatal to the relations, which then have nothing to relate. One may take the high line of Bradley that the whole scheme of terms and relations is a makeshift, but this position has been effectively discredited by Cook Wilson, J. M. E. McTaggart, and C. D. Broad. We cannot get on without terms and relations. But how can a term have a nature at all if everything in it depends on its relations? How can we say at one and the same time that it depends on its relations for being what is, and also that it has a nature of its own which may have these relations or may not have them? If we say the latter, we seem to be saying that in the term there is a solid nucleus of unchanging character which is beyond the influence of its relations.

Any such doctrine of a hard core for the term would take us back to a position which we have already abandoned on the ground that, however easy and inviting, it is not strictly true. A tone appears in a melody, and we say that the melody is made up of such tones, each of which would be what it is apart from the melody. But *is* the tone, as we hear it in the melody, wholly unaffected by its position there? I do not think so. And if it is not, can we distinguish within the tone a nuclear unchanging essence which is identical within the melody and outside it? Again I do not think so. We are in the odd position of having to say that the tone is both different and the same, different because the context in which it is heard affects it, the same because the designation "B flat" does obviously apply to both. To be sure, we never have this identity in the purity of absolute relationlessness. But it is not therefore nothing at all. We may approach it asymptotically by stripping it of special contexts, but when we are asked to single out by thought or ear the hard unchanging datum, we cannot do it. There is identity, but none that is sharply isolable. A term must have some character of its own, for to say that it is *constituted* by its relations is absurd. But neither is it wholly independent of them. It is independent in degree.

All this holds, I think, of the self. Greene would surely agree that "self" is not a sharply fixed term; indeed, it would be hard to think of anything that is more dependent on relations. Strip from Greene's own engaging self all his relations to Amherst, Princeton, and Yale, all his relations to India, Meiklejohn, and Tillich, all his contemplations of creeds, cosmologies, and works of art, and how much of the Greene we know would be left? I do not say "nothing at all," for something was clearly there, and an identical something, to undergo these experiences and persist through these changing environments. But the attempt to elicit and define it would be unprofitable, not only because the abstract identity that is sought for would never be found, but also because, if it were found, no one in his right mind would call it Greene. I must admit that on my view the only self worth having is so bound up with its relations as to be inconceivable and unimaginable without them. But how should that destroy the self or, rightly seen, reduce its significance?

WHAT DOES "EXISTENCE" MEAN? James Collins thinks that to conceive an individual as a synthesis of characters, even an infinity of them, is to leave out the most important component of all, namely, existence. He would have the support here of many philosophers whom I respect. But I can only say that when these philosophers speak about existence, I have the greatest difficulty in knowing what they mean. A pebble, they say, is not constituted by its qualities or by these plus their relations in time and space; for if the pebble is to be a real one, these qualities and relations must also exist. When one asks what "existence" means, the answer is that this is an illegitimate question, for existence is not a *what* at all; characters may have it, but it is not itself a character. It is that which distinguishes existent from nonexistent whats, the dollars in Kant's pocket from those in his fancy, and this is not another attribute; it is utterly without character, though we can still think of it with clearness and certainty.

My difficulty remains. If all the characters and relations of a thing were exhausted, I cannot see that anything would be left. Take the simplest possible example. G. E. Moore has pointed out that "this sense datum exists" is a meaningful statement, since it is conceivable that the datum should not have existed, and the statement reminds us that in fact it does. Very well; what is it exactly that is thus asserted? Presumably that the datum occurs at a certain point in a sequence of experiences; the existence of a sense datum requires its occurrence in time, though not necessarily in space. Does not its existence reduce to its having these relations to other events in time? No, the answer may come, for the event must occur in real or existing time, as opposed to imaginary time, and these two orders themselves can be distinguished only through the intuition that they exist or do not exist. But this, I think, is an error. When we distinguish a nonexistent order from a real one, the occurrences in dream, for example, from those of waking, surely it is not through the presence in one of them of an ineffable noncharacter called existence, but by their comparative vividness, steadiness, and coherence. If we dreamed for half the day, and remained awake the other half, the experiences of dream being exactly as vivid, steady, and coherent as those of waking life, which would be the "existent" objects and events, and which the nonexistent ones? I submit that there would be no difference at all.

It is idle to search beneath the surface of things for an indescribable something called existence, which is neither a quality nor a relation nor any complex of these. The existentialist pursuit of this will-o'-the-wisp has been an unprofitable quest; it has developed a baffling mysticism whose object is without content, and its dark pronouncements about existence preceding essence leave its critics curiously helpless, since nothing definite enough for a clear refutation is being said. And what would be the gain, from the philosophic point of view, if the unfindable were somehow found? One is tempted to quote William James' sardonic advice to the troubled philosopher to seize firmly on the unintelligible and make it the key to everything else. At any rate, it seems to me that if existence, in this sense—assuming it is a sense—were to vanish from the universe tomorrow, leaving all the qualities and relations of things what they are, we should never miss it. Individuals, human and other, consist for me exclusively of characters in relation. It is perhaps worth noting that Bertrand Russell, after his long history of reflection on the matter, seems to have come round to this view in his *Inquiry into Meaning and Truth*.

THE UNITY OF THE SELF. Peter A. Bertocci raises the question what holds the self together in its unique and familiar unity if it is really only a congeries of characters or qualities. Certainly no man seems to himself to be such a collection. His experiences at any moment make a curiously continuous whole; his combination of interests is that of no one else; his impulses, dispositions, and acquired capital of knowledge are organized about ends that are uniquely his own. How could a set of vagrant characters ever come together on their own motion and fuse themselves into the intimate, persisting, evolving unity that he calls his self?

The question perhaps needs to be further specified; it may refer to different kinds of unity exhibited by the self. Unity in the sense of the presence of diverse elements in one field of consciousness presents a different problem from the unity of the immanent end which governs the growth of the mind. As for unity of the first kind: each of us begins his life with a continuum of feeling and sensation in which there are differences of quality, but nothing is set off explicitly from anything else. If it is asked why we start with these feelings and sensations rather than others, the answer seems to lie in physiology; our bodies are equipped with sensory nerves such that, on stimulation, they give rise to just these impressions. If it is then asked why the impressions unite into a single field of consciousness, I suppose that the answer lies again in our brains. The brain centers that condition our consciousness are not unconnected islands, but intimately related parts of a single organism, and it is presumably for this reason that my feelings and sensations fuse into a continuum exclusive of yours. Bertocci might protest that no physiological explanation of consciousness is truly intelligible, and here I should agree. But if the question, Why? about the original contents of our minds or their peculiar unity is a demand for causal explanation, the only answer seems to lie in considerations of this kind.

Granting, however, that the materials of consciousness arise in this way, what is it that determines their organization into the particular kind of whole that ultimately emerges? In the mind of a Plato or a Hegel—to take an extreme for clearness' sake—the materials supplied it do not lie there in their original litter, but are organized more and more firmly into a whole; there is a "pressure" in and through consciousness toward a unity that is at once broader and better articulated. This inner drive is not peculiar to exceptional intellects. It is present in a degree in all of us, and compliance with it gives the meaning of intellectual growth. Now why is it that intellectual growth—to take this only—should have this immanent end rather than some quite different one? If this is Bertocci's question, it is both profound and not fully answerable. It is a question over which naturalism, in the sense of a purely scientific philosophy, goes on the rocks, though it seems to be difficult for some psychologists even to see that there is a problem. Why this demand for system, for logical or intelligible order, for the bringing of our experience into a rationally interconnected whole? Naturalists have commonly accepted a pragmatic explanation to the effect that logical thought gave biological advantage. So it did. But the drive of reason does not stop there; it presses its campaign far beyond the point at which utility ceases, in spite of the protests of James and Dewey. Such protests against the self-fulfillment of the intellect are peculiarly futile, for they are attempts to repress nature herself. But if you ask why the drive for understanding should have adopted logical unity or system as its end, rather than one of the innumerable forms of chaos, I do not think that any satisfactory answer can be given. My own answer, such as it is, is that in a genuine teleology the end governs the process of its own realization and that the intelligible order which is the real world is at work in our several minds, carrying them toward that understanding which would lie in identification with itself. But that is a long story.

Interrogation of

Paul Weiss

Conducted by Ellen S. Haring

Paul Weiss, philosopher, educator, writer, is Professor of
Philosophy at Yale University. Born in New York City in
1901, he was educated at the College of the City of New York
and Harvard University. He has taught at Harvard, Radcliffe, Bryn Mawr, and Yale. Weiss has held visiting profes-
sorships and lectureships at the Hebrew University, Aspen
Institute, the University of Denver, Indiana University, and
Grinnell College. The latter awarded him the L.H.D. in
1960. He is the founder of the Metaphysical Society of
America (and past president), the Philosophy Education
Society, and the *Review of Metaphysics* (and editor). He
is co-editor with Charles Hartshorne of the *Collected Papers*
of Charles S. Peirce. Member of the advisory board of the
Philosophy of Science and of the editorial boards of *Science
of Culture* and *Judaism*. Weiss is the author of numerous
publications, including *Nature of Systems, Reality, Nature
and Man, Man's Freedom, Modes of Being, Our Public Life,
World of Art*, and *Nine Basic Arts*.

I. METHOD

Weiss: Our initial outlook and language are, for the most part, conventional and humdrum. We attend primarily to what is evident to the senses; we are likely to believe and affirm only what is acceptable to practical, reasonable, mature members of our society. But intertwined with what we daily accept are errors and superstitions. These we must overcome if we are to know what in our ordinary life is true and objective. Within the familiar world are also to be referents, such as prayers, monuments, testimonies, sacraments, and commitments, directing us to an area outside the realm of common sense. If we are to encompass all that is real, we must look to where these referents point.

Philosophy begins with an awareness of the double dubiety of common sense. The philosopher sees that the ordinary world is routinized and incomplete. A desire to understand all being, and to grasp the principles of knowledge which make such understanding possible, leads the philosopher to try not only to focus on those familiar objects that are reliable and objective, but also to take adequate account of those which refer to a realm beyond.

The veridical elements in the common-sense world can be determined by attending to the distinctive guises which familiar items achieve when they are perceived, enjoyed, produced, and so on—particularly if these aspects are severally refined and systematized, and then synthesized. The outcome should be a purged, reconstituted version of what was initially encountered and unreflectively experienced. Take my watch as an example. At times I shake it to make it go, and even knock it against a table in the hope—occasionally justified—that it will run for a while. I habitually pace my activities in the light of the rate at which its hands move across its face. In a common-sense fashion, I know my watch. The watchmaker, the salesman, the chemist deal

261

with it in other and specialized ways. Their understanding is more precise than mine, but only of facets of the watch. To make their knowledge philosophically my own, I must note what each reports, unify my findings and recognize the result to be the nucleal truth of what I roughly grasped in daily life. The language appropriate to no one of their reports will do justice to that nucleal truth. To express it, I have no alternative except to use the language of common sense in a refined, generalized, reconstituted form.

No philosopher is concerned only with familiar objects. Even while I look at my watch, I am dimly aware of an indefinite area environing it and me. If I remember that my watch was a present from my brother on his return from the war, or if I follow the lead of my anxieties, hopes, awe, or wonder, I look beyond the common-sense world. I then attend to realities which differ in kind and in role from those with which I am daily acquainted, and from their derivates. One who takes the entire cosmos for his province—as I think the philosopher by definition must—cannot avoid inquiring about an area outside the commonsensical. He knows it is the focus of a number of his attitudes. Conceivably, of course, it may be little more than his own product, a projection of himself. This means, however, not that there is no realm beyond the common-sense one, but only that the further realm is rooted in the recesses of man—thus pointing up the need for philosophers to show why and how it originates there rather than in the familiar world. To treat properly the intent and discoveries of science, ethics, religion, and the arts—especially the meaning of tragedy and comedy—the philosopher must recognize that there is more to reality than can be distilled out of what we know as practical, conventionalized, common-sense men.

In the attempt to provide an account having maximum plausibility, intelligibility, and explanatory power, the philosopher tentatively adopts various hypotheses and categories which seem to bring order and clarity to some one area. He then proceeds to modify and generalize his initial assumptions until they become equally appropriate to whatever else is discerned—a procedure which requires constant intellectual experimentation, a search for exceptions, radical and relentless self-criticism, and a testing by hard cases. The result is then expressed in a discourse which refines and generalizes the purged common-sense language inside a system which offers reasons, illustrations, and arguments for all of its major theses.

Robert S. Cohen: What is your philosophic method?

I am chiefly concerned with two related issues, that of the attainment of conviction (i.e., how do you envision the grounds of your belief, and how do you think your reader can come to agree with you), and that of the mode and propriety of philosophical speculation via analogy and metaphor.

As to the attainment of conviction, I am frequently disturbed by your failure to argue. You say, for example, "A man has properties and behaviors not explicable in terms of what he [has] assimilated or contains,"[1] While this may be plausible at times, it has nevertheless to be demonstrated. Could not an adequate theory of properties of the parts explain the properties of the whole? At the least, you should show that this is impossible, and is so despite much evidence to the contrary.

What seem like gross anthropomorphisms are scattered throughout your writings. You attribute choices, qualities, and abilities of desire, processes of evaluation, etc., to all beings, and not to humans alone. Is the universe to be construed in terms of the human self? When you say that iron upon rusting changes its "concern,"[2] are you speaking metaphorically, or literally, or in some other way? What is the explanatory force of your remark? How can your claim be verified?

Weiss: No discipline has the right to dictate to philosophy. Philosophy has its own methods, tests, topics, and mode of discourse. It uses metaphor, analogy, allusions, polemics, and criticism—occasionally even poetry and drama, dialogue and meditation—in the attempt to convey the range, interrelation, and depth of what there is and what can be known. The reader will come to agree with the author only if he reads the work in a critical yet sympathetic spirit; he must allow his imagination to be extended at the same time that he tests the work

[1] *Reality* (Princeton: Princeton University Press, 1938), p. 200.
[2] *Nature and Man* (New York: Holt, Rinehart and Winston, 1947), p. 73.

to see if it does order, clarify, and explain in neutral, objective terms what is only partially, or under limitation, dealt with by science, religion, history, art, and the like. The entire account must be sustained by illustration and argument, though not necessarily in detail.

The passage Robert S. Cohen cites is preceded and followed by argument and illustration. And what he calls "anthropomorphisms" are but vivid technical terms, on a par with such scientifically respectable expressions as "action," "relativity," "space," "light years," "ego," "the north pole," "geologic faults," and "heredity." Philosophic terms of course are not quantified, and are not used in predictions. This does not disqualify them, for they are not designed to do the work required of terms used in the sciences. They are not therefore improper; they ought to be illuminating. Nor does their use imply that the user thinks the universe is to be construed in terms of man. The assertion that all beings have a concern—like Spinoza's comments about the conatus —is to be tested by seeing if it provides a category in terms of which all primary activities can be understood in a way not otherwise possible.

V. C. Chappell: Does the metaphysician *describe* something? If so, what? How do his descriptions differ from those made by non-metaphysicians, particularly natural scientists (insofar as they describe)? Does the metaphysician *explain* something? If so, what and how? And how does his explanation differ from those made by nonmetaphysicians, particularly natural scientists (insofar as they explain)? Also, how are good or successful explanations to be distinguished from bad or unsuccessful explanations? In similar fashion I ask: Does the metaphysician *solve problems?* Does the metaphysician construct or create anything?

Weiss: The philosopher both explains and describes how primary realities, through their interplay and by specification, ground all others. He seeks to present a categorial, comprehensive, dialectically sustained account of knowledge and being. His descriptions, tests, criteria are— because of the scope of his inquiry, the ultimacy of the truth with which he is concerned, and the critical procedure which he employs— distinct from those used in other enterprises. If "description" and "explanation" are proper characterizations of what nonphilosophers do, then it must be said that the philosopher neither explains nor describes, but explicates, articulates, categorizes, and systematizes.

A philosophic account is good to the degree that it is (1) comprehensive, (2) coherent, (3) unifying, (4) unbiased, and (5) makes provision for the occurrence of pluralities differing from each other in degree and in kind. It attends to discontinuities, paradoxes, apparent contradictions, unintelligibles, and the like, creating new categories and taking new perspectives in the attempt to achieve a single, all-encompassing whole. Its primary agency for moving from one position to another is dialectic, the logic by which one moves to what would complete a being, a thought, or a domain.

The philosopher is alert to problems which beset thinkers of the past, and to those which his own approach produces. He is not content until arbitrary discontinuities and oppositions, paradoxes and insolubilia are overcome, their roots exposed, and their meaning clarified. His is no subjective presentation, no statement of opinion, but an adventure at formulating an impersonal, cosmic story. And he claims to make the very same kind of advance on his predecessors as a Descartes claimed to make on a Ptolemy, a Newton on a Descartes, a Thomas on an Augustine, a Pollock on a Benton.

Ellen S. Haring: What is your defense of your epistemological realism, especially against the objections raised by Robert S. Cohen, Joseph Owens, Richard M. Rorty, Peter J. Caws, and Richard I. Aaron in the following questions (pp. 265–268)?

Robert S. Cohen: You say, "We are, in short, phenomenalists who are aware that there is a truth beyond phenomenalism, making it possible."[3] This promises a dialectical proof at least, but the discussion which ensues (and all your metaphysic is a footnote to this sentence) utilizes description of the behavior of either common-sense or speculative thinkers in place of a critical explanation of such behavior. We know that men are more than phenomenalists. What we want to know from the philosopher is why they are justified in so believing.

[3] *Reality,* p. 142.

Weiss: Phenomenalism takes phenomena to exhaust reality. This means it has no place for substances, and therefore cannot acknowledge potentialities. It has no room for relevant and exterior ideals, active selves or effective minds. It cannot explain self-identity, action, making, thinking, power, natural or human laws, secular or religious symbols, scientific or philosophic inquiry. It is therefore, at best, incomplete. I have tried over the years to forge a positive systematic account in which the items necessarily skipped over by a phenomenalism, as well as the phenomena on which it focuses, are interrelated in an intelligible, self-sustaining totality. It is not the task of the philosopher to create a universe, no matter how neat and inviting, but to understand what we experience and what this entails.

Joseph Owens, C.Ss.R.: How can you, without a thoroughgoing doctrine of intentionality, maintain your stand[4] that the existence of a thing in someone's cognition is a genuine existence for that thing?

Weiss: Cognition is one way in which man expresses his being, a being interrelated with other beings. There is no problem therefore as to how a mind can get to know an external world; the problem is how one can get that world into better focus, how one can understand it better than one does in unreflecting experience, and have it in a more useful form than one can in a mere encounter. In short, the epistemology in *Reality,* and in Chapter 1 of *Modes of Being,* offers a thoroughgoing "intentionality" in the sense, I think, that is intended by Father Owens. I have not used the term, partly because it is associated with certain philosophic views—those of Thomas Aquinas, Franz Brentano and Edmund Husserl—with which I am only partly in agreement.

Richard M. Rorty: Many criticisms of *Modes of Being,* like most criticisms of Hegel, stem from the conviction that—in a *cognitive* approach to being, though perhaps not in other approaches—all perspectives taken together add up to no perspective at all. The notion is, in other words, that to take both sides of every polarity with equal seriousness is to abandon seriousness altogether. You admit that cognition is perspectival and that philosophy is cognitive. In Chapter 11 of

[4] *Modes of Being* (Carbondale: Southern Illinois University Press, 1958), pp. 202–203.

Modes of Being you take up the burden of reconciling these admissions with the system's claim to neutrality among the modes of being. But the argument of this chapter turns on the enthymeme expressed by saying, "If the I could not grasp what Y [another mode of being than its own] encompassed of X [its own mode] . . . the I would not know what it was to know." [5] This is in point only if we take the first occurrence of "know" to mean "know adequately," and the second to mean "know another mode of being." But is not what is in question in this chapter precisely whether the I *does,* in this sense, know what it is to know?

Peter J. Caws: The "I" which occupies the mode X "knows himself therefore when and as he knows the import of the Y, i.e., [knows] what he himself is from the standpoint of Y," [6] But since his standpoint is irrevocably in X, he cannot know that Y *is* a standpoint, although he can imagine it to be so. Therefore may not all self-consciousness be illusory?

Weiss: I agree with Rorty that all perspectives taken together add up to no perspective at all. But this is not the same thing as to say that one ought not to deal with both sides of all polarities with equal seriousness. The great fault of modern philosophy is the insistence, by so many, on limited perspectives, and the denial of the rights of all other perspectives, with a consequent refusal to recognize realities which do not fit into the accepted partial schemes. One must make a start at some point and make use of criteria, methods, and tests which have not yet been subjected to thorough scrutiny. This ought not to be disturbing, provided that what was used in the beginning achieves justification in the end. In a philosophic system every part supports and is supported by every other, and the whole makes intelligible our common, intricate, interlaced, and multiple-faceted universe of knowledge and being.

I see no reason why I or anyone else should be persistently uncritical, biased, prejudiced, narrow. Every aspect of the universe, every mode of knowledge should be dealt with both critically and sympathetically.

[5] P. 527.
[6] *Modes of Being,* p. 527.

One of the things an adequate philosophy portrays is the fact that we know some truths and know that we know them. I know what it is to know when what I know is acknowledged as offering a position outside me. But this is only to say that when I know something, I know a being that is other than myself, though related to me, and that it occupies a position from which I can be approached.

If I say, "This is a pencil," I mean not merely that I think it is a pencil, or that it looks like a pencil to me, but that it can be known to be a pencil by others. And then someone else can take the pencil as a way of referring to me. (If I know that other as one who knows me, I know, in knowing him, that I am known.) The pencil as known by me not only stands over against me, but is related to me. It is a Y which is related to an aspect of me: I, in knowing it from position X, know it as that which faces a facet of me. Consequently, in knowing it, I know something of myself.

Perhaps the question is: Do we have any knowledge at all? But that question means that you know me, and think you can know the answer I will give. You believe that I can answer; you believe that I can know you to be a man with a mind. In asking the question you offer an answer to it: you know me as one who can know you. When you read my answer you know me as one who knows you, just as, in writing the answer, I know you as one who can know me. You are an I who assumes the position X, knowing me, a Y, as one who knows what it is to be an I in the position of an X.

Richard I. Aaron: If the concrete is a "necessary component in all knowledge," [7] and if, too, the empiricist is correct in supposing that no precise and exact knowledge of the concrete is possible, is this not a source of skepticism in your philosophy?

Weiss: A knowledge is a "knowledge of." The being which is known is not identical with the knowledge of it. Nevertheless the knowledge tells us what the being is. Those who think a precise and satisfactory knowledge of the concrete is impossible seem to suppose that such knowledge requires duplication, a representation of the concrete. But knowledge is the concrete transposed, given a new role

[7] *Reality,* p. 178.

and rationale, as part of a mind or language. That knowledge, however, is inseparable from an adumbrative grasp of the concrete as it stands outside the knowledge. The concrete is thus not a component in a knowledge, but a component in a knowing in which knowledge functions as another component.

A. H. Johnson: What specifically do you mean by "God preserves Actualities"? [8]

You support your theory of a plurality of modes by reference to observation and dialectic.[9] Dialectic itself involves observation insofar as it "infers to what would complete the already known." [10] It would be enlightening to be informed as to the observational context within which your dialectic is operating when you reach conclusions such as this one about God.

Weiss: No one observes God preserving actualities. That he does preserve them [11] follows from the fact that he reproduces them,[12] without compromising the fact that they have an exteriority,[13] and a being of their own.[14]

Peter J. Caws: If all proofs of God are circular, and all ineffectual unless supported by other evidence, what do the proofs add to our understanding? And is what they add necessary to a knowledge of God?

Weiss: All proofs—not only proofs of God—in the end turn out to be circular. Proofs must always be backed by an encounter. This is one of the reasons we seek to verify what we have correctly deduced, often from impeccable premises.

Proofs are ways of anticipating the nature of things, the worth of various assertions, the value of alternative suppositions. We use them

[8] *Modes of Being,* p. 351.
[9] *Ibid.,* p. 18.
[10] *Ibid.,* p. 82.
[11] *Ibid.,* p. 351.
[12] *Ibid.,* p. 337.
[13] *Ibid.,* pp. 337–338.
[14] *Ibid.,* pp. 288–289.

to save time and energy, to remind, to communicate, to teach, and to persuade. The circularity which haunts all proof is a consequence of the fact that a proof instances all four modes of being.[15] The circularity is not a defect; it would be one only if it were possible to refer, act, know, or prove without presupposing the modes of being in the beginning, in the structure, in the outcome, and in the activity of moving from the beginning to the outcome.

Robert W. Browning: Do you acknowledge that the inferential process of going from "I have just written something" to "Something occurred" is not parallel to the process of proceeding from "It is wrong wantonly to kill a friend" to "It is absolutely wrong to reduce value"?

And what is your procedure in the latter case? In one line of argument from "It is wrong wantonly to kill a friend" to "It is absolutely wrong to reduce value," [16] you proceed by the progressive removal of irrelevantly restrictive factors. Do you bank upon intuition in seeing their irrelevance? Is the whole a piece of midwifery for eliciting the terminal general intuition?

Weiss: Both cases cited by Browning offer generalizations; in both, restrictive details are abstracted from. Those details are relevant for some purposes, but they are not relevant if our purpose is that of formulating highly general categorial expressions. To find out if a mistake was made in the course of a generalization, we should go through the process of generalizing, again and again, preferably from different starting points and over different routes. If we come out with the same result at all times, and if no one can find that a step has been skipped or a turning point has been missed, we have a result we cannot gainsay. I think it is not incorrect to say that an undeniable result of a process which begins with true premises is an inescapable truth. And I am claiming that the cited cases are instances of such a truth.

John Wild: Will you explain what you mean by "reflects" in "The system is an explication of what lies outside it, in the sense that it reflects this. . . ." [17]

[15] *Ibid.,* pp. 325–326.
[16] *Man's Freedom* (New Haven: Yale University Press, 1950), pp. 211 f.
[17] *Modes of Being,* p. 386.

Weiss: A system of philosophy offers an articulated, systematic account of a real world. The system is that world, but generalized, articulated, ordered, known, made part of a mind. It can therefore be said to reflect that world, to report it, to re-present it to us under the limitation which its conversion into concepts and discourse imposes.

Ellen S. Haring: Please explain your "negative approach" in chapters 6–9 of *Modes of Being,* particularly your claims that "the negations of the theses . . . are part of the system"[18] and "The contentions which go counter to a system must illustrate it."[19]

Ernan McMullin: It is reasonable that a philosopher should be asked to "account for" philosophic views that differ from his own in the sense of showing how they originate and where they appear defective. But why should he be asked to "find a place" for them in the literal sense of making these denials of his claims into "muted parts" of *his own* system? In what sense, other than a psychological one, must a positivist —for example—"find room for" the "reality" of the nonsense he takes metaphysics to be?[20]

Weiss: A philosophic system claims to be complete. No truth can in principle stand outside it. Since it is true that there are philosophies which reject the system, the system must make provision for them, showing how they are in principle possible. When positivists say that metaphysics is nonsense, the product of an incorrect use of language, they are unable to take account of the assertion by metaphysicians that positivism is mistaken. When metaphysicians say this, they are not speaking meaninglessly. The metaphysicians could conceivably be in error. But positivism, since it is unable to make provision for the occurrence and intelligibility of such errors, is obviously inadequate. Positivism could, of course, insist that no denial of it is possible, that every denial of it is sheer nonsense. That would dispose of all dissenters readily. To be sure, metaphysicians, like other men, say foolish things; sometimes they contradict themselves and perhaps occasionally speak ungrammatically. But no matter how fumbling their analysis and specu-

[18] P. 385.
[19] P. 381.
[20] *Modes of Being,* p. 379.

lation, no matter how peculiar their language or how odd their views, they have something basic to discuss, and what they say has some modicum of intelligibility and truth. If not, what fools Plato, Aristotle, Kant, and Hegel must be.

Accepting as fact that Plato, Aristotle, Kant, and Hegel are speaking at least as significantly as A. J. Ayer, Rudolf Carnap and Karl Popper, I find it desirable to understand what they say, and to recognize that there are truths which they express—even in those cases where they explicitly reject such a view as I have presented. I find that in their different ways they are all correctly asserting that the present system does not exhaust reality. So far as they reject the system, they stand outside it, offering testimony to the fact that there is such an outside. To be sure, I—and others also—stand outside the system. And we can say we stand outside the system, directly and positively asserting, for example, that the system is nothing but a system. The positivists stand outside the system, but admit this fact only indirectly and in the guise of negations of what the system affirms.

They who say, "God does not exist," "the Good is not possible," "man does not have a self," "there is no cosmic time," stand outside the system I have offered. Where can they be but in the universe? What else are they saying but that they are expressing something of the universe in which they are? Supposing that the system I have offered tells us what is the case, the truth in the denial of the system is to be found only by attending to what the denial expresses and not to what it explicitly says.

An adequate philosophic system must offer a place where it is affirmed that there are denials of the system and thus that there is something outside the system.[21] The negations, the countercontentions of the system are so many specializations of an isolated part of the entire system, held apart from that system on behalf of the world outside the system.

John Wild: Does this mean that no philosopher can really disagree with your system?

Weiss: On the contrary; it explains why others do disagree with me. It even encourages others to disagree. And it has led me to pursue the

[21] *Ibid,* p. 383.

negative route. In chapters 6–9 of *Modes of Being,* I have myself offered denials of every thesis in the system. Each one of those denials expresses in a distinctive way the fact that there is a reality outside the system. On behalf of that outside reality I showed that I too could stand outside with your system?

Manley H. Thompson, Jr.: I am asking for a conceivable negative instance to your claim that the contentions which go counter to your system must illustrate it. If no such instances are conceivable, then how can we conceive of your claim as possibly wrong?

Weiss: Everything illustrates the perfect system. Is *Modes of Being* such a system? I am fallible, confused, corrupt. I am sure I have made errors. Yet I cannot but regard *Modes,* for the time being, as substantially true and adequate. Every philosophic system is and must be presented as making the claim that it is comprehensive and sound. To claim less is to pretend that one has a knowledge of philosophic truths which one has refused to make evident. Will not every occurrence, every illusion, delusion, fiction confirm it, making it therefore too amorphous to be of value? Since some items illustrate only a fragment of it and others large stretches, since some offer vivid illustrations and others overlay the illustrations with minor details, the system is significantly testable. Look to the nucleal facts of life, knowledge, and action, and see if these are not clarified and explained.

A satisfactory philosophy does not deduce a universe; it understands it. It accounts for space, action, time, causality, production, self-identity, life, mind, perception, meaning, memory, inference, science, art, religion, philosophy, education, history, politics, obligation, choice, will, guilt, possibility, ideals, communities, rights, laws, energy, motion, rest, change, passage, the past, the future, sacraments, criticism, civilization, worship, privacy, universals, and the togetherness of all these. To have less is to have a philosophy which, because it leaves unexamined what might be embarrassing to what is accepted, may turn out to be erroneous or misconstrued.

Ellen S. Haring: CONCLUDING QUESTION ON METHOD. Although you answer your interrogators carefully and well, perhaps in the very nature of the case you cannot satisfy them. We are sympathetic;

but we still, I think, harbor doubts about your presuppositions and your aims. Possibly we seek reassurance or proof where none can be had. I wish nevertheless to review your stand and to point out the occasions for uncertainty.

You seem to say: (1) Knowing is, primitively at least, an inarticulate but not unconscious rapport with a circumambient other. To know is to have the other as at once other and yet not discrete from oneself. (2) In the ordinary course of events we learn to attend to the other, and thus to discriminate, admire, fear, classify, and predict various factors in the other. (In these procedures, we are not always consistent or correct, and we are not exhaustive.) Our condition is then one of being common-sense persons in a partially familiar world. Evidently some of us may also have cultivated particular bents and *métiers,* and so have obtained the limited but comparatively clear perspectives proper to scientists, artists, and so on. (3) The job of the philosopher is to articulate fully—to obtain an adequate abstract version of—the primitively known other. The specific steps toward this end involve facing and resolving questions which arise in common-sense and in more specialized dealings with the other, questions which pertain to this or that part of it and to our common-sense or specialized devices for treating those parts. The philosopher seeks to overcome the disconnectedness and the vague fringing-off-into-the-obscure which the world exhibits as long as we face it only as common-sense persons or as specialists. (4) The philosopher must recognize, and sometimes rectify, limited versions of the other; but he must also reconcile them, one with another; above all, he must *ground* them. In short, he must warrantedly conceive the other as intelligibly giving rise to all we encounter.

Point 1 in the just-presented series seems to be the core of your realism; it is also the reason why you are sure that every thinker has something basic to discuss and something not wholly nonsignificant to say. But this very point bothers a number of the interrogators, including Richard M. Rorty, Peter J. Caws and Robert S. Cohen. In answering them, you reject solipsism and phenomenalism. Your remarks seem to combine points 1 and 2, and, also, to imply that no sound philosophy may violate the realistic categories—things-acting, self-others, inside-outside—used by common-sense men. What makes common sense so privileged? Might it not be the case that your respect for what you take to be common-sense views is nothing more in the end than an arbitrary determination, or a matter of temperament, or a pragmatically justified way of making theories to shore up our daily existence?

Granting your first and second points, one does not find the others so difficult to accept, in general; but their detailed ramifications remain somewhat obscure. You speak of the kind of sense such a notion as "conatus" makes out of a range of phenomena. I think we know the experience of illumination and clarification to which you refer. But we are more mindful than you seem to be that one can feel illuminated without really being so. Moreover you say very little about the tests and criteria by which to discriminate insight from illusion. Finally you are sublimely rationalistic, moving forward in the assurance that there is an ultimate discoverable ground—or set of interlocking grounds—for all we encounter. This is all very well as a faith or a hypothesis, but how do you choose between one tolerably consistent systematic representation of the ground and another?

If, as you seem to suggest, your philosophizing is dialectic, then what I have said here comes down to a single question: Can your dialectic validate your trust in the availability of a real and independent other, your trust in its amenability to human conceptualization, and your trust in your own sense of how that conceptualization should be completed?

Weiss: CONCLUDING ANSWER ON METHOD. Philosophy is an adventure which sooner or later critically examines even the ground and method it assumes and uses.

Philosophy is a creative enterprise, seeking to understand, clarify, and to explain every aspect of being and knowledge. The systematic account I am offering is grounded in, and eventually justifies, an affirmative answer to your threefold question. More specifically: I start with the muddled, rough-hewn objects, the interpretations, expectations, rules, and language of daily life. Just what parts of it will be retained, and in what guise, is not known until the end. I know, though, that I have gone astray if in the end I cannot say that there are men and women, art, science, good and bad acts, motion, rest, change, space, time, and becoming. I know that I have given a final answer to one of my own questions—or to one from my interlocutors—when it is on a footing with the rest of the system, which presumably has been justified by interlocked argument and by experience. I come to the end of the systematic development of the entire account when I have progressed to the beginning and am able to justify what the system initially accepted. If as a matter of fact I find that I must give up some of the beliefs of common sense which I took for granted—for example, its assurance that what it is not forced to question is true or reliable—I am forced to go through the entire system a second time, modifying what was dependent on the initial unjustified assumption. The process is repeated again and again until every part is justified by the rest, and this without abandoning common sense or denying the existence of basic forms of reality and knowledge. When some other system is shown to live up to this complex criterion better than mine does, mine ought to be abandoned. I offer my philosophy as an account which is external to, and independent of, me. I speculated, constructed, created in the course of the formulation of my philosophic view, but this does not mean that the result may not be sound. I may be mistaken in many places, and perhaps even on the whole—but now I am talking about myself, confused, fallible, and ignorant man that I am, and not about the system which is now part of a public world, claiming to be true and adequate.

II. BEING

Andrew J. Reck: Are the modes of being abstractions from concrete beings, or themselves such beings?

This question is prompted by your tendency to describe the modes as though they had needs, purposes, and inclinations of their own.

Weiss: The modes of being are; they are not abstractions. But each is in a different way. God and Ideality are primarily unities and secondarily pluralities; Actuality and Existence are primarily pluralities and secondarily unities. All, however, are both one and many. And since each is incomplete, less than all reality—for the others have a reality which it lacks—it has an ontological need for them, and they have ontological needs for it. The universe is the interlocked totality of four distinct kinds of being, each of which is a unity and a plurality, referring to and being referred to by all the others.

Ellen S. Haring: Your account of the modes and their togetherness does not make clear what the ubiquitous predicate "being" means.

Weiss: "Being" refers indiscriminately to any one of the four modes of being. It has no object of its own. If we wish to be precise we should speak only of the being of Actuality, the being of Ideality, the being of Existence, and the being of God. Each has a distinctive way of being.

Richard T. DeGeorge: Would it not be possible and profitable to give an account of being *qua* being? Is being in your system such that one can speak of its having transcendental qualities? When one attributes being to two actualities, for example, a man and a rock, is the use of the word univocal, analogical, or what? What is its use when you attribute being to several modes?

Weiss: It is neither possible nor profitable to give an account of being *qua* being, for there is no such being. All the four modes of being are to be characterized in distinct terms. When we say that two modes of being have being, the term "being" is radically ambiguous, for it has a different meaning and import in each of the modes.

Ellen S. Haring: You seem to claim that being is the togetherness of the modes, but evidently all this means is that (1) the modes are all there is, and (2) everything is related to everything else. What is the being which each mode has? What is the "is" of all there is?

Weiss: One can use the term "being" to refer to the togetherness of all four modes. But it is to be noted that there is more than one form of togetherness and that there is no underived power in the togethernesses which enable them to oppose and interplay with the modes of being. If we wish to speak impartially of all the modes, we must find a neutral position. Philosophic knowledge is achieved from such a neutral position.

There is no "is" of all there is. But there is a "cognitional is," a neutral position assumed by a discursive mind. That "is" is a position from which the four modes can be understood as distinctive, irreducible, interrelated, and interactive. There are other positions which one can adopt, from which all four modes can also be justly dealt with. One such position involves not cognition but appreciation; another involves action; a third, idealization.

Andrew J. Reck: Is a being such as a man an instance of Actuality alone, or an instance of the togetherness of the modes? If the former, then how is it that a man may be as much involved in Ideality and in Existence—and perhaps even in God—as in Actuality? If the latter, then does it not follow that the togetherness of the modes is more concretely real than the modes that are together?

Weiss: A man is an actuality. But every mode is affected by, and refers to, every other. A man exhibits this fact more conspicuously than other actualities do. Neither he nor any other being is an instance of the togetherness of the modes. Such an instance would, as Reck rightly concludes, make the togetherness of the modes more real than the modes. However, there is a whole area of reality not properly dealt with by me in my previous writings—the kind of being possessed by such specific *types* of togetherness as nature, history, institutions; nor have I been as clear as I ought to have been that ontology tells us what the modes are, not as they are in themselves, but as they are in a relation of togetherness which allows them to be maximally separated—a fact symbolized by the use of a comma.[22] The modes of being are together; but in and of themselves they also stand outside all forms of togetherness. Together they function as terms for one another; in and of themselves they are the unity of the various terms which they provide for one another. But the togethernesses of them, though dependent on the beings in and of themselves, do have roles, careers, meanings of their own. They are derivative in being, but possessed of distinctive natures. Like the types of togetherness which illustrate them, the ultimate kinds of togetherness depend for their being on what they interrelate, but have meanings not reducible to the meanings of any of the related items.

[22] *Modes of Being,* pp. 510 f.

Arnold Metzger: You say "the modes exhaust the meaning of being." [23] Does not the typology of being as you present it confront philosophy with a basic question: the problem of exhibiting the sources in which is rooted the question concerning the being of that which has being? Is it not first in the transcendental exhibition of these sources that the "meaning of being" is brought to light? Do not the analyses of the modes of being presuppose this "meaning of being"?

Weiss: One can say that the meaning of being is presupposed by the modes of being. But it would not be correct to say that the meaning of being itself has the kind of being which is had by a mode. If that were the case the modes of being would presuppose a further being; there would be beings without end, each presupposing other beings.

Arnold Metzger: How does the fundamental proposition of your metaphysics differ from the Hegelian thesis, "Pure being is identical with pure nothingness"?

You stand close to Hegel's *Logic*.[24] It is important to know the differences. For Hegel, too, the world is surely an "interlocked, unified totality." [25] In consequence, the world as a perfected system counts for Hegel as a state of realization, of self-disclosing, of Absolute Being; and the constitutive categories of Hegel's system count as modes of being. It seems to me that you do not dispute this comparison. For Hegel, being is what transcends all determination, delimitation, differentiation. It is the indeterminate, contentless, infinite—nothingness. In one of his early writings Hegel conceives of being as "the identity of the identical and the non-identical." Hegel speaks of death as the "dissolution," as the self-discordant finitude, that is, as the "negation of the differentiated or particular." For Hegel then the undifferentiated, the one being, is thus not only the ground of the possibility of the world as a system, but at the same time the ground of the dissolution of the material contents or differentiations within the system. So my question is: What is your

[23] *Ibid.,* p. 518.
[24] *Modes of Being,* pp. 378–386.
[25] *Ibid.,* p. 382.

view of the Hegelian identification of the one being with nothingness, in the sense described above, as the principle of "many beings"?

Weiss: If there were only one mode of being, namely, Ideality, we should I think be Hegelians—if only we could then show why and how Ideality has content to face and conquer. Because there are other modes of being as ultimate as Ideality, there is content with which Ideality must deal, and there are other perspectives in terms of which the cosmos can be understood. I agree with Hegel that mere being, undifferentiated being, is indistinguishable from nothing. But I disagree with him as to the nature of ultimate reality. This is not being, or a single undifferentiated totality, or a whole in which there is a plurality of distinguishable but not altogether real parts. Each mode of being is irreducibly real; together they make up a cosmos. That cosmos is at once single and multiple, with its items rationally and dynamically related—a fact which is expressed by the symbols . and , and) and ∴ .[26]

Robert S. Hartman: Can each of the modes be so formalized as to yield the other three modes? What would such formalization be in each case, and how would the other three modes appear in it? How would each mode itself appear in its own formalization? Would you please apply such formal framework to some one problem, for example, the definition of man?

Weiss: Each mode offers a vantage point in terms of which all the others can be dealt with. Each mode provides a characteristic material and encourages a particular way of referring to the others. The position of the mode of Ideality is adopted by one who formalizes. If he knows what the other modes in fact are like, he can then express what they are in formal terms. He could not derive those other modes; they are all on a footing, equally underivable. But he could provide a formalized account of them.

Robert S. Hartman is perhaps asking whether or not there could be a distinctive kind of formalization, or mode of discourse which is appropriate to each particular mode of being. I think there is. This is

[26] *Ibid.*, p. 514.

achieved by first idealizing the mode, then dealing with it as a mere possibility or universal, and then speaking of it in such a way as to do justice to its divisions, relations, and roles. When one deals with all the modes from the perspective of Ideality, one makes use of a single type of formalization or discourse, but one can also make use of subordinate types of formalization appropriate to the perspectives of the other modes of being.

Biology deals with man as a formalized ideality; as an interlocked set of molecules in space-time, he is dealt with as a formalized portion of Existence; taken as a soul with privacy and rights, he is a formalized part of the divine; treated as an object of knowledge, he is a formalized part of Actuality.

Ellen S. Haring: Why are you sure about the number of the modes?

Weiss: No student of Charles S. Peirce can avoid becoming aware of the danger of fastening on some finite number and giving this an import denied to all others. Why should the universe have a definite, limited number of categories, objects, dimensions? How can a rational account end by maintaining that out of the infinitude of numbers there is one which is the number most appropriate to the universe? I have asked myself these questions many times. The question, however, must confront everyone. Any finite reality gives preferential lodgment to some number or other.

"But," it will be said, *"Modes of Being* asserts that it is *necessary* that there be four and no more than four modes of being." True. But which is the more arbitrary or perplexing or "irrational": the claim that this or that number happens to be pertinent to the universe at some time or at all times, or the claim that this or that number is necessarily pertinent? I think the former.

My attempt to prove just how many modes of being there are is similar to Aristotle's attempt to demonstrate that there were only four elements, or to Kant's attempt to demonstrate that there were only twelve categories. They failed. Must I not fail too? Perhaps. But how can we know unless we face the purported demonstration, and show that it does not do what it claims to do. So far no one—and my students and I have tried—has succeeded in this.

A. H. Johnson: Why do you say that "what is more than all four is self-contradictory"?[27] You stress development and creativity: is it not possible that new observations and dialectic may without self-contradiction reveal new modes?

Weiss: Development and creativity characterize processes inside the modes; they do not characterize the cosmos any more than being does. They provide no warrant for the supposition that there might be new modes of being, in addition to the four. A fifth mode is possible only in the sense that it is possible that none but faulty arguments have been offered on behalf of the reality of just four modes of being.

A. H. Johnson: Have you considered with sufficient care the possibility of a one-mode or a two-mode philosophy?

Weiss: *Reality* tried to provide a philosophy which acknowledged only one mode of being. I think that is a good way for a philosopher to begin. But I soon found myself irresistibly driven to acknowledge another mode (Ideality), in order to do justice to the persistence of the self and the obligatory nature of the Good,[28] and then two other modes (Existence and God). Existence had to be acknowledged so as to do justice to the reality of a cosmic time;[29] God had to be acknowledged so as to do justice to the unity of the other three modes, and the need for normative possibilities to be prescriptive, and non-normative possibilities to be realized.[30] I tried again and again to see if I could dispense with one or the other of these, but I found that I was merely inviting the cold embrace of dead philosophies.[31] (And there are good reasons why there cannot be a fifth mode.[32])

William A. Christian: How do you look at Alfred North Whitehead's metaphysics in relation to *Modes of Being?* How would you

[27] *Ibid.,* p. 518.
[28] *Modes of Being,* pp. 10 ff. Cf. *Nature and Man; Man's Freedom.*
[29] *Modes of Being,* pp. 10–11.
[30] *Ibid.,* pp. 13 f., 116–120, 340–341.
[31] *Ibid.,* pp. 376 f.
[32] *Ibid.,* pp. 517 f.

characterize the difference between his system and yours in respect to (1) their logical forms, and (2) the visions of reality they express?

Weiss: I was a student of Whitehead's, and I have learned a great deal—far, far more than I know how to express—from him. But I think his descriptive method is too loose, and his categorial scheme too narrow. He cannot account for action, making, and the persistent self-identity of substantial men. His treatment of God is systematically ambiguous: he tries to bring him under the very categories which are appropriate to actualities, thus making him a kind of grandiose actuality, and nevertheless places him over against all actualities, exhibiting the categories in ways no actualities can. Whitehead's philosophy is, I think, too closely tied to actualities, and too much affected by fashions in current science—relativity and its associated theory of causation and its definition of the velocity of light, and to quantum theory with its associated theory of the ultimacy of atomic events—to be able to do justice to ethics, art, and religion, and what these deal with.

Peter J. Caws: Can the structure of the brain limit the range of thought? If so, might a more highly developed organism than man conceive of other modes of being than the four, or conceive those differently?

Weiss: A "possible higher organism" has two distinct meanings: it refers to an improved version of an actual human or to a mere detached possibility. An improved version of ourselves is related to us, the beings who know there are four modes of being. It could not, without—contrary to the hypothesis—destroying all relation to ourselves, know more than four modes of being. A merely possible higher organism, on the other hand, need have no relation to us. But such a possible being is radically indeterminate. Does such a conceivable higher organism have any knowledge? I think not. When a higher organism arrives on the scene and exercises its mind, it will have knowledge. What will it know? We cannot say, for what it will know is now but a possible possibility. A possible possibility is not a genuine possibility; a possibility is a possible actuality, or God or Existence. We cannot therefore say what is possible for a possible organism. Could we not then say that when the organism is actual, all kinds of things will be possible for it? Might it not prove that 1 plus 1 is 6, that yesterday is tomorrow, that round squares are green? Such possible proofs, since they presuppose the realization of a mind which is to engage in the proofs, are, once again, only possible possibilities. If you can speak intelligibly about possible possibilities you can speak intelligibly about a possible proof of what we now believe are contradictions, and a possible proof that there are more or less than four modes of being. But I think a possible possibility does not have sufficient definiteness to be affirmed or denied, accepted or rejected, entertained or dismissed, except as that which is being excluded by what is necessarily true.

Ellen S. Haring: How do you meet the following objections concerning the ultimacy of the modes?

Richard T. DeGeorge: Since each of the modes is incomplete and is unable to account for itself, though together they make up the whole, what accounts for the whole? Since each one of the modes is dependent on the others, it is not *causa sui*. (The fact that any being, if it is to be itself, must be over against the others, leaves each of them essentially dependent.) Yet the four taken together are claimed to be all there is; and so, presumably, taken together they are *causa sui*. It is not clear how togetherness supplies the requisite independence.

Weiss: Each mode is something in itself, for otherwise it could not be related; and each is related to the others, for otherwise it could not be in the same universe with them. The modes are not made independent by any form of togetherness; they are independent and also together. The universe is the four of them together. It is not a *causa sui;* it does not produce itself. Each of the modes is itself, however, a *causa sui* in the sense that it is the proper topic of a distinct and valid ontological argument. But when and as it is, the others must also be.

Richard T. DeGeorge: The difficulty is compounded, it seems, when one considers not Actuality, but the contingent actualities given in experience. These, if they were to be explained causally, would lead either to a first cause or to an infinite regress.

Weiss: We can explain the production of contingent actualities given in causal terms. This will lead us back and back. But there is time enough; the temporal world has always been.

W. Norris Clarke, S.J.: Must there not be one ultimate source or ground of the unity—of the unified system—of the four modes? Wherever there is an intrinsic unity of order, or a unified system of component elements, it seems an ineluctable metaphysical necessity that there be some single ontological source or ground to explain the unity and mutual interrelation of the elements of the system. If the components are such that they cannot exist save as correlated with the other components, then this means that component A cannot exist unless component B already exists, and vice versa. Neither principle, therefore, can be the ground of or generate the other, since the principle or component in question cannot exist itself unless the other is already given. Thus there must, it seems, be a single correlator not itself dependent on a part of the system. There seems to be none such in the system of *Modes of Being.* Hence this system of the four modes is posited as a sheer brute fact with no possibility of ultimate metaphysical grounding. In other words, we have here unity without a unifier, contrary to what most great metaphysical systems have required.

Weiss: Is unity prior to plurality? To say it is, is to assume the perspective either of Ideality or of God. If we make that assumption we will of course assume a unitary ground. That ground will be either a subjugating or an appreciative being. If instead we begin with actualities or Existence, and thus with cognizing or active beings, we will start with pluralities. We will then assume that our ground or source is irreducibly multiple, and that unity is a dependent notion.

It is desirable to overcome the bias that characterizes any view which insists on looking at the universe from one perspective alone. As thinkers we cannot avoid starting as actualities exercising a distinctive power, inescapably oriented toward the discursive, the multiple, the divided.

But as philosophers we must, by generalization and abstraction, by attending to the natures and demands of other modes, try to attain a state of neutrality. We will then adopt in our cognizing the position of a Good or the Ideal, and will treat them, as well as ourselves and Existence, as objects of our cognition. Only one who puts appreciation in place of cognition has a unifier before he has anything to unify. And even he, to do justice to what is, will have to make a place for realities which the unifier can cognize as other than himself.

Ivor Leclerc: The metaphysics of *Modes of Being* involves a fundamental departure from the tradition and, it seems to me, a basic difficulty. From Aristotle onward the major philosophers explicitly or implicitly have recognized *ousia*—a that which exists—as basic. Being in the fundamental sense is the being of *ousia,* and all other senses are derivative. Your doctrine is a rejection of this. For you, being is basic; or perhaps one should say that the four modes are basic. Successfully to maintain your rejection of *ousia,* you must at least show that the four modes are ultimate, irreducible, and co-ordinate. I do not see that they are on a level. Actuality and God might be so, but Ideality and Existence are not co-ordinate with one another, or with either of the other two modes.

Weiss: Instead of denying the reality of substance, I have insisted on it, over against the contemporary trend to take process, creativity, event as basic. But there are two kinds of substance: there is the substantiality of the four modes, each of which is ultimate, underived, and there is the substantiality of contingent actualities which, though caused and dependent for their presence on other contingent actualities, have a modicum of existence all their own, and are so far ultimate realities, not reducible to any other. The four modes of being are co-ordinate realities, but this does not mean that they exercise similar functions or are analyzable in the same way. Each has its own rationale, career, divisions, problems, and answers.

Richard I. Aaron: You do not accept the Platonic theory of universals; yet your account of universals seems more like Plato's than any other. Will you discuss this point?

Weiss: Most Platonists seem to understand the realm of possibility to be made up of a plurality of distinct, determinate possibilities. In effect they make it a domain of particulars, reduplicating the items in this world. The plurality in Ideality is, I think, a submerged plurality, a matter of creases and distinctions,[33] not one of distinct entities. Each actuality is oriented toward the realm of Ideality, and through the agency of its concern focuses on a part of that realm, thereby making it yield a distinctive, pertinent possibility for that actuality. *Distinct* possibilities, precisely because they are isolated by, and in this sense produced by, contingent, changing actualities, necessarily change in nature over the course of time.[34]

Ellen S. Haring: There are difficulties in your treatment of God as together with other beings.

Nathan Rotenstreich: You say, "God's essence is an all-inclusive essence."[35] How can one mode of being be all-inclusive in its essence? Is there a pantheistic trend in this theory of God?

Weiss: Each mode of being is primary in some respect. Each has a nature which provides a standard in terms of which the others are to be measured. God is superior to the others in the unity he embodies, in his self-expressiveness, and in the comprehensiveness of his essence. But the other modes enjoy other advantages; in terms of their virtues, He is inferior to them. He is all-inclusive in one way; they are all-inclusive in others. I have been maintaining that all beings, including God, can be seen to be instances, determinations of possibility, just as surely as all, including the Ideal, can be seen to be cases of unity. The view I have been offering is therefore no more pantheistic than it is panidealistic, and so on.

Joseph Owens, C.Ss.R.: You characterize the coexistence of God and creatures as a problem, but I am not sure that you see the problem correctly. A "fragment of existence . . . over against God"[36] does not

[33] *Modes of Being,* p. 118.
[34] *Ibid.,* p. 109.
[35] *Ibid.,* p. 335.
[36] *Ibid.,* p. 191.

seem to me to be the heart of the problem. After all, such fragmentary existence is a definitely known existence from the viewpoint of human cognition. The problem implied seems to me to lie rather in the infinite existence of God over against such fragments, and not vice versa. The solution would then be sought in an analysis of the notion "other," which applies to finite fragments but which does not seem to have any meaning when one attempts to apply it to something infinite in every respect.

Weiss: I don't think that God is infinite in every respect. And no matter how we twist and turn we surely must affirm that I am not God and God is not I. He and I are others of one another. This truth is not altered when one adds that God is superior to me. It surely is not affected when one adds that God is not infinite in all respects—since he has limitations and lacks the reality possessed by other modes and their parts—and that I am infinite in some respects, since I have a mind which can, via abstractions, encompass all being. My existence is held precariously and is but a tiny part of all existence; but it is mine, enabling me to be. "Otherness" moreover is a symmetrical relation. If I am other than God—and this surely is so, for I sin, blaspheme, err, and engage in the arts—he must be other than I. I think therefore that a problem faces all those who, with Father Owens, seem to deny the irreducible reality of themselves and other beings. I think he gets to his position because he assumes that God is not only the source of the essence and existence of everything else, but that God never lets these loose, never lets them stand completely outside himself. I see no warrant for either supposition. Ought they not to be abandoned, since they lead one to irresolvable paradoxes and make one reject obtrusive facts and other, even more important, parts of one's theoretical scheme?

W. Norris Clarke, S.J.: In a long and sympathetic review of *Modes of Being* in *Archives de Philosophie*,[37] E. Braun, S.J., makes the following criticism: "The author professes his inability to put together the existence of the Thomistic God [as creator] and the existence of creatures. The notion of participation, in fact, which is so essential in Thomism, seems to be one of the rare notions that has eluded the synthesizing

[37] XXIII (1960), 298–303, esp. 300.

genius of Professor Weiss." Would you care to comment on your attitude toward the notion of participation in general, and toward Thomistic participation in existence in particular?

Weiss: To participate is to partake of, to share, perhaps even to have features and characteristics in common with something else. Each mode of being participates in all the others. I, as a representative of Actuality, participate in God. But conversely, God participates in me. I know what unity is because of God; he knows what action is because of me. I know what it is to be *"a man"* because of God; he knows what finitude is because of me.

The Thomist identifies ultimate existence with God's existence, leaving nothing over for the rest of us but a dependent, participated-in existence. But what is it that participates? If I am not a being apart from God, how could I participate in him? The Thomist doctrine of participation is unnecessary if God never lets go of me, never lets me stand on my own two feet. And if I do so stand, I have a being and a dignity which philosophy says God must respect, and which theology should say he does respect.

Ellen S. Haring: CONCLUDING QUESTION ON BEING.   The four ultimate modes seem sometimes a luminous discovery; more often they are cloaked in paradox. For example, you claim that the word "being" applied to two modes is "radically ambiguous"; yet you are willing to assert, "Each has a distinctive way of being." The latter statement seems to me to be unambiguous. Rather than argue about what you have already said on the being of the modes, however, let us approach the matter from another angle. If you reached your conception of the modes by dialectic, then presumably you asked yourself what is requisite to complete various familiar items—living and dying actualities, moral judgments, and so on. You proceed four times over in the way that Plato did, once, with respect to the intelligibility of particulars. This type of reasoning is a quest for the unconditioned ground of evidently conditioned entities. Here in the Interrogation, however, you say that each mode is the subject of a valid ontological argument. If you are asserting that *humans* must reason from conditioned to condition, although ontological arguments can in principle be made, you are remarkably close to Thomas Aquinas, who said that "God exists" would be a necessary proposition for us if we had an adequate understanding of God. Moreover, it remains doubtful that the four modes are on a par. If I try to get a better grasp of them by telling myself that each must be the very epitome of something evident in the familiar world, then God is sheer unity, Existence is something like energy, the Ideal is order or formality, and—since unity, energy, and order are definitory of actualities—actualities do not seem to be *sui generis* at all. If this conclusion is correct, then there are alternative next steps, one rather Platonic and one Aristotelian. In the former case, actualities are less than the other three modes, are the upshot of their interplay. In the latter, actualities are the characteristic constituents of the cosmos, and the other modes are attenuated aspects or special cases of them. A. H. Johnson and Ivor Leclerc appear to incline to this alternative. Other participants present their difficulties in terms of God, not Actuality, but again emphasize the dubiousness of parity—and also of distinctness—of the modes.

Weiss: CONCLUDING ANSWER ON BEING. Each mode is demonstrable in at least two ways: It is the subject of an argument to an unconditioned ground for the other modes, and it is the subject of an ontological argument since it is a being over against the other modes. I do not think we need an "adequate" knowledge of God to know that "God exists" is necessarily true. We need only an appropriate knowledge of God.[38] I think that we do have such knowledge.

Each mode of being—not only actualities—can be dealt with as a threefold combination of the other modes. Each mode of being—not only actualities—can be dealt with as a perspective on all the other modes. Each shares features with the others; each stands over against the others. However, it is not the case that unity, etc., are definitory of actualities. Actualities are substances in space-time, and this none of the other modes is.

I do not see why this doctrine is thought to be paradoxical or to offer any difficulty to understanding. If there is more than one mode of being in the universe, either all will be merely *sui generis,* and hence not intelligible, or else each—while ultimate, and distinctive in nature—will be understandable in terms provided by the others.

[38] *Modes of Being,* chap. 4.

III. TIME, SPACE, AND ACTUALITIES

Richard T. DeGeorge: What is time? It would seem that it is neither Actuality, Ideality, Existence, nor God; nevertheless, actualities exist in it, it is related to eternity, and it seems to exist.

Weiss: Time is a dimension, an aspect of Existence. It stands out as a distinctive dimension, however, only so far as Existence is related to other modes of being. Ideality enables time to have a future, God enables it to have a persistent past, and actualities enable it to have a present. Since actualities not only exist, but are in the domain of Existence, since God is the great preserver, and since a dimension of Existence must be in Existence, "actualities exist in [time], [time] is related to eternity, and it seems to exist."

Robert S. Cohen: Will you reply to those who, with Adolph Grünbaum, object to your gulp theory of time? [39]

Weiss: My discussion of time relates to an objective time, a time ingredient in reality, apart from all measurement and scientific investigation. Grünbaum ignores this time to attend instead to an abstract order, the "time" of relativity physics. I do not see the relevance of his (or his opponents') views to the time which is a dimension of Existence and is lived through by actualities. He thinks my account is based on a reference to conscious organisms. This is not correct, though to be sure the time with which I am concerned is a time that at intervals is consciously enjoyed by some men. That I think is something in its favor.

Milic Capek: What is your view of the so-called specious present? I myself think "specious" present is a misnomer. It is not specious at all, but an immediate datum experienced in a single pulse of duration. Moreover, it is evidently contemporary with an enormous number of successive events in the physical world. How then are we to understand and accept your assertion that "the magnitude of a passing in-

[39] "Relativity and the Atomicity of Becoming," *Review of Metaphysics*, IV (1950), 143.

stant must be a constant, permitting all co-present entities to enter the future together." [40]

Weiss: I agree with Capek; the specious present is not "specious." [41] The present in the passage to which he refers is not "specious," not psychological, not physical; it is ontological, the irreducible unit of a cosmic time. If the present moments recognized by a science are smaller than this, they are evidently abstractions, obtained by dividing numbers and not by dividing time. There are, however, moments larger than those which make up cosmic time—for example, in history. This raises a number of problems with which I am currently occupied.

Robert W. Browning: In what sense are you an "epochalist"? Is your epochalism a doctrine about "crisis points" in the careers of continuants, but not—as with Charles Hartshorne—a "temporal atomism or chronological pluralism" of experient occasions?

Weiss: "Epochalism" is a broad term pointing up the fact that I think it important to be alert to crises, turning points, pivotal realities. The term is intended to make one attend to the different roles and natures of various beings, acts, outcomes, to differences among the arts, to the different rationales of science, philosophy, history, to the difference between men, animals, and inanimate beings. Epochalism refers us to the crisis points in the careers of continuants; it also acknowledges a temporal atomism. However, unlike Descartes, Whitehead, and Hartshorne, I would maintain that beings do not perish at every moment, but instead persist through a number of atomic moments. This affirmation, however, does not follow from the theory of epochalism, but from a consideration of the nature of motion and change. [42]

W. Norris Clarke, S.J.: How can genuine causal efficacy, genuine productive action of a cause, be maintained if a time gap be inserted between the act of causing and its effect? The act of causing seems to make no sense save as an intrinsically relational act. Just as every in-

---

[40] *Reality,* p. 235.
[41] *Nine Basic Arts* (Carbondale: Southern Illinois University Press, 1961), pp. 17–19.
[42] *Reality,* pp. 232 f.

tentional act of consciousness is always a consciousness of something, so it seems that every act of causing must be the causing of its effect. Thus if the effect is not given simultaneously with the act, the act is not really an act of causing at all, but only some operation preparatory to the actual act of causation. So Aristotle, Thomas Aquinas, Scotus, etc. Yet the time gap between cause and effect is insisted upon in *Modes of Being* and elsewhere.

Weiss: If Father Clarke is right, and the effect is simultaneous with the causing, how is it that anything happens because of and after something else? I agree with him that the cause and the causing are of an effect, but I would add that a cause is inseparable from a *possible* effect, and that the process of causing is the process of converting the possible into an *actual* effect. It takes time for the effect to be changed from a possible to a fully actual effect.

Ellen S. Haring: There seem to be obscurities in your treatment of space.

Nathaniel Lawrence: How can you assert both that actualities are in space and that space is brought about by the interplay of actualities? [43] You seem to mean that actualities generate the space they are in. But then what enables the actualities to do this, and what or where are actualities prior to the production of space? On the other hand, you may mean that there is a possibly abstractable space which is what it is because actualities are spatial. But then the actualities are not in any fundamental sense beings in reciprocity. Then should there not be a way in which space produces or modifies the actualities? Finally, how do you counter the contention—for example, in the General Theory of Relativity—that the space-time continuum is the basic mode, and that actualities are derivative?

Andrew J. Reck: How is cosmic space—which as Existence is distinct from actualities—consistent with space as a produced derivative of actualities? The former involves an absolute theory of space and the latter a relational one.

[43] *Modes of Being,* pp. 21, 28.

Weiss: A man and a woman marry. He gives up playing pool, drinks a little more than before; she begins to look forward to having a child. The marriage, though constituted by both, has an effect on them both. The analogy is faulty, but it does help to point up the fact that beings can be affected by what they themselves constitute.

Actualities are focal points, intensities at the center of vectors. The vectors overlap one another and other actualities. When the overlapping vectors are reciprocals of one another they together constitute a single co-ordinate space.[44] The actualities also have mutually supplementary vectors within themselves.[45] They are therefore spatial when and as they constitute an environing space. There is no space in addition to their own at the place they are; they are space intensified. They can thus be understood in terms of, but not derived from, space. But the converse is also true; actualities are the beings which provide elements out of which the comparatively empty space around them is produced. That space moreover has an extensional reality rooted in existence; actualities merely give it a geometrical nature and orientation points. The entire issue is discussed at length in *Reality*.[46]

Peter J. Caws: If the self is an actuality, it must be a being in space;[47] how then can it be the "other of whatever there be"?[48]

Weiss: To be other than all else is not to be unrelated to all else; nor is it to be denied a place inside some domain. To be the other of whatever there be is but to stand out over against all else with a distinct nature and being.

Robert S. Cohen: Will you explain indication more fully?

How can a one-to-one relation [49] pair spatially distant objects without affecting their natures? On your view this seems strange. You want both independence for each being and internal relatedness of all to all. Either such one-to-one relations are mere lists (and I think there are

[44] *Reality,* pp. 185 ff.
[45] *Ibid.,* pp. 188 f.
[46] Bk. II, chap. 3.
[47] *Modes of Being,* pp. 21, 95.
[48] *Ibid.,* p. 95.
[49] *Reality,* p. 33.

no such mere lists), or they are relations of some sort and affect the nature of the beings related. How can there be a nonspatial way of one-to-one relationship which is a component of the spatial relationship? I ask also what the act of indicating is like. If it is not spatial, what is it?

Weiss: A one-to-one relation is an abstract relation; it abstracts from the distance between objects. It relates the beings as separate from one another. Separation is an internal relation, but one which does not change the natures of what is related; it merely precludes them from being without any reference beyond themselves. The act of indicating rests on an act which is spatial, in that it relates us, via attention, action, reference, to a distant object, and then abstracts from the distance.

F. S. C. Northrop: What do you mean by reality in the essential as distinct from the radically empirical existential mode? Moreover, is essential reality ever directly known in the case of objects other than the knower? If essential reality can be directly known in such cases, what does one mean by the assertion that an event happens in Sydney, Australia, at the same moment that another event happens in New Haven, Connecticut? Certainly this simultaneity is not directly sensed. Nevertheless, without knowledge of such simultaneity there can be no knowledge either of public real objects or of public time, where real means identical for all percipients. If essential reality cannot be directly known in the case of objects other than the knower, how are such entities known in the essential mode of being?

Weiss: The simultaneity of events at different places is not directly sensed or perceived. But this does not mean that it is not directly known. Formal knowledge has an object as surely as sensing and perceiving do. The real object, which is what Professor Northrop apparently has in mind, is not reached through sensing, perceiving, or formalization. It is known as the outcome of a construction, a synthesis of the formal, the perceptual, the eventful and valuational aspects of objects.[50] These aspects are abstracted from the common-sense objects of daily life and then combined, after having been freed of irrelevancies, errors, and confusions. The outcome is directly known, unless direct knowledge

[50] *The World of Art* (Carbondale: Southern Illinois University Press, 1961), pp. 63 ff.

means a knowledge which has no place for reflection, construction, activity. But if that be the case, I do not see how direct knowledge of anything is ever possible. Yet, it may be asked, do we not directly sense the *qualia* of things? We surely encounter them by means of the senses. Such encounter yields no knowledge, however. On the other hand, when we conceptually construct an object, we can be—through the agency of thought—in direct relationship with a reality.

Ellen S. Haring: Please explain "inside" and "outside" more fully.

Robert S. Brumbaugh: Why is this metaphor never sharpened or explored further? Perhaps it is because the paired notions are spatial and static, and so not wholly suited to a dynamic system. I wonder whether there are not "one-sided" entities? A stream of energy might be thought to have an outside, but no inside. Some ideas in mathematics might have interesting analogues in this connection.

Weiss: I don't think of "inside" and "outside" as essentially spatial or static. Kant used the terms "inner" and "outer" in his discussion of the Concepts of Reflection. Though he took the outer to be spatial, he viewed the inner as "a *thinking* or analogous to thinking," [51] and the spatial was dealt with in terms of active forces.[52] However, in contrast with Kant I think both the inside and the outside have static and dynamic roles. The outside of a being is what the being is from the standpoint of others; it is the being as in some relation of togetherness; what the being is on the inside is what it is in and of itself. I have given a great deal of attention to the former and not enough to the latter. (But see *Nature and Man,* chap. 3.) The former, though, is most complex, for there are forms of togetherness which involve the merging of beings, others which involve their dynamic interplay, still others which connect them rationally, and others which allow them to stand apart from one another, as separate.[53]

The self, mind, privacy can be viewed as insides without outsides—

---

[51] *Kritik der reinen Vernunft,* trans. by Norman Kemp Smith (London: Macmillan & Co., Ltd., 1929), A266, p. 279.

[52] *Ibid.,* A265, p. 279.

[53] *Modes of Being,* p. 514.

the outside being provided by the body or other objects; energy, space, and togetherness can be viewed as outsides without insides—the inside being provided by the beings which yield or ground those outsides. In short, they are abstractions from a more complex and real occurrence in which both inside and outside have a place and role.

Robert S. Cohen: How are the public and the private, or the inside and the outside, related to one another without the use of an essentially "outside" concept?

Weiss: Inside and outside are related both on an inside and on an outside. The relations are distinct from what is related. As inside, the relation is presupposed by what it relates; as outside, the relation is derivative from the items it relates. One inside relation of the inside mind to the outside body is the will. One outside relation of the inside mind to the outside body is an object of desire. The will (which is biased toward the mind) is prior to the mind and body which it in fact activates; the object of desire (which may be neutral to both) offers a single focus for both mind and body.

Robert W. Browning: Is your inference to the insides of other things a case of reasoning by analogy?

Weiss: The reasoning to the insides of other beings is the outcome of an inference as direct and as effective as any other. We reason directly, though precariously, when we infer from the smile of the infant to the joy of the infant. When in speculation we start not with smiles or other qualities, but with highly general characteristics, we infer just as directly but less precariously to what those characteristics necessarily entail, as presuppositions, focal points, origins.

Arnold Metzger: What place has death in your system? I mean death, not dying, which is important to distinguish.

Weiss: When alive our bodies are governed by principles, essences, meanings which are not bodily in origin or import. On death the body is freed from this alien governance; it then exhibits the essence which is its own. Death is the time when a body reveals itself to be essentially inanimate, making evident that the life it exhibited depended on the presence and governance of a psyche, or self. If that psyche, or self, has an existence of its own (which existence has been hidden by the existence of the body it quickened), it will be capable of immortality.

Ellen S. Haring: CONCLUDING QUESTION ON TIME, SPACE, AND ACTUALITIES. All the questions in Section III of this Interrogation bear, one way or another, on nature. (Nature I would define roughly as the totality of actualities insofar as they are not products of technique or bearers of added cultural significances.) Your answers in this section, however, are largely either ontological or epistemic. Nature tends to be left on the periphery of discussion. You treat preponderantly the modal foundations of nature and the abstractions we make from natural objects. This is all right, but I would like to know your views on nature. You used to be a naturalistic philosopher, but *Modes of Being* marks a shift from that position. How would you now define nature and, also, how would you now defend the claim that we know it? The second half of this question is not fully answered here by your remarks to Professor Northrop. In the passage cited from *The World of Art* you say: "A unity produced by conceptually uniting the various strands [formal, perceptual, etc.] *refers* to a being which is more real than any of those strands or the common-sense object from which they were abstracted. . . . An encountered man . . . is a common-sense substance; a rationally understood man . . . as that which is at once perceptual, scientific, eventful and important, is the substantial *counterpart* of a construction. . . ."[54] You maintain that we know the real and know it directly, but it is hard to see why you are so sure that the abstraction and reunification of strands do not lead to falsification.

Weiss: CONCLUDING ANSWER ON TIME, SPACE, AND ACTUALITIES. "Nature," as Arthur O. Lovejoy and George Boas have made clear, has an enormous number of distinct meanings. We come close to the core of most of them, I think, if we take it to be the rationally clarified world of common sense—that is, our daily world, de-

[54] P. 63. Italics added.

conventionalized, reconstructed, and expanded to cosmic proportions. Were the reconstruction, through the abstraction and reunification of strands, a falsification of what is the case, then science, perception, events, and values, severally or together, would not answer to the real. But what evidence could be given for the supposition that the scientific or any other strand is untrustworthy? All our rationally certifiable evidence is provided by the different strands. And in terms of what could a combination of them be said to be in error? What other unities would we have to measure them by: Their objective unity is more real than the commonsensical object. He who claimed that there might in fact be nothing which answered to the reconstruction would have to say that clarifying the common-sense world was a way of abandoning whatever reality it contained. He would be one who told others in a common-sense world that nothing which rested on common sense could be real, or he would be one who tried to make intelligible the commonsensical claim that any attempt to make common sense intelligible was mistaken. Either answer is existentially absurd, denying the possibility of its own being or meaning.

IV. ETHICS

Nathan Rotenstreich: I have difficulty in understanding and reconciling the following assertions:

The test of a philosophy is the degree of correspondence an active moral life manifests as holding between the coherent consciously achieved scheme of things and the common-sense philosophic perspective it attempted to make clear. . . . It is through moral action that the being of a man achieves clarity and definiteness, and what he knows individuality and intensive depth. . . .
Man, however, is capable of a vicarious completion through the medium of knowledge, for to know is to possess in the mind those things which one in fact lacks.[55]

What is the nature of the relation between "practical" and "theoretical" reason? That is, between moral action and knowledge? Is knowl-

---

[55] *Reality*, pp. 14–15, 294.

edge only an incomplete completion and not the real not-yet-attained completion embodied in moral action? What makes moral action the mediating link in terms of the architectonic structure of the system?

Weiss: Knowledge is a strategy; it gets the real under a limitative condition—as something articulated, structured, conceived. Moral action, as involving mind and body in harmonious interplay, and as reaching to and doing justice to other realities, mediates and completes what is achieved in mind (and also what a mere body has or can do). There are of course other ways of completing and mediating various realities—for example, practical life, history, art. All of them share with moral action the fact that they involve a use of mind and body, directing both of these toward an end which is common to the goals of each. This end is more limited in range than the goal of mind, but it is also more concrete and determinate. It is more comprehensive than the goal of the body, but in compensation it is less determinate, less concrete.

Nathan Rotenstreich: You say also that "nature is saturated with values." [56] What is the relation between this ultimate fact and the status of moral action as indicated above? Why is it that nature is intrinsically a realm of values? Is it because every existence has the drive to be preserved, and hence has a right to be preserved, and this right is value? Or is it that every existence is in a way granted, and being granted, puts before man the demand of being acknowledged?

Weiss: Nature—every part of the universe in fact—can be dealt with from the perspective of Ideality. When it is, it is seen to be through and through rational and valuational, a fact which moral action takes account of. Nature is a realm of values, but it is also permeated by the divine, oriented toward the individual, and is a special case of Existence —an Existence bounded and qualified by the other three modes of being. Every being does have the right to be itself; that right can be understood in the light of the Ideal. But it also can be viewed in terms of Existence, when it appears as a warranted might; in terms of God, when it appears as an appreciated ultimate; and in terms of Actuality, when it appears as an other, standing over against all else. [57]

[56] *Modes of Being*, pp. 111, 183, 185.
[57] *Ibid.*, p. 515.

Ellen S. Haring: Will you discuss obligation in the light of the following queries and observations (pp. 301–303)?

Robert W. Browning: How do you conceive the source of man's obligation? In particular: Does a universal obligate? Is it not a concrete situation which obligates the agent within it (although, in case of doubt or dispute, discrimination of aspects within it is effected and reference is made to rules)? Or is the contention that in the realm of ethics universals obligate a way of saying that certain sorts of possibilities invest present action with obligation, and these sorts of possibilities are distinguished by reference to a universal?

Weiss: There is a demand made by the Ideal on man; the converse of that demand is obligation. We are obligated because we are men whose completeness requires that we adopt and make determinate the Ideal with which we are by nature concerned. We are not obligated by a particular situation, though we may have particular obligations with respect to this or that; our primary obligation is to realize the Good every place. That Good, before it is realized, is, to be sure, a possibility, an indeterminate universal. We are not, however, obligated to it *qua* universal; we are obligated to realize it, the universal, in the guise of a determinate plurality of particulars. The Good to be realized certainly makes some possibilities have more significance than others. In this sense it is true that "certain sorts of possibilities invest present action with obligation, and these are distinguished by reference to a universal."

Joseph Owens, C.Ss.R.: In *Man's Freedom* the moral good seems derived rather hastily from being. "Ethical facts come into existence when men use the absolute good, which ought to be, as a test and guide for every thing and every value," is a statement hard to reconcile with "Ethical facts are constituted by man's being, not by his attitudes, interests or knowledge." [58] *Our Public Life* does not seem to clear up this difficulty. It maintains an ethics grounded upon absolute good, yet appears willing to allow that men "could have common natures because of the pressure exerted by tradition, by the institutional patterns of their societies, by virtue of their habits, and so on." [59] The background

[58] P. 203.
[59] P. 153.

of the difficulty for me, needless to say, is the profound Aristotelian distinction between theoretical and practical science, the former obtaining its first principles from the intuition of things, while the latter obtains its principles from habituation through correct upbringing under good laws.

Weiss: That I ought to do x implies that I can do x only if I am free and strong enough to do x. That x ought to be done implies that x can be done whether or not I am free. The former assertion, since it involves a condition which may not be fulfilled, allows for the fact that there might be something I ought to do which I in fact cannot do. But the latter is an ontological matter. If the universe in any part makes an inescapable demand on any other, then that universe provides a way in which the demand is met, if not by that obligated part, then by some other part of the universe. If the demand could not be satisfied in some way, somewhere, it is a demand that cannot be met, an ought-to-be that cannot be realized. But it is irrational to ask that the impossible be done. The only things a part of the universe can be required to do are what can somehow be done, if not by it, then by something else.

Aristotle's distinction between the theoretical and practical sciences relates only tangentially to the present discussion. Aristotle was not primarily interested in the formulation of an absolute ethics for all men at all times (though what he says in Books I, VII, and IX of *Nicomachean Ethics* has application beyond Greece), but in a morality which could be inculcated by good training under good laws, to bring men to the position of being good citizens of an Athenian state. I think the ethical reaches much further than this because it specifies an ontological relation between the Good that ought to be and any part of the cosmos that could satisfy it. This ontological relation in turn is a special case of the relation which connects an ultimate, ideal ought-to-be with whatever else there is.

Andrew J. Reck: If the residuum of the Good unrealized by man is necessarily realized by the other modes of being, then should not man be released from his ontological guilt, and be allowed to enjoy an unending moral holiday? This question is sharpened by the threefold consideration: (1) For you man has obligations which he cannot possibly meet and yet he is guilty; (2) you hold that although "ought" does not imply "can" for man, it does so for the cosmos; (3) you say that, since what can be must be, cosmically what ought to be is necessarily realized, though not necessarily in time.

Weiss: The Good is realized. But man is the being who has as his *task* the realization of that Good. A man does not escape the guilt of having failed to do what he ought to have done, merely because someone else does the job. My hungry neighbor is hungry no longer because you were kind. I still am a wretch for not having fed him myself. Had I employed you, had I given you the food with which you fed him, I would escape my guilt by virtue of my identification of myself with you as feeding him.

The religious man holds that God makes good what man does not. If the religious man is right, he escapes from ethical guilt by giving up his status as a distinct being and adopting instead God's ways or being as his own. Others look elsewhere for the being or beings which make good what man does not, and with which man can identify himself. If I am right, the philosopher will intellectually identify himself with all four modes of being, and thereby intellectually see that what ought to be must be and therefore is, in fact. This does not mean that this world in which we daily struggle is as it ought to be; only the entire cosmos is this. It is only because we men seek to be representative of all mankind, of all Actuality and eventually of all there is that we have an obligation to bring about what ought to be. To be one with the ought which is realized we must in part move beyond this daily world. And philosophic speculation is one eminently desirable but often neglected way of doing this.

If men could cancel out the fact that they are men, they would become mere items inside the cosmos, having no representative role, and no duty toward the Good. They would then, with stocks and stones, have one "unending moral holiday." Because we are men we have the inescapable responsibility of trying to see that Good is realized, God enjoyed, Existence possessed, and Actuality conceptually completed.

Ellen S. Haring: How do you meet the following objections (pp. 304–306) about possibility?

Ernan McMullin: From the requirement that only those are "real possibilities" which will, in fact, be realized,[60] it follows that, if it did not rain today, it would have been in all circumstances incorrect to have said yesterday, "It is possible that it will rain tomorrow." Thus the latter statement and the statement, "It will rain tomorrow," turn out to be exactly equivalent, which seems wrong on any definition of possibility.

To say that at a given time T, "I realize the possibility (standing-or-sitting) in the guise of a sitting," [61] is doubly unhappy. It confuses the actual (sitting) with the possible, equating the coming-to-be of the actual with the defining of the possible. It confuses the hypothetically necessary (standing-or-sitting) with the possible (sitting), predicating possibility only of the former while explicitly denying it of the latter. In this way the modes of actuality, possibility, and necessity seem to be thoroughly and inextricably mixed up.

Since my sitting-or-standing at a future time T is characterized as "possible" and since this disjunction depends on my being alive at T, you will be forced to admit the legitimacy of, "It is possible that I will be alive at T." You cannot consistently restrict yourself to the unitary "alive-or-dead" brand of possibility. Moreover, one could just as easily say that "sitting-upright-or-sitting-slumped" is possible in your sense, thus making "sitting" a possibility. You wish to deny that "sitting" is a possibility, but this denial is purely arbitrary.

Amélie O. Rorty: How can you hold both that the realization of a possibility is the outcome of a free action [62] and that the possibility is "necessarily realized at some time"? [63] On the one hand, if the possible and the future are coalesced (you deny, e.g., that it was possible to have prevented World War II), the possible and the necessary become the same. On the other hand, since the free realization of a possibility is "beyond the control of the possibility or of present actualities," [64] the

---

[60] *Modes of Being,* p. 116.
[61] *Ibid.*
[62] *Modes of Being,* p. 44.
[63] *Ibid.,* p. 116.
[64] *Review of Metaphysics,* VIII (1955), 670.

actualization of the possible seems arbitrary. You appear in fact to have merged modality and temporality.

Weiss: It does not rain today. What was possible, yesterday, for today? It was not possible for it to rain today, for the course of the world, from yesterday to today, precluded the rain. But if it were not possible for it to rain, is it not necessary that it not rain? Only if possible rain and possible not-rain are two distinct entities, and the rejection of the one requires the selection of the other. Yesterday what was possible for today was "rain-or-not-rain"; today this possibility was realized in the delimited form of "not-rain." Does this confuse the actual with the possible? On the contrary, it distinguishes them. Does it confuse the hypothetically necessary with the possible? On the contrary, it identifies them. Does it merge modality and temporality? On the contrary, it relates them.

A possibility has an indeterminate range which is specified only when the possibility is realized. In speaking of "rain-or-not-rain," "sitting-or-standing" as possibilities, I am of course making use of particular illustrations. I could have used "raining light-or-hard," "sitting straight-or-slumped." If I did, I would not be referring to "raining" or "sitting" *simpliciter* as possibilities.

If it is possible for me to be standing or for me to be sitting at moment T, must I not be possibly alive at moment T? Yes. Does this not mean that there is a nondisjunctive possibility, "alive"? No. "Alive" here means only "able-to-be-sitting-or-standing." We can always call the hyphenated expression by a single name. But this will not make it determinate internally, without internal disjunctiveness. If it be said that the possibility of my being alive at moment T is actualized at T in my being alive standing, that the possible weather at moment T is actualized at T in not-rain, only a verbal alternative is offered to my position.

If it be maintained that the possible is a determinate entity in every respect like the actual except that it has a different date or place, the world is unnecessarily duplicated, and no place is left for the vital act of actualizing possibilities, of exercising freedom, of making, of living through a time in which something that was not yet able to stand over against other items, which lacked detail, was given status, power—in short, specification and determinateness.

Amélie O. Rorty: Do you really avoid an infinite regress of mediators between possibility—or Ideality—and Actuality? God assures the realization of every possibility,[65] and Existence makes every actuality strive for its possibilities.[66] But then one needs something to relate God to possibilities and Existence to actualities. If this is unnecessary because the modes are somehow internally related, no mediation was required in the first place.

Weiss: A special form of this question was stated and dealt with in *Modes of Being.*[67] There and throughout the book it was contended that a mode is related to other modes by a neutral relation of togetherness, whose being is derived from the beings of the modes. The togetherness mediates; such mediation would lead to an infinite regress only if the togetherness were another mode of being, or if the modes had to be related to the togetherness. The togetherness has a being, but a dependent one (though an independent nature); the modes are relatable to the togetherness in thought (and this leads not to an infinite regress, but to an infinite progress in analysis).

Richard H. Cox: Can you clarify your stand on rights?
You say in *Our Public Life,* "Almost all men today . . . are convinced that men have . . . native rights." [68] You appear to rely heavily on that widely shared opinion to corroborate the argument that we must grant the existence of such rights or else find it impossible to say that the state could abuse men or treat them unjustly. What is the philosophic status of the shared opinion, so far as the presumed existence of the rights is concerned? Why do you insist on rights as opposed to what is right by nature for the being, man?

Weiss: A widely held opinion is to be taken seriously. One may give it up in the end, but the reason must be that it is inconsistent with

[65] *Modes of Being,* pp. 119, 535.
[66] *Ibid.,* p. 223.
[67] P. 114.
[68] P. 46.

other truths more firmly grounded. Rights are claims which are warranted by the nature of the beings who make them. Our awareness of ourselves as like others, combined with our awareness of the warrant for our claims to personality, truth, life, and the like, grounds the common acknowledgment that there are native rights, the defiance of which testifies to the injustice of a state or of other men. The existence of such rights is consistent with "right by nature," that is, with what the Ideal demands. Indeed, both must be acknowledged, the one if the proper functioning of society is to be understood, the other if man's obligations are to be properly grounded.

Robert W. Browning: What is the transition or relation between the cores of Part II and Part III of *Man's Freedom?* Are there not two contrasting ethics here, one an ethics of individual policy with freedom to choose ultimate ends, and one an ethics which assigns man his one ultimate end as essentially grounded in his nature?

Weiss: There are distinct but related views presented in the *three* parts of *Man's Freedom*. The first relates to the freedom to prefer some means to a goal; the second relates to a freedom of choice of ends and means together; the third deals with the creative will and its production of results in consonance with the absolute Good. Strictly speaking, the last alone is the concern of ethics; the other two are the concern of societal and absolute morality. All three are limited specifications of an ultimate encompassing whole; they are related in an order of more and more adequate, more and more comprehensive, realizations of the Ideal.

Ellen S. Haring: Concluding Question on Ethics. I have the impression that you try to have too many things "both ways." Will you please deal with the following apparent conflicts in your theory?

1. You say we humans are guilty. This is, in part, because of our failures and omissions. Now, every failure and omission marks what most of us regard as a lost possibility. You, however, will not allow us to say that a possibility has been lost. Genuinely real possibilities always are realized, and a so-called lost or unrealized possibility was never genuinely real (see *Modes of Being,* p. 109, as well as your replies to

Amélie O. Rorty and Father McMullin). You can grant that today I failed to help my neighbor, but you will not say that yesterday it was possible for me to give help today. Even if the difficulty here is only verbal, why adopt a locution which requires that an act properly termed obligatory and practicable be also termed not a possible act?

2. You argue persuasively that real possibilities must be disjunctively indeterminate in order to allow for the free creative action of actualities. The Good, however—"the Ideal in its relation to Actualities," [69] a highly or the maximally general real possibility—is in some ways anything but disjunctively indeterminate. It demands, obligates, prescribes, and measures. It is not good-or-bad, but good all through.

3. How can the indeterminate Good prescribe anything? Must there not be something outside the Ideal which prescribes what aspects or incipient subdivisions of the Ideal merit realization?

4. You suggest to Nathan Rotenstreich that a philosopher should not be content merely to inquire and know; yet, in your answer to Andrew J. Reck, philosophic speculation seems to be a way as sound as any other for getting into right relation to the Good.

5. Along with Robert W. Browning I have difficulty in bringing together your treatment of ends and choice with your account of Good and will. You hold us irretrievably committed to the ends associated with our acts; [70] you also grant that ends may be evil, not what a good or wise man would have chosen.[71] It is evidently better for us to regulate our lives in the light of the Good than only to serve ends, even if we serve them conscientiously. On the basis of all this, I would expect you to say that a knowledge of the Good will enlighten our choice of ends, and that a man's discovery of the Good releases him from a commitment to poor ends previously chosen. I do not, however, find explicit assertions of this sort in your writings.

6. You wish to hold that values are both man-dependent and man-independent. Moreover, as to man-dependence you make the two claims which strike Father Owens and me as incompatible (see the first part of his question on the moral good, p. 301). Very likely it is possible

[69] *Modes of Being*, p. 120.
[70] *Man's Freedom*, p. 123.
[71] *Ibid.*, pp. 114–115; *Modes of Being*, p. 98.

to acknowledge values which are natural phenomena,[72] other values which are "a new dimension in existence" introduced natively and even unconsciously by men,[73] and still different values which depend on men deliberately dedicated to the Good. Yet I do not think that you have made fully evident just how you recognize all three without falling into contradictions.

7. In your replies you have made these two statements: "We are obligated because we are men whose completeness requires that we adopt and make determinate the Ideal with which we are by nature concerned (p. 301)." And, "It is only because we seek to be representative of all mankind, of all Actuality, and eventually of all there is, that we have an obligation to bring about what ought to be (p. 303)." According to the first assertion, we seem to be congenitally obligated, and, according to the second, we seem to be voluntarily so.

Weiss: CONCLUDING ANSWER ON ETHICS. 1. We can be obligated to do what we cannot in fact. "Never do evil," "Don't be selfish," "Pay your debts," "Be perfect as thy father in heaven is perfect," cannot be completely fulfilled; do they therefore cease to be obligatory?

Surely we do not mean by the first, "Do as little evil as you can manage to do; should you be driven by greed, desire, passion, should you be confused, ignorant, or poorly conditioned, whatever evil you then do will not be ascribable to you." Those who hold that we are obligated to do only what we can do, make the Good vary in extent according to the weaknesses or attitudes of men. In the end, for them, all men are innocent. But this surely is not the case. As for the antecedent possibility of the deed you fail to perform, I see no need to change my position. The possibility which one could have realized but did not—for example, helping one's neighbor so far as it is within one's power—is an unseparated, indeterminate component of a real distinct possibility which was realized in the form of a neglect of the neighbor's needs.

2. The fact that the Good demands, obligates, etc., that it is good all through, does not mean that its disjunctively related components are

[72] *Man's Freedom,* chap. 7.
[73] *Ibid.,* p. 203.

themselves good or determinate. Taken disjunctively, the Good is radically indeterminate; as a unity, however, it has definite, determinate features which enable it to stand over against other ultimate realities.

3. The question is twofold. It may be asking why there should be any prescriptiveness at all to the Ideal, or the Good, or it may be asking why we are obligated to do this rather than that. The answer to the first of these questions is that the Ideal (like Actuality, Existence, and God) is incomplete, demanding of other realities that it be completed by them. The answer to the second question is that the Ideal is necessarily specified by actualities in the form of distinctive subdivisions of the obligation imposed by the Ideal as such.

4. Philosophic speculation is as sound and basic and desirable an adventure as any other. But this does not mean that it can replace the others, or that a man ought not to supplement what he achieves in philosophy by what can be achieved in other ways.

5. The Good as creatively willed does and ought to make a difference to one's preferences and choices, leading one to abandon some which otherwise would be desirable.[74]

6. Apart from men, there are good and bad things—growth, decay, natural beauties, conflict, frustration. With the coming of man, some things necessarily achieve a value in relation to him; certain microbes are good, and others bad, for him. Third, man by his actions deliberately improves and mars, making some things more and others less valuable.

7. Because we are men, we are inescapably obligated. This point is threefold. First, a man is an actuality who—even without choosing or reflecting on his acts—seeks to be representative. For example, almost every assertion that I make carries with it the claim to be true not only for myself, but for all men. When I say that this sheet before me is white, I mean that it is white for any man in this position. I judge, act, plan as a representative *man*. Second, by virtue of his self and mind, a man is representative not only of men, but of all actualities; thus he is necessarily and nonvoluntarily concerned with the realization of the Good. Third, when a man comes to know himself, when he becomes more and more self-aware, when he freely seeks the Good, he does more effectively and completely what he was always trying to do.

[74] See *Man's Freedom*, pp. 221, 224 ff.

V. PERSONAL OBSERVATIONS

Joseph Owens, C.Ss.R.: What led to your deep interest in metaphysics at a time when the subject was unpopular and the term practically a term of abuse?

Weiss: I was taught by a brilliant teacher, Morris R. Cohen; I was a student of a philosophic genius, Alfred North Whitehead; I studied under a great historian of philosophy, Étienne Gilson.

Having some aptitude for logic, I began by concentrating in that area. I had hoped it would provide a clue to understanding the entire range of knowledge and being. After a number of years of concentrated work in the field I discovered that I was not singularly apt, that almost everyone working in it at the time was overly cautious and had little knowledge or understanding of the great philosophers or the perennial problems, and that at its best, logic raised problems which it was unable to solve—the nature of individuals, the risk in inference, the status of logical laws, its bearing on, and relation to, nonmathematical disciplines, and the like. I had also learned from Charles S. Peirce that the greatest intellectual crime was to block the road of inquiry. It soon became apparent to me, too, that those who forbid other strugglers toward the light to look in some direction or other are usually unprepared to deal with and uninterested in something of magnitude to be found in that direction. They prompted me to become even more alert to what was being forbidden than I had been before.

The positivists who suddenly came to the fore in the thirties and forties seemed to me to be singularly ignorant of the history of thought, and strangely innocent of the difficulties their own views raised—such as the need to acknowledge potentialities (conditionals), their incapacity to verify their own preconceptions, the limitations of the scientific method. When they stridently proclaimed that metaphysics was nonsense, I found it difficult to take their claim seriously. After all, they justified it only on the flimsy ground that the expressions of metaphysicians did not conform to those which could be formulated in the language of the *Principia Mathematica* or contemporary physics. I did not see why one should, without examination, without knowledge, without a consideration of the possibility of approaches alternative to one's own, treat Plato, Aristotle, Spinoza, Hegel as stupid men who tripped over elementary facts of grammar. A pinch of dialectic would have helped them—and might still help their successors, the analysts—to see that the positivist thesis was naïve and bankrupt.

The more I worried about the problems which I confronted in my initial studies in logic, the more I became aware that I had to face the basic, all-comprehensive issues which are traditionally associated with ontology and metaphysics. As time went on I became more and more convinced that philosophy has its own problems, methods, and tests. I am now fully persuaded that the true philosopher knows that not only philosophy, but all other basic disciplines have their own characteristic rationales, problems, procedures, and solutions, and that one ought not to use the outcomes of any to block the way of the others. I found too that if I concentrated on some special problem without having made sure of my underpinnings, I would be bothered again and again, in and outside that special problem, with difficulties I had not faced.

He who refuses to come to terms with ultimate issues refuses to carry through a philosophic quest. The fact that the relentless pursuit of philosophic inquiry is not popular, and particularly not among so-called professional philosophers, points up, I think, the difficulty of philosophy, and the sad effect which the academic world and temper have on the minds of those who are philosophically immature. To have neither interest nor knowledge in other types of thinking or in other types of study than are exhibited in logic, science, ethics, language, religion, or law is, I think, the mark of an unripe philosophic mind.

Had I not studied logic, had I not discussed issues with the dissenters, had I not read what they were affirming and denying, I would not perhaps have become so deeply involved in metaphysics and ontology so quickly. Since most of my early writings were neglected and since my presence in the academic community was largely ignored, I was perhaps freer than most to make the venture of trying to become a philosopher. And then I found that young people here and there, and a few contemporaries, were either going through a similar experience or were sympathetic with the enterprise of thinking things through to the bitter end, no matter what the current fashion, shibboleth, and sanctions. In the midst of a desert pierced by occasional shrieks of denial and dogmatism and ignorance, glimpses of a flourishing land were discerned. It is a pleasure to have lived long enough to see the desert becoming verdant, and to perceive the shrieks turning into faint echoes, hardly heard.

Robert S. Brumbaugh: What implications has *Modes of Being* for the aims of education? In other words, what practical corollaries follow for a person aiming at self-realization?

Weiss: In *Man's Freedom* and *Modes of Being,* education is discussed, and its aims indicated. But Brumbaugh perhaps intends to ask what the implications of the entire system are for education. I think it tells us to take seriously the reality of individuals, the cosmic domain of space-time-energy, the Ideal and God; it points up the importance of engaging in disciplines which rigorously and relentlessly try to understand the essential features of these realities and primary instances of them, and the value of, and need for, studying the outcome of junctures of these realities, and junctures of their instances. It makes evident that we must specialize and then supplement our specialties with an appreciative understanding of the needs and the achievements of others, and that the truly educated man has a vision of the whole, articulated in a plurality of illuminating pivotal points.

William A. Christian: Though philosophy is something more than a treatment of special problems, are there certain special problems in philosophy which are more urgent than others at the present time? What do you consider the principal growing points for philosophy in the near future?

Weiss: I do not think there are any special problems which are more urgent than others. It is as legitimate today as ever to study the nature of universals, the conditions of knowledge, the structure of the state, the aims of education, the methods of science, the claims of religion, the problems of free will, the one and the many, evil, immortality, and action. I do not think there are any principal growing points for philosophy in the near future. Whatever interests a disciplined, intelligent student of philosophy willing to carry out investigations remorselessly and pertinaciously will be the seed from which great philosophic oaks will grow.

Richard T. DeGeorge: In your opinion what is the weakest or most vulnerable or least satisfactory part of *Modes of Being?*

Weiss: The most comprehensive criticism I can make of *Modes of Being* is that it too often is naïve, crude, undetailed, that it should have been subtler and more searching in many places, and that it often fails to carry out the dialectic to the degree it could and should have been carried out. I know that a full meeting of this criticism would entail increasing the size of the book considerably, and that this would involve diminishing returns in comprehensibility. I therefore now look at *Modes of Being* as a kind of blueprint, as a locus of suggestions, reminders, and boundaries, of primary categories and inescapable conditions, needing supplementation by a whole library of works.

Modes of Being should have had an introductory chapter on Experience, in which it was made evident that the four modes of being were encountered in daily life, though in an inchoate form, and in not clearly distinguished areas. In the foreground of our experience are actualities and some part of Existence. Beyond are areas which exhibit something of the Ideal and God and the rest of Existence. The main features of the latter are remarked in hope and fear; we attend to them when we interest ourselves in the Good or the eternal; we are alert to them whenever we wish to know what would complete that which is here concentrated on.

The chapter on Actuality does not keep sufficiently in focus the difference between the mode of being, Actuality, and the particular actualities within it. It should have stressed the fact that man at his best is the representative of the mode of being, Actuality, and thereby of all other actualities.

The chapter on the Ideal strikes me, as it strikes almost everyone else, as allowing for a startling paradox—the necessary realization of possibilities. But I do not yet see that there is anything wrong here. I did not make clear that God enables normative possibilities to be exterior to actualities, and that he guarantees that non-normative possibilities will eventually be realized in Actuality. Most of the discussion on

Might needs correction, particularly Theses 2.56–62,[75] and what is said about natural and positive law must be modified in the light of the discussion in *Our Public Life*.

I cannot get into clear focus the self-divisiveness of Existence, though I think the fact cannot be gainsaid. I did not attend sufficiently to the existence of the Ideal or the existence in God; nor did I ask whether or not such existence would require them to be spatial, temporal, and dynamic, and therefore extended. I think we must say they are not extended, and thus that they subjugate the existence in themselves in a way no actualities do or can. I did not see that not only Existence but God, Actuality, and Ideality all have "existential import," [76] and that the time—and space and process—of history is quite different from that of nature.[77] I did not say, as I should have, that God relates Existence and Actuality, and Existence and the Ideal.[78]

I did not keep in clear focus the fact that separated beings (i.e., beings which are related to one another by a comma) are internally related to one another. If cosmology be thought to concern itself with the modes of being as dynamically interrelated (∴), experience as that which concerns itself with them as merging one with the other (.), and a system of the universe as that which concerns itself with them as structurally involved with one another (⊃), ontology can be said to deal with them as maximally separate. Metaphysics could then be described as being concerned with what beings are in themselves, that is, with the sources of the termini of the forms of togetherness. I did not differentiate metaphysics from ontology. I did not recognize that beings as separate are facets of what they are in and of themselves. It should have been remarked in Thesis 4.06 [79] that each feature of a being is essential to it when that being has certain relations to others. Each of the modes, it should also have been said, has four different kinds of essential features, and each of these offers a ground for a proof of the others. Nor was it clearly seen that man, to be an other of God, must be a representative of Actuality (288–289).[80] It should have been emphasized too that the

[75] *Modes of Being*, pp. 149–153.

[76] *Ibid.*, p. 201.

[77] *Ibid.*, p. 272.

[78] *Ibid.*, p. 274.

[79] *Ibid.*, pp. 280–281.

[80] *Ibid.*, pp. 288–289.

proofs of God that are offered have counterparts in proofs of the other modes, and that whatever virtues and defects are to be found in the former will also be found in the latter.[81]

Throughout I have used terms like "appreciation," "evaluation," and "co-ordination," [82] or "artist" and "mystic," [83] to refer to basic ways of dealing with the modes. But I have not held steadily to those designations, and I think that my choice of terms was not always felicitous. The negative approach (chaps. 6–9) would perhaps be more intelligible if each item were restructured by substituting in the italicized portion "but then" for "otherwise," and placing the whole at the end of the section headed "Against."

The question of the One and the Many discussed in chapter 10 of *Modes of Being* is stated in dualistic terms, and an attempt is made to give an answer in just those terms.[84] But if what is said on pages 514 ff. of *Modes of Being* about the four modes as necessarily involved with one another, and what is said on pages 517 f. on the necessity that there be four modes, is correct, the preceding discussions are seriously affected. Incidentally, it seems to me that, in *Modes of Being,* I occasionally confuse the dot and the comma—for example, page 510, lines 21, 22, where "of" and "from" ought to be interchanged, and page 513, eight lines from the bottom, where "convergence" and "self-direction" should be interchanged.

I am not yet content with the answer that there are four "ones," each uniting a distinct facet of each mode of being with a distinct facet of each of the other modes. I see that any reduction of those "ones" to a single "one" will involve a production of three additional single "ones," that any merging of the modes of being will presuppose their union in three other ways. I feel uneasy before the result, though I see nothing wrong with it. Perhaps I sense a weakness; or perhaps I am needlessly clinging to old, unexpressed beliefs which the dialectical result rightly contravenes. I do not know. If the answer given is correct, however, consideration should be given to the necessity that there be four kinds of time, four logics, four norms, and so on. One will then be driven to

---

[81] *Ibid.,* pp. 324–327.

[82] E.g., *ibid.,* p. 374.

[83] E.g., *ibid.,* pp. 543, 547.

[84] *Ibid.,* pp. 509 ff.

consider anew the question of the nature of the one comprehensive time, logic, norm, etc., which is to be adopted if we are to speak of all the modes in neutral terms.

Though I think it cannot be maintained that the forms of togetherness are modes of being, it seems quite clear that they have distinctive natures. But what is the relation of these four natures to the four modes of being that they relate? Do the four modes of being have natures of their own? Or is it the case that just as the being of a togetherness is derived from the beings which are together, the nature of a being is derived from the togetherness relating that being to others? It seems to me now that the answer to the last question is in the affirmative, but the question should have been raised, pursued, and answered in detail in *Modes of Being*.

Most important perhaps is the need to attend to the outcome of the interplay of actual men with each of the other modes. Ethics and politics relate to the interplay of men and Ideality; art and history relate to the interplay of men and Existence; religion and church relate to the interplay of men and God. The outcome of these interplays are forms of togetherness which have careers and—in the case of politics, history, and church—also have a distinctive power integral to them. But how is it possible for history, for example, to have a distinctive course, a distinctive space, time, and way of becoming, and yet be only a derivative outcome of the coming together of distinct modes of being? My tentative answer is that history takes into itself the powers which are expressed by these modes of being. It is a basic weakness of *Modes of Being* that it did not look into the question of how a togetherness could relate beings and also have a power to continue to be and to function over against the very items which helped to constitute it.

I hope that these various difficulties can be overcome. If they cannot, they reveal serious limitations in my view. I hope that what has been said on behalf of that view is of sufficient interest to make it worth the while of others to see if there are fatal flaws in what was proposed, and that therefore the day is not far off when a comprehensive and less flawed account is made available to us all.

Interrogation of

Charles Hartshorne

Conducted by William Alston

Charles Hartshorne was born in 1897 at Kittanning, Pennsylvania. He was educated at Haverford, Harvard, Freiburg and Marburg. Hartshorne has taught at Harvard, the University of Chicago, Emory University, Stanford University, the New School for Social Research, and at the Universities of Melbourne, Washington, Kyoto, Johann Wolfgang Goethe in Frankfurt, and Yale. At present he is in the Department of Philosophy at the University of Texas. He is a past president of the American Philosophical Association, Western Division, of the Charles Peirce Society, and of the Metaphysical Society of America. He is now president of the Southern Society for Philosophy of Religion and an associate of the American Ornithological Association. He was co-editor with Paul Weiss of the *Collected Papers of Charles Peirce,* editor and author, with William L. Reese, of *Philosophers Speak of God.* Among his extensive writings are *Beyond Humanism, The Philosophy and Psychology of Sensation, The Divine Relativity, Man's Vision of God, Reality as Social Process,* and *The Logic of Perfection.*

I. PROCESS

Nels F. S. Ferré: Can process as we know it be self-explanatory in any genuine sense? Is not the mystery of the blitz-emergence of process in eternity and of human history in cosmic process so staggering as to make more rational a faith-judgment which posits creative being as the source of the process?

Hartshorne: Since possibilities are infinite and include "incompossible" values, and therefore potential value is inexhaustible, one must choose between two views: There is eternal contentment (or helpless lack of contentment), with the actualization of values up to, but not beyond, some arbitrary limit; *or* there is eternal progression toward ever more value. The former seems absurd; hence I view process as the irreducible mode of reality. Absurdity of the alternative is not the only ground for my taking process to be ultimate. Another is the following: (1) Every concept depends for its meaning upon a contrast. But some concepts can expressly include the contrast upon which they depend in a sense in which others cannot include it. The former are the ultimate or self-explanatory concepts; the latter are secondary or dependent ones. Becoming or process can be so conceived that it entirely includes its own contrast with being, while being cannot be conceived to include its contrast with becoming. More precisely: What becomes and what does not become (but simply is) together constitute a total reality which becomes. (2) Again, a novel factor together with an old or non-novel factor give a novel togetherness of the two factors. The new or created, or that which becomes, is thus in principle the inclusive reality, and the uncreated, or pure being, is the included reality. To arrive at the latter, we must abstract from the total concrete reality insofar as it becomes. Philosophy's task, however, is to conceive the concrete; for the abstract has its function only in relation to the concrete. Being is in and for becoming, not conversely. (3) My third argument is pragmatic. To act is to produce the novel. The standpoint of pure being must claim to transcend entirely the practical point of view. But the defense of such transcendence is itself a piece of practice, which cannot consistently justify itself as such. On the other hand, the process of acting can perfectly well include elements of fixity, stability, permanence by the principle referred to in the previous argument. We shall see this more clearly in subsequent replies. (4) A fourth argument is from experience. Experience is a process, whose data are processes. We observe happenings—a flash, a clap of thunder, a twinge of pain. And granting, against David Hume, that an abiding self can be found in experiences, it is a self in experiences rather than experiences in a self that is found. This again illustrates the doctrine of inclusiveness referred to above. (5) A fifth argument is from natural science, which has found the concept of event indispensable, but the concept of self-identical changing substance not only dispensable but inapplicable on the ultimate microlevel. (6) I have one more rather technical argument from the definability of symmetrical relations through those not symmetrical. Beings symmetrically coexist (unless there is but one, and then "one" expresses no contrast and insofar is meaningless), while processes asymmetrically succeed one another. These, in outline, are my arguments, for process philosophy as against a philosophy of being.

If "process as we know it" means the worldly process, then it is indeed not self-explanatory. To explain it one may appeal to divine process (analogically conceived), of which the divine eternity is only an aspect (the primordial-everlasting ideal of fulfillment, but not the fulfillment iself). Process as such does not emerge, in eternity or anywhere else. It simply is, without alternative. Eternity is an abstract element of actual process, just as "different entities containing an identical aspect" stands for realities more concrete than the bare identity.[1]

Vergilius Ferm: How has the philosophy of Alfred North Whitehead influenced your own, both in general and in particular doctrines?

Hartshorne: I came to Whitehead already convinced that experience is essentially participation, that any reality we can conceive must be

[1] Concerning "creative being," see Ferré's question, pp. 344 f.

constituted of feelings in some broad sense, that reality is creative process and the future is open even for God (here William Ernest Hocking was my teacher, with William James and perhaps Henri Bergson), that metaphysical freedom is real. Each of these convictions was arrived at after I had for a time believed the contrary position. Whitehead began to influence me strongly at the same time as Charles S. Peirce (in 1925 —following two years of postdoctoral study abroad—while I graded papers in Whitehead's course at Harvard for a semester) and it is not easy to disentangle their influences. One effect of Whitehead was in making me aware of the ambiguities in the notion of predication as applied to enduring individuals or "substances." "Accidents," he enabled me to see, are not really predicated of the individual at all, but of the state he is "in." It is the states, the events, of experience which have the enduring individuality, not conversely. (The token-reflexive functioning of nouns and pronouns tends to conceal this.) Leibniz showed once for all what the converse assumption means, namely, the denial of accidental states altogether. Whitehead with sheer consistency adheres to his choice, once made. Only in application to God does he seem to waver or to fall into ambiguity in this regard.

The sources of my ideas about God are in good part elsewhere, though I enormously admire Whitehead's discussions of the theistic problem. That God must, as he says, be "dipolar," with an eternal-immutable and an accumulative-everlasting aspect, seems to me the essential correction which must be made in traditional theism. It was implicit, though probably I was not sharply aware of this, in the view which I had accepted some years before 1925. However, it is important to realize that, as Whitehead admitted (in conversation with A. H. Johnson), it will not do to think of God merely as two natures or essences; even though the second, as expressing the concrete side of God, may be thought to include the first and thereby establish the divine unity. Any essence is abstract, and the Consequent Nature is simply the abstract principle that there must always be for each new state of the world process a new Consequent State of deity by which the world totality in question is prehended or possessed. Thus there is no one entity called God *qua* consequent, but an endless accumulation of consequent states of deity, each of which sums up all its predecessors. This has some similarities and some differences with Trinitarian doctrine, and in my view it implies that God is a "personally ordered society." Whitehead's objection to this view (given only in conversation with Johnson) seems invalid. It amounts to this, that God would not be simply one more personal society, but would have a unique excellence. This must be no less true of God as identical with a single "actual entity"; indeed, this terminology seems to make God precisely that sheer exception to categorical principles which Whitehead says must be avoided. My view, on the contrary, merely explicates the sense in which God is the "supreme exemplification" of the categories. Being "supreme" has to mean being exceptional in some sense; however, the category itself should make the exception intelligible; and I cannot see that "actual entity," for God *qua* consequent, can do this. Actual entity here must rather mean a single Consequent State in the divine sequence of states.

Whitehead's views of "matter," the mind-body relations, perception, and causation have influenced me greatly. It is his, and not Kant's, "answer to Hume" that I have found intelligible.

William A. Christian: What is your present view of relations between contemporaries?

Hartshorne: Since an event can, on my view, be intrinsically related to another only by having it as datum, and it scarcely seems that two events can each be datum for the other, it appears that contemporaries (events not past or future relative to one another) cannot have intrinsic relatedness. But the relativity of simultaneity affirmed by physics, while no doubt a deep truth about the world, cannot, I incline to think, be the whole truth about temporal relations. If the past alone is actual and the future but potential (or if we are to avoid a neo-Parmenidean view of the event-manifold), then contemporaries must be in process of becoming actual; however, of two contemporaries to a given event, one subsequent to the other (physics allows this), both cannot be in process of becoming, for only when the earlier has already become can the later be in process. Thus the notion of a "creative advance of nature" seems to imply a cosmic "front" of simultaneity as short as the shortest specious present. I suppose God to have this cosmic *now* as his psychological simultaneity. His awareness not being at a distance from any-thing, no time lag is required for information to travel to him. Yet, to avoid the mutuality above excluded (two entities, each a datum for the other), the divine awareness must be viewed as always just subsequent to its data; and to square the doctrine with physics we need to deny that God's awareness of things as simultaneous has any appreciable effect in the world. As two scientists put it to me, "God must not be able to tell us" what is or was simultaneous with what we have just experienced.

In Whiteheadian terms, our prehensions of God must be "negative" with respect to his prehensions of distant contemporaries. Is this so surprising? What relevance could these have for us? Moreover, as former Emory student John Wilcox has pointed out in a Master's thesis, the assumption of a divine simultaneity need not mean that some actual perspective in the world is "right" as against others. For the divine per-spective might be "eclectic," agreeing (approximately) as to some items with one standpoint, as to others with another, and the incidence of agreement might be constantly shifting. The number of moving bodies (at least in a finite area) being finite, they constitute all together only a vanishing fraction of the possible standpoints. There is then every reason to attribute a unique standpoint, not represented in the world, to deity, and in this way the "symmetry" among inner-worldly stand-points which is affirmed by physicists may be essentially retained. On the other hand, is it not rather implausible that localized and, as such, defective perspectives could add up to the entire truth simply by virtue of a law of transformation verifiable from those perspectives? Perhaps we have no need to know the whole truth; but we may have need to believe that the whole truth can be and is known.

Newton P. Stallknecht: If we recognize that the past does not ex-haustively determine the present and future, can we argue that the present "determines" the past—that is, in the sense that it logically im-plies the past? Or can we not say that our present might have arisen as the outcome of any one of a number of pasts? If we do logically limit our present to "one possible past," do we not revive the notion of a necessary connection between past and present?

Hartshorne: My argument is: Temporal relations must be in something: if "A precedes B" expresses a relation in A, then B must be real before it becomes, which seems paradoxical; if, however, the relation is rather, and solely, in B, as a relation of following, not of preceding, the paradox vanishes, for first A alone is, and then B-following-A. But if, as the questioner seems to suggest, the relation is in *neither* A nor B, then it is a third term needing to be related to the other two—again, a paradox. It may, of course, be regarded as no less paradoxical that B should contain relation-to-A, and hence A as its predecessor, and thus the past event should still be a reality. But how could it be otherwise, considering that truth is agreement with reality, and that practically all definite truth about particular events that we can know is truth about the past? Moreover, the necessity of the earlier for the later event no more entails the converse necessity than "P entails Q" means that "Q entails P." To be sure, so far as B is causally determined by A, that is (on my view of causality), so far as *something like* B is bound to occur, A having occurred, we can say that A, just in being A, necessarily must have as its successor something or other fulfilling the causal requirements. It would not, however, do to limit ourselves to "something or other fulfilling certain requirements" for the predecessor of B, for then there would never be a pair of determinate particular events illustrating the temporal relation in either direction, and this contradicts the notion that there are "events" at all.

Albert E. Avey: What is the connection of Leibniz' monadology with your philosophy?

Hartshorne: I have always admired Leibniz for his clarity and originality. Even his mistakes are those of great genius. To be made acceptable his monads must be "toned down" into Buddhistic-Whiteheadian momentary actual entities, units of becoming; and they must be really related to preceding actual entities, units of becoming; and they must be really related to preceding actual entities by relationships intrinsic to their natures. Monads must have windows, at least toward the past of the universe relative to them. One must also tone down the doctrine that the monad involves future events as well as past. An actual entity involves a range of real potentialities for the future, both in and beyond its own personal sequence (if it belongs to such), rather than a single determinate possibility. There is not even a moral determinism or "infallible inclination" of the will, but only approximate or probabilistic causal influence.

Leibniz combined two theorems in his view of monads: (1) The most concrete or determinate thing describable in true predication must intrinsically contain all predicates attributable to it, and thus to speak of "inessential" or "accidental" qualifications is here meaningless; (2) the concrete is the common-sense "individual" or "substance" (not the event or unit-becoming as in Buddhism and some recent Western systems). Many of the paradoxes of the monadology derive from the attempt to combine these two tenets, plus (3) the attempt to explain away relations as not genuine properties ("subject-predicate logic," for which an elementary proposition typically concerns but one subject or concrete entity at a time). I entirely agree with (1), which with Leibniz I regard as analytic, explicative of what is meant by "truth," or by "concrete." But it follows that we should reject (2); for only so can we construe the indispensable common-sense meanings expressed in "inessential characters" of an individual, for example, acts which that very individual might not have performed, or experience "he" might not have had. Freedom to have done otherwise must not mean to have been born a numerically other individual. Only of the "actual entity" can this be accepted. "John might have done otherwise" means that another actual entity (also a token-reflexive referent of "John") might have self-created itself (see Wild's query, p. 330) at that point in John's personal sequence. Of course I reject (3). Leibniz' God I accept only with essential transformations: properties not admitting an absolute maximum (such as complexity) must also be applied to God—though in all-other-surpassing, self-surpassing fashion, and not as simply unsurpassable; and God must have open windows of receptivity toward the creatures, not merely they toward him.

Milic Capek: Is the existence of durationless instants compatible with the reality of process? Are not mathematical instants fictitious or ideal? If not, how do you deal with Zeno's paradoxes? If so, why do you, in *The Philosophy and Psychology of Sensation,* refer to "mathematical continuity" as one of the features of your theory of sensation?

Hartshorne: I have accepted from Whitehead the conception of a quantum of becoming. Any actual process is held to be composed of unit-events, each with finite, not zero or indefinite, time-length. Thus between waking in the morning from dreamless sleep and falling again into such sleep at night, a person has, in the course of a particular day, a definite finite number of successive experiences. That we do not clearly observe this division of experience into units is one example among many of the limitations of human consciousness or introspection (retrospection, really). Some philosophers suppose the number of experiences in a finite time to be indefinite or merely subjective, depending upon what criterion of a "single" experience we arbitrarily adopt. Charles S. Peirce argued for the "infinitesimal" present, which would seem to mean an infinite number of experiences in a finite time. This is not plausible to me. I agree with Leibniz that if there is plurality as an objective fact, and there plainly is, there must be units, each of which is one definite entity, in a sense in which the plurality is not. But with Whitehead I apply this to temporal as well as spatial plurality. Space-time being the order of interrelated events, actual and potential, there must be unit-events. Leibniz seemed not to recognize these; the Buddhists, however, have always recognized them, though perhaps without sharp focus on the question put by Professor Capek. William James, of course, took the quantum view, and Whitehead refers to this precedent. I am not sure which author I read first on the point. Only lately have I discovered that from the historical point of view it is the Buddhists, and no Western group of philosophers, who first arrived at a philosophy of process.

Within a unit-event there is no actual succession, A after B, with memory of B in A. There is but one "subject" remembering in a given event, and what it remembers are previous unit-events, not "earlier parts" (there are none) in the same event. To say that the event has duration means only that it becomes, and that while it becomes, a number of other events may occur in succession. Thus while one of us has a single experience, some other enduring individual (event-sequence) on a nonhuman level may have a thousand or a million. (This idea I first encountered in Josiah Royce, though in him the notion of unit-event seems lacking in focus.) If an event occupied a mathematical instant, this overlapping of events one-to-many would be contradictory. Time-length is relational, not an internal affair of successive parts within a single actuality. Both psychology and physics seem to support this view, though there are subtle problems in both connections.

In my first book, I was not thinking of a continuum of actual sensations, but of possible sensory qualities. It happened that I arrived at something like Peirce's notion of the continuity of possible qualities a year or two before reading Peirce. This was an example of the sort of thing which led me to feel a measure of pre-established harmony with Peirce as well as with Whitehead. For Whitehead said once, "Possibility, generality, and continuity are all the same thing." Couple this with Whitehead's "actuality is incurably atomic," a point which Peirce at times seems to forget or deny, though it is required to give his doctrine any sharp meaning, and you have a theory of continuity as the order of possibility, but not of actuality. The relation of the "continuity of possible sensory qualities" to mathematical continuity is a subject I am not competent to discuss. At that time I had some trust in Peirce's "proof" that mathematical continuity is a "multitude beyond all multitude," points being virtual rather than real parts. Persons more versed in these matters than I am have denied the validity of Peirce's demonstration. Admitting this, I still think that the continuum is no actual multitude, but an affair of the possible. The continuity of time is the order of the possible time-lengths for specious presents of various kinds; the continuity of red, orange, yellow, etc. (as sensory qualities) is the order of possible color sensations. Any actual array of sensations is finite in number of qualities, but the possible qualities (including those our introspection could not distinguish) between red and orange are neither finite nor infinite but continuous or beyond number. This is one reason why I have trouble with "eternal objects." I have here been greatly influenced by Peirce's conception of the "evolution of . . . the very Platonic forms themselves." [2]

Against the denial of quanta of process, a "Zeno argument" might take this form: In the history of a single human being, say, there would be no first experience. For the experience during the first second would not be the first, nor that during the first half-second. Thus there would

[2] See *Collected Papers of Charles S. Peirce*, ed. by Charles Hartshorne and Paul Weiss (Cambridge: Harvard University Press, 1935, 1960), Volume VI, Section 194; see Sections 185–212.

be no objectively first experience. Yet it would not do to say that there is simply one experience throughout the individual's life, or until the first sleep. For then there would be no real succession of experiences. Note that the series of events after the state of things in which the individual did not exist as an event-sequence is not simply an endless series (supposing each event to consist of subevents without end) but is also a beginningless series. Yet this series has to be entered upon. How can a beginningless series be entered upon?

In this formulation I have adapted an argument of Whitehead's, changing it slightly in an effort to avoid a difficulty which his version seems to suggest.

I hope these explanations narrow the gap, if any, between my views and those of the questioner, since I believe he has thought astutely about such matters.

John Wild: You assert in *Reality as Social Process* [3] that "the human mind, at any given moment, is not drastically different in size and shape from the pattern of activity in the nervous system . . . and as this activity moves about somewhat, it follows that the mind literally moves in brain and nerves. . . ." But do we not have to maintain the following distinctions between the *physical* and the *psychical?* The psychical is intentional in structure; it is always of something quite distinct from itself and may be double-dated in memory and anticipation, once as subject and once as object. Whereas the physical is non-intentional in structure, it is not *of* anything quite distinct from itself, and is never double-dated—one as a subject, another as an object. How would you deal with the facts on which this distinction is based?

Hartshorne: How does my questioner know that physical events contain simply no intentional structure, no intrinsic reference to past or future? On the contrary, we seem compelled to treat all events as relative to preceding causes and as involving a range of possible subsequent effects; and this is how immediate memory and anticipation must appear from without. To remember is to experience in the present the influence of the past; Whitehead (following Bergson) turns this around: to posit an influence of the past is to posit some form of mem-

[3] (Glencoe, Ill.: The Free Press, 1953), p. 36.

ory. Our human memory (especially immediate memory—for recollection after forgetting is a higher-level affair which, I agree with Wild, is not universal)—our memory is not simply evidence of influence, it is a case of it, the model for any concept of influence that goes beyond Hume's skepticism without mere verbalism.

II. FEELING

A. P. Ushenko: What are your objections, if any, against a shift of emphasis from the category of *feeling* to the category of *power*? Does not the unqualified emphasis on the category of feeling carry with it too much of a suggestion of passive receptivity?

Hartshorne: By all means, emphasize "power." But is there not an ambiguity in the word? It connotes influence, and it also suggests the capacity or potentiality for being influenced. Thus the power to enjoy music is a potency for being influenced in a certain way. In "feeling *of* feeling," the second feeling, as prehended or received, influences the first as prehending or receiving it; the receiving feeling, however, is not merely passive; for it is impossible that data should strictly dictate the manner of their reception into a new unity of feeling. The new "one" cannot be deduced from the antecedent "many"; rather, it must be "self-created." It is real only as an act; and the new creature becomes, in its turn, a "potential for becoming," a datum available for future acts of prehension, a new *power*.

William Alston: You hold that panpsychism is the only genuine metaphysical alternative because various aspects of things—intrinsic quality, temporary relations, singularity, potentiality, etc.—can only *really* be conceived in terms of feeling. But it seems that in science and in everyday life, we do often conceive temporal relations, potentialities, etc., of things, without thinking about them panpsychistically. Could you make explicit your notion of conception or thought in terms of which these everyday ways of conceptually dealing with things cannot be considered "really" conceiving or thinking them? Could it be that we are required to conceive what it would *feel* like to be temporally related, etc.? In that case, the metaphysical position is already presupposed in the criterion.

Hartshorne: The nonpanpsychistic ways of thinking tend, I believe, to be visual imaginings (our own visual feelings) taken as signs of independent reality, plus pragmatic notions of how we might act or of what it would be like (feel like) for us to bring about certain interactions between that portion of the reality which is our own bodies and the other portions. The "nonhuman" tends to be an x which must have the structure required to explain certain structures in our direct experiences, actual or predictable. Any quality, or any further structure, not thus required is normally of no concern to us—unless we are philosophers, poets, or religious persons, for whom even a very vague awareness of that which in sharp detail is perhaps humanly unknowable may yet be of interest. "How things feel" or "what it is like to be an atom" does not ordinarily matter to most of us. A general need not care at a given moment how his soldiers feel or what they are like in other respects, if only they are making the movements that are winning the battle. That is how we usually deal with crystals, or even with microbes. *Where* things are in the spatial (I say, social) system, and what our bodies will do, and what we will feel, on encountering them, are what we are concerned about. It comes down finally to inner bodily effects explained by an external structural skeleton, whose "flesh and blood," if any, we leave to mystery or to God. And physicists now tell us that the microstructure of matter cannot be visualized, but only given mathematical symbolization. What is being symbolized? Surely not bare numbers or shapes! What is left out, some of us think, could not be anything but the "ocean of feelings," including "intellectual feelings," thoughts, constituting the "life of things" (Wordsworth). There is no reason why this should be visually imaginable, for the eye is a pragmatic organ, not a clear, direct road to the fine-structure and quality of the concrete.

William Alston: Do you consider every feeling to be *of* something, to have an objective reference? If so, is not this to overcognitivize the emotional life?

Hartshorne: Yes—but no! There is nothing necessarily cognitive in my sharing the sufferings of my cells. I have a datum—but not necessarily knowledge, if that means comparison, inference, evaluation of evidence, bringing under a concept. And how much less is the cells' sharing in my feelings knowledge in the normal sense! Yet to admit even a single feeling which *merely feels itself* is to let the solipsist camel under the canvas.

Peter A. Bertocci: Apart from the mechanics of the feeling of feeling, I can find empirical evidence for the hypothesis that biological cells are to be intelligibly conceived as psychic unities. For the most reasonable interpretation of biological fact seems to me to support the view that there is telic activity, or purposive feeling, in all living cells. But is there any sense in which an electron can be considered a telic unity? In other words, can we justify, not on any purely speculative grounds, which I do not discount, but empirically, the extension of panpsychism to the inorganic realm?

Hartshorne: It may be foolish for me, knowing no more physics than I do, to discuss electrons. Yet I do not know how matter can be interpreted save by analogy with an experience as such—the only unitary concrete entity given, with any distinctness, as unitary and concrete. Also electrons undoubtedly relate themselves to their nearest environment, that is, speaking behavioristically, they take account of it; and this taking account is all that "prehension" can be to external observation. Physics does give reason for doubting that electrons pursue identical private ends from event to event in such a manner as to constitute an enduring individual. But such a "socially ordered" or linear sequence of events is a special case, not essential to "experient events." The momentary aim of self-enjoyment as contributory to future becoming of some sort, including God as analogically future, is all that is required. (See below, reply to next question.)

William Alston: Does your (and Whitehead's) "reformed subjectivism" presuppose (*contra* Peirce) that self-awareness is more basic than awareness of objects?

Hartshorne: No, I see no issue with Peirce here. Even when we observe "our own" subjectivity, a present experient occasion objectifies a prior one in immediate memory. Peirce also affirms and emphasizes immediate memory. And Whitehead and I agree with Peirce that personal subjectivity is never the sole content of experience. In that sense, it is not "more basic." It is, however (and this I call "Leibniz' greatest discovery"), the datum which is *most distinctly illustrative of concrete singularity*. In the inanimate world, entities are too insignificant, taken singly, to be worth our perceiving them as such; and hence they are not so perceived. And the subhuman entities composing the human body are likewise given only with a blurring of individual outlines. I see nothing in Peirce against all this. Indeed he rather implies it.

C. J. Ducasse: In *Philosophy and Psychology of Sensation* [4] you write: "That the cells feel individually what we vaguely feel as a blurred synthesis, is, on our theory, inevitable, for it is simply the mind-body relation." I submit on the contrary that the relation these words describe, even if it really obtains, is *not* the mind-body relation at all, but is the relation between the many cellular *minds* and the one human *mind;* and that the relation between these two implies nothing either as to the relation between the cellular body and the cellular mind, or as to the relation between the human body and the human mind.

Hartshorne: I distinguish "a mind" from "a body" (somewhat as Ramanuja did long ago) in terms of the dominance relation of the former with respect to the constituents of the latter. My body is (approximately) the totality of cells over which I have predominant influence (though—Ramanuja seems to forget this at times—they also influence me). A cell's body is the totality of its molecules; and that of a molecule, the totality of its atoms or particles. As for the particles, they apparently have no bodies, but are "disembodied minds" (or subminds, sentient events). The distinction ceases at this point, not because "mind" has faded out, leaving mere "matter," but because there is no further dominance relation. The "extension" of body is interpretable, as Peirce and Whitehead have shown, as the pattern of relationships connoted by the "of" in "feelings," or, as I like to put it, as the social structure of

[4] (Chicago: University of Chicago Press, 1934), pp. 248–249.

feelings. Particles feel other particles, their "embodiment" is in each other.

Peter A. Bertocci: It is one of your basic theses that psychic experience is extended or spatial. If this description were valid, would I not have to find extension in logical relations? Yet it seems clear that logical relationships are not a matter of any conceivable juxtaposition. Implication seems nonspatial, if anything is. Again, while I am convinced that guilt is temporal, I find the experience, as introspected, nonspatial.

Hartshorne: The question rather surprises me. A "psychic experience" as extended is concrete; "logical relations" are abstractions. There is a type problem here: triangularity is not triangular or extended. But any really concrete awareness of shapes, logical relations, or guilt, is neither (1) at a point, nor is it (2) nowhere or anywhere indifferently, but rather (3) in a region—by the same tests as we normally use to locate things regionally (by asking the question, With what other events are there direct relationships of influence?). I, at least, cannot introspect my own experiences as punctiform, nor yet as nowhere. For example, they are "here," you are "there." To be in a region is to be extended. What is extended is always an event; mere guilt is no event, but an aspect of experient events which have also other aspects.

Henry A. Finch: If God's memory contains the achievements of our lives without our being self-conscious after bodily death, does this not raise a strong suspicion that feeling is contingent in the universe, for was not the point of departure of the whole argument to panpsychism the feeling tone of self-conscious personality? In other words, how probative is the analogy argument from self-feeling to the necessary metaphysical conclusion of panpsychism, if self-feeling is contingent? Or again, if the only feeling we are acquainted with is contingent, what reason is there to believe that any other feeling was not contingent?

Hartshorne: As the reader may by this time have seen, the analogical argument is not from the enduring self, as subject of feeling, but from the momentary self, or actual experient occasion. The "achievements" consist entirely of influences upon the feelings of sentient events.

True, every particular, determinate, concrete case of feeling is contingent, even the divine feelings as concrete! It is, however, one thing to say that each feeling is contingent, and another to say that it is only contingent that there are feelings, some feelings or other. It is a favorite doctrine of mine that the non-nullity of a class can be necessary, though no particular member of the class is so. On the plane of conditional necessity this is clear: "You *must* make up your mind" does not imply that any given decision is necessary. Remove the implied condition ("if you want to avoid trouble" or to do your duty), and the same distinction can still be made. On my doctrine, the class of divine feelings, and also the class of nondivine feelings, are both necessarily non-null; but the second class does not refer to any one individual, whereas all possible divine feelings are simply possible states of the one divine individual, or "personally ordered society." This connectedness inheres in their "divinity," or perfection, for example, their all-knowingness.

Bertram Morris: What is your conception of the relevance of society to art? More specifically, how do you come to grips with the element of timeliness of aesthetic creation? Is there not a social factor different from feeling of feeling, such that "impersonal" social forces find their way through the creative spirit into works of art?

Hartshorne: Each society, and each temporal phase of each society, has a more or less different range of qualities of feeling in its members. Structural differences, "intellectual feelings," Max Wertheimer's "whole-qualities," Charles S. Peirce's "emotions of the ensemble," need to be taken into account.

Henry A. Finch: Since in *Reality as Social Process* [5] you hint that a machine is a controllable "society," why not admit that "mechanical" conceptualization is preferable to "animistic" conceptualization, for the advantage that machines can be perfected by work, whereas life can be "tragically enjoyed" but not mastered?

Hartshorne: For some purposes it may well be preferable. Note, however, that a machine is not an *absolutely* controllable society, for

[5] (Glencoe: The Free Press, 1953), p. 133.

nothing is absolutely so; and note also that the most controllable societies are so only because their members are poor in individuality and
creative power. In science we may have to abstract from individuality
and freedom, and thus view things as mechanisms. But it is important
to realize that the purpose of all this is to enhance creative power, and
thus in a very real sense to *decrease* "prediction and control" (sacred
phrase). In these days of unparalleled depth of uncertainty, this elementary truth ought to begin, at least, to gain acceptance. Science itself
is unpredictable; and we know only too well the perils in seeking to
control it.

III. MORALITY

A. C. Garnett: Would not the absolute, logical certainty of the
existence of God reduce all virtue to the level of elementary prudence?
Should not the defense of faith therefore be by logical methods which
seek to show that belief in his existence is reasonable rather than logically certain?

Hartshorne: The certainty *for us* of the divine existence is not entailed by its noncontingency, for the definitive rebuttal of positivism is
not accomplished by the ontological argument; not to mention that one
may admit the validity of one or more arguments without being certain of this validity. And in any case, certainty of the divine existence is
one thing, and the identification of virtue with prudence is a very different thing. I see no logical path from the notion of a divinely wise
and good being to that of a rewarder or punisher who sees to it that,
either in this life or another, good deeds "pay off" in future benefits to
the agent. Virtue is necessarily its own reward so far as the "actual
entity," or momentary self is concerned; beyond that, virtue is generosity of the present self for possible future selves, including those
which may continue the same personal series—all of this future good
being included in what may be termed the divine future. God alone
can reap all rewards, harvest all crops; for he alone forever survives
with unlimited power of appreciating all achievements. My future
comes (or ought to come) into this only as any other person's future in
whom I happen (or ought) to be interested comes into it.

John Wild: You say in *Reality as Social Process* [6] that "absolute identity of the concrete or particular is given in an event or occasion, not in a thing enduring through time, like a person or a body." This troubles me in two respects. First, it seems to imply that an event does not have any duration and is instantaneous. But can anything happen in an instant? Second, it would seem to deny strict identity to bodies and persons as they persist through time. How, then, does it explain the facts of moral responsibility? How can I be strictly held to account for something performed by someone else a year, or a week, or a minute ago?

Hartshorne: As explained in answer to Capek's query (p. 327), events are not instantaneous, nor are they endlessly analyzable into successive subevents (in either case, some form of Zeno's paradoxes would, I suspect, come in). The fractions of a second (or other unit of time) which fail to correspond to any actual subevents express unrealized possibilities of becoming, how process might have been quantized, but was not. This illustrates the general thesis of Peirce and Whitehead that the duality, "actual-potential," is inherent in process, and that continuity is to be assigned to the second pole in the duality.

CONCERNING RESPONSIBILITY: Suppose one of my past selves made a certain decision; we may now either commend or blame that self even though it cannot hear what we say about it. For what it did was good or bad. Suppose the latter. My present self can then take one of two attitudes. It can say (if it dares): I am not as that past self; its way of acting is not mine; for I (in some intermediate self) have repented of this way, and thus I have been "born anew." "Forgiveness of sins" thus means literal innocence of the new self. Remorse is in order only so long as repentance and forgiveness are not complete. Pity for the victims of past acts is another matter, and so is making amends. (One may also make amends for the deed of a relative or even of a friend.) The other possible, in some cases correct, attitude is for the self to confess that repentance is not complete, that there has been no rebirth in the relevant respects, and that the present self, though numerically distinct, is in character, or qualitatively, much as the past self was. Where this is so, the numerical difference affords no escape from con-

[6] P. 102.

demnation. Similarly, if a past self was good, the present self's innocence is presumptive, but is not entailed. One might almost as well boast of the saintliness of one's ancestors. For who knows that his present self has not fallen from the former height, perhaps in the very act of boasting? Thus innocence-and-guilt is a new issue every moment, as the theologian Rudolf Bultmann likes to emphasize.

Consider the legal aspect of the matter. On the preventive theory of punishment, there is no difficulty; for a momentary self does normally take account, more or less, of the probable good or evil of future selves in this same personal sequence. And the reasons lie within reach of our doctrine. So do the considerations supporting the theory that punishment is the preferable alternative to the otherwise perhaps inevitable private vengeance.

"Strictly held to account"—by whom and to what end? If by the law, this has been covered. If by neighbors who wish to censure me, they are perhaps trying to discourage certain modes of conduct, which introduces no new problem; or they are trying to fortify their own resistance to temptation. If the accounting referred to is the divine, then I grant that God judges all acts, but on the understanding that the past self alone is judged for past acts, and the present self only for its present acts or intentions. (If the resort to such unwonted expressions as "present self" is held a suspicious feature of my account, I can only reply that ordinary practical language is used contextually or *token-reflexively,* with all sorts of adjustments to the relativities involved, while philosophers and theologians have substituted illicit absolutes of identity in their theories of substance or of cosmic justice.) The purpose of the divine accounting is not, I am convinced, to give the past self its "deserts" by dealing out values or disvalues to the present or to some future self, but rather to assign the past self its permanent place in the treasury of values. If the self is content to make a poor contribution to the treasury (the divine "memory"), then "it has had its reward." The punishment for failing is—to fail. The world is not, I am convinced, a cosmically extended police court. Yet there is a sense in which the wicked are "brought to naught." For they have no rational aim which can be realized. If they merely want to enjoy themselves as they live, this is not a rational aim; for reason surveys ultimate consequences, and when our personal sequences are all in the past, then it will not be we who still profit from the pleasantness of the experiences making up the sequences. It will rather be the surviving individuals, and God. Thus the rational aim of an actual entity must be disinterested. It is not that virtue becomes rational self-interest, but that self-interest appears as an arbitrarily emphasized constituent of the only motive that can survive criticism: love.

Nels F. S. Ferré: Does personal being persist in any sense beyond physical death? If so, does it persist in such a manner as to make eschatology a more important factor than it is in the philosophy of Whitehead? If not, why is not your philosophy characterized by a more tragic sense of life?

Hartshorne: I have no more eschatology than Whitehead, but I regard his as unimaginably sublime. The tragic aspect of life derives from freedom, which in its multiplicity of self-determining acts means a degree of real chance. That the tragedy would be less if we human beings went on developing new states of self-experience immortally is not at all clear to me. In any heaven there must still be chance and conflict. Moreover, a human individuality cannot, I think, have simply unlimited possibilities of significant variations upon the theme which constitutes its identity; only God is thus unlimited. Nevertheless, I hold with Whitehead that what we are and do upon earth must have significant consequences forevermore; but it is God who will enjoy these consequences, God and future creatures. Nor do I find this particularly tragic. He will elicit the utmost value out of even our failures; and the notion that we could do this better ourselves were our personally ordered sequences to have new members after death seems to me idle speculation if not sheer arrogance. Of course, in a strict sense we do, in our personal being, persist immortally; for the actualities of earthly experience are as personal as anything can be, and in God they "live forevermore."

Peter A. Bertocci: How could we extend the notion of feeling of feeling to situations involving moral guilt (at the human level)? If I represent to myself another's feeling of moral guilt, do I "immediately participate" to some extent in the emotion or desire represented, and sympathize with it? Since his act is contrary to his ideal, the uniqueness of his feeling of guilt is unique to him. Thus I do not know how I can feel *his feeling* at that particular point.

Hartshorne: I do not insist that we can immediately (except with negligible faintness) participate in the feelings of other human beings. But I fail to see that an impossibility of this follows merely from your argument. If I feel the other's sense of an ideal, his actual decisions as partly contrary to it, and his feeling of regret concerning this, I do not thereby cease to be myself. For his "subjective forms" of feeling thus become my "objective forms"; they are my data, but not his data (except as he later reflects back upon them, and then he is, strictly speaking, another subject or actual entity). I feel the other's shame without "being" ashamed, for I feel it as expressing his will in its subjective character, not mine. Your question really denies the very notion of "feeling *of* feeling." In memory, for example, I now intuit or feel my past feeling, but no longer as mere subjective form, rather as objective form, as datum, for the present not-yet-objectified feeling.

Newton P. Stallknecht: What is the significance for the theory of freedom of a moral choice expressed, like Martin Luther's, as follows: "I cannot do [or choose] otherwise?"

Hartshorne: My view allows two interpretations here. "I cannot choose otherwise" may only indicate a near inevitability of the action or that "I could not believe in the rightness of another course" (though I might perhaps be capable of acting wrongly). Or again, the construction might be: The kind of act is indeed strictly unavoidable, given my nature and circumstances, but the moment of the action, and the details, are freely chosen, as against alternatives that I (and not just some other person) might in the circumstances have decided upon. I deny categorically that a genuine act of choice is ever the only possible act. We can like and accept the uniquely possible; we cannot choose it. It does not follow of course that we can have infallible knowledge as to the scope of our actual choosing. Why should we have such knowledge, such absolute introspection? When people say that they could not have avoided falling in love, do they claim that such falling was a free choice? Philosophers speak as though such a claim can be and commonly is made. On the contrary, people are likely to say that it is fate or destiny, not choice, in such an instance. And they are right on the assumption. It is important, too, that what is unavoidable at a given moment of time may have been avoidable at an earlier stage, and hence genuine freedom and choice cannot easily be excluded when the whole past is taken into account.

IV. GOD

Henry N. Wieman: Which of the following should command the ultimate commitment of man?

1. A cosmic mind that gathers into itself all values as they come into existence and conserves them everlastingly.

2. The process of interchange between human beings and between them and material things, by which communicable meanings are created, accumulated, and integrated into a system that can (*a*) expand beyond any known limit; (*b*) be shared with each and all to the limit of the ability of each; (*c*) be integrated into the psychosomatic individuality of each so that what the individual gets from others is creative of his own personality.

3. The abstract order of the universe which makes possible the kind of interchange just described.

Hartshorne: We should be committed to (1) taken as inclusive of (2) and (3) and still more besides! God is in creative interaction with us, and the conservation is only an aspect of the creation. How we remember the past gives character to our creative effort; and how God preserves the actualized process gives character to his ideal for the future, which, in the depths of feeling, inspires the direction of creative process both in us and in the universe at large. The abstract order simply expresses a structural feature of this ideal, and—save in its most abstract aspect—it is subject to creative alterations appropriate to what has already been actualized. God is the "organ of novelty" as well as of conservation, and the two are inseparable. Process is always creative reception of data, emergent synthesis. As John Dewey keeps insisting, "Knowing is acting"; there is no merely neutral reception of facts, but only a utilization of them, which is always itself a new fact and a new datum, hence a new influence or power. Our human interchange is indeed creative, but it is also an enrichment of deity, and it involves the divine self-creativity as well as our own in interplay. In both cases, self-creativity is how the data are incorporated. The divine form of this is needed not simply to preserve the achieved values, but to inspire all things with a tendency toward a common orderly pattern. The alternative, or pseudo alternative, I take to be sheer chance, in lieu of our real world of chance fluctuations about divine norms of order and beauty.

William A. Christian: In *The Divine Relativity,*[7] you mention three logically possible views of God and the world, namely (1) God *is* the world, (2) God is the world *and* something else, and (3) God is in all respects independent of the world. Is it not also a logical possibility that God is (*a*) different from the world (against 1 and 2), both in the sense that he is not identical with it and in the sense that he does not include it, and (*b*) in some respects conditioned by the world (against 3), and (*c*) in some respects independent of the world (against 1)?

Hartshorne: To be conditioned by *is* to include, according to my logic. (What a thing does not include, it could be without.) To be sure, if one describes things abstractly enough, they will (as thus identified) include the environment on which they depend in a generalized sense only; also, except for God, things include most of what conditions them in radically deficient ways (by faint prehensions). In God, however, inclusion is not deficient, so that what conditions him is included adequately (though of course not in his unconditioned or nonconsequent —in a sense, generalized—aspect). Thesis (2) in the trichotomy is not clearly defined. The point is the joint rejection of complete dependence *and* complete independence with respect to the system of dependent beings; or, of mere inclusion and mere exclusion of that system. God does include it; but had it not existed, he would not have included it; and yet his essential individuality, by which "he" is identified, would still have been actualized somehow. Thus this essential individuality does not include the particular world; only the actual divine state of experience does so.

[7] (New Haven: Yale University Press, 1948), p. 90.

Wm. Oliver Martin: How can "panentheism" escape falling into pantheism if, to quote from *The Divine Relativity*,[8] "a whole is not identical with its constituents" and at the same time "a whole has relation to its parts"? Is there such a thing as "relation" of a whole to a part?

Hartshorne: I fear I have sometimes used "whole" misleadingly to connote "inclusive being"; and this is more than a mere totality of included beings or "parts." God, as actual, is a whole in the way that an experience is a whole; and experience is no mere sum of its data, but yet it does possess them, include them, and this inclusion is not only *a* relation, but *the* relation! The scholastic distinction between "intentional" and real, or "entitative" inclusion I accept only for the deficient mode of experience, where the given is inadequately given. The distinction does not apply to God. The avoidance of pantheism is in the noninclusion of the world by God in his necessary individuality as well as in the mutual freedom of God and creature in relation to the other. God happens to include just this world; he did not have to in order to be himself; hence our acts are not required by the divine essence, and neither is the particular divine response to these acts. Also, the state of God which includes an act of ours is not the state which influences— without completely determining—that act.

Nels F. S. Ferré: In what sense, if any, is God a creative being? Is creation in any real sense *ex nihilo,* or is it merely the rearrangement of the ever new arrangements of flux in form?

Hartshorne: Creation is indeed no mere rearrangement, for an actuality is never simply a new aggregation of pre-existing elements. Actual entities create, first of all, themselves, as emergent unities, no less unitary than emergent, and no less unitary than each of the elements they presuppose; second, all entities help in the self-creation of subsequent entities by furnishing data for their creative synthesis. The divine creating is the eminent form of this. That the eminent creating is not and could not be the only creating is the explanation of evil, about which, curiously, no question has been put. As for *ex nihilo,* it

[8] Pp. 84, 69.

could at most apply to a hypothetical first state of creaturely actuality; for all subsequent entities, by the very meaning of "subsequent," must presuppose the first state as their set of data. One cannot create a memory *ex nihilo,* for memory is a synthesis of antecedent actualities. A created something presupposing no prior creation has no data, solves no determinate problem, and is not what we mean by an actuality. In one sense, however, perhaps God creates *ex nihilo.* At each phase of process God sums up the entire actuality of the previous phases; and thus any datum which we now, say, can use in our self-creation is "nothing" unless it be an item in the divine reality as just prior to now.

William A. Christian: If temporal process is additive and cumulative and without "perishing," how do you interpret the principle of conservation of energy?

Hartshorne: The essential cumulativeness is in the divine life. In the world, cumulativeness is indeed illustrated, but (as with all divine attributes) the worldly version is in principle inferior. We remember, but also we forget; we wax and we wane. Furthermore, since any one type of world order is arbitrary and limited in its possibilities of value, it is in the long run to be superseded by another, so that the inexhaustible possibilities of value may be drawn upon, beyond any such limitations. Both the conservation of energy and the "degradation" of energy appear compatible with, but not necessary to, these assumptions. What the world must do is to add new values not to itself, but to God, values new but harmoniously akin to the old. The stability of the bottom level of physical reality (composed of the least creative modes of individuality) makes possible our own human (and on remote planets doubtless many other types of) cumulative memory and culture, and this is a contingent intermediate step or contribution to the ultimate or divine stability and cumulativeness. But any definite system ought eventually to wear itself out and give way to another.

Paul Weiss: The things that have been do not form a simple unity of value, meaning, or power. To preserve them all within a single whole, they must be given different weights and roles. Since these weights and roles are other than what they had in this world, does not

God in preserving the past necessarily alter it? But then is it entirely correct to say that the past is perfectly preserved by God?

Hartshorne: Actual entities or events are what is preserved; they do indeed, as preserved, play diverse roles, but this does not alter them as past events; for one means by a certain actual entity that which *all possible subsequent uses of it have in common.* The common denominator of all possible wholes-containing-X, that is, prehending X, in whatever manner, is just X itself. In X is included the weights and roles of things in its past; and in any subsequent event, Y, will be included X's special role in Y, and this will then be preserved with Y as a new common denominator for further becoming. All this is what is meant by defining being through its "potentiality for every becoming." The actualization of such a potential does not change it, but only creates a new potential containing the old as datum.

Paul Weiss: Is there not a sense in which the world transcends God? Does not your panentheism require counterbalance?

Hartshorne: Alas for the forlorn hope of understanding between philosophers! The counterbalance is supposedly built into the doctrine, and is its *raison d'être,* as opposed to pantheism as well as to theism! The world transcends God in the sense that each actual entity, in becoming, is a new offering to deity which enriches him, through his creative response to it. To this extent "the world creates God," and not simply God the world—allowing for the difference in principle that God, by his infinitely more perfect response to data, sums up in himself all previous creatures, and for the difference that only the divine state, not the divine individuality, requires this or that particular world. (See pp. 344–345, replies to queries of Martin on "panentheism" and Ferré on God as a creative being.)

A. C. Garnett: You say in *Man's Vision of God,* "Thus that God's essence should imply his existential status (as contingent or necessary) is not an exception to the rule, but an example of it, since the rule is that contingency or noncontingency of existence follows from the kind of thing in question."[9] Grant the rule. But does it not imply merely

---

[9] (Chicago: Willett, Clark and Co., 1941), p. 307.

that if God exists he exists noncontingently, not that he exists noncontingently because that is the mode of existence implied in the idea of him?

Hartshorne: "If God exists, he exists noncontingently" I regard as self-contradictory; for the "if" can only mean that something which could be lacking is required for the existence, while "noncontingently" means that nothing required for the existence could possibly fail, or have failed to obtain. "If" refers to a condition, but we are speaking of unconditioned existence. Thus "if" and "necessary" do not properly combine in the manner proposed. That a necessary proposition is true is itself necessary; except in the sense that a certain combination of words in the English, or other, language might have had another meaning than the one expressive of a necessary and consistent proposition. The way to insert an "if" is to say, with Leibniz: If "God" is logically possible, he necessarily exists. The question is simply whether there be a coherent idea of "perfection" or divinity. Not the atheists, but only the positivists, have a pertinent reply to Anselm!

A. C. Garnett: In *Man's Vision of God* you say, "But clearly God . . . is the only *consistently conceivable object which must be conceived as unproduced,* a reality always existing or never existing or even capable of existing; either in essence uncaused or a mere non-entity." [10] But are not "eternal objects," if conceived at all, conceived as unproduced?

Hartshorne: "Eternal objects" are inseparable from God. Also— here I seem not to be Whiteheadian—I think there is but one eternal object; God's fixed essence, as distinct from his contingent actuality. Pure possibility is a continuum, beyond all multitude of distinct items, the continuum of possible states of divine experience. The actual states are of course not "unproduced."

V. METHOD

Huston Smith: Is human experience sufficiently alike, is our analysis of what its generic features really are sufficiently pure, and if so, is our

[10] P. 303, italics in text.

realization of what these features imply about the nature of reality sufficiently plain to warrant your assertion that when basic questions "are answered with any but one set of answers, the result is absurdity"? In other words, can the coherence theory of philosophic truth be used against alternative positions as effectively as you seem to think? Or are the differences primarily in the estimate of the elemental offerings of experience instead of in the degree of logical consistency?

Hartshorne: First, the consistency (or inconsistency) at issue is not simply logical. For, until we define our terms, there is only an *intuition* of harmony or discord in our meanings. Logic construes our concepts, not our intuitions. In the step from intuitions to conceptual formulae is where our differences mostly lie. In that sense all philosophy must be experiential—or intuitional—and more than just logic. But second, it seems to be an unsolved problem how completely logic can be purified of intuitive elements. Perhaps some day the state of logic will be so far clarified as to help us greatly in our metaphysical inquiries. I certainly hope so.

Warner A. Wick: Why insist on calling things by names that obviously belong to something else? "The Universe is an organism"—literally, of course? . . . "Reality is a social process."

> Blest be the tie that binds
> Our parts in cosmic love.
> The fellowship of microminds
> Is like to that above!

Apparently, then, nothing is what it is, but always some other thing?

Frivolous or captious as these queries may seem, they express my confidence that your practice reflects a defensible principle and my hope that we may have an explicit statement and defense of it.

Hartshorne: I am glad this delectable satire is included. R. B. Perry once accused Whitehead of stretching terms (such as "feeling") beyond any clear meaning. So far as I recall, Whitehead replied that such stretching of terms *is* speculative philosophy (which no one is compelled to engage in). As against stretching materialistic concepts (the mere "agitation of things agitated"), on the one hand, and remaining content with "being is being," on the other, Whitehead held (with Leibniz and all idealists) that the former procedure commits the "fallacy of misplaced concreteness," and the latter is useless truism. As for a dualistic procedure—"There is agitation of things agitated *and* there are experiences"—the "and" seems to cover a refusal to think. The togetherness of mind and matter is either material, mental, or a third thing; and when this is taken into account, the dualism as such vanishes.

Terms may be legitimately used in wider or narrower senses. Thus one may mean by "animal" the metozoa other than man, or one may include man. One may also include protozoa, even some with chlorophyll. A philosopher may wish to mean by "experience" just human experience, or just vertebrate experience, or some other restricted class of cases. And he may then insist upon an ultimate duality between concrete reality which contains experiences (or feelings) and that which does not. But what is he doing if not trying to get knowledge out of the absence of clarity in his own procedure? One can tie down the *word* experience, or feeling, as one wishes; but one does not thus do away with the question, What sort and degree of analogy is there between what is inside and what is outside the circle one has drawn? If analogy obtains, then a common word can be used for it. The speculative argument is that some analogies must be universal, for otherwise we could not explicate such general terms as "actuality." To do this we start with a specimen of actuality; and our own experiences as actual are the clearest, most indubitable instances (Descartes' great discovery, as Whitehead points out). From this beginning we can conceive more and more general variables of experience. Is anything gained by supposing that, however far this goes, there will still be something "simply not experience at all"? It would not be known in any positive way; for the moment something is given, it not only enters into an experience but, by virtue of the unity of feeling which constitutes experience, it presents itself as composed of feelings, or a function of feeling. My conviction on this point antedates my study of philosophy, and I still seem to "see" the feeling quality of all data.

Wm. Oliver Martin: If, as a substitute for a doctrine of analogy, we must "stretch" categories [11] to obtain "maximal flexibility of concepts," [12]

[11] *Man's Vision of God*, p. 132.
[12] *Ibid.*, p. 221.

and all metaphysical propositions are "analytic," [13] then to what kind of evidence is appeal to be made in case of disagreements arising because metaphysicians "stretch" concepts in different ways?

Hartshorne: The stretching *is* a doctrine of analogy (see p. 352). Otherwise, this seems to be Huston Smith's question. Perhaps I may add here: The final appeal is to intuition (of meaning), but on the way to the final appeal one can always insert further analysis. Nothing has to be "shot out of a pistol." One can always reason further if one is sufficiently resourceful in seeking common ground of intuitive certainty. All metaphysical concepts are in themselves equally "primitive." It is only relative to particular individuals that one starting point is "ultimate" and unarguable.

William L. Reese: It must be assumed that there does exist a valid method of inquiry in metaphysics; that this method, when successful, issues in necessary judgments; that this necessity is' gained either through demonstrating that every disjunct in a set of all logically possible disjuncts relevant to a given problem implies an identical doctrine or by demonstrating that all possibilities save one contain insuperable difficulties. Yet this method, however successful in other areas of metaphysical inquiry, yields almost equivocal results when applied to the question, What is the nature of the ontological unit? Assuming further that by a necessary argument we have been able to ascribe "sentience" to the ontological unit, the argument necessarily transforms apparent differences of kind into differences of degree of a single kind. Strict reasoning about the ontological unit has resulted curiously in something like an analogy of indefinite extent; and the univocity of meaning in reasoning about this unit has given way to analogical meanings by virtue of having specified the nature of this unit.

Hartshorne: One concrete singular, at least, must be given, if we are to know what "concreteness" and "singularity" mean. But givenness, as itself given, I find to be participatory: experience of experience, feeling of feeling (clearest case, memory). "Self-transcendence" in knowledge is always social. Now the difference between the perhaps

[13] *The Divine Relativity,* p. xiv.

"negligible feelings" of electrons and no feeling at all may seem, as you have suggested to me, a "negligible difference." Yet it is *all* the difference between what could conceivably (at least, by God) be known through participation (itself an indefinite analogy—see below) and what could not be thus known. And I find no other mode of knowing the concrete. Another argument is this: Even very simple feeling can positively exclude other modes of feeling, as an infant's feeling excludes from the infant's "subjective forms" adult modes of experience; but the sheer absence of feeling would be that absurd entity, a merely negative fact. No positive trait can logically exclude feeling as such: Extendedness will not do it, for the social structure of feeling is its spatio-temporal character. Nor will simplicity do it, though I here waive the argument. No property conceivably observable can exclude all feeling from a concrete singular; and what makes an aggregate, such as a rock or a cell colony, the singularity of which is relative to the spectator, too little integrated to feel as a whole is the positive independence of its truly singular (microscopic) members; and thus the very criterion that denies feeling to the whole makes the parts unsuitable for such denial. If the "insentience of singulars" must be a "fact" wholly negative for all possible observation, and if this is the same as no fact, then their having feeling, however slight, is the only alternative to nonsense. What metaphysics seeks to exclude is precisely and solely nonsense (or contradiction).

Is the problem before us so different from metaphysical problems in general? For example, to the question, does every process have both causal connections or necessities and open possibilities, I answer with a simple, "Yes"; but it remains true that the open possibilities become negligible from our human perspective in certain cases, as in the motions of the heavenly bodies, and uniquely important in the case of conscious human acts. Of course, if "necessity" means unconditional, absolute necessity, and "contingency" the mere denial of this, then everything is indifferently contingent except the bare necessary essence of deity (as including that of "world as such"). But still, some contingencies are conditional necessities throughout a cosmic epoch, and others only just here and now; and so again one can set up an analogy of indefinite extent. The simple Yes and No as to contingency applies only to the gap between infinite relevance to *all* process, and relevance only after some chosen stage of process. Between finities, the indefinite analogy always replaces mere dichotomy. And even the dichotomy between finite and infinite is not that between none and all, but that between some and all. (Thus the necessary is what is common to all possibilities; the contingent, to but some possibilities.) Mere Yes-and-No thinking, as Peirce held, is the last word on no fundamental subject; rather, it is always a more or less crude oversimplification.

Wm. Oliver Martin: How can a doctrine of analogy (as opposed to metaphor) in any sense be admitted if its "matter-form foundation be denied"? [14]

Hartshorne: I did not intend to reject every distinction between "form" and concrete embodiment of the form. Any doctrine which makes the contrast "abstract-concrete" ultimate, even for God (his necessary individuality is not thought of as concrete, but only as necessarily present in some concrete actualization or other), must admit a difference between the formal and the nonformal, or material (to use that venerable word). But the distinction as I make it has almost nothing to do with a contrast between mind and matter, and is otherwise different from the Aristotelian doctrine. Also I distinguish God from ordinary individuals not by altogether denying to him the material (concrete, determinate) aspect, but in a somewhat more complex manner. The formal aspect of God is A-perfect, and this means that its quality can be stated in purely categorical terms (e.g., as "adequately cognitive of all things"). Thus the divine form is the only one which is purely formal. But God has this form; he does not in his full actuality coincide with it. In his "material" (contingently determinate) aspect, he incomparably transcends all forms whatever. (This is a radically existentialist note in the panentheist doctrine.) In the divine form-transcendence, a form is nevertheless embodied, the form of R-perfection, or Transcendent Relativity, that is, self-surpassing superiority to all other individuals, as a matter of principle, or without possible exception. This form, too, is pure in that it is specified without mention of any contingent or particular determination. No other individual has

[14] *The Divine Relativity*, p. 31.

an individuality thus specifiable purely formally. Only of God can we say who he is without mention of any particular instance of any universal.

"Perfect knowledge" does not particularize "knowledge"! It refers to sheer knowing, unmixed with anything else. On the contrary, my peculiar brand of imperfect knowledge, or yours, restricts the essence of knowing, in particular or material and more or less ineffable ways. Also the actual, contingent, divine knowing of the actual, contingent world likewise particularizes knowing; but always in conformity with the general, yet individually unique, form of "perfection," in the sense of "transcending other individuals without possible exception." God is the individual who alone has universal relevance, and thus constitutes all ultimate essences or universals (if they are really plural) by his own individuality. But God as he actually is, our God, transcends any essence and any mere individuality. Our God had no relevance for Abraham, for there was no such deity coexistent with Abraham. Thus the legitimate sort of form-matter distinction applies also to God, and yet serves to distinguish him, since with us even the form itself, the essential individuality, is material, that is, particular, contingent, and knowable only *a posteriori*. "Material" here refers to a relatively determinate process of experiencing, in contrast to the "pure potential," or universal characteristic of such process. Process is not made determinate by fusing "stuff" and universal. This is mere verbalism, not an explication of the idea of experient process as unique feeling or satisfaction. It is social experience or experiencing that explains stuff, not conversely. "Experience" cannot be put together out of more ultimate conceptions. To suppose it can is the error of materialism, partly shared by traditional doctrines of form and matter.

As for the older theories of theistic analogy, they were deeply influenced and, I hold, partly ruined by "ontolatry," or worship of being (in contrast to becoming), by "etiolatry," or worship of cause (in contrast to effect), of independence or immunity to influence (in contrast to receptivity or sensitivity), and by over a thousand years of groveling before (or, if you prefer, unlimited deference to) Infinity, Absoluteness, Eternity, Necessity, Simplicity, and other plausible but, some of us think, spurious equivalents of perfection in the appropriate religious sense of "worshipful superiority in principle to all other individuals." It is, I believe, such perfection, irreducible to the categories above mentioned, that characterizes the proper object of our entire devotion, interest, or love, the Life in which we live, and with us all that we can care for.

Interrogation of

Paul Tillich

Conducted by William L. Reese

Paul Tillich characterizes himself as a professor of theology.
He was born in 1886 at Starzeddel, Kreis Guben, Prussia.
He studied at the Universities of Berlin, Tübingen, Halle
and Breslau. Since 1926 he has been awarded a great num-
ber of honorary degrees, both in this country and abroad.
He is the recipient of the Goethe Plakette award, the
Grosseverdienstkreuz of the West German Republic, and
the Goethe prize. Tillich has taught at the Universities of
Berlin, Marburg, Dresden, Leipzig, Frankfurt am Main,
Union Theological Seminary, and he was University Pro-
fessor at Harvard from 1955 to 1962. Now he is the John
Nuveen Professor at the University of Chicago Divinity
School. His works in English include *The Religious Situa-
tion, The Interpretation of History, The Protestant Era, The
Shaking of the Foundations, Systematic Theology, The
Courage to Be, Love, Power and Justice, The New Being,
Biblical Religion and the Search for Ultimate Reality, Dy-
namics of Faith, Theology of Culture, Christianity and the
Encounter of the World Religions.*

I. BACKGROUND QUESTIONS

William L. Reese: A number of questions reflect an interest in the influence upon Professor Tillich of important movements of thought to which he is, or seems to be, allied. These questions, ranging from Malebranche to contemporary existentialism, provide an appropriate opening for the interrogation; and while, in some aspects, more than historical alignment is sought, these may be regarded as background questions.

Albert C. Outler: As a historian interested in source criticism, I have often wondered whether Tillich ever read much of the Oxford Platonist, John Norris. In his *Reason and Religion* (1689), Norris has many interesting passages designed to "prove" that God is not *a* being, or even the Absolute, but rather "being in general," "being itself," "the ground of being." The general tenor of Norris' argument sounds strangely familiar to one who has been reading Tillich, or vice versa. It would be useful to know if Tillich had read and been influenced by *Reason and Religion.* Or, again, has Tillich been consciously influenced —if so, how much?—by Norris' mentors: the Cambridge Platonists and Malebranche? Finally, if Tillich never saw *Reason and Religion,* or anything else of Norris', what should the historian conclude about the life history of this sort of ontologism?

Tillich: I have never read *Reason and Religion* by John Norris. I must even confess that I do not remember that I ever before heard or read his name. Of the Cambridge Platonists and Malebranche, I had only secondary knowledge when I developed my doctrine of God. But the mentioning of Malebranche points in the right direction: The Platonic-Augustinian-Franciscan tradition and its emphasis on the principle of "immediacy" had a great influence on me. This is a point in

357

which Nicolaus Cusanus and Descartes do not contradict each other, and the way over Spinoza, Schelling I, and Schleiermacher to my own thinking can be easily traced. It is astonishing as well as reassuring for me that the same motives of thought which drove me to my formulations have driven a man more than two hundred and fifty years ago to the same ones. This may be a warning against a too-confident application of the "method of literary dependence" in historical research.

Lewis S. Ford: Tillich accepts many features of Schelling's thought. Perhaps the most significant is his emphasis upon polarity, particularly in its application to ontological concepts. Tillich's ontological elements, such as dynamics and form, are expressed in polar terms. Polar elements oppose one another, yet they remain indispensable for one another. A precarious balance between both polar elements must be maintained, for the tension between them cannot be fully resolved without eliminating one of them.

1. Schelling applies such polar concepts to the divine being as well as to finite being. Without such polarity the divine simplicity (in his terms, the "absolute indifference") would lack the differentiation and mediation necessary for self-conscious reflection and volition. In order to be the personal, intelligent, living creator of the world, God must include within his own simplicity a real polarity, a polarity requiring both time and process for its manifestation. Schelling can apply such attributes as personality and life to God only by applying them literally to this real polarity within God, while Tillich is able to apply them symbolically to the ground of being itself, that is, to the "absolute indifference," bypassing any such real polarity. Was the desire to avoid postulating a real polarity within God Tillich's chief motive for developing the symbolic approach?

2. Is the symbolic approach itself simply the application of Schelling's polar concepts to language? A symbolic expression is "one whose proper meaning is negated by that to which it points." [1] Thus both affirmation and denial are required in spite of their mutual opposition. Is this not an example of polar tension?

Tillich: I have not been influenced by Schelling's concept of polarity in my doctrine of God and in my theory of religious symbols, not even

[1] Tillich, *Systematic Theology* (Chicago: University of Chicago Press, 1951), I, 239.

in my conception of the basic ontological polarities. Potencies in the sense of Schelling are not polarities; the very term "potency" points to a kind of hierarchy, while polarities lie on the same level. I believe, but without a complete certainty, that the doctrine of ontological polarities is rooted in thought-experiences similar to those which have led to the concept of complementarity in physics: It is impossible to grasp reality with one of two contrasting concepts, for example, freedom *or* destiny, contingency *or* necessity, dynamics *or* form, vitality *or* spirituality, etc. Both are needed and even more: The two are dependent on each other in their validity—which, I believe, is a step beyond the present understanding of complementarity.

The conception of my theory of religious symbols goes far back to sources I am not able to discern in their effectiveness for my thought, to the study of Dionysius the Areopagite, of Scotus Erigena, of Meister Eckhart, of Hegel and David Friedrich Strauss and the whole development of biblical criticism from Spinoza to Albert Schweitzer and Rudolf Bultmann. Schelling and Schleiermacher are important, but not decisive in this "host of ancestors."

The symbolic theory of religious knowledge makes it impossible to attribute polarities to God in a nonsymbolic way. The polarities of being are rooted in the ground of being, but the ground of being is not subject to them. They are not "fate" for God.

Gordon D. Kaufman: It is well known that Professor Tillich is indebted to Schelling in many ways for his thought. His relationship to Hegel, however, has not been so frequently stressed, either by himself or by others. Many Tillichian concepts are reminiscent of Hegelian notions, for example, *"kairos,"* "estrangement," "dreaming innocence," love and salvation conceived of as primarily a kind of ontological reunion, Christ viewed as the principle of the relationship between God and man, the strong philosophical interest in history, etc. It would be of great interest, as well as of considerable value in the understanding of both Hegel and Tillich, to have the inner relationship between the two made explicit and clear by Tillich himself.

Tillich: Kaufman's question would be the subject matter of a whole dissertation if it were to be answered sufficiently. This rather incomplete answer emphasizes my general evaluation of Hegel as I have developed it in repeated courses in the Harvard University philosophy department. In them I have above all dealt with Hegel's early fragments (as I did twenty-seven years ago in Frankfurt). Within them I believe we discover the life blood of Hegel's system, namely, the theological and the political problem, and their common solution in a "philosophy of life." These elements are still fully visible in *Phenomenology of Mind*. This explains, for example, my "ontology of love" in *Love, Power and Justice*. The concepts of "estrangement" and "reconciliation" are important in all periods of Hegel's thinking; but I learned their realistic significance only through the attack on Hegel's belief in an already reconciled existence, as was done by his pupils, Karl Marx and Søren Kierkegaard, who used Hegel's own concepts against Hegel. (When I took the term *kairos* from the New Testament, I was not aware that Hegel had used it, as I was not aware that he had used the term "dreaming innocence.") The strong interest in history was born out of my being thrown into history in World War I and my participation in the religious-socialist movement. Theoretically, Marx, Ernst Tröltsch, and Oswald Spengler were most important, but of course the shadow of Hegel stands behind them.

Hegel's Christological solution has never influenced me, but I confess a strong dependence on Schleiermacher. This means that I could not accept Hegel's reduction of the Christological event to the main example of the universal unity of God and man. My strong existentialist bias would not have admitted that. And this leads me to a valuation of Hegel's later development. It looks to me as if the network of categories developed in his great *Logic* was put by him over the existential substance of his thinking, covering it up and producing in most parts of his *Encyclopedia* a dialectical mill of ever repeated categories. This is certainly not the whole story of his later development (cf. the Introduction to his *Philosophy of History,* the brilliance of his aesthetic theories, his philosophy of law, and his understanding of the centrality of religion). But this was the reason for the revolt of the existentialists against his philosophy and the immense consequences this revolt had and has for our own century. Although I have sometimes been called an existentialist, I agree with Schelling that there can be no "positive" (existentialist) philosophy without the frame of a "negative" (essentialist) philosophy. For this reason, I refuse to join the chorus of those for whom the name "Hegel" is an object of contempt—and is so partly because of antipathy, partly because of ignorance and misunderstanding. I still intend to learn from him.

Georges H. Tavard, A.A.:   In *The Interpretation of History,*[2] Tillich states his early readiness to adopt the existential approach. In his autobiographical reflections at the beginning of the volume, *The Theology of Paul Tillich,*[3] his account is different: "It took years before I became fully aware of the impact of this encounter on my own thinking. I resisted, I tried to learn, I accepted the new way of thinking more than the answers it gave." Elsewhere, especially in his article on "Existential Philosophy,"[4] he has identified himself with the early phase of modern existential philosophy, at least as regards the existential interpretation of history.

A question may be asked concerning an apparent inconsistency in Tillich's account of his philosophical development. Does he at times project his present "existential phase" into his own past, thus giving different accounts of his encounter with the philosophies of existence? Or does he speak of several aspects, or several depths, of existential philosophy, some of which would be more congenial to his thought than others?

These queries lead to a more basic problem. To what extent do the analyses of the conundrum of existence in *Systematic Theology,* II, draw on the theological solution which Tillich knows he is going to give to the problem of existence? Is the relevance of existential analysis mainly apologetical, in that it enables the theologian to "correlate" his answer to a question couched in modern language? Or does existential philosophy have a validity of its own, independent of any theological answer? Is it, or is it not, true that existential philosophy has revealed nothing that could not have been found by an analysis of traditional Christian doctrines?

---

[2] Trans. by N. A. Rasetzki and Elsa L. Talmey (New York: Charles Scribner's Sons, 1936).

[3] Ed. by Charles W. Kegley and Robert W. Bretall (New York: The Macmillan Co., 1952), p. 14.

[4] *Theology of Culture,* ed. by Robert C. Kimball (New York: Oxford University Press, 1959), p. 79.

Tillich: The biographical question asked by Tavard can be answered comparatively easily. The statement that "it took years before I became fully aware of the impact . . ." of existentialist philosophy refers to the philosophy of Martin Heidegger and to the novels of Franz Kafka. Actually I was, decades before, under the influence of what *today* is called existentialist thought: Kierkegaard since 1905, Boehme and Schelling II since 1910, Nietzsche since 1917, Marx's early writings since 1920, etc. But today I would go even beyond this to the early impression on me of the existentialist elements in *Hamlet,* whereby I reached an extraordinary degree of identification of my whole being with the symbol "Hamlet," which was more real to me than any "empirical" reality.

More difficult is the answer to the systematic question concerning the method of correlation. It has often been asked, though not always as clearly as here. My answer to the question: "Is it, or is it not, true that existential philosophy has revealed nothing that could not have been found by an analysis of traditional Christian doctrines?" has several facets. First, I must say emphatically that no analysis of the implications of any doctrine could have produced what Pascal and Kierkegaard, what Feuerbach, Marx, and Nietzsche, what Heidegger, Jaspers, and Sartre have brought to light.

Each of these men gives in his analysis a significant, original contribution. They have immensely enriched our insight into the human predicament. For this reason their work is an invaluable gift to theology. For theology also describes human estrangement (an existentialist term, borrowed from Hegel and used against Hegel). But existentialism as existentialism does not answer its own questions. The many answers given by existentialists to the questions of finitude, loneliness, guilt, emptiness are derived from direct or indirect religious traditions: Catholic, mystical, Protestant, Pietistic, humanist, naturalist. The theologian gives his answer on the basis of his own tradition and his personal conviction. But as always, the form of the answer is partly determined by the question, as the form of the question, if formulated in view of the answer, is partly dependent on the latter. This mixture of mutual dependence *on,* and independence *of,* question and answer characterizes all life processes. It is not a unique theological phenomenon and is not restricted to what I call the "method of correlation."

II. ON HISTORY AND THEOLOGY

William L. Reese: Much interest, and some perplexity, is evident concerning the relations intended by Professor Tillich between historical scholarship, the Christian faith, and theology.

John Baillie: 1. In his book, *The Interpretation of History*,[5] Professor Tillich writes that "outside of genuine eschatology stands the question of the individual after death." How can he say this in view of the New Testament teaching? Is not what the New Testament has to say about rising again from the dead integral to its whole outlook?

2. In the same book he writes, "To practise Christology does not mean to turn backward to an unknown historical past or to exert oneself about the applicability of questionable mythical categories to an unknown personality."[6] Tillich appears to imply that Christian faith would not be affected by however great a degree of skepticism regarding the historicity of Jesus of Nazareth. Yet he makes the idea of incarnation central in his understanding of the Christian faith. But surely the idea of incarnation is a *false* idea if no incarnation actually took place on the level of ordinary history. Or to put it otherwise, how can Christ be "the center of history" if he was not himself a real historical person, but only an idea? An idea can indeed be the center of a system of ideas, but only an actual historical figure can be the center of *history*.

Tillich: Baillie's two questions are based on an early book of mine which in no way expressed the fully developed answers to his questions. To the first question, I would today answer that it is impossible to say anything about the eternal destiny of the individual without saying everything one can say about the eternal destiny of the universe (including human history) and their participation in the eternal. It is my philological suspicion that to say this was the intention of the quoted sentence—perhaps like this: You cannot discuss the eternal destiny of the individual in terms of a doctrine of the immortality of the soul or

---

[5] P. 281.
[6] *Ibid.*, p. 265.

of life "after" death without envisaging the relation of the eternal to the temporal as a whole. This, in any case, is my present position.

The quotation on which Baillie's question is based is also superseded, in this case, by the second volume of my *Systematic Theology,* where my Christology is fully developed. Nothing is more emphasized in these chapters than the factual side of the event on which Christianity is based. But I ask the question, How can the factual element be cognitively reached so that it gives the basis for the Christian faith? And the answer is: *Not* through scholarly research in the sources, a procedure which in spite of all its great *indirect* merits can produce no more than changing degrees of probability, and which would make the faith of the church dependent on the hermeneutic skills of a group of highly specialized scholars. Instead of that, I suggest that the participation of the faith of the church and its individual member guarantees the event which has transformed old being into new being in them. This experience always was and still is the basis for the certainty that "eternal God-manhood" has appeared in a personal life under the conditions of estrangement without being conquered by them. This event is rightly called the center of history.

Gordon D. Kaufman: In many places, both in *Systematic Theology* and elsewhere, Tillich has stressed the independence of theological work from the somewhat tentative conclusions of historical scholarship. For example: ". . . that which concerns us ultimately is not linked with any special conclusion of historical and philological research." [7] "Theologians need not be afraid of any historical conjecture, for revealed truth lies in a dimension where it can neither be confirmed nor negated by historiography. Therefore, theologians should not prefer some results of historical research to others on theological grounds. . . ." [8] However, he holds that the Christian faith is somehow rooted in "the picture of Jesus as the Christ" in the New Testament.[9] But is not the claim that the New Testament portrays "Jesus as the Christ" itself a *historical* statement about the ideas, attitudes, etc., of the New Testament writers?

[7] *Systematic Theology,* I, 36.
[8] *Ibid.,* p. 130.
[9] *Systematic Theology* (Chicago: University of Chicago Press, 1957), II. The idea also appears elsewhere in Tillich's writings.

If this is not the case, what kind of statement is it? If it is, then is not theological knowledge dependent on historical research for the validation of this fundamental theological statement? And if this is so, then all the problems connected with the uncertainty of historical knowledge, which Tillich has tried to avoid, are brought right back into the center of the theological enterprise and cannot be avoided at all.

Tillich: The question of Kaufman's has been answered implicitly in my answer to Baillie. I only want to add a few remarks. The assertion that the New Testament portrays Jesus as the Christ is a matter of immediate awareness. It is actually a tautology. There is no possible doubt, conjecture, alternative to this assertion. It is logically completely different from statements about the actual occurrence of some events told in the New Testament. These statements are more or less probable or improbable and never can become certain. The stories concerning the foundation of Rome in a book which has come to us under the name of Livius are largely improbable. But that the book which I have in my hand tells these stories is a matter of immediate awareness. If "the problems connected with the uncertainty of historical knowledge" cannot be solved, Christians either must ignore them in an unconscious repression of their seriousness—which is the usual way or must give up a faith which is based on insoluble historical problems.

Allen O. Miller: My question concerns the importance of the historical in the theology of Dr. Tillich. More specifically, what is the relation of history to Christian faith? Does the assertion that "historical research can neither give nor take away the foundation of the Christian faith," [10] mean that the biblical picture of Jesus as the Christ is an abstraction that can be held in indifference to factual verification in history? If, on the other hand, the transforming power of the New Being in Jesus as the Christ is a once-for-all event, how do "the historian" and "the theologian" differ in their orientation to this event?

Tillich: To Miller's question I answer that the New Testament image of Jesus as the Christ is certainly not an "abstraction," but a portrait of a reality which is presupposed and interpreted. We have noth-

[10] *Systematic Theology,* II, 113.

ing except this portrait which is not the same in any of the first three Gospels and totally different in the Fourth Gospel. The church lived from these pictures for seventeen hundred years without scientific verification and when finally a scientific verification was tried, it proved to be a failure because the sources did not intend to give a biography. Systematic theology ever since has tried to deal with this situation. Some theologians were satisfied with the remnants called "historical Jesus," left by the process of historical criticism. So Jesus appeared as a rabbinic teacher or a prophet of the "Kingdom-of-God-at-hand"—but not as the Christ, the bringer of a new reality; and man, consequently, is still "under the law," without a reality which liberates from the law and guarantees the "good news" of this liberation. My own way of solving the problem is based on the experience the church had in all periods of the new reality which was and is mediated through the historical event: "Jesus, accepted as the Christ." This experience includes the affirmation of the event and of the way in which it is continuously effective, namely, through the biblical picture, however the event came empirically into existence as fact and in its interpretation. The immediately present event guarantees the past event; but it does not guarantee the causes and the mixture of the elements *in* the present or *in* the past event. The former are objects of psychological analysis, the latter of historical construction. But neither approach gives certainty about an experience which carries its certainty within itself.

Albert C. Outler: Tillich has said, more than once, that it is intolerable for faith, as ultimate concern, to be dependent upon the relativities and uncertainties of historical knowledge and historical reason. Yet, in the second half of the second volume of *Systematic Theology,* he says that Christianity is based on "factual events" from which the "picture" of "the New Being in Jesus as the Christ" is formed. He denies, however, that historiography affects the process by which "this factual element" is cognitively reached so that it gives the basis for Christian faith. If this means that the historian of the period—6 B.C.–A.D. 30—may remain unconverted by his researches, this is commonplace enough. If he means the Christian faith may arise without *any historical* knowledge of "the factual side of the event on which Christianity is based," this would seem to involve a contradiction. If historical knowledge is *conditio sine qua non* for Christian faith, does this not mean that faith is dependent on that knowledge to the extent that if it were falsified by historical reason, Christian faith would also be falsified thereby? To put the same point in a general form, what are the conditions in which the Christian faith would be falsified or falsifiable?

Tillich: I am glad about the interesting form into which Outler has put his question, namely: "What are the conditions in which the Christian faith would be falsified or falsifiable?" The meaning is: falsifiable by distorted historical reports. The question in this form can only refer to the first witnesses (since there are no other historical reports). It can then only mean: Are their reports so false that the faith based on them is falsified? Could such a thing have happened? To this I answer: Such kind of asking misses the unity of the event on which the Christian faith is based, namely, the unity of the fact which the disciples called Jesus of Nazareth and the reception of the fact as the appearance of the Christ by people who were grasped and transformed by this fact. Their reports show the expression of the power that has grasped them in the appearance (words and deeds) of this man Jesus. For them as for us the only unfalsifiable truth is that they encountered somebody who showed qualities that grasped and transformed them in such a way that they called it saving power or new creature or the presence of the Kingdom. Beyond this statement no historical research can go. It transcends the alternative, "falsifiable" or "verifiable," as the awareness of my own existence as a Christian in the church does. If, however, the traits of the image of Jesus to which the disciples refer are brought under the dimension of historical research, none of these traits can be verified beyond reasonable historical probability. The only thing, implied in the faith of the disciples as well as in our faith, is the immediate expression of an encounter with a personal life that has grasped and transformed us in an ultimate sense.

III. ON
THEOLOGY AND PHILOSOPHY

William L. Reese: Embarked on a program of seeking clarity among kinds of inquiry, the relation between theology and philosophy is next to be explored.

George A. Schrader: Professor Tillich expressly states that God is "being-itself beyond essence and existence." [11] The statement seems almost to entail an identification of theology and ontology, making very difficult the distinction between being and God. On what basis, then, is conversation possible between philosopher and theologian? If philosophy is theological by virtue of an existential (ultimate) concern; and if theology is ontological because it deals with being, the accommodation of one to the other may be so complete that there remains no basis for conversation, no real basis for conflict, no possibility of an antinomy between the two. Not only antinomy but, also, productive conflict and conversation may be impossible on this view. On the other hand, if there is a basis for conversation between these two disciplines, the conversation will take place either on a *neutral* and *transcendent* ground or between persons each of whose perspective is in some sense autonomous and ultimate. If it is the latter, further insight on the nature of this autonomy would be welcome. If there exists a *higher* point of view from which it is possible to assess this relationship, and adjudicate the difficulties which may arise, one is admitting implicitly the Hegelian view of "absolute knowledge" as *the* ultimate perspective. The view has much to be said for it, but the point is that it is a philosophical position. And, quite clearly, many theologians since Kierkegaard have been unhappy with it.

Tillich: The decisive sentence in Schrader's question is the one in which he says that the accommodation of the philosopher to the theologian (and vice versa) may be so perfect that there remains no basis for conversation or conflict. I simply ask: Why should that not be so? There were always theological philosophers and philosophical theologians who represented such unity. In *principle* the identity of the philosopher and the theologian is possible and even desirable because it would express the ultimate unity of truth. The "conversation" of which Schrader speaks would then take place between representatives of the different ways in which this unity was expressed (e.g., the Augustinian and the Thomistic or the Schellingian and the Hegelian way).

The formulation which has brought Schrader to his question, namely, that "God is being-itself beyond essence and existence," must be seen

[11] *Systematic Theology*, I, 205.

in the context of the whole systematic construction of the idea of God. It is the answer to the first (but by no means the last) question about God: What is the relation between God and being, or simply: What does the statement mean, that God "is"? The answer says that he is not *a* being whose existence can be affirmed or denied, but that he is *esse ipsum* or, in a metaphorical circumscription, the "power of being" in everything that is.

With respect to Schrader's question about the ground on which discussions about "ultimate perspectives" of persons take place, I want to answer that there is always a plane of possible neutrality, insofar as the rational structure of knowledge is concerned. The fact that individuals, meeting on this plane, nevertheless do not agree, has partly contingent reasons like differences in semantic connotations or in intellectual acuteness; partly it is dependent on the interference from another dimension, namely, that of "ultimate concern." The latter involves the whole person, including his will and his emotion, and is not a matter of rational argument, but of existential decision in interdependence with historical destiny. In most philosophical and theological discussions, both elements are present and often hardly separable. Hegel's "absolute knowledge" is reached through many existential decisions (as still visible in his *Phenomenology of Mind* [*Geist*]), and Kierkegaard's discussions are based on Hegelian categories turned against Hegel. Destiny, appeal, and decision determine the outcome in the encounter with forms of ultimate concern; the rational argument has a secondary, though often very influential, function: It clarifies meanings, discovers inconsistencies, shows consequences, adds experiential material, etc. The distinction of the two elements in philosophical-theological encounters is basic for the understanding of their potentialities and their limits.

Richard M. Rorty: Can philosophy, *without* invoking the theological doctrine of the logos as a paradigm, prevent the distinction between the universal and the concrete from collapsing into that between the abstract and the particular? The answer to this question is important for the distinctions between sign and symbol, and between philosophy and theology. For if the difference between signs and symbols is reducible to the difference between reference to the abstract and reference to the particular (a "naturalistic" view which many philosophers are tempted to propose), then it will become a difference of degree, and all "signs" will in some measure "participate in the reality they signify." In particular, all philosophical "concepts" (including "being-itself") will in some measure serve as theological "symbols." *All* philosophizing may then be seen as a striving, more or less unsuccessful, after "theonomous philosophy," and "dialectical realism" can be assimilated to pragmatism.

Professor Tillich's objection to this chain of reductions and assimilations is, I take it, based on an insistence that it is the concreteness of the referent in which a symbol participates, and not simply its particularity: "Particularity excludes every particular from every other one. Concreteness represents every other concrete because it includes universality." [12] But this notion of "concreteness," with the correlative that "universality includes every part because it includes concreteness," entails (as an analytic consequence, quite apart from revelation) the "identity of the absolutely concrete and the absolutely universal," which *is* the logos doctrine. To invoke this self-annihilating polarity in constructing the "receiving situation" for revelation seems to use Christ as an answer to a question which could not have been posed except through a consciousness of Christ. Professor Tillich does, indeed, sometimes suggest that only Christ can pose the questions which Christ answers. If this be so, can one then preserve the kind of independence of theology from philosophy which the method of correlation requires?

Tillich: My statements about the mutual participation of the universal in the concrete are not so much based on the paradoxical assertion that Jesus as the Christ is the logos, as they are based on the (Cusanian) dialectical doctrine of the coincidence of the infinite and the finite. This principle can be applied to the logos doctrine—though with a definite qualification, following from the existential fact of the estrangement of the infinite from the finite. But the doctrine itself is independent of this application. It can be directly derived from an analysis of the concept of the infinite (in the sense of infinite creativity): The infinite would become finite if it had the finite outside itself. On this basis the "absolutely universal" is the unity of all potentialities of

[12] *Systematic Theology,* I, 17 n.

being, and the absolutely concrete is a particular being in which is manifest the central relation of the infinite to the finite under the conditions of finite existence. The logos doctrine as the answer to the question of this relation is paradoxical and not, like the general relation of the finite to the infinite, dialectical. It is theological, while the assertion of the coincidence of the infinite and the finite is metaphysical. The former is based on a directly religious experience, the latter is only indirectly dependent on it, and directly upon ontological analysis.

James Collins: I am dubious about Professor Tillich's dualism between existentialism and the Christian faith, as stated in his contribution to *Christianity and the Existentialists.*[13] He describes the function of existentialism as that of mirroring contemporary man's predicament. Its legitimate work is restricted to describing our situation and formulating the basic questions. Any theistic answers which the existentialists may give about our alienated existence are attributed in principle by Tillich to the Christian influence and not to the existentialist analysis. Thus he distinguishes sharply between the questions a man propounds as an existentialist and the replies he gives as a Christian, a religious person, or as a mystic. But the existentialists themselves do not seem to respect this nice division. Religious-minded existentialists tend to bring their religious conviction to bear upon the original analysis of the human situation and do not reserve it for their answers. Moreover, their responses are quite continuous with, and proportioned to, their descriptive interrogation of existence, without maintaining any rigid division between the resources used in constructive theistic interpretation. A common methodology runs throughout both the analysis and the development of religious meaning. A final point is that the existentialists are more careful than is Tillich to distinguish between the Christian, the religious, and the mystical sources of theism, as well as to maintain these differences all the way through their philosophies.

Tillich: I fully agree with Collins' statement that no "nice division" between existentialist questions and theological answers is possible—not because the existentialists did not make such a division, but because the nature of the method itself makes it impossible. Questions and an-

[13] Ed. by Carl Michalson (New York: Charles Scribner's Sons, 1956).

swers determine each other in a definable way. And in the case of the theologian, both lie within the "theological circle" which is characterized by this interdependence. Nevertheless, the points of approach are different in the case of the question (the description of man's nature and predicament) and the answer (the way of living with one's finitude or the way of overcoming one's predicament). And often—as in the case of Kafka—there is no answer at all.

I do not understand Collins' last sentence. The first volume of my *Systematic Theology* and many passages in other books and articles deal expressly with the contrast of the mystical and the prophetic types of religion; and I would understand if somebody said that I make too much of it. The same I would say of the distinction of Christianity and the other religions generally. But the question whether one should refer to the distinctions must be answered on the basis of their relevance for a particular discussion. I also would like to know at what points the existentialists do more and better that which I supposedly do not do.

James Collins: In answer to the point just raised by Professor Tillich, the existentialists write as philosophers, and regard both their questions and their answers about man's situation, including his relationship with God, as lying within the domain of philosophy. The answers are theological only in the sense that they concern man's bond or lack of it with God, but not in the sense that they cease to be philosophical answers. The existentialists sometimes go on to analyze a religious response which is proportioned to what their existential philosophical inquiry about the human structure and situation uncovers. This is a contribution to theism, both as a question and as an answer, made without relying upon the claim for the Christian revelation. Thus the existentialists maintain that the theistic interpretation of human existence includes one distinct component which their philosophy can treat of in terms of answer as well as question.

Tillich: I am grateful that Collins has reformulated his last question, making it more understandable to me. In answering it, I would first say that I have never made the revelatory experiences on which Christianity is based the only source of answers to existentialist questions. Existentialist questions are universal, and answers to them appear in all religions, and all religions are based on revelatory experiences. My concept of a philosopher is that he is first of all a human being who is rooted in one of the great cultural and religious traditions which originate in revelatory experiences and their mythical expressions. On this basis the philosopher asks the radical questions which are a human possibility and constitute—with other elements—the greatness of man. In asking these questions he liberates himself from the bondage under particular questions and answers in his tradition. But he cannot liberate himself from the substance of his tradition (e.g., language) except through a complete transformation by another tradition into which destiny has thrown him. Plato remains always a "son of Apollo" and Spinoza a "successor of Amos." The answers to the ultimate questions of life are not discovered by him, but conceptualized within the context of his knowledge of the universe. This does not exclude that the philosopher may be a prophet and bearer of revelatory experiences, but in this situation he is not a philosopher. Personal union does not prevent differences of functions. No philosopher answers the ultimate questions of existence as a result of his discursive inquiries. But if he goes beyond them, he becomes a seer, a prophet, a mystic, who conceptualizes "revelatory" experiences. Therefore one should not say that theism confirms or supplies philosophical inquiries, but one should say that on the basis of a theistic or any other kind of religious experience and tradition—however unconscious this tradition may be to the particular philosopher—philosophers discover elements of the human predicament which otherwise could not have been discovered (e.g., the meaning of suffering generally, and of suffering in nature especially, in the revelatory experiences of the Buddha. The same is true of the valuation of the individual person on Christian grounds, etc.). For the myths of the nations the answers are given. The theologian is bound to one of these experiences and their expressions, and he tries to interpret it in universal terms. The philosopher is universal from the very beginning; but he can never hide his actual religious substance.

The evidence for this description in the typical existentialist philosophers from Pascal to Gabriel Marcel is overwhelming.

IV. ON GOD AND HIS ATTRIBUTES

William L. Reese: Many questions were posed concerning the nature of God on Tillich's view. We have divided these questions into two sections, "On God and His Attributes" and "More Especially, on God as Personal." In both sections the questions concern what is to be attributed to God and how these attributions are to be understood. The questions in these two sections overlap to some extent the questions concerning symbolism, which follow in a later section of the interchange.

Charles Hartshorne: Some terms applied to God are merely *metaphorical,* as when God is said to be "shepherd." Here an idea which does not even apply universally to the creation is applied to God, the Universal Reality. Thus it could not be meant literally. God is not just like any mere part of creation. Some terms applied to God are *analogical* (you would say "symbolic"), such as "God is powerful." Here a term which applies universally to the creatures is used, obviously in an eminent sense, of God. This is not a mere metaphor; but still, God is not powerful merely as we are. (Terms like "experience" or "love" are metaphorical for a nonpanpsychist, but analogical for a panpsychist.) Finally, some terms applied to God are *literal,* such as "being itself." (I should prefer "reality itself" as neutral to "being and becoming.") But does it not ensue that certain terms as abstract as "being" or "reality" also apply literally, such as "actual" and "potential"? For, God being the measure of reality, that a certain thing *might* have been real though it is not (to reject this is sheer Spinozism) can only mean that it might have been real for God though it is not, or that he *might* have "known" it as real but does not. I see no shade of difference in the literalness of the two "might-have-beens." To make God literally neutral though symbolically sensitive or differential with respect to the alternative in question is to make the alternative itself symbolic, and thus to nullify the distinction proposed.

Does not "God is the inclusive object of our concern, hence reality itself" mean that the comparisons we must make between "actual" and "possible" things in the world are really comparisons between—in the same sense—"actual" and "possible" modes, states, properties of God? Comparisons between divine knowledge or love and ours need not be literal, for perhaps we do not need to know just how God differs from us (in some respects we could not possibly know this). But comparisons which we *must* make between the creatures generally, such as "actual" and "possible," must coincide with some difference between God and God, for nothing is anything except as measured by the divine reality.

Are not differences with respect to *value* similarly universal and referrable to God? For he is the measure of value, as of reality. To say, "it is better," not meaning merely, relative to certain purposes, but relative to the totality of purposes, or the definitive purpose, is to say, it is better for God (he "cares about," "appreciates," "enjoys" the difference). "Better" is here literal if it ever has anything more than a merely relative meaning; and a merely relative meaning will not do, for what is the use of doing things better for some purposes and worse for others if there is no definitive better? Of course God cannot be better in the sense of more "holy" or "wise," but he must be better in the sense of *total* value or good, thanks to one course of action rather than another on our part. To deny this is to imply that it is only symbolically better or worse if we act one way rather than another. This seems to me to land us exactly in the position of much of Buddhism and Hinduism, that the value of concrete action and individuality is left in sheer ambiguity or is contradicted.

The previous paragraph seems to imply a qualification of our admission above that "love" in God is merely analogical. I suspect that we must hold that we have direct intuition (faint and hard to render conscious) of the divine caring, and with respect to this intuition our notion of divine love has an element of literal meaning, without which we could not understand human love and its deficiencies any better than God's superior love. The analogy then would run both ways. We know both God and creatures directly, intuitively, and we use comparisons between them to throw light on both for our conscious thought. We do not merely experience creatures, and then reach up by analogy toward God.

Tillich: Of the many problems raised by Hartshorne's questions I want to concentrate on the one which deals with the literal or symbolic character of the concepts "potential" and "actual" if applied to God. This problem has more implications than the logical structure of the question seems to admit. I believe that they are the reason for the persistent affirmation of the scholastic theologians, both of Roman Catholicism and of Protestant Orthodoxy, that the divine life transcends the difference between potentiality and actuality and that it has the character of *actus purus.* They realized that the literal application of that difference to the divine life would subject it to the structure of finitude, for example, to the temporality of finite becoming. Now I must confess that such ideas have a great attraction for me because of my own dependence on philosophers like Jakob Boehme, Friedrich Wilhelm Joseph von Schelling, Henri Bergson, who have successfully turned against the *actus-purus* doctrine; and further, because the term "divine life," even if used symbolically, necessarily implies an element of becoming in the divine ground of being and consequently an element of temporality. I am convinced that it is neither philosophically nor theologically justified to identify eternity with timelessness, and that the directing creativity of God works for what is "better" for his creature *and* for him, namely, reunion of the estranged.

But in spite of my agreement with Hartshorne in these important points, I cannot accept his assertion that these elements which characterize finite being can be applied to God "literally," because that would make God finite; and a "finite God" is a contradiction in terms. Certainly, one must say that God has the finite (and its categories) "within" himself, not alongside himself—which also would make him finite. But he is not subject to finitude; he is the infinite who comprises his infinity and his finitude. If this is denied, he becomes another name for the process of life, seen as a whole, and is subject to the tragic possibility which threatens every finite process. Then not only is the world a risk taken by God, but God himself is risk to himself, a risk which may fail.

A few more remarks to Hartshorne's questions: I prefer the term "symbolic" to "analogical" because in symbolic, the symbol-creating and -destroying activity of man's spiritual life is presupposed, while "analogy" points to a static, calculable relation between the world and

God, which can be rationally verified, as in traditional "natural theology."

The reason I prefer the term "potentiality" to "possibility" is that
possibility points to a logical structure, while potentiality points to a
"power of being," which has, so to speak, not yet used its power.

Finally, I suspect that the discussion about "being" and "becoming"
as basic concepts is merely verbal. If being means static self-identity, becoming must be the ultimate principle. But if being means the power
that conquers nonbeing in every life process, then even the process-
philosopher must acknowledge that being, namely, the negation of nonbeing, precedes in ontological dignity the polarity of the static and the
dynamic.

Peter A. Bertocci: With reference to the answer given to Professor
Hartshorne, you are convinced that to talk about God as in any sense a
being alongside other beings—which you believe to be entailed if we call
God *a* person—is to make him a finite God, which is a "contradiction
in terms." I grant that a being who depended for his being on other
beings would be different only in degree from other finite beings. But
why would "contradiction in terms" apply to an ultimate being who
(*a*) has a complex, self-sufficient, self-identifying structure that endures
along with controlled changes in its nature and (*b*) is the Creator-
Sustaining-source of all finite beings, including persons? Even if we
assume that such a finite-infinite God must be "subject to the tragic
possibility which threatens every finite person," why is this possibility
that God himself is a risk to himself, a risk that may fail, intolerable?
What is the source of your judgment here?

You have urged: "God as being-itself transcends nonbeing absolutely.
On the other hand, God as creative life includes the finite and, with it,
nonbeing, although nonbeing is eternally conquered and the finite is
eternally reunited within the infinity of the divine life." [14] I am aware
from your writings, and from your reply to Professor Hartshorne's
interrogation, that you do not wish to identify eternity with timelessness. But do you intend a real ontological and valuational difference to
take place in being *before* and *after* conquering, *before* and *after* re-
uniting? (1) Similarly, is God in *any* valuational sense "better" be-

[14] *Systematic Theology*, I, 270.

cause estrangement has been overcome? (2) If so, why not identify God as being-itself with God as the *kind of creativity that endures through change?* (3) What fact about the world, and what experience, would be necessarily denied if you took the view in (2)?

Tillich: An adequate answer to Bertocci's searching questions would require an argument which is almost identical with a fully developed philosophy of religion; and the difficulty is not diminished, but increased by the fact that our points of view are in many respects quite similar. Nevertheless, there are differences in the basic approach, as already indicated in my answer to Hartshorne.

Perhaps the basic difference is a different feeling about the unapproachable character of the divine mystery. I try, not always successfully, to avoid statements about the divine nature which transcend the merely relational, the "for us." A question such as: "Is God in *any* valuational sense 'better' *because* estrangement has been overcome?" would produce anxiety in me. (Note the quotation marks around "better" in the question.) The philosophical problem is the concept of an "eternal process." As always in the relation of the eternal to the temporal, the only way of speaking adequately is in boundary-line fixations: Eternity is *not* timelessness; and eternity is *not* endless temporality. It lies, so to speak, between them, or more correctly, above them. For this "above," however, we have no possible concept; therefore the question of a "before" or "after" in God cannot be answered, although I could accept Bertocci's statement that "God [is] that kind of creativity that endures through change."

The reason I find "intolerable" the idea that God may be a risk to himself is that it contradicts the religious experience which is expressed in Psalm 90, or in the hymn which calls God the "rock of ages." It belongs certainly to the possibility of finite freedom to fail; and therefore one can say that God may fail in what he intends to do through men and mankind. But there is the transcending certainty that in spite of every individual and group failure, an ultimate fulfillment can be expected. Beyond this expression of religious "hope," I would not go, and I would shy away from the task of finding a definite "structure" in God. Symbols, derived from particular experiences of the relation to God, do not constitute a structure.

Albert C. Outler: One cannot be sure whether, from Tillich's viewpoint, a query about the "impassibility of God" is a "philosophical interrogation" or a theological one. Nonetheless, it is a legitimate and inescapable question for any "system" that takes tragedy and redemption seriously—as Tillich's certainly does. He speaks, repeatedly, of "the New Being" entering the conditions of existence without being overcome thereby. This implies an actual participation of God in the agony and tragedy of human life. This, in turn, entails some kind of "suffering" and *some* sort of frustration of the perfect will and power of God to achieve the end or ends of his creation. How can this essentially soteriological view of God's involvement in existence be squared with Tillich's notion of the ontological transcendence of "the God above God"?

Tillich: My reply to Bertocci answers to a certain extent the question by Outler. But he raises two additional points: The phrase "God above God" is quoted in order to show that there is no possible involvement of God in the world if his transcendence is as absolute as these words indicate. But this often quoted phrase is, as the context shows, a dialogical, not a systematic formula. It answers him who is in the state of radical doubt by pointing to the fact that in the unconditional seriousness of his doubt the divine Presence is effective—though in terms of the divine "absence."

To the question of the highly symbolic phrase, that God "participates" in the agony and tragedy of human life, I have given an affirmative answer in my doctrine of atonement in *Systematic Theology,* II. But I would not dare to make structural statements about God on this basis. We do not know what divine suffering may mean, as we do not know what eternal blessedness means. We can only say that if we apply these human experiences symbolically to God, we must also apply the experience that there is no joy without an element of suffering and no suffering without an element of joy. But again, this does not lead to a conceivable structure of "a" divine being.

V. MORE ESPECIALLY,
ON GOD AS PERSONAL

William L. Reese: Three of our interrogators ask specifically about Tillich's view that God, while personal, is not a person. The identity of this interest suggests a distinct section for the posing of these questions, and the elucidation of Tillich's answers.

Helmut Thielicke: 1. Tillich says:

"Personal God" does not mean that God is *a* person. It means that God is the ground of everything personal and that he carries within himself the ontological power of personality.[15]

Why cannot the ground of all that is personal itself be personal? If one denies that, the consequence seems to be hardly avoidable, then, also to have to say: Because sacred history (*Heilsgeschichte*) (e.g., the incarnation) creates history, or makes it possible, it is by itself not historical. To me it seems to be rather this way: that the one who creates history himself becomes historical and that therein lies the mystery of the gospel.

2. Even if the person (or personality) has ontic character, the conclusion appears to me *not* to be: Therefore we must come to a synthesis of the personalistic and the ontological aspects, as Tillich wants, but rather that both become effective as categories which do not set forth realms of objects (*Gegenstandsbereiche*) that can be brought into congruence. They appear to me rather to lead to different aspects which, assuredly related to each other, yet in their capacity of expression relate to each other alternatively, like the wave-aspect and the corpuscle-aspect in microphysics. The congruity of the two aspects, as Tillich tries to see it, did not convince me. What is his reaction to this objection?

Tillich: Thielicke asks: Why cannot the ground of all that is personal itself be personal? The argument, I have stated in many places, is not that the ground of all that is personal cannot be personal, but that

[15] *Systematic Theology,* I, 245.

all the predicates which we attribute to God are incompatible with the assertion that he is *a* person. The emphasis lies on the "a," because this brings him side by side with other persons and makes him ontologically finite in relation to them. It belongs to the characteristics of a human person to be centered in himself and to exclude every other person from the center itself. My ego is always my ego, and nobody else's. But God, according to religious assertions—biblical, mystical, and Reformation ones—is nearer to my ego than I myself am to it. Similar consequences follow from symbols like omnipotence, omniscience, omnipresence. If they are taken seriously, they do not prevent one from calling God personal, but they make it impossible to call him a person.

I am very interested in how Thielicke transfers the principle of complementarity from physics to theology. I am much in sympathy with it, and went a similar way in my doctrine of the ontological polarities (e.g., freedom and destiny). But I shy away from the term "aspect," because of its nominalistic subjectivity. If, as some philosophers of science suggest, the scientific models have no objectivity at all, but are mere constructs for special purposes of calculation, their incompatibility is not a serious problem. If the models, however, are supposed to say something about reality, the acceptance of complementarity remains unsatisfactory and preliminary. In any case, if transferred to the relation between God and man, a merely subjective-nominalistic understanding of "personal" and "ontological" is neither possible nor probably intended by Thielicke. But then more than different aspects are at stake, and some objective validity must be asserted of both of them. I believe that a prayer which penetrates to God is just such an "objective realm" in which the personal and the suprapersonal in God are experienced in one and the same act of the spiritual life. The polarity, however, in the conceptualization of this experience is unavoidable, as it is in all statements about the relation of God and man.

Nels F. S. Ferré: Does not an "ontology of love" in some determinative manner involve the ultimacy of what is personal? Tillich affirms that "we need not only an ethics of love but, following Augustine, also an ontology of love." [16] Love he defines as "the power that unites

---

[16] *Biblical Religion and the Search for Ultimate Reality* (Chicago: The University of Chicago Press, 1955), p. 69.

that which is separated" [17] or "love is the power in the ground of every-thing that is," [18] driving toward reunion. This love he calls neither impersonal nor personal, but "transpersonal," the power in the ground of being for all personal existence, abetting such existence.

Lately Tillich has strongly stressed Spirit as a basic category. He objects to personality or self as ultimate on the ground that the ultimate, or God, so defined would be conditioned, related, and thus finite.

Suppose, however, that an ontology of love is best defined as personal Spirit, not spiritual Personality. Spirit, all-penetrating (co-inhering), cannot be localized or limited. Second, such a personal Spirit of love could maintain self-identity and creative purpose without suffering any limits of spatialization. Third, for love to be related in no way destroys its ultimacy; love is by nature capable of entering into relations, and indeed lives in those relations. Such love as Spirit could then be capable, as love is, of purposed passivity for the sake of the freedom of the creatures and of the necessary conditions for such freedom, and yet retain final control as the ultimate source of power.

Would not Tillich strengthen his ontology and make it more appropriate to his phenomenology by the acceptance of such a category which would be the ground of both the personal and the impersonal?

He would thereby also escape what is now a matter of conflicting ultimates in his thinking. The nature of the unconditioned allows for "no transcendent realm," and also there can be no unconditioned as such within experience. Therefore in this sense Tillich has an ultimate ontology of nonbeing, even *ouk on;* an empty category, or a limiting concept; but, on the other hand, the ground of being and even the abyss are powers that, without existing, work on existence. In some sense they *are* beyond the analysis of experience. These two analyses are contradictory: there is no transcendent realm; there is transcendent power.

Would not Professor Tillich be willing to affirm that an ontology of love in some determinative manner personal, a God of love as Spirit, best fulfills his own profound analysis?

[17] *Ibid.,* p. 68.
[18] *Dynamics of Faith* (New York: Harper & Row, 1957), p. 114.

Tillich: I am very much caught by Ferré's suggestion that I should use my ontology of love for the solution of the problem of ultimacy and personality. Love as relatedness could overcome the emptiness of the abstract unconditioned without making finite the unconditionally transcendent. There are trends in my thought pointing in this direction, for example, the "Trinitarian" idea of the ground of being separating itself from itself and returning to itself, and beyond this the symbolic description of the divine life as having the finite as potential "within" itself, but eternally conquering the negative element in finitude. But I would not identify an ontology of love with the affirmation of a personal Spirit as *archē*. Love goes beyond the personal, as we have it in our experience, in both directions—toward the natural and toward the ultimate: There is love in the mutual attraction (in spite of repulsion) of all beings and there is love in the participation of the divine Presence in everything in every moment. But in the first case, love is used metaphorically; in the second, it is used symbolically. Both ways of speaking are justified, but they show that the term "personal Spirit" is too limited to cover the phenomenon of love universally. If, however, Spirit is thought of as "all-penetrating" and "co-inhering," it cannot be distinguished from the creative ground of everything, and the adjective "personal" as a particular quality loses its meaning. If we say with the Fourth Gospel that God is Spirit, we must be aware of the demythologizing consequences which Nietzsche has sharply observed in this word. The concept of "*a* personal Spirit of love" is not compatible with the implications of the Johannine word. Neither is it compatible with the Trinitarian doctrine, which never applied the term person to God, but only spoke of *persona* in relation to the Trinitarian "faces" in God.

Peter A. Bertocci: I am puzzled by a problem issuing from your assertion, expounded elsewhere and specifically included in your reply to Thielicke, that while God can be said to be personal he cannot be called *a* person because this "brings him side by side with other persons and makes him ontologically finite in relation to them." You suggest here that since a person is centered in himself and "excludes every other person from the center itself," personhood cannot be attributed to God because God is "nearer to my ego than I myself am to it." On your view

of the relation of infinite being to finite persons, does the essence of
infinite being itself transcend any particular being, and in *some* sense,
therefore, exclude any particular finite being from the center (essence)
of itself? If the expression, "God is nearer to my ego than I myself am
to it," means that God is the creative source of my being and that I
am not in a *mere* alongside-relation to him, then a theistic position
could be defended in which the human person, though "posited"
ontologically, is a limited but creative source of change in his own and
other being. My question is: Unless God's being and my being are to
some extent and in some way ontologically distinct—at least so that the
center of my being and the center of God's being exclude each other
ontologically (without denying interaction)—can there be real individuality for me, and individual freedom in any degree? Again, I realize
that you do not wish a rationalistic Spinozistic monism, but on your
view how is the locus of personhood and personal freedom protected if
God is "nearer to my ego than I myself am to it"? (I assume that the
ontological issue is not whether persons are "alongside" or "within"
God, but whether persons are in any sense ontic individuals.)

Tillich: The question of how my criticism of traditional theism
drives me in the direction of a Spinozistic monism is certainly justified
and I have often considered it myself. My answer is the doctrine that
man *is* finite freedom. As free, he is able to turn against his own essential being, and it is a universal fact that he does so in the process of
actualizing himself. The individual is not a mere "mode" of the eternal
substance, but he has that independence which is implied in the possibility of turning against himself—and consequently against his divine
ground. But this does not make him ontologically independent. God's
sustaining creativity, as Martin Luther asserts, gives the arm of the
murderer the power to stab his victim. One cannot speak of a relation
of the divine to the human center as if they were in the same ontological dimension. If we speak of a divine center at all—symbolically—we
must say that the periphery of which one's center is the center is infinite
and includes everything that is (cf. the symbols "omnipresence" and
"omniscience"). If Bertocci removes the metaphors "within" and
"alongside," and insists on "ontic individuals," I agree with him and
interpret his concept by the term "finite freedom."

VI. ON SYMBOLISM

William L. Reese: One would hardly expect so prominent a feature of Tillich's thought as the doctrine of symbolism to be overlooked in the present interrogation. And, indeed, a vigorous patterning of questions awaits us on this issue.

George Boas: How does one discover the meaning of a symbol?

Tillich: The brief question from Boas can be aimed in several directions. It can ask for the way that one should inquire into the meaning which symbols had, or have, to those for whom they were, or are, symbols. Documents concerning their meaning, comparison with similar symbols, the framework within which a symbol appears, etc., are tools for such research. But Boas' question can also ask for the way to an existential understanding of a symbol by participation in its revealing power. In the latter case, one should not use the term "discover," because the meaning of the symbol was never hidden. It is permanently present to those who are grasped by it. If there is a larger group, as a nation or a church, which expresses its foundation in symbols, conflicts can arise about the conceptualization of symbols (church doctrines, interpretations of a political constitution); but even then the basic meaning of the symbol is sufficiently understood to keep the community together. If, however, a definite split of a group takes place (as in the Reformation), then this means that under the cover of the common symbols a new existential relation to the ultimate of meaning and being has developed and has produced either the elimination of some symbols (e.g., the Holy Virgin) or the addition of some others (e.g., the lay-priest) or the change of the meaning of some of them (e.g., divine grace). This can lead to a point where an existential understanding (by participation) has become impossible and a scholarly approach—which still requires some empathy of understanding—is necessary if members of the one group want to understand the symbols of the other group.

A third meaning that Boas' question could have is whether there is another way of knowing that which is symbolized in the symbol, so that on the basis of such nonsymbolic knowledge the meaning of the symbol could be explained. To this I have to answer that symbolic language, for example, in the arts and in religion, reveals qualities of the encountered word which cannot be grasped in any other way. It is a "confusion of dimensions" if one takes the theological conceptualization of religious symbols as a direct cognitive approach to that which is symbolized by these symbols—as some forms of philosophy of religion and natural theology have tried to do.

Walter Kaufmann: You have often argued that, except for the equation of God with being-itself, "nothing else can be said about God as God which is not symbolic" and that "the symbol participates in the reality of that for which it stands." (1) In what do propositions about God "participate"? In being-itself? Or in the quality which they ascribe to God? In either case, how can we tell whether they do? It is clearly not your point that they must be literally true to "participate." How, then, can we tell the literally false propositions which "participate" from those which do not? And have you any quarrel with the claim that most propositions about God are through and through ambiguous? (2) In what sense does the sacramental wine "participate" in Christ's blood?

Tillich: Kaufmann asks about the meaning of the participation of symbols in what they symbolize. He asks it ontologically and epistemologically. Ontologically speaking, I would answer that symbolic statements about God point to a special quality of the divine life in which it manifests itself to us in an "ecstatic" experience. If such a quality is expressed in a symbolic term like "almighty God," this phrase, which uses finite material, points to something real in that which transcends finitude—the divine. In a similar way, I could answer the question of the symbolic character of the sacramental wine. In its sacramental use (not outside of it as the Roman Church insists) the wine becomes the bearer of the presence of God, insofar as he is manifest in the cross of the Christ. It is not merely a sign for the faithful, reminding them of a past event, but it is a vehicle of the experience of the presence of God here and now.

Symbolic statements about God, his attributes, and his actions are not false or correct, but they are "demonic" or "divine," and in most cases, they are mixed (ambiguous). The criterion is whether their implications are destructive or creative for personality and community. But this criterion cannot be applied from outside in terms of detached observations (though such observations can be made in retrospect); the criterion is effective and experienced in the life-processes which are determined by a particular set of symbols, expressing a particular relation to the ultimate; the dynamics of the history of religion are largely determined by these experiences. The theologian can try to formulate the criterion, and judge in its light and the light of those experiences the validity of religious symbols in religions generally and in his particular religion.

Peter A. Bertocci: The words you favor to indicate the cognitive-ontological relation between man and God are "grasped by," "union," and "participate." Apart from their describing what you believe to be an actual experience, the epistemic monism indicated by such expressions protects against the skepticism which you believe to result from any form of epistemic dualism, in which the experient is in no way identical with what is known. On your view, I take it, in "religious awareness" we are provided with cognitive certainty issuing from union and participation. Yet does not the cognitive assurance thus given initially in your system evaporate in the later contention that none of the ("pointing") symbols can be adequate renderings of the nature of unconditioned being? If no symbolism can possibly do cognitive justice to the Unconditioned, why are the cognitive attributions ("information" or not) you make, on the basis of direct encounter or union, better *in any sense* than those attributions an epistemic dualist would base on reasonable inference? (1) Why is the venture of faith, which we must put in symbols, any more trustworthy than the reasonable probability of an epistemic dualist if no symbol is adequate to render "the point" of immediate awareness which purportedly gives "unconditioned certainty"? (2) Are the judgments about the comparative suitability of different symbols based on any noninferential cognitive relationship?

Tillich: The validity of the experience of faith (the state of being grasped by the spiritual Presence) is not diminished by the fact that our knowledge of the divine ground of our being refers to its relation to us, but not to its essence. The mystery of being itself is beyond the cognitive grasp of any finite being just because it transcends the subject-object scheme which of itself is the unquestioned presupposition of every "epistemic dualist." The attempt to do "cognitive justice to the Unconditioned" by dissolving its mystery would be the greatest cognitive injustice.

The problem is not to find a more or less trustworthy cognitive approach to the divine, either by faith or by "the reasonable probability" of inference; the problem is one of participation itself.

The cognitive expressions, based on the experience of participation, are of secondary importance and have no standing in themselves—a fact which makes it impossible to discover or to confirm them inferentially.

VII. ON UNIVERSALS

William L. Reese: Related to the problem of symbolism is Professor Tillich's attitude toward universals. One of the interrogators found it important to pose a question concerning their status.

Paul G. Kuntz: Tillich speaks often of nominalism and realism. Perhaps his clearest definition of nominalism is in *The Courage to Be:* "Without language there are no universals. . . ."[19] Does the author share the conviction that only particulars exist? It seems so to many readers, and it is therefore a shock to find Tillich's polemic against nominalism. After saying that nominalists "dissolve our world into things," the author speaks of structures in being-itself. Of love, power, and justice he writes: "They precede everything that is, and they cannot be derived from anything that is. They have ontological dignity. . . . There is no truth without the form of truth. . . ."[20] And now a

[19] New Haven: Yale University Press, 1954, p. 91.
[20] *Love, Power, and Justice: Ontological Analyses and Ethical Applications* (New York: Oxford University Press, 1954), p. 21.

more explicit non-nominalism. "Reality as a whole," of which a nominalist philosopher tries to give account, "is a *reale* (in the sense of medieval realism) and not a *nomen.*" [21] Is nominalism a stage that leads to realism? Is neither adequate to experience, in that being is prior to both particulars and universal essences? Has Tillich a less extreme position than either his existentialist nominalism or his ontological realism, perhaps a version of conceptualism that does not go to untenable extremes?

Tillich: The statement: "Without language there are no universals . . ." means, in context and intention, that the essences which constitute the structure of encountered reality cannot be grasped by beings without language. The word "universal" was supposed to point to the universal notions which liberate man from the bondage to the "here and now." This is far away from nominalism. I am usually attacked as a realist in the Platonic-Augustinian sense, and I used to tell my American students: "You are nominalists by birth," in order to make them aware of the philosophical and theological consequences which follow from this unanalyzed prejudice. Personally, I would call myself a moderate realist, believing in the inner telos (*entelecheia*) of life-processes which directs them in all particulars in a definite direction (e.g., to become a tree). I must excuse myself by saying that in the sentence quoted I took the term "universals" in a merely subjective sense, probably because I usually call the objective side "essences" (or ideas).

VIII. ON VERIFICATION

William L. Reese: The problem of verification, with reference to experimental and experiential methods, was voiced more than once, and with reference both to positivism and to pragmatism.

Bowman L. Clarke: In his discussion of truth and verification in *Systematic Theology,*[22] Professor Tillich writes: "Statements which have neither intrinsic evidence nor a way of being verified have no

[21] In "A Colloquy on the Unity of Learning," *Daedalus*, Vol. 87 (Fall, 1958), p. 161.
[22] I, 102.

cognitive value. 'Verification' means a method of deciding the truth or falsehood of a judgment." For this reason he distinguishes between an "experimental" method, which is based on repeatable experiment, and an "experiential" method, which finds verification "within the life-process itself." Theological statements are verified experientially. I certainly agree with Professor Tillich that if theology is to maintain a cognitive value for its statements, it must face this problem and make some such distinctions with regard to method. Is there not, however, a more basic question than method in the problem of verification? In any problem of verification is not the question of the "truth conditions" of the statements more basic and itself determinative of the method; that is, must not one know under what conditions a statement would be considered true before he can determine what method is best for ascertaining if these conditions are actually present? If so, can "truth conditions" be given for theological statements? If not, is there any sense in which the term "verification" can still be employed? Also, can any distinction be made between the "type" of truth conditions for literal theological statements and the "type" for symbolic theological statements?

Tillich: Bowman L. Clarke's decisive and very significant question is: "Can 'truth-conditions' be given for theological statements?" If I understand him rightly, he wants me to show that the relation of theological statements to religious experiences and to their symbolic expressions make true theological statements possible. To answer the question we must first ask whether religious symbols themselves can be true or false. The answer is No! They can be authentic or non-authentic (based on a living experience or not); they can be adequate or inadequate (fit or unfit to express the experience); they can be divine or demonic (predominantly creative or predominantly destructive); but they cannot be true or false. This is different with theological statements. They can be true if they deal with authentic and adequate symbols interpreting them, relating them to each other, comparing them with other symbols of religious experience, and judging them in the light of the divine-demonic contrast. This makes every theological statement relative to the set of symbols in which a religious group lives: the theologian must stand somehow within what I have called the "theological circle." At the same time he must "serve the logos" and criticize the existing symbols in the power of the "principle" of the particular religion to which he belongs, for example, in the Protestant principle. Although relative to a group, the theologian need not restrict himself to a merely historical report about the tenets of this group. He interprets and, in doing so, he criticizes.

This description, which can be confirmed by an analysis of what most of the classical theologians have done, implies that there are no "literal" theological statements. If a theologian tries to give a literal interpretation of a religious symbol, he makes statements which are neither true nor false, but absurd or meaningless.

William A. Christian: You say, "The verifying test belongs to the nature of truth; in this positivism is right." [23] I take this to mean, in part, that when we are dealing with genuine truth-claims it is possible to find some principles of judgment which are neither arbitrary nor purely private. Of course, when we are dealing with religious truth-claims positivistic principles of judgment are not appropriate. As you explain, the appropriate principles are experiential, not experimental. But I suppose that any "verifying test" requires principles that are, in a sense, public principles. That is to say, they must be such that *we* can be guided by them in making our personal decisions, and they must also be such that we can offer them to *others,* in good faith, as guides for decisions. My question is: Does this apply in cases where "different and perhaps contradictory examples of revelation are encountered by phenomenological intuition"? [24] Are there some principles of judgment for deciding between conflicting claims of this sort, as between Judaism and Buddhism?

Tillich: William A. Christian's question is unanswerable in general terms. Decisions for or against religion are not being made in a vacuum. There are no criteria within a particular religious tradition concerning religious truth outside religious experience. This existential character of all religious knowledge is implicit in the nature of the religious encounter. On this basis, however, a process of testing is going on, partly

[23] *Systematic Theology,* I, 102.
[24] *Ibid.,* pp. 106–107.

within the immediate religious experience, partly within theological reflection upon it. Symbols prove inadequate to express intensified or changed religious experiences; or they may become unauthentic, merely remembered. It is the task of the theologian to discover and to conceptualize the "logos" in these transformations and to formulate principles which serve as criteria for theological and even religious decisions within this particular group.

The situation is different in the mutual encounter between two living religions. First of all, there is no common religious experience out of which common criteria could be derived. As long as this is not the case, only indifference or hostility or conversion from one religion to the other one is possible. If, however, the encounter of religions creates some kind of interpenetration, religious as well as theological tests occur and common criteria of adequacy can appear. This, by the way, is the situation into which all world-religions are increasingly driven. The immediately religious test concerning the superiority of a religion is its superior power of taking the other religion into itself without losing its own particular character. If such movement has started, the theologian can support it by elaborating the principles of such reception and transformation. Within this process concepts like that of the law in Judaism or of the logos in Christianity or of the dharma in India appear. If these principles are stated, the apologetic theologian will try to show that some tensions in the encountered religion can be solved by applying concepts like those mentioned. This was the way Christian apologists worked in the ancient world. In my personal encounter with Buddhism in Japan, I also found that this is the only method which is possible today. In the confrontation of the principles of justice and *agape* with the Buddhist principles of identity and compassion, a large number of concrete problems came under discussion, and not without some impact on both sides.

Richard M. Rorty: Professor Tillich says that "the verification of the principles of ontological reason" does not have the character of a "pragmatic test," because pragmatism "lacks a criterion." "If the successful working of the principles is called the 'criterion,' the question arises, 'What is the criterion of success?' This question cannot be answered again in terms of success, that is, pragmatically." [25] But in reply to Professor Walter Kaufmann, Tillich says that the criterion of whether symbols are demonic or divine is "whether their implications are creative or destructive for personality and community." How does this invocation of "creativity" differ from the pragmatist's invocation of "success"? Surely not in that the pragmatist makes only "detached observations"; pragmatism is not committed either to "detachment" or to intersubjective verification. Granted that pragmatism requires an ontology to ground its semiotics, need this ontology be "naturalistic" in Tillich's sense? "The infinite distance between the whole of finite things and their infinite ground" [26] seems quite as compatible with pragmatism's brand of voluntarism as it was with Kant's.

Tillich's criticisms of pragmatism seem to involve the same distinction which he uses to criticize "empirical theology": that between "philosophical possibilities with the tentative character of such" and "religious necessities." [27] But is there really an existential difference between the "tentativeness" with which an empirical theologian affirms his "concepts" and the "risk" in which a Tillichian theologian affirms his "symbols"? If both enterprises can, and do, meet in "theonomous philosophy," can we find any cognitive difference between the methods they use in evaluating alternatives?

Tillich: Rorty is quite right if he points to the pragmatic element in my own thinking. And I readily accept a kind of pragmatism which seems to be implied in Rorty's examples. In my earlier German writings and in comparisons of pragmatism and existentialism, I have acknowledged my positive valuation of a pragmatism of the type of William James. My critical remarks are directed against a kind of pragmatism, as it developed in the later Dewey school, approaching scientific empiricism as the only remaining element. I consider my emphasis on the "cognitive risk" as a definitely pragmatic element in my thought.

Every theologian affirms concepts and every theologian does so in relation to symbols. And every theologian should know that his con-

[25] *Systematic Theology*, I, 105.
[26] *Ibid.*, II, 7.
[27] *Ibid.*, I, 44.

cepts are problematic and subject to rational criticism and to change. This is his scientific attitude. The "risk of faith," however, involves the whole person; and a failure in it can have destructive consequences. Therefore, I cannot see the biblical historian as historian and the Christian who accepts the Christ as his ultimate concern on the same level of risk. Theological statements are like all scholarly statements, intentionally preliminary. Religious decisions are total risks; they may change, but the change is not intended; it may or may not happen. If one uses the word pragmatic in this context, one should distinguish scientific from existential pragmatism.

IX. ON BEING AND VALUE

William L. Reese: Nor was the relation of being and value, and the nature of evil, ignored in the interrogation. Demos, Nielsen, and Outler pose distinct but related questions in this area.

Raphael Demos: 1. Tillich identifies God with being-itself exclusively, thus denying or at least ignoring value as a constituent of God's nature. So far as I understand him, he does not regard value as an ultimate reality; unlike being, value is for him something belonging to the finite order.

In some sense, Plato and Leibniz held the opposite of Tillich's doctrine. According to Plato, the idea of the good is above *ousia* and is the source of it; Leibniz maintained, speaking from the epistemic point of view, that a statement is true to the extent that it is consistent and comprehensive; thus a theory is true insofar as it explains the most with the least. But order, consistency, clarity, simplicity are values; thus both philosophers define being in terms of value.

I am not proposing that being should be reduced to value; that would be simply to reverse Tillich's procedure. But I think that being and value are so mixed up that they are co-ordinate, and co-ordinately ultimate.

To identify God with being-itself is both to demean him and to depart from Christian doctrine, according to which "God is love" is as literally true as "God is." Otherwise we have Spinozism. The progress of religious insight has consisted in an advance from the worship of mere power to that of power joined with goodness. Tillich's view of God is a regression to primitivism.

2. There seems to be a strong anticonceptualist trend in Tillich. True enough, he admits and indeed argues for a rational apprehension of God, but his logic is a dialectical logic. The essence of the latter is that it denies the law of contradiction. Consider the effect of this on Tillich's assertion that God is being-itself. Suppose that I reject this statement; then, since the law of contradiction is without force, I am just as right as Tillich is. In short, by substituting dialectical for formal logic, Tillich undermines his own theological doctrine and refutes himself.

Tillich: Demos' second question can be answered in terms of the distinction between a logical contradiction (which is not admissible in any consistent statement) and a "real" (in German, *Real*) contradiction which is stated in every adequate description of life-processes: Life goes beyond itself by partly negating itself. The element of self-negation can be expressed in statements which seem to be logically contradictory, but are not if their descriptive meaning is understood. And, certainly, one could not call Hegel "anticonceptualist." The real problem of the rationality of the theological system appears in the concept of the paradox. In a special chapter of the second volume of my *Systematic Theology,* I try to define the genuine meaning of paradox, and to distinguish it sharply from the dialectical, the irrational, the absurd, and the nonsensical. I often criticize theologians for using the "paradox" in order to escape dangerous logical consequences. The paradox is that which contradicts human expectation, but not the logos of speech.

With respect to Demos' first question, I am glad that we are more in agreement that I thought. I never have ignored what Demos calls value as "a constituent of God's nature." I have always understood the idea of the good as the point of identity of being and value, and my whole doctrine of the contrast between essence and existence implies the "goodness of essential being." My resistance against the philosophy of values stems from my early dissatisfaction with the neo-Kantian, theological as well as philosophical, use of the value theory. It appeared as a way of replacing the ontological questions in philosophy and the mystical elements in religion. But above all, it did not give any indication about the source of values or any explanation of its commanding position over against reality. Therefore, it also blurred the distinction between valuations and objectively valid values. For all these reasons, I prefer an ontology which includes value to a nonontological value theory—as Demos also seems to do.

I would hesitate, however, to call structural elements of logical language, like consistency, simplicity, etc., values. They are logos structures of the mind and correspond to the logos structures of the encountered reality; to follow them is valuable, but they are not values.

Kai Nielsen: Professor Tillich has argued in "Is a Science of Human Values Possible?" that there can be a science of value in the sense that there can be an "ontology of value." He says that values must be *derived* "from essential structures of being which appear within existence, though in a state of distortion." [28] "Ethical values," he argues, "are commands derived from the essential nature of man. . . . The moral law is man's own essential nature appearing as commanding authority. . . . Value is man's essential being . . ." [29]

1. Is the "is" ("are") in these sentences the "is" of identity or the "is" of predication?

2. If Professor Tillich says that it is the "is" of identity, would it not then be meaningless to ask, "Though man's essential nature is *x,* is *x* good or valuable?" But for whatever *x* is, it is *not* meaningless to ask if it is good or valuable. It is *not* a self-answering question like "Is a brother a male sibling?" Whenever we assert there is an *x,* we can always ask if it is a good *x.* That it is a good *x* is never established by simply asserting that it is an *x.* But if the "is" in the above-quoted statements from Professor Tillich is the "is" of identity, then the words "good" and "value" would be identical with some property or set of properties which constitute man's essential nature, and it would be the case that in discovering what an *x* really is we would *ipso facto* discover that it was good. But do not the remarks above indicate that the words "good" and "value" are not so used?

3. If the "is" is the "is" of predication, we have only attributed good-

<hr>

[28] Abraham H. Maslow (ed.), *New Knowledge in Human Values* (New York: Harper & Row, 1959), p. 193.
[29] *Ibid.,* pp. 194–195.

ness or value to a person or a type of character-trait or traits. But then have we actually found out what the nature of value is? If we understood the nature of good or value, we could make such an attribution; but such a statement, so interpreted, could not serve as our foundation for a standard of value, for would we not remain puzzled by the questions "What is value?" and "What is goodness?"

4. Thus, whether the "is" in Professor Tillich's sentences above is the "is" of identity or of predication, has he any good grounds at all for claiming that moral statements can be *derived* from statements asserting that man has such-and-such an essential nature? I can put my question in a slightly different way: If in saying that man has such-and-such an essential nature we are *not* making a normative claim, how can we deduce or derive a normative claim from it without illicitly smuggling into the conclusion what is not in the premises; and if in saying that man has such-and-such an essential nature we *are* making a normative claim, then we have not derived our values from man's essential nature, for they are already there.

Tillich: My answer to Demos is also an answer to Nielsen's basic question. I simply can state that the "is" in sentences like "Value is man's essential being" is meant as the "is of identity." Autobiographically speaking, these sentences are inspired by Augustine's assertion: *"Esse qua esse bonum est."* But this fact does not guarantee the truth of the statement, although it gives it some trans-individual weight, since Augustine's short formula is the result of a long and severe struggle of the early church against the religious-dualistic tendencies of Gnosticism, Manichaeism, etc. (and even Neoplatonism), for the "goodness of creation." I do not need to enumerate the many theoretical and practical consequences of this decision. But I may say that if we call a thing good, we always have the connotation of "fulfillment of its essential nature." We define a good tree as one in which its potentialities as pine tree or apple tree are actualized, undistorted by external or internal influences. And we describe a good man as one who actualizes humanity, namely, his essentially human potentialities. The question of how we know essentiality, and with it goodness, or goodness and with it essentiality, leads to the questions of relative and absolute ethics and to the principle of love as the unity of the absolute and the relative. It seems to me, however, that Nielsen is right when he rejects the term "deriving" for the relation of being and value.

Kai Nielsen: Professor Tillich bluntly states in answer to my question that the "is" in sentences like "Value is man's essential being" is the "is" of identity. Assuming what is not clear, namely, that we can understand the meaning of the phrase "man's essential being," it does not seem to me that Professor Tillich has at all met the problem in (2) of my question. A consideration of it should surely follow on the admission that "value is man's essential being" is an identity statement. Let me put my question again in a slightly different way. Let *x* stand for *whatever* would be the correct definition of "man's essential being." "Man's essential being" is the *definiendum,* and *x* is a variable for the *definiens* of "man's essential being." For *whatever* value we replace for the variable *x*—whatever we give as the definition of "man's essential being"—*it clearly is not meaningless to ask,* "Though man's essential being is *x,* is *x* good or valuable?" If the "is" in "Value is man's essential being" is the "is" of identity, then such a question would be meaningless; but since such a question clearly is not meaningless, Professor Tillich must be wrong in asserting that the "is" in such a statement is the "is" of identity. This argument, as the argument in (2) of my previous question, seems to show plainly that statements like "Value is man's essential being," "The moral law is man's own essential nature appearing as commanding authority," or even *"Esse qua esse bonum est"* cannot possibly be identity statements. I would like Professor Tillich at least to indicate why he does not think this is so.

Tillich: It is a consequence of the identity of goodness and essential being that the question "Though man's essential being is *x,* is *x* good or valuable?" cannot be asked. For if it were asked, it would imply the presupposition that there is another criterion of the good and the valuable than what makes a thing what it essentially is and therefore ought to be. An "ought" which stands against what a thing potentially is (e.g., humane if he is a man) would not concern him, would have to be rejected by him as heteronomous, and could not exercise power over him. Therefore, I must insist on the identity of goodness and essential being. Nielsen also indicates a lack of clarity of "essential being." Here I can

follow him if he refers to the problems implied in this term, especially
the relation of essential (or potential) to existential (or actual) being.
Essential being, for example, should not be understood as static in the
(probable) Platonic sense; on the other hand, existential being should
not be understood as a continuous change without lasting, though not
necessarily eternal, structures. It seems to me that the unity of these two
characteristics of encountered reality is given in the dynamics of love
(love in all its different qualities). Therefore I consider love both as the
universal power of essential being and as the source of all true valuation.

Albert C. Outler: I have never been satisfied with Tillich's treatment of "the problem of evil." To the classical question, *Unde malum?*
he responds with another question, "How could he [God] permit sin?" [30]
The obvious answer to this is, "Not permitting sin would mean not
permitting freedom; this would deny the very nature of man, his finite
freedom." He then turns back to the *unde malum:* "Only after *this*
answer can one describe evil as the structure of self-destruction which
is implicit in the nature of universal estrangement."

This is dark indeed. What is the meaning of "the structure of *self-
destruction*" and how is it related to other "structures" of "destruction"?
Does not "structure" imply being —*formed* being, at that? On the preceding page, Tillich had said, "Sin is seen as *one* evil beside *others.*" [31]
If evil is the structure of destruction, has it *another* ground than being-
itself? If not, how far is Tillich's notion of evil from the notion that
evil is *ingredient* in finite existence *as such?* Again, how far is Tillich's
concept of "the nature of universal estrangement" from the notion that
the *original* sin of man is simply being a man at all?

Tillich: Outler has difficulty with the term "structure of self-destruction." The term is the conceptualization of the symbol, the demonic.
The description of the demoniacs in the New Testament shows a
definite structure—one, by the way, which is confirmed by the modern
insights of psychopathology. This structural element which distinguishes the demonic from the satanic includes positive elements (both

[30] *Systematic Theology,* II, 61.
[31] *Ibid.,* p. 60.

in the New Testament and in modern psychotherapy). The term "structure of destruction" is an intended paradox pointing to the ambiguous character of the demonic.

The term "universal estrangement" is the conceptualization of the Pauline idea that in the sin of Adam everybody has sinned or that God has included all men under sin or Augustine's anti-Pelagian emphasis. The Pelagian or Erasmian question was always, Does this not identify "being man" and "being sinner"? It certainly does, but as existential fact, not as essential necessity. For every individual man affirms with finite freedom and therefore with responsibility his state of estrangement. The road between Manichaeism and Pelagianism is narrow, and ultimately it can be described only negatively: Man's predicament is neither a matter of freedom alone nor a matter of destiny alone.

To the question *"Unde malum?"* I am inclined to answer with Kierkegaard: "The Sin presupposes itself"; it is *the* irrational. But one can show the possibility of sin and the temptation to it in man's creatureliness. And one can and must state at the same time that sin is not necessary essentially and universal existentially. It is interesting that Reinhold Niebuhr, in a criticism of my assumedly ontological explanation of sin, emphasizes the historical explanation (after having demythologized the story of the fall) and then asserts that sin is not necessary but "unavoidable." I fully agree; but does this remove the *element* of necessity in what is unavoidable?

If one tries to follow up the question *"Unde malum?"* into the divine life, I would—with an important stream of thought in Western philosophy and theology—point to the element of negativity in the divine life which makes God a living God, although it is eternally conquered in him. This element of negativity (symbolically the chaos-element in biblical and nonbiblical literature) is ambiguously actualized and fragmentarily conquered in historical existence.

X. ON NONBEING

William L. Reese: The status of nonbeing in Tillich's system was the subject of two questions.

Reese: The attempt to exclude nonbeing from one's thought seems to involve, in a puzzling manner, its tacit recognition. Ordinary negations can be interpreted in a mood of Platonic "otherness" so that the category of nonbeing is not mentioned. The prefix "non-" changes a term into its complement. And the complements of ordinary terms refer as much to beings as do the terms from which the complements had been derived. The category of nonbeing is mentioned, however, when our useful prefix is joined to the high abstraction, "being." Since "being" refers to all that is, there is nothing to which its complement can refer. And "otherness" does not appear to perform adequately at this level. What is, I am certain, is other than what is not. I seem to be making reference to the *ouk on,* the nothing at all.

And yet the admission of nonbeing into the structure of ontology immediately transforms "nothing" into the name of something, and nonbeing becomes a kind of being. The existential admission, this is to say, does not eliminate the puzzle. Only relative nonbeing, the *mē on* —I should judge—can be admitted into ontology. In the act of "othering," affixing negative prefixes to ordinary terms, Tillich would find relative nonbeing already present. And possibly the "nothing at all" can be understood to be a mere extension of this act. What are we to do in this situation?

It seems to me the part of wisdom merely to grant that nonbeing has, indeed, a kind of being—namely, the being of the *mē on,* of the possible or potential. Much of the contrast between being and nonbeing can be fitted to this distinction of actual and possible being. The view would be in Tillich's terminology a type of "essentialism," but allowing an extension of Platonic "otherness" to the possible, including the possibilities of error, falsehood, and disappointed expectation. What evidence, or argument, prevents this alternative from being judged a more reasonable outcome to this exasperating problem than the ontological assertion of nonbeing?[32]

Tillich: The puzzle of nonbeing has vexed Western philosophy since Parmenides. It was, as Reese acknowledges, partly solved by the distinction between *mē on* and *ouk on,* the not-yet-being of the poten-

[32] The discussion has reference mainly to Tillich, *Systematic Theology,* I, 186–189.

tial, and the absolute not-being of the potential as well as the actual. In my analysis of the meaning of existence (in the second volume of my *Systematic Theology*) I have referred to the significance of the notion of *mē on* for my own thinking. But there is a problem not touched on by the Greek distinction, namely, the possibility of the human mind to think that there might have been nothing at all. I have called this thought the "shock of nonbeing." It is a real experience, analogous to anxiety produced by the awareness of our own individual nonbeing (before birth and after death). It can also be expressed positively as the astonishment about the fact that there is something (the *"unvordenkliche"* fact, as Schelling calls it). Kant, in his criticism of the cosmological argument, has attributed this "shock of nonbeing" symbolically to God when he makes God reflect about the where-from of his own being. I do not believe that the distinction between *mē on* and *ouk on* is the answer to this experience of nonbeing.

There is a third place where the problem of being and nonbeing appears, namely, the awareness of becoming, and with it of all life-processes, including what is symbolically called divine life. It is not the transition from essence to existence, from *dynamis* to *energeia,* which states the problem, but the "otherness," which is the negation of "sameness." It is, in Hegelian terms, the dialectical otherness which implies nonbeing in the sense of not being "this or that." The otherness in the realm of essences becomes negation in the processes of life.

This dialectical nonbeing cannot be excluded from consideration, and its ontological standing in relation to the two other ways in which nonbeing is asserted is worth inquiry.

Kai Nielsen: We recognize that we might not have existed. Upon further thought, we recognize that since the denial of an existential proposition is not self-contradictory, it could be the case (as a *purely logical possibility*) that there might be nothing at all. The recognition of this, in Professor Tillich's words, comes as a shock; it supposedly generates the ontological question of being. We wonder why it is that anything at all exists. It seems to me correct to say, as John Hick has,[33] that Tillich's statement of this problem involves a needless and mystifying hypostatization of "nonbeing" and that Bertrand Russell's theory

[33] *Scottish Journal of Theology,* XII (Sept., 1959), 291–292.

of descriptions provides an adequate way of elucidating the meaning of negative existential propositions. But granting all this, it still seems to me that "There might have been nothing at all" is an intelligible statement. It means, "All negative existential statements might be true." This is a semantically proper way of saying, "There might have been nothing at all." If, in fact, all negative existential statements were true, it would then be the case that there would be nothing at all. When we ask Tillich's question, "Why is there something rather than nothing at all?" we are asking what is the *reason* for there being something rather than nothing. But it seems to me that there is no *possible* answer to this question that would not itself generate the same type of question. If someone says, "God is the reason there is something rather than nothing" the question immediately arises, "But, why *must* there be a God rather than nothing at all? What *reason* is there for this?" Is not Professor Hick again correct in saying that Professor Tillich's basic philosophical problem is "insoluble, or rather an improperly formulated problem; there is no *conceivable* proposition that would constitute an answer to it. We can only accept with piety the fact that there is something rather than nothing." [34]

1. How would Professor Tillich reply to the above counterclaim?

2. If nothing could *conceivably* answer Tillich's basic philosophical question or problem, in what sense is it literally a question or a problem? A question or problem without a *conceivable* answer seems to me no question or no problem at all.

3. If Professor Tillich thinks his alleged question is a question because he has an answer, would he please indicate what the answer is.

Tillich: There is no doubt that the question, "Why is there something, why not nothing?" is not a question in the proper logical sense of the word. There is no answer to it, as I myself have indicated by referring to Kant's mythical God who asks this question with respect to himself and cannot answer it. But the question *has* been asked by philosophers (and by children) and is the most radical expression of the astonishment which makes the philosopher a philosopher. Expressions of a shock are not problems, but they can remind reason of that which precedes reason (*das Unvordenkliche*—Schelling), the merely given,

[34] *Ibid.*, p. 292.

the original fact, which as Professor Hick rightly says, must be "piously" accepted. And it is just this "piety" to which my description of the experience of the mystery of being was supposed to lead.

XI. ON
SOCIALISM AND THE *KAIROS*

William L. Reese: Most of the questions posed have had metaphysical or theological issues at their focus. The following question, however, turns our attention to Tillich's analysis of contemporary society.

James Luther Adams: Tillich's religious socialism has combined theological and sociological elements. The questions to be posed here have to do primarily with sociological elements, namely, with his conception of the structure and dynamics of society.

Tillich has interpreted modern Western society in terms of a theory of periodization, each period exhibiting characteristic preliminary concerns and characteristic forms of social structure; for example, he has spoken of the period of capitalism (with its developing phases) and of a period of postcapitalism, of a Protestant and a post-Protestant era. The dynamics in the change of structures he has interpreted in terms of a dialectical conception according to which each period exhibits characteristic contradictions that drive toward their own dissolution and, through "directed tensions," to a new period demanding new structures. Accordingly, he has asserted that "there is no other way out" of the contradictions and crises of capitalism than through the overcoming of competition; the socialization of heavy industry, banking, and foreign trade; the exclusion of endless parliamentarian discussion; a centralized power and authority, not only with respect to economic and political organization, but also with reference to education and religion.[35]

Recently, however, Tillich has spoken of the present period as inducing the experience of "a sacred void," a *kairos,* when we must "wait for a new reality, not produced by better methods or more knowledge, or severer human toil"; we are in "a holy vacuum which is holy if it is

[35] *Die sozialistische Entscheidung* (Potsdam: Alfred Protte, 1933), p. 197. *The Protestant Era*, trans. and with a Concluding Essay by James Luther Adams (Chicago: University of Chicago Press, 1948), pp. 225–226.

patiently experienced and not filled with activities and short-cut solutions." The demands for a socialist reorganization of society seem to be relinquished (cf. the articles entitled "Religion and Secular Culture," [36] "Beyond Religious Socialism," [37] and "Beyond the Dilemma of Our Period").[38]

How are we to understand the divergence between the earlier and the later formulations? Does Tillich still hold to the earlier dialectical theory which envisaged sharp discontinuity between the capitalist period and a postcapitalist collective system? Has he abandoned the dialectical theory which appeared to demand sharp disjunction between periods and between their respective types of social structure? In going "beyond socialism" does he now agree substantially with Reinhold Niebuhr's postsocialist, pragmatic outlook? In face of the present "sacred void," do the earlier "epochal" conceptions and the earlier dialectical methods require revision? And in face of "the holy vacuum," does "ultimate seriousness" demand any sort of structurally conceived program of social change for our day?

Tillich: Adams' questions can be brought down to the one with which I happened to deal in the week preceding my writing this answer, when delivering four Rauschenbusch Lectures on "Kairos and Utopia" in a half-autobiographical, half-systematic way. I tried in these lectures to show that the prophetic spirit, the "spirit of utopia," hardly ever avoids becoming "utopianism," namely, an objective description of a future state of things in which the aspirations of the spirit of utopia are supposed to be fulfilled; and I make it quite clear that I believe in the unavoidable "existential disappointment" which follows every utopianism. On the other hand, I warned against the danger of a conservative-conformist reaction to such a disappointment, and I demanded the continuous presence of the spirit of utopia, whether in religious or in secular symbols.

It is indeed my belief that the element of utopianism, into which we fell in the awareness of the *kairos* after World War I in Central Europe, had to be removed, but that the pronouncement of the *kairos,* the begin-

[36] (Lecture given at the University of Chicago, January, 1946, on the Hiram W. Thomas Foundation), *Journal of Religion,* XXVI, No. 2 (April, 1946), pp. 79–86 (included in *The Protestant Era,* pp. 55–65).

[37] *The Christian Century,* LXVI, No. 24 (June 15, 1949), pp. 732–733.

[38] *The Cambridge Review,* No. 4 (November, 1955), pp. 209–215.

ning of a new period in thinking and acting, was justified, objectively as well as subjectively. Both sides belong to the experience of a *kairos:* Something objective must happen, and some minds must grasp it and interpret it as a moment in which a new answer to the question of the meaning of existence breaks into existence. In the years after World War II, in which I spoke of the "void" (the lack of prophetic spirit), the objective side was different from that after World War I and was not understood as a *kairos* by any group with symbol-creating power. Instead of that, despair and cynicism prevailed; they continue to prevail in the present feeling that contemporary history is almost completely determined by trends and that the chances of breaking the control of these trends is minimal. Conformism and the search for security have become the burial place of the prophetic spirit.

From these facts I do not derive the rejection of the spirit of utopia or of the idea of *kairos.* But they are lacking and cannot be forced. In no way do I deny the great *kairoi* of the past, including the central *kairos,* the appearance of the New Being in Jesus as the Christ. I do not deny the *kairos* of which the men of the early Renaissance and the early Reformation were aware, as they brought a new period into existence. I do not even deny the *kairos* character of the proletarian revolution as expressed in the *Communist Manifesto,* in spite of the utopianism and demonic distortion of the original prophetic element in it.

For our present situation, the demonic danger to be fought is the destruction of the humanity in man by the cultural structure of the industrial mass society—on both sides of the great split. What we can and must do is to analyze and denounce the structures of destruction in our society and in this way prepare the prophetic spirit which may rise again and show the image of a new "theonomy," even if it cannot avoid the pitfall into utopianism—which has never been completely avoided in any of the great *kairoi* (including that of which the New Testament speaks).

XII. ON ART

William L. Reese: Our final question touches upon aesthetic analysis and is concerned with certain distinctions of terminology employed by Professor Tillich.

J. Herman Randall, Jr.: How do you distinguish "painting" from *Kitsch?* How do you distinguish *Kunst* from other forms of making? Why is it not easier to distinguish "better" and "worse" art and painting than to set both off sharply from the Worse?

Tillich: The question from Randall is a repercussion of a paper I gave at the Philosophy Club in New York City about the "Revelatory Character of Style and the Contemporary Visual Arts." One of the problems which arose in the discussion was the question of how non-art can be distinguished from art in cases in which the production of art is intended. In my paper I dealt with this problem only briefly, but I used the untranslatable German word *Kitsch* for a special kind of a beautifying, sentimental naturalism, as it appears in disastrous quantities in ecclesiastical magazines and inside church buildings. The word *Kitsch* points not to poor art, based on the incompetence of the painter, but on a particular form of deteriorated idealism (which I like to call "beautifying naturalism"). The necessary fight against the predominance of such art in the churches during the last hundred years leads me to the frequent use of the word *Kitsch* (which I even applied to describe the face of Jesus in Dali's famous "Last Supper" in the National Gallery of Art in Washington).

The question of the quality in art is most difficult because of the character of the aesthetic encounter. It is an "involved" encounter, insofar as the result—the aesthetic vision—always contains elements coming from the encountered object, and elements coming from the encountering subject. In this point the aesthetic and the religious encounter are similar: Both of them create symbols and require participation in these symbols in order to be understood.

This situation makes it impossible to establish general objective criteria of artistic quality which can be applied by an outside observer. Certainly it is possible to formulate negative criteria (as the teacher in "creative writing" uses them in his class); and it is also possible to point in a work of art to those qualities which express an overcoming of these negative possibilities. But beyond this one cannot go. Every academic rule ever formulated has been broken by creative artists. This does not mean that the rule was completely wrong, but it means that the rule was only partly true and had to be restated in a larger context, which again may prove to be too small. The actual decisions about the quality of works of art are not being made in this way. They are made in terms of encounters by individuals or groups with them in acts of aesthetic participation.

The other question Randall asks is whether one should distinguish *Kunst* from other forms of making. Certainly not, insofar as they all are forms of making (technical, educational, political). But these kinds of making are so different in ends and means that the fact that they all "make" something is not of great significance. If, as Randall suggests, the word "art" be vastly enlarged, beyond "the arts" in the conventional sense, a new word must be found for the latter, perhaps "aesthetic art" or "expressive art," that is, a kind of making in which aesthetic symbols are produced or in which a special dimension of man's encounter with reality is expressed in directly sensory or imaginary-sensory symbols. The question whether there is a sharp, definable distinction between non-art, which claims to be art, and actual art, is perhaps not very important, since even if one asserted such a distinction, the actual mixture between merely intended and real art would be so overwhelming that the establishment of a boundary line would have little practical value.

XIII. CONCLUDING STATEMENT

Tillich: I feel greatly honored that such an elite group of scholars has deemed it worthwhile to deal with my thought; and I am grateful for the incisiveness of the questions and the fairness in which they are presented. I learned much from them, and I hope that some misunderstandings are removed and some difficulties are eased by better formulations in my answers.

The systematic thinker—and I cannot deny that this is my natural inclination—is more vulnerable than the essayist. For the criticism of each point has implications for the whole system—if it is worthy to be called a system. Therefore, the systematic thinker must defend himself in all directions into which his system reaches; and he often is inferior in his defense to critics who are thoroughly expert in one or several fields. The systematic thinker, on the other hand, has the advantage of envisaging his field as a whole and, consequently, the interrelations of every problem with every other problem. It is my experience that this possibility—and necessity—is an excellent heuristic principle. It shows connections which otherwise one never would have discovered. But above all, it forces strict consistency upon the systematic thinker. And this is especially important in theology where the complex relation between religious symbol and theological concept makes clarity and consistency especially difficult. Therefore, I believe that the *telos*, the inner aim of all thinking, is the system, the unity in which every statement is under the critical control of every other statement.

NOTES ON THE
EDITORS AND INTERROGATORS

SYDNEY AND BEATRICE ROME are social scientists at the Center for Research in System Sciences in the Research Directorate of the System Development Corporation of Santa Monica, California. They are, together, the Joint Principal Investigators of the Leviathan Research Studies, a program which is conducting theoretical and laboratory investigations of large, intentionally structured social hierarchies. They have published jointly in the areas of intentional logic, system simulation, non-quantitative (qualitative) computer modeling, and large-group theory.

Sydney Rome was given the doctorate by Harvard University. He has served as Special Research Associate at Harvard, head of the Project Information Section of Polaroid Corporation's research laboratories, a lecturer on the Graduate Faculty of the New School for Social Research, a philosophy professor at the College of William and Mary, and a social scientist at the RAND Corporation.

Beatrice Rome was granted the doctorate by Radcliffe College and Harvard, and studied at the Sorbonne and the Collège de France. She was a professor of philosophy at William and Mary and a social scientist at the RAND Corporation. Besides her joint publications with Sydney Rome, she has written in the areas of crisis management, political strategy, computerization of military intelligence, theory of command and control, and has published *The Philosophy of Malebranche.*

RICHARD I. AARON, past president of Mind Association and the Aristotelian Society, has written philosophical articles in English and Welsh and is editor of the Welsh philosophical journal, *Efrydiau Athronyddol.*

JAMES LUTHER ADAMS, Professor of Christian Ethics, Harvard Divinity School, is the author of *The Changing Reputation of Human Nature and Religious Orientation,* among other works, and has translated and written an introduction to Paul Tillich's *The Protestant Era.*

JACOB B. AGUS, Rabbi of Beth El Congregation, Baltimore, is the author of *Modern Philosophies of Judaism* and *The Evolution of Jewish Thought,* among other works.

WILLIAM ALSTON, Professor of Philosophy, University of Michigan, is the author of numerous essays on problems of philosophy.

ROBERT ASSAGIOLI, founder and director of the Institute for Psychosynthesis, is the author of numerous essays and studies in the fields of psychology and philosophy.

ALBERT E. AVEY, Professor of Philosophy, Emeritus, Ohio State University, is the author of *Rethinking Religion, Basic Religious Questions,* and *Handbook in the History of Philosophy,* among other works.

JOHN BAILLIE, late Professor of Divinity, University of Edinburgh, was the author of *Our Knowledge of God, Belief in Progress, The Place of Jesus Christ in Modern Christianity,* among other works.

WILLIAM BARRETT, Professor of Philosophy, New York University, is the author of *Irrational Man,* and editor (with H. D. Aiken) of *Philosophy in the Twentieth Century.*

DAVID BAUMGARDT, the author of numerous works including *Jeremy Bentham and the Ethics of Today, Maimonides: The Conciliator of Eastern and Western Thought, Spinoza und Mendelssohn,* died during the summer of 1963.

SAMUEL HUGO BERGMAN, Professor of Philosophy at the Hebrew University, Jerusalem, is the author of *Faith and Reason: An Introduction to Modern Jewish Thought,* among other works. Professor Bergman is editor of the section on philosophy of the *Encyclopedia Hebraica.*

PETER A. BERTOCCI, Borden Parker Bowne Professor of Philosophy, Boston University, is the author of *The Empirical Argument for God in Late British Thought, Introduction to the Philosophy of Religion,* and *Religion as Creative Insecurity,* among other works.

BRAND BLANSHARD, formerly Sterling Professor of Philosophy and Chairman of the Department of Philosophy at Yale University, is the author of *Reason and Goodness, The Nature of Thought,* and *Reason and Analysis,* among other works.

WALTER BLUMENFELD, Professor of Psychology, Emeritus, Universidad Nacional Mayer de San Marcos, Lima, Peru, is the author of numerous studies in psychology and philosophy. Among his most recent publications are *La antropología filosófica de Martin Buber y la filosofía antropológica* and *Valor y valoración.*

GEORGE BOAS, Professor of the History of Philosophy, Emeritus, Johns Hopkins University, Baltimore, Maryland, is the author of *Dominant Themes of Modern Philosophy, Some Assumptions of Aristotle,* and *The Limits of Reason,* among other works.

GERD BRAND has occupied distinguished posts in the West German government at Bonn. He is presently Director General of the German Foundation for the Developing Countries. Among his publications is *Welt, Ich und Zeit,* based on unpublished manuscripts of Edmund Husserl.

RICHARD B. BRANDT, Chairman of the Department of Philosophy, Swarthmore College, and its McDowell Professor of Philosophy, is the author of *The Philosophy of Schleiermacher, Ethical Theory,* and *The Problems of Ethics,* among other works.

ROBERT W. BROWNING is presently Professor of Philosophy at Northwestern University, and has published studies on the philosophy of C. I. Lewis and Paul Weiss.

ROBERT S. BRUMBAUGH, Professor of Philosophy, Yale University, is the author of *Plato's Mathematical Imagination* and *Plato for the Modern Age,* as well as co-author (with Newton P. Stallknecht) of *The Spirit of Western Philosophy* and *The Compass of Philosophy.*

MILIC CAPEK, Professor of Philosophy, Boston University, is the author of *Bergson and the Trends of Contemporary Physics* and *The Philosophical Impact of Contemporary Physics.*

PETER J. CAWS, presently Executive Associate of the Carnegie Corporation of New York, is the author of articles in the history and philosophy of science and the forthcoming *Philosophy of Science: A Systematic Account.*

ROBERT CHAMPIGNY teaches in the Department of French at Indiana University. He is the author of *Stages on Sartre's Way* and *Le Genre romanesque.*

V. C. CHAPPELL, Associate Professor of Philosophy, the University of Chicago, is the editor of the Modern Library edition of the works of David Hume and editor of *The Philosophy of Mind* and *Philosophy and Ordinary Language.*

E. LA B. CHERBONNIER, Professor of Religion, Trinity College, Hartford, Connecticut, is the author of *Hardness of Heart.*

WILLIAM A. CHRISTIAN, Professor of Religion, Yale University, is the author of *An Interpretation of Whitehead's Metaphysics.*

BOWMAN L. CLARKE, Assistant Professor of Philosophy, the University of Georgia, has contributed essays to the *Journal of Religion* and the *Anglican Theological Review.*

W. NORRIS CLARKE, S.J., Associate Professor of Philosophy, Fordham University, is the American Editor in Chief of the *International Philosophical Quarterly* and contributor of essays to *Religious Experience and Truth: A Symposium; Experience, Existence and the Good: Essays in Honor of Paul Weiss,* and *Ethical Aftermath of Automation,* among others.

ARTHUR A. COHEN, Editor in Chief, Trade Department, Holt, Rinehart and Winston, Inc., New York City, is the author of *Martin Buber; The Natural and the Supernatural Jew: An Historical and Theological Introduction,* and the forthcoming *The Myth of the Judeo-Christian Tradition.*

ROBERT S. COHEN, Professor and Chairman of the Department of Physics, Boston University, is the author of numerous books and articles in the related disciplines of philosophy and science.

JAMES COLLINS, Professor of Philosophy, St. Louis University, St. Louis, Missouri, is the author of *The Existentialists: A Critical Study, The Mind of Kierkegaard, God in Modern Philosophy,* and *Three Paths in Philosophy,* among other works.

FREDERICK CHARLES COPLESTON, S.J., Professor of the History of Philosophy, the Pontifical Gregorian University, Rome, and Heythrop College, Oxford, is the author of *A History of Philosophy* (six volumes to date), *Nietzsche, Schopenhauer, Aquinas,* and *Contemporary Philosophy,* among other works.

RICHARD H. COX, Associate Professor of Political Science, the University of California, Berkeley, is the author of *Locke on War and Peace.*

G. WATTS CUNNINGHAM, Professor of Philosophy, Emeritus, Cornell University, is the author of *A Study in the Philosophy of Bergson, The Idealistic Argument in Recent British and American Philosophy,* and *Context in the Meaning Situation,* among numerous works.

VIANNEY DÉCARIE, Professor of Philosophy and Director of the École Normale Supérieure, the University of Montreal, is the author of *L'Objet de la Métáphysique selon Aristote.*

RICHARD T. DEGEORGE, Associate Professor of Philosophy, the University of Kansas, is the author of *Classical and Contemporary Metaphysics: A Source Book.*

RAPHAEL DEMOS, Professor of Philosophy, Vanderbilt University, is the author of *The Philosophy of Plato* and editor of the *Complete Works of Plato.*

WILFRID DESAN, Professor of Philosophy, Georgetown University, Washington, D.C., is author of *The Tragic Finale, An Essay on the Philosophy of J-P Sartre* and *A Noetic Prelude to a United World,* among other works.

MALCOLM L. DIAMOND, Assistant Professor, Department of Religion, Princeton University, is the author of *Martin Buber: Jewish Existentialist.*

FRANK B. DILLEY, Associate Professor of Philosophy, Millikin University, Decatur, Illinois, is a contributor to *Masterpieces of Christian Literature.*

C. J. DUCASSE, Professor of Philosophy, Emeritus, Brown University, is the author of *The Philosophy of Art, Philosophy as a Science, Nature, Mind, and Death,* and *A Critical Examination of the Belief in a Life After Death,* among other works.

A. C. EWING, Fellow of Jesus College, Cambridge, is the author of *Idealism, A Short Commentary on Kant's Critique of Pure Reason* and *Second Thoughts in Moral Philosophy,* among other works.

VERGILIUS FERM, Compton Professor of Philosophy and Chairman of the Department of Philosophy, the College of Wooster, Wooster, Ohio, is the author of *Pastoral Psychology, Pictorial History of Protestantism,* and *A Brief Dictionary of American Superstitions,* among other works.

NELS F. S. FERRÉ, Abbot Professor of Christian Theology, Andover Newton Theological School, Newton Center, Massachusetts, is the author of *Faith and Reason, Evil and the Christian Faith, Christ and the Christian,* and *Searchlights on Contemporary Theology,* among other works.

HENRY A. FINCH, Professor of Philosophy, Pennsylvania State University, has contributed articles on philosophy and the history of ideas to learned journals.

LEWIS S. FORD, Assistant Professor of Humanities (Philosophy and Religion), Raymond College, University of the Pacific, wrote his doctoral dissertation on "The Ontological Foundations of Paul Tillich's Theory of the Religious Symbol."

MAURICE S. FRIEDMAN, Associate Professor of Philosophy, Sarah Lawrence College, is the author of *The Problematic Rebel, Martin Buber: The Life of Dialogue* and translator and editor of many works of Martin Buber, among which are *Pointing the Way, The Origin and Meaning of Hasidism, The Legend of the Baal-Shem,* and *Daniel: Dialogues on Realization.*

LON L. FULLER, Carter Professor of General Jurisprudence, Harvard University Law School, is the author of *The Law in Quest of Itself.*

A. C. GARNETT, Professor of Philosophy, University of Wisconsin, is the author of *The Moral Nature of Man, Freedom and Planning in Australia, Religion and the Moral Life,* among other books.

WALTER GOLDSTEIN, who has lived in Israel since 1934, is the author of books on Jakob Wassermann, Carl Hauptmann, Hermann Cohen, and Martin Buber.

THEODORE M. GREENE, until recently Henry Burr Alexander Professor in Humanities, Scripps College, Claremont, California, is the author of *Our*

Cultural Heritage and *Moral Aesthetic and Religious Insight,* among other works.

ADOLF GRÜNBAUM, Andrew Mellon Professor of Philosophy and Director of the Center for Philosophy of Science, the University of Pittsburgh, is the author of *Philosophical Problems of Space and Time.*

ELLEN S. HARING, Chairman of the Department of Philosophy, Wellesley College, is the author of numerous articles for philosophic journals in the United States and Europe.

ROBERT S. HARTMAN, Research Professor of Philosophy, the National University of Mexico, is the author of *The Structure of Value* and co-author of *The Language of Value,* among other works.

CHARLES HARTSHORNE, presently in the Department of Philosophy, the University of Texas, was the editor (with Paul Weiss) of *The Collected Papers of Charles S. Peirce* (Vols. I–VI) and author of *The Divine Relativity, Reality as Social Process,* and *The Logic of Perfection,* among other works.

F. H. HEINEMANN, who has taught at the University of Frankfurt and Oxford University, is the author of *New Pathways in Philosophy* and *Existentialism and the Modern Predicament,* among other works.

HEINZ-JOACHIM HEYDORN, educator and social philosopher, makes his home in Germany.

WILLIAM ERNEST HOCKING, Chairman of the Department of Philosophy, Harvard University, until his retirement in 1943, is the author of numerous distinguished works, among which the most recent are *The Coming World Civilization* and *The Meaning of Immortality in Human Experience.*

ROBERT M. HUTCHINS, President of the Center for the Study of Democratic Institutions, Santa Barbara, California, is the author of numerous books and articles on education and democratic values.

VLADIMIR JANKÉLÉVITCH, of the University of Paris, is the author of numerous works, including *Le Mal* and *L'odyssée de la conscience dans la derniere philosophie de Schelling.*

A. H. JOHNSON, Professor and Chairman of the Department of Philosophy, University College, University of Western Ontario, is the author of *Whitehead's Theory of Reality, Whitehead's Philosophy of Civilization,* and editor of several books on Whitehead and Dewey.

GORDON D. KAUFMAN, Associate Professor of Theology, Vanderbilt University, is the author of *Relativism, Knowledge and Faith,* and *The Context of Decision.*

WALTER KAUFMANN, Professor of Philosophy, Princeton University, is the author of *Nietzsche, Critique of Philosophy and Religion, From Shakespeare to Existentialism, The Faith of a Heretic,* and other works.

NORMAN KELMAN, a practicing psychoanalyst and former Associate Dean of the American Institute for Psychoanalysis, is the author of numerous articles which have appeared in such periodicals as the *American Journal of Psychoanalysis* and the *American Scholar.*

GEORGE P. KLUBERTANZ, S.J., Dean of the College of Philosophy and Letters, St. Louis University, St. Louis, Missouri, has been editor of *The Modern Schoolman,* and is author of *The Discursive Power, Introduction to the Philosophy of Being,* and *St. Thomas Aquinas on Analogy,* among other works.

TAKEHIKO KOJIMA, Executive Director of the International Philosophical Research Association of Japan, is the author of *The Concept of Kinesis in Aristotle* and *Diary of a Philosopher in Africa,* among other works, as well as the translator into Japanese of works by Gabriel Marcel, O. F. Bollnow, and Diez del Corral.

S. KÖRNER, University of Bristol, England, is the author of *Conceptual Thinking, Kant, Philosophy of Mathematics,* and the editor of *Ratio.*

HELMUT KUHN, Professor of Philosophy, the University of Munich, is the author of *A History of Esthetics* (with K. E. Gilbert) and *Encounter with Nothingness,* among other works.

PAUL G. KUNTZ, Professor of Philosophy, Grinnell College, Grinnell, Iowa, is co-author of *Philosophy, the Study of Alternative Beliefs.*

HERBERT LAMM, Associate Professor of Philosophy, the University of Chicago, has contributed studies to many philosophical journals both in the United States and in Europe.

NATHANIEL LAWRENCE, Professor of Philosophy at Williams College, is co-author (with Robert S. Brumbaugh) of *Philosophy of Education* and author of *Whitehead's Philosophical Development.*

IVOR LECLERC, Senior Lecturer in Logic and Metaphysics, the University of Glasgow, is the author of *Whitehead's Metaphysics* and editor of *The Relevance of Whitehead.*

PERRY LEFEVRE, Dean and Professor of Constructive Theology, Chicago Theological Seminary, is the author of *The Prayers of Kierkegaard* and *The Christian Teacher.*

ALBERT WILLIAM LEVI, Professor of Philosophy, Washington University, St. Louis, Missouri, is the author of *Philosophy and the Modern World* and *Literature, Philosophy and the Imagination.*

EMMANUEL LEVINAS, Director of the École Normale Israélite Orientale de l'Alliance Israélite Universelle, is the author of *De l'existence a l'existant,*

En découvrant l'existence avec Husserl et Heidegger, and *Totalité et Infini,* among other works.

CHARLES MALIK, University Professor at the School of International Service, the American University, Washington, D.C., and former President of the General Assembly of the United Nations, is the author of numerous books and articles on questions of morals and philosophy.

WM. OLIVER MARTIN, Professor and Chairman of the Department of Philosophy, University of Rhode Island, is the author of *Metaphysics and Ideology* and *The Order and Integration of Knowledge.*

ROLLO MAY is the author of numerous works, among which are *The Meaning of Anxiety, Man's Search for Himself, Existence: A New Dimension in Psychiatry and Psychology,* and *Existential Psychology.*

ERNAN McMULLIN, a member of the Department of Philosophy at the University of Notre Dame, is editor of *The Concept of Matter* and contributor to numerous general and Catholic periodicals.

Y. P. MEI, Professor of Oriental Studies, State University of Iowa, is the translator of *The Ethical and Political Works of Motse* and author of *Motse, the Neglected Rival of Confucius.*

PHILIP MERLAN, Professor of German Philosophy and Literature, Scripps College, Claremont, California, is the author of *Monopsychism, Mysticism, Metaconsciousness.*

ARNOLD METZGER, Professor of Philosophy at the University of Munich, Germany, is the author of *Der Gegenstand der Ernkenntnis, Freiheit und Tod,* and *Das Umweltproblem,* among other works.

ALLAN O. MILLER, Professor of Systematic Theology and Philosophy, Eden Theological Seminary, Webster Groves, Missouri, is the author of *Invitation to Theology* and editor of *The Heidelberg Catechism.*

LOUIS O. MINK, Associate Professor of Philosophy, Wesleyan University, is the author of numerous articles and reviews in major journals of philosophy in the United States and Europe.

BERTRAM MORRIS, Professor of Philosophy, University of Colorado, is the author of *Philosophical Aspects of Culture.*

ERNEST NAGEL, John Dewey Professor of Philosophy, Columbia University, is the author of *The Logic of Measurement, Principles of the Theory of Probability, Logic without Metaphysics, Structure of Science,* among other works.

MAURICE NÉDONCELLE, member of the Faculty of Theology, University of Strasbourg since 1945 and its Dean since 1956, is the author of *De la fidélite, Existe-t-il une philosophie chrétienne, Conscience et Logos,* and *Prière humaine, prière divine,* among other works.

REINHOLD NIEBUHR, the distinguished theologian, is the author of numerous books, the most recent being *The Self and the Dramas of History* and *Pious and Secular America*. He is co-chairman of the Editorial Board of the biweekly journal, *Christianity and Crisis*.

KAI NIELSEN, Associate Professor of Philosophy, New York University, is author of many essays on ethics and the philosophy of religion for learned journals.

F. S. C. NORTHROP, Sterling Professor of Philosophy and Law, Yale University, is the author of *The Meeting of East and West, The Logic of the Sciences and the Humanities,* and *The Complexities of Legal and Ethical Theory,* among other works.

ALBERT C. OUTLER, Professor of Theology, Perkins School of Theology, Southern Methodist University, Dallas, Texas, is author of *Psychotherapy and the Christian Message, The Christian Tradition and the Unity We Seek,* among other works.

J. OWENS, C.Sr.R., Professor in the Pontifical Institute of Medieval Studies, Toronto, is the author of *The Doctrine of Being in the Aristotelian Metaphysics, Saint Thomas and the Future of Metaphysics, A History of Ancient Western Philosophy,* and *An Elementary Christian Metaphysics.*

FRANCIS H. PARKER, Professor of Philosophy, Haverford College, Haverford, Pennsylvania, is co-author (with Henry B. Veatch) of *Logic as a Human Instrument* and contributor to *The Return to Reason* and *Philosophy of Knowledge.*

PAUL E. PFUETZE, Professor of Religion and Chairman of the Department of Religion, Vassar College, is the author of *The Social Self* and *Self, Society, Existence.*

WILLIAM H. POTEAT, Associate Professor of Christianity and Culture, Duke University, is the contributor of articles to such journals as *Mind, Philosophical Quarterly, Hibbert Journal,* and the *Journal of Religion.*

FRANCIS V. RAAB, Associate Professor of Philosophy at the University of Minnesota, has contributed to the *Review of Metaphysics,* the *Philosophical Review* and *Philosophy of Science.*

P. T. RAJU, Professor of Philosophy and Psychology, Emeritus, the University of Rajasthan, Jaipur, India, and visiting Professor at a number of American and European universities, is the author of numerous books and articles on philosophical questions.

J. HERMAN RANDALL, JR., F. J. E. Woolbridge Professor of Philosophy, Columbia University, is the author of *The Making of the Modern Mind* and other works in philosophy and the history of ideas.

ANDREW J. RECK, Associate Professor of Philosophy, Tulane University,

New Orleans, Louisiana, is the author of a number of studies on the history of American philosophy.

WILLIAM L. REESE, Chairman of the Department of Philosophy, University of Delaware, is the general editor of *Philosophy of Science: The Delaware Seminar,* co-author (with Charles Hartshorne) of *Philosophers Speak of God,* and author of *The Ascent from Below.*

AMÉLIE O. RORTY has taught at Wheaton College, Princeton University, and Barnard College in New York City. She is presently Assistant Professor of Philosophy at Douglass College of Rutgers University.

RICHARD M. RORTY is presently Assistant Professor of Philosophy at Princeton University, and has contributed articles to various philosophical journals.

EUGEN ROSENSTOCK-HUESSY, Professor of Social Philosophy, Emeritus, Dartmouth College, is the author of *Out of Revolution, The Christian Future,* and *The Multiformity of Man,* among other works.

NATHAN ROTENSTREICH, Professor of Philosophy, the Hebrew University, Jerusalem, is the author of *Spirit and Man, The Recurring Pattern,* and *Humanism in the Technological Era,* among other works.

MEYER SCHAPIRO, Professor in the Department of Art History and Archaeology, Columbia University, is the author of numerous studies in medieval and modern art.

PAUL F. SCHMIDT, Associate Professor of Philosophy, Oberlin College, is the author of *Religious Knowledge.*

GEORGE A. SCHRADER, Professor of Philosophy, Yale University and Master of Branford College, Yale University, is the author of numerous articles on philosophy for journals in the United States, England, and Europe.

HUSTON SMITH, Professor of Philosophy, the Massachusetts Institute of Technology, is the author of *The Religions of Man* and *The Purposes of Higher Education.*

HERBERT SPIEGELBERG, Professor of Philosophy, Lawrence College, Appleton, Wisconsin, is the author of *Antirelativismus, Gesetz und Sittengesetz,* and *The Phenomenological Movement.*

NEWTON P. STALLKNECHT, Professor of Philosophy and Director of the School of Letters, Indiana University, is the author of *Studies in the Philosophy of Creation* and *Strange Seas of Thought, William Wordsworth's Philosophy of Man and Nature.*

GEORGES H. TAVARD, A.A., Chairman of the Department of Theology, Mount Mercy College, Pittsburgh, Pennsylvania, is the author of *Paul Tillich and the Christian Message,* among other works.

FRIEDRICH THIEBERGER, who died in Jerusalem in 1958 shortly after the completion of the present exchange with Martin Buber, was the author, among other works, of the standard *Jüdisches Fest-Jüdischer Brauch* and *King Solomon.*

HELMUT THIELECKE, Professor of Systematic Theology and Social Ethics, University of Hamburg, is the author of *Nihilism,* among other works.

KARL THIEME, Professor of European History, the University of Mainz, and co-editor of the *Freiburger Rundbrief,* is the author of *Biblische Religion Heute* and numerous other studies describing the relation of Christianity and Judaism.

MANLEY H. THOMPSON, JR., Professor of Philosophy, the University of Chicago, is the author of the *Pragmatic Philosophy of C. S. Peirce* and various articles for journals of philosophy in the United States and England.

PAUL TILLICH, the distinguished theologian, is the author of numerous works, among which the most recent are *Biblical Religion and the Search for Ultimate Reality, Dynamics of Faith,* and *Theology of Culture.*

A. P. USHENKO, late Professor of Philosophy, Indiana University, was the author of numerous works on logic, the metaphysical background of modern science, and the philosophy of art.

HENRY B. VEATCH, Distinguished Service Professor of Philosophy, Indiana University, is the author of *Logic as a Human Instrument* (with Francis H. Parker), *Realism and Nominalism Revisited,* and *Rational Man.*

EWALD WAÉMÜTH is the author of *Der Mensch in der Mitte, Die Philosophie Pascals, Vom Sinn des Todes,* and *Der unbekannte Pascal,* among other works.

HERMANN WEIN, Professor of Philosophy and Lecturer on Philosophical Anthropology, the University of Göttingen, Germany, is the author of *Untersuchungen über das Problembewusstsein* and *Das Problem des Relativismus,* among other works.

PAUL WEISS, Professor of Philosophy, Yale University, is the author of *Modes of Being, Our Public Life, Nature and Man,* among other works.

WARNER A. WICK, Professor of Philosophy and Dean of Students in the Division of the Humanities, the University of Chicago, is the author of *Metaphysics and the New Logic.*

HENRY N. WIEMAN, Professor of Philosophy, of Religion, Emeritus, Divinity School, the University of Chicago, and presently Professor of Philosophy, Southern Illinois University, Carbondale, Illinois, is the author of numerous books, including *The Sources of Human Good.*

JOHN WILD, Professor of Philosophy, Yale University, is the author of *Philosophy East and West, Plato's Theory of Man, Challenge of Existentialism,* among other works.

HELEN WODEHOUSE, Mistress of Girton College, Cambridge, is the author of *One Kind of Religion*.

KURT H. WOLFF, Professor and Chairman of the Department of Sociology, Brandeis University, is the author of numerous essays and studies in the history of modern sociology and the translator and editor of works by Georg Simmel.